Josiah

Worlds of the Ancient Near East and Mediterranean

Series editor: Diana Edelman, University of Oslo

Worlds of the Ancient Near East and Ancient Mediterranean brings alive the texts, archaeology and history of the cultures of the regions around the Mediterranean Sea and eastward to ancient Iran and Iraq, from the Neolithic through the Roman periods (ca 10,000 BCE–393 CE). Studies of one or more aspects of a single culture or of a subject across cultures in the regions outlined will form the foundation of this series, in which interdisciplinary approaches are encouraged. Studies can be based on texts, on material remains, or a combination of the two, where appropriate. In the case of a project that focuses on either the memory or the reception history of a place, person, myth, practice, or idea that arose or existed within the prescribed time, chapters that trace ongoing relevance to the present are welcome. The volumes are meant to be accessible to a wide audience interested in how the inhabitants of these parts of the world lived or how they understood their own pasts, presents, and futures, as well as how current scholars are understanding and recreating their pasts or their future aspirations.

Published titles:

A History of Biblical Israel: The Fate of the Tribes and Kingdoms from Merenptah to Bar Kochba
Axel Knauf and Philippe Guillaume

Ancient Cookware from the Levant: An Ethnoarchaeological Perspective
Gloria A. London

Leadership, Social Memory and Judean Discourse in the 5th–2nd Centuries BCE
Edited by Diana V. Edelman and Ehud Ben Zvi

New Light on Canaanite-Phoenician Pottery
Dalit Regev

Forthcoming titles

Burial Practices in Ancient Israel and the Neighboring Cultures (c. 1500–330 BCE)
Jürg Hutzli and Stefan Münger

Painting the Mediterranean Phoenician: On Canaanite-Phoenician Trade-nets
Dalit Regev

Recovering Women's Rituals in the Ancient Near East
Julye Bidmead

Josiah

From Improbable Stories to Inventive Historiography

Lowell K. Handy

SHEFFIELD UK   BRISTOL CT

Published by Equinox Publishing Ltd.

UK: Office 415, The Workstation, 15 Paternoster Row, Sheffield, South Yorkshire S1 2BX

USA: ISD, 70 Enterprise Drive, Bristol, CT 06010

www.equinoxpub.com

First published 2020

© Lowell K. Handy 2020

All rights reserved. No part of this publication may be reproduced or transmitted in any form or by any means, electronic or mechanical, including photocopying, recording or any information storage or retrieval system, without prior permission in writing from the publishers.

British Library Cataloguing-in-Publication Data

A catalogue record for this book is available from the British Library.

ISBN-13 978 1 78179 857 7 (hardback)
978 1 78179 858 4 (paperback)
978 1 78179 859 1 (ePDF)

Library of Congress Cataloging-in-Publication Data

Names: Handy, Lowell K., 1949- author.
Title: Josiah : from improbable stories to inventive historiography / Lowell K Handy.
Description: Bristol : Equinox Publishing Ltd., 2020. | Series: Worlds of the ancient Near East and Mediterranean | Includes bibliographical references and index.
Identifiers: LCCN 2019011194 (print) | LCCN 2019015889 (ebook) | ISBN 9781781798591 (ePDF) | ISBN 9781781798577 (hb) | ISBN 9781781798584 (pb)
Subjects: LCSH: Josiah, King of Judah.
Classification: LCC BS580.J75 (ebook) | LCC BS580.J75 H36 2020 (print) | DDC 222/.54092--dc23
LC record available at https://lccn.loc.gov/2019011194

Typeset by ISB Typesetting, Sheffield, UK

In Memory of
Philip R. Davies

Table of Contents

Preface	ix
Abbreviations	xiii
Josiah: An Introduction	1
1. Josiah Was Dead to Begin With	17
2. The Wise Man: Josiah's Busy Scribes	42
3. Josiah Is Not Jeroboam and Other Kingly Questions	69
4. A Man of God and Huldah: Prophets in the Tale of Josiah	99
5. Religion at the Time of Josiah: Reconstruction, Text, and Invention	121
6. Time for a Change (er, um, a 'Reform')?	157
7. An Invitation to Dinner: Josiah and His Passover Narratives	189
8. The Popular Afterlife of Josiah: The King in World Histories	208
9. Art of the Story of the King	235
10. Creating Memories of Josiah	260
Bibliography	276
Index of Scripture References	331
Index of Authors	335
Index of Subjects	345

Preface

This volume began as an idea for inclusion in a series of volumes on the rulers of Judah and Israel. Of the original start-up titles and authors, death and career moves eliminated all of the projected authors save myself for Josiah and the series was dropped. Twelve years ago, Philip Davies and Diana Edelman inquired about the book and I said I would return to work on it. Full time employment kept that work to a minimum—I 'poked' at it as Philip continually encouraged me to keep at it, with "no deadline." Papers were presented along the way at the Chicago Society of Biblical Research, the Midwest Region of the Society of Biblical Literature, and the annual Society of Biblical Literature meetings, but a 20-minute paper with minimal documentation is a long way from a book. Some of those papers saw print. Retirement has provided time to take to the task in earnest. This volume is the result of 50 years in the field, starting with my first undergraduate term paper entitled "David the Rat" for an Introduction to the Old Testament course. I held the David of the book of Samuel to the standards of Torah legislation. The professor was impressed enough to suggest I might want to take up the field. You may blame him.

The original series, as envisioned by Steve Wiggins, was to concentrate on individual rulers of the Hebrew Bible/Old Testament/ancient Judah and Israel from Rehoboam up to, but excluding, Herod the Great. The Josiah volume was planned as a one-stop survey of the history and current state of scholarship, with deliberation of literary, historical, and ideological influences on the reading of King Josiah. A glance down the bibliography for this volume will supply the beginner in the area with as much of that as anyone might need, so the purpose of the work has shifted in this volume to Josiah as a 'memory' captured in 'literary' prose and an entire smorgasbord of 'imaginations' through time and traditions. I think of the work as a place to begin Josianic studies, not an end. I have for years told entering scholars that this is a field where the more you learn the less you know; if one thinks one has it all figured out and knows all there is to know about the topic, one has not yet started in the field. This I offer as background to cogitation [a good Dickens word] concerning Josiah and the invention of a biblical reign-to-end-all-reigns.

My interest in Josiah did not arise until my doctoral work at the University of Chicago. As my dissertation committee could attest, this was not your usual crank-it-out production, as I needed to reconsider a number of underlying problems in order to deal with Josiah's reform. In the course of my research I realized Josiah could not have carried out the reforms recorded for him; however, having by then expended much time and effort, I 'wisely' kept that thought to myself until after the project had been signed. Gösta Ahlström, Walter Michel, and Frank Reynolds were all quite helpful in the writing of the dissertation and, more importantly, were kindly amused about my change of mind concerning Josiah and his religious proclivities without informing them until it was too late. They were also instrumental in supporting my decision not to publish the dissertation as written; once the book is published the thesis is yours forever, but their mutual observation was that nobody reads dissertations. It was at this juncture that Philip Davies entered this narrative. He offered to publish the dissertation "as written." The book that resulted was an elaboration of one of the underlying problems covered in the dissertation. I would like to note that the most supportive faculty member at Chicago for that dissertation was the late Joseph Kitagawa, Professor of History of Religions, who forever kept my spirits up through its writing.

The entire tradition of Josianic studies, of course, has been helpful, but many people have been especially generous in this project over the years. A few colleagues from my days at the University of Chicago have kept abreast of the development from dissertation to book: Elaine J. Ramshaw, Mary Patrick, Diana V. Edelman, and Steven W. Holloway have been, and remain, supportive friends with helpful suggestions. Many members of the CSBR, ASOR, and SBL have continued to inquire about and encourage the project. Several members have, over the years, graciously provided me with copies of papers presented before, or in lieu of, publishing. My appreciation is warmly extended to each of them.

Before submitting the dissertation proposal, the topic had come up in conversations with now departed distinguished scholars who had visited the Disciples Divinity House of the University of Chicago. John Gammie and Leo Perdue both urged me to pursue the subject. I must include the late W. Boyd Barrick, who asked permission to refer to me in his book on 'the cemeteries' as neither a minimalist nor a maximalist but a nihilist in studying biblical historiographical narratives; I consider myself honored. (Boyd was working on the Manasseh volume for the projected Kings series when he died unexpectedly.) The scholars who passed through the American Theological Library Association during my years employed on the Religion Index deserve special thanks. This group of intelligent staffers reported articles, essays, books, and off-hand references to Josiah through the decades, many of which have found their way into this volume. I extend many gracious thanks to Tom Blanton, Steven Holloway, Ginny Landgraf, John Meeks†, Suzie Park, Nina Shultz, as well as the many others who toiled there in the endless succession of articles, essays, and book reviews.

For supplying items I would never have had in hand otherwise, three people deserve special thanks. Bob Mowery kindly loaned me a very old comic book, which I hope I returned in the same condition I received it. Elaine Ramshaw sent me a Lutheran story picture book on Josiah (and referred me to another). Nina Shultz graciously informed me of her copy of a Russian Orthodox Bible commentary and proceeded to translate the extensive passages on Josiah from Russian for me.

My alma mater, the University of Iowa School of Religion [now: Department of Religious Studies], supplied an indispensable background upon which to build; special recognition is deserved by Jonathan Goldstein, Helen Goldstein, Fred Bargebuhr, Ken Kuntz, George Nickelsburg, Jay Holstein, James McCue, and Bob Baird for excellence in teaching and scholarship. At the University of Chicago Divinity School, I was privileged to work for a time with Jay Wilcoxen, Jon Levenson, Gösta Ahlström, David Wilmot, Hans Dieter Betz, Wendy Doniger, Frank Reynolds, and Joseph Kitagawa. I also worked at the Oriental Institute with Norman Gelb, Dennis Pardee, Walter Farber, Robert Biggs, and Ed Wente. Whether they like it or not, they have all contributed to the composition of this volume.

Libraries remain indispensable, even as internet resources expand. I have been happy to make use of public libraries in Fort Dodge, Iowa, Des Plaines, Illinois, Park Ridge, Illinois, and Evanston, Illinois, all of which have been most helpful. I thank the people of these cities for maintaining such valuable institutions. University libraries, of course, form the backbone of research materials. Over the years, I have made ample use of the University of Iowa Library; Regenstein Library, Herbert L. Willett Library of the Disciples Divinity House, and the Oriental Institute Archives (all of the University of Chicago); Cudahy Library (Loyola University Chicago); Styberg Library and Main Library (both Northwestern University); Henry C. Crowell Library (Moody Bible Institute); and JKM Library (located at the Lutheran School of Theology at Chicago). I wish to thank the librarians and staff at each of these institutions. For general research it is hard to beat the resources of the Newberry Library in Chicago and I thank the staff for hauling many a heavy and disintegrating tome out of the stacks for me to look through, most of which went back without my having use for them. It would be a thankless task, save that I made certain to thank them then and do so again here.

Diana Edelman has been of invaluable assistance in the production of the volume. Not only was she there when the dissertation was written, but she has followed the writing of this particular book for many years. As editor at Equinox, she ably steered the manuscript through to its completion. Equinox has been diligent in handling the manuscript from author to book, no doubt making much obscure text intelligible in the process. I extend many thanks to Sarah Lee, Sarah Hussell, and Iain Beswick for carrying on their jobs so well. The continued publishing production despite restrictive and personal difficulties during the 2020 pandemic is greatly appreciated.

As always, it is impossible to thank my wife Erica enough. I sit and key away hours at end and then she sits patiently listening as I read chapters or long selections to her, some of which I completely rewrite so that she ends up having to sit through it again.

The book was written with continuous enthusiastic encouragement from Philip Davies. At the last Society of Biblical Literature annual meeting he attended, he urged me to finish the book quickly, because, "I'm getting old." He had read and commented on three of the chapters late in 2017 and I promised him a completed manuscript by the following summer. I emailed that manuscript to him in May 2018 and received his warm thanks. Two weeks later I received an email that Philip had died suddenly. It is with deep thanks and fond memories that I dedicate this book to Philip R. Davies.

Abbreviations

ÄAT	Ägypten und Altes Testament
AB	Anchor Bible
ABD	*Anchor Bible Dictionary*
ABG	Arbeiten zur Bibel und ihrer Geschichte
ABRL	Anchor Bible Reference Library
ABS	Archaeology and Biblical Studies
ACCSOT	Ancient Christian Commentary on Scripture: Old Testament
ADPV	Abhandlungen des Deutschen Palästina-Vereins
AFN	Anthropology of Food & Nutrition
AHR	*American Historical Review*
AIL	Ancient Israel and Its Literature
AJBI	*Annual of the Japanese Biblical Institute*
AJBS	*African Journal of Biblical Studies*
AJSL	*American Journal of Semitic Languages and Literature*
ALGHJ	Arbeiten zur Literatur und Geschichte des hellenistischen Judentums
AMD	Ancient Magic and Divination
ANEm	Ancient Near East monograph
ANESSup	Ancient Near Eastern Studies Supplement
AOAT	Alter Orient und Altes Testament
AOS	American Oriental Series
APOT	*The Apocrypha and Pseudepigrapha of the Old Testament*. Edited by Robert H. Charles. 2 vols. Oxford: Clarendon, 1913.
ARech	Actes et Recherches
ASE	*Annali di storia dell'esegesi*
ASORBS	American Schools of Oriental Research Books Series
ATANT	Abhandlungen der Theologie des Alten und Neuen Testaments
AYBRL	Anchor Yale Bible Reference Library
BA	*Biblical Archaeologist*
BASOR	*Bulletin of the American Schools of Oriental Research*
BBB	Bonner biblische Beiträge
BBHR	Blackwell Brief Histories of Religion Series
BBR	*Bulletin for Biblical Research*
BCT	*The Bible and Critical Theory*
BeO	*Bibbia e oriente*
BEJH	Bibliothèque d'Études Juives. Série Histoire
BETL	Bibliotheca ephemeridum theologicarum lovaniensium
BFCT	Beiträge zur Förderung christlicher Theologie
Bib	*Biblica*
BibB	Biblische Beiträge

BibEnc	Biblical Encyclopedia
BibInt	*Biblical Interpretation*
BibIntS	Biblical Interpretation Series
BibThS	Biblisch-Theologische Studien
BibW	*The Biblical World*
BLib	Bible and Liberation
BlMan	Blackwell Manifestos
BMW	Bible in the Modern World
BN	*Biblische Notizen*
BR	*Biblical Research*
BSS	Biblical Seminar Series
BTT	Bible de tous les temps
BZ	*Biblische Zeitschrift*
BZABR	Beihefte zur Zeitschrift für Altorientalische und Biblische Rechtsgeschichte
BZAW	Beihefte zur Zeitschrift für die alttestamentliche Wissenschaft
CBC	Cambridge Bible Commentary
CBET	Contributions to Biblical Exegesis and Theology
CBQ	*Catholic Biblical Quarterly*
CBQMS	Catholic Biblical Quarterly Monograph Series
ChrSt	Christian Studies
CJR	Christian Jewish Relations
ConBOT	Coniectanea biblica: Old Testament Series
CrCur	*Cross Currents*
CTh	Cuadernos de Teológia
CurTM	Currents in Theology and Mission
CV	*Communio viatorum*
DBAT	Dielheimer Blätter zum Alten Testament und seiner Rezeption in der Alten Kirche
DDD	Dictionary of Deities and Demons in the Bible [First edition, 1995]
DTT	Dansk Teologisk Tidsskrift
EBib	Etudes bibliques
EDB	Eerdmans Dictionary of the Bible (2000)
EmSch	Emerging Scholars
EncBrit[11]	Encyclopedia Britanica eleventh edition (1910–1911)
ERE	Encyclopedia of Religion and Ethics (1908–1922)
EDRS	Encyclopédie, ou Dictionnaire raisonné des sciences, des arts et des métiers (1780)
EMH	Early Music History
ERH	Erev-Rav-Hefte: Biblische-feministische Texte
ESHM	European Seminar in Historical Methodology
EssBib	Essais Bibliques
EstBib	*Estudios bíblicos*
EstOr	Estudios Orientales
ETL	*Ephemerides Theologicae Lovanienses*
FAT	Forschungen zum Alten Testament
FCB	Feminist Companions to the Bible
FCBib	Fuentes de la ciencia Bíblica

FOTL	Forms of the Old Testament Literature
FRLANT	Forschungen zur Religion und Literatur des Alten und Neuen Testaments
GBSOT	Guides to Biblical Scholarship: Old Testament Series
GUS	Gorgias Ugaritic Studies
HANE/M	History of the Ancient Near East / Monographs
HAT	Handbuch zum Alten Testament
HBAI	*Hebrew Bible and Ancient Israel*
HBM	Hebrew Bible Monographs
HBT	*Horizons in Biblical Theology*
HC	Handy Commentary
HCS	Hellenistic Culture and Society
HdO	Handbuch der Orientalistik
HDR	Harvard Dissertations in Religion
HeBAI	*Hebrew Bible and Ancient Israel*
HoSo	Horae Soederblomianae
HR	*History of Religions*
HRel	Histoire des Religions
HSM	Harvard Semitic Monographs
HTIBS	Historic Texts and Interpreters in Biblical Scholarship
HTR	*Harvard Theological Review*
HUCA	*Hebrew Union College Annual*
ICC	International Critical Commentary
IEJ	*Israel Exploration Journal*
IJOURELS	Ilorin Journal of Religious Studies
Int	Interpretation
JAJ	Journal of Ancient Judaism
JAJSup	Journal of Ancient Judaism Supplements
JANER	Journal of Ancient Near Eastern Religions
JapanRel	Japanese Religions
JATS	Journal of the Adventist Theological Society
JBL	Journal of Biblical Literature
JBLMS	Journal of Biblical Literature Monograph Series
JBQ	Jewish Bible Quarterly
JBR	Journal of Bible and Religion
JEBS	Journal of European Baptist Studies
JFSR	Journal of Feminist Studies in Religion
JHNES	Johns Hopkins Near Eastern Studies
JHS	Journal of Hebrew Scriptures
JJL	Judaism and Jewish Life
JNES	Journal of Near Eastern Studies
JNSL	Journal of Northwest Semitic Languages
JPSTC	Jewish Publication Society Torah Commentary
JQR	Jewish Quarterly Review
JRitSt	Journal of Ritual Studies
JSJ	Journal for the Study of Judaism in the Persian, Hellenistic, and Roman Periods
JSJS	Supplements to the Journal for the Study of Judaism

JSOT	*Journal for the Study of the Old Testament*
JSOTSup	*Journal for the Study of the Old Testament: Supplement Series*
JSP	*Journal for the Study of the Pseudepigrapha*
KTAH	Key Themes in Ancient History
LAI	Library of Ancient Israel
LASBF	*Liber Annus: Studium Biblicum Franciscanum*
LDif	*Lectio difficilior*
LED	Library of Early Christianity
LHBOTS	Library of Hebrew Bible/Old Testament Studies
LS	*Louvain Studies*
MC	Mesopotamian Civilizations
MCAAS	Memoirs of the Connecticut Academy of Arts and Sciences
MdB	Le Monde de la Bible
ModC	*The Modern Churchman*
MTSR	*Method and Theory in the Study of Religion*
MSAR	Monographs of The School of American Research
NBEH	Nueva Biblia Española. Historia
NBEN	Nueva Biblia Española. Narraciones
NCB	New Century Bible
NCBC	New Collegeville Bible Commentary
NCBOT	New Clarendon Bible: Old Testament
NEAEHL	*The New Encyclopedia of Archaeological Excavations in the Holy Land*
NEArch	*Near Eastern Archaeology*
NICOT	The New International Commentary on the Old Testament
NovTSup	Supplements to Novum Testamentum
NSKAT	Neuer Stuttgarter Kommentar—Altes Testament
OBO	Orbis biblicus et orientalis
OBT	Overtures to Biblical Theology
OIS	Oriental Institute Seminars
OLA	Orientalia Lovaniensia Analecta
OPBF	Occasional Papers of the Babylonian Fund
OPIAC	Occasional Papers of the Institute for Antiquity and Christianity
OR	*Orientalia* (NS)
ORA	Orientalische Religionen in der Antike
ÖSAW	Öikumene Studien zur antiken Weltgeschichte
OTL	Old Testament Library
OTP	*Old Testament Pseudepigrapha* (James H. Charlesworth, 1983, 1985)
OTRM	Oxford Theology & Religion Monographs
OtSt	Oudtestamentische Studien
PAe	Probleme der Ägyptologie
PCHCOT	Preachers Complete Homiletical Commentary on the Old Testament
PCS	*Proceedings, Central States, Society of Biblical Literature and American Schools of Oriental Research*
PEGLAMBS	*Proceedings: Eastern Great Lakes and Midwest Bible Societies*
PFES	Publications of the Finnish Exegetical Society
PittTM	Pittsburgh Theological Monograph

PJBR	*The Polish Journal of Biblical Research*
PTMS	Princeton Theological Monograph Series
QS	Qué se sabe de …
RB	*Revue biblique*
RCSS	Records of Civilization: Sources and Studies
REJ	*Revue des etudes juives*
RelArts	Religion and the Arts
RGRW	Religions in the Graeco-Roman World
RILMA	Répertoire Iconographique de la Littérature du Moyen Age: Le Corpus de RILMA
RRB	*Review of Rabbinic Judaism*
RRR	*Reformation and Renaissance Review*
SAA	State Archives of Assyria
SAAS	State Archives of Assyria Studies
SBJT	*The Southern Baptist Journal of Theology*
SBLANEM	Society of Biblical Literature Ancient Near East Monographs
SBLDS	Society of Biblical Literature Dissertation Series
SBLMS	Society of Biblical Literature Monograph Series
SBLSP	*Society of Biblical Literature Seminar Papers*
SBLSymS	Society of Biblical Literature Symposium Series
SBLWAW	Society of Biblical Literature Writings from the Ancient World
SBT	Studies in Biblical Theology
SBTS	Sources for Biblical and Theological Study
SCJ	*The Stone-Campbell Journal*
SCS	Septuagint and Cognate Studies
SEÅ	*Svensk exegetisk årsbok*
SemeiaSt	Semeia Studies
SEMGH	Studies in Early Modern German History
SeptCom	Septuagint Commentary Series
SFSMD	Studia Francisci Scholten Memoriae Dicata
SGWB	Studien zur Geschichte der Wissenschaften in Basel. Neue Folge
SHANE	Studies in the History of the Ancient Near East
SHBC	Smyth & Helwys Bible Commentary
SHCANE	Studies in the History and Culture of the Ancient Near East
SJud	Studies in Judaism
SJOT	*Scandinavian Journal of the Old Testament*
SJT	*Scottish Journal of Theology*
SLTHS	Siphrut: Literature and Theology of the Hebrew Scriptures
SMRT	Studies in Medieval and Reformation Traditions
SOTSMS	Society for Old Testament Studies Monograph Series
SPOT	Studies on Personalities of the Old Testament
SR	*Studies in Religion/Sciences religieuses*
SSA	Social Sciences in Asia
SSSA	Stockholm Studies in Social Anthropology
StASRH	St. Andrews Studies in Reformation History
StCS	Studies in Church and State
StHCWC	Studies in the History and Culture of World Christianities
StPhon	Studia Phoenicia

StudOr	Studia orientalia
SWBA	The Social World of Biblical Antiquity
TA	Tel Aviv
TBT	The Bible Today
TCBAI	Transactions of the Casco Bay Assyriological Institute
ThA	Theologische Akademie
ThRev	Theological Review
TOTC	Tyndale Old Testament Commentaries
TSHB	Textpragmatische Studien zur Hebräischen Bibel
TSS	Themes in the Social Sciences
TTCSGOT	T&T Clark Study Guides to the Old Testament
TwnJTh	Taiwan Journal of Theology
TZ	Theologische Zeitschrift
UBSJ	Union Biblical Seminary Journal
UCOP	University of Cambridge Oriental Publications
UF	Ugarit-Forschungen
UMSR	University of Manitoba Studies in Religion
VFLUS	Veröffentlichungen der Forschungsstelle Ludwigsburg der Universität Stuttgart
Viator	Viator: Medieval and Renaissance Studies
VS	Vox Scripturae
VT	Vetus Testamentum
VTSup	Supplements to Vetus Testamentum
WANM	Worlds of the Ancient Near East and Mediterranean
WATSA	What Are They Saying about...?
WB^{2018}	World Book Encyclopedia (2018 edition)
WBC	Word Biblical Commentary
WBCom	Westminster Bible Companion
WMANT	Wissenschaftliche Monographien zum Alten und Neuen Testament
YNER	Yale Near Eastern Researches
ZABR	Zeitschrift für altorientalische und biblische Rectgeschichte
ZAW	Zeitschrift für die alttestamentliche Wissenschaft
ZRGG	Zeitschrift für Religions- und Geistesgeschichte
ZTK	Zeitschrift für Theologie und Kirche

Josiah: An Introduction

King Josiah of ancient Judah has caught the attention of the academic world in the past two centuries in a manner that was previously restricted to the kings David and Solomon. It is not that King Josiah was not always a noted biblical character; it is just that he was, as a general rule, a secondary player upon the scholarly stage.[1] What we know of the king and his rule is a lot less than any scholar would like and significantly less than an academic would need to write a biography, history, or character study of any historical (let alone living) human being.[2] The narratives in the Bible make no pretense of providing an account of Josiah's life.[3] This does not, and will never, stop people from writing biographies, histories, and psychological makeups of the figure, but these texts will also always be modern inventions; there is almost no data.[4] This study is the story of

---

1   It is interesting that in earliest Christian literature outside the New Testament, not only Josiah but the kings of the separate polities Judah and Israel are not generally brought up as exemplars of good or bad behavior: Philip F. Esler, "Prototypes, Antitypes and Social Identity in *First Clement*: Outlining a New Interpretative Model," ASE 24 (2007): 136. Byzantine literature may be a bit more inclusive, but still no Josiah: Claudia Rapp, "Old Testament Models for Emperors in Early Byzantium," in *The Old Testament in Byzantium*, ed. P. Magdaline and R. Nelson (Washington, DC: Dumbarton Oaks Research Library and Collection, 2010), 175–97.

2   Indeed, despite near agreement on the very dates of Josiah's life, even these are not certain (641/639–610/609). See John H. Hayes and Paul K. Hooker, *A New Chronology for the Kings of Israel and Judah and Its Implications for Biblical History and Literature* (Atlanta: John Knox, 1988), 70; Jeremy Hughes, *Secrets of the Times: Myth and History in Biblical Chronology*, JSOTSup 66 (Sheffield: JSOT Press, 1990), 223; Gershon Galil, *The Chronology of the Kings of Israel and Judah*, SHCANE 9 (Leiden: Brill, 1996), 104, 119–21; Jack Finegan, *Handbook of Biblical Chronology: Principles of Time Reckoning in the Ancient World and Problems of Chronology in the Bible*, rev. ed. (Peabody, MA: Hendrickson, 1998), 252–53; John W. Rogerson, *Chronicle of the Old Testament Kings: The Reign-by-Reign Record of the Rulers of Ancient Israel* (London: Thames and Hudson, 1999), 146. Any dates remotely related to the Jerusalem temple should be considered suspect: see Klaus Koenen, "1200 Jahre von Abrahams Geburt bis zum Tempelbau," ZAW 126 (2014): 494–505. Koenen sets out the literary stylization of biblical chronology regarding the temple, concluding it cannot be used for dating.

3   This is long observed by, for example, Donald W. B. Robinson, *Josiah's Reform and the Book of the Law* (London: Tyndale Press, 1951), 5.

4   A standard biblical dictionary entry can more than cover the available

a historiographical figure.⁵ It is of no importance whether Josiah was a historical, real-life person or the figment of someone's imagination.⁶ To this point in time there has neither been anything excavated from the ancient Near East nor discovered in ancient extrabiblical documentation confirming the existence of a Judahite King Josiah—at least not anything that is not dependent on the Bible itself to make that connection.⁷ There

---

information: see Robert Althann, "Josiah," *ABD* 3.1015-18 or Marvin A. Sweeney, "Josiah," in *Dictionary of the Old Testament: Historical Books*, ed. B. T. Arnold and H. G. M. Williamson (Downers Grove, IL: InterVarsity, 2005), 575–79. Even shorter, Lowell K. Handy, "Josiah," *EDB* 471; or shorter yet, Carole R. Fontaine, "Josiah," *WB²⁰¹⁸* 11.169.

5   Terje Stordalen ("Imagined and Forgotten Communities: Othering in the Story of Josiah's Reform [2 Kings 23]," in *Imagining the Other and Constructing Israelite Identity in the Early Second Temple Period*, ed. E. Ben Zvi and D. V. Edelman, LHBOTS 456 [London: Bloomsbury, 2014], 189) divides the Josianic material into three types: historical, narrative, and contextual. The creation of all three of these "Josiahs" derives from early Persian recreations of the memory of Josiah and an imagined past (see 182, 187–89). It is not entirely impossible that the old notion that these narratives were composed in the Hellenistic era has some merit, but I opt, on debatable grounds, for a Persian origin. For a Hellenistic dating, see Niels Peter Lemche, "Historie og kulturel erindring I Det Ganle Testamente," *DTT* 76 (2013): 25–30.

6   Most scholars posit a historical person, though the extent to which the material in either Kings or Chronicles reflects actual events in a real Josiah's life extends from very little (as with W. Boyd Barrick, *The King and the Cemeteries: Toward a New Understanding of Josiah's Reform*, VTSup 88 [Leiden: Brill, 2002] or Lauren A. S. Monroe, *Josiah's Reform and the Dynamics of Defilement: Israelite Rites of Violence and the Making of a Biblical Text* [Oxford: Oxford University Press, 2011]), to essentially everything (see Mark Leuchter, *Josiah's Reform and Jeremiah's Scroll: Historical Calamity and Prophetic Response*, HBM 6 [Sheffield: Sheffield Phoenix, 2006] or Kenneth A. Kitchen, *On the Reliability of the Old Testament* [Grand Rapids: Eerdmans, 2003], 29–32). At the other extreme are Thomas Thompson and several other academics who view the material in Kings as a late invention not only of the events but of the king himself. For these scholars, Josiah is an "aetiology" used for narrative purposes. See Thomas L. Thompson, *The Mythic Past: Biblical Archaeology and the Myth of Israel* (New York: Basic Books, 1999), 306–7 (and this in a decidedly non-historical work [60]). Karin Finsterbusch allows that the finding of the scroll story may have been solely an aetiological tale without historical basis ("Modelle schriftgestützten religiösen Lehrens und Lernens in der Hebräischen Bibel," *BZ* 52 [2008]: 231).

7   This takes into account the "relevant" signet rings and impressions, all of which are often presented as showing Josiah's rule, but are in themselves mute about Josiah. Michael Heltzer ("Some Questions Concerning the Economic Policy of Josiah, King of Judah," *IEJ* 50 [2000]: 106–7) and John Strange ("Solomon and His Empire: Fact or Fiction?," *SJOT* 29 [2015]: 19) take such items as legitimate evidence for Josiah's existence, but others are more suspicious. See, for example, Israel Finkelstein and Neil Asher Silberman, *The Bible Unearthed: Archaeology's New Vision of Ancient Israel and the Origin of Its Sacred Texts* (New York: Free Press), 288. Even Kitchen (*On the Reliability*, 20) notes that the archaeological evidence is at best questionable.

may well be reasons to doubt the existence of a historical Josiah, but the track record of rulers in Kings being documented in ancient contemporary inscriptions, when excavated, should weigh in favor of accepting this ruler in a time of geopolitical change and the assumption herein will be that a King Josiah reigned in ancient Judah during the last half of the seventh century BCE.[8] The historical Josiah is not, however, the object of the majority of this volume. It is quite clear that the historical Josiah has been completely re-envisioned for the literary texts from which modern studies must take their information.[9]

In writing about Josiah, Kings, Chronicles, First Esdras, and even Josephus did not produce 'history' in anything like what has been meant since the European Enlightenment.[10] These texts are representations of historical events as reimagined by later scribes and for use in their own times.[11] Retelling these stories in different words does not produce a history but puts a historical patina on essentially ahistorical narratives. Historians, literary theorists, sociologists, anthropologists, archaeologists, political scientists, historical theologians, and philosophers, not to mention

---

8   Wilfred G. Lambert ("Mesopotamian Sources and Pre-Exilic Israel," in *In Search of Pre-exilic Israel: Proceedings of the Oxford Old Testament Seminar*, ed. J. Day, JSOTSup 406 [London: T&T Clark, 2004], 357–78) lists the rulers of Samaria and Judah recorded in Mesopotamian documents; Josiah, of course, is not among those that appear. The list clearly demonstrates knowledge of the Neo-Assyrian period yet it does not demonstrate knowledge of any Judahite documents written in that period.

9   My previous contention that the narrative of Josiah's reform is neither contemporary nor reliable still stands. See Lowell K. Handy, "Historical Probability and the Narrative of Josiah's Reform in 2 Kings," in *The Pitcher Is Broken: Memorial Essays for Gösta W. Ahlström*, ed. S. W. Holloway and L. K. Handy, JSOTSup 190 (Sheffield: Sheffield Academic, 1995), 274–75. See also Ehud Ben Zvi, "Imagining Josiah's Book and the Implications of Imagining It in Early Persian Yehud," in *Berührungspunkte: Studien zur Szial- und Religionsgeschichte Israels und seiner Umwelt: Festschrift für Rainer Albertz zu seinem 65. Geburtstag*, ed. Ingo Kottsieper, Rüdiger Schmitt and Jakob Wöhrle, AOAT 350 (Münster: Ugarit-Verlag, 2008), 197.

10   The use of 'history' for biblical narrative has been suspect in some scholarly circles for a couple of centuries and as history itself becomes a more complex notion, equating what the Bible records and what might have actually happened becomes ever less likely. See the survey in Jens Bruun Kofoed, *Text and History: Historiography and the Study of the Biblical Text* (Winona Lake, IN: Eisenbrauns, 2005), 1–28, 242–27. Nevertheless, "history" remains popular as a genre term for some, e.g., Baruch Halpern, *The First Historians: The Hebrew Bible and History* (New York: Harper & Row, 1988), 3–15. Halpern is clearly aware that writing "history" is not the same as recording events that actually happened—in the case of Josiah, stories knowingly entering known untruths (249–53).

11   This is not to say that the authors of these texts did not believe they were recording events that had taken place. See Ben Zvi, "Imagining Josiah's Book," 196–97.

psychologists and semanticists, have all attempted 'historical reconstructions' of Israelite history and even Josiah in particular.[12] By this time it should be well known to anyone working in the field of biblical studies that all of these approaches are inadequate to deal with Josiah; the data is too slim. When it comes to King Josiah in particular, the sources are hopelessly inadequate. A history of Josiah cannot be written, but attempts at historiographical reconstructions can and will continue to be devised.[13] There is some relation between events that happened in a real world, events that were recorded in the distant past, reading and using the texts previously written, and modern attempts to make any sense out of Josiah at all.[14] Such is the confusion over this 'lesser' king at the base of this volume.

There have been times and situations when Josiah has emerged from relative obscurity to play an important part in history. He, of course, could always be used to remember a ruler considered just and pious in a good funeral sermon.[15] His example as a destroyer of idols and his insistence on

---

12   There have been plenty of essays produced to document the trouble with methodology in biblical 'history' writing. For an easy to understand quartet, see J. Maxwell Miller's *The Old Testament and the Historian*, GBSOT (Philadelphia: Fortress, 1976), 40–48, which is especially nice in clearly explaining the problem of doing "archaeology with Bible in hand"; on the problem of attempting to think in terms of what was written then as opposed to what "we" want the texts to say now, see Jacob Licht's "Biblical Historicism," in *History, Historiography and Interpretation: Studies in Biblical and Cuneiform Literatures*, ed. H. Tadmor and M. Weinfeld (Jerusalem: Magnes, 1986), 117–20; Marc Zvi Brettler (*The Creation of History in Ancient Israel* [London: Routledge, 1995], 2–6) presents the shift from seeking history to seeking ideology; and Garrett Galvin's *David's Successors: Kingship in the Old Testament* ([Collegeville, MN: Liturgical Press, 2016], 1–18), urges an eclectic approach that takes into consideration more than ancient and modern ideology as well as a broad reading of culture.

13   Licht ("Biblical Historicism," 119) correctly observes "We are historicists ourselves." Historiography, as the present author uses the term, can be used in a vastly broader sense than most historians (biblical or otherwise) use it: any literary narrative using real or supposed events in a narrative formation, which includes fiction novels and counter-factual imaginings. Lemche ("Historie," 23–25) correctly notes that the biblical narratives are historiography, creating memory of a past useful for the author's present.

14   Philip R. Davies ("'1 Samuel and the 'Deuteronomistic History,'" in *Is Samuel among the Deuteronomists? Current Views on the Place of Samuel in a Deuteronomistic History*, ed. C. Edenburg and J. Pakkala, AIL 16 [Atlanta: Society of Biblical Literature, 2013], 141) no doubt overstates the case "that the scribes did not care about the past," but he is correct that they could, like Euripides, throw a vial of oil in anywhere (Aristophanes, *Av.* Act 2). Their past was indeed creative and for their own time; it was not intended or immediately useful for modern historians.

15   Graeme Murdock, "Death, Prophecy and Judgement in Transylvania," in *The*

enforcing the 'true religion' has proven useful at times and places including the pivotal reign of Charlemagne.[16] As an exemplar of repentance and adhering to God's law, he has been used as a model for monastic behavior.[17] During the Protestant Reformation in Europe, Josiah became a paradigm for, and religious ancestor of, Protestant rulers and reformers.[18] The hopes for the very model of the true and just king found expression in tract and even drama.[19] Josiah appears even as a proof-text example for allowing the woman, and Protestant, Elizabeth to reign in England.[20] A good

---

Place of the Dead: Death and Remembrance in Late Medieval and Early Modern Europe, ed. B. Gordon and P. Marshall (Cambridge: Cambridge University Press, 2000), 222. See Joseph Powell, *The Death of Good Josiah Lamented: A Sermon Occasioned by the Death of Our Late Most Gracious Soveraign Queen Mary, of Ever Blessed Memory, Preach'd at Balsham in Cambridgshire, March 3, 1695* (London: Three Crowns, 1695). This text was delivered in honor of Mary II, Queen of England, and presents Josiah as the model on which her great wisdom, virtue, piety, and uncommon goodness was properly based in a proper "prince" (5).

16 Mary Alberi, "'Like the Army of God's Camp': Political Theology and Apocalyptic Warfare at Charlemagne's Court," *Viator* 41, no. 2 (2010): 9–10. It might be noted that medieval political philosophy, essentially based on Cicero, noted Moses as a hero-founder who sets out the rules and establishes a way to maintain them, but in such a system Josiah (not specifically noted) would have been an "orator" who is responsible for a well-run society, ensuring justice and maintaining the contract formed by the founder. The population itself must accept the customs and laws. See Vasileios Syros, "Founders and Kings versus Orators: Medieval and Early Modern Views on the Origins of Social Life," *Viator* 42 (2011): 386, 393, 400, 402.

17 Derek Krueger, "The Old Testament and Monasticism," in Magdalina and Nelson, *The Old Testament in Byzantium*, 205–6.

18 Christopher Bradshaw, "David or Josiah? Old Testament Kings as Exemplars in Edwardian Religious Polemic," in *Protestant History and Identity in Sixteenth-Century Europe. Vol. 2: The Later Reformation*, ed. B. Gordon, StASRH (Aldershot: Ashgate, 1996), 77–90; Margaret Aston, *The King's Bedpost: Reformation and Iconography in a Tudor Group Portrait* (Cambridge: Cambridge University Press, 1993), 26–36; R. Gerald Hobbs, "Bucer's Use of King David as Mirror of the Christian Prince," *RRR* 5 (2003): 102–4.

19 The tragedy *Josias*, attributed to Philone (1566), included dramatic choruses who chanted advice to the character Josiah concerning the characteristics Huguenot partisans wished to find in King Charles IX. See Frank Dobbins, "Music in French Theatre of the Late Sixteenth Century," *EMH* 13 (1994): 101; J. S. Street, *French Sacred Drama from Bèze to Corneille: Dramatic Forms and Their Purposes in the Early Modern Theatre* (Cambridge: Cambridge University Press, 1983), 52. However, note that Jeremiah takes center-stage in this Protestant rendition of Josiah. See Samuel Junod, "'Maintenant moi, Jérémie": De l'exposition de Jérémie a l'exploitation de Jérémie,' in *Las paraphrases bibliques aux XVIᵉ et XVIIᵉ siècles: Actes du Colloque de Bordeaux des 22, 23 et 24 septembre 2004*, ed. V. Ferrer and A. Mantero (Geneva: Droz, 2006), 183–87.

20 The model for the Protestant (Anglican) church was grounded not on Rome but the Old Testament, including Josiah, in the theology of Thomas Cranmer. See

sermon could equate the time of Josiah with the time of the Reformation, when superstition, idolatry, and "great pretenders to devotion" needed a good ruler to remove the "rotten men."[21] Josiah provided a perfect example for the suppression of witches as the "Modern Era" commenced.[22] The specifics of idol-smashing and that the book found by Josiah was Deuteronomy became standard understandings of Josiah's story for biblical use by Protestants.[23]

'Reform,' not surprisingly, became the default reference word for Josiah's religious activities, as it remains to this day.[24] In the narrative itself, however, it does not seem to warrant the term 'reform' so much as liquidation of other forms of worship than of Yahweh.[25] But as an example of 'reforming' a supposed purer worship community, Josiah has been seen

---

Joan Lockwood O'Donovan, "The Church of England and the Anglican Communion: A Timely Engagement with the National Church Tradition?," *SJT* 57 (2004): 321. On Elizabeth and Josiah, see John Jewel, "View of a Seditious Bull Sent into Englande, from Pius Quintus of Rome, anno, 1569," in *Works of John Hewel*, ed. J. Ayre (Cambridge: Cambridge University Press, 1850), 4.1153 [text available at: http://anglicanhistory.org/jewel/seditious.html]. As authorities for Elizabeth's right to rule, Jewel cites a series of biblical kings (Moses, Joshua, David, Solomon, Josiah, and Jehoshaphat) before submitting a string of Christian rulers. The Josiah/Elizabeth connection also played out in an anonymous polemical volume entitled *The Reformation of Religion by Josiah, a commendable example for all princes professing the GOSPELL to followe: With a warnige to all faithful and truehearted Subiects, to encourage theire Princes in so happie a course* (1590), cited in Aston, *The King's Bedpost*, 126.

21 As presented in a Long Parliament sermon by Cornelius Burges. See Achsah Guibbory, "Israel and English Protestant Nationalism: 'Fast Sermons' during the English Revolution," in *Early Modern Nationalism and Milton's England*, ed. D. Loewenstein and P. Stevens (Toronto: University of Toronto, 2008), 121.

22 Matthew Michael, "The Prophet, the Witch and the Ghost: Understanding the Parody of Saul as a 'Prophet' and the Purpose of Endor in the Deuteronomistic History," *JSOT* 38 (2014): 339; Stuart Clark, *Thinking with Demons: The Idea of Witchcraft in Early Modern Europe* (Oxford: Oxford University Press, 1997), 567.

23 Marginal notes printed in the Geneva Bible and the Bishops' Bible—Protestant staples—for the narrative of Josiah in 2 Kings stress both of these aspects of Josiah's reign for the good Protestant.

24 Duly noted in Lowell K. Handy, "The Good, Bad, Insignificant, Indispensable King Josiah: A Brief Historical Survey of Josiah Studies in the Church," in *Restoring the First-century Church in the Twenty-first Century: Essays on the Stone-Campbell Restoration Movement in Honor of Don Haymes*, ed. W. Lewis and H. Rollmann, StHCWC (Eugene, OR: Wipf and Stock, 2005), 46.

25 On the dubious nomenclature of 'reform' with Josiah, see James Richard Linville, *Israel in the Book of Kings: The Past as a Project of Social Identity*, JSOTSup 272 (Sheffield: Sheffield Academic, 1998), 23n16. On the restricted intent of Josiah's actions, see Frederick E. Greenspahn, "Deuteronomy and Centralization," *VT* 64 (2014): 230, 232–34, expanding on earlier work by Adam C. Welch.

as a pattern for, say, the American Restoration Movement.²⁶ In the late twentieth- and early twenty-first centuries, Josiah and his story have been offered as prime models for Christians in sub-Saharan Africa: Josiah is a model of a monotheist emerging from polytheism and a loyal follower of God. Josiah's story has even been used as a model for women's political responsibilities.²⁷ Josiah also serves to exemplify the evils of concentrating power (economic, political, cultural) in a centralized despot.²⁸ Then, again, Josiah has been lifted up as an example of a minority affirming its right to its own religion and history in the face of cultural imperialism.²⁹ And, for some, the story has become a model for assertiveness by women in patriarchal cultural and religious establishments.³⁰

The biblical data recorded for Josiah runs the gamut in terms of probability from fairly certain to totally unlikely.³¹ While much of this material is noted throughout the volume, some basic contentions might best be noted at the start.³² I assume the historical reality of a Judahite king

---

26   R. Mark Shipp, "The First Restoration Movement: The Chronicler's Program of Restoration and Churches of Christ Today," *ChrSt* 27 (2015): 27.

27   Caleb O. Ogunkunle, "Josiah's Reform as a Model for Religious and Political Rebranding in Nigeria," *IJOURELS* 2 (2012): 11-12; Jonathan Ola Ojo, "Prophetess Huldah as a Principal Strategist of Josiah's Reforms (2 Kings 22): Lessons for Women in Political and Religious Leadership in Africa," *AJBS* 31 (2013): 132.

28   Shigeyuki Nakanose, *Josiah's Passover: Sociology and the Liberating Bible* (Maryknoll, NY: Orbis, 1993), 91-92; Hieronymus Cruz, "Centralisation of Cult by Josiah: A Biblical Perspective in Relation to Globalisation," *Jeevadhara* 55 (1995): 65-71. Josiah as destroyer of popular/rural religion and culture is no new idea; however, see Ernst Renan, "The History of the People of Israel," in *Studies of Religious History and Criticism*, trans. O. B. Frothingham (New York: Carleton, 1864), 117, 129.

29   Uriah Y. Kim, *Decolonizing Josiah: Toward a Postcolonial Reading of the Deuteronomistic History*, BMW 5 (Sheffield: Sheffield Phoenix, 2005): 241-42.

30   Husazulu Chuzho, "Women as Agents of Transformation," *UBS Journal* 4, no. 1 (2006): 44-45.

31   Several recent studies have concentrated on what is historically probable in the Bible. For Josiah, see, among many, Kitchen, *On the Reliability*, 43; John Van Seters, *In Search of History: Historiography in the Ancient World and the Origins of Biblical History* (New Haven: Yale, 1983), 317-19; Lester L. Grabbe, *Ancient Israel: What Do We Know and How Do We Know It?* (London: T&T Clark, 2007), 204-7; Victor P. Hamilton, *Handbook on the Historical Books: Joshua, Judges, Ruth, Samuel, Kings, Chronicles, Ezra-Nehemiah, Esther* (Grand Rapids: Baker Academic, 2001), 463-68. On Josiah in particular, see Luciano Lepore, "La storicità del 'manifesto' di Giosia," *BeO* 45 (2003): 3-33. Needless to say, these, as with numerous specialized Josianic studies, do not agree on what is historically reliable, what is literary interpretation, and what is literary fiction. Some scholars see in Chronicles a reliable, independent version divorced from Kings. See, for example, H. Neil Richardson, "The Historical Reliability of Chronicles," *JBR* 26 (1958): 12.

32   In my "Josiah as Religious Peg for Persian-Period Jews and Judaism," in

8   *Josiah*

named Josiah; I believe he was neither Joshua nor ruler of any extensive geographical area as displayed in the book of Joshua.³³ With less certitude I assume that Josiah was indeed the son of Amon by Jedidah and grandson of Manasseh.³⁴ It seems highly reasonable to conclude that Josiah tinkered with the cult of Judah (which forms the shaky basis for the 'reform' narratives in Kings and Chronicles, noting duly and significantly that First Esdras sees no need to mention such an event at all);³⁵ the thoroughgoing religious change presented in the Bible never took place in the First Temple period.³⁶ The biblical sources for Josiah are Persian-era narratives at the earliest and no written material can seriously be extracted from these surviving narratives to be posited as deriving from the time of Josiah.³⁷ By extension, Deuteronomy cannot seriously be used as a source for

---

Religion in the Achaemenid Persian Empire: Emerging Judaisms and Trends, ed. D V. Edelman, A. Fitzpatrick-McKinley and P. Guillaume, ORA 17 (Tübingen: Mohr Siebeck, 2016), 73–74, I set out three basic positions merely listed here. I would note at the outset that "monotheism" is a notion I doubt Josiah or any of his peers would have understood, and centralization of cult had to have been somebody's utopian vision, certainly not a successful historical event.

33   Josiah's 'national policies,' whatever they may have been, are not those of the post-exilic authors of Kings and Chronicles (and certainly not the territory of Joshua geography). See Steven Grosby, *Biblical Ideas of Nationality: Ancient and Modern* (Winona Lake, IN: Eisenbrauns, 2002), 95. No "greater Israel" existed under Josiah. See Lester L. Grabbe, *1 & 2 Kings: History and Story in Ancient Israel*, TTCSGOT 5 (London: Bloomsbury T&T Clark, 2017), 73–74.

34   The political situation under Manasseh and Amon makes for fruitful interpretations of the royal marriages in Judah. See Jay A. Wilcoxen, "The Political Background of Jeremiah's Temple Sermon," in *Scripture in History and Theology: Essays in Honor of J. C. Rylaarsdam*, ed. A. L. Merrill and T. W. Overholt, PittTM 17 (Pittsburgh: Pickwick, 1977),153–58; W. Boyd Barrick, "Dynastic Politics, Priestly Succession, and Josiah's Eighth Year," *ZAW* 112 (2000): 566–70.

35   Uehlinger is optimistic about the Kings text reflecting Josianic activity but recognizes that the Josiah narratives are indeed secondary sources that provide no contemporary rationale for a far-reaching "reform,": Christoph Uehlinger, "Was There a Cult Reform under King Josiah? The Case for a Well-grounded Minimum," in *Good Kings and Bad Kings*, ed. L. L. Grabbe, LHBOTS 393; ESHM 5 (London: T&T Clark, 2005), 281, 297, 306.

36   There was certainly no creation of a monotheistic religious region under Josiah. See Christoph Auffarth, "Justice, the King and the Gods: Polytheism and Emerging Monotheism in the Ancient World," in *One God—One Cult—One Nation: Archaeological and Biblical Perspectives*, ed. R. G. Kratz and H. Spiekermann, BZAW 405 (Berlin: de Gruyter, 2010), 445.

37   Stordalen ("Imagined and Forgotten Communities," 191–95) correctly assumes the Josiah story is an imagined past identity (highly selective of remaining Judahites) useful for Persian-period Jerusalem-Samaria arguments. Both Kurt L. Noll ("Was there Doctrinal Dissemination in Early Yahweh Religion?," *BibInt* 16 [2008]: 421) and Lemche ("Historie," 29–30) see the same goal in the text, but date it to the

Josiah, not in religious matters, nor in state centralization,[38] nor in legal procedure.[39] This is not to say there were not active scribes during Josiah's reign;[40] I simply find no reason to assume that the modern world retains any of it (some excavation may at some point recover something, but it is not known as of yet).

As for the historical background to the king, a few items are posited, but since the historical events of that time period are so poorly evident in the archaeological record, these remain conjecture. The major power in the region of Judah at the time of Josiah's ascendancy was Assyria; however, the Judean territory was recognized by both Assyria and Egypt as having been traditionally in the Egyptian sphere[41] (and King Amon's name was no

---

Hellenistic era. In *Hasmonean Realities behind Ezra, Nehemiah, and Chronicles: Archaeological and Historical Perspectives*, AIL 34 (Atlanta: Society of Biblical Literature, 2018), 161–62, Israel Finkelstein argues for a period in the time of the Maccabees on the basis of surviving Hebrew inscriptions, though clearly Hebrew continued to be used throughout the period. Note that the textual transmission does not reflect any sense of an early sacredness to the narratives.

38   Yoshihide Suzuki, "Deuteronomic Reformation in View of the Centralization of the Administration of Justice," *AJBI* 13 (1987): 24, 49.

39   Vast amounts of scholarship have defined Josiah's reign by the legal sections of Deuteronomy: see the small bibliographical selection listed in Rainer Albertz, *A History of Israelite Religion in the Old Testament Period*, trans. J. Bowden, OTL (Louisville: Westminster John Knox, 1994), 1.195–97. From such studies, even more tangential Josiah studies are capable of being invented. See W. Eugene Claburn's "The Fiscal Basis of Josiah's Reforms" (*JBL* 92 [1973]: 11–22) and Philip J. Nel's "Social Justice as Religious Responsibility in Near Easter Religions: Historical Ideal and Ideological Illusion" (*JNSL*, no. 2 [2000]: 149–51), which produce an entire economic world from Deuteronomy and posits it for the king.

40   The beleaguered question of literacy is not terribly relevant here. It should be a given that literacy in Judah had a long history by the end of the seventh century, as effectively surveyed in André Lemaire, "Levantine Literacy ca. 1000–750 BCE," in *Contextualizing Israel's Sacred Writings: Ancient Literacy, Orality, and Literary Production*, ed. B. Schmidt, AIL 22 (Atlanta: Society of Biblical Literature, 2015), 15–23; Nadav Na'aman, "Literacy in the Negev in the Late Monarchical Period," in Schmidt, *Contextualizing Israel's Sacred Writings*, 64–66; and Christopher A. Rollston, "Scribal Curriculum During the First Temple Period: Epigraphic Hebrew and Biblical Evidence," in Schmidt, *Contextualizing Israel's Sacred Writings*, 76–78. Scribes, some priests, and some of the elite were undoubtedly literate, but general literacy is unlikely (see Lowell K. Handy, *Jonah's World: Social Science and the Reading of Prophetic Story*, BibleWorld [London: Equinox, 2007], 117–19, 137–38nn4-6) or basically nonexistent (Noll, "Was there Doctrinal Dissemination in Early Yahweh Religion?," 422). This does not mean non-official literacy was restricted to Jerusalem or Samaria. See Nadav Na'aman, "A Sapiential Composition from Horvat 'Usa," *HeBAI* 2, no. 2 (2013): 221–33.

41   Ernst Axel Knauf, *Die Umwelt des Alten Testaments*, NSKAT 29 (Stuttgart: Katholisches Bibelwerk, 1994), 173.

homonymic fluke).⁴² At the end of Josiah's reign, the power in the region was Egypt.⁴³ There was no Josianic 'empire.'⁴⁴ Josiah was a minor lord (*mlk*) of a minor tract of land on the periphery of a major disputed territory along the east coast of the Mediterranean;⁴⁵ Judah itself was of tangential value to the expanding powers save as a possible source of soldiers, human labor, and possibly foodstuffs (Judah was not a major production

---

42   The name should be connected to the god of Egypt. See John Jarick, "The Stings in the Tales of the Kings of Judah," in *Far from Minimal: Celebrating the Work and Influence of Philip R. Davies*, ed. D. Burns and J. Rogerson, LHBOTS 484 (London: T&T Clark, 2012), 233–34. The name is decidedly significant if provided at birth when, possibly, Assyria was "at its zenith" when Meshullemeth bore Amon to Manasseh. See Wilcoxen, "Political Background," 156.

43   In "Judah in the Seventh Century: From the Aftermath of Sennacherib's Invasion to the Beginning of Jehoiakim's Rebellion," in *Ancient Israel's History: An Introduction to Issues and Sources*, ed. B. T. Arnold and R. S. Hess (Grand Rapids: Baker Academic, 2014), 372–78, Brad E. Kelle surveys the debate on Assyrian/Egyptian overlordship of Judah. Lester L. Grabbe (*Ancient Israel*, 207) evaluates the evidence in favor of Egyptian control. In "The Late Period [664–332 BC]," in *The Oxford History of Ancient Egypt*, ed. I. Shaw (Oxford: Oxford University Press, 2000), 378–81, Alan B. Lloyd describes Egyptian activities well north and east of Judah at the time of Josiah. In "Judean Auxiliaries in Egypt's Wars against Kush," *JAOS* 127 (2007): 513–14, Dan'el Kahn concludes that Josiah must have been an Egyptian vassal no later than 616 BCE, and Judahite soldiers were used by Psamtik I in his assault on Kush. In this he takes Let. Aris. 13 as a historical reference to Psamtik I. The passage has been taken to refer to Psamtik II and to be totally fictitious. See Herbert T. Andrews, "The Letter of Aristeas," APOT 2.96.

44   Megan Bishop Moore and Brad E. Kelle, *Biblical History and Israel's Past: The Changing Study of the Bible and History* (Grand Rapids: Eerdmans, 2011), 320 and n116. Inventive attempts to map Josiah's territory as an empire have, on occasion, extended well north into Syria and south into Egypt. See, for example, Yohanan Aharoni and Michael Avi-Yonah, *The Macmillan Bible Atlas* (New York: Macmillan, 1968), 102. Use of the term 'empire' is based on the notion that it consists of territorial expansion under centralized control of peoples and resources; attempts to redefine the term as a modern innovation should be treated as contemporary political polemic. See the survey in Mario Liverani, *Assyria: The Imperial Mission*, MC 21 (Winona Lake, IN: Eisenbrauns, 2017), 1–9, 240–46.

45   Some general histories have duly noted the essential insignificance of Judah and Israel in their time: "little country in between" (H. G. Wells, *The Outline of History*, Vol. 1: *Prehistory to the Roman Empire*, Barnes & Noble Library of Essential Reading [New York: Macmillan, 1920; repr. New York: Barnes & Noble, 2004], 209) and "modest kingdom" under Solomon (Frank Welsh, *The History of the World: From the Dawn of Humanity to the Modern Age* [London: Quercus, 2011], 40). In *The Fall and Rise of Jerusalem: Judah under Babylonian Rule* (Winona Lake, IN: Eisenbrauns, 2005), 2, 4, Oded Lipschits notes that Assyria "obliterated and annexed" the large, important areas of *eber nari*, meaning for the biblical territories, Israel; Judah was not so considered.

center for anything highly valued in that time or place).⁴⁶ That there were minor fluctuations in the territory of Jerusalem⁴⁷ or Ramat Rahel under Manasseh and Josiah is no doubt true, but a massive expansion movement in any given direction is unlikely.⁴⁸ It is also highly unlikely that Assyria, Egypt, or Babylonia spent much thought on Judah or Jerusalem,⁴⁹ save for the clearly important town of Lachish (which Assyrian reliefs treated as *the* major city of Judah).⁵⁰

Other cultic changes in the ancient Near East have been used for comparative studies of Josiah's cult changes as they appear in Kings: Akhenaton, Nebuchadnezzar I and II, Nabonidus, Tukulti-Ninurta I, Xerxes I,

---

46 Liverani (*Assyria*, 61–64) notes timber and stone as primary materials desired from conquests by Assyria; Judah would not have been a good source for either. Avraham Faust finds late seventh-century remains reflecting a decline in political and economic status from earlier periods. See Avraham Faust, "The Shephelah in the Iron Age: A New Look on the Settlement of Judah," *PEQ* 145 (2013): 214–15.

47 Lipschits (*The Fall and Rise of Jerusalem*, 10) sees Jerusalem established as a central city in the seventh century BCE, as Judah prospers within the Assyrian sphere.

48 The enormous kingdom of Josiah envisioned by, for example, John Bright (*A History of Israel* [Philadelphia: Fortress, 1959], 295), is clearly a fiction; lesser expansions, however, fall within the range of possibility. See Ephraim Stern, *Archaeology of the Land of the Bible: The Assyrian, Babylonian, and Persian Periods (732–332 B.C.E.)*, ABRL (New York: Doubleday, 2001), 134–65. That Josiah controlled territory to the Mediterranean, including the tiny outpost of Mezad Hashavyahu (140–42), seems highly unlikely. The still-popular notion that Josiah's 'empire' included Megiddo, a fortress he needed to defend, is unrealistic. See Jacob Milgrom, "Did Josiah Control Megiddo?" *Beit Mikrah* 16 (1971): 26–27 [Hebrew]; Kelle, "Judah in the Seventh Century," 375.

49 This, to be quite honest, means that some reform work by Josiah could have been carried out after the reigns of Psamtik I and Ashurbanipal. This assumes Neco did not care what Josiah did with the cult and Sin-shar-ish-kun being elsewhere involved. See Grabbe, *1 & 2 Kings*, 75.

50 For over a century it has been known that Assyria deemed Lachish a suitable conquest to display Assyrian might. Its use in the murals in Sennacherib's Nineveh palace for victories in the 'west' suggests it sufficed as the major city of Judah not only for Assyria, but for others as well, since its display was clearly to impress the viewer with Assyrian power. See further Julian Reade, *Assyrian Sculpture* (Cambridge, MA: Harvard University Press, 1983), 46–52. It may safely be assumed that Lachish also had a sanctuary dedicated to Yahweh (and perhaps other deities). See David Ussishkin, *The Conquest of Lachish by Sennacherib* (Tel Aviv: Tel Aviv University Press, 1982), 105; Ephraim Stern, "From Many Gods to the One God: The Archaeological Evidence," in Kratz and Spiekermann, *One God—One Cult—One Nation*, 396–67. Archaeology of its defenses suggests it was *the* most important Judean town. On this, see Sandra Richter, "Eighth-Century Issues: The World of Jeroboam II, the Fall of Samaria, and the Reign of Hezekiah," in Arnold and Hess, *Ancient Israel's History*, 345–49.

even Zarathustra, among others.⁵¹ However, sufficient data does not survive from any of these events to understand their motivation, implementation, or consequences. Significant studies have been devoted to these 'cult reforms' that they will not be considered here.⁵² Perhaps the most commonly cited parallel is to the restoration of the cult of Sin by Nabonidus; however, Nabonidus was clearly not making much of a change in the Neo-Babylonian religious traditions and was certainly not reducing the pantheon or attempting to centralize religious cultic activity.⁵³ Moreover, texts sponsored by Nabonidus and the history behind them are not necessarily compatible.⁵⁴ A heavy reliance on the Cyrus Cylinder for the religious activities of either Nabonidus or Cyrus has proven unreliable.⁵⁵ Akhenaten and Zarathustra have both been seen as promoting a single deity; there are decided problems with both figures and their religious proclivities.⁵⁶

---

51   As I did in my dissertation: Lowell K. Handy, "A Realignment in Heaven: An Investigation into the Ideology of the Josianic Reform" (PhD diss., University of Chicago, 1987), 290–308, 327–33; idem, "Historical Probability," 264–74. See also Reinhard G. Kratz, "The Idea of Cultic Centralization and Its Supposed Ancient Near Eastern Analogies," in Kratz and Spiekermann, *One God—One Cult—One Nation*, 130–36; Hanspeter Schaudig, "Cult Centralization in the Ancient Near East? Conceptions of the Ideal Capital in the Ancient Near East," in Kratz and Spiekermann, *One God—One Cult—One Nation*, 147–63.

52   This is not to say that there are not significant parallels to biblical texts in these religious changes. See J. J. M. Roberts, "Nebuchadnezzar I's Elamite Crisis in Theological Perspective," in *Essays on the Ancient Near East in Memory of Jacob Joel Finkelstein*, ed. M. de Jong Ellis, MCAAS 19 (Hamden, CT: Archon Books, 1977), 184–87.

53   From voluminous studies on Nabonidus, e.g., Paul-Alain Beaulieu, *The Reign of Nabonidus, King of Babylon 556–539 B.C.*, YNER 10 (New Haven: Yale University Press, 1989), 43–65; idem, "Nabonidus the Mad King: A Reconsideration of His Steles from Harran and Babylon," in *Representations of Political Power: Case Histories from Times of Change and Dissolving Order in the Ancient Near East*, ed. M. Heinz and M. H. Feldman (Winona Lake, IN: Eisenbrauns, 2007), 148–63; Alexa Bartelmus and Jon Taylor, "Collecting and Connecting History: Nabonidus and the Kassite Rebuilding of the E(ul)maš of (Ištar)-Annunitu in Sippar-Annunitu," *JCS* 66 (2014): 113–28.

54   Bartelmus and Taylor, "Collecting and Connecting History," 118, 125.

55   Amélie Kuhrt, "Cyrus the Great of Persia: Images and Realities," in Heinz and Feldman, *Representations of Political Power*, 171–72, 180–81.

56   For Akhenaten, see Donald B. Redford, *Akhenaten: The Heretic King* (Princeton: Princeton University Press, 1984), 59, 172; Jan Assmann, Ägypten-Theologie und Frömigkeit einer frühen Hochkultur (Stuttgart: Kohlhammer, 1984), 233–39; Emily Teeter, *Religion and Ritual in Ancient Egypt* (Cambridge: Cambridge University Press, 2011), 182–96. Aten shared its divinity with the king, something Josiah, in the biblical texts, did not; however, Akhenaten certainly destroyed rival temples. For Zarathustra, see William W. Malandra, *An Introduction to Ancient Iranian Religion: Readings from the Avesta and the Achaemenid Inscriptions* (Minneapolis: University of Minnesota

Josiah's fame as a 'conservative' religious ruler is legitimate in so far as 'conservative,' politically speaking, is a post-Josiah literary invented memory for the last semi-independent king of Judah.[57] The historical narrative in which Josiah's story is embedded must be viewed as an attempt to create a memory of a distant past that held significance for the present.[58] Myth, legend, history, and creative imagination combined to produce a useable past for the Persian Yehud community.[59] The effort has had parallels in the modern world that have been much easier to reconstruct.[60] The rise of the *Kojiki* to the status of a 'sacred text' promoting a Japan essentially created by a single ruler Jimmu [read for the Hebrew Bible: David] has been adequately described as a series of adaptations made of a 712 CE text.[61] The evolution in the importance of the document can be correlated to a series of known personalities. Ō no Yasumaro (†723) was the compiler of remembrances recited by Hieda no Are forming the narrative. This text was made a central aspect of Japanese ethnocentrism by the renowned Japanese scholar Motoori Norinaga (1730–1801). In turn the tradition was given an authoritative textual format by Kinoshita Iwao (1894–1980). Finally, the *Kojiki* was romanticized for the 'West' by Lafcadio Hearn (1850–1904), an

---

Press, 1983), 16–23; Prods Oktor Skjærvø, "Zarathustra: A Revolutionary Monotheist?" in *Reconsidering the Concept of Revolutionary Monotheism*, ed. B. Pongratz-Leisten (Winona Lake, IN: Eisenbrauns, 2011), 317–37. Zarathustra, whose dates and even existence are debated, was at best a dualist and appears to have remained a polytheist; he certainly did not close down regional cultic sites.

57 However, the religious actions accredited to him in Kings and Chronicles do not reflect 'conservative' behavior, and Deuteronomy is not Josiah's game-plan. Thus, attempts to define Josiah as a conservative reactionary are more inventive than insightful. See Ferdinand E. Deist, "Conservative Rebound in Deuteronomy: A Case Study in Social Values," *JNSL* 22 (1996): 18, 28, though note Deist assumes Deuteronomy as Josiah's blue-print and as an older functioning legal document developed in the class-struggle of the Omrides (19).

58 "...take control of the interpretation of tradition" (Deist, "Conservative Rebound," 28).

59 Linville, *Israel in the Book of Kings*, 163–64. See also Niels Peter Lemche, "Did a Reform Like Josiah's Happen?" in *The Historian and the Bible: Essays in Honour of Lester L. Grabbe*, ed. P. R. Davies and D. V. Edelman, LHBOTS 530 (New York: T&T Clark, 2010), 17–18. Lemche posits a Hellenistic origin to the Josiah narrative.

60 Klaus Antoni, "Creating a Sacred Narrative: *Kojiki* Studies and Shinto Nationalism," *JapanRel* 36 (2011): 3–30. A comparative study of the "ancient histories" envisioned for centralized Meiji Japan and centralized Judah appeared in Marvin A. Sweeney, *The Origins of Kingship in Israel and Japan: A Comparative Analysis*, ed. J. M. Asgeirsson, OPIAC 33 (Claremont: Institute for Antiquity and Christianity, 1995).

61 See Antoni, "Creating a Sacred Narrative," 5, 12, 18, 21, 24. On the centrality of the *Kojiki* for the Japanese identity movement as an academic enterprise, see John Breen and Mark Teeuwen, *A New History of Shinto*, BBHR (Chichester: Wiley-Blackwell, 2010), 60–65.

American expatriate newsman in Japan, who passed on the then current Meiji Era understanding of the narrative. Like the Josiah narrative, the *Kojiki* was envisioned by a Japan that sought to stand out from other cultures and to reconstruct a cultic-religious-political state uniquely and divinely Japanese. In origin and in later rereading, the *Kojiki* was useful for centralized political and cultic leaders to promote antiquity and a conservatism that did not in fact relate to anything that had existed.[62] The major difference for Josiah's narratives is that the construction of the narrative sought to create a conservatism that had not existed, while inventing a *new*, never existing before, 'old' centralized cultic-religious-political system (Josiah's independent Judah) useful for a later period (Yehud *and* Hasmonaean Judah). Would there were such a wealth of information about Josiah and his narratives! However, it is worth noting that even with 'modern' centralized planning and effort, Meiji Japan could neither succeed in reducing the pantheon to those mentioned in the *Kojiki* nor in restricting ritual to 'ancient Japanese' rites of record.[63] Meiji Japan sought to impress upon its citizens the centrality, divinity, and authority of the Emperor.[64]

The figure of King Josiah has been, and can be, read in many ways. I tend to be suspicious of historiographical renditions as accurate representations of past events. Ancient texts used by modern scholars for, and

---

[62] Joseph M. Kitakawa, in a conversation with the author in the mid-1980s, suggested that the use of the *Kojiki* in Japan may well have been, like many other movements in the Meiji Period, an attempt to replicate western traditions, making Josiah's narrative indirectly the cause for the promotion of a parallel authority in Japan thereby investing in created ancient and lost traditions.

[63] The imposition of State Shinto was neither easy nor successful; the Japanese populace could be made to go through the rituals, but traditional practices continued unabated as political authorities continually revamped attempts to control 'tradition' to their purposes. See Trent Maxey, "The Crisis of 'Conversion' and Search for National Doctrine in Early Japan," in *Converting Cultures: Religion, Ideology and Transformations of Modernity*, ed. D. Washburn and A. K. Reinhart, SSA 14 (Leiden: Brill, 2007), 5–25; Helen Hardacre, *Shinto and the State, 1868–1988*, StCS (Princeton: Princeton University Press, 1989), 74, 101–2.

[64] I would hasten to note that a comparative study of Meiji Japan with biblical Josiah is useful for raising questions, but contexts preclude easy parallels. The interesting observation of Jewish Torah arks and Shinto/Buddhist household shrines does suggest a divine status for Torah in Jewish tradition, which would be connected to the Josiah narratives but not to the time of Josiah. See Jeffrey H. Tigay, "The Torah Scroll and God's Presence," in *Built by Wisdom, Established by Understanding: Essays on Biblical and Near Eastern Literature in Honor of Adele Berlin*, ed. M. L. Grossman (Bethesda: University Press of Maryland, 2013), 323–25. As for the reconstruction from an ancient source timely discovered, there is even a Japanese counterpoint for that; see Ola Wikander, "Finding Indra, Finding Torah: The Story of Shibamata Taishakuten and Josiah's Renovation," *SEÅ* 80 (2015): 71–72.

written about, the past have purposes beyond historical verisimilitude. Assigning ancient contemporary status for existing textual items to the reign of Josiah is done as a matter of opinion rather than as a demonstrable fact. Rewriting extant texts in a manner to recover earlier versions that would be more helpful in recovering Josiah's history are, at the very best, dubious undertakings.[65] It is impossible to recover the mental state of the scribes or those for whom they wrote, but any guesses, academic or otherwise, might have some insight. Just remember that outside necromancy (which Josiah in theory abolished), neither you nor I can converse with the authors. However, I find the plurality of approaches and conclusions by modern authors not only interesting but significant. If a scholar wishes to believe all of the biblical stories of Josiah and study them as historical verity, I wish her well; however, if one wishes to reject the biblical stories out-of-hand, I wish him well also. Cogent observations continue to be made from both camps and from the spectrum between. I would simply note that in the long history of reading Josiah, the repetition of 'discoveries' continues apace; this work would hope to provide a glimpse into the past of the field for those engaged in it and for laity interested in texts about King Josiah.

I would end this introduction with a note about my guess as to the early scribe's intentions. The Josiah narratives clearly set out to reduce, if not remove altogether, the importance of the king. Often represented as a centralization of control of politics, economics, and religion within Judah in the figure of Josiah,[66] the text removes authority from Josiah to a scroll that predates him and supersedes him. The narratives emphasize that Josiah is not divine; he takes orders from Yahweh. Moreover, Josiah is not in command; he is subservient to ancient rules (they are not elaborated upon save that no god but Yahweh is to be worshiped in Judah and Israel). Josiah cannot make up rules or change the *proper* religious world. The center that is demanded by the narrative is not in the palace but in the temple; it centralizes power and authority, but it is the deity not the king who has this authority. Kings can obey the God or disobey the God, but

---

65 Reconstructing "earlier" forms of texts is very common in biblical studies, but in Assyriology, where reuse of earlier material is common enough, it has been shown that the redaction critical methods of biblical scholars to "write backwards" do not conform to known ancient practices. See Steven W. Holloway, "Sargon II and His Redactors Repair Eanna of Uruk," *BR* 43 (1998): 27–48; JoAnn Scurlock, "Sins of Omission or Commission or What Can Assyrian Scribes Teach Us about the Bible as an Edited Book" (paper presented at the Spring Meeting of the Chicago Society of Biblical Research, Chicago, 7 April 2018).

66 Albert Ten Eyck Olmstead, "The Reform of Josiah and Its Secular Aspects," *AHR* 20 (1915): 568–69; Claburn, "Fiscal Basis," 14; Roger S. Nam, *Portrayals of Economic Exchange in the Book of Kings*, BibIntS 112 (Leiden: Brill, 2012), 137, 141.

they cannot replace the deity either by themselves or by another deity. Indeed, the king and the monarchy itself can be removed, but the temple and the reign of Yahweh will continue. This is the tale of Josiah: a transition from an independent monarchy to a province without a king at all.[67]

---

[67] Yoshihide Suzuki, "A New Aspect on Occupation Policy by King Josiah," *AJBI* 18 (1992): 59–61, though assuming Deuteronomy as the scroll found by Josiah nonetheless correctly reads the Josiah story as replacing the Davidic kings as an authority with a greater authority beyond their manipulation.

CHAPTER ONE
JOSIAH WAS DEAD TO BEGIN WITH

For a king of Judah with a particularly cult-centered narrative, Josiah's biblical text deals with a lot of death. There are, of course, the usual stereotypical, literary opening statements (2 Kgs 21:26–22:1//2 Chr 33:25–34:1); however, the closing of Josiah's reign does not provide stereotypical death and succession pericopes. The first introduction to Josiah in Kings (1 Kgs 13:2), in a perfectly fine prophetic speech, presents Josiah as a future, predicted slaughterer of priests.[1] The prophet making this prognostication is thereafter killed by a lion for disobeying Yahweh's directions (1 Kgs 13:21–26). The burial of the man of God from Judah is then described (1 Kgs 13:29–31) so that, in the reign of Josiah, the memorial tomb still existing for the man of God from Judah could be recognized and honored by Josiah (2 Kgs 23:16–18).[2] Huldah's prophecy includes threats against all of Judah (2 Kgs 22:16–17; 2 Chr 34:24–25) that probably imply death but do not directly promise death, save for Josiah himself (2 Kgs 22:20; 2 Chr

---

1   It is rather immaterial to the Josiah narrative whether or not the name Josiah (1 Kgs 13:2) was added to an earlier version of the prophetic story. It is unlikely that the narrative about the prophet from Judah would have appeared in Kings without the Josianic reference to it in 2 Kgs 23:16–18. In *1 Kings: with an Introduction to Historical Literature*, FOTL 9 (Grand Rapids: Eerdmans, 1984), 145, Burke O. Long notes the problem of dating this legendary material as early as, or as part of, the Deuteronomistic History. See also Terence E. Fretheim, *First and Second Kings*, WBC (Louisville: Westminster John Knox, 1999), 77–78; Walter Brueggemann, *1 & 2 Kings*, SHBC 8 (Macon, GA: Smyth & Helwys, 2000), 167–68. The standard explanation for naming Josiah has been that the narrative concerning the man of God, prophet from Judah, is an "early" prophetic legend into which the king's name has been inserted (as argued by John Gray, *I & II Kings: A Commentary*, 2nd ed., OTL [Philadelphia: Westminster, 1970], 325–26), or that an original prophecy has had Josiah's name inserted at a much later time (see Pedro Zamora García, *Reyes I: La fuerza de la narración*, NBEH [Estella: Verbo Divino, 2011], 266–67). There is no literary reason for removing the name Josiah from the prophecy since it forms a literary formula for emphasizing an aspect of the speech.

2   Both Fretheim (*First and Second Kings*, 78) and Brueggemann (*1 & 2 Kings*, 168) emphasize the importance of the relation of the two passages in Kings as a whole. On the "conjectural" nature of Deuteronomic redactions of these tales, see Nakanose, *Josiah's Passover*, 26–27.

34:28). Then, in the portrayal of the overthrow of the religious tradition, there is reference (probably) to the execution/sacrifice of certain priests and certainly to ritual dealings with the dead relating to the bones on the altars (2 Kgs 23:5, 8, 16 [with reference to 1 Kgs 13:2]; 2 Chr 34:5). The memory of Josiah after his death rounds out this litany of mortality in the reign of a king who was recorded as fighting no battles prior to his death (a military event not recorded in Kings, but appearing in Chronicles and First Esdras).

The narrative of Josiah properly begins with an assassination.[3] He comes to the throne through the palace murder carried out by "servants/slaves" of King Amon (2 Kgs 21:23; 2 Chr 33:24).[4] There is no reason given for this regicide, allowing for no end of speculation. Not surprisingly, the rendition of Josiah's reign in terms of a religious reformation has led to descriptions of royal family infighting between traditionalists (the exact meaning of which is malleable) and reformers (planners, backers, and implementers of Josiah's 'reform'), often enough simultaneously related to an international alliance with Egypt or Assyria, leading to the removal of King Amon.[5] Internal struggles for the throne, family rivalry, political control of the area of Judah, an independence movement in Jerusalem, and religious definition have all been proposed as explanations of the infighting.[6] There is no reason to assume the murder was related to

---

3   It is not quite correct that Josiah's story is 'framed' with death narratives (Amon's and Josiah's) since Josiah's memory clearly ends the story. However, both death-dealing texts are important, significant literary phases of Josiah's biblical portrayal. See Kim, *Decolonizing Josiah*, 182, 217. However, Kim's sense of liminality permeating Josiah's narrative seems an astute observation; I would just argue that it was as valid an observation for the Persian Empire or under the Seleucids, if not more so.

4   In Kings, this death event appears as a coda for Josiah's life; it is interesting that Ristau does not include it among the "palls" that prefigure Josiah's sad end, since it would appear to fit well into his list of ominous precursors. See Kenneth A. Ristau, "Reading and Rereading Josiah: The Chronicler's Representation of Josiah for the Postexilic Community," in *Community Identity in Judean Historiography: Biblical and Comparative Perspectives*, ed. G. N. Knoppers and K. A. Ristau (Winona Lake, IN: Eisenbrauns, 2009) 224–47.

5   In "The Historical Background of the Assassination of Amon," *IEJ* 3 (1953): 26–29, Abraham Malamat conveys the lack of information in the biblical texts and the theoretical connection to Egypt; idem, "The Twilight of Judah: In the Egyptian-Babylonian Maelstrom," in *Congress Volume: Edinburgh 1974*, ed. G. W. Anderson et al., VTSup 28 (Leiden: Brill, 1975), 126; Wilcoxen, "Political Background," 153–58.

6   See surveys in Gösta W. Ahlström, *The History of Ancient Palestine from the Palaeolithic Period to Alexander's Conquest*, ed. D. V. Edelman, JSOTSup 146 (Sheffield: JSOT Press, 1993), 739–40; J. Maxwell Miller and John H. Hayes, *A History of Ancient Israel and Judah*, 2nd ed. (Louisville: Westminster John Knox, 2006), 437.

any religious adaptations that appear in the biblical story of Josiah.[7] Nor is it clear that the assassination was even popular within royal circles; the number of court conspirators is as ambiguous as the cause for conspiracy itself. One thing is quite clear, however: this was not an attempt to remove and replace the existing monarchical status quo. Josiah's staff appears to be retained from the scribes, priests, and courtiers already in place and, according to the text, Josiah himself is the rightful heir to Amon and the Davidic lineage.

According to the narrative (2 Kgs 21:24), Josiah's backers immediately slew the conspirators. There is no notion supplied here that there was any sort of legal function related to this enforcement of 'justice.' Apparently, the "people of the land" were neither opposed to Amon nor the Davidic lineage as it had been for the past generation. There should be no arguments made that somehow this was a popular revolt since the assassins were court people and the murder took place in the "house" of Amon.[8] Given that there is no relation of a civil war, or any description of general conflict at all, the "people of the land" are here seen as supporting their king, revenging his death on those who committed the homicide, and restoring the monarchy with its rightful heir.[9] The phrase "people of the land" has provided much debate among scholars over the years,[10] but not

7 A religious purpose for the assassination has long had its promoters. George Sale (*An Universal History from the Earliest Account of Time to the Present* [Dublin: George Franklin, 1744], 1.841) assumes Amon was young enough only to have known Manasseh's reformed rule and so was not continuing the religious cult he had grown up with, but was reverting to the religion of his father's early reign. A religious motive continues to appear among scholars: see Bustenay Oded, "Judah and the Exile," in *Israelite and Judaean History*, ed. John H. Hayes and J. Maxwell Miller, OTL (Philadelphia: Westminster, 1977), 456. In *First and Second Kings*, NCBC 9 (Collegeville, MN: Liturgical Press, 2010), 156, Alice L. Laffey leaves the cause of the murder unclear while suggesting the Deuteronomistic author inferred a religious motivation.

8 Nor is there reason to assume there was a historical basis for a popular uprising against the assassins as posited by Nakanose, *Josiah's Passover*, 71–72.

9 As the narrative stands, this regicide cannot be twisted into a popular uprising by the populace or a political coup against kings in general. Nor do the phrases used for the murderers and the murderers of the murderers imply definable political positions, even though scholarly imagination may attempt to show that they do (see Brueggemann, *1 & 2 Kings*, 535–36). Nor do they provide modern political reconstructions a motive for these events. See Steven W. Holloway, "Smart Mobs, Bad Crowds, Godly People and Dead Priests: Crowd Symbols in the Josianic Narrative and Some Mesopotamian Parallels," *BR* 51 (2006): 49–50. Holloway sees Assyrian control at work. See also Richard D. Nelson's *Historical Roots of the Old Testament (1200–63 BCE)*, BibEnc 13 (Atlanta: Society of Biblical Literature, 2014), 153, which sees nationalists opposing Assyrian control.

10 Joseph P. Healey ("Am ha'areṣ," *ABD* 1.168–69) provides a succinct survey of the debate. The observation that the Bible uses the phrase in various ambiguous

too much specificity should be attached to it in the Amon-Josiah narrative.[11] It is a literary/propagandistic designation for the acceptance of the populace for the legitimacy of the new king and has its ideological counterpart in Egypt, as well as a parallel phrase in Akkadian royal ideology (*niše mat aššur*).[12] The use of the phrase should not be taken as evidence for any actual popular backing by the populace; it is a political trope only. It might suggest a certain amount of unease with the manner in which the ruler has attained the throne or the right of said king to hold the position.[13] Moreover, the courtiers and priests that are shown in Josiah's court are an apparent continuation of those of the court of Manasseh and Amon.[14] So, unlike almost all other Judahite kings presented in the book of Kings, Josiah enters his reign with multiple violent deaths.

This has its counterpart in Josiah's violent end. The narratives of Josiah's death in the biblical texts are a fascinating study of retouching a written tradition.[15] Perhaps, however, it is more interesting to ask why Josiah's

---

manners holds true. See John Tracy Thames, Jr., "A New Discussion of the Meaning of the phrase '*am ha'ares* in the Hebrew Bible," *JBL* 130 (2011): 109–10. In 2 Kgs 21:24, "people of the land" is not an expression for any particular group or party, but the theological/political notion that kings are enthroned and dethroned by the gods and the "people of the land." For biblical monarchy, see Geoffrey P. Miller, *The Ways of a King: Legal and Political Ideas in the Bible*, JAJSup 7 (Göttingen: Vandenhoeck & Ruprecht, 2011), 252. Further attempts to define the group that put Josiah on the throne would appear to be a hopeless endeavor.

11 There was, of course, much written about these "people of the land" in rabbinic literature, but this cannot be used to argue backward into the middle of the first millennium BCE. For rabbinic use of the term, see Sigalit Ben-Zion, *A Roadmap to the Heavens: An Anthropological Study of Hegemony among Priests, Sages, and Laymen*, JJL (Boston: Academic Studies, 2009).

12 Handy, "A Realignment in Heaven," 282n2. For Egypt, see Donald Redford, "Some Observations on the Traditions Surrounding 'Israel in Egypt,'" in *Judah and the Judeans in the Achaemenid Period: Negotiating Identity in an International Context*, ed. O. Lipschits, G. N. Knoppers, and M. Oemeng (Winona Lake, IN: Eisenbrauns, 2011), 281–82.

13 Handy, "A Realignment in Heaven," 282; the survey of Mesopotamian examples in Holloway, "Smart Mobs," 28–35, and for applicability in the case of Josiah (35).

14 As noted by Heltzer, "Some Questions," 105–6. The continuation of the court may well have led earlier scholars to the conclusion that these were a faction in "the nation's leadership." See Aharon Oppenheimer, *The 'Am Ha-Aretz: A Study in the Social History of the Jewish People in the Hellenistic-Roman Period*, trans. I. H. Levine, ALGHJ 8 (Leiden: Brill, 1977), 10; Abraham Malamat, "The Last Kings of Judah and the Fall of Jerusalem: An Historical-Chronological Study," *IEJ* 18 (1968): 140.

15 It is assumed here that the various renditions of Josiah's death were written using the sequence: Kings, Chronicles, First Esdras, midrash. Aside from midrash, it is certainly possible that any given reader may not have read the other texts, these being individual scrolls. See further Raymond E. Person, Jr., *The Deuteronomic History*

death is recorded in narrative form at all; it appears in variant forms in Kings, Chronicles, First Esdras, and, interestingly enough, in a narrative rendition in Midrash Rabbah Deuteronomy.[16] The actual death of Judahite rulers is not a standard topic in Kings. The usual reign ends simply with a variation on the bracket notation that the king died and was buried.[17] The particulars of the death are seldom recorded.[18]

There are exceptions, and it is to these exceptions that Josiah belongs. All seven of the narratives concerning Judean rulers' deaths entail homicide. Unlike the northern kingdom's narratives, however, the historiography of Judah does not record a single instance of the assassin of a sitting ruler taking the throne.[19] While Israel appears in the narrative of Kings as a continuing cycle of would-be-dynasty overthrown by would-be dynasty, Judah [one is tempted to write: miraculously] remains the single Davidic dynasty presented as having been preserved in a straight, unbroken

---

and the Book of Chronicles: Scribal Works in an Oral World, AIL 6 (Atlanta: Society of Biblical Literature, 2010), 126.

16 The variations on the story have been admirably discussed several times. See Adam C. Welch, "The Death of Josiah," ZAW 43 (1925): 255–60; Zipora Talshir, "The Three Deaths of Josiah and the State of Biblical Historiography (2 Kings xxiii 29–30, 2 Chronicles xxxv 20–25, 1 Esdras I 23–31)," VT 46 (1996): 213–36; Steve Delamarter, "The Death of Josiah in Scripture and Tradition: Wrestling with the Problems of Evil," VT 54 (2004): 29–60. With more specificity, see Leslie J. Hoppe, "The Death of Josiah and the Meaning of Deuteronomy," SBFLA 48 (1998): 31–47. Also, Michael Avioz, "What Happened at Megiddo? Josiah's Death as Described in the Book of Kings," BN 142 (2009): 5–11; Joseph Rabbinowitz, trans., Midrash Rabbah: Deuteronomy, 3rd ed. (London: Soncino, 1983), 142–43. The midrash combines biblical text, Talmudic traditions, and an independent pericope to explain Josiah's death as righteous.

17 Matthew J. Suriano, The Politics of Dead Kings, FAT 2.48 (Tübingen: Mohr Siebeck, 2010), 22–50, 90 (on Josiah's lack of formula), provides a useful and cogent survey of the scholarship on these passages.

18 Seven of twenty-one rulers have narratives concerning their deaths recorded for Judah from Rehoboam through Gedaliah. Five of these are assassinations: Athaliah, Jehoash, Amaziah, Amon, and Gedaliah. For the Israelite rulers there are ten death narratives for twenty rulers from Jeroboam through Hoshea. Seven of these are assassinations; however, it is of interest that five of these Israelite deaths are predicted by prophetic statements.

19 However much other death she may be presented as having caused, Athaliah (2 Kgs 11:1–3), who comes to the throne through assassination (but not by her own hand), would be an exception were it not for the literary convention that she was never really a ruler of Judah; historical probability would suggest she was, but the historiography needs to avoid her as ever having been the Judahite ruler because she was not of the Davidic line. So, a wee babe in direct line appears hidden away to be the real descendant all the time she rules. Probability suggests the direct royal lineage of David was broken at this point: Lowell K. Handy, "Speaking of Babies in the Temple," PEGLAMBS 8 (1988): 162–63.

genealogical lineage. Josiah's story is the sole narrative to be related to a prophetic prediction of the death of a specific particular sitting ruler of Judah, a narrative format common in stories of the northern kingdom.[20] Josiah's narrative in several ways parallels that of Ahaziah's recorded in 2 Kgs 9:27-28, not the least of which is that both deaths are related to prophetic pronouncements and are the sole examples of prophetic references to reigning rulers' deaths in the Judean realm in Kings. True, Ahaziah is not specifically addressed in Elisha's missive, sent via messenger (a "son of the prophets") to Jehu in 2 Kgs 9:3-10, but Jehu's command in v. 27 connects the death of Ahaziah to the prophetic command to destroy the entire "house of Ahab." It is also worth noting that Elisha does not deliver this message from Yahweh directly to the person for whom it is intended, Jehu, but to the intermediate son of the prophets who will deliver the message as though directly from Yahweh, beginning with the stock phrase: "Thus says Yahweh...". In a similar manner, Huldah delivers the message from God not to Josiah, but to his delegation, who, in turn, we are led to suppose (2 Kgs 22:20) delivers it verbatim to the king. She, too, begins with "Thus says Yahweh..." but then prefaces the actual message to Josiah with a brief statement made by Yahweh to her. As for the prophetic pronouncements delivered for these two Judahite kings, Josiah's is directed to him and delivered to him while Ahaziah's only tangentially refers to him and is directed to Jehu, who is to kill the house of Ahab, Ahaziah included.

The prophetic proclamations concerning the deaths of both Ahaziah and Josiah are not recorded as a preface to the deaths as recorded, but are divided from the death narratives by intervening stories about the kings' lives. In both cases the death story itself is quite short. Essentially, they are the same length and appear in the same literary format: Ahaziah's (2 Kgs 9:27-28) consists of four short sentences, while Josiah's consists of two compound sentences (2 Kgs 23:29-30a).[21] This said, it is interesting that these two Judahite kings happen to be in Israelite territory when they die. Ahaziah had gone to the aid of his in-law, Joram, in a military capacity in the latter's war with Aram. Josiah had set out to "meet" Pharaoh Neco, the reason for which the text leaves unstated. In the story of Ahaziah, it is made very clear that the Judahite king is not only in Israel—clearly foreign territory—but has allied himself both politically and religiously with Israel

---

20   Prophetic death notices are recorded specifically for Nadab (1 Kgs 14:6-14; 15:27-28), Elah (1 Kgs 16:1-4, 9-10), Ahab (1 Kgs 22:17, 29-38), Joram (2 Kgs 9:1-10, 14-27), and Zechariah (2 Kgs 15:12).

21   Thirty-six and twenty-three words, respectively. In both cases, the prophetic statements that include the reference to the impending deaths are much longer than the death narratives, though the prophetic statements both include more than the announcement of the ruler's death.

so as to make his death in the northern kingdom at the hand of Yahweh's anointed, Jehu, a theologically significant event. Josiah's death in Israel provides a much more confusing scene because he has consistently been presented in Kings as the anti-Israelite religious ruler of Judah, and no political alliances with any foreign powers, great or small, are recorded of him. While Ahaziah is in war mode in the story of his reign and, therefore, rationally dies in a chariot, the text concerning Josiah merely states that he is going to "meet" Neco. Whether this is as ally, subordinate, or enemy is not stated, and the text has been interpreted in all ways.[22] However, the historiographical story makes no mention of warfare at all, so Josiah's military death appears more like a parallel to Ahaziah's death than anything related to the story having been told of Josiah in his own narrative. In Kings, Ahaziah is killed in his chariot by an arrow shot by the soldiers of Jehu as Ahaziah seeks to escape the coup.[23] While this looks surprisingly like Second Chronicle's rendition of the death event of Josiah (2 Chr 35:23–24), the author of Kings renders a distinctly shorter and less explicit version of the king's demise. In both cases, the death of the king is ordered by a foreign ruler, takes place near Megiddo, the corpse is transferred to Jerusalem, and the king is buried.[24] In many a translation, Ahaziah's chariot

---

22 Early modern scholars thought Josiah might have been allied with Assyria and may, therefore, have been going out to fight Neco. See, for example, Samuel Kinns, *Graven in the Rock: or, The Historical Accuracy of the Bible Confirmed by Reference to the Assyrian and Egyptian Monuments in the British Museum and Elsewhere* (London: Cassell, 1891), 615; Ira Maurice Price, Ovid R. Sellers, and E. Leslie Carlson, *The Monuments and the Old Testament: Light from the Near East on the Scriptures*, rev. ed. (Philadelphia: Judson, 1958), 45 [1st ed. 1899]; Arthur Penrhyn Stanley, *Lectures on the History of the Jewish Church*, Vol. 2: *Samuel to the Captivity*, new ed. (New York: Scribner's Sons, 1901), 435. Later, it was generally assumed that Josiah was going out with an army to join Neco in an attack on Assyria until the discovery, translation, and publication of the "Babylonian Chronicle" (C. J. Gadd, *The Fall of Nineveh* [London: British Museum, 1923]), wherein it was recorded that Egypt was allied with Assyria. Subsequently, it was assumed that Josiah must have been going out to stop Neco from aiding Assyria in accordance with the stories of the Chronicler and First Esdras, or at least to be defending Judah from an Egyptian encroachment. See Charles F. Pfeiffer, *Old Testament History* (Grand Rapids: Baker Books, 1973), 343; Shimon Bakon, "Egypt: The Nemesis of Israel and Judah," *JBQ* 40 (2012): 13. Finally, Nadav Na'aman ("Josiah and the Kingdom of Judah," in Grabbe, *Good Kings and Bad Kings*, 227–29, 232) posits that Josiah owed fealty or tribute to Neco and failed to comply, but notes that the circumstances are quite unclear. The execution for disloyalty, however, has proven a popular explanation. See Nelson, *Historical Roots*, 160; Grabbe, *1 & 2 Kings*, 76.

23 Reading with variant manuscripts where he is shot in his chariot; the MT is quite unclear here. See further James A. Montgomery, *A Critical and Exegetical Commentary on the Books of Kings*, ICC (Edinburgh: T&T Clark, 1951), 402, 407.

24 Christopher B. Hays, *A Covenant with Death: Death in the Iron Age II and Its Rhetorical Uses in Proto-Isaiah* (Grand Rapids: Eerdmans, 2015), 156–60.

as mode of transport for the corpse finds its way into the Josiah narrative without appearing in the Masoretic text of Kings.[25] The addition of the chariot to the narrative of Josiah's demise by the Chronicler may have been intentional and related to the refusal of Josiah to harken to the word of Yahweh spoken by Neco.[26] Perhaps it is also no accident that both kings have parallel death and burial summations, though, for reasons unknown, Josiah receives his own tomb.[27]

So, two question arise: Why tell a story of Josiah's death? And why tell *this particular* story? An answer like "because his death happened this way" is nonsensical in this context. Josiah was not one of the assassinated kings of Judah and no other ruler's death except Josiah's is an expanded narrative. Ahaziah's death, which clearly has several affinities to Josiah's, is in fact part and parcel of the long narration of the death of Joram, the last king of the house of Ahab. As such, it is a narrative to the northern kingdom. Indeed, the only extended narratives of rulers' deaths in Kings concern northern rulers.[28] This leaves Josiah's story unique among the

---

25 So, among others, NEB, NRSV, NJBS NAB, but note translations from MT in Montgomery, *A Critical and Exegetical Commentary*, 537, and by Mordechai Cogan and Hayim Tadmor, *II Kings: A New Translation with Introduction and Commentary*, AB 11 (Garden City, NY: Doubleday, 1988), 280. However, also note that 2 Chr 35:23–24 has two chariots in the same narrative, one in which Josiah is wounded and one in which he is transported to Jerusalem. In Chronicles, Josiah is permitted to die in Jerusalem and not in foreign territory. Some point this out without explaining why it would be so, e.g., Sara Japhet, *I & II Chronicles: A Commentary*, OTL (Louisville: Westminster John Knox, 1993), 1044; Ralph W. Klein, *2 Chronicles*, Hermeneia (Minneapolis: Fortress, 2012), 525–26. In the theology of the Chronicler, it was no doubt highly significant that Josiah, good cultic king that he is portrayed as being (even if he disobeys God, at least as explained by Neco in Chronicles; First Esdras has the more impressive Jeremiah), should not die in "exile" but in Jerusalem.

26 Peter M. Sensenig ("Chariots on Fire: Military Dominance in the Old Testament," *HBT* 34 [2012]: 77–78) notes that the Hebrew Bible often contrasts chariots with prophetic Yahwism. The Chronicler explicitly records that the word given to Neco by Yahweh is Yahweh's message (2 Chr 35:22) and Josiah ignores it in his chariot. This would then reflect a position of trusting military might (chariot) rather than the word of Yahweh (however strange Yahweh's message might sound). The chariot may simply symbolize Josiah's self-importance in light of late Neo-Assyrian use of the chariot (Liverani, *Assyria*, 127). This would still reflect a certain amount of hubris.

27 Jeffrey Zorn, "The Burials of the Judean Kings: Sociohistorical Considerations and Suggestions," in *"I Will Speak of the Riddles of Ancient Times": Archaeological and Historical Studies in Honor of Amihai Mazar on the Occasion of His Sixtieth Birthday*, ed. A. M. Maier and P. de Miroschedji (Winona Lake, IN: Eisenbrauns, 2006), 801.

28 Moreover, they are all stories about Omrides: Ahab, Ahaziah, Joram, and Athaliah. Athaliah has to be judged among the Omrides in Kings and it is important to remember that no matter how modern academics view her seven-year reign (see,

narratives of Judahite kings. Curiously, the story told of Josiah's death in Kings is not much of a story and contains very little information. If the manner of death were related to the manner of reigning, Ahaziah (whom the text insists did evil and was explicitly declared a member of the house of that trilogy of 'villains' Omri, Ahab, and Athaliah [2 Kgs 8:26–27]) seems a very strange model for the 'straight-arrow,' goody-two-shoes, true-blue descendant of David, Josiah (2 Kgs 22:2).[29] However, Hezekiah, rated as righteous and as a good Davidic ruler (2 Kgs 18:3), had one hellish end to his life: despite Yahweh saving Jerusalem, it was a horrible siege, he was afflicted with a terminal disease (but got a reprieve), and Isaiah promised him that his family and all the wealth of Judah would be hauled to Babylon. Nonetheless, Manasseh, a totally despicable ruler in Kings (2 Kgs 21:2), reigns for fifty-five years in which he does nothing but wicked things, yet Yahweh only threatens to destroy Judah and Jerusalem—not him—and he dies in peace.[30] Being a good king does not, in these late narratives of Kings, have anything to do with the manner of one's death.[31]

Nothing in the Kings rendition of Josiah's reign would suggest a coming death for the king of Judah in Israel and at the hand of an Egyptian

---

for example, Linda S. Schearing, "Models, Monarchs and Misconceptions: Athaliah and Joash of Judah" [PhD diss., Emory University, 1992]), Kings does not portray her as having ruled Judah at all; it would have broken the Davidic lineage so beloved by the historiographer of Kings. One should not extrapolate a source for Israelite death stories from this! Clearly, the authors of Kings had a much happier time detailing the demise of those northern, non-Davidic rulers.

29   Note, however, that Josiah's response to the reading of the scroll appears to have been paralleled by that paradigm of wickedness, Ahab. See Marvin A. Sweeney, *I & II Kings: A Commentary*, OTL (Louisville: Westminster John Knox, 2007), 440–41. In the literary composition, Josiah's relationship to wicked kings is even more extensive. Christine Mitchell focuses on four such rulers: Saul, Ahab, Amaziah, and Ahaziah. See Mitchell, "The Ironic Death of Josiah in 2 Chronicles," *CBQ* 68 (2006): 431–34; so also, Mark J. Boda, "Identity and Empire, Reality and Hope in the Chronicler's Perspective," in Knoppers and Ristau, *Community Identity in Judean Historiography*, 251–52.

30   Manasseh's reign makes a mockery of the wisdom tradition about good people enjoying long lives and evil people having short ones. See Richard W. Medina, "Life and Death Viewed as Physical and Lived Spaces: Some Preliminary Thoughts from Proverbs," *ZAW* 122 (2010): 206–7.

31   Stanley Brice Frost ("The Death of Josiah: A Conspiracy of Silence," *JBL* 87 [1968]: 280–81) argues that the righteousness of Josiah's reform having been written during Josiah's reign left his death unexplainable so that it was left in "silence." Robert North ("Theology of the Chronicler," *JBL* 82 [1963]: 372) notes that the Chronicler's notions that good things happen to good rulers and bad things happen to bad rulers needed to be explained for the less-than-peaceful end for good King Josiah. Of course, both could have left Josiah's death out of the story were this a major problem.

pharaoh.³² Indeed, the sudden, unexplained appearance of Egypt and Assyria at the end of his rule has no narrative connection in the story of Josiah.³³ The last mention of Assyria or Egypt in the history presented within Kings was during the reign of Josiah's great-grandfather, Hezekiah, when Egypt was inept and Assyria defeated. Suddenly, at the end of Kings, Egypt is powerful and Assyria unimportant, but they appear back in the narrative just long enough to be replaced by Babylonia. A historical reality behind Josiah's reign may be reflected in this material, but why mention it? In particular, why mention it at his death if there is nothing mentioned in his life to lead the reader toward such an end, or even any reason for Egypt and Assyria to 'rise from the dead,' literarily speaking. Manasseh is recorded without reference to either of the major political powers for a reign of 55 years, even though the Assyrians were mighty in the neighborhood of Judah and their Egyptian campaigns would unquestionably have drained resources from Judah.³⁴ Josiah's 31 years are recorded without a single reference to any major external political power. The empire of Assyria that bordered Judah to the north with its province Samerina is totally absent, the northern neighbor is always referred to as "Israel," a political entity that had ceased to exist in 721 BCE.³⁵ The silence of the texts of Kings (Chronicles and First Esdras also) regarding Ashurbanipal, the last and arguably very important Assyrian king for historical Judah, is remarkable.³⁶ Were Kings attempting to relate a serious history of Josiah's reign (let alone Hezekiah's, Manasseh's, or Amon's), Assyria and its last

---

32 Philip R. Davies ("Josiah and the Law Book," in Grabbe, *Good Kings and Bad Kings*, 75–76) suggests a connection between Bethel and Neco's execution of Josiah. However, there is no textual or historical reason to relate Egypt with Bethel in the late seventh century.

33 Both Chronicles and 1 Esdras provide a minimal rationale for Josiah going out to meet Neco, while Kings provides that the Egyptians were going up to meet the Assyrians when Josiah decided to go to meet Neco. The ambiguity of the event is overt in the Kings account. See Robert L. Cohn, *2 Kings*, Berit Olam (Collegeville, MN: Liturgical Press, 2000), 162. For years, commentators on the Kings passage have merely "filled in" ostensibly missing data to explain the passage. See, for example, Gray, *I & II Kings*, 747–48; T. Raymond Hobbs, *2 Kings*, WBC 13 (Waco, TX: Word, 1985), 339–40; Sweeney, *I & II Kings*, 450.

34 Ariel M. Bagg, "Palestine under Assyrian Rule: A New Look at the Assyrian Imperial Policy in the West," *JAOS* 133 (2013): 122–23.

35 2 Kgs 23:15, 22, 27. Note that Israel is a Judahite concept for the area of the Assyrian Empire known as Samerina. See Israel Finkelstein, *The Forgotten Kingdom: The Archaeology and History of Northern Israel*, SBLANEM 5 (Atlanta: Society of Biblical Literature, 2013), 157, 163.

36 Lowell K. Handy, "Josiah in a New Light: Assyriology Touches the Reforming King," in *Orientalism, Assyriology and the Bible*, ed. S. W. Holloway, HBM 10 (Sheffield: Sheffield Phoenix, 2006), 422–24.

powerful king would not be absent. Why relate the death of Josiah and bring these two powers back?

Egypt may well be explained by the apparent fact that it was to play a significant role in the subsequent Babylonian conquest of Judah. Kings ends with the double exile of Davidic rulers, Jehoahaz to Egypt and Jehoiachin to Babylon. Egypt became the default refugee destination for those unwilling to live in Judah once it became Yehud of the Babylonian Empire. As in the case of King Jehoahaz, Kings presumes that one goes to Egypt to die. The better option, it would seem, was to follow King Jehoiachin by going to Babylon, where, after initial captive status, one becomes not only honored but honored above other captives. In Kings, upon Josiah's death, Egypt controls Judah until Babylonia arrives, but Assyria just disappears. This is strange since Kings does not present any circumstances concerning Assyria's disappearance at this time, nor does it make a case for Assyria doing so. Indeed, Assyria disappeared in Kings with Sennacherib's defeat by the might of Yahweh.[37] Assyria does not even appear in the passage dealing with the death of Josiah, but is mentioned solely as the reason for Egypt being present in the text. Perhaps Assyria's last appearance and Josiah's death are not such strange companions. Historically, Judah, as vassal state to Assyria, passed first into Egyptian control then into Babylonia proper when, as part and parcel of Assyria's greater empire, Assyria ceased to exist. Judah was not an independent state expanding into sections of Assyria's dying territory; Judah was a dying Assyrian peripheral territory up for grabs by the real expanding powers. David's kingdom *revivdus* is a modern reconstruction known neither in the biblical historiography of Kings nor in the last years of the seventh century BCE.[38] The real death of Judah is the death of Josiah.[39] It was worth telling, even if

---

37   2 Kgs 19:35–37 swiftly details the destruction of Sennacherib's army by Yahweh's angel, the prompt flight of Sennacherib, his assassination with the escape of his assassins, and the rise of Sennacherib's heir to the throne, not to be heard of again in this work. The sudden loss of Assyria as an active player in the narrative of Kings remains curiously unmentioned in commentaries on this passage.

38   It is quite acceptable to assume that when Josephus was patterning Josiah on David in his *Jewish Antiquities*, he envisioned a recreation of the Davidic kingdom as well (*Ant.* 10.49)—remember that Josephus was writing a Jewish history that made Judahite kings look like good (stereotypical) Roman rulers. For a thorough survey of more modern notions of Josiah as a Davidic figure, see Antti Laato, *Josiah and David Redivivas: The Historical Josiah and the Messianic Expectations of Exilic and Postexilic Times*, ConBOT 33 (Stockholm: Almqvist & Wiksell, 1992).

39   See John Brian Job, *Jeremiah's Kings: A Study of the Monarchy in Jeremiah*, SOTSMS (Aldershot: Ashgate, 2006), 45; Boda, "Identity and Empire," 252. This end includes a "consummation of the cult" in Judah as well (Ristau, "Reading and Rereading Josiah," 228) and a shift to a religious practice connected to torah rather than temple cult (Axel Knauf, "Kings among the Prophets," in *The Production of Prophecy: Constructing*

obliquely. The death narrative is more of a metaphor than a historical event.[40] Chronicles, First Esdras, and Josephus (not to mention thousands of later commentators) will attempt to create history of the death, but it appears as a literary device in Kings to present the death of Judah at the hands of Egypt, the birth-mother of Israel/Judah. Chronicles explains the less than peaceful death that had not been promised Josiah by Huldah.[41]

What about the actual death of Josiah the king? By this is meant simply, what did it mean to be a dead ruler in Judah?[42] It has long been known that the Hebrew Bible does not present a pleasant vision of the afterlife.[43] However much the region of Judah may have been within the orbit of Egypt in the second millennium BCE and returned to it late in the first millennium BCE, the biblical record does not reflect Egyptian notions of afterlife.[44] Nor do archaeological remains suggest that Assyria had an effect on Judahite notions of the dead.[45] One did not wish to be dead in biblical

---

Prophecy and Prophets in Yehud, ed. D. V. Edelman and E. Ben Zvi, BibleWorld [London: Equinox, 2009], 143). If not pointed out by many commentators, it has been noted in modern novel narrative. e.g., Frederick John Foakes-Jackson, *The Biblical History of the Hebrews to the Christian Era*, 3rd enlarged ed. (New York: George H. Doran, 1920), 304; James A. Michener, *The Source* (New York: Fawcett Crest, 1967), 334.

40 Both Josiah's death and his reign become post-exilic symbolic tales. See Axel Knauf, *Die Umwelt*, 84, 155. In "Die Reform des Jeschija: Methodische, historische und religionsgeschichtliche Aspekte," in *Jeremia und die "deuteronomistische Bewegung*, ed. W. Groß, BBB 98 (Weinheim: Beltz Athenäum, 1995), 52, Herbert Niehr sees Josiah as a symbolic mediating figure between the First Temple and the Second Temple. Using Georg Lukács as a model, Roland Boer (*Marxist Criticism of the Bible* [London: T&T Clark, 2003], 121, 130) sees Josiah's reform as "national allegory" and Huldah's prophecy of doom as the literary end of the state.

41 Joaquim Azevedo, "El concepto de lo malo en la teodicea del Cronista," *Theologika* 28 (2013): 28–29; David Janzen, "The Sins of Josiah and Hezekiah: A Synchronic Reading of the Final Chapters of Kings," *JSOT* 37 (2013): 366–67.

42 Lloyd R. Bailey, Sr. (*Biblical Perspectives on Death*, OBT [Philadelphia: Fortress, 1979], 25) correctly notes that the Hebrew Bible is lacking in detail about the dead but assumes different notions about the dead.

43 The standard scholarly vision of Sheol in ancient Judah is surveyed in Robin L. Routledge's "Death and Afterlife in the Old Testament," *JEBS* 9 (2008): 24–25. The ambiguity of the origin of the word *sheol* is surveyed in Richard Elliott Friedman and Shawna Dolansky Overton's "Death and Afterlife: The Biblical Silence," in *Judaism in Late Antiquity. Part 4: Death, Life-after-Death, Resurrection and the World-to-Come in the Judaisms of Antiquity*, ed. A. J. Avery-Peck and J. Neusner, HdO 1 49.4 (Leiden: Brill, 2000), 41–42.

44 Routledge, "Death and Afterlife," 36. Nor were Egyptian notions of the afterlife consistent; see Alec Basson, "Death as Deliverance in Job 3:11–26," in *"From Ebla to Stellenbosch": Syro-Palestinian Religios and the Hebrew Bible*, ed. I. Cornelius and L. Jonker, ADPV 37 (Wiesbaden: Harrassowitz, 2008), 67–69.

45 Elizabeth Bloch-Smith, "From Womb to Tomb: The Israelite Family in Death

Judah.⁴⁶ One did not cease to exist, but the existence the dead endured left much to be desired. While the Bible presents numerous clipped glimpses of the abode of the dead, it has been to the texts of the surrounding cultures that scholars have turned to recreate the afterlife as presented in the Hebrew Bible.⁴⁷ In Kings there is little to suggest a cult of the dead kings.⁴⁸ However, the Bible is clearly aware of the "Canaanite" cult of dead rulers and/or the mighty deceased known as the *rephaim*, a group known also from surrounding cultures.⁴⁹ While it seems likely that the dead kings of Judah were seen to have passed into some existence after death, they do not appear to have been a powerful or commanding presence as individual entities among the living.⁵⁰ Their existence is assumed to be in the

---

as in Life," in *The Family in Life and Death: The Family in Ancient Israel: Sociological and Archaeological Perspectives*, ed. P. Dutcher-Walls, LHBOTS 504 (New York: T&T Clark, 2009), 131.

46 Basson ("Death as Deliverance," 75) posits an afterlife of calm after a life of trauma. However, in Job the wish for death is merely that the horrible place of the dead is preferable to the agony of the life being led by the protagonist. See further Susan Niditch, "Experiencing the Divine: Heavenly Visits, Earthly Encounters and the Land of the Dead," in *Religious Diversity in Ancient Israel and Judah*, ed. F. Stavrakopoulou and J. Barton (London: T&T Clark, 2010), 20.

47 Concise presentations of this biblical netherworld and its dead can be found in several studies: Robert Martin-Achard, *La Mort en face: Selon la Bible hébraïque*, EssBib 15 (Geneva: Labor et Fides, 1988), 72-75; Theodore J. Lewis, "Dead, Abode of the," *ABD* 2.102-4; Paolo Xella, "Death and the Afterlife in Canaanite and Hebrew Thought," in *Civilizations of the Ancient Near East*, ed. J. Sasson (New York: Scribner's Sons, 1995), 3.2067-70; John J. Collins, "Death, the Afterlife, and Other Last Things: Israel," in *Religions of the Ancient World: A Guide*, ed. S. Johnston (Cambridge, MA: Belknap, 2004), 480-82.

48 Gregorio del Olmo Lete, "La religion cananea de los antiguos Hebreos," in *Mitología y Religión del Oriente Antiguo II/2: Semiticas occidentales*, ed by D. Arnaud, F. Bron, G. del Olmo Lete and J. Teixidor, EO 9 (Sabadell: AUSA, 1995), 305. Bailey (*Biblical Perspectives*, 32-36) perhaps overconfidently dismisses any possible cult of the dead in the Hebrew Bible, however possible it is that a popular folk tradition may have existed in ancient Judah/Israel. See Naomi Steinberg, "Exodus 12 in Light of Ancestral Practices," in Dutcher-Walls, *The Family in Life and in Death*, 92. In "Funerary Rites for Infants and Children in the Hebrew Bible in Light of Ancient Near Eastern Practice," in *Feasts and Festivals*, ed. C. Tuckett, CBET 53 (Leuven: Peeters, 2009), 26, Carly L. Crouch hypothesizes that even infants and children were incorporated into a cult of the dead in ancient Israel/Judah.

49 Manfred Dietrich, Oswald Loretz, and Joaquín Sanmartín, "Die ugaritischen Totengeister *rpu(m)* und die biblischen Rephaim," *UF* 8 (1976): 45-52; del Olmo Lete, "La religion cananea," 299-301; Hedwige Rouillard, "Rephaim," *DDD*¹ cols. 1307-24; Suriano, *Politics*, 149-65; Hays, *A Covenant with Death*, 167-68. Nicolas Wyatt, "Royal Religion in Ancient Judah," in Stavrakopoulou and Barton, *Religious Diversity in Ancient Israel and Judah*, 73-75.

50 Suriano, *Politics*, 166; Richard S. Hess, *Israelite Religions: An Archaeological and*

netherworld, Sheol, where, if there is a relationship with a deity, it is not with Yahweh but Mot (Death).[51] The extent to which the deity Mot was understood to be an actual existing deity in which the people of Judah or Israel believed (let alone the populace of Ugarit, where he plays a major part in the myths) remains a debated question.[52] Clearly, however, Mot was known in Judah as a divine embodiment, or ruler, of the dead.[53] There is, however, sufficient evidence to posit that Judah retained an idea that the deceased kings of the Davidic lineage formed some kind of unit in the netherworld that supported the legitimacy of the living king in Jerusalem.[54]

Biblical Survey (Grand Rapids: Baker Academic, 2007), 294-95. The significantly more active dead/ghosts of Mesopotamian tradition do not seem to have influenced the biblical authors, since the Mesopotamian dead want their recognition, meals, remembrance days, and, if not properly honored, their revenge. See Dina Katz, "Death, the Afterlife and Other Last Things: Mesopotamia," in Johnston, *Religions of the Ancient World*, 477-78. In a culture that saw ghosts as vengeful, the need to keep the dead away from the living is evident in both Mesopotamian and Egyptian traditions. See further JoAnn Scurlock, *Magico-Medical Means of Treating Ghost-Induced Illnesses in Ancient Mesopotamia*, AMD 3 (Leiden: Brill, 2006), 5-8; John Taylor, "Death, the Afterlife and Other Last Things: Egypt," in Johnston, *Religions of the Ancient World*, 474, 476.

51   Hays (*A Covenant with Death*, 184-89) and Edward Noort ("Der Tod und die Gerechtigkeit im alten Israel: Zwei Rollenspiele," in Kottsieper, Schmitt and Wöhrle, *Berührungspunkte*, 372-73) survey notions about Yahweh and Sheol. Apparently, Yahweh can raise souls up from the dead while being a deity of the living. See Ziony Zevit, *The Religions of Ancient Israel: A Synthesis of Parallactic Approaches* (London: Continuum, 2001), 664. Note that any clearly defined notion of the geography of the netherworld in Judean/Jewish literature only appears well after not only the death of Josiah but any reasonable date for the writing of the book of Kings. See Richard Bauckham, *The Fate of the Dead: Studies on the Jewish and Christian Apocalypses*, NovTSup 93 (Atlanta: Society of Biblical Literature, 1998), 49-80. However, it appears that divine 'travel' into the netherworld in the ancient Near East was not normally considered to be possible and the gates thereof kept in those intended to be there whilst keeping locked out those who were not: Samuel A. Meier, "Granting God a Passport: Transporting Deities across International Boundaries" in *Moving across Borders: Foreign Relations, Religion and Cultural Interactions in the Ancient Mediterranean*, ed. P. Kousoulis and K. Magliveras (Louvain: Peeters, 2007),186-87.

52   Stefanie Ulrike Gulde, *Der Tod als Herrscher in Ugarit und Israel*, FAT 22 (Tübingen: Mohr Siebeck, 2007), 156-236. See Lowell K. Handy, *Among the Host of Heaven: The Syro-Palestinian Pantheon as Bureaucracy* (Winona Lake, IN: Eisenbrauns, 1994), 105-6; John F. Healey, "Mot," *DDD* cols. 1128-31.

53   Hays, *A Covenant with Death*, 122-24, 179-80. In *The Early History of God: Yahweh and the Other Deities in Ancient Israel*, 2nd ed. (Grand Rapids: Eerdmans, 2002), 87-88, Mark S. Smith notes that Mot appears in biblical texts as a "demon." However, as has been noted for a long time, it is more likely that "Death/Mot" had been a deity for the duration of the entity called Judah: W. Carleton Wood, *The Religion of Canaan: From the Earliest Times to the Hebrew Conquest* (Ontario: Newmarket, 1916), 268-69.

54   Suriano, *Politics*, 21, 165. Stephen L. Cook ("Death, Kinship, and Community:

There is very little (and that being very obscure) in the biblical texts to suggest any afterlife with Yahweh, even for royalty or the righteous.[55] This does not mean that these dead kings had any part to play in the living world; there is simply no evidence for that in the canonical biblical texts.[56]

There may have been a belief, formal or popular, that the graves and/or tombs of the significant dead bore numinous aspects of the deceased.[57] Certainly, the burial places of the kings of Judah were recorded and remembered.[58] Prophets, who carried the presence of deities in their words, were also seen to carry what modern social scientists would call magical power in their persons and bones after burial.[59] The man of God from Judah is buried with care by the 'lying' prophet from Bethel in the latter's grave with a mourning ritual and the request that the 'lying' prophet should be buried with the 'truthful' prophet when the former dies (1 Kgs 13:29–31). There was something about the very bones of the prophets of God that had numinous powers which were still effective long after their death (2 Kgs 13:20–21). That the bones of the Judahite man of God were so revered even by those who hated his message and by the prophet who drew him to his death that his place of burial was preserved and memorialized beside the temple he condemned would have been extraordinary.[60] The very

---

Afterlife and the דמה ideal in Israel," in Dutcher-Walls, *The Family in Life and in Death*, 112–13, 117) would see a ghostly reception of family groups, at least for elite families, and certainly for the royal family.

55 J. Kenneth Kuntz, "'In Sheol, Who Can Give You Praise?': Death and 'Immortality' in the Hebrew Psalter," *PCS* 3 (2000): 77, 82; Cook, "Death, Kinship, and Community," 110–11.

56 For all the material on ghosts and necromancy, the common notion appears to have been that death was a one-way street—one did not return. For more on this, see Salom M. Paul, "Two Notes on Biblical and Mesopotamian Imagery," in Grossman, *Built by Wisdom*, 174–77.

57 Alice Mandell and Jeremy Smoak ("Reading and Writing in the Dark at Khirbet el-Qom: The Literacies of Ancient Subterranean Judah," *NEArch* 80 [2017]: 193–95) describe tomb inscriptions and artifacts as being related to family ritual in conjunction with the dead buried there.

58 It is quite possible that the "garden of Uzza" as the resting place for Manasseh and Amon carried an unfavorable commentary on these rulers for the author of Kings. See Bob Becking, "The Enigmatic Garden of Uzza: A Religio-Historical Footnote to 2 Kings 21:18, 26," in Kottsieper, Schmitt and Wöhrle, *Berührungspunkte*, 388–89.

59 Johannes Lindblom, *Prophecy in Ancient Israel* (Philadelphia: Fortress, 1962), 50–51. See also James F. Osborne ("Secondary Mortuary Practice and the Bench Tomb: Structure and Practice in Iron Age Judah," *JNES* 70 [2011]: 44), who defines such a notion with regard to Josiah as "spiritual significance."

60 Long (*1 Kings*, 150–52) defines the narrative of the burial and commemoration as a "prophetic legend" with an oral history. However, the text need not be "old" nor "oral." In any case, it displays a belief in the Judean scribal circles that a

notion that there was a prominent memorial highly visible for anyone near the temple seems strange.⁶¹ Assuming that the story is based on a historical event, which is not to be taken as a certainty, the tomb would certainly have been remembered in Bethel for the 'other,' 'lying' prophet and only later remembered by Judahites for the prophet from Judah. However, there simply has not been a wealth of highly visible memorial tombs excavated in the time and place of ancient Judah and Israel to support the story as it survives.⁶² The story reflects a belief acceptable in a literary text of a historiographical nature that the deceased remained in some fashion around their grave.⁶³

In the case of Josiah proper, as with all kings of Judah or Israel, there is no reference to his continuing individual existence after death.⁶⁴ He is car-

---

true prophet—one that defends the Jerusalem temple—should be recognized by all people with any interest in Yahweh. It begs credulity that Bethel, the home town of the false prophet (according to 1 Kgs 13:11; not, obviously, Samaria [2 Kgs 23:18], save as a reference to the northern kingdom), would maintain for almost 300 years the tomb (NRSV: "monument" and clearly a visible and impressive one) that was so evidently a false prophet in their own tradition, who desecrated and delegitimatized their premier temple. The story suits the agenda of Kings. It has to be taken as having at the very most a minimal amount of historical anchoring either in 1 Kgs 13: 29–31 or in 2 Kgs 23:16–18. The stories themselves have absolutely no possibility of having taken place.

61   Hobbs (*2 Kings*, 336) notes the narrative necessity of the "monument" being big enough to see from a distance and impressive enough to catch the eye of Josiah in a way that suggests it was more than just another tomb.

62   Johannes Thon ("Das Grab des 'Lügenpropheten' im Dienste Wahrheit [1 Kön 13,11–32; 2 Kön 23,15–18]," in *Die unwiderstehliche Wahrheit: Studien zur alttestamentlichen Prophetie*, ed. R. Lux and E. J. Waschke, ABG 23 [Leipzig: Evangelische, 2006], 473) observes that the concern about grave sites for biblical prophets seems to be a later concern of "early Judaism."

63   This was certainly a belief held in ancient Greece. See Walter Burkert, *Greek Religion* (Cambridge, MA: Harvard University Press, 1985) 194–95; Ronald C. Finucane, *Ghosts: Appearances of the Dead & Cultural Transformation* (Amherst, NY: Prometheus, 1996), 7–8. A proper burial was seen as necessary to keep Greek ghosts from visiting the living; in the tomb they could rest. For more on this, see Debbie Felton, *Haunted Greece and Rome: Ghost Stories from Classical Antiquity* (Austin: University of Texas Press, 1999), 9–11. However, the Mesopotamian dead seem to have separated from their graves according to Katz, "Death, the Afterlife and Other Last Things," 479.

64   Samuel is an important example. The raising of the ghost [*ob*] of Samuel by the woman of Endor (1 Sam 28:7–20) provides examples of two relevant beliefs: 1) necromancy was part and parcel of Judahite thought about the dead and was assumed to be effective; and 2) dead rulers (Samuel was prophet, priest, judge, and ruler) could be contacted from Sheol for consultation, even if this displayed the ineptitude of the king in this case. See further, Esther J. Hamori, *Women's Divination in Biblical Literature: Prophecy, Necromancy, and Other Arts of Knowledge*, AYBRL (New Haven: Yale

ried by his subordinates from (apparently) Megiddo, where he was killed by Pharaoh Neco, to Jerusalem. In Kings he is buried in his own tomb, in a fashion that diverges from the usual burial notices found for the kings of Judah prior to Hezekiah.[65] Whether this is as immensely significant as often suggested is open to debate. Chronicles renders the parallel version with the notice that Josiah is returned to Jerusalem and is buried with his ancestors, which would conform to the 'standard' rendition of the formula found in Kings. The burial in Jerusalem would have been significant in that it placed the ruler in the city of his reign and provided a symbolic sense of the continuity of the reign of the dynasty of David, a central concern of both Kings and Chronicles.

Any existence of King Josiah in an afterlife is not a concern of any of the biblical renditions of Josiah's reign. Both Chronicles and First Esdras, however, carry the memory of Josiah not only beyond his death and burial, but as something to be continued in perpetuity (2 Chr 35:24-25; 1 Esd 1:30).[66] Thereafter, no record is provided of any actual official remembrance commemoration for Josiah, which likely suggests a literary rather than a historical event. Indeed, these texts themselves provide the memory of the king and the proposed reason for why he should be remembered.[67] At no point here, or anywhere, is there any suggestion that ritual events are to be involved in this remembrance. Philip Johnston and Jon Levenson appear to be quite correct that the historical narratives of the Hebrew Bible have a distinct disinterest in the dead as dead persons.[68] Unlike some cultures and literatures, the biblical historical texts do not have the dead traversing the world of the living; neither do the dead appear as intrusive honored ancestors nor as beings that inhabit the twilight edges of human existence;[69] in fact, they do not ever appear as 'creatures' needing to be

---

University Press, 2015), 128, 130. However, Kings (as also Chronicles) does not deal with deceased royalty.

65 Zorn, "The Burials of the Judean Kings," 801, 812; Suriano, *Politics*, 121-23.

66 Note that the numbering system for 1 Esdras follows that of the Göttingen edition. Aleksandr Aleksandrovich Glagolev et al., "Chetvertaia Tsarstv," in Lopukhin, *Tolkovaia Biblia*, 2.574. The memory of Josiah is emphasized in the Greek and Latin of Sirach. See Patrick W. Skehan and Alexander Di Lella, *The Wisdom of Ben Sira: A New Translation with Notes*, AB 39 (New York: Doubleday, 1987), 543.

67 Medina ("Life and Death," 209) suggests that the memory of the righteous keeps them alive forever, unlike the wicked who are forgotten and perish. Of course, Kings and Chronicles would keep alive the memories of both sorts of rulers.

68 Philip S. Johnston, *Shadows of Sheol: Death and Afterlife in the Old Testament* (Downers Grove, IL: InterVarsity Press, 2002), 127, 217; Jon D. Levenson, *Resurrection and the Restoration of Israel: The Ultimate Victory of the God of Life* (New Haven: Yale University Press, 2006), 65.

69 Bloch-Smith ("From Womb to Tomb," 128-29) presents the few possible biblical citations that might reflect the notion of a divine dead.

fed or provisioned, even though burial excavations suggest the practice of both existed historically.[70] There may well be a gap between the literary notion of the existence of the dead and that practiced by the general populace, but the practice of the populace is impossible to reconstruct accurately.[71] Josephus claims the mourning for Josiah lasted for many days and that Jeremiah wrote a lament on the occasion that was preserved to Josephus's present day (*Ant.* 10.78–79); there is no doubt that it was intended to impress the reading audience of the Roman Empire.[72] Attempts to discover memorial passages related to Josiah in the biblical corpus, however, are not convincing.[73] Nevertheless, the notion that Josiah should be remembered is clear from Chronicles (2 Chr 35:25), a text reflecting concerns of the late Persian period.[74] It is interesting, if not necessarily significant, that while the unnamed prophet from Judah is recorded as having a prominent physical memorial in Bethel, no such memorial monuments are recorded for the kings of Judah, Josiah included.[75]

---

70 Elizabeth Bloch-Smith, *Judahite Burial Practices and Beliefs about the Dead*, JSOTSup 123 (Sheffield: JSOT Press, 1992), 81–86, 141. In "Death in the Life of Israel" (in *Sacred Time, Sacred Space: Archaeology and the Religion of Israel*, ed. B. M. Gittlen [Winona Lake, IN: Eisenbrauns, 2002], 140–42), Bloch-Smith swiftly outlines the debate for and against any "cult of the dead" in ancient Israel or Judah. It seems clear that the biblical authors were aware of such practices: Osborne, "Secondary Mortuary Practice," 44–45.

71 Wayne T. Pitard, "Tombs and Offerings: Archaeological Data and Comparative Methodology in the Study of Death in Israel," in Gittlen, *Sacred Time, Sacred Space*, 155, 163. The absence of biblical data for a literary belief in something other than Sheol is decidedly rare and ambiguous. See Routledge, "Death and Afterlife," 38. That excavated burials reflect post-mortem existence is, however, fairly clear. See Hermann Spieckermann, "'YHWH Bless You and Keep You': The Relation of History of Israelite Religion and Old Testament Theology Reconsidered," *SJOT* 23 (2009): 174–49. Friedman and Overton ("Death and Afterlife," 55) correctly urge great caution on deriving notions of the dead from biblical texts.

72 The Roman populace had a long tradition of mourning for the dead, as well as retaining respect and provision for them, even if the practice of burial had given way to cremation by Josephus's time. For more on this, see Robert Maxwell Ogilvie, *The Romans and Their Gods in the Age of Augustus*, Ancient Culture and Society (New York: Norton, 1969), 75–76; John Bodel, "Death, the Afterlife, and Other Last Things: Rome," in Johnston, *Religions of the Ancient World*, 490–92.

73 Antti Laato, "Beloved and Lovely! Despised and Rejected: Some Reflections on the Death of Josiah," in *Houses Full of All Good Things: Essays in Memory of Timo Veijola*, ed. J. Pakkala and M. Nissinen, PFES 95 (Helsinki: Finnish Exegetical Society; Göttingen: Vandenhoeck & Ruprecht, 2008), 123–27.

74 Latto, "Beloved and Lovely!," 116, 124.

75 Osborne ("Secondary Mortuary Practice," 48), citing Isa 14:18, suggests there was special burial for Judean kings, but it is less than clear what was meant by burying them in their own house.

That Josiah killed priests at the altar of Bethel is usually assumed, though the text of Kings—the sole narrative that records the defilement of Bethel's altar—makes mention of it only in the prophecy of the unnamed man of God from Judah (1 Kgs 13:2), not in the narrative of the destruction of the altar at Bethel (2 Kgs 23:18). However, according to 2 Kgs 23:20, the priests whom Josiah found at the rest of the sacred sites of Israel he "slaughtered." This passage claims this was the manner of dealing with Bethel. A decided distinction is made between the priests removed from Judahite sanctuaries and those of Israelite shrines.[76] King Josiah is recorded as having removed from their positions the priests in Jerusalem and throughout Judah who served deities other than Yahweh (2 Kgs 23:5, 8) at the same time that he destroyed their religious sites. These priests, the narrative explains, were merely sent home (2 Kgs 23:9). Demotion from a priestly post to the status of mere commoner was probably shameful enough; however, a dedicated devotee of Baal or Shemesh (or whatever deity) who found the god and sanctuary of their devotion now extinct would have suffered more than just a loss of social status.

Meanwhile, the biblical text notes that bones were burned on the altars (2 Kgs 23:16, 20; 2 Chr 34:5), reflecting some notion of the significance of the remains of the dead. Bones were meaningful if for no other reason than that they were the last remaining physical elements of the deceased.[77] First of all, in the case of Josiah, Kings restricts this bone-burning behavior to sanctuaries of the northern kingdom—clearly a designation of Israel's inferior status in the estimation of Judah and Jerusalem in the author's opinion—while Chronicles restricts the burning of bones by Josiah's reformers to Jerusalem and Judah. Moreover, in Chronicles it appears that the priests of the various deities (with Baal and Asherah being specifically mentioned) and sacred places not being or belonging to Yahweh are those whose remains are destroyed. Neither Kings nor Chronicles explicitly states that the bones being burned in Judah or Israel were those of priests.[78] Even so, the proximity of the comment on the priests and the human bones could easily have been intentional. What is significant about the burning of human bones on the altars? The biblical passages suggest that the intent was to defile the altars by making abominable sacrifices on them that would desecrate their use forever (were it not that they seem also to be destroyed at the same time).[79] Simple contact with dead human

---

76 Cogan and Tadmor, *II Kings*, 290.
77 Bailey, *Biblical Perspectives*, 46.
78 Klein, *2 Chronicles*, 497.
79 Joseph Robinson, *The First Book of Kings*, CBC (Cambridge: Cambridge University Press, 1972), 159; Japhet, *I & II Chronicles*, 1023; Cogan and Tadmor, *II Kings*, 299. See discussion in W. Boyd Barrick, "Burning Bones at Bethel: A Closer Look at 2 Kings

bodies would accomplish that (Lev 21:1-4; Num 5:2-4).[80] In an ancient Near Eastern context, the burning of the bones would more likely have been a demolition of the deceased and a horrific example of the destruction of those deemed impious.[81] The intention in these passages would appear to have been to make it clear to the reader that those who engaged themselves in the cultic ritual of 'other' deities (and, perhaps, at any sacred site other than the temple in Jerusalem) deserved to be totally annihilated in this life and the next, and Josiah took ritually proper vengeance on them.[82] The total annihilation of any 'existing' aspect of 'life' in a dead person would not be unique to these biblical narratives; aside from the Mesopotamian examples, Egypt's wicked faced the usual prospect of simply being 'eaten-dead,' having no part in the afterlife at all, which was reserved for the righteous (of any social rank, wealth, or position).[83] Being a meal

---

23:16a," *SJOT* 14 (2000): 5-12. Barrick probably provides more information about cremation at low temperatures than any biblical scholar wants to know. Nevertheless, he decisively clarifies that the contact of dead human bodies with an altar was more than enough to defile the sanctity of the object.

80   Barrick, "Burning Bones at Bethel," 6-7; Gregorio del Olmo Lete, "Antecedentes y concomitants del culto hebreo-biblico" in *Los caminos inexhauribles de la Palabra (Las relecturas creativas en la Biblia y de la Biblia)*, ed. G. Hansen (Buenos Aires: Lumen – ISEDET, 2000), 121.

81   See del Olmo Lete ("Antecedentes," 121-22), who sees the burning of the bones of the dead as a way of demolishing the "cult of the dead" (the *rephaim*); JoAnn Scurlock, "Josiah: The View from Mesopotamia," *BR* 51 (2006): 17, 21. In "Theorizing Circumstantially Dependent Rites in and out of War Contexts," in *Warfare, Ritual, and Symbol in Biblical and Modern Contexts*, ed. B. E. Kelle, F. R. Ames and J. L. Wright, AIL 18 (Atlanta: Society of Biblical Literature, 2014), 20-21, Saul M. Olyan notes that Josiah is intending to "demonstrate malevolent intent" in burning these bones and is no doubt correct that destroying the bones was intended to disturb the afterlife of those persons. However, Josiah's actions are neither represented as, nor likely to have been part of, warfare. Hostility, yes; a military campaign, no.

82   Complete annihilation is the just desert of the wicked and the land must be rid of the ungodly. See Medina, "Life and Death," 203-5. Political and religious leaders of one's enemies were open to postmortem destruction in the ancient world; the postmortem had actual and symbolic significance. See John A. Brinkman, *Prelude to Empire: Babylonian Society and Politics, 747-626 B.C.*, OPBF 7 (Philadelphia: Babylonian Fund, University Museum, 1984), 102.

83   Egyptian traditions had extensive notions about the future life of the soul differing by time and location, but best known from the Book of the Dead. See Siegfried Morenz, *Egyptian Religion*, trans. Ann E. Keep (Ithaca, NY: Cornell University Press, 1973), 126-27, 207; Teeter, *Religion and Ritual*, 120-21. Matthew J. Suriano ("Sheol, the Tomb, and the Problem of Postmortem Existence," *JHS* 16 [2016], doi:10.5508/jhs.2016.v16.a11) posits the interesting notion of Sheol as a limbo area, where one's dead self may find itself stranded if not accepted into the collective afterlife of one's ancestors, more in line with an Egyptian testing of the 'soul.'

for Ammut ended any form of existence in the afterlife of the wicked.[84] Apparently, the burning of the bones of the deceased in Judah fulfilled the same objective.[85] In both Egypt and the Bible, the cause for complete destruction of the individual is related to being evil (or at least impious). It should be noted in this context that it is likely the death of the man of God from Judah at the jaws and paws of a lion (1 Kgs 13:21–26) is also explicitly related to his having broken the directions given him by Yahweh.[86] It would seem that the conduct of one's life along good/evil lines was considered connected to the form of one's death and of the persistence of one's soul.[87] In Egypt, the decision about non-existence was in the hands (so-to-speak) of the gods; in the Josiah narrative, however, the decision is in the hands of Josiah and his enforcers.

Given that the biblical narrative proposes that human agency determines the fate of the priests at Bethel, it is somewhat odd that Huldah's prophecy does not relate Josiah's fate to how he lived his life and is not connected by the author to his death. Presented in Kings as the 'double-check' on the authority of the *torah* of Moses, Huldah acts as the voice of Yahweh.[88] Only tangentially does she confirm the authority of the scroll (2 Kgs 22:18b–19; 2 Chr 34:27): Yahweh speaks only of the reaction of Josiah to hearing its words. It may be assumed that the words Josiah heard were legitimate, then, and yet Yahweh never says any such thing. What Yahweh says through Huldah is an unleashing of the wrath of God upon the inhabitants of this place (2 Kgs 22:16, 19; 2 Chr 34:24, 27). Given the context, it must be assumed that "this place" refers to Jerusalem and Judah. Deuteronomy this

---

84 At the weigh-in of the soul (*ba*) in the afterlife came the end of the line for the wicked, as that last vestige of their individual existence (heart) was devoured (serpent early, Ammut late); Morenz, *Egyptian Religion*, 127; Veronica Ions, *Egyptian Mythology*, 2nd ed. (London: Hamlyn, 1968), 42, 136.

85 Mordecai Cogan (*1 Kings: A New Translation with Introduction and Commentary*, AB 10 [New York: Doubleday, 2001], 367) suggests that the burning of the bones is an act of disrespect towards the dead and defiles the altar; it would appear that the burning of the bones to ash was intended to do more than just "disrespect" the dead.

86 Of course, taunting a prophet could get one mauled if not eaten (2 Kgs 2:24). Fretheim (*First and Second Kings*, 139) theorizes this use of animals to carry out divine justice may actually be connected to a possible prophetic rebuttal of the temple at Bethel. The location of the bear attack is nonetheless clearly significant, See Cohn, *2 Kings*, 17.

87 This becomes common enough in Jewish traditions in early Judaisms. See Noort, "Der Tod," 375–78.

88 On Huldah's literary persona, see Lowell K. Handy, "The Role of Huldah in Josiah's Cult Reform," *ZAW* 106 (1994): 95–103. On prophets being used to check on the veracity of other prophets in the ancient Near East, see Thomas Römer, "Von Maulwürfen und verhinderten Propheten: Einige Anmerkungen zum prophetischen Buch," *CV* 51 (2009): 182.

is not. There is nothing in this harangue that would identify the coming doom to the scroll just read save that, somehow, whatever Josiah and his fellow Judahites have been doing is not what makes Yahweh happy. Herein are the problems, and they decidedly relate to death, both symbolically and physically. The inhabitants are doomed; they are promised in pure, prophetic, irredeemable vindictive declaration that they will suffer disaster, desolation, and curse (2 Kgs 22:16, 19–20; 2 Chr 34:24, 28 [NRSV]).[89] In both Kings and Chronicles, these punishments are all related to not worshiping Yahweh properly and solely. If the biblical historiography were to be believed, Josiah himself had not worshipped Yahweh properly or solely for years. Josiah, however, receives a full reprieve because, upon hearing the words of the scroll, he tore his garment and felt terrible. Yahweh is to let him die without him seeing the coming demise of the people. The elders of Judah and Jerusalem get to hear the words of the scroll; indeed, all of the population of Jerusalem and Judah hear the scroll (it should be pointed out that the historical probability of this event is nil)[90] and everyone there (that is to say, all the inhabitants of "this place") joins in a covenant to keep the commandments of Yahweh (2 Kgs 23:1–3; 2 Chr 34:29–32).[91] Nevertheless, Yahweh's promise to demolish them stands.

The disjuncture between Yahweh's judgment of the Judahites and of Josiah may not be a modern conundrum; the Chronicler changes verbal

---

[89] Klein (*2 Chronicles*, 505) provides a possible explanation for the absence of "curse" in Chronicles' rendition of Huldah's speech as a copying error, while Japhet (*I & II Chronicles*, 1035) sees the absence as an example of the Chronicler's theology with a softer, kinder, more lenient Yahweh.

[90] Bringing the entire population of Judah before Josiah is clearly a literary trope; the obstacles to moving the entire population to Jerusalem and getting them within hearing distance of the king standing at the temple are about as enormous as getting every descendant of David after a thousand years to Bethlehem for a census (Lk 2:1–5). It has been noted that the story has literary connections to material before and after it in the biblical historiography. See, for example, Marvin A. Sweeney's *King Josiah of Judah: The Lost Messiah of Israel* (Oxford: Oxford University Press, 2001), 25–26, 123, where it is suggested that Josiah is supposed to be channeling Joshua, and Gary N. Knoppers's "Ethnicity, Genealogy, Geography, and Change: The Judean Communities of Babylon and Jerusalem in the Story of Ezra" in Knoppers and Ristau, *Community Identity in Judean Historiography*, 170, where Josiah prefigures Ezra. See Table 3.1 in Monroe's *Josiah's Reform and the Dynamics of Defilement*, 64.

[91] Note that Chronicles adds Levites and Benjaminites to this crowd of listeners and then adds that the residents of Jerusalem thereafter acted exactly as Yahweh wanted them to (2 Chr 34:32b). Noll ("Was there Doctrinal Dissemination in Early Yahweh Religion?," 398) is no doubt correct that there was no general knowledge of any material from scrolls in the monarchic period and may well be right that it was (late) in the Hellenistic period that many Jews would even have known who Moses was supposed to have been (427).

tenses to make the Kings' passage read that the king caused (made/forced) the people to conform, which may reflect an ancient observation that Yahweh was not playing fair.⁹² Having Josiah as the only person who really cares about the change in behavior and who makes the people, priests, and Levites behave allows Yahweh to spare Josiah while raining catastrophe on the heads of the people, priests, and Levites. Of course, Chronicles then changes the story of the death of Josiah, who is shown to be disobedient towards Yahweh and thus deserving of his death at the hand of Neco, regardless of there being good reason for Josiah to assume Neco was not a true prophet of Yahweh.⁹³ First Esdras expands on the Chronicler's narrative to include Jeremiah as the prophet whom Josiah refused to obey, stopping Josiah from being able to dismiss Neco as a true prophet; how could he not obey the word of Yahweh from the true prophet Jeremiah?⁹⁴

In Kings, Huldah's prophecy makes little sense on an ethical/righteousness level. Neither Judah nor Josiah have been anything but polytheists for a good decade and yet Yahweh, through Huldah, finds cause to bring death and destruction upon the Judahites. Josiah, however, will not live to see such a punishment. Death is coming for everyone in this prophetic speech; however, it is not equal. For the populace, who went after other gods and ignored Yahweh, it is desolation. Desolation is, as it appears in Lamentations, the death of a people, a culture, and a city. It is a proclamation of doom on an entire ethnic/political/religious entity without any possibility to change or escape from this horrific future. King Josiah, on the other hand, has been doing the exact same things, but having heard the scroll read to him by intermediaries, and having reacted in proper

---

92   Japhet (*I & II Chronicles*, 1036–37) and Klein (*2 Chronicles*, 506–7) note the change.

93   This disobedience of Josiah has often been read back into Kings. However, it is simply not there in the narrative. See Michael Avioz, "Josiah's Death in the Book of Kings: A New Solution to an Old Theological Conundrum," *ETL* 83 (2007): 362–65. It has also been asserted that Egyptians would have been quite open to divine oracles, thus Neco being the voice of one would seem rational, e.g., Aleksandr Aleksandrovich Glagolev et al., "Vtoraia Kniga Paralipomenon," in Lopukhin, *Tolkovaia Biblia*, 188. David J. Chalcraft ("Sociology and the Book of Chronicles: Risk, Ontological Security, Moral Panics, and Types of Narrative," in *What Was Authoritative for Chronicles?*, ed. E. Ben Zvi and D. V. Edelman [Winona Lake, IN: Eisenbrauns, 2011], 215) places Josiah's death in Chronicles in the category of "retribution narrative" of swift moral panic and divine retribution.

94   Ralph W. Klein ("The Rendering of 2 Chronicles 35–36 in 1 Esdras," in *Was 1 Esdras First? An Investigation into the Priority and Nature of 1 Esdras*, ed. L. S. Fried, AIL 7 [Atlanta: Society of Biblical Literature, 2011]: 222) sees First Esdras shifting the prophetic authority to Jeremiah from Neco. It was an interesting idea that Jeremiah was distraught to discover that Josiah was not the avenger for Yahweh against the Assyrians rather than the Babylonians—a dubious historical reality. For more on this, see Michael B. Rowton, "Jeremiah and the Death of Josiah," *JNES* 10 (1951): 130.

mourning ritual fashion, Yahweh gives him a pass. Again, in Kings, when the people finally get to hear the same scroll (supposedly), they similarly clamor to do exactly what Yahweh commands, but their demise is already sealed. There is no way out regardless of whether they are sorry, or whether they change behavior, or whether they sing all 150 psalms (some of which are not yet written); it makes no difference. Huldah's prophecy is one of death all around.[95] And, of course, it is entirely post-exilic.

Death permeates Josiah's narratives. He, himself, is prophesied about in death-dealing terms; he is prophesied to in his lifetime in a death-coming forecast. While the kings all proceed to the throne with the death of their fathers and die to pass on the kingship to their sons (at least as a literary motif), Josiah dies to pass on control of Judah to Egypt and Babylon. He is presented as bringing about the death of a traditional religion of Judah and of the Solomonic temple in Jerusalem. It has been noted that Josiah brings an end to legitimate monarchy in Judah; however, the narratives do not establish prophetic 'possibility,' but a written authority above kings and beyond prophets.[96] Huldah pronounces the end of Judah; it comes with the end of Josiah.[97] The ancient world knew the death of rulers meant the ever-possible end of the polity over which they ruled or the return to chaos within it, which would be the same thing.[98] Such a situation is the content of the prophecy given through Huldah. None of these major

---

[95] In "Observations on Josiah's Account in Chronicles and Implications for Reconstructing the Worldview of the Chronicler," in *Essays on Ancient Israel in Its Near Eastern Context: A Tribute to Nadav Na'aman*, ed. Yairah Amit et al. (Winona Lake, IN: Eisenbrauns, 2006), 97–98, Ehud Ben Zvi comments on the presentation of oracles of coming destruction of Judah, and of Huldah's pronouncement concerning Josiah explicitly, both in Kings and Chronicles. The object of the promise of destruction is shifted from one text to the next.

[96] Walter Brueggemann and Davis Hankins ("The Affirmation of Prophetic Power and Deconstruction of Royal Authority in the Elisha Narratives," *CBQ* 76 [2014]: 76) correctly envision Kings as a text that does not endorse monarchy, but fail to note that in the Josiah narrative the end of Kings also supplants prophets. Clearly, prophets have not been terribly successful correcting kings or Israelites/Judahites in the story.

[97] Duane L. Christensen, "Huldah and the Men of Anathoth: Women in Leadership in the Deuteronomistic History," *SBLSP* 23 (1984): 402; Marianne Grohmann, "Hulda, die Prophetin (2 Kön 22,14–20)," *CV* 45 (2003) 213; Alice L. Laffey, *Wives, Harlots and Concubines: The Old Testament in Feminist Perspective* (London: SPCK, 1990), 142. Grohmann and Laffey note Huldah's literary function of ending prophetic voices in Kings (or the Deuteronomic History for some scholars).

[98] Ellen F. Morris, "Sacrifice for the State: First Dynasty Royal Funerals and the Rites at Macramallah's Rectangle," in *Performing Death: Social Analyses of Funerary Traditions in the Ancient Near East and Mediterranean*, ed. N. Laneri, OIS 3 (Chicago: Oriental Institute of the University of Chicago, 2007), 15.

events are likely to have taken place in the reign of a historical Josiah, but they do occur in the reign of the literary Josiah.[99] By the time his story was told, Josiah was dead (as a doornail).

---

99   The impossibility of discerning a historical event behind the Josiah narrative has long been recognized. Note, for example, Norbert Lohfink, "The Cult Reform of Josiah of Judah: 2 Kings 22-23 as a Source for the History of Israelite Religion," trans. C. R. Seitz, in *Ancient Israelite Religion*, ed. P. D. Miller, Jr., P. D. Hanson and S. D. McBride (Philadelphia: Fortress, 1987), 465 (though Lohfink is hopeful of some basically unrecoverable earlier and reliable source); Richard H. Lowery, *The Reforming Kings: Cult and Society in First Temple Judah*, JSOTSup 120 (Sheffield: JSOT Press, 1991), 18-19; and Ronny M. Zorn, "The Pre-Josianic Reforms of Judah" (PhD diss., Southern Baptist Theological Seminary, 1977). The unlikelihood of any "reformation" as described in 2 Kings or 2 Chronicles having taken place is discussed here in Chapter 6. The very format of the narrative should preclude anyone from simply assuming a historical event as described: Handy, "Historical Probability," 253-61, 274-75.

CHAPTER TWO
THE WISE MAN:
JOSIAH'S BUSY SCRIBES[1]

In December of 1979, Norman Whybray read a paper at the International Symposium for Biblical Studies in Tokyo in which he cast doubt upon the long-held notion of an explosion of literary wisdom composition in the period of the united monarchy.[2] Modestly, Whybray simply sought to demonstrate that the wisdom literature ascribed to Solomon was incapable of being shown to have derived from Solomon's court. Though Whybray was very careful to couch his conclusions in speculative language, the paper began an unraveling of a tapestry of traditions that dated many biblical texts to the court scribes of David and Solomon.[3] In succeeding studies, biblical scholars proceeded to remove Proverbs, the Song of Songs, Ecclesiastes (though many prior to Whybray had already assigned Ecclesiastes to the Hellenistic era),[4] the Psalms with the *ldwd* headings, Joshua, Judges, Ruth, the 'Succession Narrative,' and the Yahwistic source from the theoretical explosion of canonical-level literary activity of the scribal circles during the united monarchy, re-dating them throughout later periods. The end of this trajectory may be seen in the rise of an

---

1   This chapter is a complete revision of a conference paper, "The Busy Scribes of Josiah's Court," presented at the 2000 Midwest Regional Meeting of the Society of Biblical Literature.
2   R. N. Whybray, "Wisdom Literature in the Reigns of David and Solomon," in *Studies in the Period of David and Solomon and Other Essays*, ed. T. Ishida (Winona Lake, IN: Eisenbrauns, 1982), 25–26.
3   The notion of a vast literary output at the beginning of the states of Israel and Judah was widely accepted well into the final quarter of the twentieth century. See E. W. Heaton, *Solomon's New Men: The Emergence of Ancient Israel as a National State* (New York: Pica, 1974), 129–65 (and citations there). It needs to be noted that the rise of biblical texts in the reign of David has not disappeared. Peter Feinman (*Jerusalem Throne Games: The Battle of Bible Stories after the Death of David* [Oxford: Oxbow, 2017], 184–85) posits a decidedly political/ritual origin of biblical narrative that then saw constant revision by feuding/competitive succeeding authors.
4   See discussions in James L. Crenshaw, *Ecclesiastes: A Commentary*, OTL (Philadelphia: Westminster, 1987), 49–50; and Leo G. Perdue, *Wisdom Literature: A Theological History* (Louisville: Westminster John Knox, 2007), 161–79.

entire branch of biblical scholars who not only dismiss the writing frenzy of the united monarchy, but the united monarchy itself.[5]

However, it sometimes seems that by the end of the twentieth century, the notion of a massive creative explosion of literary biblical data had merely shifted from the beginning of the political entity of Judah to the end of the independent existence of Judah. There has been extensive literature proposing this explosion of biblical texts during the reign of Josiah, just as there had previously been a theory of a large body of literature consigned to the reigns of David and Solomon.[6] Much of the literature discussed as arising from either the united monarchy or the reign of Josiah has been the same biblical books or sections of the texts. Simultaneously, scholars have added texts to the corpus proposed for Josiah's scribes as other scholars have reconstructed a vast scribal editing community busy rewriting or expanding earlier written material.[7] This chapter seeks to note some of the material proposed to have derived from the Josianic period in order to suggest that there is as little to connect most of this vast literary output with Josiah's court as the antecedent academics had to connect, say, Joshua or Proverbs with the court of David and Solomon.

One should begin, therefore, with the obvious: only one book of the Bible claims to have been composed during Josiah's reign, or is claimed by any biblical reference to have been composed at this time.[8] The editorial introduction to the prophecy of Zephaniah (Zeph 1:1) in the Book of the Twelve explains that the material following the note of its origin was the "word of Yahweh which was to Zephaniah…in the days of Josiah son of Amon king of Judah."[9] It needs to be noted that the headings for the individual Minor Prophets are editorial notations and are now generally agreed to belong

---

5   See Niels Peter Lemche, "On Doing Sociology with 'Solomon,'" in *The Age of Solomon: Scholarship at the Turn of the Millennium*, ed. L. K. Handy, SHCANE 11 (Leiden: Brill, 1997), 312n1.

6   See, for example, Michael Fishbane, *Biblical Interpretation in Ancient Israel* (Oxford: Clarendon, 1985), 33–36. Recently, much of this work was discussed with the determination that it was again edited post-Josiah in order to reformat it for the Babylonian and Persian empires in Marvin A. Sweeney's *King Josiah of Judah*, 315–23 (for his conclusion). The vast majority of the volume is his understanding of the origins and edits of Josiah's scribal writings.

7   John Van Seters (*The Edited Bible: The Curious History of the "Editor" in Biblical Criticism* [Winona Lake, IN: Eisenbrauns, 2006], 400–401) concludes his massive study on the history of "modern" notions of ancient biblical editors/redactors by doubting the entire ancient enterprise. This is a possible conclusion.

8   Klaus Koch (*The Prophets: The Assyrian Period*, trans. M. Kohl [Philadelphia: Fortress, 1982], 158) posits Joel, Nahum, and Zephaniah as prophets of the last days of Assyria and of Josiah.

9   John D. W. Watts, *The Books of Joel, Obadiah, Jonah, Nahum, Habakkuk and Zephaniah*, CBC (Cambridge: Cambridge University Press, 1975), 153–54; J. J. M. Roberts,

to the time when the editing of the collection of selected prophetic texts was being carried out. In the case of Zephaniah, the heading provided for the sayings of this prophet stating that he was active in the time of Josiah might possibly date to an early collection of prophetic sayings garnered from only four of the Minor Prophets. Subsequent editors continued to include additional prophetic collections until the scroll now known as the Book of Twelve reached its present form. The assignment of Zephaniah to the reign of Josiah can arguably be deemed the work of those engaged in the formation of the Book of the Twelve scroll and, therefore, both post-exilic and debatable.[10] It cannot be automatically assumed that the 'dates' assigned to the prophetic texts by the editors actually fix the time when the words were spoken, and even less that they reflect the time of the writing down of those words. The dates are certainly not a reflection of the time of the editing of the prophets' proclamations.[11]

Interestingly, the prophetic material of Zephaniah does not present a Jerusalem that shows any signs of a Josianic reformation of the religious cult.[12] This anomaly is usually explained by dating the prophetic utterances of Zephaniah to the very early years of Josiah's reign.[13] As a result, Zephaniah can be, and has been, included in a great conspiracy dedicated to instigating Josiah's religious changes, making the book, like Deuteronomy, a primary text for the written rules of the reform itself.[14] The notion of this series of prophetic statements instigating any action on the part of Josiah is unwarranted, either from the text itself or from any description of the cultic activities taken by Josiah.[15] There was a long period when this

---

Nahum, Habakkuk and Zephaniah, OTL (Louisville: Westminster John Knox, 1991), 163–66.

10   See the succinct summary in Anselm C. Hagedorn, "When Did Zephaniah Become a Supporter of Josiah's Reform?," *JTS* 62 (2011): 459–62.

11   Diana Edelman, "From Prophets to Prophetic Books: The Fixing of the Divine Word," in Edelman and Ben Zvi, *The Production of Prophecy*, 42. There is no compelling reason to move these texts and their headings as late as the end of the Ptolemaic period in Palestine, though such a date has been suggested: Louise Pettibone Smith and Ernest R. Lacheman, "The Authorship of the Book of Zephaniah," *JNES* 9 (1950): 137–42.

12   Ehud Ben Zvi, "Josiah and the Prophetic Books: Some Observations," in Grabbe, *Good Kings and Bad Kings*, 53.

13   Watts, *The Books of Joel*, 154; Roberts, *Nahum, Habakkuk and Zephaniah*, 163; John S. Kselman, "Zephaniah, Book of," *ABD* 6:1077.

14   Ernest Renan (*History of the People of Israel. 3: From the Time of Hezekiah till the Return from Babylon* [Boston: Roberts Brothers, 1896], 146), presents Zephaniah as one of a potent political group that presses the reform on Josiah; shadows of this line of thought remain popular. See Sweeney, *King Josiah*, 197.

15   Hagedorn, "When Did Zephaniah Become a Supporter of Josiah's Reform?," 470–74.

collection of prophecies was cited as proof that Josiah's religious changes were ineffectual and ignored by the general populace.[16] It has been argued that Zephaniah's oracles against the nations (Zeph 2:4–15) reflect the regions Josiah intended to conquer and formed some basis for such an expansion.[17] Though the regions can be defended as surrounding Josiah's Judah, they do not reflect the territory which Kings associates with Josiah and so cannot be assumed to have anything at all to do with Josiah.[18] In the end, the content of Zephaniah reflects a social, political, and religious world not unlike that of Jeremiah, most of whose sayings are dated by scholars to well after the death of Josiah.

Zephaniah, however, can be regarded as the only book of the Bible to be attributed to the reign of Josiah within the biblical texts themselves. That said, it has rationally been argued that the original core of the scroll was perhaps Zeph 2:5–15, which constituted a short section of oracles against the nations spoken in support of Josiah's relations with Assyria and Egypt. These would have been related to political events reconstructed by modern scholars and, aside from Neco's short note, were not recorded in Kings or Chronicles.[19] This is not to claim that some, or all, of these oracles may not have derived from the time of Josiah, but it is hard to extend that claim to any historical reconstruction of Josiah.[20] The relation of Zephaniah to Josiah becomes, therefore, somewhat tenuous as Josiah's political positions and international relations remain obscured by a lack of data and the suppositions of modern historical reconstruction and theory.

---

16   See Lowell K. Handy, "Josiah and the History of the World," BR 62 (2017): 33, 36, 37. Note that Zephaniah had been cited as proof of the failure of Josiah's religious adaptations well before its citation in Sale, *An Universal History*, 845.

17   Duane L. Christensen, "Zephaniah 2:4–15: A Theological Basis for Josiah's Program of Political Expansion," CBQ 46 (1984): 669–82.

18   Sweeney (*King Josiah*, 192–95) argues for all the oracles being genuine Josianic proclamations, but does note the relation to Jeremiah's post-exilic (post-Josiah) passages (194).

19   So Dan'el Kahn, "The Historical Setting of Zephaniah's Oracles against the Nations (Zeph 2:4–15)," in *Homeland and Exile: Biblical and Ancient Near Eastern Studies in Honour of Busteney Oded*, ed. G. Galil, M. Geller and A. Millard, VTSup 130 (Leiden: Brill, 2009), 450. See Hagedorn, "When Did Zephaniah Become a Supporter of Josiah's Reform?," 465. Hagedorn includes other assorted political oracles as probably original to the time of Josiah but the biblical book is the product of the post-exilic world and may contain as many as three prophets' sayings as well as the additions of (various) editors.

20   Eric Lee Welch ("The Roots of Anger: An Economic Perspective on Zephaniah's Oracle Against the Philistines," VT 63 [2013]: 484–85) argues for a Josianic date for Zeph 2:4 on the basis of seventh-century economic rivalry and rejects the *ex eventu* posit used to date the Philistine oracles after their Babylonian capture.

The book of Nahum has no such internal claim to derive from the time of Josiah. Its editorial heading (Nah 1:1) is not at all curious in lacking a fixed reign (the dating accorded Zephaniah is the minority format). Nonetheless, Nahum has been dated almost universally not only to the time of Josiah but explicitly to 614–613 on the grounds that the impinging destruction of Nineveh in 612 would surely have prodded such a prophetic prediction,[21] or to 612–611 upon the actual destruction of Nineveh, which is then seen as an event that influenced someone to create the 'prophecy' after the fact in view of the jubilation over the fall of a hated Assyrian Empire.[22] Yet, in the case of Nahum, there has been a substantial minority of scholars who have used the internal reference to the destruction of Thebes in 663 (Nah 3:8) to posit the possibility that the prophecy was a product of the reign of one of the pre-Josianic rulers.[23] The prophetic poetry could have been written years or decades after the fall of Nineveh. Christensen is certainly accurate in stating that the literary form displays a very liturgical appearance and should probably be considered as a part of the religious cult. This is likely after the fall of Nineveh, and Nahum is clearly not a ritual text that would have bothered a Neo-Babylonian imperial milieu in any way.[24] However, Nahum attained its current form after Josiah's reign and probably after the existence of an independent Judah altogether. The heading, at least, would have been added at the time of Nahum's incorporation into the Book of the Twelve, but to what extent any textual changes were made aside from copy divergences is unclear.

In a similar manner, the book of Jonah has been assigned to the years immediately prior to the destruction of Nineveh and has therefore been

---

21 See Julius A. Bewer, *The Literature of the Old Testament*, 3rd ed., rev. Emil G. Kraeling, RCSS 5 (New York: Columbia University Press, 1962), 147–48, "imminent fall"; Otto Eissfeldt, *The Old Testament: An Introduction*, trans. Peter R. Ackroyd (New York: Harper & Row, 1965), 414–15: "after 662 and before 612." Even H. H. Rowley, noted for Hellenistic dating of Hebrew Scripture texts, assumes a Josianic date for Nahum, see Rowley, *The Growth of the Old Testament*, Hutchinson University Library (London: Hutchinson, 1950; repr., Cloister Library; New York: Harper & Row, 1963), 116–17.

22 Ernst Sellin and Georg Fohrer, *Introduction to the Old Testament*, trans. David E. Green (Nashville: Abingdon: 1968), 448; Watts, *The Books of Joel*, 99–100; Roberts, *Nahum, Habakkuk and Zephaniah*, 38–39; Mario Liverani, *Israel's History and the History of Israel*, trans. C. Peri and P. R. Davies, BibleWorld (London: Equinox, 2005), 168–70.

23 Eissfeldt, *The Old Testament*, 415; Kevin J. Cathcart, "Nahum, Book of," *ABD* 4.999; Gregory D. Cook, "Naqia and Nineveh in Nahum: Ambiguity and the Prostitute Queen," *JBL* 136 (2017): 902 and 902n44; see Edwin M. Yamauchi, *Africa and the Bible* (Grand Rapids: Baker Academic, 2004), 140.

24 Duane L. Christensen, *Transformations of the War Oracle in Old Testament Prophecy: Studies in the Oracles Against the Nations*, HDR 3 (Missoula, MT: Scholars Press, 1975), 166–67.

seen as a product of Josiah's court.[25] The argument still in existence that the story would carry more force with Nineveh does not carry much conviction, and Jonah is now almost universally dated to the era of Persian domination.[26] Traditionally, Jonah has been dated to the prophet Jonah mentioned in Second Kings during the reign of Jeroboam II (2 Kgs 14:25), but this date has long since been abandoned.[27] The text presumes a single deity ruling the entire heavens and earth, which could be related to Josiah's 'reform' if biblical monotheism were all one had for chronology. Nevertheless, Jonah could have been, and undoubtedly was, written any time after this view of Yahweh developed. Jonah's Yahweh has more in common with the deity found in Job and Ecclesiastes than in Kings, and this understanding would appear to postdate Judah as an independent entity.[28] It has long been observed that the Nineveh in the book of Jonah is a literary invention with little to nothing to do with the historical Assyrian city.[29] Currently there is no notable attempt to date Jonah to Josiah's reign. However, it has been suggested that another short story of the Bible, Ruth, was not a product of the post-exilic controversy over ethnic lineage, but a tale told of the Davidic dynasty as part of the Davidic revival.[30] While this view may not be widely held, it includes Ruth among the suggested literary production of Josiah's busy scribes.

Of course, the eighth-century prophets, whose editorial headings in the Book of the Twelve claim the reigns of earlier Judahite kings for their chronological origins, have uniformly been assigned to Josianic editing. First Isaiah has had a proposed Josianic edition created by circles seeking to conform the Isaianic prophetic tradition from the time of Hezekiah to the Josianic reform. This theory has had a number of supporters who then date the text of First Isaiah as passed on to the Exilic community

---

25   See comment on B. Eerdman in Leslie C. Allen, *The Books of Joel, Obadiah, Jonah and Micah*, NICOT (Grand Rapids: Eerdmans, 1976), 186.

26   Jack M. Sasson, *Jonah: A New Translation with Introduction and Commentary*, AB 24B (New York: Doubleday, 1990), 20–21; Ehud Ben Zvi, *Signs of Jonah: Reading and Rereading in Ancient Yehud*, JSOTSup 367 (London: Sheffield Academic, 2003), 7–9n19.

27   Cunningham Geikie (*Old Testament Characters* [New York: James Pott, 1885], 360–61) reflects the traditional dating in his sketch of the life of Jonah.

28   Handy, *Jonah's World*, 54, 58; Yahweh may be the only god recognized by the author, but it is a Wisdom on Its Head vision of that deity.

29   Bewer, *The Literature of the Old Testament*, 423; Sellin and Fohrer, *Introduction*, 442. The book of Jonah deals in miraculous events and the city of Nineveh has little relation to the historical Assyrian capital; it is an "imaginary real world" literary setting. See further, Handy, *Jonah's World*, 31–33.

30   Jack M. Sasson, *Ruth: A New Translation with a Philological Commentary and a Formalist-Folklorist Interpretation*, JHNES (Baltimore: Johns Hopkins University Press, 1979), 251.

to the later years of the seventh century.³¹ Whether this edition of Isaiah included chapters 2–32 or some more modest contents, like chapters 5–12, 14–23, 27–32, 36–37,³² or some other configuration, is immaterial; what is interesting is that many scholars envision a need by Josianic scribal circles to edit previous prophetic texts by a noted and prolific prophet to support a religious reform and to condemn a collapsing Assyrian Empire.³³ In short, the presumed need for a scribal rewrite of First Isaiah in the time of Josiah rests on the historicity of the 'Josianic Reform' as it appears in Kings and the assumption that the collapse of Assyria was dealt with by Josiah in a manner that can be grasped two and a half millennia later. Neither of these assumptions should be presumed. This observation applies to the rest of the Minor Prophets currently seen as having a Josianic edition.

In the same way, it has been argued by Wolff (and others who follow his lead) that a Josianic edition was made to Amos that supplemented the received text with newly devised passages suitable to Josiah's needs. Amos 4:4–13 would have been useful for the demolition of Bethel, for example.³⁴ Since Bethel had been a continuing rival cultic center in the northern kingdom for the temple in Jerusalem, there is no particular need to have an anti-Bethel passage added during the reign of Josiah simply because there is a Bethel destruction tale told of Josiah. Cult site rivalry would have sufficed for an earlier such passage and even a post-exilic date would not be improbable on the basis of cultic rivalry.³⁵ Undoubtedly, scribes

---

31   Among the champions of this editorial activity for Isaiah: Hermann Barth, *Die Jesaja-Worte in der Josiazeit: Israel und Assur als Thema einer produktiven Neuinterpretation der Jesaja*, WMANT 48 (Neukirchen-Vluyn: Neukirchener Verlag, 1977); Jacques Vermeylen, *Du Prophète Isaïe à l'apocalyptique: Isaïe 1–35*, 2 vols., Ebib (Paris: Gabalda, 1977–1978); idem, "L'unité du livre d'Isaïe," in *The Book of Isaiah*, ed. J. Vermeylen, BETL 81 (Leuven: Leuven University, 1989), 28–33; Ronald E. Clements, *Isaiah 1–39*, NCB (Grand Rapids: Eerdmans, 1980), 6; Marvin A. Sweeney, *Isaiah 1–39 with an Introduction to Prophetic Literature*, FOTL 16 (Grand Rapids: Eerdmans, 1996), 51, 57–58.

32   These are the reconstructions of Clements (*Isaiah*, 5) and Sweeney (*Isaiah*, 57), respectively. Mark Leuchter ("Tyre's '70 Year's' in Isaiah 23,15–18," *Bib* 87 [2006]: 416) envisions a passage datable by Judean release from Assyrian control after the death of Ashurbanipal during Josiah's reign and directly related to Judean writers being familiar with the Texts of Esarhaddon (414–15).

33   Jonathan Goldstein, for example, sees Isa 10:27 as a text written to reflect Josiah's reign, see Goldstein, *Peoples of an Almighty God: Competing Religions in the Ancient World*, ABRL (New York: Doubleday, 2002), 91. This is, however, not necessary.

34   Hans Walter Wolff, *Amos the Prophet: The Man and His Background*, trans. F. McCurley (Philadelphia: Fortress, 1973), 215–17, 222; idem, *Joel and Amos*, trans. W. Janzen, S. McBride, Jr., and C. Muenchow, Hermeneia (Philadelphia: Fortress, 1977), 111–12. The language chart is on p. 113.

35   James Luther Mays sees no reason to doubt a Jerusalem-Bethel rivalry in the eighth century in *Amos: A Commentary*, OTL (Philadelphia: Westminster, 1969), 73–76.

worked on these passed-down prophecies. There is no particular reason to assume that their copying did not involve making changes in the text or even adding additional sayings that the scribe/s deemed relevant, but there is nothing about Amos itself to tie any specific edition to the time of Josiah.

In the 1980s, Hosea was posited a similar Josianic edition by Emmerson and Yee; both based their renditions of the edited scroll on the presumed attacks by Josiah's forces on the Israelite temples at Dan and Bethel.[36] Yee's Josianic edition of Hosea is a decidedly cut-up version of the Masoretic Text's version, implying that the editing of this prophetic material had a very long history and that the exact words of the historical prophet were not sacrosanct but were constantly malleable.[37] This raises the possibility that any given prophet from the 'past' was available to the scribes for rewriting into whatever form the 'current' religious needs of the ruler, or of his scribes, deemed necessary at the time. What one gets in these 'edited and expanded' renditions of Hosea is an entirely new Hosea. Central to the proposed rewritten book is the notion that traditional prophetic material needed to be adapted to religious changes implemented by Josiah. Among these innovations was the notion of a faithful 'elected' populace.[38] When the certainty of the "reform narrative" in Kings becomes questionable and the dating of Deuteronomy is removed from Josiah's realm, the need for dating almost all of the changes proposed for Hosea disappears. What the scroll of Hosea looked like at the beginning or the end of Josiah's reign is not recoverable, and theories dependent on the complete realignment of religious thought along Deuteronomistic lines should not be taken seriously. The text is certainly not to be dated to the whims of King Josiah.

Micah, famous in Jer 26:18 for providing the textual tradition of releasing the later prophet from a precarious situation, is often argued to have had an edition of denunciations embodied in chapters 1–3, minus the introduction composed for the Book of the Twelve along with a smattering of later additions, including chapters 4–6, which it has been assumed were produced by scribes involved with Josiah's cultic reform.[39]

See also Philip J. King, *Amos, Hosea, Micah: An Archaeological Commentary* (Philadelphia: Westminster, 1988), 40–41.

36 Grace I. Emmerson, *Hosea: An Israelite Prophet in Judean Perspective*, JSOTSup 28 (Sheffield: JSOT Press, 1984) 138; Gale A. Yee, *Composition and Tradition in the Book of Hosea: A Redactional Critical Investigation*, SBLDS 102 (Atlanta: Scholars Press, 1987), 120.

37 Yee (*Composition and Tradition in the Book of Hosea*, 315–17) outlines the detailed description of the reconstituted Hosea text posited for the scribes of Josiah's court.

38 See Erasmus Gaß ("Hosea zwischen Tradition und Innovation am Beispiel von Hos 2,16f," ZAW 122 [2010]: 183), who sees Hos 2:16 as reflecting the Josianic reform.

39 James Luther Mays, *Micah: A Commentary*, OTL (Philadelphia: Westminster, 1976), 23; Delbert R. Hillers, *Micah*, Hermeneia (Philadelphia: Fortress, 1986), 3.

Essentially, the Micah text cited in the Jeremiah narrative (Jer 3:12) would have supposed a prophet who spoke doom without reprieve.[40] The alleged additions of Josiah's scribes mollify the doom and, in the present book, provide hope in the long run. How an edited version of Micah's official prophetic words created in the time of Josiah would then be of aid to the dire straits of Jeremiah becomes a question in that Jehoiakim is condemning Jeremiah for proclaiming doom alone with no hope. Did the friends of Jeremiah know that Jehoiakim had a copy of the earlier edition of Micah or did they assume the king knew the words of Micah from the scribal addenda? Did both the king and Jeremiah's supporters ignore the scribal work of Josiah's court? A more rational answer is that the Jeremiah story is one of many post-exilic legends circulating concerned with the then famous prophet.[41] This explanation does not explain a Josianic era adaptation of the prophecies of Micah since a post-exilic scribe writing such a tale, even if only creatively rewriting an early story, should have known that the scroll of Micah was not one of irrefutable doom, but one pulsating between punishment and retrieval. On the other hand, it would be absurd to posit that Josiah's faithful followers burned all the scrolls from which they had adapted, enlarged, and edited previous prophetic material. If the redemptive texts of Micah are not all post-exilic additions (when a series of hopeful repentant comments would allow the doom texts to be retained without being invalid), there would appear to have been two versions of the scroll after Josiah. This is not impossible, but it begs the question: was one authoritative and one not? Or, better, can there be content evidence here of a Josianic adaptation at all?

Two later prophets have also been assigned Josianic material. Habakkuk was popularly dated to the reign of Josiah in the late nineteenth and early twentieth centuries. This is now an unpopular view among scholars, who tend to date the book in the decade after Josiah's death.[42] The questioning of actions taken by Yahweh could have been recorded at any time, and the notion that the righteous are being abused by the godless could have reflected either internal or external dismay. The current idea that this reflects Jehoiakim or Babylonians, but not Josiah, is common, but

---

40 Mays, *Micah*, 23. See the short summary in Claude F. Mariottini, "The Trial of Jeremiah and the Killing of Uriah the Prophet," *JBQ* 42 (2014): 30–31.

41 Robert P. Carroll sees the earliest possible date for this material as after the fall of Jerusalem in 587 BCE in *Jeremiah: A Commentary*, OTL (Philadelphia: Westminster, 1986), 518.

42 See Rowley, *Growth*, 118; the surveys in Roberts, *Nahum, Habakkuk and Zephaniah*, 83; Peter Jöcken, *Das Buch Habakuk: Darstellung der Geschichte seiner kritischen Erforschung mit einer eigenen Beurteilung*, BBB 48 (Cologne: Peter Hanstein, 1977), 14–40. However, note Robert D. Haak, *Habakkuk*, VTSup 44 (Leiden: Brill, 1992), 132.

in previous scholarship the distant rise of the 'Chaldeans' at the time of Josiah was used to date part of Habakkuk to the reign of Josiah.[43]

Jeremiah is recorded as having begun his prophetic career in Josiah's thirteenth year without claiming that the following book contains Josianic era texts (Jer 1:2).[44] Only at Jeremiah 3:6 does the book claim a prophetic saying from the Josianic period. This prophetic text appears to consist of verses 6b–10, a prose passage steeped in Deuteronomistic language condemning the religious activities of Israel and, only secondarily, of Judah. The prose format has caused most scholars to posit a late date for the passage over an early one.[45] However, Holladay, following Lohfink, is certain that Jer 1:4–10 derives from early in Jeremiah's prophetic activity and should be considered one of the prophecies delivered in the time of Josiah.[46] John Bright agrees with the Josianic date for that passage, including more material in the Josianic corpus of Jeremiah: Jer 2:1–37 and 3:1–4:4.[47] Finally, Jeremiah 30–31 has been taken by several Jeremiah scholars as being the ur-text for a double redaction of the material into the so-called Book of Consolation and then into the book of Jeremiah.[48] That none of Jeremiah's recorded sayings derive from the time of Josiah remains quite reasonable.[49] More interesting is that the reign of Josiah that appears to be presented in Jeremiah is one of unmitigated apostasy.

---

43 Bewer (*The Literature of the Old Testament*, 149, 152) proposes an early date, 625 BCE, for the earliest possible prophecies of Habakkuk, but see the survey in Eissfeldt, *Old Testament*, 417–20.

44 Indeed, even commentaries that assume some Josianic-era material in Jeremiah note that it is difficult to assign any passages to that time; Norbert Lohfink, "Die Gattung der 'Historischen Kurzgeschichte' in den letzten Jahren von Judah und in der Zeit des Babylonischen Exils," *ZAW* 90 (1978): 339–41. See too Ernest W. Nicholson (*Jeremiah 1-25*, CBC [Cambridge: Cambridge University Press, 1973], 4–5), who also contends that the superscription dating is not accurate (21).

45 William McKane, *A Critical and Exegetical Commentary on Jeremiah*, ICC (Edinburgh: T&T Clark, 1986), 1.68–69; Carroll, *Jeremiah*, 145; Marvin H. Sweeney, *King Josiah*, 209 and 209n6. Nicholson (*Jeremiah 1-25*, 44) assumes it is a late editor's comment.

46 William Lee Holladay, *Jeremiah 1*, Hermeneia (Philadelphia: Fortress, 1986), 2.

47 John Bright, *Jeremiah: A New Translation with Introduction and Commentary*, AB 21 (Garden City, NY: Doubleday, 1965), 6–8, 16–18.

48 See Holladay, *Jeremiah*, 2, and discussion by Sweeney, *King Josiah*, 225–32. Sweeney connects an even more restricted *ur-ur*-text to the destruction of Bethel and the desire to reconstruct the united monarchy in Josiah's reform and, thus, to be dated to that time (231–32).

49 C. F. Whitley, "The Date of Jeremiah's Call," *VT* 14 (1964): 467, 483; McKane, *Jeremiah*, 3–5. See especially John Brian Job (*Jeremiah's Kings*, 39–52), who surveys the current attempts to correlate Jeremiah with Josiah's reign and concludes that there is no credible reason to assign any pericope of the book of Jeremiah to the time of Josiah. The best arguments that can possibly be made for any part of Jeremiah

The book of Jeremiah knows of no positive cultic reform for this king.[50] This does not mean that there is not much to draw out from the book of Jeremiah on the creation of a remembered Josiah, only that these passages are probably not materials derived from the reign of Josiah.[51] The depiction of Josiah in the book of Jeremiah is a creation of the compilers of the prophet's sayings, the legends surrounding him, and the material ascribed to (if not written specifically for) Jeremiah and then attached to a king credited with pristine religious behavior.[52] Similarities between the scroll of Jeremiah and the Former Prophets may well signify compositions relatively congruent in time, but content suggests a very late, post-monarchic, date.[53]

The description of Josiah's reign as it currently appears in Second Kings cannot be a product of Josiah's reign.[54] It could conceivably have been written by his scribes in the wake of his death, but this also seems unlikely.[55] What has been taken by most scholars to be a genuine product

---

deriving from the time of Josiah are internally circular and highly suspect. See further Ben Zvi, "Josiah and the Prophetic Books," 64.

50 Ben Zvi, "Josiah and the Prophetic Books," 50–51, 53; Grabbe, *1 & 2 Kings*, 74.

51 Sweeney (*King Josiah*, 208) correctly insists the book is a good source for studying Josiah in the Hebrew Bible, but he is overly optimistic that the book contains anything directly from Jeremiah in the time of Josiah (233).

52 The pro-Babylonian leanings envisaged for Jeremiah, even related to the Assyrian-era death of Josiah, suggest exilic dating at the earliest. See Rowton, "Jeremiah and the Death of Josiah," 128–30.

53 Thomas Römer, "The Formation of the Book of Jeremiah as a Supplement to the So-called Deuteronomistic History," in Edelman and Ben Zvi, *The Production of Prophecy*, 169–71, 179.

54 So the theory that Josiah's story in Kings was produced by Josiah's court (Cogan, *1 Kings*, 97). It was observed long ago that the entire 'Josianic Reform' narrative was reliant on the reform conditions already being in existence in order to make any sense and could therefore not have been contemporary descriptions. See the summary of several earlier articles in *The Jewish Quarterly Review* by Cook in his encyclopedia entries; Stanley Arthur Cook, "Josiah," *EncBrit*[11], 15.520; idem, "Kings, First and Second Books of," 15.813. One example of many contributions: idem, "Biblical Criticism 'Moderate' and 'Advanced,'" *JQR* 20 (1907): 161. Cook was a widely published scholar whose observation of Judean religious "evolution" also appeared in popular periodicals: idem, "The 'Evolution' of Biblical Religion," *ModC* 24 (1934): 475. The observation that the rationale of the "reform" narrative is an internally circular argument has reappeared (see Philip R. Davies, *In Search of 'Ancient Israel'*, 2nd ed., JSOTSup 148 [Sheffield: Sheffield Academic, 1995], 38–39), and has the idea that it appears to be internally incoherent and must be a story after the supposed events described. See David Henige, "Found but Not Lost: A Skeptical Note on the Document Discovered in the Temple under Josiah," *JHS* 7 (2007): 16.

55 See Colby Dickinson ("Canons and Canonicity: Late Modern Reflections on Cultural and Religious Canonical Texts," *ASE* 30 [2013]: 384–85), whose statement

of Josiah's reign is the prophecy recorded of Huldah in 2 Kgs 22:15b-20a. That some of the Huldah material has been edited to conform to the defeat of Jerusalem by the Babylonians has not dampened the notion that the declaration of Josiah's death *beshalom* must somehow have been a genuine recorded prophecy that could only be reproduced precisely as it had been recited.[56] That the prophecy was tampered with would seem to dispel that argument and should have caused such contentions to disappear from the academic world long ago. The argument that Huldah's oracle (in full or in part) is received in an original form from the time of Josiah can no longer be taken as obvious or probable.[57] The historical context of Huldah's prophecy depends entirely on how much a given scholar accepts the narrative of Josiah's reign in 2 Kings as an unedited historical report. It is possible that the semi-miraculous discovery of the scroll and its authentication by Huldah was a fictitious short story written by scribes during Josiah's reign[58]—possible, but unlikely. A number of current studies of the oracle agree that it is more likely that the oracle is, at the earliest, an exilic creation, but that it is probably a literary construction of the compiler of the book of Kings during the Persian Empire.[59] It is less clear that the bracketing material for Josiah, or any of the kings in the book of Kings, derives from some official court document; the theory is very popular, but is not demonstrable.[60]

---

that the canonization is most associated with Ezra should be considered in consort with the "fiction" of Josiah's narrative. Becker (among others) has argued that the "monotheism" and idealized temple cult of the Josiah narratives derive from early Judaism and not from the late Judah monarchy. See Uwe Becker, "Von der Staatsreligion zum Monotheismus: Ein Kapital israelitisch-jüdischer Religionsgeschichte," ZTK 102 (2005): 7-8, 13-14.

56   Bewer, *The Literature of the Old Testament*, 244; also Montgomery (*A Critical and Exegetical Commentary*, 545), who sees two prophecies: one before the reform and one after, but both genuine and both by Huldah in the time of Josiah. John Gray finds the prophecy a muddled edited confusion but decides that the prediction of Josiah's death was part of the original prophecy by Huldah, see *I & II Kings*, 727.

57   Sweeney suggests the current prophecy written for Huldah is a later literary creation, see *I & II Kings*, 442-43.

58   So Arthur J. Droge ("'The Lying Pen of the Scribes': Of Holy Books and Pious Frauds," *MTSR* 15 [2003]: 118-19), who terms the entire discovery narrative a self-serving fraud, but of the time of Josiah. More recently, Nadav Na'aman, "The 'Discovered Book' and the Legitimation of Josiah's Reform," *JBL* 130 (2011): 62.

59   Ahlström, *The History of Ancient Palestine*, 773-74; Thomas Römer, *The So-Called Deuteronomistic History: A Sociological, Historical and Literary Introduction* (London: T&T Clark, 2007), 50-51; Michael Pietsch, *Die Kultrefom Josias: Studien zur Religionsgeschichte Israels in der späten Königszeit*, FAT 86 (Tübingen: Mohr Siebeck, 2013), 159.

60   Helga Weippert, "Die 'deuteromischtischen' Beurteilungen der Könige von Israel und Juda und das Problem der Redaktion der Königbucher," *Bib* 53 (1972): 332.

The Deuteronomistic History has widely been assumed to have more or less reached its modern form during the reign of Josiah. These hypothetical histories of the Deuteronomistic History have usually been understood to be minus the death of Josiah, perhaps lacking the death of David, and, occasionally, missing the entire reign of Solomon. The continuing references to the destruction of the land of Judah, and possibly the several references to all of the prophets in the book of the Former Prophets, have also been suggested as post-Josianic redactions of the tome. The exclusion of prophetic material is a theory of those who see the original text as an official court history of the Jerusalem monarchy, therefore presuming the original book to be interested in political and chronological matters.[61] According to this theory, the Deuteronomistic History may have begun as court records as early as the time of David or Solomon, but is usually ascribed, if not to Josiah, to Hezekiah.[62] There is, however, no evidence for such a court history. If the Deuteronomistic History were the product of the Josianic court, this would put the bulk of Joshua, Judges, Samuel, and Kings among the scribal activities of Josiah's faithful corps. Frank Moore Cross's Dtr[1] in fact includes almost everything from Deuteronomy to 2 Kgs 22:20 in the Josianic rendition.[63] In contrast to the theory of Martin Noth that the Deuteronomistic History was essentially a post-exilic, or, at best, an exilic production,[64] Cross's theory has held sway over the latter quarter

---

[61] The use of official court annals is usually asserted, asserting that Josiah's Judah would provide the latest possible time for such a composition. See Christoph Levin, "Das synchronistische Exzerpt aus den Annalen der Könige von Israel und Juda," *VT* 61 (2011): 626. It is then argued that a post-monarchic rewrite changed the emphasis from court to temple (secular to religious), creating a different genre of text, so John W. Rogerson, *The So-called Deuteronomistic History: A Sociological, Historical and Literary Introduction* (London: T&T Clark, 2007), 19.

[62] As noted in summary fashion in William M. Schniedewind, "Jerusalem, the Late Judahite Monarchy, and the Composition of the Biblical Texts," in A. G. Vaughn and A. E. Killebrew, *Jerusalem in Bible and Archaeology: The First Temple Period*, SBLSymS 18 (Atlanta: Society of Biblical Literature), 388–89. Because of Prov 25:1, Schniedewind adduces "good reason to believe" that the collecting and writing of biblical literature began in Hezekiah's reign (387), a position that seems incapable of being demonstrated.

[63] Frank Moore Cross, *Canaanite Myth and Hebrew Epic: Essays in the History of the Religion of Israel* (Cambridge, MA: Harvard University Press, 1973), 274–85. For a survey of this theory, see Steven L. McKenzie, *The Trouble with Kings: The Composition of the Book of Kings in the Deuteronomistic History*, VTSup 42 (Leiden: Brill, 1991), 1–19.

[64] Martin Noth, *Überlieferungsgeschichtliche Studien I: Die sammelnden und bearbeitenden Geschichtswerke im Alten Testament* (Halle: Max Niemeyer, 1943). Noth's dating of the material continues to have support, e.g., John Van Seters, "The Deuteronomist—Historian or Redactor? From Simon to the Present," in Amit et al., *Essays on Ancient Israel in Its Near Eastern Context*, 372.

of the twentieth century. It is unlikely that the several 'books' of the Bible, each of which has its own structure and its own view on historical people and events, were the product of a single author. Much more likely is the possibility that Joshua, Judges, Samuel, and Kings were independent scrolls that at some point in time may (or may not) have been edited into a continuous rendition of a historical record of Judah and Israel.[65]

Deuteronomy had been connected to the book of the Torah found by Josiah's workmen at least since the time of Jerome and Chrysostom.[66] This equation was accepted as historical fact by Alfonso X, the Geneva Bible, Sir Walter Raleigh, John Hobbs, and the often-cited authority de Wette.[67] If this were the scroll found by Hilkiah, this is not clear from the author of the text of Kings, who uses the generic *torah* to define it as a work of Moses—and even then only slightly connected to Moses (2 Kgs 23:25 is the only Kings citation relating this scroll to Moses). Certainly, the oracle ascribed to Huldah does nothing to define the work in the Kings story

---

[65] Ernst Axel Knauf, "'L'Historiographie deutéronomiste' (DTRG) exist-t-elle?," in *Israël construit son histoire: L'historiographie deutéronomiste à la lumière des recherches récentes*, ed. Albert de Pury, Thomas Römer, and Jean-Daniel Macchi, MdB 34 (Genève: Labor et Fides, 1996), 413–18. Note the distinct literary difference, composition, and concern of Samuel from the other three scrolls: Michael Avioz, "The Motif of Beauty in the Books of Samuel and Kings," VT 59 (2009): 359; Davies, "I Samuel and the 'Deuteronomistic History,'" 114–16; and Kurt L. Noll, "Is the Scroll of Samuel Deuteronomistic?," in Edenberg and Pakkala, *Samuel among the Deuteronomists*, 138–39. The four 'histories' in the 'Deuteronomistic history' all have their own literary and theological cohesiveness; the example of Samuel will suffice here.

[66] As noted by the often-cited James A. Kelso, "Theodoret and the Law Book of Josiah," JBL 22 (1903): 51. Still popular is Bernard M. Levinson, "Die neuassyrischen Ursprünge der Kanonformel in Deuteronomium 13,1," in *Viele Wege zu dem Einen: Historische Bibelkritik—Die Vitalität der Glaubensüberlieferung in der Moderne*, ed. S. Beyerle, A. Graupner, and U. Rüterswörden, BibThS 121 (Neukirchen-Vluyn: Neukirchener Verlag, 2012), 38–39.

[67] On the early and continuing assumption that Deuteronomy was the book found in Josiah's reign within the Christian tradition, see Lowell K. Handy, "Josiah after the Chronicler," PEGLAMBS 14 (1994): 100; and idem, "The Good, Bad, Insignificant, Indispensable King Josiah," 44; Hans-Peter Mathys, "Wilhelm Martin Lebrecht de Wette's *Dissertatio critic-exegetica* von 1805," in *Biblische Theologie und Historisches Denken: Wissenschaftsgeschichtliche Studien*, ed. M. Kessler and M. Wallraff, SGWB n.f. 5 (Basel: Schwabe, 2008), 174–81. On the significance of de Wette, see John W. Rogerson, *W. M. L. de Wette, Founder of Modern Biblical Criticism: An Intellectual Biography*, JSOTSup 126 (Sheffield: JSOT Press, 1992). On Jewish assumption that the Josiah scroll was Deuteronomy, see Eran Viezel, "Un precedent juif de De Wette: Un commentaire attribué à Rashi sur le livre des Chroniques, autour du livre trouvé au Temple par le prêtre Hilkiyyahou," trans. R. Klein, REJ 170 (2011): 523–24. Midrashic and Talmudic references that suggest Josiah knew Deuteronomy are also noted (524–27).

as having anything to do with the book of Deuteronomy.[68] However, that the book shown to Josiah was Deuteronomy has increasingly come under suspicion.[69] Nonetheless, there has been, and continues to be, a contingent of scholars who propose that Deuteronomy was written in the time of Josiah in order to legitimate the religious changes he instigated.[70] Various attempts have been made to discern which parts of Deuteronomy may have been original to Josiah. These attempts become moot when the currently popular urge to date the work backward to Hezekiah is accepted.[71] This would still allow for a Josianic edition that revamps the text. There are, however, problems with connecting Deuteronomy in any form with the Josiah represented in Kings or Chronicles.[72] In any case, there is reason to doubt that Deuteronomy derived from before the fall of the state of Judah.[73] Indeed, there is reasonable doubt that any scroll intended to be

---

68 Ahlström, *The History of Ancient Palestine*, 775–77. This is in opposition to the conclusion of de Wette, see Mathys, "Wilhelm Martin Lebrecht de Wettes," 210–11.

69 This suspicion is not particularly new. See, for example, Kjeld Jensen, "Om de moaiske Lovskriters Alder," *DTT* 5 (1942): 3-4, 14.

70 This was already a popular theory in the eighteenth century; Sale, *Universal History*, 483–84n.E. Moshe Weinfeld, *Deuteronomy and the Deuteronomic School* (Oxford: Oxford University Press, 1972), 1; Baruch Halpern, "Between Elective Autocracy and Democracy: Formalizing Biblical Constitutional Theory," in *Literature as Politics, Politics as Literature: Essays on the Ancient Near East in Honor of Peter Machinist*, ed. D. S. Vanderhooft and A. Winitzer (Winona Lake, IN: Eisenbrauns, 2013), 174. It retains its popularity: Dale Patrick, *Old Testament Law* (Atlanta: John Knox, 1985), 15–16.

71 It was often suggested that Deuteronomy had a long gestation that predated Josiah. See, for example, Weinfeld, *Deuteronomy*, 9; Norbert Lohfink, "Zur neuen Diskussion über 2 Kön 22–23," in *Das Deuteronomium: Entstehung, Gestalt und Botschaft*, ed. N. Lohfink, BETL 68 (Leuven: Leuven University Press; Peeters, 1985), 24–48.

72 Davies, *In Search*, 38–40. It is worth noting that some 'conservative' biblical scholars have little trouble seeing Deuteronomy as a post-Judean product, citing it as an example of a text written in the name of an ancient figure. As one example, see Christopher B. Ansberry and Jerry Hwang, "No Covenant before the Exile? The Deuteronomic Torah and Israel's Covenant Theology," in *Evangelical Faith and the Challenge of Historical Criticism*, ed. C. M. Hays and C. B. Ansberry (Grand Rapids: Baker Academic, 2013), 78–89.

73 See Edward Day, "The Promulgation of Deuteronomy," *JBL* 21 (1902): 213; Gustav Hölscher, "Komposition und Ursprung des Deuteronomiums," *ZAW* 40 (1922): 228–29; Juha Pakkala, "Why the Cult Reforms in Judah Probably Did Not Happen," in Kratz and Spieckermann, *One God—One Cult—One Nation*, 210–11; Rainer Albertz, "A Possible *terminus ad quem* for the Deuteronomistic Legislation: A Fresh Look at Deut 17:16," in Galil, Geller, and Millard, *Homeland and Exile*, 292. It is interesting that Schniedewind ("Jerusalem," 387–93) does not even discuss Deuteronomy in his list of publications of late-Judean Jerusalem.

followed (let alone read) by an extended populace would make literary sense before the Persian Period at the earliest.[74]

Each of these 'Deuteronomic History' books of the Bible has had scholarly studies determining its Deuteronomistic qualities, but for the reign of Josiah none has had more importance, aside from the rendition of Josiah's reign in the book of Kings itself (2 Kgs 21:26–23:30),[75] than Joshua. However, the near identification of Joshua's conquest of Canaan with Josiah's reign rests on the unlikely basis that King Josiah recreated the kingdom of David, as David's realm is reported in Samuel, thereby providing the geography appearing in Joshua.[76] In this reconstruction, Josiah would historically have finished off the conquest narrative begun in Joshua.[77] That there is little to no evidence for anything except a very small Judah, from Jerusalem southward, makes this hypothesis highly unlikely.[78] Neither is there reason to equate the geography in Joshua with a hypothetical Josiah empire.[79] Nor can sub-sections of Joshua's territory lists reasonably be assumed to derive from Josiah's state papers.[80] Nonetheless,

---

74 Or even later: Finsterbusch, "Modelle," 230, 242, though note that attempts to include both Hezekiah and Josiah in dating Deuteronomy by having it composed *between* their reigns do exist. This would appear to be an unlikely compromise. See further Robert R. Wilson, "Deuteronomy, Ethnicity, and Reform: Reflections on the Social Setting of the Book of Deuteronomy," in *Constituting the Community: Studies on the Polity of Ancient Israel in Honor of S. Dean McBride Jr*, ed. J. T. Strong and S. S. Tuell (Winona Lake, IN: Eisenbrauns, 2005), 119, 123.

75 The description of Josiah's reign as it appears in Kings has to post-date Josiah's death and reasonably does not pre-date the Persian Empire. Knauf, "Kings among the Prophets," 142.

76 J. Alberto Soggin (*Joshua: A Commentary*, trans. R. A. Wilson, OTL [Philadelphia: Westminster, 1972], 11–14) provides a short survey of the dating of the geographical conquest of Canaan noting G. Albrecht Alt as the instigator of the notion that Josiah's territory provided the textual geography of Joshua. See also J. Maxwell Miller and Gene M. Tucker's *The Book of Joshua*, CBC (Cambridge: Cambridge University Press, 1974), 9–10.

77 Yehezkel Kaufmann, "The Biblical Age," in *Great Ages and Ideas of the Jewish People*, ed. Leo W. Schwarz (New York: Modern Library, 1956), 56.

78 See Nadav Na'aman, "The Kingdom of Judah under Josiah," *Tel Aviv* 18 (1991): 41–51. On the wide disparity of reconstructions of Josiah's realm, see Handy, "Josiah in a New Light," 425–30.

79 Ahlström, *The History of Ancient Palestine*, 768–69; Ching-Wen Chen, "The Asylum Cities: A Reconsideration," *TwnJTh* 20 (1998): 109–10.

80 Under the influence of Albrecht Alt, see Martin Noth, *The History of Israel*, 2nd rev. ed., trans. P. R. Ackroyd (New York: Harper & Row, 1960), 273; Nadav Na'aman, "Josiah and the Kingdom of Judah," in Grabbe, *Good Kings and Bad Kings*, 191–92. That a section of Joshua's political geography can be excerpted as genuinely Josianic while dismissing the rest remains popular; see Ernst Axel Knauf and Philippe

a complete fusion of Joshua with Josiah has been proposed.⁸¹ However, the military commander that is Joshua's portrayal in Joshua is unlikely for Josiah and is certainly not reflected in the biblical texts of Kings, Chronicles, or First Esdras, or in any archaeological material.⁸² In addition, it has been duly noted that the 'priestly' Josiah of Kings is less Joshua-like than the Josiah of Chronicles.⁸³ That there might be intentional parallel items at the beginning (Joshua) and the end (Josiah) of a 'Deuteronomistic History' is possible, but is less clear than an intentional literary parallel construction might have produced.⁸⁴ Finally, the supposition that Joshua was written as a warning to political insiders that Josiah and his cohorts could make them outsiders with their governing power still in flux stretches the theoretical purpose of the book of Joshua too far.⁸⁵

Given the Deuteronomistic references that he finds throughout the Pentateuch, Rolf Rendtroff has suggested that there was no discernable unified Pentateuchal narrative until the Deuteronomistic circle created their edition of Torah from disparate earlier traditions.⁸⁶ In this he follows Schmid, who connects J and D.⁸⁷ Rendtroff and Schmid claim that there are strong reasons for dating the Deuteronomistic Pentateuch-cre-

---

Guillaume, *A History of Biblical Israel: The Fate of the Tribes and Kingdoms from Merenptah to Bar Kochba*, WANEM (Sheffield: Equinox, 2016), 127.

81   Richard D. Nelson sets out the reasons for assuming an equation of Joshua with King Josiah: Nelson, "Josiah in the Book of Joshua," *JBL* 100 (1981): 531–40. The link between Joshua and King Josiah has been a popular academic idea, see Jeffrey C. Geoghegan, "The Levites and the Literature of the Late-Seventh Century," *JHS* 7 (2007): 34–80, doi:10.5508/jhs.2007.v7.a10. This notion was picked up on in Alex Woolf's *A History of the World: The Story of Mankind from Prehistory to the Modern Day* (London: Arcturus, 2015), 33.

82   Nadav Na'aman, "The Sanctuary of the Gibeonites Revisited," *JANER* 9 (2009): 114. See also the discussion in Grabbe, *Ancient Israel*, 204–6.

83   Giovanni Garbini, *History and Ideology in Ancient Israel*, trans. J. Bowden (New York: Crossroad, 1988) 130.

84   David A. Glatt-Gilad, "Revealed and Concealed: The Status of the Law (Book) of Moses within the Deuteronomistic History," in *Mishneh Todah: Studies in Deuteronomy and Its Cultural Environment in Honor of Jeffrey H. Tigay*, ed. N. Sacher, D. A. Glatt-Gilad and M. J. Williams (Winona Lake, IN: Eisenbrauns, 2009), 196–97. Nelson ("Josiah in the Book of Joshua," 534–36) presents four such parallels: obedience to the law, covenant mediation, a Passover, and a civilian army. The first three might be intentional parallels, the fourth is questionable.

85   Lori Rowlett works hard to come up with a reason for writing Joshua during the reign of Josiah in "Inclusion, Exclusion and Monarchy in the Book of Joshua," in *Social-Scientific Old Testament Criticism*, ed. D. J. Chalcraft, BibSem 47 (Sheffield: Sheffield Academic, 1997), 373, 380.

86   Rolf Rendtorff, *The Problem of the Process of Transmission in the Pentateuch*, JSOTSup 89 (Sheffield: Sheffield Academic, 1990), 60, 197–99, 201–3.

87   Hans Heinrich Schmid, *Der sogenannte Jahwist: Beobachtungen und Fragen zur*

ating circle to the eighth century at the earliest, but that it more probably existed in the time of Josiah. For the present purposes, it suffices to note that the scribes of Josiah are credited with the production of the entire Pentateuch, minus a few random passages and possibly some of the Priestly material (Rendtorff hesitated to date these five scrolls before or after the Josianic compilation). Clearly this would make the Pentateuch itself a product of the Deuteronomic world of Josiah's reign.[88] That there are many studies of individual Pentateuchal passages dating them to Josiah's time need not be considered here as these two studies encompass the entire Torah.[89] If, however, Deuteronomy was not the book found by Josiah's priest, Hilkiah, and it was not written at the time of Josiah, the dating of the Pentateuch to the reign of Josiah collapses.[90] Certainly the Pentateuch is not deemed "scriptural" until long after the independent state of Judah ceased to exist.[91]

Finally, there is the question of dating psalms to the time of Josiah. Over the years, a scattering of psalms have been assigned to the reign of Josiah. Most of the reasons given for dating the psalms as such are theologically related to the notion of their having been composed as part of the religious reform. Others are dated to the time of Josiah for reasons of political international relations, providing a rationale or a theory that there was a sizable Nubian contingent in Judah due to Psamtik I's (in Greek: Psammetichus I) control of Egypt and Egypt's traditional lands in the Levant.[92] A survey of select scholarship on the psalms produced the following psalm

---

Pentateuchforschungen (1976), summarized in Joseph Blenkinsopp, *The Pentateuch: An Introduction to the First Five Books of the Bible*, ABRL (New York: Doubleday, 1992), 23.

88   The notion that the Pentateuch as a whole was the text discovered by Hilkiah is not solely a Jewish tradition. Note, too, the Russian Orthodox position: Glagolev et al., "Chetvertaia Tsarstv," 2.565.

89   A pair of examples: Axel Graupner, "Exodus 18,13-27: Ätiologie einer Justizreform in Israel?" in *Recht und Ethos im Alten Testament—Gestalt und Wirkung: Festschrift für Horst Seebass zum 65. Geburtstag*, ed. Stefan Beyerle, Günter Mayer and Hans Strauß (Neukirchen-Vluyn: Neukirchener Verlag, 1999), 20; Bill T. Arnold, "Deuteronomy 12 and the Law of the Central Sanctuary *noch einmal*," VT 64 (2014): 237, 248.

90   Though dating the Pentateuch as late as the Hellenistic period seems extreme. See Gerhard Larsson, "The Documentary Hypothesis and the Chronological Structure of the Old Testament," ZAW 97 (1985): 331-32. It needs to be noted that Finkelstein and Silberman (*Bible Unearthed*, 14) see both the Pentateuch and the Deuteronomic History as being supported by archaeological evidence for having been composed in the late seventh century.

91   James W. Watts, "Scripturalization and the Aaronide Dynasties," JHS 13 (2013): 6-7, https://doi.org/10.5508/jhs.20ll.v11.a7.

92   See Donald Redford, *Egypt, Canaan, and Israel in Ancient Times* (Princeton: Princeton University Press, 1992), 434. Redford sees Egyptian economic power throughout the region, even if not necessarily direct political control.

lyrics as potential candidates composed for Josiah's cultic liturgy: 8, 19[A], 20, 21, 78, 82, 104, and the Korahite collection of 42–49.[93] It is left open as to whether the designated first two books of Psalms (the Davidic and Elohistic) existed as collections by the time of Josiah or not, so those psalms will not be considered as Josianic scribal compositions or copies.

When these suggestions for Josianic scribal work are tallied, we have from the canonical, biblical texts major parts or whole books of the following as products of Josiah's reign: Genesis, Exodus, Leviticus, Numbers, Deuteronomy, Joshua, Judges, Ruth, Samuel, Kings, First Isaiah, Amos, Hosea, Micah, Jonah, Zephaniah, Nahum, Habakkuk, the Korah Psalms, and assorted other Psalms (ten per cent of the entire Psalter all told). If all of these texts were actually produced or copied by Josiah's scribes, it is safe to say they were a very busy group. Assuming that the main occupation of scribes was not the creation of literary or liturgical work, they would have produced most of the Hebrew Bible in their spare time. It is true that *all* of the canonical books *could* have been written in that period of time—indeed, even the entire Ethiopian canon *could* have been written in that length of time. Nevertheless, it is doubtful that they were. There are good reasons *not* to date texts to Josiah's reign.

Major reasons given by scholars for dating the composition of biblical texts to within the Josianic reign reduce to a few. The most common four, in ascending order of likelihood, relate to the following: 1. Josiah's military reconstruction of the Davidic empire; 2. The collapse of the Assyrian Empire; 3. The great monotheistic/single temple cultic reform; 4. Finding/Composing/ Editing Deuteronomy. Problems arise when each of these hypotheses are investigated.

The first thing to say is that the attempt by, or success of, Josiah to reconstruct the Davidic empire is not a biblical event. Though the notion that Josiah created an extensive empire is not new, current scholarly constructs of such a kingdom rely primarily on a single modern academic article by Cross and Freedman in 1953,[94] but in fact Josiah never attempted to recreate David's world at all. The texts on Josiah in Kings and Chroni-

---

93 Moses Buttenwieser, *The Psalms: Chronologically Treated with a New Translation* (Chicago: University of Chicago Press, 1938), 135, 163, 176, 180; Leopold Sabourin, *The Psalms: Their Origin and Meaning* (Staten Island, NY: Alba House, 1969), 21–22; Susan E. Gillingham, *The Poems of the Hebrew Bible*, Oxford Bible Series (Oxford: Oxford University Press, 1994), 239; Lowell K. Handy, "Sounds, Words and Meanings in Psalm 82," *JSOT* 47 (1990): 63n1; Leslie J. Hoppe, "Vengeance and Forgiveness: The Two Faces of Psalm 79," in *Imagery and Imagination in Biblical Literature: Essays in Honor of Aloysius Fitzgerald, F.S.C.*, ed. L. Boadt and M. S. Smith, CBQMS 32 (Washington, DC: Catholic Biblical Association of America, 2001), 11.

94 Frank Moore Cross and David Noel Freedman, "Josiah's Revolt against Assyria," *JNES* 12 (1953): 56–68.

cles make no parallels to a military David; the comments on the destruction of cult centers in Israel/Samerina contend neither that Josiah has taken territory nor controls the region. The activity is pure vandalism in the texts. Indeed, the biblical Josiah has no interest in former Assyrian territory at all. Assyria dropped out of Kings with the retreat of Sennacherib, last heard of in a speech by Isaiah (2 Kgs 20:6); in Chronicles, the Assyrians make their last appearance as an army hauling off Manasseh as a captive to Babylon (2 Chronicles 11). According to the biblical narratives, the foreign power of the moment for both of these rulers at the end of their reigns is Babylon. The biblical passages from which scholars assume a great concern for things David on the part of Josiah are 2 Kgs 22:2, where the claim is made that Josiah did what was right in the eyes of Yahweh in the way of David his father, and 2 Kgs 23:25, where it is posited that no king of Judah before or after Josiah was as good as he, a follower of Moses's *torah*. From this it has been divined that the author was attempting to show Josiah as the new David. It only needs to be pointed out that the narrative of Josiah does nothing to parallel Josiah with David. There are no battles, there is no intrigue, there is no family dysfunction, there is no lust (or any other kind of emotion, save overt piety). If Josiah is carefully paralleled with any early ruler, it is Solomon, and those references are overt and display both positive and negative relations between the two kings. The notion that Josiah had run roughshod over the former Israel to recreate David's united monarchy derives from the notion that Josiah must have had control of all those cities wherein he destroyed their sanctuaries and slaughtered their religious leaders. The underlying supposition is that, in war, one destroys what one controls, while in actual wars one destroys what one does not—or even cannot—control. However, this is all mute, since it is doubtful that the Josianic campaign in Samerina ever took place; even the central narrative of the desecration of the temple of Bethel is, by archaeological evidence, dubious.[95] Both *lmlk* seals and a petition in Hebrew on a pot sherd have been marshaled to suggest the Josianic new Davidic empire; however, both have been dismissed as irrelevant to the argument. The seals would reflect a much smaller territory if they could be related to Josiah rather than Hezekiah (or, perhaps more rationally, to Manasseh), and a Hebrew text found in a multilingual outpost is not evidence of Judean control.[96]

---

95   James L. Kelso, "Bethel," *NEAEHL* 1.194.
96   Joseph Naveh, "The Excavations at Mesad Hashavyahu: Preliminary Report," *IEJ* 12 (1962): 89–113; André Lemaire, "Remarques sur la datation des estampiles lmlk," *VT* 25 (1975): 678–82; Nadav Na'aman, "Hezekiah's Fortified Cities and the *lmlk* Stamps," *BASOR* 261 (1986): 5–21. On both items, see Raz Kletter, "Pots and Politics:

The second point to make is that while the collapse of the Assyrian Empire after the death of Ashurbanipal is very clear to scholars today, the picture was not so clear even a hundred years ago, and it may not have been very clear to ancient Judah in the second half of the seventh century BCE. Unfortunately, the ancient records for that time and region are quite sketchy. It appears from the available artifacts that Egypt had gained its independence from Assyrian control under Psamtik I ±653 BCE, about halfway through the reign of Ashurbanipal in Assyria. It is unclear whether or not this independence for Egypt was politically acceptable to both Assyrian and Egyptian ruling elites. This is uncertain since it was Ashurbanipal who had established the Twenty-Sixth Dynasty in Egypt with Assyrian forces helping to dislodge Nubian control thereby apparently giving Assyrian assent to Psamtik's Egyptian control of Egypt.[97] Therefore, it is not strange that Egypt was still allied with Assyria in 616 and 609, even with its military forces.[98] The question arises as to whether Judah and the adroit Judahite leaders saw any useful signs for siding against both Egypt and Assyria prior to the actual fall of Nineveh in 612. Judah might have hoped for a Nabopolassar victory in 627 at Ashdod, especially if, as seems to have been the case, Judah was under Egyptian control. Nevertheless, the victory was Psamtik's, and the Babylonians would not be back in the vicinity until after Josiah's death. There was no realistic reason to hope for independence from that direction. The biblical abandonment of Assyria as an enemy before Josiah's time could signify many things, but a large independent state would not seem to be one of them. To the end, Assyria and/or Egypt assumed control over the territory of Samerina and, apparently, Judah.[99]

Thirdly, a great religious reform is recorded in both Kings and Chronicles. It is true that the two reports are essentially of two different cultic changes, Chronicles having ascribed the major temple reform to Hezekiah rather than to Josiah. Here, actual biblical texts may be consulted, rather than conjectures, but no contemporary documents exist to confirm these literary changes. There is simply no primary data for these reforms. As a historical event, the biblical texts can only be cited as some scribe's vision of what such a reform should have been like; however, those scholars who posit that no reform at all took place are probably overly optimistic. Any king in the ancient Near East who reigned for three decades (Josiah for

---

Material Remains of Late Iron Age Judah in Relation to Its Political Borders," *BASOR* 314 (1999): 37–38, 42.

97 Redford, *Egypt, Canaan*, 195–96.

98 This was recorded in the Neo-Babylonian chronicle. See Jean-Jacques Glassner, *Mesopotamian Chronicles*, ed. B. R. Foster, SBLWAW 19 (Atlanta: Society of Biblical Literature, 2004), 222–25.

99 Ahlstöm, *The History of Ancient Palestine*, 768, 780.

31 years according to 2 Kgs 22:1 and 2 Chr 34:1) fiddled with the religious cult under their control. Surely Josiah dealt in some way with the religious and political elements of his kingdom, but it was not the total religious upheaval of either 2 Kgs 23:1–25 (unlikely) or 2 Chr 34:29–35:19 (more unlikely).

The major problem with taking the great cult reform seriously is simply that the prophetic texts ascribed to Zephaniah (dated to Josiah's reign) and Jeremiah (dating to immediately after Josiah's reign) know nothing about such a thorough religious reform. There are other problems. That Josiah was raised to have a theology totally different from the theology of his father and grandfather is unlikely; so unlikely, indeed, that the Chronicler made an attempt to rectify this problem by having Manasseh repent.[100] The biblical narrative leaves a religious continuity of Manasseh-Amon-Josiah, at least through his eighteenth year (2 Kgs 22:3), while Chronicles moves Josiah's religious "awakening" back ten years 2 Chr 34:3).[101] The priests that are posited to have swayed Josiah would have been priests in this traditional cult, none of whom would have reached their positions prior to the rise of Manasseh some 57 years earlier and who would have been the priests of the allegedly corrupt generations.[102] Until almost two-thirds of the way through Josiah's reign, no one would have assumed that a Judah (or Israel, for that matter) with several sanctuaries would have been a problem. Less likely still would be a Judahite or Jerusalemite who saw anything wrong with maintaining the Solomonic religious cult instigated by Solomon; Solomon himself built the temples to many gods (1 Kgs 11:1–8).[103] Indeed, he worshiped many gods at these temples. There may have been reasons like priestly jealousy for instituting such a reform, but the biblical text of the three reigns does not support any need for major cultic centralization or reduction of the pantheon. Why Josiah would wish to change the religious traditions of Samerina to be subject to Jerusalem without taking the entirety of ancient Israel makes little religious or political sense. Moreover, the populace of Samerina, whatever its ethnic background by the time of Josiah, would not have stood by and enthusiastically destroyed their own religious tradition of two centuries just when

---

100 It is a half-hearted attempt. See Japhet, *I & II Chronicles*, 1001–4, 1014. Note that the Amon material is left unchanged.

101 Klein, *2 Chronicles*, 495–96.

102 Japhat (*I & II Chronicles*, 1019) notes the impossibility of this passage in Chronicles. It would stand as well for Kings.

103 A possibility of ±1000 temples if each wife had her own beloved deity. The text goes out of its way to make certain that the reader knows these are not the real religion of Jerusalem (the king is old, the king is sex-crazed, the king is in love, his wives made him do it, his wives were not Judeans, he turned away from the true religion). Zamora García, *Reyes I*, 225–30.

the Assyrian grip on power was loosening simply because a rival, the king of Judah, read a book found in Jerusalem's temple to Yahweh.[104] What the biblical reform narratives mostly resemble is the retro-installation of the theology of Second Isaiah, as encapsulated in the book of Isaiah, not necessarily as and when Deutero-Isaiah spoke them.[105] The extension of this literary cultic reformulation northward into an Israel—the Josianic contemporary status of which we have only the slightest notion, save that the Bible insists that it was *not* Judahite territory—more clearly reflects the vision of Ezekiel of the reunited Judah and Israel under the control of Jerusalem. It would appear that Noth was right: this Deuteronomic History, at the very least of the reign of Josiah, postdates Josiah.[106]

A fourth consideration is that Deuteronomy as the "Book of Instruction" read by Josiah has been the Christian understanding of 2 Kgs 22:8, 11, 13, 16 and 23:2, 21, 25 from at least the fourth century CE.[107] It is to this equation that almost all literary texts ascribed to the time of Josiah are tied directly or indirectly. When de Wette and Wellhausen made Deuteronomy the one securely fixed datable text of all of the books in the Hebrew Bible, other documents were then dated in relation to it.[108] From

---

104 Adam C. Welch ("The Death of Josiah," 257–58) envisioned a religious rivalry between the established (and Assyrian-deity-inclusive) Bethel and a late upstart Jerusalem cultic site that Josiah forcefully imposed on Israelites in favor of Jerusalem. This was also deemed a political move to reunite the Divided Kingdom; see idem, *Deuteronomy: The Framework to the Code* (London: Oxford University Press, 1932), 205. It needs to be noted that Welch read the centralization material as post-Josiah and as an invention of the Kings' Josiah narrative historian (if still pre-exilic in his recreation); Welch, *The Code of Deuteronomy: A New Theory of Its Origin* (London: James Clarke, 1924), 196; idem, "When Was the Worship of Israel Centralized at the Temple?," ZAW 43 (1925): 252. The relation of the book of Deuteronomy to Josiah and to a centralization of the cult has often been related to some such conflict, e.g., Walter Dietrich, "Josia und das Gesetzbuch (2 Reg. XXII)," VT 27 (1977): 33.

105 Albertz, *A History of Israelite Religion*, 2.417. This is much the same as the biblical narratives retro-writing an idealized vision of the Jerusalem temple into the wilderness-wandering stories in the guise of the tabernacle. See Brevard S. Childs, *The Book of Exodus: A Critical Theological Commentary*, OTL (Philadelphia: Westminster John Knox, 1974), 537. It should not be assumed that "Deutero-Isaiah" was a single prophet; several scribes may have composed prophecies in Isaiah's name.

106 Knauf ("Kings," 142) dates the Josianic reform narrative in Kings no earlier than the reconstruction period of Jerusalem and the construction of the Second Temple.

107 For early attestations, see Handy, "Josiah after the Chronicler," 100–103. For the idea that it has been accepted as fact by the Middle Ages, see Handy, "Josiah and History," 33–34.

108 See Julius Wellhausen's *Prolegomena to the History of Ancient Israel* (trans. S. Black and A. Menzies [Cleveland, OH: Meridian, 1957], 9), which recognizes de Wette as the origin of this exact dating (10).

that point onwards, the history of Deuteronomy studies has been an interesting, if not always enlightening, endeavor.[109] Some argue that a book of instruction (*torah*) was indeed found by the workmen, which led to a progression by which an original Deuteronomy was written in the time of Hosea in Israel and then brought to Hezekiah's court by refugees fleeing before or during the Assyrian invasion since their capital of Samaria had fallen.[110] Others opted for the theory that Josiah's henchmen or the priests of the temple in Jerusalem (maybe Yahweh-Alone purists) composed the volume and passed it off as an old text to support Josiah in enacting his (or their) ideas for religious reformation.[111] There were also those who insisted that Deuteronomy was *not* the book found at the time of Josiah, but was only the book placed in the extended narrative to serve the purpose of being the book found. Some do not believe there was a law book found at all, and that the entire tale is creative historiography.[112] It was realized early on that the current book of Deuteronomy could not have been the Deuteronomy of the Josianic reform.[113] If the beginning and end of Deuteronomy were removed, it was argued, then the legislation would do nicely for that reforming book. Deuteronomy's sections on the need to remove all deities who were not Yahweh, along with their devotees, as well as needing to worship Yahweh only in the place Yahweh will make

---

109 See surveys in Ernest W. Nicholson, *Deuteronomy and Tradition* (Philadelphia: Fortress, 1967), 1–17; Jeffrey H. Tigay, *Deuteronomy*, JPSTC 5 (Philadelphia: Jewish Publication Society of America, 1996), xix–xxvi.

110 Nicholson, *Deuteronomy and Tradition*, 58–82, 122–24; Ziony Zevit, "Deuteronomy in the Temple: An Exercise in Historical Imagining," in Fox, Glatt-Gilad, and Williams, *Mishneh*, 216–17. Though why Josiah, hero against Israelite religious apostasy, would use a guidebook from Israel should have raised a few red flags. Variations of this notion include the original text of Deuteronomy having been written in the reign of Hezekiah and of the numerous copies of Deuteronomy having been destroyed by the evil King Manasseh—a single copy surviving to be found by Hilkiah. This is a very old hypothesis: Powell, *The Death of Good Josiah Lamented*, 6 (from 1695).

111 So Droge, "Lying Pen," 118–20. It is an old theory: Arthur Penrhyn Stanley, *Lectures on the History of the Jewish Church*, 428 (from 1901).

112 Hans-Detlef Hoffmann, *Reform und Reformen: Untersuchungen zu einem Grunthema der deuteronomistischen Geschichtsschreibung*, ATANT 66 (Zurich: Theologische, 1980), 208–26.

113 Indeed, only the curses of Deuteronomy 28–29 are referenced in Huldah's speech and it has been suggested that this small section of Deuteronomy was all that was found: Herbert Edward Ryle, *The Canon of the Old Testament: An Essay on the Gradual Growth and Formation of the Hebrew Canon of Scripture*, 2nd ed. (London: Macmillan, 1914), 50. Johannes Pedersen (*Israel: Its Life and Culture, III-IV*, trans. A. I. Fausbøll [London: Oxford University Press, 1940], 587) postulated that *if* there had been a version of Deuteronomy connected to Josiah, the current book has been changed beyond recognition soon after the Exile.

known to "you,"[114] are cited as reflecting Josiah's activities. These passages are short enough, though one would not know it from reading introductions and commentaries on Deuteronomy or histories of Josiah. In this way, Deuteronomy 5–28 becomes associated in some scholars' minds with the book promulgated by Josiah's scribes. Deriving from this comes the dating of the Deuteronomistic History, the Josianic rendering of the Pentateuch, the notion of recreating a golden past not only of David, but also of Moses, and even the notion that King Josiah was a savior from the tyranny of all those kings who preceded him, though this last is a thought now mostly dead.

Seeing Deuteronomy as the book of the reform has fallen on hard times. Though most scholars would still hold that there is an intended parallel between the passages on one worship site and eliminating the non-Yahwists, the Deuteronomistic history itself is collapsing back into a series of independent books rather lightly edited together, none of which seem to have had Deuteronomy as a model. More to the point, the portion of Deuteronomy usually assigned to the reform is slowly being taken apart and disposed of as having to do with Josiah.[115] If the text found by the workmen was supposed to have been the foundation of the reign of Josiah, it is strange, Gary Knoppers has noted, that the laws of the king make little sense in relation to what is written about the reign of Josiah (thus removing 17:14–20); a king who takes on the entire religious world hardly seems one to write vast restrictions on the role of the king.[116] It has long been noted that the Passover/ Feast of Weeks material of Deuteronomy 16 reflects Persian-era material.[117] Christophe Nihan has made a case for Deuteronomy 18 (+ 34:10–12) as the product of late-Persian era circles,

---

114 Mount Gerizim was replaced by Jerusalem if one posits a northern provenance, unless one assumes that Israelites really did love Jerusalem as their one-and-only place to worship, as in the book of Tobit.

115 Even such a large section as Deuteronomy 19–25 has been deemed impossible as a Josianic-era text by those who otherwise find Deuteronomy viable as "the found scroll." See Lohfink, "The Cult Reform of Josiah of Judah," 474n43.

116 Gary N. Knoppers, "The Deuteronomist and the Deuteronomic Law of the King: A Reexamination of a Relationship," ZAW 108 (1996): 329–46. See also Ronald E. Clements, "A Dialogue with Gordon McConville on Deuteronomy: I. The Origins of Deuteronomy: What Are the Clues?," SJT 56 (2003): 515–16. Aspects of the laws concerning kings were noted as illogical during the monarchy long ago. On foreign rulers for Israel (Deut 17:15), see, for example, Francis C. Burkitt, "The Code Found in the Temple," JBL 40 (1921): 167.

117 See discussion in Otto Kaiser, *Gott, Mensch und Geschichte: Studien zum Verständnis des Menschen und seiner Geschichte in der klassischen, biblischen und nachbiblischen Literatur*, BZAW 413 (Berlin: de Gruyter, 2010), 44–47. A short survey of options that insinuates a possible Josianic time for the Passover in Deuteronomy is found in Steinberg, "Exodus 12 in Light of Ancestral Practices," 95–96, 102–3.

pushing a prophetic authority dependent on a Moses "exclusive revelation."[118] Ching-Wen Chen asserts with some persuasion that the asylum cities could not have been in use until after Josiah (taking out 19:1–13).[119] Yair Hoffman takes up the action of holy war and finds it unreasonable to have been connected in any way to Josiah (leaving aside 20).[120] William Morrow, considering the "police state" legislation while assuming some possible antecedent in the Josianic reform, acknowledges that the existing text is at best exilic (deleting Deuteronomy 13).[121] Indeed, the notion that Deuteronomy could have been envisioned as the law book of a functioning ancient Near Eastern state—Judah specifically—is unconvincing.[122] In short, Deuteronomy as the theoretical tome found in Josiah's reign has dissolved. The more the contents of Deuteronomy are compared to the biblical narrative of Josiah, or the modern reconstructions of a historical Josiah, the less likely it becomes that Deuteronomy could have been a book found or used by Josiah.[123] Neither Deuteronomy nor any part of that scroll appear to have been a product of the court of Josiah; nonetheless, it does serve as a literary device for a later work.[124] Deuteronomy's composition in all likelihood comes after Jehoiachin was among Judahite exiles and not before or during Josiah's reign among immigrant Israelites or disgruntled Jerusalemites, as has been concluded by Ernest Nicholson, whose earlier work helped establish much of the groundwork for the theory of pre-Josianic renditions of Deuteronomy, which he has now abandoned.[125]

---

118 Christophe Nihan, "'Moses and the Prophets': Deuteronomy 18 and the Emergence of the Pentateuch as Torah," *SEÅ* 75 (2010): 53.

119 Chen, "Asylum Cities," 103–22.

120 Yair Hoffman, "The Deuteronomistic Concept of the Herem," *ZAW* 111 (1999): 196–210.

121 William S. Morrow, "The Paradox of Deuteronomy 13: A Post-Colonial Reading," in *"Gerechtigkeit und Recht zu üben" (Gen 18,19): Studien zur alt orientalischen und biblischen Rechtsgeschichte, zur Religionsgeschichte Israels und zur Religionssoziologie: Festschrift für Eckart Otto zum 65. Geburtstag*, ed. R. Achenbach and M. Arneth, BZABR 13 (Wiesbaden: Harrassowitz, 2009), 227, 233. The author of Kings simply could not have known Deuteronomy 13 according to Noll ("Was there Doctrinal Dissemination," 414).

122 Ernest W. Nicholson, "Reconsidering the Provenance of Deuteronomy," *ZAW* 124 (2012): 539–40. Clements sees Deuteronomy as a text and a theology designed for a post-monarchic Yehud after 587 BCE ("Dialogue with Gordon McConville," 516).

123 Davies, *In Search*, 39.

124 Pedersen, *Israel*, 587–88.

125 Nicholson, "Reconsidering the Provenance of Deuteronomy," 531–32. It should be noted that the parallels made between the death of Moses in Deuteronomy and of Josiah in Kings are not sufficient to suggest any close correlation and are certainly not useful for dating either story. See Philippe Guillaume, "Did Moses Die before Entering Canaan?," *ThRev* 24 (2003): 50–51.

What, then, of the canonical corpus can reasonably be dated to the reign of Josiah? Part of Zephaniah might derive from that king's realm. It is probably not the case that Nahum was sung in Josiah's temple. At present, the Deuteronomistic History is often dated by many, on dubious grounds, backward from Josiah's reign to the time of Hezekiah. In any case, those who do so do not consider it a product of Josiah's court. The narrative of Josiah found in Kings can only postdate his death. Zephaniah proclamations exist alone of possible Josianic era compositions, and serious scholars doubt that chronology.[126] The scribes of Josiah had plenty of their official duties to perform, none of which remains; they cannot also be credited with most of the Hebrew Bible. That the Bible does not present Josiah or his court as a fount of wisdom seems to be a silence worthy of respect.

---

[126] Donald L. Williams, "The Date of Zephaniah," *JBL* 82 (1963): 85; Ehud Ben Zvi, *A Historical-Critical Study of the Book of Zephaniah*, BZAW 198 (Berlin: de Gruyter, 1992), 33–42; Joseph Blenkinsopp, *A History of Prophecy in Israel* (Philadelphia: Westminster, 1983), 140.

Chapter Three
Josiah Is Not Jeroboam and Other Kingly Questions

Whatever the redaction of Kings and Chronicles, Josiah remains in both texts the last of the ruling kings of an even slightly independent Judah; the stories of the kings that precede him make up the bulk of the scrolls. Josiah is more closely related to some of these rulers than he is to others. He is explicitly connected to seven Judahite kings in the narrative of Kings: Amon (his father), David (his "father"), Ahaz (builder of an upper room in the temple), Manasseh (constructor of improper altars to the temple and purported bringer of doom on Judah [2 Kgs 23:26]),[1] Solomon (builder of *bamoth* to assorted deities), Jehoahaz[2] (his son), and Jehoiakim (his son). In addition, reference is made more generically to kings of Judah: 2 Kgs 22:20 "your fathers"; 23:5, 11, 12, 22 "kings of Judah"; 23:25 "no king like him"; 23:28 "scroll of the records of the kings of Judah."[3] In Chronicles, Josiah's father and sons appear much as they did in Kings, but the other Judahite rulers drop out of sight, with the exception of David and Solomon. The creator and installer, respectively, of the proper cult of the Jerusalemite temple, they are cited as the foundational figures for Josiah's Passover. Both rulers become more important through Chronicles to First Esdras. The Chronicler's rendition of Josiah also makes sparing reference to Judahite kings generically: 2 Chr 34:11 "kings of Judah" ["kings of

---

1 The question of Manasseh's guilt is not dealt with here. See Baruch Halpern, "Why Manasseh Is Blamed for the Babylonian Exile: The Evolution of a Biblical Tradition," VT 48 (1998): 473-514. On this topic it should be noted that there is a contrast between Kings and Chronicles; Galvin, *David's Successors*, 104-12. Michael ("The Prophet, the Witch and the Ghost," 321, 339-40) posits a relation within the Deuteronomistic History between Saul and the final destruction of Judah and Israel, making him indirectly responsible for the exile.

2 The problem with both of Josiah's ruling sons and their multiple names is explained concisely by Garbini in *History and Ideology in Ancient Israel*, 47-49.

3 It might be noted that the treatment of monarchy in Kings suggests the author finds the institution less than satisfactory as a whole and, indeed, notes that prophecy is less than ideal. See Gershon Hepner, "Three's a Crowd in Shunem: Elisha's Misconduct with the Shunamite Reflects a Polemic against Prophetism," ZAW 122 (2010): 399. This anti-prophetic bias might also reflect on the last prophet of the scroll, Huldah.

Israel" appears in 35:18]; 34:28, 35:24 "your/his fathers"; and 35:27 "scroll of the kings of Israel and Judah." The texts are clear about how they serve to link Josiah's story to the depiction of royal dynasties in Judah and Israel in the larger narrative.[4] More interesting are a pair of kings who should be considered in relation with Josiah: Jeroboam (who is mentioned) and Ahab (who is not).[5] These two kings, neither of whom are held in high repute by the biblical historiographers, are closely tied to Josiah.

The most enthusiastic royal connection is to Josiah's genealogical ancestor (according to biblical reckoning) and founder of the dynasty, David.[6] For Kings, Josiah's comparison to David is restricted solely to David's rectitude (2 Kgs 22:2);[7] there is no other Davidic attribute even suggested in the text.[8] The David of the fabulously edited Deuteronomistic History, or even

---

4   The inventive notion that the Josianic material was composed (or edited) as edifying material for Jehoiachin in the Babylonian exile seems more fantastic than reasonable. That it was composed for general edification in the Persian era for some literate level of society in Yehud would be more likely. See David Janzen, "Sins of Josiah and Hezekiah," 350, 355, 362.

5   Mitchell notes literary parallels to four "evil" kings ("Ironic Death," 431–34).

6   Christoph Levin, "Die Frömmigkeit der Könige von Israel und Juda," in Pakkala and Nissinen, *Houses Full of All Good Things*, 149. This may, in fact, be the single most important reason for mentioning David in the Josiah narrative. See S. Min Chun, *Ethics and Biblical Narrative: A Literary and Discourse-Analytical Approach to the Story of Josiah*, OTRM (Oxford: Oxford University Press, 2014), 189. The David being referenced, however, is more "mythical" than real (whether or not there was a historical King David). See Luciano Lepore, "L'umanità in camino dall'enoteismo al monoteismo: l'evoluzione della religione di Israele," *BeO* 47 (2005): 41.

7   In "Comparison with David as a Means of Evaluating Character in the Book of Kings," *JHS* 11 (2011): 6–7, doi:10.5508/jhs.2011.v11.a7, Amos Frisch points out that the reference to David in the Josiah comparison deals solely with righteousness and does not include the comparative items used elsewhere in these non-standardized Davidic comparisons. In Kings, Josiah and David fulfill only the first of Frisch's list of seven types of comparison (19–20).

8   Hobbs notes that it is all a question of piety and cites Hezekiah as Josiah's match (*2 Kings*, 323,). See also Chun, *Ethics and Biblical Narrative*, 184–85; David M. Howard, Jr., "David," *ABD* 2.46. A couple of studies compare Josiah and Hezekiah, finding Kings and Chronicles opting for Josiah as at least slightly better. In *Reflections of King Josiah in Chronicles: Late Stages of the Josiah Reception in 2 Chr 34f*, TSHB 2 (Gütersloh: Gütersloher, 2003), 50–54, Louis C. Jonker finds Josiah to be more proper in his performance of the Passover. In *Hezekiah and the Dialogue of Memory*, EmSch (Minneapolis: Fortress, 2015), 21, Song-Mi Park stresses the uniquely David-related status of Hezekiah (2 Kgs 18:3) and Josiah among kings in the Kings narratives. For a concise comparison of the kings Hezekiah and Josiah, see the latter at pp. 71–77. There, Park discerns a series of Deuteronomistic Histories with at least one of them composed in the reign of Hezekiah. Even if one does not share the certainty of such an early text, the contrasts between Hezekiah and Josiah in the existing narrative are instructive, and the author's intention to make Josiah the greater of the two rulers seems a cogent observation.

just the one in the beginning of the book of Kings, is not being referenced; only a religiously rigorous ruler, more known in Chronicles than in 1 Kings 1-2 or, heaven forefend, the book of Samuel.[9] It has been suggested that in the book of Samuel, David's obedience to Yahweh is reflected in the portrait of Josiah in Kings.[10] Moreover, the scroll of Kings reflects and probably knows no Josianic version of the Davidic empire.[11] Attempts made to see David's united kingdom in Josiah's cultic destruction in Israel bear little correlation to the political aspects favored in the Davidic narrative in Kings, short as it is, with the totally religious vision of Josiah.[12] There is little to no reason to postulate that this restricted vision of David provides evidence that this line of comparison derived from the court of Josiah.[13]

The scroll of Chronicles uses a parallel narrative to that in Kings in order to display Josiah walking in a straight Davidic line (2 Chr 34:2).[14] It is prob-

---

9   George Barlow comes up with three parallels between Josiah and David, but two of them are explicitly made to the David in Chronicles, and even his "attachment to God's house and devotion to God's service" reflects the David in Chronicles more than that in Kings. See Barlow, *A Homiletical Commentary on the Book of Kings*, PCHCOT (New York: Funk & Wagnalls, 1892), 630-31. See also Sweeney, *King Josiah of Judah*, 27. Reconstructing an earlier form of David narratives does not reduce the anomaly in the least.

10   Karl Deenick, "Priest and King: Or Priest-King in 1 Samuel 2:35," WTJ 73 (2011): 338.

11   Antti Laato centers his entire Josiah/David relationship to the recreation of the Davidic empire. See Laato, *Josiah and David Redivivas*, 58-59. Joseph Blenkinsopp extrapolates a faint thought of such a reign backward from Chronicles; however, the text knows no such empire. See Blenkinsopp, *David Remembered: Kingship and National Identity in Ancient Israel* (Grand Rapids: Eerdmans, 2013), 7. See also Marti J. Steussy (*David: Biblical Portraits of Power*, SPOT [Columbia: University of South Carolina Press, 1999], 47, 94), who recognizes the problem of equating the way of David with the way of Yahweh even in her short note on David in Kings.

12   The comparison remains common enough, but continues to be less than convincing: Monroe, *Josiah's Reform and the Dynamics of Defilement*, 87-88. Alison L. Joseph (*Portrait of the Kings: The Davidic Prototype in Deuteronomistic Poetics* [Minneapolis: Fortress, 2015], 27, 148, 152) relies much too heavily on the notion that a prototype David for the author of Kings is one the modern reader can reconstruct, despite the single citation to David in the Josiah story bearing none of the Davidic traditions 'remembered' by ancient Jews as reconstructed by Robert Alter in *The Art of Biblical Narrative* ([New York: Basic Books, 1981], 47, 114-26), who is aware of this relational problem.

13   This view was postulated by Cross, *Canaanite Myth and Hebrew Epic*, 283-85; Manfred Weipert, "Fragen des israelitischen Geschichtsbewustseins," VT 23 (1973): 439-40; and Israel Finkelstein, "A Great United Monarchy? Archaeological and Historical Perspectives," in Kratz and Spieckermann, *One God—One Cult—One Nation*, 20. Finkelstein sees tenth-century Israel/Judah as a tiny territory made into an imaginary former empire at the time of Josiah.

14   Jacob M. Myers, *II Chronicles: A New Translation with Introduction and Commentary*, AB 13 (Garden City, NY: Doubleday, 1965), 205; Japhet, *I & II Chronicles*, 1021.

able that the notion of being ethical is also the intention here; however, the text dealing with David in Chronicles contains no great blemish on his character, save that he shed a lot of blood as a military man (1 Chr 28:3), providing a shinier burnish for both David and his descendent, Josiah. The religious piety of David is more heavily foregrounded in Chronicles than in Kings, and is the main obsession of citing David in the Josianic material as well: David drew up the plans for the temple, its cult, its provision, its personnel, and its hymns;[15] Josiah implements it all, some for the first time![16] While it has often been argued that Josiah reconstructs the Davidic united monarchy in some manner, this is not stated in Kings or in Chronicles.[17] Indeed, there is nothing that indicates evidence of the existence of an empire controlled by David or Solomon in the archaeological record.[18] What is mentioned is the importance of *religious* control of the "North" by the southern religious personnel, as demonstrated by Josiah following the way of David (and Solomon).[19]

In the biblical renditions of Josiah's reign, Solomon comes out at opposite ends of the evil/righteous continuum. Even though he is remembered in both narratives specifically as the king of "Israel" (2 Kgs 23:13; 24:13; 2

---

15   In "Identity Coherence in the Chronicler's Narrative: King Josiah as a Second David and a Second Saul," *JHS* 17 (2017): 5, doi:10.5508/jhs.2017.v17.a4, Brendan G. Youngberg sees the Davidic connection essentially in the Passover preparations. Youngberg's parallels to Saul are less impressive: use of disguise and death by arrows in death passage (3), consulting a woman (6), and the Benjamin connection (9).

16   Park notes not only the use of David and Solomon as prefigurations of kings Hezekiah and Josiah, but the two as a unit for the invention and implementation of the Jerusalemite temple cult. See Park, *Hezekiah and the Dialogue of Memory*, 203–6.

17   Intentional resumption of a Davidic empire by Josiah has been a popular thesis. See, for example, E. W. Heaton, *The Hebrew Kingdoms*, NCBOT (Oxford: Oxford University Press, 1968), 118–19. The notion of a 'second David,' popular in many Josianic studies, has found its way backward in time to the figure of Hezekiah. However, this modern reading of the king is problematic for both kings. In "The Relationship of Hezekiah to David and Solomon in the Books of Chronicles," in *The Chronicler as Theologian: Essays in Honor of Ralph W. Klein*, ed. M. P. Graham, S. L. McKenzie and G. N. Knoppers, JSOTSup 371 (London: T&T Clark, 2003), 107–13, Mark A. Throntveit sees four valid points for Hezekiah, none of which the Chronicler used as relationships between Josiah and David, and yet none of them appear to have been substantial characteristics to make Hezekiah superior (113).

18   See Israel Finkelstein, "State Formation in Israel and Judah: A Contrast in Context, A Contrast in Trajectory," *NEArch* 62 (1999): 39–40.

19   It is interesting to note that, in earlier days of scholarship, thought was given to a cultural relationship between Israel and Judah that Josiah resumed in which the Jerusalem cult of David was admired by both Israelites and Judeans: Adam C. Welch, *Post-Exilic Judaism* (Edinburgh: Blackwood & Sons, 1935), 48–49. This notion stands behind more modern recreation of David's empire theories as well, e.g., Laato, *Josiah and David Redivivas*, 59.

Chr 35:4), this title appears to have different meanings for the different renditions of Josiah's relation to Solomon.[20] In Kings, Solomon appears as an antithesis to Josiah; "King Solomon" is recorded in the story of Josiah only in a list of evil practitioners of the temple cult (2 Kgs 23:13). In this he joins Ahaz, whose upper room was used by "kings of Judah" for their altars, and Manasseh, who made altars in the courtyards of the temple. Solomon does only "evil" things: establishing the worship of Astarte, Chemosh, and Milcom. There is no hint that the temple that Josiah was rectifying was the product of this heretical creator of apostasy. What Solomon is recorded as having built are "foreign shrines," abominations to the author of Kings.[21] All the works of Solomon mentioned in the Josianic narrative of Kings need necessarily to be destroyed by the good, pious Josiah who walks in the way of David.[22]

For Chronicles, however, Solomon is an ideal, of whom Josiah is an embodiment. This has much to do with the polished, romanticized, squeaky-clean Solomon that appears in the Chronicler's narration of David's son.[23] Josiah still destroys the *bamoth* of Jerusalem, but here there is no mention of Solomon, who, after all, did not build them in the Chronicler's world. Solomon did, however, build the temple to Yahweh, and Josiah's story in Chronicles manages to credit this seminal and central edifice to the deeds of Solomon in no uncertain terms (2 Chr 35:3). This does not make Josiah a "second Solomon," however.[24] Moreover, Solomon is credited with writing out the directions for the proper worship of Yahweh according to the houses of the fathers and their divisions as written down by David and Solomon, reflecting the importance in Chronicles of obeying written texts of the past.[25] Both Kings and Chronicles record a form of Solomon's dedicatory sermon in which the founding king of the temple

---

20 Linville, *Israel in the Book of Kings*, 191.

21 Yaron Z. Eliav (*God's Mountain: The Temple Mount in Time, Place, and Memory* [Baltimore: Johns Hopkins University Press, 2005], 85, 87) notes that, in early Judaism, the placement of any shrines in Jerusalem to deities other than Yahweh caused violent revolt (citing Cassius Dio, *Hist.* 69.12.1), so the earlier use of multiple shrines in the Solomon/Josiah stories may also have been intended to raise spirited emotions against apostasy and in favor of Josiah.

22 Joseph, *Portrait of the Kings*, 158–61. The notion that "the Law of the King" (Deuteronomy 17) was written as a counter to the evil Solomon as viewed at the time of Josiah (155–58) seems a theory which is more than either text will bear, but it is an interesting observation nonetheless.

23 Adrien-M. Brunet, "Le Chroniste et ses Sources," *RB* 61 (1954): 351, 374.

24 Throntveit ("The Relationship of Hezekiah," 113–16) compiles a hefty number of reasons to consider Hezekiah a "second Solomon," but these should only be taken as tokens of Hezekiah's faithfulness to Yahweh; the same needs to be noted regarding Josiah.

25 Klein, *2 Chronicles*, 519–20.

explains the coming desertion of Judah, Jerusalem, and the temple by a miffed Yahweh.[26]

As for Solomon's place in the Kings' account of Josiah, it is among the vile rulers that have sullied the cult of Jerusalem. Ahaz explicitly did not behave righteously nor walk in the way of David (2 Kgs 16:2-3), but walked instead in the way of those kings of Israel; the flow of the narrative in Kings here shifts to emphasize the villainy of King Ahaz.[27] The Josiah reference, curiously, refers to altars made by kings of Judah but not the altar made by Ahaz to replace the proper altar already at the Jerusalem temple (2 Kgs 16:10-16). More cultic reform work by Ahaz at the insistence of the Assyrians, who had not even incorporated Judah into Assyria, goes unnoted (2 Kgs 16:17-18). There is, however, no doubt that the author of the Josiah story in Kings named Ahaz because he was such a fine example of malevolency. His grandson Manasseh, who was Josiah's grandfather, is also named in this trio of infamous kings in Jerusalem. Manasseh, of course, built a series of altars in Jerusalem, and Kings presents this as exquisitely evil (2 Kgs 21:3-5) while Josiah is presented destroying all these improper altars. The recitation of other sacrilegious deeds committed by Manasseh are passed over in the Josiah narrative. It was undoubtedly enough to point out that Manasseh was so evil that Josiah's righteousness was insufficient to save the region (2 Kgs 23:26-27); just how evil do you want a king to be?[28] That both Ahaz (2 Kgs 16:3) and Manasseh (2 Kgs 21:6) "passed their sons through fire" may be covered in the Josianic rectification without naming them by noting that Josiah destroyed the *tophet* where Molech was worshiped (2 Kgs 23:10). These three previous kings form a named trilogy of rulers who are offensive to the author of Kings; they corrupt the cult of Jerusalem and none of them worship Yahweh as their only deity. They are the antithesis of Josiah.

A final comment on the Judahite rulers should deal with Josiah's sons, Jehoahaz and Jehoiakim.[29] While Josiah's father and sons are mentioned

---

26 On 1 Kgs 9:4-9, see, Gary N. Knoppers, "Yhwh's Rejection of the House Built for His Name: On the Significance of Anti-temple Rhetoric in the Deuteronomistic History," in Amit, Ben Zvi and Finkelstein, *Essays on Ancient Israel*, 226-33. See also 2 Chr 7:17-22.

27 Cogan and Tadmor, *II Kings*, 190.

28 Apparently sinful enough even to bring Yahweh's wrath upon the temple in Jerusalem (Knoppers, "Yhwh's Rejection," 232).

29 The observation that the story of Josiah's reaction to the scroll is retold in Kings and Chronicles with diametrically reversed reactions from those of Jehoiakim in Jeremiah was clearly a literary device (Jeremiah 36), but must be read as a comment by the author of the Jeremianic prose rather than an aspect of Kings or Chronicles: Stephen Dempster, "'A Light in a Dark Place': A Tale of Two Kings and Theological Interpretation of the Old Testament," *SBJT* 14, no. 2 (2010): 19, 24.

only in the transitional passages of Josiah's reign, it is worth noting that none of the three receive 'good' report cards from the author of Kings. They all do what their evil ancestors had done before them. Amon comes across in Kings as a footnote to Manasseh and is graded accordingly.[30] The two sons, however, are also marked as wicked rulers.[31] It is a characteristic of the book of Samuel that heirs apparent are not only not their parents but, indeed, seem to be the opposite of what their respective fathers had been.[32] The literary formula of good kings/bad kings moves through Josiah's story, coming to an end with Josiah and his sons. From Ahaz onward, the pattern would, in fact, be: bad—good—bad—bad—good—bad—bad, and not a rapid repeat from one to the other, but ending with two evil kings suitable to be leaders of a tiny territory swallowed by expanding empires.[33]

Unstated in the narratives of the reigns of any king is how poorly these rulers had raised their heirs to rule in their stead. The notion, however, appears to have occurred to the author of Kings [as of Samuel]. Indeed, if Josiah's poor handling of his boys tends to pass unnoticed, Amon's lack of positive influence on Josiah has long been observed. Usually, the explanation has been that Amon's wife, the Queen Mother Jedidah, had clearly been the one who had raised her son and brought him up in a proper manner.[34] That Josiah's wives, Hamutal, mother of Jehoahaz, and Zebidah, mother of Jehoiakim, can be seen to have exerted evil parental influence on their wicked sons should raise serious questions about the entire 'goodness' of Josiah, as well as the role of Queen Mothers in

---

30 Duly noted by Hobbs, *2 Kings*, 311–12. Chronicles repeats Kings without making any change, given Manasseh's repentance in its own narrative. See Klein, *2 Chronicles*, 486–87.

31 In *History and Ideology in the Old Testament Prophetic Literature: A Semiotic Approach to the Reconstruction of the Proclamation of the Historical Prophets*, ConBOT 41 (Stockholm: Almquist & Wiksell, 1996), 360, Antti Laato sees the book of Jeremiah using Jehoiakim as the antithesis of Josiah.

32 In my "The Characters of Heirs Apparent in the Book of Samuel," *BR* 38 (1993): 5–22, I observe that all the sons of the central characters reverse the characteristics of their fathers; this cannot have been an accident and undoubtedly reflects a negative opinion on inherited kingship (and priesthood). Kings is less obvious about this aspect of dynasty, but the material from Ahaz to the end of the monarchy clearly reflects this literary/theological/political ideology.

33 The good king/bad king progression is more pronounced in Chronicles than in Kings which would explain a repentant Manasseh: Wilhelm Rudolph, "Problems of the Books of Chronicles," *VT* 4 (1954): 405.

34 Barlow, *Homiletical Commentary*, 629; Annie Russell Marble, *Women of the Bible: Their Services in Home and State* (New York: Century, 1927), 206; Wilda C. Gafney, *Daughters of Miriam: Women Prophets and Ancient Israel* (Minneapolis: Fortress, 2008), 144–45. This theory is the guiding plot device of the novella by Lois Nordling Erickson, *Huldah* (Hagerstown, MD: Review and Herald, 1991).

shaping the behavior of "my son(s), the king(s)."³⁵ Both of Josiah's wives are "from the provinces,"³⁶ but of Judean extraction; whether they were selected by Josiah and/or Jedidah, who was herself from the "provinces," is unknown, though Josiah would have needed to take some responsibility for how his sons were raised. The mothers may be a source of influence on the princes, but knowledge of the education of the heirs apparent of Judah remains about as close to nil as it can get.³⁷ Ezekiel 19:1–14 insists on the influence of Hamutal on her sons but provides no concrete information.³⁸

Josiah has been related to two kings of Israel, both in terms of their activities and as literary construction. The more significant of the two is Jeroboam, king of Israel. According to the historiography of Kings, Jeroboam was the innovative and apostate creator of the cultic and religious culture of Israel, abandoning the temple and ritual of Jerusalem so dear to the author of Kings. Less obvious at first glance is King Ahab, a ruler of dubious élan in Kings, whose wife, Jezebel, is presented as being in control. He provides a parallel to, and a literary sibling for, the repentant king as well.³⁹

Two drastic cultic changes bracket the narrative of the divided monarchy in Kings. The first is that introduced by Jeroboam, king of Israel, and the last by Josiah, king of Judah. Whoever constructed the overall narrative of Kings viewed them in diametrically opposite manners but clearly linked these two rulers.⁴⁰ Jeroboam is presented as a character embodying

---

35   Additional information on Josiah's wives needs to be sought from somewhere other than Kings or Chronicles. The short citations to them as queen mothers in Jeremiah and Ezekiel suggest that the compilers of those prophetic books took these women to be responsible for their sons' apostasy: Ginny Brewer-Boydston, *Good Queen Mothers, Bad Queen Mothers: The Theological Presentation of the Queen Mother in 1 and 2 Kings*, CBQMS 54 (Washington, DC: Catholic Biblical Association of America, 2016), 123, 128–89, 130, 132–34.

36   Linda S. Schearing, "Queen," *ABD* 5.585.

37   James L. Crenshaw (*Education in Ancient Israel: Across the Deadening Silence*, ABRL [New York: Doubleday, 1998], 4–5) acknowledges the minimal amount of information available for education of any kind in the states of Israel and Judah; there is nothing about teaching kings-to-be. See also Finsterbusch ("Modelle schriftgestützten," 224) on the lack of religious education data. Brewer-Boydston (*Good Queen Mothers*, 137) presumes queen mothers were responsible for their sons' education. However, the evidence in support of this is miniscule.

38   Brewer-Boydston, *Good Queen Mothers*, 130.

39   The following derives, with major adaptations, from two of my papers presented at the Midwest Society of Biblical Literature: "'I'm Sorry, So Sorry': Ahab and Josiah Escape Destruction," Calvin College, Grand Rapids, Feb. 2003, and "Josiah Is Not Jeroboam and Other Uncertainties," Olivet Nazarene University, Bourbonnais, Feb. 17, 2007.

40   Galvin, *David's Successors*, 131. See also Joseph (*Portrait of the Kings*, 26–27), who

the very definition of the evil ruler, allowing him to be used as the paradigm of wicked kings throughout the work.⁴¹ Josiah, on the other hand, is promulgated as the embodiment of the faithful ruler, characterized by the perfect example of King David (2 Kgs 22:2).⁴² For both kings it is their activities related to the cultic traditions of their respective territories that is central to the narratives written about them. The religious involvement of the two literary figures would appear to be a significant aspect of the rendition of their respective reigns. Moreover, the current text explicitly relates their reigns to each other (1 Kgs 13:2).

The religious activities of Jeroboam and Josiah can only be studied as presented in the literary production of Kings. Neither archaeological excavations nor modern social sciences provide data; the only sources are segments of biblical historiography. However, it is possible to compare the religious activities of the two rulers either as textual events (as they are presented in the biblical narratives), or as material for modern social scientific reconstructions. The following analysis is divided into two sections. The first assumes that the narratives in Kings about Jeroboam and Josiah were intentionally related and that this is reflected in the parallel materials used to construct the stories. The second section makes use of select, popular, modern socio-political theories to demonstrate that the notion of a 'good' or a 'bad' ruler, both in the ancient world and in the modern, is highly subjective.

Kings includes a number of items related to both the first king of the independent polity of post-Davidic Israel⁴³ and the last independent ruler of Judah. According to the Kings' narrative, the respective right to rule

---

understands Jeroboam as the "anti-David" and Josiah as the "second David" in literary contrast.

41 An observation perhaps too common to warrant citation; however, see Carl D. Evans, "Jeroboam 1," *ABD* 3.744; Juha Pakkala, "Jeroboam without Bulls," *ZAW* 120 (2008): 521, 523; Finkelstein, *Forgotten Kingdom*, 4. A survey of the impious kings of Israel is compiled in Levin, "Frömmigkeit," 138–42.

42 So, for example, Cogan and Tadmor, *II Kings*, 281, and Cohn, *2 Kings*, 152; but note Fretheim (*First and Second Kings*, 211), who sees Hezekiah as the embodiment of David, and Josiah as the new Moses, which is creative and reasonable from the narrative but not actually present in the textual reference, and is therefore a modern reading.

43 It is important to disavow any technical terminology for the term 'state,' here being used as any socio-anthropological collection of human beings larger than a couple villages. Also, there was clearly a social entity entitled 'Israel' prior to that created for, or by, Jeroboam (or Saul). The appearance of the designation in the Merneptah inscription would seem to substantiate such a 'place/people' while not connecting it to the biblical 'Israel,' other than by modern equation. See Redford (*Egypt, Canaan, and Israel in Ancient Times*, 275–80), who defines Israel at that time with the Shasu; also Liverani, *Israel's History*, 25.

and the manner in which they ruled is significant. Taking the textual narrative as a historiographical referent, the characters of these two men may be examined, keeping in mind that any relation to historical facticity is not here assumed.[44] While not exactly forming an *inclusio* for any narrative structure, the disparity between the presentations of Jeroboam and of Josiah is interesting for a variety of themes.

Their very right to be leaders, let alone rulers, of Israel and Judah respectively might well be the most significant comparison. Jeroboam's position of authority derives directly from Solomon (1 Kgs 11:28). There is a formal list of Solomon's three adversaries in the larger passage of 1 Kgs 11:14–40 that highlights the irony that he appointed his own "adversary." Both of the other adversaries were rulers in their own right of significant kingdoms to the south and north of David's Israel. Hadad was of the royal house of Edom, an independent region with a monarchical history. David, according to the text, had commanded Joab to exterminate the entire male population of Edom and, according to the narrative tradition recorded, succeeded in this genocidal endeavor, with the exception of one man. In contrast to Moses and the Hebrews/Israelites, who escaped the slaughter of males by fleeing from an Egyptian king, Hadad escapes the slaughter of Edomite males carried out by a Hebrew/Israelite king by fleeing to Egypt. The reversal was probably a literary inversion meant to contrast the approved Moses with the despised Hadad. Rezon, at the other end of David's kingdom, was essentially son-of-a-nobody. His father was an underling of the king of Zobah who escaped his master. Rezon's rise to power resembles nothing less than that of the rise of David himself. He raised a band of 'mighty thugs' to terrorize the country in the wake of David's genocidal slaughter. Removing themselves to Damascus, this gang overwhelms the city, making Rezon the king of Aram. He will hold this position for the length of Solomon's reign, continuously being a royal pain to King Solomon. Along with Jeroboam, all three rulers were active during Solomon's reign and, according to the received narrative, all three were deemed by Solomon to be problems.[45]

Jeroboam is clearly described as being of no royal lineage; his father is said to have been the Ephrathite Nebat and his mother was Zeruah, both names having potentially purposeful denigrations connected to them.[46] In

---

44 So, for example, Finkelstein's *Forgotten Kingdom*, 81–82, which recreates a historical rise of Jeroboam much more related to Egyptian concerns in the region and centered on an imposing Tirzah, a 'capital' more significant than Jerusalem and without monumental architecture.

45 Diana V. Edelman, "Solomon's Adversaries Hadad, Rezon and Jeroboam: A Trio of 'Bad Guy' Characters Illustrating the Theology of Immediate Retribution," in Holloway and Handy, *The Pitcher Is Broken*, 169. Literally, these are three *satans*.

46 J. R. Soza, "Jeroboam" in Arnold and Williamson, *Dictionary of the Old Testament*,

this way, it is made clear that Jeroboam, as opposed to Rehoboam, son of Solomon, is a 'son-of-a-nobody,' much like Rezon. Jeroboam is first designated as a servant of Solomon. He is observed by the king to be industrious and, apparently, a born leader. Solomon, therefore, appoints him as head of *corvée* labor in the district of "Joseph" (1 Kgs 11:28), which would have been deemed an important region of Israel and a plum appointment if it does not represent the territory of Israel itself.[47] It is most likely that the phrase "house of Joseph" is used for literary reasons related to Egyptian captivity and other unsavory implications.[48] In his rebellion against Solomon, Jeroboam, like Hadad, flees for protection to Egypt and returns from there to rule the northern breakaway kingdom, as the author of Kings understands Jeroboam's Israel.

In contrast, Josiah derives from the lineage of David through Solomon, as the legal heir apparent of the Davidic King Amon. Despicable as this assassinated king is portrayed to be in Kings, he is recorded to be of the direct Davidic lineage.[49] He had a reigning monarch for a father and Jedidah, daughter of Adaiah, for a mother, a perfectly Judean woman from Bozkath in a region of both economic and strategic importance to Judah.[50] Josiah was the legitimate ruler with no immediate foreign parentage.[51] The fact that his father's name is also the name of a major Egyptian deity may have had some significance historically but makes no impression on the

---

544-45; Jerome T. Walsh, "Nebat," *ABD* 4.1054. See also Linda Schearing ("Zeruah," *ABD* 6.1084), who notes that the LXX renders the name Sarira and designates her as a prostitute, while the MT name merely means "skin rash" or "leper."

47 It cannot be certain exactly what the author meant by *bet yosef*, even if the designation changed between pre-independent Israel and the independent kingdom of Israel. In this situation, it could mean either Ephraim and Manasseh or "all the Northern tribes" (Gray, *I & II Kings*, 294). It may have retained a restricted regional designation even after independence. See further Yohanan Aharoni, *The Archaeology of the Land of Israel*, trans. A. S. Rainey (Philadelphia: Westminster, 1982), 321.

48 Sweeney, *I & II Kings*, 159-60.

49 The importance of the direct royal family connection for Josiah, as with Assyrian kings, is set out in Karen Radner, "Assyrian and Non-Assyrian Kingship in the First Millennium BC," in *Concepts of Kingship in Antiquity: Proceedings of the European Science Foundation Exploratory Workshop: Held in Padova, November 28th-December 1st, 2007*, ed. G. B. Lanfranchi and R. Rollinger, HANE/M 11 (Padua: S.A.R.G.O.N. Editrice e Libereria, 2010), 26-27. Josiah is significant as the "last great descendant of David to occupy the throne" (Blenkinsopp, *David Remembered*, 110).

50 Denis Baly, *The Geography of the Bible*, new and rev. ed. (New York: Harper & Row, 1974), 142.

51 'Foreign' queen mothers are deemed a problem in Kings. See Schearing's "Queen," 586, which fits in with the sociological notion of 'folk devils' as causers of disaster in the Bible; also Chalcraft, "Sociology and the Book of Chronicles," 217-19.

narrative, unless it is very subtle.[52] That his mother's name is so clearly a variant of the name given to Solomon by Nathan (2 Sam 12:25) begs the question of whether it was significant in designating Josiah's mother as literally (if not otherwise) related to the proper Davidic lineage. Being of the Davidic lineage, Josiah shares with other Judahite kings the eternal promise of God to David (2 Sam 7:11–16) that seems to be understood, if not mentioned explicitly, throughout Kings.[53] Josiah's immediate reason for taking the throne is the death of his father in a bloody assassination during Josiah's minority. Nonetheless, Josiah takes the throne at the age of eight and there is no acknowledgment that he is not the acting monarch.

A couple of correspondences link Josiah and Jeroboam in the narratives concerning their reigns. First, both attain their rule through violent revolts. Jeroboam is recalled by the Israelites to lead them in their newly formed kingdom independent of David's son Solomon. Josiah is placed upon the throne by the Judahites after the assassination of his father and the rounding up and execution of the perpetrators of the royal murder. Violent revolts bring both to their position as king. Both are inextricably related to Solomon: Josiah by direct descent and Jeroboam by appointment and then recall by the very people he had been placed over by the iron-fisted Solomon. On a theological level that was important to the author of Kings, both are highly regarded by Yahweh for countering the cultic improprieties of Solomon. According to the narrative, Jeroboam is selected by God because Solomon worshiped other gods, made idols, and built a lot of shrines or temples to deities other than Yahweh. Yahweh creates the kingdom of Israel for Jeroboam to rule over for this reason, separated from the apostasy of the Solomonic court. The irony of this divine blunder cannot have been lost on the author and readers of Kings. Josiah

---

52 Giving the king the name of an Egyptian deity that was well known to the populace of Judah would certainly have connected the god and the king in a territory assumed by the author of Kings to have been exclusively dedicated to Yahweh, Zevit (*The Religions of Ancient Israel*, 590) and Assmann ("Amun," DDD 53) notwithstanding. Variations in the versions seem to suggest the scribal tradition was aware of the Egyptian divine name of a Jerusalemite king; see Montgomery, *Critical and Exegetical Commentary*, 522; Hobbs, *2 Kings*, 299n18b.

53 Steussy (*David*, 89–90) notes the ambiguity in this promise to David and its relation to descendants to come. Long assumed to date back somehow to David himself, the Davidic 'covenant' and this tale of Nathan's prophetic announcement, need not be dated so early: Leonhard Rost, *The Succession to the Throne of David*, trans. M. D. Rutter and D. M. Gunn, HTIBS 1 (Sheffield: Almond Press, 1982), 40–41. Rost argues for a Davidic origin for the theological propaganda. However, a much later date for the passage that still acknowledges the presence of theological propaganda seems more reasonable, even if the historical Judah would have embraced the notion. See Van Seters (*In Search of History*, 271–77, 290–91), who surveys the discussion concerning that later date.

belongs to that Solomonic dynasty but is emphatically related to David, prior to Solomon's heresies. It is Josiah who not only listens to the words of the book of Moses, which predates David and Solomon by generations in the biblical chronology, but who also acts upon it even though there has been no obedience to its cultic tradition since there has been a king in Israel or Judah. Ironically, Josiah, who occupies the throne after two generations of "idolaters," rectifies the cult of Judah *and* Israel in short order. In both cases the writer goes out of his way to mention that the ruler had both divine and popular support, a staple of the ideal of the proper ruler throughout the ancient Near East. Both of these kings are presented in the theological narrative of Kings as having had the right derived from Yahweh to rule their respective kingdoms.

The book of Kings now forms the final section of the Former Prophets; the prophetic character of the texts should not be forgotten. The narratives concerning both kings contain prophets of some importance and share one prophet that ties the tales together explicitly. Jeroboam is declared king by the actions of Ahijah, who explains the reasons why Solomon, despite being David's son and legal heir to the promise of David's eternal reign, has lost the right for his family to rule and why Solomon's descendants are going to retain Judah in any case. The speech by Ahijah in 1 Kgs 11:31-39 stresses the list of offenses committed by Solomon, the most serious being that he has gone after other gods. He warns Jeroboam to walk in the way of David in faithfulness to Yahweh. It is necessary to understand that this is the David of the book of Kings and not the David of the book of Samuel. His characterization in Kings is much more in line with that of the David of Chronicles.[54]

The appearance of Shemaiah, prophet of Yahweh, to King Rehoboam in order to confirm the divine sanction of Jeroboam as king of Israel cements Jeroboam's legitimacy with regard to Jerusalem's monarch. The counterpart to this prophetic statement is the one of Huldah. Her message may have been relayed to the king through yet more mundane human messengers than had been Ahijah's message to Jeroboam, but Josiah is led to know that Judah, if not Josiah himself, has gone after other gods and thereby disobeyed Yahweh. Huldah reports that Josiah will live out his reign before his kingdom is demolished (2 Kgs 22:19-20), in line with a similar statement made to Jeroboam by Ahijah (1 Kgs 14:13).

---

54 On the varieties of 'David' to choose from even within Kings, see Steussy, *David*, 94-95. There, Josiah is shown to be clearly adhering to the first part of David's double instructions to Solomon (92-93) and not the bloodbath from the second part of the instructions, unless killing off non-Yahwistic priests forms that parallel (93). A quite different and more congregational David appears in Chronicles (125).

The unnamed prophet who appears in the story at the beginning of the tale of the Israelite temple at Bethel appears in the narrative of both kings. This prophet serves to predict the coming of Josiah to destroy the altar at Bethel just established by Jeroboam (1 Kgs 13:2). In the story of Josiah, he appears as an unseen corpse, demonstrating the overt piety of Josiah, when Josiah goes to Bethel to destroy the Israelite cultic center (2 Kgs 23:16–18). In addition to this honest prophet, there is also the lying prophet living in Bethel. He uses perfectly proper prophetic speech to detour "the man of God" to his death at the hands of Yahweh. This allows the true prophet to be buried in Bethel via the intercession of the lying prophet, who nonetheless wishes to be associated with the honest prophet. Only the 'true' prophet is retained in the Josianic tale; the lying perpetrator of the honest prophet having been buried at Bethel remains unmentioned in the Josiah story.

Ahijah returns in the story of Jeroboam to predict the death of the royal child and condemn the king for behaving as Solomon had before him. The conditions for Jeroboam's right to reign have not been met, and his legitimacy on the throne is lost. The catch-phrase that he had done more evil than all those preceding him (1 Kgs 14:9) is slightly odd, given that there were no kings of an independent Israel prior to Jeroboam, unless Saul is counted. Otherwise, the referents could only be David and Solomon. Given that Josiah is credited with having been perfect in every way, just like David, his ancestor (2 Kgs 22:2), the villain who is surpassed by Jeroboam must be Solomon, who lusted after foreign gods and women. Jeroboam's behavior becomes the literary norm for all of the succeeding rulers of Israel and a fair number of the rulers of Judah.

If it is made clear that Yahweh has provided divine support for the rule of these two kings, the text of Kings also makes it clear that the general populations of their respective kingdoms were supportive of their kings. The text reads that all the people of the northern breakaway kingdom of Israel not only declared Jeroboam to be their king (1 Kgs 12:20a) but willingly followed him without exception (1 Kgs 12:20b). Moreover, his religious policies were universally accepted throughout Israel (1 Kgs 12:30; 14:15–16). Josiah's popular support came from all the people of Judah, the priests, the prophets, and the residents of Jerusalem (2 Kgs 22:2–3). The text clearly intends for the reader to accept the Judahites under Josiah as good, repentant Yahwists and the Israelites under Jeroboam as heretics. In both cases, the general population of the two kingdoms follow the lead of their respective kings and, moreover, support them.

The narrative geography of the two kingdoms is of some interest. When Rehoboam's kingdom is split by Yahweh, the Davidic lineage receives only the former tribe of Judah as a sop to the memory of the promise made to David. For the infractions of Solomon and the intransigence of Rehoboam,

Jeroboam gets almost all of David's mini-empire: ten of the former tribes (1 Kgs 11:30–37).[55] While the extent of Josiah's realm is defined, Jeroboam's is not. Geba to Beer Sheba (2 Kgs 23:8) delineates Josiah's rather small territory, itself somewhat conforming to a possible geography of Judah.[56] For Josiah there is a royal capital, or royal residence, which is the Jerusalem around which much of Kings centers.[57] As ruler of Jerusalem, Josiah appears as a cultic official in charge of clearing out all the improper 'evil stuff' in the city and dumping the religious rubbish outside the limits of the city. The boundaries of Jerusalem are clearly marked as separating the refuse of idolatrous worship from the newly purified city itself.

In like manner, and in accordance with the prophecy made in the reign of Jeroboam, Josiah also destroys the sanctuary at Bethel and its accouterments. This defines the narrative stage upon which Josiah acts. Jeroboam's Israel is defined solely as those ten tribes taken from Solomon at the time of Rehoboam. It is not explicitly defined by topographical or urban locales; however, ten tribes would be perceived as larger and more important than one. Jerusalem was the cultic center for Josiah precisely because it had been the center of Solomon's temple, which the text assures the reader was selected by David on divine commission. The cultic centers for Jeroboam were meant precisely to distance themselves and their worshipers from Jerusalem (1 Kgs 12:28–29) and are reported to be Bethel and Dan. Unlike Josiah, Jeroboam recognized no such centralized cultic center but instead allowed shrines/temples all over Israel and personally appointed cultic officials for them (1 Kgs 13:33). The author of Kings defines all of these activities as apostasy for not retaining Jerusalem as the religious center of a kingdom now separated from that location. While ignoring Jerusalem as the center of religious attention is defined

---

55 The extent of any historical kingdom of Jeroboam is less clear. Liverani (*Israel's History*, 105) speculates that the original territory of Jeroboam's Israel was not much larger than the Joseph tribes. Similar, but with the possible addition of Gilead, is Finkelstein, *Forgotten Kingdom*, 78. In any case, the cities assigned to Rehoboam in Chronicles appear to reflect the time of John Hyrcanus in the Hellenistic era; see Israel Finkelstein, "Rehoboam's Fortified-Cities (II Chr 11,5–12): A Hasmonean Reality?," ZAW 123 (2011): 105–6, though the list of cities has been formerly associated with the time of Josiah (92).

56 On the debate over the actual possible territory of Josiah's kingdom, see Handy, "Judah in a New Light," 425–29; Finkelstein and Silberman, *Bible Unearthed*, 347–53.

57 Where Josiah actually resided is unimportant here since the text places all the legitimate kings in Jerusalem. Ramat Rahel, from excavation, appears a likely location for the residence of the Judahite ruler at the end of the seventh century. See Aharoni, *Archaeology of the Land*, 204. See also Stern, *Archaeology of the Land of the Bible*, 34–35, 215, who notes the Assyrian aspects of the palace most reasonably, placing its construction while Assyria remained the power in the region.

as "sin," Jeroboam's building of his own capital for the royal palace at Shechem is not defined as an evil act (1 Kgs 12:25). The reason for the locations of the two major religious cultic centers for Israel being established at the ends of the territory rather than in the same location as the royal residence remains unexplained. The temples are considered evil because they are not Jerusalem; however, the palace is apparently legitimate. Jeroboam's cultic activity takes place almost exclusively at Bethel; though Dan is clearly defined as a place of religious activity, activities undertaken there are not recorded. The only other site mentioned as important for Jeroboam is Penuel, which he ordered to be built (1 Kgs 12:25).[58]

Of these locations, none has more importance for the current narrative than the stories of Jerusalem and, in particular, Solomon's palace temple. It is the focal point of the stories of both kings. In Jeroboam's case, it is the sacred place to which he does not wish his subjects to go to or to align themselves with (1 Kgs 12:28). For Josiah's restitution of the proper Yahwistic cultus, it is the center of all proper cultic activity for both his own kingdom, Judah, and for the neighboring territory of Israel. Jeroboam's desire to eliminate the former practice of his populace, which saw them traveling to Jerusalem for cultic activities, would likely be seen by modern readers to reflect political concerns, with these cultic acts portrayed as evidence of allegiance to David's royal house. The various temples or shrines (often translated *high places*) that Solomon built for his wives and for his own worship activities are among the many reasons for Solomon to lose territory to Jeroboam in this narrative. The individual deities for which these establishments had been constructed are given in order to illustrate the apostasy of Solomon himself, leading to Yahweh's seeking out Jeroboam (1 Kgs 11:33). Josiah makes use of a proper manual, written by the hoary, pre-monarchic, shadowy figure of Moses, to purify the temple in Jerusalem and to remove all the temples and shrines built by Solomon for those same named deities (2 Kgs 23:13). While Jeroboam supports major national shrines in Bethel and Dan, Josiah deals only with Bethel. The former builds and encourages participation in the worship services at the religious center in Bethel; the latter destroys the same religious center and apparently violently removes the cultic personnel who

---

58 The narrative of Jeroboam's wife includes other locations, but they are not directly related to the reign of Jeroboam by the story except as fulfillment of the curse laid upon the king by Yahweh through Ahijah. Shiloh (1 Kgs 14:4) has clear prophetic affinities with Samuel and legitimacy for the throne: Sweeney, *I & II Kings*, 185. The place name Tirzah in 1 Kgs 14:17 remains questionable on several grounds. See Montgomery, *Critical and Exegetical Commentary*, 266; Gray, *I & II Kings*, 339; Robinson, *The First Book of Kings*, 168–69. Most of these commentators assume the passage on Jeroboam's wife is somehow clumsily incorporated into the narrative of Kings from an earlier folk literature tale: Long, *1 Kings*, 154–57.

serve the site. Finally, Jeroboam builds and enthusiastically maintains the *bamoth* everywhere in his Israel, while Josiah destroys the shrines and forbids religious practice at all such former sacred sites.⁵⁹

The theological import of the narrative of Kings is quite explicit both in what the respective religious changes enforced by the two kings entail and what they portend. The two major items of reform ascribed to Jeroboam are the fashioning of golden images of young bovine as objects of worship and the declaration that henceforth the sacred sites for pilgrimage in the northern kingdom will be Dan and Bethel, where building operations for temples are instigated. Neither of these acts is presented as being entirely new; they are intended to pry the people away from Yahweh, Jerusalem, and Judah. Josiah, in counterpoint, destroyed all the images accrued over the centuries in Jerusalem, Judah, and Israel while declaring Jerusalem the only place of proper worship for Judah, Jerusalem, and with a bit of force, Israel. If Jeroboam permitted the worship of many deities, as had Solomon, Josiah restricted worship to Yahweh alone.

Interestingly, both kings make speeches at the beginning of their religious reform activities. Jeroboam announces to his people that the golden calves he has had manufactured are the gods who brought them out of Egypt. They may now worship them at the respective sites in Dan and Bethel. Josiah, on the other hand, reads the entire scroll found in the temple to the crowd in Jerusalem as the preface to his reforming activities that make Jerusalem the sole acceptable place for the worship of Yahweh. Both kings also proclaim festivals that no one knew anything about previously. Jeroboam (1 Kgs 12:32) institutes an unnamed festival, usually assumed to be a form of Tabernacles moved to another month for observation.⁶⁰ To the author of Kings, Jeroboam's festival is considered an invention of an evil king having no validity.⁶¹ Josiah is presented as recovering and reinstituting the Passover described in the scroll of the covenant found in the temple (2 Kgs 23:21-23). Unlike Jeroboam's invented and, therefore, invalid festival, Josiah faithfully enacts the true religious ritual that should have been practiced throughout the monarchic period but that had been forgotten even before the time of David. For both Jeroboam and Josiah the narrative relates the connection of their cultic upheavals to the Exodus narrative: Jeroboam negatively with the golden

---

59 On 'high places,' see W. Boyd Barrick, "What Do We Really Know about 'High Places'?," *SEÅ* 45 (1980): 51-57; idem, "The Word *bmh* in the Old Testament" (PhD diss., University of Chicago, 1977).
60 Gray, *I & II Kings*, 317-18; Sweeney, *I & II Kings*, 178-79
61 Robinson, *First Book of Kings*, 158; Laffey, *First and Second Kings*, 56.

calves[62] and Josiah positively with the Mosianic Passover.[63] For the author of Kings, Jeroboam knows the historiography but abuses it, while Josiah does not know the historiography but, when appraised of it, makes all necessary corrections to a woefully errant past.

As far as the priesthood goes, Jeroboam is presented as being loose and indifferent to proper priestly lineage. He establishes a priesthood that, according to the writer of Kings, would not have existed for an independent kingdom of Israel at the time. Josiah, however, rectifies this situation in his day by exterminating these families of newly-minted priests invented originally by King Jeroboam. Indeed, Jeroboam had made many priests from the general public, filling the sanctuaries and the temples at Dan and Bethel with personnel that the author of Kings does not deem to be priestly at all. While anybody might wind up as a priest at the whim of Jeroboam and his religious descendants, Josiah is presented as restricting the priesthood to properly Torah-instructed Levitical families and those who are in or are allowed to move into Jerusalem.

In the end, Jeroboam is shown rejecting Yahweh. He puts Yahweh behind his back (1 Kgs 14:9) by seeking "other" deities, creating forbidden images, and recognizing many legitimate sanctuaries when there should be, according to Kings, one aniconic deity and one official temple in Jerusalem. Josiah, to the contrary, is presented as obeying Yahweh in every manner and executing a purification of the cultic life of Jerusalem and Judah perfectly; the text is less sanguine about how thorough Josiah was in Israel. Jeroboam is just religiously evil and Josiah righteous.

To complete the narrative contrast of these two biblical characters, there are the summary statements, the death and burial notations, and the predictions given to each concerning their heirs. Needless to say, in both summary clauses (1 Kgs 12:20b and 14:7–14) Jeroboam is all evil while Josiah is all good (2 Kgs 22:2 and 23:25). The contrast is as stark as possible; as Gösta Ahlström used to phrase it: "There is the man in the white hat and the man in the black hat and you know who is who!"[64] Here, that is part of the narrative strategy.

If reigning a long time was deemed a sign of acceptance and good will from the gods, or, in this case, Yahweh, it is interesting to note that both Jeroboam and Josiah had long reigns. Although, according to the text, he went rather astray, Jeroboam ruled for 22 years before sleeping with his

---

62   Long observed by S. R. Driver, *The Book of Exodus*, Cambridge Bible for Schools and Colleges (Cambridge: University Press, 1918), 347–48; Miller and Hayes, *A History of Ancient Israel and Judah*, 275–76.

63   Hobbs, *2 Kings*, 337; Sweeney, *I & II Kings*, 439.

64   Oral communication repeated at various times through several lectures and office conferences at the Divinity School of the University of Chicago, 1980–1987.

fathers; the phrase is generally taken to mean that the king died peacefully and was buried in his family's tomb. Having ruled for 31 years and having been assured by Yahweh's prophet, Huldah, that he would die in peace, Josiah was killed by King Neco of Egypt; he nonetheless was buried in his own tomb in Jerusalem. The predictions for the heirs of each ruler are not good. The political system by which rule is passed on from father to son is not highly regarded in the biblical narratives. Jeroboam and Josiah provide classic examples: while the former king is portrayed as all wicked and the latter as all righteous, nonetheless, both receive prophecies that their heirs are doomed. Clearly, Yahweh found something good in Jeroboam and much good in Josiah and therefore both are to be allowed to continue their reigns. Nevertheless, the son and immediate heir of Jeroboam will die violently, his dynasty will be wiped out quickly, and his kingdom itself will end later. Josiah's heirs will not rule peacefully or for long, and the kingdom will come to an end with them. For the very different presentations of these two rulers, the prophecies regarding their respective children and kingdoms are markedly similar. Indeed, they both seem quite like the prophecy made to Ahab (1 Kgs 21:20-29).

If the Kings' narrative presents a historiographical message of an evil king forming an evil kingdom and a righteous king attempting to salvage a legitimate kingdom, critical modern scholars take quite different views of the rulers. Still, there is much in common with the two kings. The biblical text remains the basic working material for 'modern'/'postmodern' approaches, but biblical hermeneutics tend toward a hermeneutics of political polemic.[65] A short view of these two kings through more current study is at least interesting.[66] Divorcing the view from a Jerusalemite and Josianic perspective, the rulers appear both more similar and more distinct.

---

65 Roland Boer, "National Allegory in the Hebrew Bible," *JSOT* 74 (1997): 106-112. One can also read the biblical narratives in radical revolutionary manners, e.g., Roland Boer, *Rescuing the Bible*, BlMan (Malden, MA: Blackwell, 2007), 105-27.

66 "Interesting" because it ceases to be a study of texts and becomes much more a study of overlaying popular theories-of-the-moment on ancient texts. This has been a major and serious concern for those interested in both a religious tradition, whether their own or another's, and modern trends in scholarship. In *Revealed Texts, Hidden Meanings: Finding the Religious Significance in Tanakh* (New York: KTAV, 2009), 19-26, Hayyim J. Angel contrasts the study of a text (as a unit) and the microdivision of artifacts for modern theory. Herbert W. Basser ("The Butchering of Jewish Texts to Feed the Masses," in *Judaism in Late Antiquity. Part 3: Where We Stand: Issues and Debates in Ancient Judaism*, ed. J. Neusner and A. J. Avery-Peck, HdO 40/3.1 [Leiden: Brill, 1999], 241) justly warns about scholarly populism, trendy academia, and "The cursing of the careful work of those few who endeavor to represent the texts and traditions as in fact they are." The following material on Jeroboam and Josiah falls under these observations, but I would contend it has indeed ceased to be a study of a text, and has instead become a rendition of theories of possible pasts.

To begin again, both Jeroboam and Josiah are presented as rulers who were breaking with the traditional religion of their respective territorial regions. The religious cult that is being defied in both cases is that of the Jerusalem temple, the cultic center of their immediate predecessors. In the case of Jeroboam, this is emphasized as an immediate plan of distancing himself and his people from Solomon's dynasty (1 Kgs 12:26–27), while for Josiah it is deemed an attempt to curb improper worship extending backwards in time to the age of the Judges. There is nothing in the text about either king attempting to restore Davidic traditions regardless of how popular that theory may have become in some circles.[67] It appears that both rulers were attempting to relate their cultic reforms to earlier religious traditions and locations, whether real or creatively invented for the purpose of legitimation.[68] In both cases, the religious 'reform' was presented as being instigated by royal fiat. It is the king, not priests, prophets, or the populace at large, who had the authority to declare new religious institutions. Both Jeroboam (the Exodus, 1 Kgs 12:28) and Josiah (Moses, 2 Kgs 23:2–3) appealed to antiquity for the right to create a proper religious environment for their people.[69] In both cases, the manner of moving forward to future proper relations with Yahweh was by looking backward to events performed by Yahweh in a time before a physical, landed, political body existed. Moreover, they used the same general, pre-kingdom, Mosianic narrative for their authority.

The right for the current king to make these claims upon the population is spelled out in each case. In Jeroboam's instance, Solomon's incapacity to refrain from apostasy set the stage for the need for a better ruler. The instigation of his reign and his reform was made by Yahweh through prophetic speech and action. He was to stop behaving like Solomon and not emulate the manner in which he had been running the religious activities of the kingdom. He was instead going to do it better; this was a call for religious reform. For Josiah, the instigation is by Yahweh through the *torah* of Moses in which the desires of the deity are recorded.

The religious lives of the kings of Judah and Israel through the first 18 years of the reign of Josiah had been improper. Yahweh spoke directly to Jeroboam through the prophetic mouthpiece and indirectly to Josiah

---

67 Cross and Freedman, "Josiah's Revolt against Assyria," 56–58; Mark Leuchter, "Jeroboam the Ephraitite," *JBL* (2006): 52, 65. Note that some perceive the literary David 'prototype' to be based on Josiah, e.g., Joseph, *Portrait of the Kings*, 185.

68 See Wyatt, "Royal Religion in Ancient Judah," 66, for Jeroboam's 'reform.'

69 In "The Exodus Story: Between Historical Memory and Historiographical Composition," *JANER* 11 (2011): 39–69, Nadav Na'aman rationally envisions the Exodus tradition as creative recasting of the exit of Egypt from Canaan rather than the exit of Israel from Egypt and as an inventive historiography in both the northern and southern Yahwistic territories.

through a textual record that no one seemed to remember. Jeroboam consulted with his human advisors as to what he should do, while Josiah consulted with Yahweh through his human advisors via the prophet Huldah. As presented, Jeroboam checked the word of Yahweh through humans and Josiah checked the word of a human through Yahweh. In the end, Jeroboam acted as part of a group decision, however empowered and elite it may have been, and the general population accepted the reform that he devised. Josiah, on the other hand, presents the 'covenant' to the population as a *fait accompli*, and the crowd accepted it by acclamation.[70] The reform is from the top down in both instances.

Jeroboam's reform is the product of the monarch. Though he may have consulted with advisors, he is shown instigating the cultic changes by himself. That said, Jeroboam does not centralize the worship of his people in his private chapel or in his capital at Shechem but builds his major temples at the margins of his political state, Dan in the north and Bethel in the south. Moreover, the local sanctuaries, shrines, or cult places, where the Israelites had been used to engaging in religious activities, remained and were acknowledged by Jeroboam as legitimate, authorized religious institutions. Local religious tradition was encouraged, distanced from the king's immediate control. One needs to keep in mind, however, that even in small, rural settlements 'local' did not necessarily mean popular or people-oriented; these sites would have had their own hierarchies and regulations. Democracy and anarchy were never a part of ancient social life; the almost universal equation of local autonomy with freedom and popular support is a fiction of modern academic minds.

Nonetheless, Jeroboam is envisioned as consulting authorities or advisors, decentralizing state shrines, and allowing numerous established local cultic sites to form his religious polity. Josiah, who also reformed his cult by royal mandate, claiming to be the conduit for the will of Yahweh, orders the centralization of all worship in his own private sanctuary in his own royal palace. This would have been a centralization that not only required the physical acknowledgment of the reign of Yahweh but also, and more so, the reign of Josiah.[71] In the age of political proletarian democracy and religious options for the poor, Jeroboam, while no shining beacon of liberation theology, would come out far ahead of Josiah.[72]

---

70 Tradition has assumed in some instances that the scroll is presented to the populace devoid of passing through Huldah and the comments by Yahweh: Stanley, *Lectures on the History of the Jewish Church*, 429.

71 Olmstead presents Josiah's reform as a power grab by the king and the peasant "robbed of his religion." See Olmstead, "The Reform of Josiah and Its Secular Aspects," 568. See also Nakanose, *Josiah's Passover*, 111-12. Nakanose's views are endorsed by Sally Brown, "2 Kings 23:1-20," *Int* 60 (2006): 69.

72 To be honest, however, most biblical studies that claim to be liberating from

If religion as cultic activity needs to be performed in a particular way in a particular location, how was this enforced by these two kings creating 'new' traditions? Jeroboam built up the pre-existing holy sites of Bethel and Dan into pilgrimage destinations while encouraging continued worship at innumerable local shrines. His reformation was enforcement by construction and the promotion of diversity. Josiah enforced his reform by the destruction of any religious sites outside of his own carefully controlled sanctuary, and by demoting any religious or quasi-religious personnel who might have practiced public or private religious traditions that were not under his direct control. Acceptable cultic activity would have to have meant a trip to Josiah's residence in order to be acknowledged. Jeroboam raised up a 'center' from the periphery while Josiah suppressed the periphery around 'a center.'[73]

As far as who was allowed to participate in this newly constructed religious world, the personnel seem quite different for the two kings. Jeroboam cast a wide net. All the people of Israel follow his lead (1 Kgs 12:30) and continue to do so for as long as there is an Israel (2 Kgs 17:21–23). Moreover, a respectable number of the Judeans and their rulers also followed the lead of Jeroboam (2 Kgs 17:19). For Josiah, public participation was restricted by three things: space, since only the Jerusalem temple might properly be utilized; time, since one must go "up" to Jerusalem at appointed times; and personnel, since the ritual might only be performed by Levites and, of those, only ones allowed into Jerusalem by Josiah. As for the performance of the cult, there were two levels in both states: the king and the priests. In Jeroboam's case, the king acted as the high priest, performing the sacrifice at Bethel. The entire religious world of Israel was promoted under his

---

the hegemony of elitist ideology simply posit an alternative mandate which is equally arbitrary, but which has the decided advantage of having themselves as the new elite. Norman K. Gottwald (*The Politics of Ancient Israel*, LAI [Louisville: Westminster John Knox, 2001], 3–6, 27–31) and Walter Brueggemann (*Truth Speaks to Power: The Countercultural Nature of Scripture* [Louisville: Westminster John Knox, 2013], 2–8) both appear to recognize the situation without wishing to acknowledge themselves as an academic elite positing new socially hegemonic dicta.

73 On several occasions in conversation with the author at the Divinity School of the University of Chicago, Joseph Kitakawa commented on the opposing approaches taken by Josiah's Judah and Meiji Japan; his observation, as best as I can condense it from several repetitions, is as follows: Josiah sought to centralize a national religion by suppressing everything except the temple in Jerusalem while Meiji attempted to centralize a national religion by raising Ise above the myriad of shrines. This he did with accompanying hand movements. Kitakawa was (properly) convinced that, in this narrative, Josiah was attempting to create a 'super-religious cult' in Judah comparable to State Shinto in Japan, with heavy political/state/religion entanglement. For Meiji, see Joseph M. Kitakawa, *Religion in Japanese History* (New York: Columbia University, 1966), 286–87.

sponsorship. Jeroboam made the office of priest open to everyone (1 Kgs 12:31). The possibility of being a priest under Jeroboam allowed for a vast number of professional and even part-time priests—a notion not especially bizarre for a territory which had not long since been under Egyptian control.[74] Whether this also meant priestesses is not mentioned, but is not an unreasonable suggestion.[75]

Josiah, on the other hand, demoted any priests not under his control and restricted the office to Levites living in his capital Jerusalem. Slaughtering of the various priests of the outlying sanctuaries suggests Josiah had a tight grip on the office and intended to maintain it.[76] Thus, if Jeroboam opened religious orders to the population as a whole, Josiah restricted it to the one family of Levites and apparently to males who were physically unblemished and with their genitalia intact. It was probably the case that the priests were beholden to the king who appointed them so that the priestly office should be seen as the equivalent of the modern patronage political office. In the texts, Jeroboam acts as king and priest and is so represented, while Josiah is king and appoints priests but has cultic control that is explicit in the text but covert in literary representation. Josiah is king but not priest, yet he is shown as having absolute control of the priesthood in Jerusalem.

Two final comparisons are relevant. First, in both cases the general public is represented as supporting each reformer's new cult. Jeroboam is shown divesting no one in Israel and his brand of cult (in market theory) clearly attracted a lot of Judahites as well. Josiah, on the other hand, dismisses whole ranks of cultic personnel and the devotees of non-Yahwistic religious traditions. These people are not included in the phrase "all Judah"; they are, apparently, non-people or, at best, really Israelites, although they may have "all" acquiesced to Josiah's reform for devotional, strategic, or political reasons, or, indeed, as a result of sheer terror. Secondly, Josiah moves out of his own territory to force Israel (which was still a part of Assyria historically) to conform to his own religious ideal through savage means. Josiah could not defend, historically or literarily, an argument that

---

74 See Byron E. Shafer ("Temples, Priests, and Rituals: An Overview," in *Temples of Ancient Egypt*, ed. B. E. Shafer [Ithaca, NY: Cornell University Press, 1997], 9–10), who notes that the priesthood in Egypt was the domain of the king as primary priest and appointer of the lower echelons of priests, but any male adult of standing could serve for a time as a priest.

75 Shafer, "Temples," 11–16. The "holy woman" (*qedesha*) who appears in temples and shrines might have been a priestess, but her role is not defined in the Bible, only condemned: Phyllis A. Bird, *Missing Persons and Mistaken Identities: Women and Gender in Ancient Israel*, OBT (Minneapolis: Fortress, 1997), 96–97.

76 Exhuming the bones of already deceased priests probably suggested that the lineage, if inheritable, was now defunct.

he was returning Israel to a religious world it had ever known. That he is acting on these grounds is good biblical propaganda that was no doubt aimed directly at Samaria.[77] Josiah comes across here as a ruthless political invader concerned with his own hegemony of the cultic world of Israel. The text assures the reader that the action was for Israel's own good, but objectively it would have been religious usurpation of power for the benefit of Josiah and the religious elite of Jerusalem. Jeroboam never leaves his own kingdom; he may have been a cold, calculating religious reformer, but his was not an expansionist program to influence territories beyond his borders.

If the narratives of Jeroboam and Josiah are bookends for the divided monarchy, the stories of Ahab and Josiah intersect literarily in the rendition of repentance.[78] According to the Kings account, when Josiah heard the contents of the scroll found in the temple, he tore his clothes (2 Kgs 22:11). Yahweh perceived this action (2 Kgs 22:19) as penance and humility, and also saw that Josiah wept, which the reader did not get to observe back in v. 11. The reward for penitence and humility was that Josiah would not live to see the coming destruction of Judah (2 Kgs 22:20). For traditional commentators Josiah's repentance reflects the author's estimation of Josiah as the truly great, good, and pious ruler of Judah. The 'reform' that follows is assumed to be proof that Josiah deserved a reprieve from the coming defeat of Judah that leads to the final positive 'report card' for Josiah (2 Kgs 23:25).[79] The notice of Josiah's evaluation in 2 Kgs 22:2 is very positive. He did what was right in the eyes of Yahweh; he did not get an evaluation like the one found in 1 Kgs 16:30: Ahab son of Omri did evil in the eyes of Yahweh more than all who were before him. This is interesting because, in the larger Kings narrative, both Josiah and Ahab were kings who repented before Yahweh and both were rewarded with the promise that they would not live to see the destruction prophesied or hinted at in both cases.[80] Both stories form part of the book of Kings.

---

77   Ernst Würthwein ("Die Josianische Reform und das Deuteronomium," ZTK 73 [1976]: 417) sees mostly propaganda with some historical material.

78   Other connections between Josiah and Ahab have been suggested: the battle at Megiddo in 2 Chr 35:20-24 has been compared to Ahab's battle at Ramoth-Gilead by Welch, "The Death of Josiah," 255; Elijah's destruction of a Baal altar has been related to the destruction of altars by Josiah in Nam's *Portrayals of Economic Exchange*, 100.

79   Hobbs, *2 Kings*, 326; Cohn, *2 Kings*, 153; Laffey, *First and Second Kings*, 157; Brueggemann, *1 & 2 Kings*, 547; Janzen, "Sins of Josiah and Hezekiah," 361-62.

80   H. G. M. Williamson, "The Death of Josiah and the Continuing Development of the Deuteronomic History," VT 32 (1982): 246. Isaac Kalimi sees the demise of Josiah rewritten in Chronicles as specifically related to the demise of Ahab in Kings in that both kings disobey Yahweh and are justly punished for such behavior. See Kalimi,

To begin, it is interesting that these two episodes of repentance are not generally connected to the same author or redactor. A survey of the dates proposed in the scholarly literature for the composition of the two stories ranges from the ninth-century reign of Ahab to the last major redaction of the 'Genesis through Kings' texts in the Hellenistic era. The literary episode of Josiah rending his clothes has been dated variously, from the time of the "Deuteronomistic Historian" in Josiah's court, who had quite possibly been on hand at the consultation with Huldah according to Steven McKenzie,[81] to the first editing of the text post-Josiah. Interestingly, Josiah's rending of his clothes is almost universally agreed to have been an early story in these reconstructions; they all assume that the prophecy of Josiah's reprieve delivered by Huldah is late. Marvin Sweeney connects the narratives of Ahab and Josiah as an intentional literary construct, without assuming they were contemporary renditions.[82]

Though numerous commentaries disclose a high level of belief in the early record of Josiah's reaction to the discovered scroll, they also tend to assume a late redaction for the second part of Huldah's oracle in which Josiah's reaction is referenced. Perhaps, as Yair Hoffmann suggests and as Gary Knoppers agrees, the reprieve by Yahweh announced through Huldah (2 Kgs 22:19–20) was unconnected to the rending of clothes in v. 11, being instead a reference to some unrecorded reaction to Huldah's oracle itself. It is, however, more likely that the rending of the clothes and the reprieve were intentionally connected and derive from the same post-Josianic author. The date of these humiliations of Ahab and Josiah is not as important as the fact that the two instances are clearly related vignettes in the text of Kings. This should be seen as a curious occurrence, given the assessments in Kings of each of these rulers.

The two stories share a fair amount of material. Some of the commonalities are transparent: the two are men, they are kings, their two countries are the focus of Kings, and this interest in Kings is heavily concerned with religious matters. In comparison to most of the kings dealt with in the book of Kings, both Ahab and Josiah have extended accounts of their respective reigns, during which the author posits major religious changes in their respective cults. Indeed, in the historiography of the author of Kings, Josiah and Ahab are selected as representatives of moral religious conduct; the former is portrayed as 'good' and the latter as 'evil.'

More specifically, each repentance includes the hearing of a divine proclamation. In Ahab's case, the message is delivered more clearly and more

---

The Reshaping of Ancient Israelite History in Chronicles (Winona Lake, IN: Eisenbrauns, 2005), 23.

81   McKenzie, *The Trouble with Kings*, 110.
82   Sweeney, *I & II Kings*, 440–41.

directly by the prophet Elijah, who apparently speaks the very words of Yahweh, although the text goes out of its way to demonstrate that the words Elijah actually speaks to Ahab are not those Yahweh had told him to speak.

God says to say:	"Thus says Yahweh: 'In the place where dogs lick up the blood of Naboth, dogs will also lick up your blood!'"
Elijah says:	"I have found you. Because you have sold yourself to do what is evil in the eyes of Yahweh, I will bring disaster against you; I will eat you and will cut off from Ahab every male, bond or free, in Israel, and I will make your house like the house of Jeroboam son of Nebat, and like the house of Baasha son of Ahijah, because you have infuriated me and caused Israel to sin." (1 Kgs 21:19-22)

The dogs' dinner described by Yahweh follows but is presented by Elijah as a speech by Yahweh about Jezebel. In any case, whatever the oracle was, it was not good news for Ahab. When Josiah hears the scroll of instruction in 2 Kgs 22:11, he is not hearing the word of Yahweh; the text is quite clear that this is the work of a Moses (2 Kgs 23:25) who, interestingly, is only tangentially mentioned as being related to the scroll in any way and *not* at its finding, its reading to Josiah, or its reading to the people. Instead, the actual word of Yahweh came to Josiah, as it came to Ahab, through a named prophet,[83] although this did not happen directly in Josiah's case. Huldah's oracle is decidedly more broken:

Huldah to delegation:	"Thus says Yahweh, God of Israel, 'Tell the man who sent you to me: 'Thus says Yahweh:'"
Yahweh to Josiah:	"I certainly will bring disaster...and it will not be quenched."
Yahweh to delegation:	"And for the king of Judah...thus you will tell him:"
Yahweh to Josiah:	"Thus says Yahweh...the disaster I will rain on this place." (2 Kgs 22:15-20)

Huldah's declaration tells Josiah that "this place" is to be destroyed because the words in the scroll are true, not that they are Yahweh's words, and that, at that juncture, the anger of Yahweh was unquenchable. The words in the scroll are clearly related to Yahweh, but Huldah merely reports that Yahweh says that Josiah's reaction to the hearing of those words was well received. For Josiah, the message provided by Yahweh through Huldah was not good news.

---

83 On the history of dealing with the prophet/prophetess irrelevance for the book of Kings, as opposed to the relevance found in it by later traditions, see Lowell K. Handy, "Reading Huldah as Being a Woman," *BR* 55 (2010): 6-7nn5-8.

The reaction of both kings is presented in the narratives as a series of actions. Ahab's immediate response to the proclamation by Elijah is fivefold:

1. He tore his clothes.
2. He put on sackcloth over his bare flesh.
3. He fasted.
4. He lay in sackcloth.
5. He went about aimlessly/dejectedly.[84]

He is presented as repenting in a big way. The story has Ahab engaging in all of this activity at once; this is narrative time and makes no sense as a reflection of historical action taking place as the events unfold in the story. Josiah's response to the scroll is much simpler:

1. He tore his clothes.[85]
2. He sent Hilkiah, Achbor, Shaphan, and Asaiah to check with Huldah.[86]

How much time passed between Josiah hearing the scroll and his sending a delegation to check on it is unclear from the text (*waw* can be a connective or a temporal conjunction). As with Ahab, Josiah's reaction is collapsed into a single literary time.

It is significant that Yahweh perceives both kings as being genuinely contrite. Both responses are followed by proclamations by the respective prophets of Yahweh. Ahab's reply comes from the prophet who brought the condemnation but who now reports that Yahweh will allow Ahab to avoid the destruction to come, while Josiah's reply comes from Huldah, who was not the cause of his repentance at all. Josiah had sought out Yahweh and sent a delegation in his stead to confirm the words of the scroll that had been read to him. They went to Huldah, who reports that Yahweh will also allow him to avoid the destruction to come. There is no real reason to assume that either of the 'reprieve' statements on behalf of Yahweh were somehow a late addition to a previous prophecy. There is little reason to assume that either prophecy was ever anything but a literary creation of the author of Kings.

---

84   Cogan (*1 Kings*, 483) suggests that Ahab was more than just dejected, but became as a "ghost," using Akkadian *eteema* as a cognate.
85   The phrase is the same as for Ahab, with the exception of a missing particle.
86   The narrative of Josiah's repentance contains a third act—weeping (2 Kgs 22:19). However, Josiah is never actually described as doing this; it is only Yahweh who comments on it. The same phenomenon occurs in Chronicles (2 Chr 34:19, 27).

The content of the replies from Yahweh center on the deity taking notice of the behavior of the respective kings. In both cases, Yahweh is presented as being fairly impressed by the humiliation of the kings. Regarding Ahab, God says to Elijah: "Have you seen how Ahab has humbled himself before me?" Regarding Josiah, God says to Huldah: "But to the king of Judah, who sent you to inquire of Yahweh, thus you will say to him: 'Thus says Yahweh, the God of Israel: "Concerning the words you had heard, since your heart repented and you were humbled before Yahweh... you will not see the destruction I will rain on this place."' Neither Ahab nor Josiah heard directly from Yahweh that their repentance has touched the deity; neither is informed of this directly by their prophets. It is an interesting detail in the Kings narrative.

Alongside all the parallels, the stories also have significant differences. First among them is that Ahab is king of Israel, a country seen by the author of Kings as apostate with nothing but evil rulers, and, with the exception of the founder Jeroboam, Ahab is the most evil of all of them. This is made abundantly clear in the mouth of Elijah (1 Kgs 21:25–26). Since Josiah is king of Judah, the good, legitimate, ruler of pure Davidic lineage over the 'good' kingdom, he is presented as the most pious of all these good, righteous rulers of Judah. The bulk of Elijah's prophecy precedes Ahab's repentance; all of Huldah's prophecy follows Josiah's repentance. Ahab has no scroll, and what religious changes he had made in Israel were all seen in Kings as evil and as a turning away from Yahweh. He also made those adaptations long before his confrontation with Elijah. Josiah had a written text, a word from his advisors, a word from God, a word from Huldah, and all this after making repairs to the temple, which was a good thing for kings to do anywhere in the ancient Near East. They were not a part of the religious reform, however. Josiah's religious changes came after his repentance.

It should be noted that the condemnations of the two kings are not the same. In the case of Ahab, the promises are aimed directly at Ahab himself in a three-fold flourish: bring disaster against you, eat you, destroy your house. In Josiah's case, the condemnation is directed against "this place" and against its inhabitants. It has been customary to relate these prophecies to the ensuing destruction of the respective kingdoms; however, the narratives clearly avoid relating the prophecies to the demise of Israel and Judah. Ahab is declared the cause of Yahweh's wrath, but, because he repents, it will be his descendants who are the ones to be consumed. The dog meal of Jezebel is unaffected by Ahab's action. Josiah hears that "this place" and its inhabitants are doomed, but not while he will be alive; his cultic activities appear to be of little or no importance in the prophecy. The same result arises with Josiah as with Ahab; Josiah's repentance saves him but no one else. His descendants are not mentioned.

Moving slightly further from the central tale, Ahab's wife, the very powerful and influential Queen Jezebel, is instrumental in the story of the events precipitating the repentance of Ahab. Therefore, the evil of the king is not just his alone—a point that Elijah makes as part of the prophetic message, even if Yahweh had not (1 Kgs 21:25).[87] Josiah, on the other hand, is alone in his repentance. Not even the advisory committee had taken serious note of the contents of the scroll prior to having read it to their king. Needless to say, Josiah's wives are not implicated. Ahab may share the blame for the evil he has done, but Josiah himself is not accused of having done any evil at all. It is irrelevant to the story that the reader could see Josiah as being as responsible for the corrupt cult during his reign as Ahab and Jezebel had been of theirs. In Huldah's speech to Josiah, the condemnation by Yahweh is of "this place" and its inhabitants, not of Josiah! The proclamation of destruction is explicitly for the people and is explicitly not aimed at Josiah according to Yahweh, to Huldah, to the (literary) narrator, and to the author. Unlike Ahab, Josiah is not dodging an attack personally directed toward him by Yahweh; rather, he is missing an attack by Yahweh on the people around him.

Finally, in view of the final assessments of the two kings, Ahab was not being genuine in his repentance, even if Yahweh thought so at the time. Josiah, however, was truly repentant. The inclusion of the stories probably has more to do with a good tale than a heavily theological object. They both deal with repentance and the possibility of Yahweh taking such emotional shifts into account, but the stories also clearly demonstrate that once Yahweh decides to destroy a lineage or a people, it is going to happen. It has been proposed that the narratives show Yahweh's flexibility.[88] However, they merely demonstrate a slight delaying action in an intractable divine desire for destroying somebody, no matter what. Certainly, the repentance of a king neither demonstrates that the king is good (or else Ahab would get a better 'grade') nor that they will have a better death (or else Josiah would not have been shot by Egyptians).[89]

In the end, the literary figure of Josiah is used as a final stop on the independent kingdom of Judah. Relations developed with other kings that

---

87   See Sweeney, *I & II Kings*, 252; Fretheim, *First and Second Kings*, 120. It is a text that may or may not have been a late addition to an earlier version of the prophetic story: Gray, *I & II Kings*, 443.

88   Fretheim, *First and Second Kings*, 218; Brueggemann, *1 & 2 Kings*, 263.

89   It is useful to note that the notion of 'repentance' became more important for Chronicles and early Judaism, even though for Josiah it appears already in the Kings account of Josiah: Norman Burrows Johnson, *Prayer in the Apocrypha and Pseudepigrapha*, SBLMS 2 (Philadelphia: Society of Biblical Literature and Exegesis, 1948), 54–61; Mika S. Pajunen, "The Saga of Judah's Kings Continues: The Reception of Chronicles in the Late Second Temple Period," *JBL* 136 (2017): 571.

appear in the scroll of Kings are many, and religious tinkering by Judahite rulers is often noted.[90] Josiah is also related to the kings of Israel. For the scroll, Josiah is the final king of any independent political or religious entity founded by, sustained through, and worshipful of Yahweh.

---

[90] There seemed no particular reason to deal with Josiah's reform among the many other biblical 'reform' stories about Judahite kings; there has been plenty written that may be consulted. See, for example, Zorn's "The Pre-Josianic Reforms of Judah" and Lowery's *The Reforming Kings*.

CHAPTER FOUR
A MAN OF GOD AND HULDAH:
PROPHETS IN THE TALE OF JOSIAH

There are two major 'true' prophets in the biblical story of Josiah. One is the unnamed "man of God" appearing to Jeroboam in 1 Kings 13[1] and the other is the named prophet Huldah appearing to Josiah's delegation in 2 Kgs 22:14–20 and its parallel, derivative text in 2 Chr 34:22–28.[2] It is immediately apparent that these two prophets do not have a great deal in common, some of which is unimportant in these narratives: unnamed/named, "man of God"/"prophetess," male/female, or Judahite/Jerusalemite.[3] The differences which might be of significance include: sent by Yahweh/sent for by the king; teller of the distant future/teller of the near future; prophet to an Israelite ruler/prophet to a Judahite ruler; and, specifically for the Josianic

---

1   Significantly, this man of God makes no appearance in Chronicles. It is assumed the Chronicler simply dropped the material from Kings, dealing as the scroll does more with the malevolence of Judah's Rehoboam and not so much with Israel's Jeroboam. See Klein, *2 Chronicles*, 181. In 2 Chr 13:4–12, Abijah's speech makes clear the villainy of Jeroboam for the Chronicler. However, the man of God narration in Kings finds no place in Chronicles, but Yahweh insists on the rule of David's family over Israel. See Myers, *II Chronicles*, 80.

2   With very few and minor alterations, Chronicles follows Kings quite closely in the Huldah passage; Myers, *II Chronicles*, 208. On the differences, see Japhet, *I & II Chronicles*, 1035. Nonetheless, the Chronicler needed to change Huldah's role in Chronicles from that in Kings due to the reform predating the finding of the book of the law. See David A. Glatt-Gilad, "The Role of Huldah's Prophecy in the Chronicler's Portrayal of Josiah's Reform," *Bib* 77 (1996): 19.

3   In biblical narratives these particular distinctions appear to have no religious or literary distinctions. A true spokesperson for Yahweh can have several titles or none at all. See Blenkinsopp, *A History of Prophecy in Israel*, 36–37. Male and female prophets are not biblically distinguished as far as their trustworthiness is concerned: Lester L. Grabbe, *Priests, Prophets, Diviners, Sages: A Socio-historical Study of Religious Specialists in Ancient Israel* (Valley Forge, PA: Trinity, 1995), 115; H, G. M. Williamson, "Prophetesses in the Hebrew Bible," in *Prophecy and Prophets in Ancient Israel: Proceedings of the Oxford Old Testament Seminar*, ed. J. Day, LHBOTS 531 (New York: T&T Clark, 2010), 76. This is not to say that commentators on the gender of the prophets did not have lots to say about gender distinctions; it is just that the Huldah text assumes the reality of Huldah's prophetic status.

tale, dead/alive. In terms of the type of prophetic activity in which they are engaged, it is interesting, and potentially significant, that the man of God represents an 'inspired' proclamation while Huldah represents 'technical' consultation.[4] However, it is central to the literary narratives, whether in Kings or in Chronicles, that the authors understand that the prophets are aware of the will of Yahweh and properly expound it.[5] It should also be noted that both of these minor characters do not appear elsewhere outside these specific Josiah-related stories in the biblical texts.[6]

Except for the reference in First Esdras 1:26,[7] neither Jeremiah nor Zephaniah—prophets with their own biblical books who are internally dated to the time of Josiah (Jer 1:2; Zeph 1:1)[8]—take any part in the respective biblical narratives of Josiah's reign. This is not the case in the book of Kings in the Former Prophets or in the book of Chronicles in the Writings.[9] This is not to say that some early form of the book of Jeremiah did

---

4   A distinction made for ancient Near Eastern divination in general. See Karel van der Toorn, "L'Oracle de victoire comme expression prophétique au Proche-Orient ancient," *RB* 94 (1987): 67; Handy, *Jonah's World*, 62–64.

5   Ehud Ben Zvi, "Are There Any Bridges Out There? How Wide Was the Conceptual Gap between the Deuteronomistic History and Chronicles?," in Knoppers and Ristau, *Community Identity in Judean Historiography*, 69.

6   Gafney presumes there must have been a collection of Huldah sayings collected and then forgotten, in Gafney, *Daughters of Miriam*, 102. This cannot be posited from the Josianic narratives. Neither can the possibility that the phrases in both Huldah's oracle and Jeremiah be shown to belong originally to Huldah, in some unknown prophetic record. See Tal Ilan, "Huldah, the Deuteronomic Prophetess of the Book of Kings," *LDif* 10, no. 1 (2015), 9.

7   The numbering system for First Esdras follows that of the Göttingen edition. See the note in Jacob M. Myers, *I & II Esdras: A New Translation with Commentary*, AB 42 (Garden City, NY: Doubleday, 1974), 29. See also Dieter Böhler, *1 Esdras*, trans. L. M. Maloney, IECOT (Stuttgart: Kohlhammer, 2016), 41–42.

8   Nor is there any reason to include Ezekiel in the question of Josiah's narrative, even if his birth can be determined to have taken place in Josiah's reign. See Marvin A. Sweeney, "Ezekiel's Debate with Isaiah," in *Congress Volume Ljubljana 2007*, ed. A. Lemaire, VTSup 133 (Leiden: Brill, 2010), 558. Supposed allusions to Josiah in Ezekiel 17–18 are at best weak and unconvincing. See Daniel I. Block, "Transformation of Royal Ideology in Ezekiel," in *Transforming Visions: Transformations of Text, Tradition, and Theology in Ezekiel*, ed. W. A. Tooman and M. A. Lyons, PTMS 127 (Eugene, OR: Pickwick, 2010), 213–14. Nahum and Habakkuk, also mentioned as possible characters for the stories, do not appear. See Francesc Ramis Darder, *Qué se sabe de Los profetas*, QS (Esella: Verbo Divino, 2010), 219.

9   Theodore H. Robinson posits the theory that Jeremiah was too young to be considered a serious prophetic source in the estimation of Josiah in Robinson, *A History of Israel. Volume I: From the Exodus to the Fall of Jerusalem, 586 B.C.* (Oxford: Clarendon, 1932), 417. Many explanations have been posited for why Huldah and not some male prophet of more renown to later Jewish tradition was consulted beginning

not influence the Chronicler's historiography, but Jeremiah as a character is absent from the reign of Josiah.[10] This is more curious because of Jeremiah's appearance after the death of Josiah in Chronicles.[11] Interestingly, the Chronicler's narrative brings Jeremiah into the story in order to join in the laments for the fallen king (2 Chr 35:25).[12] Undoubtedly based on the passage in Chronicles, 1 Esd 1:30 also records the postmortem lament of Jeremiah for Josiah, if not quite telling the same story.[13] That lament, however, does not appear in any biblical passage;[14] traditional attestations of it being a reference to Lamentations make little sense, as Jeremiah is not a likely candidate for authoring Lamentations, despite the preface found within the book in the Septuagint.[15] Moreover, the actual contents of the laments in Lamentations make no reference to Josiah, his reign, or to Judah prior to the capture of Jerusalem well after Josiah's death.[16] The scattered references to Josiah in the current Masoretic Text of Jeremiah cannot, in fact, be used to date Jeremiah's prophetic ministry to the time of Josiah in any case, and must be taken as part of the history of interpretation of the king, not as sources for Josiah.[17]

---

already in the Talmud (*Meg.* 14b), none of them germane. See Jonathan Stökl, "Deborah, Huldah, and Innibana: Considerations of Female Prophecy in the Ancient Near East and the Hebrew Bible," *JAJ* 6 (2016): 331.

10 See Louis Jonker, "The Chronicler and the Prophets: Who Were His Authoritative Sources?," in Ben Zvi and Edelman, *What Was Authoritative for Chronicles?*, 162–63.

11 Amber K. Warhurst, "The Chronicler's Use of the Prophets," in Ben Zvi and Edelman, *What Was Authoritative for Chronicles?*, 180.

12 See Gary N. Knoppers, who sees Jeremiah as the "bracket" for the Judean Babylonian captivity in Knoppers, "Democratizing Revelation? Prophets, Seers and Visionaries in Chronicles," in Day, *Prophecy and Prophets*, 396.

13 Böhler, *1 Esdras*, 43; Leuchter, *Josiah's Reform and Jeremiah's Scroll*, 106–7.

14 The book of Jeremiah makes no notice of any such lament, as well as making little note of Josiah at all. One manner of circumventing this lack of a citation is to posit an unknown repository of imagined Jeremiah materials. See Williamson, "The Death of Josiah," 246–47; Leuchter, *Josiah's Reform*, 171. Josephus's comment that the lament existed even unto his time does not, however, mean that it actually did or even that it ever actually existed (*Ant.* X.78).

15 On the long tradition in both Jewish and Christian literature of the authorship by Jeremiah, see Delbert R. Hillers, *Lamentations: A New Translation with Introduction and Commentary*, 2nd rev. ed., AB 7 (New York: Doubleday, 1992), 10–15. Anne James notes the complications of the Lamentations/Jeremiah/Josiah connection in the seventeenth-century citation by John Donne in James, *Poets, Players, and Preachers: Remembering the Gunpowder Plot in Seventeenth-Century England* (Toronto: University of Toronto, 2016), 205.

16 See Williamson, "Death of Josiah," 12n9, for references to the Targum of Lamentations and a note by Jerome.

17 See Rowton, "Jeremiah and the Death of Josiah," 130; Job, *Jeremiah's Kings*, 43–52.

Not called a prophet, or any title designating one, but bearing the word of Yahweh in Chronicles and First Esdras is Neco, king of Egypt (2 Chr 35:21-22; 1 Esd 1:24-25), whom Josiah ignores to his doom. First Esdras is clearly following the lead of the Chronicler, who uses Neco as a conveyer of the word of Yahweh through a foreign ruler; he is one of two such foreign kings in Chronicles.[18] It has long been common practice to presume that Neco was indeed speaking a true thought from Yahweh, but that Josiah, being less wise in this instance than he had been upon hearing the scroll, did not seek any but his own counsel and chose to ignore the very word of Yahweh.[19] Commentators have refrained from using a 'prophetic' title to describe Neco, though they agree that the Egyptian was acting on behalf of Yahweh and properly announced so to Josiah, at least in the minds of the biblical authors.[20] The Chronicler certainly believed that Yahweh, as divine ruler of the cosmos, used 'foreign' kings and alien peoples when dealing with Israel and Judah.[21] Neco serves as a prophetic figure but Josiah does not treat him as one. He is significant for the death of Josiah but not for narratives of his life.

The first of the prophetic narratives in the Josiah tale concerns the "man of God" who appears at the beginning of the apostasy of the northern kingdom (1 Kgs 12:32-13:10).[22] There is a long scholarly tradition that the tale is an adapted folkloric story with a heavy-handed Judahite polemic against Israel dating from early in the divided monarchy.[23] The 'legend'

---

18 According to Knoppers ("Democratizing Revelation?," 398), Neco and Cyrus serve as "temporary prophets."

19 Joseph Hall, *Contemplations on the Historical Passages of the Old and New Testaments*, Christian Family Library 3 (Glasgow: Blackie and Sons, 1835), 1.118.

20 Myers (*II Chronicles* 216) sees Neco as having understood he was being advised by an Egyptian deity, but the Chronicler understands it to be Yahweh. By the time 1 Esdras adapts the material, the author clearly intended Yahweh. See Klein, "The Rendering of 2 Chronicles 35-36 in 1 Esdras," 221; Myers, *I & II Esdras*, 17, 29; Böhler, *1 Esdras*, 41.

21 Neco among them. See Matthew Lynch, *Monotheism and Institutions in the Book of Chronicles: Temple, Priesthood, and Kingship in Post-Exilic Perspective*, FAT 2.64 (Tübingen: Mohr Siebeck, 2014), 254-55.

22 On attempts to put a name on these nameless characters, see Johannes Thon, "Das Grab des 'Lügenpropheten,'" 471-73.

23 See the survey in Montgomery, *A Critical and Exegetical Commentary*, 260-61; Gray, *I & II Kings*, 318-20. Ronald A. Geobey hypothesizes a date of origin in the reign of Jeroboam II, adapted in the time of Josiah in Geobey, "The Jeroboam Story in the (Re)Formulation of Israelite Identity: Evaluating the Literary-Ideological Purposes of 1 Kings 11-14," *JHS* 16 (2016): 23, doi:10.5508/jhs.2016.v16.2. Burke O. Long is very cautious about dating the legend or the date of its "final" form in the Masoretic Text. He does, however, see the Josiah reference as a late addition (Long, *1 Kings*, 145-52).

of the condemnation of Bethel and Jeroboam, however, could easily have been invented at any time in the history of Judah, even when Israel and Judah were on politically friendly terms; there is no reason to assume that rival cultic personnel held each other in alliance, even if their rulers were getting along. Indeed, as the story now appears, it was clearly included in Kings precisely because it has the reference to Josiah and could, conceivably, have had no earlier formulation than as a marker for the desecration of Bethel's altar and the story of the true prophet's grave at the time of Josiah.[24] The entire parallel construction could have been written after Josiah's death.[25]

The theology behind the passage deals with the evil of the king, in this case Jeroboam, leaving the proper laws and worship of Yahweh. It is interesting and significant for the Chronicler that this story does not appear in Chronicles, but the 'fact' of royal abandonment by Yahweh is retained, with Rehoboam being abandoned in this case (1 Chr 12:1-2).[26] Jeroboam is not forgotten or forgiven by the Chronicler; however, the condemnation of Jeroboam's abandonment of Yahweh and the Davidic lineage is pronounced not by a prophet, but by King Abijah of the Davidic lineage of Judah (2 Chr 13:4-12).[27] In Abijah's speech, the two-fold villainy of Jeroboam is expressed in an explanation of why a war between Judah and Israel will result in defeat for Israel: wrong king and wrong cult. Thus, Chronicles covers the propaganda of the "man of God" passage, but omits its prophetic authority as well as decidedly leaving out any mention of Josiah. This speech is a battle taunt and not a prophetic promise, which constitutes a major distinction between Chronicles and its source.

For Kings, the significance of the story clearly lies in the dismissal of any legitimacy attributed to the altar in Bethel. That the man came from

---

24 Halpern notes the importance of Josiah being in the story for its being included in Kings: Halpern, *The First Historians*, 249. Jonathan Goldstein cites this passage as a classic example of a *vaticinium ex eventu*, a fabricated story no earlier than Josiah's reign itself, see Goldstein, *Peoples of an Almighty God*, 10.

25 See Joseph Robinson, *The First Book of Kings*, 159; Long, *1 Kings*, 152. Geobey ("The Jeroboam Story," 25) considers the two narratives to reflect a contrast between the creator of an old Israel and a new Israel.

26 Ehud Ben Zvi notes the Chronicler's conveyance of Rehoboam's inclination toward "wrong" from early in his appearance in Chronicles, and he relates this to events in late Persian or Hellenistic times: Ben Zvi, "The Secession of the Northern Kingdom in Chronicles: Accepted 'Facts' and New Meanings," in Graham, McKenzie, and Knoppers, *The Chronicler as Theologian*, 64-66, 86-88.

27 Klein (*2 Chronicles*, 200-204) emphasizes the royal speech as having been composed to be directed at Israelites in general and insists that Jeroboam is a "son of a nobody," who has broken compacts with both humans (Davidic lineage, the only legitimate ruling house) and Yahweh (apostasy, bulls, and non-Levites). However, it is a royal declaration, not one from a spokesperson for Yahweh.

Judah literarily allows the author to contrast Israelite disobedience with the Judahite obedience in both religion and politics.[28] This prophet was instigated by Yahweh; no human sent for him or inquired of him. His residence being the faithful "Judah" contrasts nicely with the wicked mockery of Yahweh-worship being depicted here for "Israel" as an invention by Jeroboam. The message delivered, according to the story, was a direct proclamation of Yahweh prompted by the actions of Jeroboam in settling on a contrasting temple to Jerusalem, establishing a festival/sacrifice against the regulations understood by the author to be those of the proper cult of Yahweh, a differing cultic calendar,[29] and, no doubt, the actual involvement of the king in the religious ceremony that ought to be left for the proper priests.[30] The run of corrupt rulers in Israel and in Judah, unfortunately, does not begin with this tale, even though it is now clearly the inclusio for Josiah. Instead, for the Josiah narrative in Kings, the first of the evil kings whose activities need to be rectified is Solomon, as Josiah's activities are so clearly designated (2 Kgs 23:13). What this story of the unnamed prophet does is invalidate the religious viability of Bethel and the northern cultic tradition as an alternative to Solomon's Jerusalem impieties. For Josiah, this Judahite prophet makes the king's destructive religious tactics in Samerina *and* Jerusalem right and honorable.

The biblical narrative repeatedly insists on the validity of the message of this prophetic figure. The intent, of course, is to make it quite clear that the Bethel cult site is an abomination to Yahweh and that Josiah's desecration and/or destruction of it is not only laudable but the very embodiment of righteousness and justice. In his introduction, the man is doubly connected to Yahweh: Yahweh sent him out of Judah to Bethel,[31] and the word that he spoke is indeed the word of Yahweh for Bethel's altar (1 Kgs 13:1–2).

After his prophetic speech at Bethel, Jeroboam attempts to have the prophet seized, only to have his own hand paralyzed, the altar destroyed,

---

28 Pedro Zamora García, *Reyes I*, 265; Sweeney, *I & II Kings*, 180.

29 Geobey ("The Jeroboam Story," 22) emphasizes the repetition in the text of the variant celebration dates.

30 The impurity of the king's hand seems appropriate for stopping anyone from engaging in an acceptable sacrifice; see Zamora García, *Reyes I*, 267. The implication that kings should not be involved in priestly business would be clear only at 2 Kgs 23:4–5, where the 'good' priests handle all the religious objects (defiled or holy) and 'bad' priests are summarily removed from all places where they have been performing.

31 A Judahite prophetic figure going north to condemn Bethel parallels Amos (Amos 1:1; 7:10–15), but it is a religious/political trope and cannot make the man of God in any way the prophet Amos.

and its ashes strewn, desecrating the ground.³² Jeroboam himself thus knows the words are true and instantly binding. This is emphasized in the tale by the king's plea for the man to intercede with Yahweh to restore his hand, which is done. It provides more proof that Yahweh is working through this man of God. Jeroboam, apparently not intending evil, wishes to acknowledge, or at least show appreciation to, the prophet by eating with him and presenting him a gift. Since the man had been told not to eat or drink in "this place" and to return by a different route, the man of God refused Jeroboam's offers and set off back to Judah by a different route. Moreover, the recognition by Josiah of the truth of the true prophet is clear in the Josianic narrative itself (2 Kgs 23:16-18).

More to the point, however, is the story told of the 'old prophet' of Bethel. It is not important for the validation of the true prophet's message that this 'prophet' is, here, a lying, deceitful personage. His son sends him to waylay the man of God as he insists that he has received word from Yahweh reversing the latter's previous word. This is a lie. However, the very Yahweh for whom they both serve as prophets orders the lying prophet to speak to the true prophet and inform him that he has broken the word of Yahweh in a true prophecy (1 Kgs 13:20-22). This may be incredibly confusing, but even the death of the man of God by lion consumption emphasizes the truth of the word of Yahweh against Bethel and Jeroboam. The human voice of Yahweh may not be trustworthy, but the word of Yahweh spoken by these untrustworthy mortals is true nonetheless.³³ The lying prophet recognizes the truth spoken by the man of God and buried him in his own tomb.

That Jeroboam continues his wicked ways is here driven home as a literary proof of the honest word of the man of God to the Bethel sanctuary. The human is curiously slain for believing the false word of God spoken through the prophet of Bethel, who speaks a real prophecy directly to the man of God. The man believes the word of Yahweh even when it is a lie.

---

32 Cogan correctly notes that the withering of Jeroboam's hand by Yahweh is punishment for attempting to arrest or harm the man of God; it just happens to be appropriate for stopping a cultic activity on the part of the king as well. See Cogan, *1 Kings*, 368.

33 It is equally important to remember that prophets can speak the very word of Yahweh and still be lying since the words given to them by Yahweh are lies (1 Kgs 22:5-28). This is not the same as 'lying prophets,' who simply make up their oracles whole cloth. Johannes Lindblom (*Prophecy in Ancient Israel*, 210-15) notes that who was truthful and who was lying would have been determined not by a deity but by the personages hearing them. See also David Noel Freedman ("Between God and Man: Prophets in Ancient Israel," in *Prophecy and Prophets*, ed. Y. Gitay, SemeiaSt [Atlanta: Scholars Press, 1997], 67), who posits that all prophets could be deemed false in different times and places.

It is a curious tale, but a significant one in the theology of Kings: prophets are fallible, the word of Yahweh is not. The story clearly demonstrates that this particular prophet, honored for centuries by Bethel devotees and Josiah alike, was a less than perfect discerner of the word of Yahweh, but delivered a true message that connected directly to the king of Judah, Josiah by name, long in the future.

This direct connection to Josiah in the man of God's speech explicitly condemns the altar of Bethel and predicts the act of its destruction by Josiah. Interestingly enough, it makes no comment on the righteousness of Josiah and clearly makes no assessment of the reward or punishment of the king who will destroy the altar. This true prophet is directly connected to Josiah only in the king's recognition of the respect due to the prophet through not disrupting his burial memorial. The prophecy itself is all about the illegitimacy of Bethel as a religious site in the eyes of Jerusalem and is only tangentially related to Josiah. Josiah's respect for the prophet reinforces the authority of the man of God but only tangentially displays the piety of Josiah.

The narrative concerning the delegation sent by Josiah to consult with the prophetess Huldah in 2 Kgs 22:14-20 and in the parallel story in 2 Chr 34:22-28 has held a fascinatingly central interest to commentators of the reign of Josiah.[34] It is rather needless to remark that, outside of the parallel passages in 2 Kgs 22:14 and 2 Chr 34:22, Huldah makes no appearance of any kind in any other biblical text or in any literature of early Judaism or Christianity that is not based on her mention in 2 Kgs 22:14.[35] On this basis it is very difficult to declare with any certainty whether or not she was a historical person.[36] For current purposes, her actual existence in

---

34 This, of course, is related to the premise that her prophetic statement was actually delivered to Josiah during his lifetime and the terrible trauma this has caused for many a commentator attempting to correlate that part of the very short speech that is historical with that which is a later addition; see Sweeney (*I & II Kings*, 440, 442-43), who notes that the passage provides major difficulties. The double (or even triple) redaction of an "original" prophecy is highly popular among commentators: Walter Dietrich, "Josia und das Gesetzbuch (2 Reg. xxii)," 27; Cogan and Tadmor, *II Kings*, 295. For an extended proposal for the construction of the speech by Huldah as a Josianic prophecy with later additions, see Baruch Halpern and D. S. Vanderhooft, "The Editions of Kings in the 7th-6th Centuries BCE," *HUCA* 62 (1991): 221-30. Note that Norbert Lohfink does "not have the courage to reconstruct Huldah's oracle as composed by Dtr 1," see Lohfink, "The Cult Reform of Josiah of Judah," 471n12.

35 Knoppers ("Democratizing Revelation?," 400) notes that biographies of prophets are not common and are lacking from Chronicles altogether.

36 Esther J. Hamori finds that what little is recorded of Huldah fits well into sociological/anthropological models of women prophets in the ancient western world in Hamori, "Childless Female Diviners in the Bible and Beyond," in *Prophets*

worldly form is not important.³⁷ It is also unimportant for the narrative that she was a woman, which is not to say that her gender has not been the very central aspect of her existence that has captivated commentators for two millennia. It is just not important here.³⁸ What *is* important is what Huldah does in the narratives of Kings and Chronicles. Only three interrelated aspects of her appearance in Josiah's story are to be considered here: 1) Huldah as a prophet in this book of the Former Prophets and its replication in Chronicles; 2) the consultation concerning a received word of Yahweh; and 3) the conundrum of the contents of her message. These points are, in fact, aspects of each other.

A great aura of importance about the person Huldah has evolved within the Jewish and Christian traditions over the past couple of centuries.³⁹ It

---

Male and Female: Gender and Prophecy in the Hebrew Bible, the Eastern Mediterranean, and the Ancient Near East, ed. J. Stöki and C. L. Carvalho, AIIL 15 (Atlanta: Society of Biblical Literature, 2013), 169-91. Robert R. Wilson finds no reason to deny Huldah's existence or the narrative concerning her in Kings and Chronicles: Wilson, *Prophecy and Society in Ancient Israel* (Philadelphia: Fortress, 1980), 221, 223.

37   The text presents little to form any notion of a historical woman, and attempts are fairly circumspect; see, for example, Karel van der Toorn, *From Her Cradle to Her Grave: The Role of Religion in the Life of the Israelite and the Babylonian Woman*, trans. S. J. Denning-Bolle, BSS 23 (Sheffield: JSOT Press, 1994), 131; Gafney, *Daughters of Miriam*, 98-99; Jeanie C. Crain, *Reading the Bible as Literature: An Introduction* (Cambridge: Polity, 2010), 119-20. Esther J. Hamori presents several alternative reconstructions in Hamori, *Women's Divination in Biblical Literature*, 148-52.

38   A survey of the history of the importance of Huldah's having been female appears in my "Reading Huldah as Being a Woman." It has, of course, been very important for women prophetesses (and other religious leaders) in Judaism and Christianity that she was a woman: Adriana Valerio, "Il profetismo femminile Cristiano nel II secolo: Bilancio storiografico e questioni aperte," in *Profeti e profezia: Figure profetiche nel christianismo del ii secolo*, ed. A. Carfora and E. Cattaneo, Oi Christianoi 6 (Trapani: Pozzo di Giacobbe, 2007), 164.

39   Among the many studies of individual women in the Bible, Huldah has not been the subject of a great many academic works dedicated explicitly to her; she has appeared more often in texts devoted to women in the Bible or the Hebrew Scriptures in general. A few works dedicated specifically to Huldah have been exceptionally influential for the past half a century, including Arlene Swidler, "In Search of Huldah," *TBT* 98 (1978): 1780-85; Christensen, "Huldah and the Men of Anathoth," 399-404; Diana V. Edelman, "Huldah the Prophet—of Yahweh or Asherah?," in *A Feminist Companion to Samuel and Kings*, ed. A. Brenner, FCB 5 (Sheffield: Sheffield Academic, 1994), 231-50; Udo Rüterswörden, "Die Prophetin Hulda," in *Meilenstein: Festgabe für Herbert Donner zum 16. Februar 1995*, ed. M. Weippert and S. Timm, ÄAT 30 (Wiesbaden: Harrassowitz, 1995), 234-42; Renita J. Weems, "Huldah, the Prophet: Reading a (Deuteronomistic) Woman's Identity," in *A God So Near: Essays on Old Testament Theology in Honour of Patrick D. Miller*, ed. B. Strawn and N. Bowen (Winona Lake, IN: Eisenbrauns, 2003), 321-39. A few other significant works devoted to her have had less exposure, including Phyllis Trible, "Huldah's Holy Writ: On Women

needs to be understood that while much of this material is inventive, it is difficult to correlate a great deal of it with the Huldah of the Kings account from which all of our knowledge about Huldah derives.[40] Her status in Jerusalem is quite unknown, though she has been portrayed as everything from the most famous prophet of her day to a virtual unknown.[41] The narratives of both Kings and Chronicles simply do not contain the relevant data on this question to provide anything to decide one way or the other, which legitimately leaves scholars with cause for conjecture.[42] What is of importance to the narratives themselves is that Huldah was a

---

and Biblical Authority," *Touchstone* (Canada) 3 (1985): 6-13; Marianne Grohmann, "Hulda, die Prophetin (2Kön 22,14–20)," *CV* 45 (2003): 209–16. A few books have extended sections on Huldah, most notably Klara Butting, *Prophetinnen gefragt: Die Bedeutung der Prophetinnen im Kanon aus Tora und Prophetie*, ERH 3 (Wittingen: Erev-Rav, 2001), 131–62; Gafney, *Daughters of Miriam*, 94–103.

40 Grace I. Emmerson, "Women in Ancient Israel," in *The World of Ancient Israel: Sociological, Anthropological and Political Perspectives*, ed. R. E. Clements (Cambridge: Cambridge University Press, 1989), 375: she "bursts suddenly upon the scene ... and as quickly disappears."

41 That Huldah was a famous—possibly the most famous—prophet of her day in Jerusalem has been a popular supposition for a long time: Heinrich Graetz, *History of the Jews I: From the Earliest Period to the Death of Simon the Maccabee (135 B.C.E.)* (Philadelphia: Jewish Publication Society of America, 1891), 286; Foakes-Jackson, *The Biblical History of the Hebrews*, 302. For the past two centuries, among women commentators this has tended to be the default: Grace Aguilar, *The Women of Israel: or Characters and Sketches from the Holy Scriptures and Jewish History*, 8th ed. (London: Groombridge and Sons, 1873), 324; Sydney Morgan, *Woman and Her Master* (Philadelphia: Carey and Hart, 1840), 118; Kyung Sook Lee, "Books of Kings: Images of Women without Women's Reality," in *Feminist Biblical Interpretation: A Compendium of Bible and Related Literature*, ed. L. Schottroff and M.-T. Wacker (Grand Rapids: Eerdmans, 2012), 175; if most often cited from Elizabeth Cady Stanton, *The Woman's Bible. Part II: Comments on the Old and New Testaments from Joshua to Revelation* (New York: European Publishing, 1898), 81–82. However, note that Isho'dad of Merv, *Books of Sessions 2 Kings* 22.14, cited in Marco Conti, ed., *1-2 Kings, 1-2 Chronicles, Ezra, Nehemiah, Esther*, ACCSOT 5 (Downers Grove, IL: InterVarsity Press, 2008), 230, had already suggested this in the ninth century. For other scholars, Huldah was basically unknown, or, at best, "obscure," e,g., Suriano, *The Politics of Kings*, 89. Butting (*Prophetinnen gefragt*, 139–40) suggests that if Huldah had any fame, it came after the incident with Josiah's prophecy and not before.

42 Robert L. Cohn emphasizes the lack of personal characterization of Huldah and sets this in the context of prophets in the book of Kings in general: see Cohn, "Characterization in Kings," in *The Books of Kings: Sources, Composition, Historiography, and Reception*, ed. A. Lemaire and B. Halpern, VTSup 129 (Atlanta: Society of Biblical Literature, 2010), 94. However, note that she is the sole named woman prophet in Kings: Grohmann, "Hulda," 210. Generalizations that all prophets were closely related to the cult cannot be assumed, though they are popular: John Priest, "Huldah's Oracle," *VT* 30 (1980): 367–68; Gafney, *Daughters of Miriam*, 103.

prophet.⁴³ That she was a prophet of Yahweh and that Josiah believed her to be speaking for Yahweh are central to the narrative, but, even so, her words from Yahweh are the items of interest, not Huldah herself. Here, "the medium is not the message; the message is the message."⁴⁴ Alternative theories about Huldah's appearance have been proposed, but the text is silent.⁴⁵

As prophets go in the biblical narratives, Huldah cannot be classified as a hopeful messenger from Yahweh. Her speech, rendered entirely as provided by Yahweh,⁴⁶ concerns the doom of Judah and Jerusalem, with a small exception made for Josiah. There is no inkling of hope for Judah,

---

43   William Johnstone stretches way beyond the textual comments to argue that Shallum, since he handled vestments for the Levitical priests, must have been a Levite (which would certainly suit the Chronicler) and one would suppose that his wife was also a Levite by extension and priestly lineage. See Johnstone, *1 and 2 Chronicles. Volume 2: 2 Chronicles 10-36: Guilt and Atonement*, JSOTSup 254 (Sheffield: Sheffield Academic, 1987), 241. However, were a Levitic lineage important, it would not have been couched in such an indirect fashion. So, Huldah and Shallum *may* have been Levites, but for this narrative it simply does not matter. Indeed, Shallum's relationship with the temple or court is not important either. See Donald J. Wiseman, *1 and 2 Kings: An Introduction and Commentary*, TOTC 9 (Leicester: Inter-Varsity Press, 1993), 298.

44   Knoppers, "Democratizing Revelation?," 400. This is true of Huldah in Kings as well as in Chronicles.

45   Among the many interpretations of Huldah, there is Robert Wilson's invention of essentially a Jeremiah clone as a "typical" northern "Ephraimite prophet" wholly a part of the establishment; Wilson, *Prophecy*, 219-23, 298. Wilson is followed closely by others like Christensen ("Huldah," 403) and Weems ("Huldah," 334). Robert F. Horton devises a Huldah who essentially educated Josiah and invented the religious reform in Horton, *Women of the Old Testament: Studies in* Womanhood (New York: E. R. Herrick, 1897), 243-53. Also note the theory that Huldah was brought forth by Josiah in order to subvert the status of women by having a woman authenticate his patriarchal reform which would make the media the message. On this, see, for example, Judith E. McKinlay, "Gazing at Huldah," *BCT* 1, no. 3 (2005): 4-5; Karin Achtelstetter, "Huldah at the Table: Reflections on Leadership and the Leadership of Women," *CurTM* 37 (2010): 181-82. This hypothesis presupposes a historical Huldah and a heavy-handed grab for power on the part of the historical Josiah, aimed directly at his female subjects.

46   Sections of vv. 15 and 18 have sometimes been accorded to Huldah's own speech, but the stereotypical prophetic form seems to imply that this is Yahweh speaking through her, and it is Yahweh who is being sent to by Josiah, Huldah being the prophet through whom Yahweh speaks. It has also been suggested by Christof Hardmeier that the entire speech was of Huldah's invention: Hardmeier, "King Josiah in the Climax of the Deuteronomistic History (2 Kings 22-23) and the Pre-Deuteronomic Document of a Cult Reform at the Place of Residence (23.4-15): Criticism of Sources, Reconstruction of Literary Pre-Stages and the Theology of History in 2 Kings 22-23," in Grabbe, *Good Kings and Bad Kings*, 138-39.

while Josiah is promised death; the entire prophetic quotation presages ruin all around.⁴⁷ If one chooses to hold that Huldah was a historical person who was consulted by Josiah whilst denying the existence of a non-materialistic supernature, Huldah would have to have made up her own words presented by her as her God's. It would also have been possible that Huldah 'heard voices,' believed personally in a divine possession, or followed some established formula to get her delivery of Yahweh's response. However, it is most likely, given the literary nature of the story, that the prophecy was the construct of the author of Kings as though they were the very words of Yahweh; putting speeches in character's mouths was a standard feature of historiographical writing in the ancient world.⁴⁸ To assume that a narrative quoting a deity would need actual antique quotations any more than quotes attributed to a famous king would be unreasonable; speeches, as well as the characters delivering them, were the province of the author.

It is imperative to understand from the beginning that while 'modern,' 'materialist' scholars and those influenced by them do not believe that any communications from a divine world actually exist, this was not the case in the ancient world. Indeed, this is not the case for most of the people currently living in the modern world either. Any attempt to deal seriously with a narrative of an ancient prophetic speech and the prophet who delivers it must also seriously take into account the context in which the event is supposed to have taken place. In dealing with ritual efficacy, it has been noted recently that too many 'scholars' dismiss the efficacy of divination because it does not belong in their narrow vision of how the world functions. This attitude results in the scholarly dismissal of divination as ineffective and, indeed, it is usually posited as really doing something else.⁴⁹ Certainly, the efficacy of divination does not work for a scholar who believes there is nothing beyond material meaninglessness, but a scholar who does not recognize that divination does in fact 'work' for those who believe differently than they do is not doing any form of scientific study but is engaging in the time-honored sport of polemics. Divination works for those who believe it works.⁵⁰ So, for Josiah and Huldah,

---

47 Ristau, "Reading and Rereading Josiah," 227.

48 See Mark A. Throntveit, "The Chronicler's Speeches and Historical Reconstruction," in *The Chronicler as Historian*, ed. M. P. Graham, K. G. Hoglund, and S. L. McKenzie, JSOTSup 238 (Sheffield: Sheffield Academic, 1997), 225–27; and Halpern, *First Historians*, 269. Note the imaginative speech writing used by ancient 'historians.'

49 This has been part of the sociological approach to religious ritual from the beginning of the field, see Johannes Quack and Paul Töbelmann, "Questioning 'Ritual Efficacy,'" *JRit St* 24 (2010): 14–23.

50 Joachim Friedrich Quack, "Postulated and Real Efficacy in Late Antique Divination Rituals," *JRit St* 24 (2010): 56.

if only in the world for whom the narrative was written, Yahweh existed and spoke through prophets.[51]

According to the text of Kings, Josiah had received and understood the scroll found in the temple. What exactly was supposed by the author to have been written on that scroll is unknown, but that Josiah saw it as a condemnation of his reign and all those kings of Judah who preceded him is clear from his reaction. His tearing of his clothes also informs the reader that Josiah knew what he had been doing was wrong and that it was wrong in the sight of Yahweh. What he did about it, however, is interesting. He did not move directly to correct the offenses but instead sent a delegation to check on the scroll's contents.[52] This is where Huldah appears in the story. Huldah is a prophet; the text states this, but the narrative clearly describes her acting as a prophet in almost outline form.[53] That she is designated by the female form of the noun does not appear to have had any resonance in the biblical narrative. The text reflects an ancient Near Eastern prophetic tradition that did not categorize divine pronouncements by whether their source in the human world was male or female.[54] She was the word of Yahweh for Josiah and it was as a legitimate diviner of

---

51 Cristiano Grottanelli psychologizes Huldah's inspired speech into a trance recitation, but one acceptable to Josiah. See Grottanelli, *Kings and Prophets: Monarchic Power, Inspired Leadership, and Sacred Text in Biblical Literature* (New York: Oxford University Press, 1999), 190.

52 This action taken by Josiah is particularly significant in that several studies of Josiah's reform in the twentieth century simply skip over it and make the next step in the institution of the reform measures a referendum by the general public. See Daniel Jeremy Silver, *A History of Judaism. Volume I: From Abraham to Maimonides* (New York: Basic Books, 1974), 74. In "Josiah and the History of the World," I survey histories that skip Huldah altogether.

53 See Martti Nissinen, *References of Prophecy in Neo-Assyrian Sources*, SAAS 7 (Helsinki: Neo-Assyrian Text Corpus Project, 1998), 6. His four-part component list for a prophet consists of: 1. a divinity sending a communication (explicitly identified as Yahweh); 2. the message (2 Kgs 22:15-20, though some of this material may be the human speaker's formatting the message in standard prophetic speech); 3. the prophet (Huldah); 4. the recipient (in this case, the immediate recipients are Hilkiah, Ahikam, Achbor, Shappan, and Asaiah, though the intentional recipient is Josiah, and to complicate matters slightly more, it is the people of Jerusalem, Judah and Israel who are to bear the brunt of the message once Josiah receives it). Van der Toorn (*From Her Cradle*, 131) notes that Huldah is the only female in the Bible who in fact acts like an actual prophetess.

54 This is a standard observation of long standing. See, for example, Milton S. Terry, *Commentary on the Old Testament: Kings to Esther*, Whedon's Commentary 4 (New York: Phillips & Hunt, 1875), 301; Emmerson, "Women in Ancient Israel," 376; Swidler, "In Search of Huldah," 1782-83; Rütersworden, 236-37; Bruggemann, *1 & 2 Kings*, 562n324.

Yahweh's will and word that she was consulted.⁵⁵ It needs to be noted that Josiah does not send to her; Josiah sends to Yahweh and it is his delegation that goes to her. There is no textual evidence that Josiah knew of her, let alone knew her; the delegation knew her as a prophet of Yahweh. Aside from being a true prophet of Yahweh, it is less clear what position, if any, she held in Jerusalem or the royal court.⁵⁶ She has been described as a priestess, a court or temple prophet, a teacher in her own school, a keeper of the wardrobe (usually assigned to her husband), a woman in the service of Jedidiah, or the wife of Shallum (as stated in 2 Kgs 22:14).⁵⁷

The story of the delegation that was sent to her forms an important part of the narrative from the point of view of the biblical world; it is unnecessary for the narrative flow as read in the modern world. That is, Huldah confirms what Josiah has already been shown to have known. This should not be seen as some source-critical redaction or later insertion into the narrative because it does not flow neatly in notions of modern literary composition;⁵⁸ this is an ancient Near Eastern text and needs to be read in that context. Huldah performs a form of divination in which the

---

55 Esther J. Hamori, "The Prophet and the Necromancer: Women's Divination for Kings," *JBL* 132 (2013): 843. It may be of some interest that, as the texts now read, Huldah was a prophet commenting on the work of the prophet Moses. See Zevit, "Deuteronomy in the Temple," 209. This would conform to the theory of Former Prophets books being devised to accord Moses a privileged status. For more on this, see Grohmann, "Hulda," 211; Christophe Nihan, "'Moses and the Prophets,'" 53–54.

56 However, the narratives make it clear that Huldah lived in the second quarter of Jerusalem, whatever that may have meant at the time of writing. See Ramis, *Profetas*, 220–21.

57 For being a priestess, see Athalya Brenner, "Gender Prophecy, Magic and Priesthood: From Sumer to Ancient Israel," in *Embroidered Garments: Priests and Gender in Biblical Israel*, ed. Deborah W. Rooke, HBM 25 (Sheffield: Sheffield Phoenix, 2009), 10. For being a court/temple prophet, see Priest, "Huldah's Oracle," 367–68; Zevit, *The Religions of Ancient Israel*, 440. For being a teacher of women, see *Pesiqta Rabbati* 26.129. For being a teacher of men, see Trible, "Huldah's Holy Writ," 10. For being "wardrobe-mistress," see Alexander Rofé, "The Scribal Concern for the Torah as Evidenced by the Textual Witnesses of the Hebrew Bible," in *Mishneh Todah: Studies in Deuteronomy and Its Cultural Environment in Honor of Jeffrey H. Tigay*, ed. N. Sacher Fox, D. A. Glatt-Gilad, and M. J. Williams (Winona Lake, IN: Eisenbrauns, 2009), 240–41; and Hamori, *Women's Divination*, 149. For Jedidah's service, see Gafney, *Daughters of Miriam*, 98.

58 As has been suggested by Michael Pietsch, "Prophetess of Doom: Hermeneutical Reflections on the Huldah Oracle (2 Kings 22)," in *Soundings in Kings: Perspectives and Methods in Contemporary Scholarship*, ed. M. Leuchter and K.-P. Adam (Minneapolis: Fortress, 2010), 78–79. See the survey in Friedrich-Emanuel Focken, "Joschijas Gesetzesschrift: Eine literarkritische und redaktionsgeschichtliche Analyse von 2Kön 22,1–23,3; 23,21–30," *BN* 163 (2014): 36–43. Focken finds a final form no earlier than the exilic period.

deity is asked for information, rather than one where the deity instigates the communication; she is, here, a technical prophet.[59] Huldah is serving to 'double-check' the revelation from a deity to a ruler concerning the requirement to change a religious cult—in this particular case, to radically change a long-standing religious cult. This behavior had its counterparts in Assyrian, Babylonian, Hittite, and even Greek traditions.[60] What is so striking about the Huldah narrative in Kings is that Josiah immediately sends a delegation to check with Yahweh about this scroll. For finding the truth directly from Yahweh, Josiah needs to have it come from Yahweh's mouthpiece, not from any of the officials holding impressive titles. It must come from a genuine prophet, the prophetess Huldah. Huldah holds a position in terms of divine communication that none of the men in office can claim.[61]

It has long been observed that the entire story of Josiah's reformation of the cult presupposes the cult as it is envisioned to result from the reform Josiah is yet to make as the narrative now exists. Simply stated: the understanding of the Jerusalem cult prior to the reform had to be that of the Josianic reform itself.[62] That is, in contrast to what his counterparts in Mesopotamia or Greece would have done, Josiah does not seek the advice of another deity in the local pantheon to corroborate the message just received by a single god. Instead, Josiah acts exactly as though Yahweh were the only deity to whom he could make an inquiry. Here, the biblical story of Josiah's request for confirmation diverges from its ancient Near Eastern parallels, which undoubtedly stand as the models for the

---

59 She would appear to be in the category of professional technical prophets: Handy, *Jonah's World*, 62.

60 On Esarhaddon and Nabonidus, see Handy, "The Role of Huldah in Josiah's Cult Reform," 40–45; on Murshili II, see Na'aman, "The 'Discovered Book' and the Legitimation of Josiah's Reform," 55–56; on Greek inquiries of the gods made multiple times, see Michael Attyah Flower, *The Seer in Ancient Greece* (Berkeley: University of California, 2008), 101.

61 See Hamori ("Prophet and the Necromancer," 838), who stresses the need for this consultation. Hamori also points out the emphasis the Kings text places on the officials and their titles, yet they are not capable of authenticating the scroll. See Hamori, *Women's Divination*, 152–53. This actually stresses the need for a proper 'double-check' on the matter at hand, which can only be accomplished by a deity, here by a true prophet who speaks the very words of the god, meaning, as Hamori correctly notes, not high priests, scribes, or kings, but Yahweh. It might also be noted that the elders of Judah/Israel are presented as being even further removed from the divine word. See Jean Riaud, "Les Anciens," in *Les élites dans le monde biblique*, ed. J. Riaud, BEJH 32 (Paris: Honoré Champion, 2008), 38–39. Ramis (*Profetas*, 219) suggests that the men in the delegation have little to no idea of what they are doing.

62 Cook, "Josiah," 15.520.

narrative. In this case, they can only support the literary historiographical narrative; they cannot substantiate a historical event.[63]

Assuming that the biblical texts, historical and prophetic, reflect anything like reality on the ground, the Jerusalem cult at the time of Josiah's delegation to Huldah would have been made up of several deities.[64] If one was attempting to discern whether the scroll just discovered in the temple wished one to reduce the pantheon to a single deity and one had been brought up in the firm belief that there were several gods and goddesses to worship, a double-check on this document would seem most reasonable. It more likely would have been made to one of the other deities. This is where Diana Edelman's suggestion that, as a historical person, Huldah might have been a prophetess of Asherah would make eminent sense.[65] However, if Josiah inquired of Asherah or Baal or any other named or unnamed deity and received a reply of any kind, it would pretty much have invalidated dismissing as unreal the rest of the religious establishment.[66] No, Stanley Cook was right a century ago: both the prophecy and the reform pictured as deriving from Josiah came from an established Jerusalem cult that already brooked no gods other than Yahweh. The inclusion of Huldah in this biblical scene should also suggest that the author of Kings, let alone Chronicles, was quite certain that Huldah was a prophet for Yahweh and not Asherah or any other deity that once held a place in Judah's religious world.[67]

---

63 And at this point Na'aman's conclusion that this reflects a historical event, or at least a tale told at the beginning of a cult reform by Josiah or his courtiers ("Discovered Book," 62), fails to convince.

64 It has been noted that biblical prophetic texts, unlike Assyrian or Egyptian ones, do not include a pantheon supporting the king. See, for example, John W. Hilber, "Royal Cultic Prophecy in Assyria, Judah, and Egypt," in *"Thus Speaks Ishtar of Arbela": Prophecy in Israel, Assyria, and Egypt in the Neo-Assyrian Period*, ed. R. P. Gordon and H. M. Barstad (Winona Lake, IN: Eisenbrauns, 2013), 182. Such support was a standard component of ancient Near Eastern prophetic tradition that, if it existed in ancient Judah, was excised from the tradition.

65 Edelman, "Huldah the Prophet," 243–48. This possibility is sternly denied by Jill Hammer in *Sisters at Sinai: New Tales of Biblical Women* (Philadelphia: Jewish Publication Society of America, 2001), 237–38, but is presumed possible by McKinlay in "Gazing at Huldah," 5.

66 Isaac Kalimi makes note of 2 Chr 17:3–5, where Jehoshaphat does *not* seek/inquire of the Baals, nor act like an Israelite. If Kalimi correctly reads the passage, there was knowledge of seeking the message of other gods in Chronicles. See Kalimi, *The Reshaping of Ancient Israelite History in Chronicles*, 339.

67 This does not disallow the personage of Huldah having derived from some historical person intentionally divorced from some other deity, only that the authors of Kings and Chronicles would have known her as a true prophet of Yahweh with unelaborated status: Hamori, *Women's Divination*, 151.

Huldah confirms that the message from Yahweh contained in the scroll presented by Shaphan (the scribe) to Josiah (the king) is true. However, the narrative never actually informs the reader as to what the scroll was supposed to have contained.[68] The book of Deuteronomy known from the Bible is not a reasonable candidate for the scroll Huldah considers.[69] Nor would her speech affirm the Holiness Code, or any other fragment of current canons of the Bible for that matter.[70] What Huldah does is affirm the seriousness of the king's reaction. As Lohfink noted long ago, Huldah's speech is all about the king.[71] Her words concern the contrast between the actions of Josiah and the actions of the population. While the population is castigated for the many terrible things it has done up to the point of the prophetic speech, Josiah's acceptance by Yahweh is grounded in the single act of repentance and his proper protestations of observable grief (tearing his garment). What connection Josiah's tearing his garment has to any possible content of the scroll is left decidedly unstated.

In the rendition of Kings, Huldah does something else as well; she shifts the authority for the kings' religious duties from spoken prophetic proclamations to that of a written scroll.[72] She does not create a canon, as the narratives now read.[73] Neither does she have a copy of the scroll

---

68 Huldah's oracle says remarkably little: Handy, "Role of Huldah," 50; Hamori, *Women's Divination*, 151.

69 On this, see Ivan Engnell, *A Rigid Scrutiny: Critical Essays on the Old Testament*, trans. J. T. Willis (Nashville: Vanderbilt University Press, 1969), 57; Handy, "A Realignment in Heaven," 274–78. Assorted reasons for the scroll not being Deuteronomy are listed in Ahlström, *The History of Ancient Palestine*, 775–77.

70 George Ricker Berry, "The Code Found in the Temple," *JBL* 39 (1920): 44, 51; William A. Irwin, "On Objective Criterion for the Dating of Deuteronomy," *AJSL* 56 (1939): 339; Lauren A. S. Monroe, "A 'Holiness' Substratum in the Deuteronomistic Account of Josiah's Reform," *JHS* 7 (2007): 44–45, doi:10.5508/jhs.2007.v7.a10. The unlikely case of the Holiness Code being Josiah's book has been long argued; see, for example, Alexander Freed, "The Code Spoken of in II Kings 22–23," *JBL* 40 (1921): 76–80. The entire Torah is unlikely, though it remains a consideration among some traditionalists, e.g., Angel, *Revealed Texts, Hidden Meanings*, 250, 253.

71 Norbert Lohfink, "Die Bundesunrkunde des Königs Josias," 276. Indeed, the entire Josianic passage in both Kings and Chronicles is about the king. See Ben Zvi ("Imagining Josiah's Book," 199), who would connect Josiah to the promise of disaster made by Yahweh through Huldah.

72 Esther Menn, "Inner-Biblical Exegesis in the Tanak," in *A History of Biblical Interpretation*, vol. 1: *The Ancient Period*, ed. A. J. Hauser and D. F. Watson (Grand Rapids: Eerdmans, 2003), 59; Hamori, *Women's Divination*, 153 and 153n11; Ben Zvi, "Imagining," 200.

73 As sometimes asserted by, for example, Crain, *Reading the Bible*, 120; Achtelstetter, "Huldah at the Table," 182–83; Ojo, "Prophetess Huldah as a Principal Strategist," 118.

with which to compare 'Hilkiah's' text.[74] Nor does she instigate the tradition of biblical commentary, as is often proposed.[75] All of her words to the delegation from Josiah come from Yahweh, "Thus says Yahweh" being standard opening lines from Yahweh in prophetic speech.[76] In Kings and Chronicles, Huldah is a prophet, but she serves solely as the mouthpiece for Yahweh. She says nothing on her own; everything she says, even that which is directed to her from Yahweh, is the quotation of Yahweh's proclamation.[77] There is no follow-up story concerning Huldah as there was to the man of God.[78] She is essentially the word of Yahweh for her story and needs no confirmation in her status; it is a given. This is driven home to the reader in at least three significant ways. First, Josiah does not, as sometimes stated, send to Huldah herself; Josiah sends a delegation to ask Yahweh about the words of the scroll and about the wrath of Yahweh (2 Kgs 22:12-13). Second, Huldah is the prophetess whom the delegation seeks out;[79] that she has the proper 'credentials' to be the mouthpiece of Yahweh is clearly documented by the author simply from the fact that she is *called* the prophetess *and* that, in order to ask something of Yahweh, they turn to her (2 Kgs 22:14). Third, her entire speech is the reply from Yahweh to the delegation to, in turn, recite to Josiah.

---

74 It has been posited by, for example, Ojo, "Prophetess Huldah," 125.

75 And this aside from the question of whether there was a 'Scripture' to comment on in the monarchic period of Judah; see Kurt L. Noll ("Did 'Scripturalization' Take Place in Second Temple Judaism?," *SJOT* 25 [2011]: 208-9, 215-16), who sees no biblical scriptural texts at all prior to the Hellenistic period. Huldah as ur-commentator has had a lot of support, but the narrative does not support it: Morgan, *Woman and Her Master*, 118-19; Rütersworden, "Prophetin Hulda," 241; Rose Sallberg Kam, *Their Stories, Our Stories: Women of the Bible* (New York: Continuum, 1995), 144-45; Weems, "Huldah, the Prophet," 322; Gafney, *Daughters of Miriam*, 98.

76 William M. Schniedewind, "Prophets and Prophecy in the Books of Chronicles," in Graham, Hoglund, and McKenzie, *The Chronicler as Historian*, 215-16. Yahweh speaks directly to Huldah (2 Kgs 22:15) and to the delegation (2 Kgs 22:18), but Huldah is recorded solely as the voice of Yahweh.

77 Stökl, "Deborah, Huldah," 334. Huldah is used by the author of Kings to sum up the theology of the scroll of Kings. See Lee, "Books of Kings," 174-75.

78 This is not to say that later traditions have not created stories about Huldah and her memory; see Glagolev et al., "Vtoraia Kniga Paralipomenon," 183.

79 That the delegation goes to Huldah is clear, but why they went to her is not; it cannot be argued that she held "the position of 'the' exclusive spokeswoman of Yahweh" from 2 Kgs 22:13-20 or from anything else, contra Erhard S. Gerstenberger, "Persian-Empire Spirituality and the Genesis of Prophetic Books," in Edelman and Ben Zvi, *The Production of Prophecy*, 128n24. Nor, it seems, does her being a resident of Jerusalem have any bearing, other than that she was convenient; see James M. Gray, *Christian Workers' Commentary on the Old and New Testaments* (New York: Fleming H. Revell, 1915), 193.

The speech of Yahweh spoken by Huldah does not suggest any future action on the part of the king or anyone else. All that is mentioned on the part of the populace and the ruler are actions already taken. The result of these events has been set and is not going to change. The people have cursed themselves, so to speak, and there is no hope for Judah or Jerusalem (2 Kgs 22:16–17, 19–20).[80] The wrath of Yahweh here is not going to be changed (this is not Jonah); the past has been so evil in Yahweh's sight that there is no possible mediation for its redemption.[81] Huldah's prophecy is pure prediction based on activities already engaged in by the people and noted by the deity as due cause, but it is Yahweh's determination of that future that provides the thrust of the speech.[82]

Indeed, Huldah's oracle is not presented as instigating Josiah's cultic activities but only as instigating the acknowledgment by Yahweh that the scroll read by Josiah was a truthful document.[83] Although often presented as a (or the) founder of the 'reform,' Huldah does not appear in either of the biblical narratives in that position.[84] The Kings narrative never suggests that Huldah has anything to do with the wholesale religious change that follows, so the shift of chronology of the events in Chronicles is less of a mystery than sometimes supposed. Nor does her message from Yahweh extend any hope of escaping from the destruction that was coming, a destruction clearly in the past by the time the entire Josiah narrative was composed.[85]

The character of most importance in both of these narratives is, of course, Yahweh. Whatever the ancient Judeans may have thought about their patron deity, Yahweh is written in terms of a literary character like other characters that appear in the biblical texts.[86] For the narratives of

---

80 Herbert Chanan Brichto notes that the exact fate of Judah is not really clear, but it is a curse and it is not good. See Brichto, *The Problem of "Curse" in the Hebrew Bible*, corrected repr., JBLMS 13 (Philadelphia: Society of Biblical Literature, 1968), 197,

81 Terence E. Fretheim, *What Kind of God? Collected Essays of Terence E. Fretheim*, ed. M. J. Chan, SLTHS (Winona Lake, IN: Eisenbrauns, 2015), 148, 152.

82 Emmerson, "Women in Ancient Israel," 376.

83 Pietsch, "Prophetess of Doom," 79; Ojo, "Prophetess Huldah," 119.

84 Huldah as founder of the cult renovation is common enough: Lee, "Books of Kings," 174. One might note that early modern commentators assumed Jeremiah, not Huldah, was the source of the 'reform': Sarah Trimmer, *Sacred History, Selected from the Holy Scriptures; with Annotations and Reflections, Particularly to Facilitate the Study of the Bible in Schools and Families*, 9th ed. (London: J. G. F. & J. Rivington, 1840) 3.216 [first published in 1782–1785].

85 Robinson, *Josiah's Reform and the Book of the Law*, 12–13; Linville, *Israel in the Book of Kings*, 190.

86 See Dale Patrick, *The Rendering of God in the Old Testament*, OBT 10 (Philadelphia: Fortress, 1981), 2–5. Patrick notes that all such *dramatis persona* are "imaginary

both of these prophets Yahweh is at best a shadowy figure. The word of Yahweh is what they proclaim, but the actual deliverance of that word to the prophets is not described. When Jeroboam is confronted by the prophet, the narrator of the story informs the reader that this is the word of Yahweh, but the speech by Yahweh to the man of God is in the past of the flow of the story by then. The man of God *says* he speaks a "sign" of Yahweh (1 Kgs 13:3), but the word of Yahweh is simply the speech-act of the prophet himself. More interesting is that the withering and restoration of the hand of Jeroboam presupposes that Yahweh is acting in each case, but the text itself only infers it. The lying prophet is reported by his son to have received word from the "angel of Yahweh." However, the story makes it clear that that is a lie. But, the word of Yahweh really comes to the lying prophet with a real prophecy informing the man of God that he will be doomed to a burial distant from his home (1 Kgs 13:21-22). Furthermore, Yahweh does not appear in the punishment of the man of God, which is carried out by a lion; only the lying prophet, appearing to speak the truth, *claims* that Yahweh fed the man to the lion (1 Kgs 13:26). In this entire narrative Yahweh makes no appearance as a functioning character.

From the speeches/prophecies written as the words of Yahweh, some sense of the character of this deity in this material may be extracted. Yahweh does not like the altar at Bethel; why this is the case is not stated by the deity but must be inferred from the preceding narration. Moreover, the God is not going to destroy the altar; there is no promise of divine destruction by fire and brimstone. The altar will be demolished, much later, by a Davidic king not to be born for a long time, whose name will be Josiah. Yahweh acts through proper royalty. With respect to Jeroboam's arm, we learn that Yahweh is approachable, can work miraculous deeds on the human anatomy (1 Kgs 13:6), can be petitioned to reverse actions already made by himself, and can apparently be conned by a falsely repentant Jeroboam (1 Kgs 13:6, 33). In addition, with the lying prophet, the references suggest that Yahweh brooks no deviance from the prophets. The man of God knows eating with Jeroboam is forbidden; indeed, he knows eating at all is forbidden (1 Kgs 13:8-9, 16-17, 22) but does so anyway. For this he is mauled to death by a lion and buried in the location he was sent to denounce. In this prophetic story, Yahweh declares destruction, death, and punishment. The reader would conclude that Yahweh is demanding and vengeful but lenient with kings while wishy-washy with prophets; the lying prophet lives through this tale unscathed while the truthful prophet is destroyed by his deity and buried in a location Yahweh condemned. One

---

beings" in that they exist in the imagination of the reader only so long as they are being read. The author and the reader imagine the character (26).

might suggest the antithesis of 'holy ground' in later Christian burial 'theology.' Better to be an apostate king than a truthful prophet.

In the case of Huldah, Yahweh makes even less of an appearance. Josiah has heard the word of Yahweh read from a scroll and commands Hilkiah, Ahikam, Shaphan, Achbor, and Asaiah to check on this material with Yahweh. It is the delegation that seeks out Huldah, but Huldah as the voice of Yahweh. Yahweh is not a character in this narrative any more than in the man of God story. What does appear is the speech, spoken by Huldah and ascribed to Yahweh, that includes several references to an acting deity. In this, Yahweh is subsumed within the character of Huldah; she may be speaking, but, in the rationale of the time, it is actually Yahweh who speaks.

In this speech, Yahweh is an angry deity. Not fixated on Bethel or the northern kingdom, Yahweh condemns the populace of Judah and Jerusalem explicitly for the apparently inexcusable crime of worshiping deities other than Yahweh and, as reported, leaving Yahweh altogether.[87] Here, Yahweh is infuriated to the point that there is no recourse for the Judahite people or society; Yahweh declares the destruction of both as an event that cannot be changed (2 Kgs 22:16-17; 2 Chr 34:24-25). As for Josiah, Yahweh makes an exception; since the king has already gone through the motions of lament and repentance, the deity allows that Josiah may live without seeing the destruction. The oddity that, at that moment, Josiah was checking whether the word of Yahweh he had heard was actually Yahweh's true will is made explicit in that Yahweh has already reacted to Josiah as if the king had already discerned its truth and had moved to correct the situation vis-à-vis Yahweh. It is notable that the Chronicler's rendition of Josiah's Passover does not include any action by Yahweh or any reference to any action performed in the past by Yahweh that the ritual celebrates. Only the command made by Yahweh in the hoary past that the Passover ought to be kept connects this event with God—an event the king and the people had never celebrated (2 Chr 35:6; 1 Esd 1:18-19). Yahweh appears solely in his own prophecy.

Yahweh comes across in Huldah's speech as a wrathful character, consumed with jealousy and a need for absolute loyalty.[88] When crossed, he behaves not so much in a threatening manner, but with violence and, inevitably, in a manner of 'anti-creation' against Judah in its entirety.

---

87 Fretheim (*First and Second Kings*, 89, 214) properly connects the wrath of Yahweh against Jeroboam with that against Judah, tying these two episodes together.

88 Deena E. Grant defines two forms of divine anger: one more related to the provocation by the Judeans and one the wrathful response of Yahweh. See Grant, *Divine Anger in the Hebrew Bible*, CBQMS 52 (Washington, DC: Catholic Biblical Association of America, 2014), 25, 29, 32.

One could make a very long list of characteristics biblically attributed to Yahweh that are not in these passages, but what holds the Huldah passages together is the wrath of Yahweh concerning the lack of proper ritual fidelity to himself. In the end, the prophets of Josiah are the voice of Judah's God and for both prophets the deity has exhausted its patience with the people whom Yahweh deems should be loyal to him and his proper cult ritual. It is doom for the people, then, while the king gets a 'pass' for the rest of his life.

CHAPTER FIVE
RELIGION AT THE TIME OF JOSIAH:
RECONSTRUCTION, TEXT, AND INVENTION

The religion of ancient Judah at the time of the ascendancy of Josiah should not be a matter of question, but it has been a highly debated topic for millennia.[1] The biblical texts and the archaeological records more or less support each other in the basic notion that the religious cult of Jerusalem was based on a pantheon.[2] What the general Judean population believed appears to have been similar.[3] Moreover, most religious activities in either

---

1   See, for example, Crawford H. Toy, "The Triumph of Josiah," *JBL* 24 (1905): 94. One needs to keep in mind that Toy's century-old observation remains accurate: "Of the religious conditions in Judah between the dates of the reformation (622) and the death of Josiah (609-8) we have no immediate information."

2   This has been a constant among recent biblical scholars: William Foxwell Albright, *From the Stone Age to Christianity: Monotheism and the Historical Process*, 2nd ed. (Garden City, NY: Doubleday Anchor Books 1957), 309-12; Norbert Lohfink, "Gott und die Götter im Alten Testament," *ThA* 6 (1969): 58-64; Fritz Stolz, "Monotheism in Israel," in *Monotheismus im Alten Israel und seiner Umwelt*, ed. O. Keel, BibB 14 (Fribourg: Schweizerisches Katholisches Bibelwerk, 1980), 163-74. See also Smith, *The Early History of God*, 11, 113, 186. For biblical references, see the chart in Zevit, *The Religions of Ancient Israel*, 478. On the archaeology of ancient Judean and Israelite religion, see Gösta W. Ahlström, *An Archaeological Picture of Iron Age Religions in Ancient Palestine*, StudOr 55.3 (Helsinki: Societas Orientalis Fennica, 1984); Othmar Keel and Christopher Uehlinger, *Gods, Goddesses, and Images of God in Ancient Israel*, trans. T. H. Trapp (Minneapolis: Fortress: 1998), 398-405; Rüdiger Schmitt, "Elements of Domestic Cult in Ancient Israel," in *Family and Household Religion in Ancient Israel and the Levant*, ed. Rainer Albertz and Rüdiger Schmitt (Winona Lake, IN: Eisenbrauns, 2012), 175; James Anderson, "Creating Dialectical Tensions: Religious Developments in Persian-Period Yehud Reflected in Biblical Texts," in Edelman, Fitzpatrick-McKinley, and Guillaume, *Religion in the Achaemenid Persian Empire*, 10.

3   Susan Niditch notes properly that the data available is much too fragmentary to reconstruct religious thought in ancient Israel or Judah, but clearly there were variations through time and location; this includes the pantheon worshiped. See Niditch, *Ancient Israelite Religion* (Oxford: Oxford University Press, 1997), 25, 120. Rainer Albertz ("Methodological Reflections," in Albertz and Schmitt, *Family and Household Religion in Ancient Israel*, 55) posits three levels of religious life for ancient Judah/Israel (family, local, and state) that were interconnected. It is no longer possible to maintain a statement like "the people of Israel did not know polytheism," as

Judah or Israel would have been local, traditional events officiated by heads of households or regional distinguished personnel.[4] It would also appear that the regional patron deity for Judah was Yahweh, often equated with, or a regional name for, the Syro-Palestinian ruling deity, El.[5] There is, however, no archaeological evidence that Yahweh was considered the sole deity of Judah or of Israel in either region.[6] The Jewish military community in Egypt under the Persians supports the notion of a Judean polytheistic cult.[7] Clearly, elements of the greater Syro-Palestinian religious region were retained in the biblical accounts and in Judean cultic tradition itself.[8]

---

per Yehezkel Kaufmann, "The Bible and Mythological Polytheism," trans. M. Greenberg, *ZAW* 70 (1951): 195. Nor is it possible to maintain his theory that the Bible knew nothing of mythology (180).

4   See Ziony Zevit, "The Textual and Social Embeddedness of Israelite Family Religion: Who Were the Players? Where Were the Stages?," in *Family and Household Religion: Toward a Synthesis of Old Testament Studies, Archaeology, Epigraphy, and Cultural Studies*, ed. R. Albertz, B. A. Nakhal, S. Olyan, and R. Schmitt (Winona Lake, IN: Eisenbrauns, 2014), 301–11; William G. Dever, *The Lives of Ordinary People in Ancient Israel: Where Archaeology and the Bible Intersect* (Winona Lake, IN: Eisenbrauns, 2012), 249–93.

5   Jeffrey H. Tigay, *You Shall Have No Other Gods: Israelite Religion in the Light of Hebrew Inscriptions*, HSS 31 (Atlanta: Scholars, 1986); however, see the critique by Ernst Axel Knauf in "'You Shall Have No Other Gods': Eine notwendige Notiz zu einer überflüssigen Diskussion," *DBAT* 26 (1989–1990): 238–45, and the conclusions in Rainer Albertz, "Personal Names and Family Religion," in Albertz and Schmitt, *Family and Household Religion in Ancient Israel*, 340–44.

6   Textually, it is unclear whether or not the authors of the biblical literature understood anything like 'monotheism' prior to Second Isaiah, and narratives of Hezekiah and Josiah assume many deities. See Enzo Cortese, "I tentative di una teologia (Cristiana) dell'Antico Testamento," *LASBF* 56 (2006): 19. Indeed, the archaeological evidence is clear that there were other gods worshiped in addition to Yahweh. See, for example, Daniel I. Block, *The Gods of the Nations: Studies in Ancient Near Eastern National Theology*, 2nd ed. (Grand Rapids: Baker Academic, 2000), 65–69; Dever, *Lives of Ordinary People*, 264–45; Spieckermann, "'YHWH Bless You and Keep You,'" 173–74. See the general overview by William G. Dever, "Folk Religion in Ancient Israel: The Disconnect between Text and Artifact," in Kottsieper, Schmitt, and Wöhrle, *Berührungspunkte*, 425–39.

7   Paul-Eugène Dion, "La religion des papyrus d'Éléphantine: un reflet du Juda d'avant l'exil," in *Kein Land für sich allein: Studien zum Kulturkontakt in Kanaan, Israel/Palästina und Ebirnâri für Manfred Weippert zum 65. Geburtstag*, ed. U. Hübner and E. A. Knauf, OBO 186 (Freiburg: Universitätsverlag; Göttingen: Vandenhoeck & Ruprecht, 2002), 244; Collin Cornell properly notes that the Yeb colony of Judeans would naturally diverge from Yehud since time and distance separate the two religious cultic centers, see Cornell, "Cult Statuary in the Judean Temple at Yeb," *JSJ* 47 (2016): 298.

8   Herbert Niehr, "'Israelite' Religion and 'Canaanite' Religion," in Stavrakopoulou and Barton, *Religious Diversity in Ancient Israel and Judah*, 30–32. See the survey of turn of the millennium studies in Bertram Herr, "Jhwh und die Götter:

Arguments that Israel and Judah somehow formed totally unique political or religious entities in Syria-Palestine in the early first millennium BCE should not be given credence.⁹

Babylonian and Assyrian cultic material may have been incorporated into the Judean cult during times of Assyrian control of Judah and into the Israelite cult during the period of Samerina being annexed into Assyria. However, it is clear from archaeological data that some Egyptian religious traditions, so common in Syria-Palestine generally, continued unabated through the period of Judah.¹⁰ That the region had been Egyptian territory for over a millennium and would continue throughout the ancient world to be so understood explains the presence of Egyptian deities and Egyptianized versions of local deities.¹¹ Bes figures imply this minor god (or demon) was widely acknowledged.¹² Indeed, this character Bes was so

---

Ein Querschnitt durch die Forschung zum syrisch-palästinischen Gottesversändnis," *ZRGG* 52 (2000): 167–74. Roy Gane concedes that Judah and Israel were both lands with rulers open to many deities, even if there were a few rulers who made some efforts to raise Yahweh above others. See Gane, "The End of the Israelite Monarchy," *JATS* 10 (1999): 342. The populace appears to have blamed this "interruption of their idolatry" for the disasters of their land (349).

9   As duly noted by Garbini, *History and Ideology in Ancient Israel*, 64. Toy ("Triumph," 102) long ago presumed, in fact, that through the sixth century BCE, Yahweh was not the "prevailing popular worship" among the people of Israel. Knauf and Guillaume turn to surrounding territories for illustrations of the religion of the period. See Knauf and Guillaume, *A History of Biblical Israel*, 128–32.

10   Egyptian deities can be found among the excavated items throughout the 'biblical' period. For more on this, see Stern, *Archaeology of the Land of the Bible*, 478–88, 507–9; Handy, *Among the Host of Heaven*, 37–44. On the Bible as a source for a pantheon of Yahweh, see Ellen White, *Yahweh's Council: Its Structure and Membership*, FAT 2. Riehe 65 (Tübingen: Mohr Siebeck, 2014). White considers how this divine structure appears in biblical texts and notes that the Bible carefully avoids naming any members of Yahweh's council (47). For short summaries, see John L. McLaughlin, *What Are They Saying about Ancient Israelite Religion?*, WATSA (New York: Paulist, 2016), 72–78, 81–85. The notion of a divine council in ancient Israelite or Judahite thought cannot be distinguished as a "great" [official] or "small" [unofficial] tradition, but would seem to be pervasive; see Niditch, "Experiencing the Divine," 17.

11   On the Egyptian presence in the area until the end of the eighth and into the beginning of the seventh century, see Shirly Ben-Dor Evian, "Egypt and Israel: The Never-Ending Story," *NEA* 80 (2017): 37. On Egyptian motifs, see Keel and Uehlinger, *Gods, Goddesses*, 49–97, and on the notion of *ma'at* in the Bible, see Nel, "Social Justice as Religious Responsibility in Near Eastern Religions," 144. Egyptian influence on the area's cultures extends to literary materials in the Persian Empire as well. See Joachim Friedrich Quack, "The Interaction of Egyptian and Aramaic Literature," in Lipschits, Knoppers, and Oeming, *Judah and Judeans in the Achaemenid Period*, 375–76, 383–84, 393.

12   Keel and Uehlinger, *Gods, Goddesses*, 219–23, 259. See the extensive note in Zevit, *Religions of Ancient Israel*, 381–90.

important in birthing rituals and the safeguarding of the family unit that attempts at reducing a pantheon would not discontinue his existence in the religious realm; this was true in Egypt during the Amarna period and was clearly the case in ancient Judah.[13] However, if Egyptian deities continued to be recognized in ancient Judah and Israel, they were not incorporated into the biblical notion of a pantheon as they had been in the Phoenician cultus.[14] The sharp distinction between Judah's deity and the pantheon of Egypt continued into Roman times, suggesting Egyptian gods offered a continuous pull on peoples from Judah long after Judah ceased to exist.[15] The names appearing in the Hebrew Bible for divinities incorporated into the official cults of either Israel or Judah are decidedly Syro-Palestinian: Asherah, Astarte, Baal, Mot, Molech, Resheph, and so on.[16] If Josiah's Judahite temple in Jerusalem ever incorporated Egyptian, Assyrian, or Babylonian deities as such, the authors of the biblical texts either refused to recognize their existence or subsumed them under Northwest Semitic deity forms.[17] There is, however, no reason to assume

---

13   The mere fact that Bes figurines continue to appear in the region of ancient Judah and Israel reflects Bes's popularity throughout the biblical period; the god even appears in theophoric names at that time in the region: see Block, *Gods of the Nations*, 66, citing Jeffrey H. Tigay, "Israelite Religion: The Onomastic and Epigraphic Evidence," in Miller, Hanson, and McBride, *Ancient Israelite Religion*, 164. In Egypt, Bes and Hathor were retained in family faith from the Old Kingdom to the Roman era. See Teeter, *Religion and Ritual in Ancient Egypt*, 90, 173, Fig. 73. On Bes and Hathor appearing through the Amarna Period, see p. 194.

14   Stern, *Archaeology*, 492–505. However, Egyptian deities may appear in the biblical texts without being so designated (Ma'at being significant, among others). See Klaus Koch, *Der Gott Israels und die Götter des Orients: Religionsgeschichtliche Studien II: zum 80. Geburtstag von Klaus Koch*, ed. F. Hartenstein and M Rösel, FRLANT 216 (Göttingen: Vandenhoek & Ruprecht, 2007), 210–40.

15   See Rivka Ulmer, "The Egyptian Gods in Midrashic Texts," *HTR* 107 (2010): 202–3. Ulmer sees a struggle with Egyptian deities for biblical-era Judahites perceiving them to be imbedded in the Bible narratives. This also is reflected in rabbinic interpretation (183–201).

16   Matthias Delcor provides a preliminary survey of deities mentioned in the Bible as possibly worshiped at the time of Josiah, see Delcor, "Les cultes étrangers en Israël au moment de la réforme de Josias d'après 2R 23: Étude de religions sémitique comparés," in *Mélanges bibliques et orientaux en l'honneur de M. Henri Cazelles*, ed. A. Caquot and M. Delcor, AOAT 212 (Kevelaer: Butzon & Bercker; Neukirchen-Vluyn: Neukirchener, 1981), 91–23. For the wider Syro-Palestinian environment, see Mitchell Dahood, "Ancient Semitic Deities in Syria and Palestine," in *Le antiche divinita semitiche*, ed. S. Moscati (Rome: Centro di Studi Semitici, 1958), 65–94; Gregorio del Olmo Lete, *Mitos y leyendas de Canaan segun la tradición de Ugarit: Textos, version y estudio*, FCBib 1 (Madrid: Cristiandad, 1986).

17   It is certain that Egyptians incorporated Syro-Palestinian deities into their pantheon and identified them with both their Egyptian names and their Northwest

the Jerusalem temple had need of Assyrian deities, especially since it was never technically a province of Assyria proper, and the latter, however concerned it may have been about the cultic traditions of is core territory, was not obsessed with manipulating the religious cults of its periphery or its territories, let alone its treaty partners.[18]

Moreover, while it may or may not have been the case that the temple to Yahweh in Jerusalem was the major temple-site in Judah, the many references to the *bamot* throughout Kings imply that there were several localized sanctuaries for worshiping some deity or another.[19] Certainly, it would have been an unimportant and weak deity that was confined to a single temple in any mythological vision of the divine world, even if there was one residence recognized as being the most important for a deity.[20]

Semitic names: Rainer Stadelmann, *Syrisch-Palästinensische Gottheiten in Ägypten*, PAe 5 (Leiden: Brill, 1967), 21–27; Stephanie L. Budin, "A Reconsideration of the Aphrodite-Ashtart Syncretism," *Numen* 51 (2004): 100. Egyptian deities were incorporated into Syro-Palestinian polytheism (Stern, *Archaeology*, 484). That Assyria imposed Assyrian gods on Israel and Judah such that the deities being removed by Josiah were those of the overlord empire has had a fairly short but popular history. Theodor Östreicher (*Das deuteronomische Grundgesetz*, BFCT 27.4 [Gütersloh: Bertelsmann, 1923] 30) is often credited with popularizing this thesis. See also Welch, "The Death of Josiah," 257; Georg Fohrer, *History of Israelite Religion*, trans. D. E. Green (Nashville: Abingdon, 1972), 292; Bright, *A History of Israel*, 290; Hermann Spieckermann, *Juda unter Assur in der Sargonidenzeit*, FRLANT 129 (Göttingen: Vandenhoeck & Ruprecht, 1982), 322–44.

18   That Assyria did not impose its religious pantheon on its subject vassals has been sufficiently argued by, for example, John McKay in *Religion in Judah under the Assyrians*, SBT 2nd series 26 (Naperville, IL: Alec R. Allenson, 1973), 72. McKay leaves open the possibility that some Assyrian deities were in the temple, but were not particularly important. See also Morton Cogan [Mordecai Cogan], *Imperialism and Religion: Assyria, Judah and Israel in the Eighth and Seventh Centuries B.C.E.*, SBLMS 19 (Missoula, MT: Scholars Press, 1974), 112–13; Steven W. Holloway, *Aššur Is King! Aššur Is King! Religion in the Exercise of Power in the Neo-Assyrian Empire*, CHANE 10 (Brill: Leiden, 2002), 78–79. Assyrian religion does not seem to have infused the regional cult of Ekron, also in the Assyrian Empire; see William S. Morrow, "Were There Neo-Assyrian Influences in Manasseh's Temple? Comparative Evidence from Tel-Miqne/Ekron," *CBQ* 75 (2013): 72–73 (this is the case even if his example is not a palace complex). It seems highly unlikely that promoting Yahweh in Judah would have concerned Assyria at all, as opposed to the popular notion that acknowledging a deity would be seen as "treason" to a king of Assyria: Knauf and Guillaume, *History of Biblical Israel*, 127.

19   On the meaning of the *bamot*, see Barrick, "The Word *bmh* in the Old Testament"; idem, "What Do We Really Know about 'High Places'?" Exactly what *bamah* meant to either the ancient population or the biblical writers, by necessity, remains speculative: John A. Emerton, "The Biblical High Places in the Light of Recent Study," *PEQ* 129 (1997): 129–30.

20   Meier, "Granting God a Passport," 197–98. It is significant that the narrative

The polemic in the Bible against these regional religious centers does not contain an explanation as to which goddess or god these shrine-places were dedicated. It remains possible that they were places to worship Yahweh, though the account in Kings of Solomon building sanctuaries for his wives is explicit that shrines to a (very large) variety of deities existed in and/or around Jerusalem itself (1 Kgs 11:3–8).[21] Evidence for these non-Yahwistic shrines is, at best, minimal.[22] There are certainly several excavated edifices which have been interpreted as sacred shrine sites.[23] As for the temple in Jerusalem, of which the biblical text has much to say and for which there is no other acceptable cultic site, there is nothing in the archaeological record of Jerusalem by which to document this edifice.[24]

---

in Kings assumes the Jerusalem temple remained perpetually a temple for Yahweh. Even Athaliah leaves it alone, and apparently built other temples rather than move 'her' deities into Yahweh's home. See Tomoo Ishida, *The Royal Dynasties in Ancient Israel: A Study on the Formation and Development of Royal-Dynastic Ideology*, BZAW 142 (Berlin: de Gruyter, 1977), 160.

21   Zevit (*Religions of Ancient Israel*, 458) restricts the shrines to the deities listed in the text and not to all the deities of the one-thousand wives, which is undoubtedly a legendary tale in any case. He continues to contend that they were only for Solomon's wives and their personal religious activities. That these shrines remained until the reign of Josiah would counter this interpretation. Someone was worshiping at these Solomonic temples for 200 years. Of course, the entire tradition is polemical and perhaps the invention of the author, which is quite possible. See Zamora García (*Reyes I*, 229), who sets out the literary polemic but does not suggest it is not based on historical data. The entire passage is no doubt late historiography; see Linda S. Schearing, "A Wealth of Women: Looking Behind, Within, and Beyond Solomon's Story," in Handy, *The Age of Solomon*, 431, 437–38.

22   For Jerusalem proper, figurines were certainly found in the area for the period but evidence of shrines, let alone cultic centers, is lacking in Jerusalem in the early first millennium; Kathleen M. Kenyon, *Jerusalem: Excavating 3000 Years of History* (London: Thames & Hudson, 1967), 101. As for cultic sites during the era of the 'divided monarchy,' there are several possible, but still ambiguous, remains implying a sizeable number of local holy places. See Diana V. Edelman, "Cultic Sites and Complexes beyond the Jerusalem Temple," in Stavrakopoulou and Barton, *Religious Diversity in Ancient Israel and Judah*, 89–98. Figurines in Judahite regions continued until the region was incorporated into the Persian Empire: Izaak de Hulster, "Figurines from Persian Period Jerusalem?," *ZAW* 124 (2012): 85–86.

23   See the short surveys in Amihai Mazar, *Archaeology of the Land of the Bible: 10,000–586 B.C.E.*, ABRL (New York: Doubleday, 1990), 447–50, 492–502; Rüdiger Schmitt, "Kultinventare aus Wohnhäusern als materielle Elemente familiärer Religion im Alten Israel," in Kottsieper, Schmitt, and Wöhrle, *Berührungspunkte*, 444–74. On gates as religious sacred sites, see Dale W. Manor, "Gates and Gods: High Places in the Gates," *SCJ* 2 (1999): 244–50.

24   The modern city of Jerusalem precludes extensive excavations where the temple might have existed and Temple Mount is occupied by a mosque that would have removed any earlier religious sites where it stands, leaving nothing of the

It is not even certain that the Temple Mount was yet part of the city in the tenth century BCE.[25] This leaves open any attempt to reconstruct the temple itself as conjecture based on Syro-Palestinian excavations in concert with biblical texts of debatable date and reliability.[26]

The description of the temple as built by King Solomon (1 Kgs 5:3; 6:1–7:51; 2 Chr 3:1–5:1) is a more extensive narrative devoted to one subject than most stories told in Kings.[27] In Kings, this temple construction appears to be a joint effort by Solomon and King Hiram of Tyre (Huram in Chronicles);[28] in the Chronicler's rendition, Solomon plays more of a secondary role to David, who is presented as the selector of the site and the architect of record (2 Chr 3:1; 1 Chr 29:1–5).[29] It is not at all certain, however, that the temple described ever existed in Judah;[30] in any event,

---

earlier temples to excavate. For more on this, see, for example, Yohanan Aharoni, *The Archaeology of the Land of Israel*, 192–94; David Ussishkin, "Solomon's Jerusalem: The Text and the Facts on the Ground," in Vaughn and Killebrew, *Jerusalem in Bible and Archaeology*, 113–14; Elizabeth Bloch-Smith, "Solomon's Temple: The Politics of Ritual Space," in Gitten, *Sacred Time, Sacred Space*, 83.

25 Amihai Mazar, "Archaeology and the Biblical Narrative: The Case of the United Monarchy," in Kratz and Spieckermann, *One God—One Cult—One Nation*, 48. There is even reason to wonder if Temple Mount was the site of an early temple, according to Eliav, *God's Mountain*, 2–3.

26 Jean Ouellette, "The Basic Structure of Solomon's Temple and Archaeological Research," in *The Temple of Solomon: Archaeological Fact and Medieval Tradition in Christian, Islamic and Jewish Art*, ed. J. Gutmann, RelArts 3 (Missoula, MT: Scholars Press, 1976), 1–5. The standard two-volume work on archaeology and the Jerusalem temple and its relation to excavated parallels for many decades remains worth consulting: Theodor A. Busink, *Der Tempel von Jerusalem von Salomo bis Herodes: Eine archäologisch-historische Studie unter Berücksichtigung des westsemitischen Tempelbaus*, SFSMD 3 (Leiden: Brill, 1970, 1980).

27 Sara Japhet notes that the parallel temple construction narrative in Chronicles is decidedly more concise, despite the importance given to the temple in the work as a whole, see Japhet, *I & II Chronicles*, 549. See also Brunet, "Le Chroniste et ses Sources," 355.

28 The problems of the relation of Hiram of Tyre with the united monarchy are many and murky, but the biblical historiographer was clearly impressed with the relationship, fact or fiction: Garbini, *History and Ideology*, 22–25.

29 Steussy, *David: Biblical Portraits of Power*, 114: "David makes all arrangements ... Solomon meekly cooperates." Eliav (*God's Mountain*, 5) notes the centrality of Solomon's temple for both Kings and Chronicles, as well as noting that it may well have been a creation of the much later authors.

30 Nadav Na'aman suggests the Solomonic temple described was that of the author writing after modifications by Jehoash and Josiah in Na'aman, "Notes on the Temple 'Restorations' of Jehoash and Josiah," *VT* 63 (2013): 641–43. Oded Lipschits concludes that the two repair stories are related literary constructs of the first edition of the Deuteronomistic History and are no earlier than Josiah. See Lipschits, "On Cash-Boxes and Finding or Not Finding Books: Jehoash's and Josiah's Decisions

it would be unlikely to have been one built by Solomon in the tenth century BCE.[31] Neither is the interior of the temple in Jerusalem, as described, anything unusual for Syria-Palestine in the early first millennium BCE. It is replete with Egyptianized decorative devices probably to be explained as typical Levantine royal/cultic motifs of the time.[32] The exterior formation, however, is unique.

The central distinguishing feature of the sanctuary of this literary temple from those excavated in the kingdoms around and about Judah is the absence of an artistic representation of the god dwelling therein.[33] The extent to which Jerusalem (or Samaria) supported temples without

---

to Repair the Temple," in Amit et al., *Essays on Ancient Israel in Its Near Eastern Context*, 251.

31 Miller and Hayes (*A History of Ancient Israel and Judah*, 217) note the imaginary details which they suspect were added centuries after Solomon that incorporated notions of 'temple' from Mesopotamia and Egypt. Mario Liverani properly notes the unlikely dimensions of this edifice in David's city, the legendary nature of having Solomon build it rather than David, and posits the Persian era as the time for this utopian temple vision: Liverani, *Israel's History and the History of Israel*, 99–100. Clearly, the speech written for Solomon in 1 Kgs 8:22–53 was composed long after Solomon and likely long after Josiah. See Montgomery, *A Critical and Exegetical Commentary*, 194–95. Hermann-Josef Stipp ("Die sechste und siebte Fürbitte des Tempelweihegebets [1 Kön 8,44–51] in der Diskussion um das deuteronomistische Geschichtswerk," *JNSL* 24 [1998]: 3n13) compiles a short list of those holding a late date for 1 Kgs 8:44–51, whom he wishes to contradict, but he only demonstrates that the material is not datable (210–11).

32 See, for example, Heaton, *Solomon's New Men*, 77–90; Elizabeth Bloch-Smith, "'Who Is the King of Glory?' Solomon's Temple and Its Symbolism," in *Scripture and Other Artifacts: Essays on the Bible and Archaeology in Honor of Philip J. King*, ed. M. D. Coogan, J. C. Exum, and L. E. Stager (Louisville: Westminster John Knox, 1994), 25.

33 Bloch-Smith, "Solomon's Temple, Politics," 90; Tryggve N. D. Mettinger argues both that Israel/Judah maintained a cult-long tradition of having no image of Yahweh, but that the lack of an image was contextually acceptable religious practice beyond "Israelite" religion. See Mettinger, *No Graven Image? Israelite Aniconism in Its Ancient Near Eastern Context*, ConBOT 42 (Stockholm: Almquist & Wiksell International, 1995), 16, 195. However, in addition to the possibility that some Judahites may have had images for Yahweh, it has been suggested by Cornell ("Cult Statuary," 307–9) that the Judahites stationed at Elephantine in Egypt had deity statues in their temple. On the debate over a Yahweh image in Jerusalem, see Theodore J. Lewis, "Syro-Palestinian Iconography and Divine Images," in *Cult Image and Divine Representation in the Ancient Near East*, ed. N. H. Walls, ASORBS 10 (Boston: American Schools of Oriental Research, 2005), 103–5; Tryggve N. D. Mettinger, "A Conversation with My Critics: Cultic Image or Aniconism in the First Temple?," in Amit et al., *Essays on Ancient Israel in Its Near Eastern Context*, 276–81; Spieckermann, "Yahweh Bless You and Keep You," 172. There are possible references to Yahweh images in the biblical texts themselves. See Bob Becking, "The Return of the Deity: Iconic or Aniconic?," in Amit et al., *Essays on Ancient Israel in Its Near Eastern Context*, 56–57.

divine images is less than clear, but anthropomorphic images of Yahweh are decidedly hard to defend.³⁴ The Josiah story in Kings has Josiah's priests and doorkeepers, under the care of Hilkiah, remove Asherah from the temple (2 Kgs 23:6), an object that was apparently an anthropomorphic idol for which woven apparel was traditionally made on site (2 Kgs 23:7). In addition, there were votive items to be removed that had served in the worship of Asherah, Baal, and the host of heaven (2 Kgs 23:4), not to mention the priests who had served Baal, Shemesh, Yareah, and assorted celestial deities around Jerusalem and Judah (2 Kgs 23:5). These deities in the temple and in Judah's traditional cult may well have been creative polemic in these texts, but it is clear that images of them existed in Judah and probably in the Jerusalem temple in the time of Josiah.³⁵ Like those of surrounding socio-political entities, the temple served as the repository of wealth (the bank), and in the narrative this is where Josiah deals with monetary transactions.³⁶ That the banking aspect of the temple would have been known seems most reasonable. So, gods and goods define this edifice.

It is most likely that the central cultic activity of the temple in Jerusalem was ritual sacrifice. However, it is unclear what exactly that meant in a shrine of multiple deities. If the religious site were dedicated to Yahweh, were the sacrifices to this one god and the other deities in attendance

---

34 Mettinger, *No Graven Image?*, 195–97; Nadav Na'aman, "No Anthropomorphic Graven Images: Notes on the Assumed Anthropomorphic Cult Statues in the Temples of YHWH in the Pre-exilic Period," *UF* 31 (1999): 396–97, 413–15. On the possibility of there having been such an idol of Yahweh in the temple, see Diana V. Edelman, "God Rhetoric: Reconceptualizing YHWH Sebaot as YHWH Elohim in the Hebrew Bible," in *A Palimpsest: Rhetoric, Ideology, Stylistics, and Language Relating to Persian Israel*, ed. E. Ben Zvi, D. V. Edelman, and F. Polak, PHSC 5 (Piscataway, NJ: Gorgias, 2009), 85–86.

35 Taking the narrative seriously that the cultic accessories of the various deities removed by Josiah from the temple reflect actual temple life at the time. For more on this, see J. Andrew Dearman, *Religion and Culture in Ancient Israel* (Peabody, MA: Hendrickson, 1992), 87; Garbini, *History and Ideology*, 108; Niels Peter Lemche, *Ancient Israel: A New History of Israelite Society*, trans. F. Cryer, BibSem 5 (Sheffield: JSOT Press, 1990), 229. In the world of Josiah, and for two millennia prior and half a millennium afterward, iconographic representations of deities were the norm for the area and well beyond: Hanspeter Schaudig, "Death of Statues and Rebirth of Gods," in *Iconoclasm and Text Destruction in the Ancient Near East and Beyond*, ed. N. N. May, OIS 8 (Chicago: Oriental Institute of the University of Chicago, 2012), 125.

36 On the temple and temples as banks, see Marty E. Stevens, *Temples, Tithes, and Taxes: The Temple and the Economic Life of Ancient Israel* (Peabody, MA: Hendrickson, 2006), 136–62. On Josiah and the temple-bank, see pp. 73, 76, 79. For Mesopotamia, see Mukhammed A. Dandamayev, "State and Temple in Babylonia in the First Millennium B.C.," in *State and Temple Economy in the Ancient Near East*, ed. E. Lipinski, OLA 6 (Leuven: Departement Orientalistiek, 1979), 2.592, noting temples as palace economy.

presumed to combine in the Yahweh feast, so-to-speak? The Josiah narratives, which reference a Passover for this king, suggest that no such feast ever took place in the Jerusalemite temple prior to Josiah (2 Kgs 23:22; 2 Chr 35:18).[37] Whatever Pesach might have meant prior to the writing of Kings, it was not a part of the Jerusalemite sacrificial tradition. It is most likely that a variety of local agricultural feasts had latterly been combined with a perhaps newly minted historical commemorative meaning and spliced onto the *Second* Temple calendar.[38]

A minimal amount of liturgical training must have been part of the Jerusalemite temple complex. The 'high priest,' often debated as a figure prior to the Second Temple, is a term so generic that it is likely that there had always been one priest considered superior in knowledge of the cultic functions, most experienced in cultic activity, and responsible for seeing to the proper continuation of a traditional sacrificial cult.[39] The education of priests in Jerusalem at the many *bamot* would have been from one generation to another. Whether or not this included literacy is unclear from the Bible but, at least in Jerusalem, would make sense for a major shrine of the kingdom, however small. Basic ritual memorization, knowledge of the ritual calendar, feast preparation, and probably basic magic would have been a minimal course.[40] It cannot be assumed from the biblical texts, however, that a full-blown school system existed in Judah.[41]

---

37 Volker Wagner notes the emphasis Kings places on the nonexistence of Passover in the monarchical era of Judah or Israel: Wagner, "Eine antike Notiz zur Geschichte des Pesach (2 Kön 23,21–23)," *BZ* 54 (2010): 34.

38 Even a good history of Pesach accepting the biblical traditions needs to acknowledge that the monarchy celebrated nothing that could be called 'Passover/Pesach.' See Abraham P. Bloch, *The Biblical and Historical Background of the Jewish Holy Days* (New York: KTAV, 1978), 119–20. The agricultural background of the Pesach/Passover has long been recognized, as well as the combination of traditions into the rabbinic notion of Pesach. See, for example, Hayyim Schauss, *The Jewish Festivals: History and Observance*, trans. S. Jaffe (New York: Schocken Books, 1962), 38–47.

39 Wolfgang Zwickel acknowledges that pre-exilic temples would have needed a hierarchy and a priest in a "leading position." See Zwickel, "Priesthood and the Development of Cult in the Books of Kings," in Lemaire and Halpern, *The Books of Kings*, 425. Christopher R. North debates the use of various terms that might have been used for a most authoritative priest, see North, "The Religious Aspects of Hebrew Kingship," *ZAW* 50 (1932), 21.

40 James L. Crenshaw (*Education in Ancient Israel*, 279–83) summarizes ancient Near Eastern education for "sages." In Egypt and Mesopotamia, temples also served as instructional facilities, so it is not irrational to assume that some priests were fully educated. However, they would need to know a good deal more about the religious minutia than an accountant would need to know. Stevens (*Temples, Tithes*, 75–77) sees scribal accountants as regular temple staff in Jerusalem.

41 The interesting, but hypothetical, school system during the monarchy,

Perhaps of more interest because it plays such a central part in the creative story of Josiah's piety in Kings is the *bamah*/altar at Bethel (1 Kgs 12:29–13:1; 2 Kgs 23:15, 17). In commentaries and historical reconstructions, this sacred space is usually designated as a "shrine," "holy place," "sanctuary," "cultic center," or some similar designation, though the biblical narrative certainly implies Jeroboam believed it was a rival temple to the ('true') temple in Jerusalem.[42] Thus, it is only tangentially called a temple ("house") and, at that, one made out of a *bamah* (1 Kgs 12:31). The usual referent for the Bethel religious site appearing in the Kings narrative is simply "altar," which keeps the status of the establishment far below that of the temple in Jerusalem. This was necessary if, as is often assumed, Bethel was a religious site also dedicated to Yahweh.[43]

For Kings, it is immaterial that Bethel (or Dan, for that matter) would have had religious traditions stretching backward for centuries, although it is possible that the author could have suspected his readers might know of such a thing. We do not know if they knew of such a past.[44] What Kings makes very clear is that Jeroboam created an altar on an earlier sacred site just to keep people away from Jerusalem's temple. That may well have been a real motivation, but it raises questions about Bethel.

---

similar to that in ancient Egypt that existed in first-century CE Jerusalem, seems unlikely; such a wholesale education program was posited by E. W. Heaton, *The School Tradition of the Old Testament*, Bampton Lectures 1994 (Oxford: Oxford University Press, 1994).

42 Commentators and biblical historians continue to avoid the term 'temple' for either Bethel or Dan: Robinson, *A History of Israel*, 277–78; Montgomery, *A Critical and Exegetical Commentary*, 255–57; Miller and Hayes, *History of Ancient Israel and Judah*, 275; Sweeney, *I & II Kings*, 178.

43 That Jeroboam was dedicating an altar to Yahweh in his kingdom has long been suspected. Simultaneously, connections to a Northwest Semitic pantheon have been proposed. See, for example, Driver, *The Book of Exodus*, 348; Montgomery, *A Critical and Exegetical Commentary*, 255. On the historical, literary, theological, and reader-response problems with Jeroboam's calves and Aaron's calf (Exodus 32), see Nicolas Wyatt, *The Mythic Mind: Essays on Cosmology and Religion in Ugarit and Old Testament Literature*, BibleWorld (London: Equinox, 2005), 72–88.

44 Most histories and commentaries make a note of the traditions, even in the Bible, of earlier religious associations with Bethel and Dan. See the previous note above and Albertz, *A History of Israelite Religion*, 1.143, who contends that Jeroboam was more attuned to the regional formation of religion in the area than David or Solomon had been. See Rocco Scibona ("Betel e le tradizioni cananaiche e orientali dell'Antico Testamento anteriore," *BeO* 196 [1998]: 77–86), who details the biblical citations and adds hypothetical Mesopotamian connections as well; also Zamora García, *Reyes I*, 255–56; Trevor Cochell, "The Religious Establishments of Jeroboam I," *SCJ* 8 (2005): 87–89.

There has been a long debate about whether the territory of Benjamin was a part of Judah or of Israel and, if so, when this was the case.⁴⁵ A notion which is currently popular is that Josiah must have been king of a Judah that included, at the very least, Benjamin. If this notion is a reliable construction, Josiah's attacking the altar at Bethel would not have been an action against Israel/Samerina but an internal affair. It would suggest that the altar at Bethel had continued to be a highly popular alternate temple/worship site to Jerusalem—one inside Josiah's domain that had functioned for at least a decade under his patronage. Kings is very clear, however, that Bethel had been instigated by Jeroboam as a rival temple to Jerusalem and was definitely part of the renegade northern Israel; it is only through scholarly speculation that the area has been considered to have been absorbed into Judah by the time of Josiah.⁴⁶ However, if Finkelstein's notion that the conquest of Benjamin took place under King Jehoash were to be accepted, the altar at Bethel would have been a 200-year old institution within Judah with its own Judahite religious history extending before Josiah and probably its own traditions from before Jeroboam's alleged addition of an altar to the site.

This is not what Kings suggests at all. Unless there was a great deal of particularly poor editing, which is always possible and, in the view of many scholars, always probable, 2 Kgs 23:15–20 is supposed to have taken place in "Israel"/"Samaria" (2 Kgs 23:15, 17, 19).⁴⁷ It is a central foundation for the entire Josiah-as-the-new-David empire builder tradition,⁴⁸ but, if Benjamin had been part of Judah, the passage would clearly not support that assessment. Textually, it shows that Josiah reached beyond his kingdom

---

45   See the concise argument made by Israel Finkelstein that Benjamin was originally the southern region in the independent kingdom of Israel lost to Judah in the reign of Jehoash: Finkelstein, *Forgotten Kingdom*, 46–47. There has been much speculation that Benjamin was the northern portion of Judah at the time of Josiah's reign. See the concise argument from Na'aman, "Josiah and the Kingdom of Judah," in Grabbe, *Good Kings and Bad Kings*, 193–210.

46   The Masoretic Text uniformly includes the Benjaminites at the proclamation of Josiah (2 Chr 34:32), which would place Benjamin under Josiah's rule, though they are notably absent from actually following Josiah's law book. See Myers, *II Chronicles*, 204. Textual emendation to remove the Benjaminites has been fairly standard practice: Japhet, *I & II Chronicles*, 1016; and Klein, *2 Chronicles*, 492.

47   The passage is a quagmire of textual problems and dating conjectures: Gary N. Knoppers, *Two Nations under God: The Deuteronomistic History of Solomon and the Dual Monarchies. Volume 2: The Reign of Jeroboam, the Fall of Israel, and the Reign of Josiah*, HSM 53 (Atlanta: Scholars Press, 1994), 197–207; Barrick, *The King and the Cemeteries*, 46–60; Erik Eynikel, "The Reform of King Josiah 2 Kings 23:1–24," in *Die Septuaginta—Texte, Kontexte, Lebenswelten*, ed. M. Karrer and W. Kraus, WUNT 219 (Tübingen: Mohr Siebeck, 2008), 415–22. Succinctly: Friedrich-Emanuel Focken, "Joschijas Gesetzesschrift," 43.

48   Vincenzo Lopasso, "La riforma di Giosia nel nord," *BeO* 199 (1999): 37–39.

to rectify Yahwistic religion into the adjoining Assyrian province. In this, Josiah retains his literary character as a religious entity. There is no mention in Kings or Chronicles of Josiah militarily (or otherwise) annexing Samerina (read "Israel"), only of his destroying cultic sites and demolishing the images of deities that were not Yahweh.[49] There is always the possibility that the entire Bethel story is a symbolic notation that Jerusalem should be in charge of 'Jewish' religion wherever it is. If so, this would suggest an audience in the diaspora.

The biblical account of Josiah's religious world is fairly consistent. Both Kings and Chronicles concur that Manasseh had been a ferociously idolatrous ruler. Whether one reads the rendition in Kings in which Josiah's grandfather dies an unrepentant apostate to the true deity Yahweh, or whether one opts for the Chronicler's repentant Manasseh, who late in life replicates the cultic changes the Chronicler credits to his father Hezekiah and presages the third edition of this same cultic maneuvering under Josiah, King Amon replicates the religious world of his father's early reign (2 Kgs 21:20-22).

The reality of this religious world in some historical past is not the question here; it is the narrative agreed upon by the authors of Kings and of Chronicles which is questioned. Extended literary adaptations of both renditions of Manasseh's reign continued to be produced in Jewish and Christian traditions, even to the point of making Manasseh and his religious activities demonic.[50] Needless to say, the author of First Esdras, concerned about the proper Passover observance, presents no text on the reduction of the number of deities in Judah. By the time of First Esdras, the religious center of Josiah no longer concerned a pantheon, but only the proper worship of the one deity, Yahweh, thereby reflecting the canonical theology of the Hebrew Bible reflected from early Judaism.[51] For First

---

49 Lopasso, "Riforma," 34-36. Israel Finkelstein suggests that Chronicles does not even imply Josiah expanded territory because that growth was covered already in Hezekiah: Finkelstein, "The Expansion of Judah in II Chronicles: Territorial Legitimation for the Hasmoneans?," ZAW 127 (2015): 688. He sees the entire notion as a late second-century BCE rewrite of the text in Chronicles' text (694).

50 On the continuity of an unrepentant Manasseh, see Lowell K. Handy, "Rehabilitating Manasseh: Remembering King Manasseh in the Persian and Hellenistic Periods," in *Remembering Biblical Figures in the Late Persian and Early Hellenistic Periods: Social Memory and Imagination*, ed. D. V. Edelman and E. Ben Zvi (Oxford: Oxford University Press, 2013), 222-23, 233-34.

51 Dieter Böhler (*1Esdras*, 38-40) discusses the distinction the author of First Esdras delineates between the good, pious Josiah and the sinful Judahites who brought him such sorrow (1 Esd 1:21-22). David Penchansky succinctly notes the tension between the "monotheistic" theology of the Hebrew Bible and biblical texts that refer to those other deities, see Penchansky, *Twilight of the Gods: Polytheism in the Hebrew Bible* (Louisville: Westminster John Knox, 2005), ix-xii.

Esdras, there is no account of Josiah reducing a pantheon and, interestingly, no mention of it. The reference to the earlier works that one could consult might possibly have led the author of First Esdras to infer such an event, but clearly it was of no importance to him. In that work there is no evil cultic material of Asherah, Baal, and host of heaven left from Manasseh and Amon; there is only the worship of Yahweh itself that needs some clarification by Josiah. For Kings and Chronicles, however, the religious world of early Manasseh and of Josiah's father, Amon, was the functioning cult of Josiah's early kingship.

It is safe to argue that modern academics have little idea of how Judah's wealth of deities interacted on either the cultic or mythological levels. Archaeology supplies tantalizingly little physical evidence of the religious world of the time. The gods were understood to have been there, clearly, but what people thought of them is unclear.[52] If there had been shrines and sanctuaries, what remains is of particularly uninformative data as to specific ritual or belief.[53] Clearly, the biblical rendition of 'real' religion is vastly less vibrant than what was practiced at the time.[54]

While modern scholars have devised numerous theories about how Judah, a culture steeped in many deities, might have reconfigured its divine plane into a single functioning deity, actual polytheistic cultures reflect a multitude of theory-frustrating religious traditions relating their own deities' relationships to each other. Two simple examples are useful for consideration. These are from cultures far removed from the ancient Near East, but aspects of a living cultic world should confuse rather than simplify any understanding of Judahite or Israelite gods.

If one were to take a cultural summary of the deities of, say, Aztec religion in a given place and at a given time, it is rather obvious that the populace knew their gods and knew what they stood for, what they represented, what/who they had control over, what could be expected from each, and where and how they were to be worshiped.[55] It is significant

---

52   That there were images of deities is clear but it cannot be argued that there was no polemic against them at all prior to Josiah or Ezekiel, as contended by Robert J. Pfeiffer, "The Polemic against Idolatry in the Old Testament," *JBL* 43 (1924): 229–34. It is also unclear whether or not there were bull images in use in Israel and Judah: Pakkala, "Jeroboam without Bulls," 511–16. There is simply insufficient data for such conclusions.

53   See the survey in Rüdiger Schmitt, "Typology of Iron Age Cult Places," in Albertz and Schmitt, *Family and Household Religion*, 220–44.

54   Renatus Porath, "Dois textos, duas leituras: Um diálogo crítico entre a exegese e a arqueologia," *VS* 13 (2005): 64.

55   Such is the impressive compilation of Bernardino de Sahagún, *Florentine Codex: General History of the Things of New Spain. Part 2: Book One: The Gods*, trans. Arthur J. O. Anderson and Charles E. Dibble, 2nd ed., MSAR 14.2 (Santa Fe: School of American

that by the time de Sahagún recorded these deities and their descriptions, there was known to be a history in which the various deities had changed or had simply been displaced by Catholic decree. What is significant for ancient Judah is that the deities of the Aztecs did not disappear exactly, but, at least in the case of the goddesses, local aspects of the Aztec goddesses—quite distinctive deities at the time of the arrival of the Spanish—became the descriptive representations of the Spanish version of Mary, mother of Jesus.[56] Gods, quite recognizable as individual divinities with their own range of authority and cultic regalia, became transfigured into local Madonnas for regions in Mexico.[57] The theological fact that Mary is a single saint and not a goddess within formal Catholic theology—whatever social scientists might theorize—means that an established pantheon can and has combined characteristics of a number of deities into a single, heavenly Mary. The distinctions of localized saint worship also need to be taken into account as devotees can and do distinguish among the various and sundry Virgin Marys. This particular area of study has provided one comparative social example of how a pantheon devolved into a theoretically/theologically defined single entity. In the case of Aztec religion, the transformation took place in a traumatic conquest of culture by another culture, in which the former infused the latter.

More useful for attempting to understand ancient Judah's deities might well be the study of Buddhist deities in medieval Japan.[58] This religious plurality of deities encompassed a fairly short period of time (±400 years) in a fairly small political state with a myriad of gods, some indigenous and many inherited from a long Buddhist history. Indeed, Chinese Buddhists adopted Indic deities along with Taoist and local Chinese deities, where they underwent a certain degree of transformation, and then carried the deities to Korea where they were again reimagined. Subsequently, they were introduced to Japan where they were redefined and syncretized yet again with native Japanese *kami* traditions.[59] In this relatively short period of time, the myriad Buddhist deities appear in numerous forms (animal,

---

Research, 1970), 1-51. De Sahagún devotes a single chapter of varying lengths to each of the deities that have been explained to him.

56   Joseph Kroger and Patrizia Granziera, *Aztec Goddesses and Christian Madonnas: Images of the Divine in Mexico* (Farnham: Ashgate, 2012), 119-61.

57   Kroger and Granziera, *Aztec Goddesses*, 221-84.

58   For the following, see Bernard Faure, *Gods of Medieval Japan*, Vol. 1: *The Fluid Pantheon* (Honolulu: University of Hawai'i Press, 2016) and *Gods of Medieval Japan*, Vol. 2: *Protectors and Predators* (Honolulu: University of Hawai'i Press, 2016).

59   In addition to Faure's *Gods of Medieval Japan*, Vol. 1, 1-4, for the history behind medieval Japanese Buddhism, see Daigan Matsunaga and Alicia Matsunaga, *Foundation of Japanese Buddhism*, Vol. 1: *The Aristocratic Age* (Los Angeles: Buddhist Books International, 1974), 9-23, and *Foundation of Japanese Buddhism*, Vol. 2: *The Mass*

human, abstract symbolic, utensils, color patterns, astral objects) for any given deity. This plurality allowed devotees to incorporate other deities with similar identifications into any god with like markers. Moreover, deities of the local indigenous cults were widely identified with the politically patronized Buddhist gods, slightly changing the Buddhist deities in the process.[60] The capacity of human beings to easily and quickly adapt notions of the divine world, or laws of socio-economic processes for that matter, are evident from this study of Buddhist spiritual beings. That a similar adaptation in the 200+ years of Judah's cults took place should be considered likely.

The bottom line on considering this pair of parallel cultures is that, with the data currently at our command, scholars at present can only make highly theoretical assessments regarding Judahite religious thought, let alone how the ancients perceived machinations of the mythical world. Three such approaches concerning the deities of Judah/Israel may be quickly surveyed.[61] First, for centuries the various gods mentioned in the Bible were taken by scholars to be random localized primitive objects of worship. It was the default position that the various deities that appear in Israel and Judah alongside Yahweh were 'foreign,' often referred to as "pagan" introductions into an already existing 'monotheistic' Yahwism. In the Bible, baals were understood as a sort of generic fertility/rain/patron deity that referred to any number of local, unrelated, and essentially ahistorical religious entities. The term *ba'al* was simply the title of whatever deity was foremost in any given place.[62]

Movement (Kamakura & Muromachi Periods) (Los Angeles: Buddhist Books International, 1976), 1–10.

60   The relationship between 'Shinto' cultic religion and 'Buddhist' cultic tradition remains a debated issue, not made any easier by the Meiji 'Restoration,' wherein Shinto became the official religion of Japan while still retaining massive amounts of Buddhist ritual and philosophy. See Breen and Teeuwen, *A New History of Shinto*, 7–13, 221–28; *Gods of Medieval Japan*, Vol. 2, 134–36.

61   At times, more than one of these hypotheses appear in a single reconstruction. Note Lewis B. Paton, who manages to have localized indigenous *baals*, foreign deities, and Judahite Yahwism indistinct from Semitic cultures surrounding Judah, as well as a unique morally based religion; these combinations remained common throughout the twentieth century. See Paton, "The Religion of Judah from Josiah to Ezra," *BibW* 11 (1898): 410–12.

62   The assumption of numerous local deities called baal was widely accepted. See, for example, W. A. Hauser, *The Fabulous Gods Denounced in the Bible: Translated from Seldon's "Syrian Deities"* (Philadelphia: Lippincott, 1880), 72, 77 (John Seldon's book was printed in 1613); W. Robertson Smith, *The Religion of the Semites: The Fundamental Institutions* (New York: Schocken, 1972), 93–94, 98–110 (first published in 1891); Johannes Hehn, *Die biblische und die babylonische Gottesidee* (Leipzig: Hinrichs, 1913), 115–16; Lewis B. Paton, "Baal, Beel, Bel," *ERE* 2.283–84.

In the same way, the goddesses Asherah, Astarte, and Anat, all appearing in one way or another in biblical texts, tended to be lumped together under headings like "Great Goddess," "Mother Goddess," or "Fertility Goddess."[63] This approach also led to the improbable notion that, in the ancient world itself, these three goddesses had been confused with each other, or were aspects of the same deity.[64] Aside from the fact that this approach reflected a notion that the ancients were somewhat sloppy about their deities (a notion that academics tend to believe about ancient and modern humans generally), it also reflected a modern male bias about the sole use for a goddess in any case.[65] To a large degree this approach rested on the evolutionary theory of human thought moving from the primitive mytho-poetic, where everything in nature had a spirit or fetish of its own, to the rise of biblical monotheistic thought. This monotheism was posited to have existed already in the temple 'theology' of Solomon, if not earlier, in nomadic 'Judaism.'

The modern embodiment of this first thesis lies in the notion of a unique Hebrew community of [pick your beloved characteristics] egalitarian, pastoral, communal, gender-neutral, proletarian, agricultural, ecologically embedded, mutually helpful, life-affirming, and peaceful (save for annihilating those who don't share their lifestyle) humble folk. That such a community appears nowhere in the biblical texts or in the archaeological excavations appears to have no effect on holders of this message. However, for this branch of scholars, the deities of Baal, Asherah,

---

63 On Asherah, Astarte, and Anat as fertility/mother/great goddess, see Hehn, *Biblische und babylonische*, 106; Helmer Ringgren, *Israelite Religion*, trans. D. E, Green (Philadelphia: Fortress, 1966), 157; William G. Dever, *Recent Archaeological Discoveries and Biblical Research* (Seattle: University of Washington, 1990), 84; Umberto Cassuto, *The Goddess Anath: Canaanite Epics of the Patriarchal Age*, trans. I. Abrahams (Jerusalem: Magnes, 1971), 58; del Olmo Lete, "La religión cananea de los antiguos hebreos," 248-49. The confusion of goddesses is plain enough even from the title of Paton's encyclopedic entry, Paton, "Ashtart (Ashtoreth), Astarte." See discussion by Joan B. Townsend, "The Goddess: Fact, Fallacy and Revitalization Movement," in *Goddesses in Religion and Modern Debate*, ed. Larry W. Hurtado, UMSR 1 (Atlanta: Scholars Press, 1990),182; Steve A. Wiggins, "The Myth of Asherah: Lion Lady and Serpent Goddess," *UF* 23 (1991): 392.

64 Cassuto, *Goddess Anath*, 58; Robert A. Oden, "The Persistence of Canaanite Religion," *BA* 39 (1976): 34-36; David Noel Freedman, "Yahweh of Samaria and His Asherah," *BA* 50 (1987): 246.

65 The reduction to a single mind-set fits nicely with Jungian psychology: Erich Neumann, *The Great Mother: An Analysis of the Archetype*, trans. R. Manheim, Bollingen Series 47 (Princeton: Princeton University Press, 1963), 128, 259. This notion should have ceased long ago, at the very least with the insightful study by JoAnn Hackett, "Can a Sexist Model Liberate Us? Ancient Near Eastern 'Fertility' Goddesses," *JFSR* 5 (1989): 71-75.

and Anat represent the just cause for genocide in revolting against the Canaanites who, at the very least, were militant capitalists, providing for a biblical justification for yet another historical call for genocidal activities among Bible readers. Baal is "political power," Asherah is "political economy," and Anat is "war profit."[66] It is fairly obvious that these designations are twentieth-century social-scientific and political sloganeering phrases. They have little to do with any religious/mythical world that the ancients would recognize. However, if Josiah removed these deities from the mythology/theology/ideology of Judah, it probably had no effect on Judahite royal interest in controlling power, economics, or warfare.[67]

The second approach that is often taken, unlike that which assumes local, primitive spirits, is that there was a marked divide in Judah's religious world. Rural or popular religion held a polytheistic worldview while the monarchy centered in the palace cult had a theological/philosophical/ideological monotheistic tradition throughout the history of Judah, though not necessarily in Israel.[68] In this notion, there is an understanding that the single deity Yahweh conformed to the single ruler (king of Judah) and concentrated all power in a single controlling entity. This allowed the king of Jerusalem to be the privileged vassal of the single deity that ruled the world and the one who carried out the very commands of that single authority.[69]

For Judah and Israel, there was a theological stratum of the population that continually embodied the notion that Yahweh was the only god, or at least the only god that mattered. Some priests, prophets, scribes, and administrators belonged to this royal cult. Usually, this portion of the population is assumed to have been the elite in Jerusalem and is often presumed to have included the scribes and wisdom circles. For the rest of the population, there was popular religion that allowed house rituals,

---

66 Norman K. Gottwald, *The Tribes of Yahweh: A Sociology of the Tribes of Liberated Israel 1250-1050 B.C.E.* (Maryknoll, NY: Orbis, 1979) 694–96; George E. Mendenhall, "The Worship of Baal and Asherah: A Study in the Social Bonding Functions of Religious Systems," in *Biblical and Related Studies Presented to Samuel Iwry*, ed. Ann Kort and Scott Morschauser (Winona Lake, IN: Eisenbrauns, 1985) 157–58.

67 Gottwald, *The Politics of Ancient Israel*, 230, 248.

68 John S. Holladay, Jr., "Religion in Israel and Judah under the Monarchy: An Explicitly Archaeological Approach," in Miller, Hanson, and McBride, *Ancient Israelite Religion*, 268–80. This is not a new idea: Adolphe Lods, *La Religion d'Israël*, HRel (Paris: Librairie Hachette, 1939), 101–2. Nevertheless, it remains popular. See, for example, Bryan D. Bibb, "'Be Mindful, Yah Gracious God': Extra Biblical Evidence and Josiah's Religious Reform," *Koinonia* 12 (2000): 167–68.

69 Concerning patron deities and rulers, see Rocio Da Riva, "Dynastic Gods and Favourite Gods in the Neo-Babylonian Period," in Lanfranchi and Rollinger, *Concepts of Kingship in Antiquity*, 45–61.

superstition, magic, flights of fancy, amusing mythology (perhaps like Baal the mighty, yet simple-minded, action figure), and any number of gods and goddesses.[70] This Great/Small tradition perpetrated a social scientific model that at one point was immensely popular but basically pitted smart social scientists against credulous, uneducated masses.

That a kingdom as small and rural as Judah would have had so clearly a defined division in its religious world seems unlikely. The distinction between rural/popular/small religious tradition and urban/official/great tradition would entail a drastic divide in the populace, with an elite so divorced from the population as to be unrelated and unconcerned with the agricultural people who made up the vast majority of the demography. This is possible, of course, but Judah was not a major political entity. Jerusalem was small and surrounded with barley and wheat fields that made up the overwhelming majority of the economy.[71] Moreover, at the time of Josiah, it is possible that the administration and a royal residence were in Ramat Rahel, while Jerusalem had become primarily a temple town that barely constituted a 'city' even in that time and place.[72]

It is probable that there was no great divide between the 'official' temple religion and that practiced by the general population; daily rituals could carry on without higher authorities, and temple festivals could be entered into by anyone.[73] It was necessarily a continuum of religious practices and beliefs that need not have fitted together neatly for modern academics.[74]

---

70 For ancient Israel and Judah, the popularity of this theory is surveyed in Rainer Albertz, "Introduction," in Albertz and Schmitt, *Family and Household Religion*, 6-8. Albertz concludes that levels of religious belief can be distinguished, but they do function together (16).

71 Oded Borowski, *Agriculture in Iron Age Israel* (Boston: American Schools of Oriental Research, 2002), 163-65.

72 Ann E. Killebrew ("Biblical Jerusalem: An Archaeological Assessment," in Vaughn and Killebrew, *Jerusalem in Bible and Archaeology*, 337-38) concludes that, in the late seventh century, Jerusalem was a major administrative center and definable as a "city," but whether it was the main center of government or mostly a religious center at that time is unclear from the archaeological record. It is less than clear what the status of Jerusalem was at the time of Josiah: Hillel Geva, "Western Jerusalem at the End of the First Temple Period in Light of the Excavations in the Jewish Quarter," in Vaughn and Killebrew, *Jerusalem in Bible and Archaeology*, 208. The status of Ramat Rahel in the time of Josiah remains unknown.

73 The likelihood of a cultural divide between 'urban' (probably a useless term for Judah at the time) and rural culture is minimal if extant; Grabbe, "Sup-urbs or only Hyp-urbs?," 122-23; Spieckermann, "'Yahweh Bless You and Keep You,'" 180.

74 On the unrealistic distinction between elitist urban religious thought and popular rural religious behavior in ancient Judah, see Philip R. Davies, "Urban Religion and Rural Religion," in Stavrakopoulou and Barton, *Religious Diversity in Ancient Israel and Judah*, 114. Although perceived as dealing with foreign "other gods," the

140 Josiah

No doubt the official 'monotheism' of the Josiah narrative was held by some people, though whether it was in practice, and by whom, is unrecoverable. Apparently, it was necessary for the author of Kings that Yahweh and Josiah dwell in the same village (2 Kgs 22:1; 23:6, 9), though the Josiah story makes no particular mention of this. For the Josiah narrative, all of Judah and Israel needs to conform to the 'official' form of Judahite religion.

In the third option, assumed here, taking a more cultural contextual stance, the cultic world of ancient Judah would conform to the wider civilization of the Levant of the first half of the first millennium BCE. This was a territory heavily influenced by a thousand years of Egyptian cultural and intermittent political domination.[75] The Syro-Palestinian world of the early first millennium provides a temple sanctuary floorplan that corresponds to that presented in the biblical texts, cultural parallels for the rituals described in biblical legal texts, the names of the deities that appear in the polemical statements about apostasy in ancient Judah and Israel, as written about by scribes perceiving themselves to be the descendants of Judahites, and texts from which to define cultic personnel. Numerous sacred spaces and domestic religious life permeated the region. A bevy of minor political polities[76] appeared in the wake of Egyptian retreat and before Assyrian expansion. The Josiah narrative concerns itself with cultic sites and a number of deities. The former are generically referenced aside from mentioning Jerusalem and Bethel; the latter are identified in a very restricted manner.

Given that Yahweh would have been the highest divine authority of the Jerusalemite pantheon, it is fair to ask what the other deities were perceived as doing/being/representing in a Judahite religious worldview.[77] Of

---

continuity of people, temple, and king in a cultic world of many deities and their many priests has long been acknowledged by, for example, Beatrice L. Goff, "Syncretism in the Religion of Israel," *JBL* 58 (1939): 152-54.

75 Redford, *Egypt, Canaan, and Israel in Ancient Times*, 76-93, 192-213; Miller and Hayes, *History of Ancient Israel and Judah*, 447-48.

76 By the time of Josiah, it would seem fair to call Judah a 'state' in so far as it was a recognized political entity, even if in a subservient status of Assyria and then Egypt. In other words, the term 'state' is used in a general political manner denoting an observable government (monarchy) of a discernable territory (of which we moderns are decidedly unclear, but Judahites, Phoenicians, Sidonians, Arameans, and certainly Assyrians, and Egyptians would have had their own definitive notions—not likely the same). What they may properly be called before Josiah is not germane here. Megan Bishop Moore and Brad E. Kelle note the quagmire currently drowning scholars in terminology; they opt for "kingdom." See Moore and Kelle, *Biblical History and Israel's Past*, 324. However, that has vastly more anachronistic connotations than the rather generic 'state' or the even more generic 'polity.'

77 Herbert Niehr, "The Rise of YHWH in Judahite and Israelite Religion: Methodological and Religio-Historical Aspects," in *The Triumph of Elohim: From Yahwisms*

the several deities mentioned in the Bible, the goddess Asherah has been the most famously recovered in archaeological finds.[78] Asherah clearly held a place of high importance,[79] if for no other reason than that the *gebirah* appears, at least at times noted in the biblical text, to have been her devotee, if not priestess.[80] In terms of royal hierarchy, Asherah would most likely have been the wife of the ruling deity,[81] in this case Yahweh, which

---

to *Judaisms*, ed. D. V. Edelman (Grand Rapids: Eerdmans, 1995), 54-55 ,71. It needs noting that the Bible itself reflects this polytheism, but uses fairly generic terminology and reflects what is often called "monolatry" (polytheism with an emphasized ruling deity, for all practical purposes). See White, *Yahweh's Council*, 59-144. On Judah's worship as monolatry, see p. 165. On the distinction between monotheism and a pantheon of any kind, see McLaughlin, *Ancient Israelite Religion?*, 87. Monotheism and monolatry remain confusing and conjoined notions in biblical studies; see Hermann Spieckermann, "God and His People: The Concept of Kingship and Cult in the Ancient Near East," in Kratz and Spieckermann, *One God—One Cult—One Nation*, 347; and Matthias Köckert, "YHWH in the Northern and Southern Kingdom," in Kratz and Spieckermann, *One God—One Cult—One Nation*, 387.

78 The el-Qom and 'Ajrud inscriptions were early recognized as referring to a goddess: Ziony Zevit, "The Khirbet el-Qom Inscription Mentioning a Goddess, *BASOR* 255 (1984): 46; Richard J. Pettey, "Asherah: Goddess of Israel?" (PhD diss., Marquette University, 1985), 106, 263, 248-49; Saul M. Olyan, "Problems in the History of the Cult of the Priesthood in Ancient Israel" (PhD diss., Harvard University, 1985), 51-52, 62, 108; John A. Emerton, "New Light on Israelite Religion: The Implications of the Inscriptions from Kuntillet 'Ajrud," *ZAW* 94 (1982): 17-18. For a concise presentation of the Kuntillet 'Ajrud inscription and art interpretations by biblical scholars, see Richter, "Eighth-Century Issues," 334-35.

79 The continuing confusion about who, or what, or if Asherah was in Israel or Judah is aptly summarized in Nicholas Wyatt, "Asherah," *DDD* cols. 187-93; Penchansky, *Twilight of the Gods*, 75-89; John J. Collins, *The Bible after Babel: Historical Criticism in a Postmodern Age* (Grand Rapids: Eerdmans, 2005), 110-20. However, it is clear that Asherah was, in fact, a goddess included in the cultic worlds of Judah and Israel, see Saul M. Olyan, *Asherah and the Cult of Yahweh in Israel*, SBLMS34 (Atlanta: Scholars Press, 1988), 74.

80 On the queen mother as a particularly important court woman, see Phyllis A. Bird, *Missing Persons and Mistaken Identities: Women and Gender in Ancient Israel*, OBT (Minneapolis: Fortress, 1997): 36; on the queen mother as cultic manipulator and worshiper of goddesses, see p. 92. For the queen mother as the second most important person in Judah, see Georg Molin, "Die Stellung der Gebira im Staate Juda," *TZ* 10 (1954): 161. On the relationship between the queen mother and Asherah, see Wyatt, "Royal Religion in Ancient Judah," 75; Lee, "Books of Kings," 166-67; Brewer-Boydston, *Good Queen Mothers, Bad Queen Mothers*, 9-12. Elna K. Solvang surveys the use of the term in *A Woman's Place Is in the House: Royal Women of Judah and their Involvement in the House of David*, JSOTSup 49 (London: Sheffield Academic, 2003), 73-78.

81 Recognized as early as 1949 by William L. Reed, *The Asherah in the Old Testament* (Fort Worth: Texas Christian University, 1949). See also Handy, *Among the Host*, 73-74. Note that Smith (*Early History of God*, 47-54, 202) contends that the biblical and archaeological references to asherah refer to items incorporated into the worship of

would explain certain cryptic inscriptions.[82] As a divine royal queen, Asherah would have been expected to have had parallel importance in the world of deities to that of a mortal queen among humans,[83] with significant influence on the ruling king.[84] This would also explain her worship in the Jerusalem temple dedicated to Yahweh.[85] Clearly, a goddess who was nurturing towards the king, which is one of her roles that appeared in Ugarit, would have been an asset for a king's chapel.[86]

If Manasseh and Amon had been devotees of Asherah, would this have suggested that the wife chosen for Amon should be assumed to have been a devotee too? There is no evidence with which to answer this question, but the influence of the *gebirah* on a ruling king might have been important, one way or another, to the status of Asherah.[87] That she was some kind of tree goddess—a long-standing and popular idea based on little evidence—still has avid support but cannot be sustained with certitude from

---

Yahweh, but are not evidence of a goddess. This view is highly popular among Christian and Jewish scholars, but is unlikely. See William G. Dever, "The Silence of the Text: An Archaeological Commentary on 2 Kings 23," in Coogan, Exum, and Stager, *Scripture and Other Artifacts*, 147, 149–51; Hess, *Israelite Religions*, 73–74.

82 See Zevit's *Religions of Ancient Israel* (389–92, 653–54) on the 'Ajrud inscription and the probability of Asherah in the Yahweh temple in Jerusalem. For a strange conclusion that, in the biblical texts, Asherah somehow refers to the symbol of the goddess without necessarily meaning the goddess and that the Yahweh and his Asherah reflects a trend toward "monotheism," see Brian A. Mastin, "Yahweh's Asherah, Inclusive Monotheism and the Question of Dating," in Day, *In Search of Pre-Exilic Israel*, 345–46. However, Mastin provides a clear survey of the 'Yahweh and his Asherah' debate. For a survey of Asherah in the temple as symbol, see John Day, "Asherah in the Hebrew Bible and Northwest Semitic Literature," *JBL* 105 (1986): 397–404.

83 William G. Dever sets out an extensive rational for understanding Asherah as having been understood as the divine spouse of Yahweh in Dever, *Did God Have a Wife? Archaeology and Folk Religion in Ancient Israel* (Grand Rapids: Eerdmans, 2005): 176–251.

84 Molin, "Stellung der Gebira," 161; Niels-Erik Andreasen, "The Role of the Queen Mother in Israelite Society," *CBQ* 45 (1983): 182, 191.

85 Francesca Stavrakopoulou, "'Popular' Religion and 'Official' Religion: Practice, Perception, Portrayal," in Stavrakopoulou and Barton, *Religious Diversity in Ancient Israel and Judah*, 42.

86 Ivan Engnell, *Studies in Divine Kingship in the Ancient Near East* (Oxford: Basil Blackwell, 1967), 170.

87 Solvang, *A Woman's Place is in the House*, 84–85; Zafrira Ben-Barak, "The Status and Right of the *Gebira*," *JBL* 110 (1991): 33–34. See also Nadav Na'aman ("Queen Mothers and Ancestors Cult in Judah in the First Temple Period," in Kottsieper, Schmitt and Wöhrle, *Berührungspunkte*, 481–84), who also notes the possibility of queen mothers usurping the king's authority in religious matters (483–84), though the direct dependence on Hittite practice seems unlikely (486).

any biblical or archaeological text.⁸⁸ It can be argued that Asherah would have held a position as the spouse/consort/co-ruler with Yahweh prior to the reduction of the pantheon. There is no evidence, however slim, for Asherah acting in any divine council in the Bible.⁸⁹ It cannot seriously be argued that there was a "May Pole" celebration in her worship.⁹⁰ The evidence of so-called Asherah figures remains a debate in the field.⁹¹ There is very little evidence outside of the Bible proper for Asherah as a goddess in Judah, and none that is certain from Yehud onward, which has led some to argue that Josiah's reform must have removed Asherah from the temple for good.⁹² However, it seems safe to presume Asherah devotees really existed in ancient Judah, most probably in the temple in Jerusalem at the time of Josiah.⁹³

---

88   Confusion in interpreting inscriptions from the time period needs to be acknowledged: Steve A. Wiggins, *A Reassessment of 'Asherah': A Study According to the Textual Sources of the First Two Millenia B.C.E.*, AOAT 235 (Kevelaer: Butzon & Berker; Neukirchener-Vluyn: Neukirchener, 1993), 171, 180; Judith M. Hadley, *The Cult of Asherah in Ancient Israel and Judah: Evidence for a Hebrew Goddess* (Cambridge: University of Cambridge Press, 2000), 105. On Asherah as a sacred tree, see the latter, p. 153. Samuel Horsley was already arguing for a goddess instead of a grove of trees in 1844: Horsley, *Biblical Criticism on the First Fourteen Historical Books of the Old Testament: Also, On the First Nine Prophetical Books*, 2nd ed. (London: Longman, Brown, Green & Longmans, 1844), 1.222. The sacred tree theory, keeping Yahweh celibate and alone, continues to have enthusiastic support, e.g., André Lemaire, *The Birth of Monotheism: The Rise and Disappearance of Yahwism*, ed. and trans. J. Meinhardt (Washington, DC: Biblical Archaeology Society, 2007), 59–62.

89   White, *Yahweh's Council*, 176–77, there being no evidence of any goddess actually acting as a deity in the Hebrew Bible.

90   See Neumann (*Great Mother*, 259), who makes use of earlier equations of Asherah with groves and poles and Greek alleged parallels, none of which can be confirmed. Second Sam 5:24 as proof of an Israelite tree "numinous-feminine character" tradition is good imagination, but poor scholarship: Day, "Asherah," *ABD* 1.485–86. Other aspects ascribed to Asherah also remain questionable; Wiggins, "Myth of Asherah," 392. Nonetheless, Asherah as a tree remains popular, e.g., Wyatt, "Royal Religion," 76. On Ištar and the tree, see Porter, *Trees, Kings, and Politics: Studies in Assyrian Iconography*, OBO 197 (Fribourg: Academic; Göttingen: Vandenhoeck & Ruprecht, 2003), 18.

91   Melody D. Knowles succinctly presents both the hypothesis of Asherah worship and the debate about figurines considered to be Asherah. See Knowles, *Centrality Practiced: Jerusalem in the Religious Practice of Yehud and the Diaspora in the Persian Period*, ABS 16 (Atlanta: Society of Biblical Literature, 2006), 73–74.

92   Uehlinger, "Was There a Cult Reform under King Josiah?," 307.

93   See early studies by Olyan, *Asherah and the Cult*; Richard J. Pettey, "Asherah: Goddess of Israel?,"; Baruch Margalit, "The Meaning and Significance of Asherah," *VT* 40 (1990): 284–85.

The other deity that appears repeatedly in the biblical texts as being popular in Israel and in Judah is the god Baal.[94] The deity appears to have been a long-established object of veneration in the region of Judah. Therefore, it is perfectly reasonable that Judahites or Israelites would have adopted the god with the territory.[95] In the Ugaritic texts, Baal is the storm deity and protagonist of the known mythological texts. Since Yahweh clearly has storm-god qualities, it is not certain why one would need another storm deity, though Yahweh and the god El are clearly equated in biblical texts. It is reasonable to assume that some conflation of Yahweh and Baal took place in Judah itself but the author of Kings clearly imagined no such connection. The northern kingdom of Israel is presented in the biblical narratives as always recognizing Baal as an independent deity.[96] Aside from the possible rain-bringing aspect of the deity,[97] Baal might well have been an entertaining figure of the divine world, as he was in Ugarit a few centuries prior to Judah's existence.[98] In any case, Baal is presented as a recurring fixture of the Jerusalem religious world, even if it is not as clear how significant Baal was for Judah in the biblical record in contrast to Asherah.[99] The cult of Baal in Judah is not as clearly evidenced in archaeology in comparison to that of Asherah; however, the use of the

---

94 Brian Paul Irwin notes that the Hebrew Scriptures avoid using 'Baal' as a divine name, though at times that is clearly what is intended: Irwin, "Baal and Yahweh in the Old Testament: A Fresh Examination of the Biblical and Extra-biblical Data" (PhD diss., Toronto School of Theology, 1999), 223–26.

95 Frank E. Eakin, Jr., "Yahwism and Baalism before the Exile," *JBL* 84 (1965): 409.

96 See Dany Nocquet, *Le "livret noir de Baal": La polémique contre le dieu Baal dans la Bible hébraïque et l'ancien Israël*, ARech (Geneva: Labor et Fides, 2004), 340–41; Smith, *Early History of God*, 47, 65–79. Irwin ("Baal and Yahweh," 146–50) argues for Ahab, at least, seeing Baal and Yahweh as manifestations of the same deity (whether Jezebel did or not is much less clear), but Elijah definitely did not. See also Rainer Albertz ("Monotheism and Violence: How to Handle a Dangerous Biblical Tradition," in *The Land of Israel in Bible, History, and Theology: Studies in Honour of Ed Noort*, ed. J. van Ruiten and J. C. de Vos, VTSup 124 [Leiden: Brill, 2009], 379–80), who sees Ahab creating a dualistic cult with Yahweh and Baal. Neither cultic position is retrievable from text or archaeology.

97 So clearly mocked in 1 Kgs 18. See Sweeney, *I & II Kings*, 226–30; Zamora García, *Reyes I*, 348–60. Norman C. Habel assumes ancient Judah (Israel) continually promoted Yahweh as superior to Baal, see Habel, *Yahweh Versus Baal: A Conflict of Religious Cultures* (New York: Bookman, 1964), 64, 66, 87, 102. Irwin ("Baal and Yahweh," 152–53) notes that Israel (the Northern Kingdom) is mocked at the same time.

98 In *Among the Host* (102), I emphasize the entertainment value of this deity, who is strong and virile but as dumb as a rock. Baal's myths are entertaining narratives that would not be nearly so interesting were the god victorious *and* intelligent.

99 Nocquet, "Livret noir de Baal," 34–35. In the Bible, Baal is always opposed to Yahweh (26). We have no evidence about what the religious life on the ground was in ancient Judah.

name *ba'al* in personal names was common.[100] If there had been a real concern about not affirming deities other than Yahweh, *ba'al* would not have been such a prominent naming element, even in its generic definition.

The trio of divinities for which Solomon is credited as establishing the worship of, and for which Josiah is praised for abolishing, are all declared to be foreign to Judah (1 Kgs 11:5, 7, 11; 2 Kgs 23:13).[101] This is interesting only in so far as Asherah and Baal are not declared foreign abominations in the Josiah narratives. It is unlikely that any of the three were 'foreign' in the sense that the Judahites or Israelites would not have assumed they were their own deities. In the narrative, all three are presented as patron deities of lands which were important to David's empire, and the reason underlying their mention in the Solomonic passage might be related to demonstrating Solomon's empire and its corroding influence.[102] It is possible that some form of agreement among these political entities was enshrined in a physical religious item; this would still have made them part of the religious world of Judah.

Certainly, for the Josiah narrative, it was important to mention that they had been in Jerusalem since the foundation of the religious cult there by Solomon, the founder of the temple. This makes the literary Josiah a redeemer of a Jerusalem cult prior to the apostasy of Solomon and, hence, closer to David. The most amazing aspect of this trio is simply that it is not a significantly longer list of deities. Solomon is recorded as having 1,000 paramours, each wanting her own deity, though his Egyptian wife settles for her own house. Historically, one would have expected the small village of Solomon's Jerusalem to have exploded into the religious capital of the ancient Near East (1 Kgs 11:8), but, of course, Kings is denigrating Solomon and applauding Josiah, not recording the historical foundations of religious centers.[103]

Astarte was clearly very popular among the northwest Semitic peoples of the first millennium BCE and the cultures in contact with them, but little is actually known about this goddess.[104] What is ascribed to her

---

100 Albertz and Schmitt, *Family and Household Religion*, 508.

101 Baruch Halpern notes the textual insistence on the foreignness of Solomon's piety, ascribing it to the age of Josiah's reform (or maybe later). See Halpern, *The First Historians*, 154–55.

102 Siegfried Herrmann, *A History of Israel in Old Testament Times*, trans. J. Bowden (Philadelphia: Fortress, 1975), 181–82.

103 It is possible, but not provable, that there is a tradition of reusing this trio of deity references to praise or condemn Solomon; in this, the theory of constant rewriting/retelling/reinventing traditional historical material for new situations is a very compelling one. See Feinman, *Jerusalem Throne Games*, 363, though I would not want to argue a Solomonic origin for the surviving biblical tradition.

104 Handy, *Among the Host*, 108; Nicholas Wyatt, "Astarte," *DDD*, col. 204.

has been derived from Egypt, Mesopotamia, and especially Cyprus and Greece.[105] In Phoenician culture, Astarte appears to have been closely aligned with the royal family, priestesses of royal lineage being common.[106] The Kings passages restrict this goddess to the cult of Sidon (1 Kgs 11:5; 2 Kgs 23:14). It is interesting that the former passage defines her as a goddess while the latter simply as an abomination. By designating a single city for Astarte, the biblical author manages to diminish the expansive devotion to this popular Semitic deity. However, here, she was probably originally intended to signify the Phoenicians in general by using the city name Sidon, whether in a real cultic setting or one of the literary invention of the author of Kings.[107] As a temptation for Solomon, Sidon suits the purpose better than Tyre. As the first of the named deities, Astarte signals the cosmopolitan grandeur of Solomon and its heinous companion: religious infidelity. However, as a popular goddess of the first millennium BCE in the Levant, there is no reason to assume that Astarte's place in the religious world of Judah was not historical.

Chemosh is well known from the Mesha stele as the patron deity of Moab.[108] It has been established that Chemosh also existed in other pantheons but with no clearly discerned characteristics.[109] This suggests that Chemosh might have held a minor position in an extended pantheon in Jerusalem. However, it would seem to be more reasonable to assume that the inclusion of this deity in the stories of Solomon and of Josiah was connected to the region of Moab. In the storyline of Kings, Solomon presumably inherited the regions controlled by David, including Moab (2 Sam 8:2;

---

105 Budin ("Reconsideration," 96–97) notes that Greeks tended to equate many of the Near Eastern goddesses with Aphrodite (134), so Aphrodite is probably not a good choice for attempting to define the role of Astarte in the Levantine states. See Wyatt, "Astarte," cols. 205–2.

106 Budin, "Reconsideration," 108.

107 Solomon's reign, as a biblical event, was much more related to Tyre than Sidon, Tyre's "mother city." The use of Sidon rather than Tyre in these parallel polemics no doubt relates to the presentation of Sidon and Tyre respectively in the Hebrew Bible; Sidon is routinely presented as a problem for Judah/Israel while Tyre is Solomon's (even David's) beneficent helper. See Scott B. Noegel, "Phoenicia, Phoenicians," in Arnold and Williamson, *Dictionary of the Old Testament*, 794–95.

108 See Helmer Ringgren (*Religions of the Ancient Near East*, trans. J. Sturdy [Philadelphia: Westminster, 1973], 139), who notes that Chemosh appears in the inscription as a warrior deity. However, it should be remembered that any patron god could fight for their territory.

109 Gerald L. Mattingly, "Chemosh," *ABD* 1.896; Hans-Peter Müller, "Chemosh," *DDD¹* cols. 357–58.

1 Kgs 4:21, 24),[110] so a marriage to a Moabite wife would not have been unusual in a world in which marriages were political activities.[111]

While it is claimed in the narrative about Solomon's apostasy that his Moabite wife/wives (1 Kgs 11:1) encouraged him to build them a holy place for Chemosh (1 Kgs 11:7), it is at least plausible that the insistence that there was a Chemosh sanctuary in Jerusalem was intended to represent Judah's conquest of Moab. In that case, a patron deity of a subjected people sitting in subservience to Yahweh, God of Judah, would serve a nice political function. The historicity of idols/symbols/objects representing Chemosh in Jerusalem would not be necessary for the literary allusion to be effective. Whether or not David ever actually defeated Moab, it is clear that Omri had done so, and a shift of a Moabite loss to Israel being remembered as a Davidic event would not be unusual in biblical historiography.[112] In composing the narrative of Josiah it would have been easy for the author of Kings to add this deity to the material on Solomon and Josiah, whether or not the god had anything to do with either of their reigns. If there had been a remembrance of a deity Chemosh in the region, even in the latest period of Judah's existence, its Moabite connection may well have caused it to be included in a literary production.[113]

On the god Milcom (2 Kgs 23:14; Molech in 1 Kgs 11:7) there is precious little known. Like b'l, the Semitic root mlk provides the possibility of a title for deities or humans, as well as for divine names.[114] Despite lengthy studies, this god, whose worship in Jerusalem according to the biblical narratives was established by Solomon and removed by Josiah, remains pretty much a mystery.[115] Even the form of the deity's name remains a puzzle.[116]

---

110 As literary history, this territory of David works well; as reflection of historical events, it leaves much to be desired. See Garbini, *History and Ideology*, 25–26.

111 Solvang, *A Woman's Place is in the House*, 23–30, 46–50.

112 Garbini (*History and Ideology*, 33–37) lays out the hazy historiography even of the Omri-Mesha relationship.

113 Smith (*Early History of God*, 183, 190) hypothesizes that Chemosh as a deity in Judah may have appeared very late in the monarchic period.

114 However, it is sometimes argued that the Josianic passage in 2 Kgs 23:10 reflects a ritual and not a deity; see, for example, Monroe, "A 'Holiness' Substratum in the Deuteronomistic Account of Josiah's Reform," 49–50. This would still leave the deity of 2 Kgs 23:13.

115 A pair of scholarly works will provide sufficient information to grasp the academic sense of a lack of information: George C. Heider, *The Cult of Molek: A Reassessment*, JSOTSup 43 (Sheffield: JSOT Press, 1985); John Day, *Molech: A God of Human Sacrifice in the Old Testament*, UCOP 41 (Cambridge: Cambridge University Press, 1989). However, Ringgren's conclusion that, aside from being mentioned in the Bible as the god of the Ammonites, nothing is known about "Milkom" remains essentially accurate: Ringgren, *Religions*, 139.

116 Heider, *Cult*, 223–28, 401.

It is possible, however unlikely, that Milcom/Molech had been seen as an aspect of Yahweh or at one time had been worshiped in the Jerusalem temple.[117] It is usually assumed that the sacrifice of children was performed near Jerusalem and that there was a shrine for Milcom/Melek/Molech established by Solomon for his Ammonite wife.[118] Like Moab, Ammon is recorded as having been subjected to David (2 Sam 12:26–31). A deity *MLK* is well attested for the region in the second millennium, less so for the first; but, again, it is quite reasonable for it to have been worshiped in Judah.[119]

Of the other deities reported to have been removed by Josiah, it can now be stated with assurance that the astral deities (2 Kgs 23:5) were not Mesopotamian imports but reflect Syro-Palestinian traditions that predate Josiah.[120] A long academic tradition had held that the worship of the heavens or deities as astral objects displayed Assyrian influence on Judah's Yahwism.[121] It would seem that the heavenly bodies carried significance across the ancient Near East, with Syria-Palestine enjoying regional adaptations of celestial worship that was common religious practice from Egypt through Mesopotamia.[122] The actual worship of heavenly bodies already seems to have been an ancient misunderstanding of the Mesopotamian associations of certain celestial objects with particular deities; the stars were not the gods.[123] Whether Jerusalem's roof-top worship/viewing sites had any relation to astral objects or were connected in any way to

---

117 Brian B. Schmidt, "Canaanite Magic vs. Israelite Religion: Deuteronomy 18 and the Taxonomy of Taboo," in *Magic and Ritual in the Ancient World*, ed. P. Mirecki and M. Meyer, RGRW 141 (Leiden: Brill, 2002), 249–50.

118 The practice appears in the Bible to horrify and may or may not reflect actual religious ritual. See Joseph J. Azize, "Was There Regular Child Sacrifice in Phoenicia and Carthage?," in *Gilgameš and the World of Assyria: Proceedings of the Conference Held at Mandelbaum House, The University of Sydney, 21-23 July 2004*, ed. J. Azize and N. Weeks, ANESSup 21 (Leuven: Peeters, 2007), 186, 201. The sacrifice of children is long assumed to have been a regular practice in Israel. See Smith, *Early History*, 180.

119 The debate is surveyed in McKay, *Religion in Judah*, 39–41. On Classical allusions to such a deity, see Azize, "Was There Regular Child Sacrifice in Phoenicia and Carthage?," 187

120 K. Lawson Younger, "Another Look at an Aramaic Astral Bowl," *JNES* 71 (2012): 229. See, already, McKay, *Religion in Judah*, 36, 42–43.

121 Östreicher, *Deuteronomische Grundgesetz* 42; Albertz, *History of Israelite Religion*, 133, 189; Theodoor Christiaan Vriezen, *The Religion of Ancient Israel*, trans. H. Hoskins (Philadelphia: Westminster, 1967), 228; Lemaire, *Birth of Monotheism*, 97.

122 Younger, "Another Look," 228–30.

123 Francesca Rochberg, "'The Stars Their Likenesses': Perspectives on the Relation between Celestial Bodies and Gods in Ancient Mesopotamia," in *What Is a God? Anthropomorphic and Non-Anthropomorphic Aspects of Deity in Ancient Mesopotamia*, ed. B. N. Porter, TCBAI 2 (Winona Lake, IN: Eisenbrauns, 2009), 90.

Assyrian practice is impossible to determine; the text (2 Kgs 23:12) simply refers to altars and accuses Ahaz of this impropriety.[124]

Exactly what the horses and chariots of Shemesh ["the sun"] were in the temple of Yahweh is not really clear (2 Kgs 23:11). Nevertheless, the importance of Josiah having removed them is explicitly denoted as important in Kings.[125] In fact, Shemesh is mentioned three times in the short notices about the removal of non-Yahwistic gods (2 Kgs 23:5, 11), equal to the number of mentions of Asherah. It is possible that these were cultic paraphernalia of a sun deity, as many commentators have assumed.[126] The sun deity was unquestionably popular throughout the ancient Near East, Syria-Palestine included.[127] On the other hand, Hebrew names do not suggest parents vested in a popular solar cult.[128] Theories have been posited that the horses and chariots were functioning units used to transport images of Yahweh or other gods in procession,[129] an event not otherwise hinted at in biblical literature. It has also been posited that the horses and chariot were figurines kept in the temple as images of Shemesh's conveyance through the skies and the netherworld.[130] Solar worship in Jerusalem would have made good sense in the time of Josiah as being part and parcel of Syro-Palestinian religious tradition. Yet, it is also possible that these items formed the war wagon of a militant Yahweh[131] that, retrospectively, were envisioned as the paraphernalia of another deity by the later author of Kings. This, however, would depend on different presumptions from seeing Shemesh-worship as an integral part of Yahweh's pantheon.[132]

---

124 Albertz (*History of Israelite Religion*, 189) connects the rooftop altars to Assyrio-Babylonian astral worship, but note that there is no real reason to connect a rooftop shrine to any particular deity. See Gray, *I & II Kings*, 737.

125 Sweeney, *I & II Kings*, 441.

126 See Montgomery, *Critical and Exegetical Commentary*, 532-33; Gray, *I & II Kings*, 736-37; McKay, *Religion in Judah*, 32. All see some relation to Assyrian solar cultic items. Dever ("Silence of the Text," 152-53) would see the sun deity to be of indigenous Syro-Palestinian origin.

127 A long tradition of Egyptian solar figures in Judah extended to the end of Judean independence; Keel and Uehlinger, *Gods and Goddesses*, 350-54; Handy, *Among the Host*, 107-8 and n63; Karel van der Toorn, "Sun," *ABD* 6.238.

128 See Albertz and Schmitt, *Family and Household Religion*, 508, where only a single Hebrew Shamash name appears.

129 For citations, see McKay, *Religion in Judah*, 32, 99, nn30-31; Glagolev et al., "Chetviortaia Kniga Tsarstv," 570-71.

130 Hobbs, *2 Kings*, 334-35; Dearman, *Religion and Culture*, 90.

131 Peter M. Sensenig emphasizes the military connotations of chariots and the existence of chariots of the sun in Josiah's destruction of idols: Sensenig, "Chariots on Fire," 75-77 and 77n40. The warrior aspect of Yahweh in Josiah's cult changes is also noted in Keel and Uehlinger, *Gods, Goddesses*, 345, 347.

132 Smith (*Early History of God*, 154-58) sees the solar aspects of various deities

150   Josiah

The removal of Yareah's officiants (2 Kgs 23:5) is as close as the text comes to calling the moon a deity.[133] However, the reference confirms what is known from archaeological excavations.[134] There was considerable interest in the moon; whether it was seen as a full-bodied deity, as in Ugarit, or simply as the lunar orb is less clear. This comment in Kings is clearly intended to be reference to yet another non-god worshiped as a deity in addition to Yahweh. Given the ubiquity of lunar gods in the surrounding regions, it would be unlikely that a pantheon in Judah would not have included Yareah among its cultic deities.[135]

Undoubtedly, there were many gods of various importance worshiped by both the elite and the general populace in Judah.[136] There is no list of the gods Josiah was assumed to have removed. For most of them, we have no record and no material remains which identify them. Of those we know something about, their divine position or cultic significance remains unclear. The textual evidence of the surrounding cultures tells us much more about these biblical references than the biblical texts themselves do.

A classic example would be the god Resheph.[137] While it is obvious that the biblical writers knew the deity and presumed it was connected to Yahweh, it appears in a fairly demonized form by the Yahweh-worshiping authors.[138] In the one passage where Resheph is presented as actually doing something (Hab 3:5), he is a subservient military figure to the advancing Yahweh.[139] There is ample reason to assume that Resheph was accepted as

---

incorporated into a vision of Yahweh as having solar deity characteristics and cultic objects. With the chariots in the Josiah passage he distinguishes between Shemesh and Yahweh (82).

133 For the few references in the Hebrew Bible to the moon as a god, see McKay, *Religion in Judah*, 53, and Handy, *Among the Host*, 110n78.

134 Crescent symbols, corresponding to those in the surrounding regions, also appear in Judah and Israel. See Keel and Uehlinger, *Gods, Goddesses*, 298–300; Albertz, "Personal Names," 370–71.

135 Mario Provera, "Il culto lunare nella tradizione biblica e profana," *BeO* 33 (1993): 65–68.

136 Some are pretty obscure guesses on the part of modern scholars, like Uzza. For a survey, see Becking, "The Enigmatic Garden of Uzza," 384, 388.

137 Plenty of material remains from the ancient Near East to produce hefty studies on the deity. See William J. Fulco, *The Canaanite God Reshep*, AOS 8 (New Haven: American Oriental Society, 1976); Edward Lipinski, *Resheph: A Syro-Canaanite Deity*, OLA 181; StPhon 19 (Louvain: Peeters, 2009); Maciej Münnich, *The God Resheph in the Ancient Near East*, ORA 11 (Tübingen: Mohr Siebeck, 2013).

138 Paolo Xella, "Resheph," *DDD* cols. 1328–30. Münnich (*The God Resheph*, 222) sees Resheph as demoted to a demon. Fulco (*The Canaanite God Reshep*, 60–61) opts for Israelite "demythologizing" of the Canaanite deity.

139 Lipinski, *Resheph*, 243; Haak, *Habakkuk*, 90–91. However, this passage may intend Resheph as a natural phenomenon (Xella, "Resheph," col. 1329) or merely

a warrior deity suitable to propitiate in times of war, though this may not have been his primary area of expertise.[140] It was long held that Resheph was a 'chthonic' deity, which would explain his presentation as a demon in the biblical passages.[141] However, Resheph's status as a healing deity would explain his long-term following and, along with a military aspect, would explain a connection to the dead and the netherworld without making his worshipers seem predisposed to an obsession with death.[142] Of course, gods who brought plague and disease could also heal these diseases, which made them valuable.[143] On Cyprus, it should be noted, Resheph was more revered for metallurgy.[144] In the cult of Judah, Resheph should be understood in a much more positive light than the way the biblical texts portray the god.[145] It is simply not clear exactly how the god served in a pantheon or in popular belief. It is enough to note here that Josiah's reign began in a polytheistic society and probably ended in one as well.[146]

If Resheph may have been a minor deity in the area, the "Queen of Heaven," who appears in Jeremiah as a popular and central goddess to the general populace (Jer 7:18; 44:17), appears to have had a wide following.[147] According to Jeremiah, the Queen of Heaven was worshiped throughout

---

as a poetic use of mythology by someone who no longer believed in the deity itself (Haak, *Habakkuk*, 147-48).

140 For more on this, see William Kelly Simpson, "Reshep in Egypt," *Or* 29 (1960): 71; Diethelm Conrad, "Der Gott Reschef," *ZAW* 83 (1971): 161 (whatever Resheph's relation to a sun deity); Smith, *Early History*, 81.

141 Xella, "Resheph," cols. 1329-30; Fulco, *The Canaanite God Reshep*, 69; Klaas Spronk, *Beatific Afterlife in Ancient Israel and in the Ancient Near East*, AOAT 219 (Kevelaer: Butzon & Bercker; Neukirchen-Vluyn: Neukirchener, 1986), 140, 157, 261. Resheph's equation with Nergal on deity lists has colored the underworld aspect, though Nergal was clearly responsible for a number of useful aspects of human life as well; Conrad, "Der Gott Reschef," 160. Lipinski (*Resheph*) and Münnich (*The God Resheph*, 265) find no reason to associate Resheph with the netherworld at all.

142 Along with Resheph's military prowess, Egyptians also called upon the god for recovery from diseases and the god was popular for a lengthy period of time: Stadelmann, *Syrisch-Palästinensische Gottheiten*, 56-76; Fulco, *The Canaanite God Reshep*, 1-32.

143 Conrad, "Der Gott Reschef," 158.

144 Stephanie Dalley, "Near Eastern Patron Deities of Mining and Smelting in the Late Bronze and Early Iron Ages," in *Report of the Department of Antiquities, Cyprus, 1987* (Nicosia: Zavallis, 1987): 62-65.

145 The deity Resheph was clearly popular in the third and second millennia BCE but then tends to have few remains outside of Cyprus. On Resheph as a protective deity, see Lipinski, *Resheph*, 226-27. On disease and war, see Münnich, *God Resheph*, 265.

146 Susan Ackerman points out that Josiah's 'reform' was neither a turning point nor a very major incident in Judah's religious life: Ackerman, *Under Every Green Tree: Popular Religion in Sixth-Century Judah*, HSM 46 (Atlanta: Scholars, 1992): 213.

147 Philip C. Schmitz ("Queen of Heaven," *ABD* 5.586-87) notes the variety of vocalization used to distort the title.

the settlements of Judah and was carried into the displaced residences of Judahites who fled to Egypt. There is frustratingly little that can be determined about the goddess. Clearly, she was central to the religious life of women in Judah.[148] She was not a goddess whose worship was perceived to belong to the temple in Jerusalem.[149] And her devotees baked something in her honor, whether a sacrifice or festal food is unclear. Since the deity is unnamed in the Josiah narratives, it is uncertain whether or not Josiah had anything to do with the allegation in the book of Jeremiah concerning the termination of her worship.[150] Exactly what goddess was meant by the title remains unknown.[151] Astarte, Anat, Asherah, and Ištar have all been proposed.[152]

Interestingly, nowhere in the entire Josianic material is the topic of angels broached. It is not certain that messenger deities would have concerned the authors. Messenger gods in earlier texts from the Levant have no independent volition and so pose no problem for a cult that claimed allegiance to a single ruling deity. Moreover, it is clear that the angels that appear in the biblical texts represent for the authors the presence of Yahweh among human beings.[153] That messenger deities were a common aspect of Syro-Palestinian cosmology well before and after the existence of Judah or Israel should assure us that they were known during that time period as well.[154] As messenger deities, the "angels" would have

---

148 Karel J. H. Vriezen, "Cakes and Figurines: Related Women's Cultic Offerings in Ancient Israel?," in *On Reading Prophetic Texts: Gender-Specific and Related Studies in Memory of Fokkelien van Dijk-Hemmes*, ed. B. Becking and M. Dijkstra, BibIntS 18 (Leiden: Brill, 1996), 252–53; Zevit (*Religions of Ancient Israel*, 554–55) stresses that the devotion to this deity was home-based and probably orchestrated by the males of the family.

149 But perhaps was conceived as needing a temple in other places. See Cornelis Houtman, "Queen of Heaven," DDD col. 1281. Margaret Barker identifies the Queen of Heaven with Wisdom and with Asherah, thereby having Josiah remove wisdom from the Jerusalemite temple in which she was worshiped. See Barker, *The Hidden Tradition of the Kingdom of God* (London: SPCK, 2007), 34.

150 Eliya Mohol presupposes that Jer 44:18 alludes to Josiah's removal of "other" gods, but this is a theory, however popular. See Mohol, "Prophetic and Popular Responses to Religious Pluralism in Jeremiah 44," UBSJ 6, no. 2 (2009): 35–36.

151 Houtman ("Queen," cols. 1279–80) demonstrates both the spread and popularity of the title for goddesses across the ancient Near East.

152 Ackerman (*Under Every Green Tree*, 8–34), Houtman ("Queen," cols. 1280–81), and Schmitz ("Queen of Heaven," 587) cover the academic discussion. Of course, some see her as Wisdom personified/deified, e.g., Barker, *Hidden Tradition*, 34, 123.

153 Handy, *Among the Host*, 159–63; Meier, "Granting God," 203.

154 Jesus-Luis Cunchillos, "Étude philogique de *mal'ak*: Perspectives sur la *mal'ak* de la divinité dans la Bible hébraïqe," in *Congress Volume: Vienna, 1980*, ed. J. A. Emerton, VTSup 32 (Leiden: Brill, 1981), 50; Handy, *Among the Host*, 151–52.

been denizens of the heavenly realm in the time of Josiah, not demoted deities after his theological revision or aspects of Zoroastrianism during the era of Yehud, as previously posited.[155] As part of the divine world, the existence of angels was no doubt taken for granted. However, they play no part in the narratives of Josiah and may be considered of little to no importance to the authors for their vision of Josiah.

Every temple, shrine, and sacred site would have had some personnel. For the present purposes, it suffices to say that any officiating which was being carried out at an altar in a temple or sanctuary would have been undertaken by someone authorized to perform the appropriate ritual in a proper manner. The existence of priests throughout Judah was a staple of the religious world of Josiah.[156] That Josiah is credited with removing vast numbers of them may or may not reflect reality, but the reference certainly reflects a religious world that employed a large number of priests of various levels of competence and notoriety. The restrictions on who could perform priestly activities, which are presumed because of Josiah's reduction of acceptable priests, may well reflect priestly infighting of the Persian period.[157] Late traditions in both the northern and southern cultic establishments "remembered" Aaron as the founder of the proper ritual.[158] Nonetheless, Judah would have contained a lively and diverse priesthood at a number of religious locations.

Josiah is credited with removing the *komer*, *qedeshim*, and the *qedeshoth* (2 Kgs 23:5, 7). Since these positions are presented as wicked and sinful, tradition has converted what appear to be simple terms designating holy-site personnel into people engaged in behavior deemed illicit by the commentators.[159] The terms would have defined some level of priest or sacred personnel that could probably have been found at any shrine, sanctuary,

---

155 Jesus Luis Cunchillos, *Cuando los angeles eran dioses* (Salamanca: Universidad Pontificia, 1976), 158-59; Vriezen, *The Religion of Ancient Israel*, 268, 273.

156 Grabbe provides a concise discussion of priests in Judah/Israel as reflected in the Bible and contextualized in the ancient Levant: Grabbe, *Priests, Prophets, Diviners, Sages*, 57-62.

157 Joseph Blenkinsopp, *Judaism: The First Phase: The Place of Ezra and Nehemiah in the Origins of Judaism* (Grand Rapids: Eerdmans, 2009), 149.

158 Gary N. Knoppers, *Jews and Samaritans: The Origins and History of Their Early Relations* (Oxford: Oxford University Press, 2013), 192.

159 The behavior is presented in 2 Macc 6:4 to define the very evil behavior of Antiochus IV and his cronies in the temple itself: Marie-Theres Wacker, "'Kultprostitution' im Alten Israel? Forschungsmythen, Spuren, Thesen," in *Tempelprostitution im Altertum: Faten und Fiktionen*, ed. T. S. Scheer, ÖSAW 6 (Berlin: Antike, 2009), 68-69. Here, it is rendered precisely to show how foreign such activity is to the Jerusalem temple and that it is *not* part of temple ritual. On the literary background of the Maccabees passage, see Jonathan A. Goldstein, *II Maccabees: A New Translation with Introduction and Commentary*, AB41A (Garden City: Doubleday, 1983), 274-75.

or temple. *Komer* was simply a common Semitic term for 'priest' (Aramaic *kumra'*, Akkadian *kumru*) that became in Biblical Hebrew usage the means of designating priests of the wrong cult.[160] Whether this meant they were of the wrong deity or of non-Levitical genealogy, or just incompetent officiates, is neither clear nor terribly relevant for the narrative. It might be fair to translate the term 'idolatrous priest' in context, since the Bible is attempting to denigrate them, but, in Josiah's world, they would have just been 'priests.'[161]

The *qedešim* and *qedešoth* have been cited as proof of officially sanctioned prostitution not only in the 'fertility' cult of Canaan but in the temple in Jerusalem as well.[162] That later generations of scholars decided that the "holy/sacred ones" were male and female prostitutes is clearly a 'modern' fancy.[163] Despite the common translation of these terms as variations of 'male cult prostitute' and 'female cult prostitute,' there is no reason to assume that *qedeš* meant anything other than one set aside for serving the cult site or deity.[164] It would be better to translate the terms 'holy man' and 'holy woman.' Undoubtedly, they were cultic personnel, but it is there where knowledge about them ends.[165] Cult prostitution is undocumented for Judah.[166]

---

160 Cogan and Tadmor, *II Kings*, 285-56; Sweeney, *I & II Kings*, 447; Hardmeier ("King Josiah in the Climax of the Deuteronomic History," 154, 157) uses "foreign priests."

161 Edelman, "Cultic Sites," 86-87. Gray (*I & II Kings*, 730) uses "priests." Hobbs (*2 Kings*, 328), Cogan and Tadmor (*II Kings*, 278-79), and Sweeney (*I & II Kings*, 436) all use a form of "idolatrous priests." Laffey (*First and Second Kings*, 158) opts for "pseudo-priests."

162 Beatrice A. Brooks, "Fertility Cult Functionaries in the Old Testament," *JBL* 60 (1941): 235.

163 The defining of these obscure terms has produced a vast literature. The following supply references to this scholarship: Budin, "Reconsideration," 102-4; Tikva Frymer-Kensky, *In the Wake of the Goddess: Women, Culture, and the Biblical Transformation of Pagan Myth* (New York: Free Press, 1992) 200-202. This interpretation remains highly popular: van der Toorn, *From Her Cradle to Her Grave*, 102-10. In addition, see the comment on van der Toorn's position in Phyllis A. Bird, "The End of Male Cult Prostitutes: A Literary-Historical and Sociological Analysis of Hebrew *qadeš/qedešim*," in Emerton, *Congress Volume Cambridge 1995*, 38-39n5. However, the actual practice in Judah is slightly more obscure than merely ambiguous: Sweeney, *I & II Kings*, 447.

164 Wacker ("Kultprostitution," 70-71) notes the ambiguity of what was intended in the 2 Kgs 23:7 passage and the possibility that this was a reference to the cult of Asherah, whatever that may have meant to the author.

165 Zevit, *Religions of Ancient Israel*, 463; Bird, "End of Male Prostitutes," 44-46.

166 Bird, *Missing Persons*, 96-97; Wacker, "Kultprostitution," 80-81. However, note van der Toorn, *From Her Cradle to Her Grave*, 109.

Josiah is also credited in Kings with removing from the land a series of quasi-religious personnel, spiritual beings, and ritual objects that need not have been related to any religious site (2 Kgs 23:24).[167] The *obot* were for a long period of time considered to be witches, but for several centuries most scholars have dismissed this association.[168] The usual translation is simply "medium"—one who contacts the spirits of the dead.[169] The *yidd'onim* are even less understood. Often the term is loosely translated and understood to mean 'wizards,' the male counterpart to the female 'mediums,' but perhaps it refers to 'knowledgeable spirits' that are not ghosts and, by extension, to those who consult them.[170] Since the other two items mentioned in the list of four are known to have been figures of deities, or spirits, or maybe just family totems, they were solid objects that could be moved or destroyed physically. The former pair, if humans, were not necessarily connected to any religious site but could easily have been known to the public as people to consult for access to ghosts and ephemeral denizens of the spirit-world. However, it could possibly have meant that Josiah managed to remove ghosts and spirits from Judah. In any case, all four are claimed to have been removed by Josiah from the entirety of Judah. All of these items together suggest that there were a lot of private images of supernatural creatures and beliefs in spiritual beings among the populace in Josiah's time.[171] For the author of the tale of their removal, there is an intention to reflect the reduction of venues for discerning occult knowledge. Huldah's presence in the Josianic narrative establishes male and female prophets as legitimate channels of divine speech. The elimination of mediums and their spirits or ghosts also removes the potential to consult other persons.[172] For understanding religious traditions at the time, this is sufficient.

---

167 Schmidt ("Canaanite Magic," 250–55) lists several "magic" practitioners that he notes do not appear in pre-exilic prophetic texts and are condemned as foreign imports by the biblical texts, while noting that, at times, the extra-biblical evidence suggests that they are neither foreign nor absent from the time of Judah and Israel.

168 Reginald Scot insists these were ventriloquists who traded on the gullible. See Scot, *The Discoverie of Witchcraft* (London: John Rodker, 1930; repr. New York: Dover, 1972), 72 [originally published 1584].

169 The *oboth* in fact appear to be the ghosts themselves. However, it has usually been taken to refer to necromancers who call up and inquire of ghosts, as well as to the ghosts themselves; see, for example, Hamori, *Women's Divination in Biblical Literature*, 105–10; Gray, *I & II Kings*, 707; Sweeney, *I & II Kings*, 450.

170 Bird, "End of Male Prostitutes," 65; Hamori, *Women's Divination in Biblical Literature*, 110. Or, see Scot, *Discoverie*, 217. Scot refers to the "soothsayer," or one who tells the future by means of a spirit (Scot assumes they also are con artists).

171 Or, in short, Judah was part of Syro-Palestine, including idols and images of supernatural beings. See Lewis, "Syro-Palestinian Iconography," 71.

172 Attempts to undermine or remove rival seers by banishing or demeaning

Beyond the mentioned items in the stories about Josiah, there would have been magic. In addition to the numerous references to magic in the Bible itself, this would have included the many amulets that have been discovered.[173] Certainly, magic in the ancient Mediterranean and Near East relied on the belief that entities beyond the physical world could be coaxed, cajoled, or threatened into doing the will of the individual engaged in magical practices. The extent to which legerdemain concerned anyone in bureaucratic positions is unknown; divination, however, seems to have been deemed by the biblical authors as the sole realm of Yahweh and his priesthood, whatever the actual practice entailed.

In the end, there is no reason to assume that the basic religious world of Judah changed significantly under the rule of Josiah. Even the biblical texts purporting to reflect the religious activities of both the elite and the general populace before and after Josiah demonstrate no sense that anything had changed. The narratives of Josiah's 'reform,' like those invented for the biblical narrative concerning other 'reforming kings,' present a nice vision of an ideal for the Second Temple but do not reflect the religious world of the time of Josiah. Josiah's religious world looked pretty much like that of his grandfather and that of his sons.

---

their professions is not unheard of. See Kathryn Gin Lum (*Damned Nation: Hell in America from the Revolution to Reconstruction* [Oxford: Oxford University Press, 2014], 131–12), who cites such a move by Tenskwatawa, a Shawnee prophet, who uses Christian sermonizing to discredit his rivals. On the related question of demeaning rival prophets, see the survey in Hans Harald Mallau, "Las diversas reacciones al mensaje profético en Israel y su Ambiente: Una contribución al problema de los profetas verdaderos y los profetas falsos," *CTh* 2 (1972): 42–55.

173 Spieckermann, "'Yahweh Bless You and Keep You,'" 174, 181.

CHAPTER SIX
TIME FOR A CHANGE (ER, UM, A 'REFORM')?

Josiah reigned, it is written, for 31 years in Jerusalem (2 Kgs 22:1; 2 Chr 34:1). This is a fairly long period of time for a reign in the ancient world. Since it was generally considered a good activity for rulers to make repairs and assorted other changes in their religious establishments in their domains in those days,[1] it would have been surprising indeed if Josiah did not 'tinker' with the temple in Jerusalem as well as whatever religious establishments the rest of Judah contained at the time of his reign. The biblical text provides two rather different motivations for Josiah's 'reform,' a term which is now generally used in relation to Josiah's religious activities but which was made popular in the West in connection with his status as an example for Protestants in the European Reformation.[2] The book of Kings is quite clear that Josiah set off to rectify all things religious and cultic upon hearing a reading of the lost-and-found scroll of instructions [*torah*] in his eighteenth year (2 Kgs 22:3, 8).[3] Chronicles, on the other hand, insists that Josiah had been a pious child, devoted to cleaning up the religious world of Judah for his deity Yahweh since his minority.[4] Eight years

---

1   Dandamayev, "State and Temple in Babylonia in the First Millennium B.C.," in Lipinski, *State and Temple Economy in the Ancient Near East*, 591; Tammi J. Schneider, *An Introduction to Ancient Mesopotamian Religion* (Grand Rapids: Eerdmans, 2011), 68, noting the almost (when not) divine status of Mesopotamian kings that would allow them to 'tinker' with the cult as they wished; Engnell, *Studies in Divine Kingship in the Ancient Near East*, 155, 117–21. Spieckermann ("God and His People: The Concept of Kingship and Cult in the Ancient Near East," in Kratz and Spieckermann, *One God — One Cult — One Nation*, 347–51) emphasizes the importance of the religious world for Mesopotamian rulers and their connection to the cult, its ritual, *and* building edifices for it.
2   See Bradshaw, "David or Josiah? Old Testament Kings as Exemplars in Edwardian Religious Polemic," in Gordon, *Protestant History and Identity in Sixteenth-Century Europe*, 77–90. Indeed, John Donne and his contemporaries equated Josiah with the Protestant kings battling Rome (Babylon) and Spain (Egypt), see James, *Poets, Players, and Preachers*, 213.
3   Sweeney (*I & II Kings*, 443) assumes the Chronicler has more accurate chronological data. Klein (*2 Chronicles*, 492, 495) more reasonably sees the Chronicler adapting Kings to make the egregious period of Josiah's apostasy less damning.
4   Chronicle's rendition of the early years of Josiah's reign are probably

after he came to the throne, he had become a devotee of Yahweh in the manner of his ancestor, David, and four years later, he began a conscious program of eliminating any local shrines, sanctuaries, and cultic implements which were not dedicated to Yahweh, removing anything related to Asherahs and Baals, and any other religious images (2 Chr 34:3). In Chronicles, he does not come across the scroll of Moses[5] until four years into his religious cleansing program (2 Chr 34:8); in this way, the Chronicler demonstrates that Josiah was pious at a much younger age than had been portrayed in Kings.[6] The importance of the centralization of Yahweh's cult is more emphatic in the Chronicler than in Kings.[7] The intention of both renditions of Josiah's devotion to Yahweh is to display a religious awakening and a change of religious orientation; in neither case is it related to any international politics.[8] It ought to be clear that the two biblical

---

inventions of the Chronicler, see Lester L. Grabbe, "The Kingdom of Judah from Sennacherib's Invasion to the Fall of Jerusalem: If We Had only the Bible...," in Grabbe, *Good Kings and Bad King*, 115. The Chronicler's image of Josiah as a pious child has been popular in the renditions of some historians, e.g., Pfeiffer, *Old Testament History*, 372–73. Nonetheless, the image of Josiah in Chronicles has been a boon for religious leaders seeking good biblical children to use as role models; consider the sermon "Josiah" by Joseph Hammond, *The Boys and Girls of the Bible: Sermons to Children and Adults*, Volume 1: Old Testament (London: Skeffington & Son, 1898), 265–66, or, for religious storybooks for very young children, Mervin Marquardt, *Good Little King Josiah*, Arch Books (St. Louis: Concordia, 1978), 4, 10 [unpaginated].

5   It needs to be emphasized that Chronicles makes a much greater effort than Kings to connect the scroll to Moses. This begins with its first mention (2 Chr 34:14), where Moses is named as the source—a connection not made in Kings at that point or anywhere else until the summation statement (2 Kgs 23:25), see Japhet, *I & II Chronicles*, 1030. It has been common for scholars of biblical law simply to assume the connection of Josiah's Deuteronomy with Moses. See, for example, Patrick, *Old Testament Law*, 98–99.

6   The contention that the scroll of Moses had nothing to do with Josiah's 'reform' is an old and established scholarly notion. See, for example, Östreicher, *Das deuteronomische Grundgesetz*, 40.

7   Yong Ho Jeon, *Impeccable Solomon? A Study of Solomon's Faults in Chronicles* (Eugene, OR: Pickwick, 2013), 194.

8   A cause still accepted mostly by religiously motivated readers: Bibb, "'Be Mindful, Yah Gracious God,'" 157. Note that Lynn Tatum contends that any social changes at the end of the seventh century were due to something other than religion, but not to Assyrian nationalism, and no doubt ought to conform to a sociological model of "secondary state collapse." See Lynn Tatum, "Jerusalem in Conflict: The Evidence for the Seventh-Century B.C.E. Religious Struggle over Jerusalem," in Vaughn and Killebrew, *Jerusalem in Bible and Archaeology*, 292–94, 305. However, our data is miniscule and written texts insist it *was* religious, so one must begin by dismissing the written data for other popular theoretical adaptations.

narratives of Josiah's cultic interferences are not based on any historical archives that could be or were consulted.⁹

The account in Kings is fairly straightforward: Josiah was having repairs carried out on the Jerusalem temple. There is nothing in the text at this juncture about religious changes other than building work by the king on a palace chapel.¹⁰ It was the duty of a good king to at least profess to keep cultic centers of state importance in good repair.¹¹ As with all good kings, Josiah had a chain of command so he was not involved directly in the construction. Indeed, as he was not the founder of the temple, a position the book of Kings delegates to Solomon, Josiah would have no hands-on dealings with the actual repair work.¹² The high priest Hilkiah finds a scroll in the temple, hands it to the scribe Shaphan who reads it and then, as an addendum to his report to King Josiah, reads the scroll to Josiah. It

---

9   Porath ("Dois textos, duas leituras," 66) notes the problem with attempting to derive historical facts out of two differing stories, both of which reflect a later era. The lack of data for reconstructing historical events has long been noted. See, for example, Adam C. Welch, *The Work of the Chronicler: Its Purpose and Its Date*, Schweich Lectures 1938 (London: Oxford University Press, 1939), 121. Jules Francis Gomes (*The Sanctuary of Bethel and the Configurations of Israelite Identity*, BZAW 368 [Berlin: de Gruyter, 2006], 49) accurately notes that there is a paucity of evidence for Josiah's reforms.

10   Lods, *La Religion d'Israël*, 93; Ringgren, *Israelite Religion*, 211; Gösta W. Ahlström, "Administration of the State in Canaan and Ancient Israel," in Sasson, *Civilizations of the Ancient Near East*, 1.595. It has long been observed that the Jerusalem temple was, according to the construction narrative in Kings, an out-building of the palace (1 Kings 5–7). If the time given for the construction of the various buildings matters in terms of either duration or the order of construction, the temple was of less importance to Solomon than his own lavish housing and that of his Egyptian wife (1 Kgs 7:8); Gösta W. Ahlström, *Royal Administration and National Religion in Ancient Palestine*, SHANE 1 (Leiden: Brill, 1982), 34.

11   Assyrian kings proudly record their temple reconstruction, though claims of recreating ancient temple plans were rarer than claims to making improvements. See Jamie Novotny, "'I Did Not Alter the Site Where That Temple Stood': Thoughts on Esarhaddon's Rebuilding of the Assur Temple," *JCS* 66 (2014): 108; Schneider, *Introduction*, 68. Indeed, some early scholars argued that Jerusalem's temple had not been repaired since Joash demonstrated the "wickedness and idolatry" of the intervening kings, e.g., Gray, *Christian Workers' Commentary*, 193.

12   As opposed to kings as founders of temples. See Arvid S. Kapelrud, "Temple Building, a Task for Gods and Kings," in *God and His Friends in the Old Testament* (Oslo: Universitetsforlaget, 1979), 56–62. Ritual actions by rulers at temple dedications, foundation-laying, and construction are reasonable, but actual construction work by kings is unlikely. For more on this, see Handy, "Historical Probability and the Narrative of Josiah's Reform in 2 Kings," in Holloway and Handy, *The Pitcher Is Broken*, 266–67. That Assyrian kings memorialized their temple repairs, however, even as laborers, is well known. See Porter, *Trees, Kings, and Politics*, 47–58.

might be significant that the story as told in Kings does not make the finding of the scroll a part of the temple repairs. In other words, this is not a book found hidden away in the walls of the sanctuary; it is only something Hilkiah hands to Shaphan since he is there on other business anyway. It is the content of this scroll that produces King Josiah's desire to make major changes to the religion of Jerusalem and Judah.

Other, more political events have been posited as the cause of Josiah's sudden and drastic religious changes to Judah's culture. One of the stranger arguments for Josiah making a great religious reform stems from the inclusion of Herodotus' record of the Scythian invasions into a history of Israel.[13] In this rendition, the vast sweep of Scythians through Assyria, Babylonia, Phoenicia, and Philistia, with no perceptible serious opposition, convinced young King Josiah that the gods of Assyria, Babylonia, the Phoenician cities, and Philistia were helpless against these invaders; therefore, he turned to Yahweh for help. As all other deities had proven themselves to be useless as patron deities, only Yahweh should be worshiped and trusted. In this decision, Josiah had the confidence of a party of Jerusalemites devoted to prophetic interference and a 'Yahweh-alone' mentality. The danger of the situation, it was claimed, caused the general population of Judah to listen to Zephaniah and Jeremiah and accept Josiah's solution.[14] That the Scythian invasion at the time of Josiah was a popular historical event in biblical studies well into the twentieth century allowed scholars to use this traumatic and sudden catastrophe to explain the background for Josiah's drastic action against the religion he had known for all of his life.[15] The certainty of such an invasion has become greatly weakened in the past half-century,[16] though it continues to appear in both scholarly and popular histories of Josiah's reign.[17] Nonetheless,

---

13   Graetz, *History of the Jews*, 287–88. See also Lewis B. Paton, "The Religion of Judah from Josiah to Ezra," *BibW* 11 (1898): 412–15; Aleksandr Aleksandrovich Glagolev et al., "Chetvertaia Kniga Tsarstv," in Lopukhin, *Tolkovaia Biblia*, 2.566. Stanley (*Lectures*, 432–33) suggested the Scythians were left out by the biblical authors simply because they were swiftly recording the demise of the kingdom.

14   See the rousing depiction in Geikie, *Old Testament Characters*, 389–92 (391 for public reaction).

15   Adolphe Lods, *The Prophets and the Rise of Judaism*, trans. S. Hooke (London: Kegal Paul, Trench, Trubner, 1937), 142.

16   Redford (*Egypt, Canaan, and Israel in Ancient Times*, 438–41) surveys the pros and cons of a Scythian swoop through the Levant at the time of Josiah. Williams ("The Date of Zephaniah," 80–81) observes that there is no evidence for a Scythian invasion of Palestine itself. See also Na'aman, "Josiah and the Kingdom of Judah," in Grabbe, *Good Kings and Bad Kings*, 213.

17   See, among others, Robinson, *History of Israel*, 416–17; Geo Widengren, "The Persians," in *Peoples of Old Testament Times*, ed. D. J. Wiseman (Oxford: Clarendon, 1973), 315; B. S. J. Isserlin, *The Israelites* (Minneapolis: Fortress, 2001), 89; Norman

Josiah is presented as paying off the Scythians with a huge treasure as tribute before enthroning Yahweh as the sole deity in Judah.[18] For Graetz, the two most effective influences on Josiah in this cultic reaction to the Scythian invasion were the prophet Jeremiah and the finding of the book of Deuteronomy. Thus, Josiah was moved to action by prophetic proclamation (Jeremiah gets prime of place, but Zephaniah and Huldah are credited with support) and by a scroll claimed by the high priest Hilkiah to have been of hoary antiquity and written by the authoritative Moses.[19]

Since the middle of the twentieth century, the notion that Josiah was reacting to the decline of the Assyrian Empire as a catalyst for the great religious changes he made throughout Jerusalem, Judah, and, more significantly, Israel has become a more popular theory.[20] After Ashurbanipal's spectacular reign, Assyria crumbled, apparently through a combination of poor Assyrian leadership and a capable alliance of Medes and Babylonians.[21] According to this theory, Josiah rises up as a viable ruler who takes Samerina from the disintegrating Assyria and proceeds to demolish any religious activity not carried out in Jerusalem in devotion to Yahweh. Assyria, unmentioned in the entire renditions of Josiah's cultic activities in either Kings or Chronicles, becomes the major motive for Josiah.

Gelb, *Kings of the Jews: The Origins of the Jewish Nation* (Philadelphia: Jewish Publication Society of America, 2010), 131. Note that some scholars mention the Scythians, but are careful not to connect them directly with Judah or Josiah. Among highly respected scholars who include the Scythian invasion as a major Judean event in the time of Josiah are Miller and Hayes, *History of Ancient Israel and Judah*, 450, 454.

18 Graetz, *History of the Jews*, 288. This sort of made sense since Herodotus records the Egyptian king Psamtik as having paid off the Scythians (*Hist.* 1.105).

19 Another short-lived theory that caught scholars' attention early in the twentieth century involved Josiah's reaction to an Arabian-Israelite war that made an argument for the existence of "North Arabian" deities in Jerusalem's temple, e.g., Thomas Kelly Cheyne, *The Decline and Fall of the Kingdom of Judah* (London: Black, 1908), 22–25. The Ras Shamra tablets have demonstrated rather conclusively that the deities need not have originated in Arabia.

20 Generally dated from the article by Cross and Freedman, "Josiah's Revolt against Assyria," 56–58, the notion predates the article. Robinson (*History of Israel*, 419) restricts only part of the temple reforms to ridding it of Assyrian additions; see also Noth, *The History of Israel*. Cross and Freedman's Assyrian response theory was widely dispersed through general histories of ancient Israel: Bright, *History of Israel*, 295; George Wishart Anderson, *The History and Religion of Israel*, NCBOT (Oxford: Oxford University Press, 1966), 124.

21 Herrmann (*History of Israel*, 263–65) presents a concise rendition of the international relations at the time. Sarah C. Melville ("A New Look at the End of the Assyrian Empire," in Galil, Geller, and Millard, *Homeland and Exile*, 179–201) posits a failure by Assyria to consider the need for defensive strategy, expending all its military strategies on offensive warfare.

Usually it is posited that Assyria left a vacuum of power that Josiah moved into to fill. Other scenarios have been suggested, however, including the unlikely theory that Assyria itself was supportive of Josiah's expansion.[22] Again, the theory is proposed that the scroll of Deuteronomy was found, written, or rough-drafted to be the blueprint for the wholesale reformulation of the Jerusalemite cult, purporting that this would return the religious establishment to that which it had been before the apparent corruption by Assyrian imperialism.[23] Deuteronomy has been heavily understood as a treaty between Josiah's Judah and Yahweh and promoted as Josiah's rendition of an Assyrian treaty document superseded by Yahweh.[24] This now unlikely scenario of Deuteronomy being somehow a text written in parallel to Assyrian treaties is, at best, seen to have produced a post-Josianic document.[25] In any event, it is difficult to discern any Assyrian context for Deuteronomy.[26] However, the Judahite anti-Assyrian cultic

---

22 Bright (*A History of Israel*, 294–95) and Isserlin (*The Israelites*, 90) assume Josiah expanded Judah into collapsed Samerina territory of the Assyrian Empire. In *Ancient Israel*, 2nd ed., Development of Western Civilization (Ithaca, NY: Cornell University Press, 1960), 94, Harry M. Orlinsky suggests Assyrian knowledge.

23 Fishbane (*Biblical Interpretation*, 34–35) sees a vast, and newly mentioned, scribal interest in religious matters.

24 Weinfeld (*Deuteronomy and the Deuteronomic School*, 58–81) presents an extensive argument for the Assyrian treaty form in Deuteronomy. However, on the 'treaty formulation' and the problem of using it for dating biblical texts, see Birgit Christiansen and Elena Devecchi, "Die hethitischen Vasallenverträge und die biblische Bundeskonzeption," *BN* 156 (2013): 67–82.

25 Voluminous literature on dating the 'treaty' can be found elsewhere, but see Rintje Frankena, "The Vassal-Treaties of Esarhaddon and the Dating of Deuteronomy," *OtSt* 14 (1965): 152–53. The very notion that Deuteronomy had a form-critical construction was dubious from the beginning; it has phrases (and curses) that can be compared to suzerainty treaties, but the entire form of the book lies outside any treaty form. A starting point for Deuteronomy as a Josianic 'treaty' may be dated to George E. Mendenhall, "Covenant Forms in Israelite Tradition," *BA* 17 (1954): 50–76. Even extensive attempts to parallel Assyrian treaty texts with chapters of Deuteronomy are fairly forced; see, for example, Levinson, "Die neuassyrischen Ursprünge der Kanonformel in Deuteronomium 13,1," in Beyerle, Graupner, and Rüterswörden, *Viele Wege zu dem Einenung in der Moderne*, 41–53. Later attempts to specify the date of Deuteronomy by these treaties to the time of Josiah have been unsuccessful, as the generic formula has too long a history and the contents of Deuteronomy are not terribly relevant to dating it. See the extensive study by Markus Zehnder, "Building on Stone? Deuteronomy and Esarhaddon's Loyalty Oaths (Part One): Some Preliminary Observations," *BBR* 19 (2009): 341–74; idem, "Building on Stone? Deuteronomy and Esarhaddon's Loyalty Oaths (Part 2): Some Additional Observations," *BBR* 19 (2009): 511–35; Juha Pakkala, "The Date of the Oldest Edition of Deuteronomy," *ZAW* 121 (2009): 400.

26 Carly L. Crouch, *Israel and the Assyrians: Deuteronomy, the Succession Treaty of*

reform has been suggested to have been an adaptation of Assyrian cultic activity toward Babylon.²⁷

None of this happened, of course.²⁸ The reasons why Josiah's religious activities as presented in Kings and, to a lesser extent, Chronicles are unlikely to have happened in the late seventh century preclude the likelihood that this particular religious ideal predated the Persian takeover.²⁹ Some temple manipulation by Josiah undoubtedly took place. What this involved cannot be recovered from the biblical texts.³⁰ It is quite possible that Hezekiah's literary narrative of a 'reform,' which explodes in importance and extent from Kings to Chronicles,³¹ derived solely from simple royal tinkering with the accouterments of the Jerusalem temple; namely, for reasons unknown, he had the antiquated stick-figure designated in the text as Moses' brazen serpent removed.³² Maybe it had corroded, maybe it was broken, maybe Hezekiah did not know it had any connotation with Moses; a bronze snake in ancient Syria-Palestine would not automatically bring Moses to mind unless the magical story of Num 21:6–9 was indeed a local legend.³³ Maybe this action on the part of Hezekiah did not happen

---

Esarhaddon, and the Nature of Subversion, SBLANEM 8 (Atlanta: Society of Biblical Literature, 2014), 183.

27 Martin Arneth, "Die antiassyrische Reform Josias von Juda: Überlegungen zur Komposition und Intention von 2 Reg 23,4–15," ZABR 7 (2001): 209–15. Assyria's demolition of Babylon is not reflected in the less extensive damage recorded for Israel. See Brinkman, *Prelude to Empire*, 102, 67–68.

28 One always needs to remember that the religious world of the Hebrew Bible and the religion of ancient Judah (or Israel) have little in common and a history of Josiah's religious world should actually avoid the biblical texts, were that possible. See Spieckermann, "'YHWH Bless You and Keep You,'" 181. It has long been noted that even if such an event as ascribed to Josiah took place, it was superficial and did not last long. See Toy, "Triumph of Yahwism," 94 [a comment that extends back to the earliest histories of Josiah].

29 Victor Maag ("Erwägungen zur deuteronomischen Kultzentralisation," VT 6 [1956]: 18) asserts that it is the post-exilic Judah that needs a religious change, not Judah in the Josianic era.

30 Incidental items connected by scholars to Josiah's activities yet unmentioned in the narratives should not be attributed to this king; so Étienne Nodet, "On the Biblical 'Hidden' Calendar," ZAW 124 (2012): 583, 592.

31 Welch, *Work of the Chronicler*, 97.

32 "Nehustan" may well be a pejorative pun; what the object actually was or was called is unrecoverable, but it was no doubt related to the wider Canaanite religious world. Gray, *I & II Kings*, 670–71; Sweeney, *I & II Kings*, 403; Lowell K. Handy, "Serpent, Bronze," ABD 5.1117.

33 H. H. Rowley, "Zadok and Nehushtan," JBL 58 (1939): 124–28, 137. The serpent symbol was plentiful throughout the ancient Near East from Egypt to Mesopotamia. It was also prevalent in Syro-Palestinian iconography; see concluding section of Leslie S. Wilson, *The Serpent Symbol in the Ancient Near East*, SJud (Lanham, MD:

at all. It makes no appearance in Chronicles.[34] Of course, the destruction of Nehushtan has been viewed as a misplaced activity of Josiah—a position that is textually unsustainable.[35]

It is highly unlikely that Hezekiah oversaw a religious reformation, though he may have made major changes in religious accouterments as part of a defensive military strategy.[36] The single most probable scenario that was useful in creating a literary cultic reform during the reign of Hezekiah is simply that Hezekiah had no more Judah to govern than Jerusalem.[37] One might note that Kings does not include the removal of Solomon's Jerusalem *bamot* among Hezekiah's accomplishments, even though to do so would have taken only a few simple pen strokes. The exclusion of this allows for the possibility that Josiah was intended to be a 'better' king than Hezekiah in the rendition of Kings simply because Hezekiah does not

---

University Press of America, 2001), 211–16; Lewis, "Syro-Palestinian Iconography and Divine Images," in Walls, *Cult Image and Divine Representation in the Ancient Near East*, 98–99.

34   The Chronicler may have intended it to be included in the unclean filth removed by priests from the temple, handing them to the Levites for disposal (2 Chr 29:5, 16); Klein, *2 Chronicles*, 419. Nehushtan is, nonetheless, conspicuous in its absence from Chronicles.

35   Knauf and Guillaume, *History of Biblical Israel*, 132.

36   I have not changed my mind in the past three decades about Hezekiah not having a cultic reform of the type rendered in the biblical text: Lowell K. Handy, "Hezekiah's Unlikely Reform," *ZAW* 100 (1988): 111–15. However, it does make a certain amount of sense that the removal of local shrines would not have been beneficial in holding the allegiance of the populace against the Assyrians. See Diana V. Edelman, "Hezekiah's Alleged Cultic Centralization," *JSOT* 32 (2008): 427–28. Nevertheless, I would still give the Hezekian loyalists the possibility of having made a run for it at the last possible moment before the siege made it impossible. Hezekiah paid a very large tribute, which, according to the Bible, included stripping the temple of Yahweh, so stripping any other shrines to other deities for the ransom metals does not seem unreasonable. Josette Elayi (*Sennacherib, King of Assyria*, ABS 24 [Atlanta: Society of Biblical Literature, 2018], 79–80) notes the enormity of the payment and the need to turn over temple materials. Knauf and Guillaume (*History of Biblical Israel*, 115) presume that the list of tributes is a hefty exaggeration or a total for the entire Assyrian western campaign.

37   Edelman, "Hezekiah's Alleged Cultic Centralization," 435. However, the equation of Judah with Jerusalem as all that was left to Hezekiah politically or religiously in connection to "centralizing" has been well established in scholarship: Ernest Nicholson, "The Centralization of the Cult in Deuteronomy," *VT* 13 (1963): 386; Lynn Tatum, "Jerusalem in Conflict: The Evidence for the Seventh-Century B.C.E. Religious Struggle over Jerusalem," in Vaughn and Killebrew, *Jerusalem in Bible and Archaeology*, 304. However, Tatum believes Hezekiah was centralizing before his state was "in ruins." This would be true whether Sennacherib was "besieging" or "blockading" Jerusalem. Hezekiah controlled only the city itself. See Elayi, *Sennacherib, King of Assyria*, 76.

correct the evils of the 'bad' Solomon while Josiah does.³⁸ The Chronicler's vision of Hezekiah as the great reformer places the cultic activity amongst a flurry of political and construction activities culminating in the embarrassment of Sennacherib.³⁹

Josiah, in this literary religious endeavor, corrects not only the blandishments of Solomon's last impious years but the additions of the various and sundry "evil" kings of Judah.⁴⁰ But did any of this happen? Who knows? People do strange things, but there are several reasons to doubt that, in the final quarter of seventh-century Judah (let alone Israel), the reforms as described in Kings, Chronicles, or First Esdras would have been religious events to have been put into practice.

To begin with, the reforms instituted by Josiah in Kings and Chronicles are massive reorientations of long-established state-sponsored and social-identity traditions. The Passover that is described in First Esdras is clearly dependent on the text in Chronicles and essentially ignores Kings. Notably, First Esdras does not mention any major cultic shift, only an adaptation or creation of a single feast.⁴¹ First Esdras will not be used as information about a Josianic religious reconstruction since it does not actually record one. Kings and Chronicles, however, portray Josiah as a religious coordinator unlike any before him. It has been argued that the sudden independence from Assyrian overrule caused a massive nationalistic movement of independence. Needless to say, this idea clearly reflects post-Reformation/French Revolution/Liberation euphoria in commentators.⁴²

---

38 Laato (*Josiah and David Redivivas*, 59) sees this as somehow appealing to Israel as a Davidic entity devoid of the corrupting influence of Solomon. This is a somewhat dubious extension on the insightful notion that Solomon does not come out well in the Kings narrative. Solomon's negative presentation by the author of Kings has been well detailed by W. Boyd Barrick, "Loving too Well: The Negative Portrayal of Solomon and the Composition of the King's History," *EstBib* 59 (2001): 419–50.

39 Gary N. Knoppers, "History and Historiography: The Royal Reforms," in *Israel's Past in Present Research: Essays on Ancient Israelite Historiography*, ed. V. P. Long, SBTS 7 (Winona Lake, IN: Eisenbrauns, 1999), 573–74, 576–78.

40 In "'He Erected Altars to the Baal' (2 Kgs 21,3): The Absence of Iconic Objects in Cultic Sites for 'Other Gods' in the Biblical Narrative," *BN* 145 (2010): 31, Shlomo Bahar emphasizes the activities of Josiah that did not appear in Solomon's apostasy in 1 Kgs 11:1–10.

41 Böhler, *1 Esdras*, 33–35.

42 Not to mention the obsession with 'land' in twentieth-century national socialism: Aaron Schart, "Martin Noth: Auf dem Hindergrund der NS-Zeit gelesen," in *Kontexe: Biografische und forschungsgeschichtliche Schnittpunkte der alttestamentlichen Wissenschaft: Festschrift für Hans Jochen Boecker zum 80. Geburtstag*, ed. T. Wagner, D. Vieweger, and K. Erlemann (Neukirchen-Vluyn: Neukirchener, 2008), 248–49. Recent concern for Josiah's nationalism or state-building might also be connected to the

It is highly unlikely that the historical Judah would have noticed a great change in its international status in the last half of the seventh century BCE. Judah had never been incorporated into Assyria, so it would not have had a marked change in either its political or religious identity. While Samerina was, politically and legally, a subdivision within the Assyrian Empire during Josiah's reign, what was going on in the "northern" Yahwistic state as Assyria imploded remains virtually unknown.[43] Clearly, having *been* Assyria for the greater part of a century over more than three generations, it would be difficult for the residents of "Israel" simply to assume they needed to look to Jerusalem for anything: government, sustenance, and least of all religious instruction.[44] It is more likely that Judah had looked to Israel for political and religious ideas; Israel had been a major player in international dealings in the backwater of ancient Near Eastern empires and had existed for longer.[45] This is reflected in the use

---

social science addiction to 'states' in the last two centuries. On the united monarchy and modern Israelite archaeology, see Rolf Rendtorff, "The Jewish Bible and Its Anti-Jewish Interpretation," *CJR* 16 (1983): 13; Neil Asher Silberman, "Archaeology, Ideology, and the Search for David and Solomon," in Vaughn and Killebrew, *Jerusalem in Bible and Archaeology*, 397–403.

43 After surveying the archaeological data, Knoppers (*Jews and Samaritans*, 42–44) concludes that the heartland of Samerina pretty much maintained its own traditions through its Assyrian Empire years. Though it was clearly a product of the Persian period, the Chronicler's speech spoken through Hezekiah (2 Chr 30:6–9) reflects a Judean notion that, when it was a part of Assyria, the religion of Samerina remained essentially Yahwistic and traditional. However, the term used is 'Israel' and not 'Samerina' or 'Assyria' (*Jews and Samaritans*, 85–86, 91–92). Lipschits (*Fall and Rise of Jerusalem*, 2) suggests that the culture of Eber-Nari remained fairly steady throughout the Persian period.

44 As far as Assyria would have been concerned, Samerina would have been Assyria and 'Israelites' would have been Assyrians. See Liverani, *Assyria*, 203–4. Finkelstein (*Forgotten Kingdom*, 139) posits an Israelite centralization project in the early eighth century that would have been the religious base of the Assyrian Samerina.

45 In "The Importance of the Archaeology of the Seventh Century," in Grabbe, *Good Kings and Bad Kings*, 318, 328–29, David A. Warburton argues for a strong monarchical kingdom in Israel; only after Samaria fell to the Assyrians was there a strong monarchy in Judah ('capital' city uncertain) and only a significant one in the seventh century BCE. The reconstruction is highly theoretical, but the relative importance of Judah and Israel for most of the first half of the first millennium BCE rings true. On the different cultural contexts and the relative formation eras of Israel and Judah, see Finkelstein, "State Formation in Israel and Judah," 39–40, 42–43, who also notes the existence of a "small and poor" Jerusalem in the tenth and ninth centuries BCE, not an impressive administrative center. Jerusalem only expanded after Manasseh. See Israel Finkelstein, "The Archaeology of the Days of Manasseh," in Coogan, Exum, and Stager, *Scripture and Other Artifacts*, 177.

of the name "Israel" in Kings and Chronicles.⁴⁶ Certainly, the appearance of "Israel" for Samerina, the name of the Assyrian province that incorporated the core area of the former kingdom of Israel, reflects notions of Judahite wishful thinking about its own previous importance. However, the introduction of the notion of Israel for Judah + Israel probably derives from Persian-Empire Yehud and is then imagined backward into the reign of Josiah.⁴⁷ It would be highly unlikely that, were (the literary) Josiah attempting to assert Judahite independence, he would have looked to material from Samerina for guidance, and clearly, the author of Kings displays an abhorrence for all things cultic and Israelite, such that the notion that a "northern" Israelite document would be used for a major cultic reform in Jerusalem makes no sense either as a literary ploy or a historical event.⁴⁸ Nor would Josiah have been wishing to endear himself or his cult to the Israelites; the wholesale slaughter of the traditional priesthood of the territory would have been genocidal political bullying, and to restrict the murders to the priests (and not the populace) would have left a veritable army of malcontents in the area.

As for Judah in the time of Josiah, it is reasonable to assume it remained under international control.⁴⁹ Certainly under Ashurbanipal it remained

---

46 However, the long-held notion that some thundering herd of refugees, hauling scrolls of Ur-Deuteronomy with them as they fled before the Assyrian army toward Jerusalem, must be abandoned. On the northern origin theory, see Tigay, *Deuteronomy*, xxiii–iv. This theory stands behind Wolfgang Schütte ("Wie wurde Juda israelitisiert?," ZAW 124 [2012]: 62–63, 71), who dates the Judahite use of 'Israel' to the influx of Israelites in 720 BCE, but the Judean adaptation of the name to the post-exilic period (70–71). There is little reason to defend such an emigration of Israelites to Judah: Nadav Na'aman, "Dismissing the Myth of a Flood of Israelite Refugees in the Late Eighth Century BCE," ZAW (126 (2014): 1–14. It has long been known that the exilic book of Ezekiel uses the term 'Israel' for the combined Judahite and Israelite traditions: Walther Zimmerli, *Ezekiel 1*, Hermeneia (Philadelphia: Fortress, 1979), 41–42. Also, the Chronicler makes use of Israelite immigrants to Judah to emphasize the covenant with Jerusalem and the Davidic tradition: Knoppers, "History and Historiography: The Royal Reforms," in Long, *Israel's Past in Present Research*, 575.

47 Nadav Na'aman ("The Israelite-Judahite Struggle for the Patrimony of Ancient Israel," *Bib* 91 [2010]: 21–22) supports the use of Israel by Judah as part and parcel of Josiah's reign; however, the construction of this 'reform' itself should be dated to after the Persian incorporation of Judah. Nonetheless, Na'aman correctly outlines the reasons for Judah to absorb Israel as a designation.

48 Ronald E. Clements ("Deuteronomy and the Jerusalem Cult Tradition," *VT* 15 [1965]: 301, 310) posits Josiah's reform as being the application of northern Levitical tradition to Jerusalem, which he deems "remarkable." Indeed, if such a provenance were known it would be improbable at the very least.

49 Hayes and Hooker (*New Chronology*, 85) state this clearly: "Thus there was no period when Judah enjoyed independence from foreign domination during the reign of Josiah."

a tributary region to the Assyrian Empire, still the power in the region. Ashurbanipal had established an Egyptian ruler in 664 BCE (Psamtik I, Assyrian vassal, King of the West), removing the Nubian dynasty from the Egyptian Delta. Once enthroned, through warfare, family connections, and no doubt Assyrian cooperation, Psamtik I was swiftly able to solidify his position as king of all of northern Egypt and turn his attention to the south, uniting Egypt by 654 BCE.[50] In the same year, he declared himself independent of Assyria but continued Egypt's alliance with Assyria, Ashurbanipal having troubles of his own on the eastern front.[51]

It remains unclear whether Judah, a location of little, if any, strategic importance, remained directly under Assyrian tributary jurisdiction or whether this piece of real estate was ceded to the international control of Psamtik I; Egypt had certainly gained control of the trade and produce of the Phoenician cities of the southern Levant.[52] During the reign of Manasseh, Judah probably found itself having to shift its own allegiances to incorporate the reality of Egyptian pressure or indirect control while maintaining loyalty to Assyria.[53] In any case, Judah would not have envisioned itself as having attained a position much different from that which it had held with Assyria for a century; whether Judah ceased to pay tribute directly to Assyria or was then paying tribute to Egypt would not have changed the impact on the Jerusalem treasury.

The theory that Manasseh or Josiah had been acting as if they had gained total independence from the influence of larger empires makes absolutely no sense in this period. Ashurbanipal was a powerful and commanding king of Assyria well into Josiah's reign. By the time he was engaged in the Elamite War, the region of Judah was not devoid of a powerful and commanding regional authority; Psamtik I was fully established in a united Egypt and exploiting his influence west and east of his home

---

50 Robert K. Ritner argues that Psamtik I is often underestimated by modern historians. See his *The Libyan Anarchy: Inscriptions from Egypt's Third Intermediate Period*, ed. E. Wente, SBLWAW 21 (Atlanta: Society of Biblical Literature, 2009), 8, 575–76. See also Vassilis I. Chrysikopoulos, "The Statue of Padihor, General of the Army of Psammetichus I, at the National Archaeological Museum of Athens," in Kousoulis and Magliveras, *Moving across Borders*, 166.

51 Kenneth A. Kitchen, *The Third Intermediate Period in Egypt (1100-650 BC)*, 2nd ed. (Warminster: Aris & Phillips, 1995), 400–406; Redford, *Egypt, Canaan, and Israel*, 430–33; Lloyd, "The Late Period (664–332 BC)," in Shaw, *The Oxford History of Ancient Egypt*, 380; Yamauchi, *Africa and the Bible*, 140–41, 145.

52 Kitchen, *Third Intermediate Period*, 406–7; Redford, *Egypt, Canaan and Israel*, 434–47. Herbert Niehr ("Die Reform des Jeschija," in Groß, *Jeremia und die deuteronomistische Bewegung*, 43–44) certainly believes Josiah was a vassal to Egypt.

53 Nelson (*Historical Roots of the Old Testament*, 154) succinctly presents the international situation for Judah.

base, including the Levantine coast and *probably* Judah through most of the time of Josiah.⁵⁴ The suggestion that the rulers and advisors of Judah were politically stupid can be made, but the level of ignorance that would have been required to assume Judah was now free from imperial relations is unrealistic.⁵⁵ The international situation in Josiah's early reign was not conducive to setting up an independent polity needing a newly improved 'ancient-traditional' religious cult.⁵⁶

The next problem with the Josianic religious reformulation narratives of Kings and Chronicles is concerned with the argument that this was somehow the reestablishing of some ancient but proper cultic religion for both Judah and Israel. The book of Kings has argued from the beginning that Israel was a breakaway faction from the Davidic royal house of Judah. It should be pointed out that this makes narrative sense of the united (pre) history of the united monarchy that itself is not recorded in this scroll. That Judah and Israel were clearly and transparently understood to be two separate entities with their own political, social, and religious histories is clear in Samuel. In Kings, however, it is repeatedly referenced that Jerusalem and David's royal lineage were the real, honest social kingdom; Israel was a political and religious apostasy. Chronicles, on the other hand, essentially ignores Israel altogether in favor of Judah, the one and only serious Yahwistic land. Concerning the Josiah narratives, both scrolls presuppose that Jerusalem and the proper Davidic-lineage king embody the proper religious tradition for both Judah and Israel.⁵⁷ The political aspect has essentially dropped out of both Josianic histories, if there ever had been one, in favor of the question of proper religious procedure. It is certain that there was a lot of political activity in Yehud, but neither of these renditions of Josiah's reign focuses on politics, internal or external. They

---

54   Bernd Ulrich Schipper, *Israel und Ägyptien in der Königszeit: Die kulturellen Kontexte von Solomo bis zum Fall Jerusalems*, OBO 170 (Freiberg: Univeritätsverlag; Göttingen: Vandenhoeck & Ruprecht, 1999), 230, 235–36, 241; Na'aman ("Josiah and the Kingdom of Judah," in Grabbe, *Good Kings and Bad Kings*, 216) determines that Psamtik I was in control of Judah. Lipschits (*Fall and Rise of Jerusalem*, 24–25) notes that Psamtik I solidified his northern border at the Euphrates, which would mean Israel would have been under his control as well.

55   The assassination of Amon could conceivably be due to such political ignorance, but that also seems unlikely. See Chapter 1, above, on international entanglements proposed as underlying Amon's assassination.

56   Arneth ("Antiassyrische Reform," 216) sees the Judean reform as a reaction to Judah passing from Assyrian control to Egyptian dominance.

57   Knoppers ("'The City Yhwh Has Chosen': The Chronicler's Promotion of Jerusalem in Light of Recent Archaeology," in Vaughn and Killebrew, *Jerusalem in Bible and Archaeology*, 316–21) notes that, in Yehud, Jerusalem's temple would have had rivals, and Chronicles stresses the importance of Jerusalem in the face of alternatives.

focus solely on the religious aspects of this reign that lasted thirty-one years.

'Antiquity' in religious rites and norms was highly prized in the ancient world. This idea is sometimes difficult to grasp in twenty-first century, globalized youth culture. This attitude did not prevent innovation, though it was best if one made changes in religious matters by arguing that they stemmed from a distant past authority, preferably from the divine world. The Josianic reform narratives play this game well. The Josiah story has been constructed with a series of seven recognizable literary formulaic building-blocks of the ancient world that can be outlined as follows (designated here by Parts A to G).

Part A) Things are going along fine, but with a terrible corruption of the proper religious cult and the worship of improper deities. Part B) A proper religious cleric discovers directions from a written text. Part C) Fortunately, the text was biding its time in the very temple in which the populace should be sacrificing. Part D) A legitimate king, who, in Chronicles, is already a pious and devout Yahwist king, recognizes the apostasy the cult has been perpetuating. Part E) This legitimate and humbled king calls to double-check that the gods (that, in both of these cases, is the single god Yahweh) really meant what was in the first material presented to the king as being from the deities. Part F) It is all true, and the legitimate king proclaims that changes will be made to "correct" the religious conditions! Part G) Changes are made by proper cultic personnel, not by the king himself, according to the very word of the ancient and proper religious rites and rules. That is how it reads, but there are several nagging questions concerned with each of these parts.

All aspects of the entire story are known literary tropes. This does not mean that the events happened or that they are fictitious. Unfortunately, real events would be written using these formulas to conform to traditional renditions of such events, and fictitious historiography would be written using these formulas to give the story verisimilitude. Arguments that Josiah's religious changes are standard narrative devices do not, in themselves, demonstrate the material is either based on historically occurring events or that they are entirely literary fictions. In addition, it is not safe to assume that contemporary texts were written as accurate records of real events or that later texts were necessarily inaccurate or false reports.[58] The argument about the possibility of the Josiah narrative

---

58 See Uehlinger, "Was There a Cult Reform under King Josiah? The Case for a Well-Grounded Minimum," in Grabbe, *Good Kings and Bad Kings*, 283, who opts for accepting the possibility of a real event behind the narratives.

reflecting a historical event continues unabated, but without clear 'hard facts' it can neither confirm nor deny the event.[59]

From both literary and historical perspectives, the parts of the narrative about Josiah's religious change may be considered in relation to the world of their time. Starting with the opening setting (Part A), the entire book of Kings has relayed a non-stop cultic life in Jerusalem, from the time of Solomon building the temple there to the early years of Amon's child, and this is a religious world that is nothing if not malleable. Solomon's Jerusalem was a site of many shrines to many deities beyond the central palace chapel or temple to Yahweh, clearly the patron deity of Solomon and his 'kingdom.'[60] For Kings, upon which Chronicles builds, there is no official religious world mentioned for Jerusalem before Solomon, and in Chronicles the Jerusalem religious world before Solomon is the 'plan' of David, who instructs Solomon on what his religious world and edifices are to be.

Neither biblical text nor archaeological excavation reflects a Judah other than that which Josiah inherited from his father, Amon, and his grandfather, Manasseh. Judah's religious world starts with Solomon; Israel's religious world starts with Jeroboam. There is no religious tradition in either territory that the population would recognize as being their cultic world that corresponds to the tradition of one temple, one god, one religion for Judah and Israel. The stories of antiquity for the changes imputed to Josiah in Kings and Chronicles are good literature, but they would have been laughable as contemporary policy statements. The author of Kings can call the authoritative text "the scroll of *torah*" and "the scroll of the covenant," but its antiquity is not mentioned explicitly until 2 Kgs 23:25,

---

59 The term "hard facts" is from Rainer Albertz ("Why a Reform like Josiah's Must Have Happened," in Grabbe, *Good Kings and Bad Kings*, 43), and is used in defense of a "conservative maximalist" position (28) in dialogue with the 'minimalist' position of Philip Davies in his *In Search of 'Ancient Israel'*, 39. Davies saw Josiah's reform as "possible, but extremely improbable." Davies replied to Albertz in "Josiah and the Law Book," in Grabbe, *Good Kings and Bad Kings*, 70–75, seeing no need to accept Albertz's Josianic dating. Niels Peter Lemche ("Did a Reform Like Josiah's Happen?," in Davies and Edelman, *The Historian and the Bible*, 17–18) presumes the entire Josiah tale is a late invention of early Judaism, correctly noting that the Chronicler saw no need to take seriously King's rendition of events, even moving the reform itself back to Hezekiah.

60 In *Aspects of Syncretism in Israelite Religion*, trans. E. J. Sharpe, HoSo 5 (Lund: Gleerup, 1963), 45–46, Gösta W. Ahlström argues for deity idols in the temple from its foundation. It might be added that rather amorphous stones or stelae representing deities would have served the same purpose as a finely carved or molded figurine. See also Mettinger, "A Conversation with My Critics: Cultic Image or Aniconism in the First Temple?," in Amit, Ben Zvi, Finkelstein, and Lipschits, *Essays on Ancient Israel*, 284–89. Were such stones used to represent Yahweh, they would still have been "images."

when it is connected with Moses, who is not an active character in Kings at all. A written *torah* of Moses makes its sole previous appearance in Kings in David's death speech (1 Kgs 2:3); the hidden scroll, indeed, makes no sense in the book of Kings as a historical account.[61] On the other hand, Chronicles attaches "the scroll of the law of Moses" to antiquity immediately upon Hilkiah finding it (2 Chr 34:14). In both Kings and Chronicles, Moses is not an active character upon whom this scroll may internally be authorized; that must have been left to the general knowledge of the audience, and we can only guess at what that was concerning Moses. There is nothing in the book of Kings to prepare the reader for the sudden appearance of this written text; there was plenty of condemnation by the narrator of the religious life of Israel and, to a lesser extent, Judah, but the scroll comes out of nowhere.[62]

All possible fraud is literarily disposed of (Part B) by having the text found by the high priest. That the title *kohen harosh* appears to some scholars to be anachronistic in the case of Hilkiah may or may not have been the case. There needed to be a priest in charge of the ritual activities of a major temple. Whether he bore this official title or it was simply a later way to designate the most authoritative priest in the clergy in Jerusalem, Hilkiah is "the priest, head priest, or high priest" for Josiah.[63] The king may make the proclamation, but Josiah is responding to a higher authority, as all good rulers in the ancient world were supposed to be doing. These are cultic matters, and cultic personnel should be looking out for them. Of course, this has long raised the question of why Hilkiah, the high priest, had been running a temple in Jerusalem at odds with the proper worship of his God if all this information was not only written down in antiquity but was sitting in his own temple all this time. The popular argument that Hilkiah was in some way the instigator of the religious change

---

61 See Knauf, "Kings among the Prophets," in Edelman and Ben Zvi, *Production of Prophecy*, 142, who believes the *torah* is included to connect the Second Temple with the literary First Temple.

62 In various ways, the sudden appearance of this written record in the Kings account has caught the attention of scholars. Jon D. Levenson ("Who Inserted the Book of the Torah?," *HTR* 68 [1975]: 203–33) argues for its late, post-exilic insertion into a previously existing text. It is mentioned only once previously in Kings but as a referent, not as an object in itself (2 Kgs 14:6); see also Yvan Mathieu, "À la recherche du livre retrouvé! Le 'Livre de la loi' et son autorité en 2 R 22–23," in Écritures et réécritures: La reprise interpretative des traditions fondatrices par la literature biblique et extra-biblique, ed. C. Clivaz, C. Combet-Galland, J.-D. Macchi, and C. Nihan, BETL 248 (Leuven: Peeters, 2012), 68.

63 Roland de Vaux (*Ancient Israel*, vol. 2: *Religious Institutions* [New York: McGraw-Hill, 1965], 378) notes its use for Hilkiah and Siraiah; the title *kohen gadol* is used only in post-exilic passages (397), but probably also means the priest in control or with the final authority.

implemented by Josiah begs the question as to why he would run a cult for decades (or longer) in a fashion that he, as authoritative religious figure, deemed wrong.

What better place is there for an authoritative text relaying information vital to the proper worship of a deity to be found than in that deity's temple (Part C)?[64] This observation has a long history in biblical studies and has been a central aspect of the Josiah story for a century.[65] However, it needs to be understood as a rhetorical device of historiographical invention.[66] It has been easy to consider the found text to be the 'deposit copy' of some authoritative cultic text or, of course, Deuteronomy.[67] There is no reason to doubt that the Jerusalem temple had a high priest, at least one that was in charge of seeing that cultic functions were carried out correctly and in a timely fashion. What is highly unlikely is that the priest in charge had no idea that he was an apostate. Hilkiah appears suddenly in the texts when his character is needed to find the scroll; he fulfills a literary need. The narratives do not need to ask why the high priest was running a corrupt cult. It would seem safe to assume that Hilkiah had been a priest for some time, even before Josiah became king, and that he had

---

64 Zevit, "Deuteronomy in the Temple: An Exercise in Historical Imagining," in Fox, Glatt-Gilad, and Williams, *Mishneh Torah*, 210–12.

65 The citation of similar ancient Near Eastern events, the finding of ancient texts in temples, has been commonly noted: Anton Jirku, *Altorientalischer Kommentar zum Alten Testament* (Leipzig: A. Deichert, 1923), 184–85; Ahlström, *History of Ancient Palestine*, 773; Thomas Römer, "Transformations in Deuteronomistic and Biblical Historiography: On 'Book-Finding' and Other Literary Strategies," *ZAW* 109 (1997): 7–9; Lipschits, "On Cash-Boxes and Finding or Not Finding Books: Jehoash's and Josiah's Decisions to Repair the Temple," in Amit, Ben Zvi, Finkelstein, and Lipschits, *Essays on Ancient Israel*, 243. The literary device extends into classical literature for those who would like to date Josiah's tale that late: Katherine Stott, "Finding the Lost Book of the Law: Re-Reading the Story of 'The Book of the Law' (Deuteronomy–2 Kings) in Light of Classical Literature," *JSOT* 30 (2005): 153–69. However, the finding of 'ancient' religious items while refurbishing a temple is a widespread narrative trope: Wikander, "Finding Indra, Finding Torah," 71–72.

66 Mathieu, "À la recherché du livre retrouvé!," 68–69; Thomas Römer, "L'Autorité du livre dans les trois partes de la Bible hébraïque," in Clivaz, Combet-Galland, Macchi, and Nihan, *Écritures et réécritures*, 93, who notes Nabonidus as an example. Four Mesopotamian examples are discussed in Handy, "A Realignment in Heaven," 290–307: Tukulti-Ninurta I, Esarhaddon, Nabonidus, Xerxes I. See also Nadav Na'aman, "The King Leading Cult Reforms in His Kingdom: Josiah and Other Kings in the Ancient Near East," *ZABR* 12 (2006): 131–68.

67 See Glagolev et al. ("Chetvertaia Kniga Tsarstv," 565–66), who also suggest that there may have been different versions of the book at that time. The theory of a secret hiding place in the temple has had its proponents as well, though this might well reflect the popularity of Gothic fiction; see Kinns, *Graven in the Rock*, 385, who himself posits the "book" lay beside the ark of the covenant (389).

held a position of chief priest, a position that might have been inherited. Being the chief priest, Hilkiah would have been the final authority on ritual matters; his passing of the material to Shaphan to hand to Josiah lends authority to the religious changes about to be described. As a historical inquiry, Hilkiah's position in the religious world of ancient Judah appears much more literary than antiquarian. Exactly where in the house of Yahweh Hilkiah found this document is not part of the story. It has at times been assumed that it was found while repairing a wall, so that it had been hidden, but it seems temples had libraries, and it may just as well have been 'on the shelf' or mis-shelved, as so many volumes in university libraries seem to be.[68] It is notable that the document delivered to Josiah is not quoted or even summarized in this narrative; what is considered important are the actions taken by Josiah. They are credited to Josiah first and foremost as examples of his good behavior, and are provided with a written authority solely as a foundation for legitimating what Josiah does.[69]

Since what is done is quite a change from business as usual in Jerusalem, it is necessary that the person orchestrating this activity is legitimate and aware of the correctness of what is being carried out in the religious world (Part D). Josiah is portrayed as a legitimate ruler by the lineage recounted at the beginning of this section, whereby he is the legitimate son and heir of Amon, who, in turn, is the legitimate son and heir of Manasseh, and by being connected favorably with David, the titular head of the "house" (dynasty) of David. As king of Judah, Josiah has ruling authority. It seems, at least by this story's logic, that Josiah also has authority over the religious beliefs and ritual cult of Jerusalem and Judah. His right to undermine the religious traditions of Israel is assumed

---

68 It has been suggested that the Jerusalemite temple would have had a library: Jan N. Bremmer, "From Holy Books to Holy Bible: An Itinerary from Ancient Greece to Modern Islam via Second Temple Judaism and Early Christianity," in *Authoritative Scriptures in Ancient Judaism*, ed. M. Popovic, JSJSup 141 (Leiden: Brill, 2010), 344 and 344n88. Certainly, Egyptian temples included libraries in their complexes: Redford, "Some Observations on the Traditions Surrounding 'Israel in Egypt,'" in Lipschits, Knoppers, and Oeming, *Judah and Judeans in the Achaemenid Period*, 287. There is some evidence for libraries in Second Temple Jerusalem: Watts, "Scripturalization and the Aaronide Dynasties," 14. Noll ("Was there Doctrinal Dissemination?," 419) supposes that perhaps all the scrolls later to become Scripture were housed in the temple in Jerusalem until Roman times.

69 There is ample precedent for kings being portrayed as righteous for finding these deposit texts: Richard S. Ellis, *Foundation Deposits in Ancient Mesopotamia*, YNER 2 (New Haven: Yale University, 1968), 111, 156–57, 161, 166–67. In the Persian-era portrayals, Josiah is important because he follows the directions of the written "book": Ben Zvi, "Imagining Josiah's Book and the Implications of Imagining It in Early Persian Yehud," in Kottsieper, Schmitt, and Wöhrle, *Berührungspunkte*, 204.

because Yahweh is worshiped in both tiny territories. The extent to which a king of Judah would have been a priest of Yahweh is unclear.[70] The Pentateuchal laws (Num 16:40) seem to forbid such a combination, and the book of Chronicles presents the crossing of the line between king and priest as an abomination to Yahweh (2 Chr 26:16–21).[71] For Josiah's narrative to have validity in the world of Deuteronomy, and even in Kings itself, Josiah would have to have priestly authority.[72] In both narrative worlds, kings were acting on behalf of their gods by definition.[73]

Since one does not make an entire theological and ritual shift of momentous proportions on flimsy evidence, the ancient world had a method for verifying that the directives sent by the gods to humans were legitimate (Part E). This is the purpose of Huldah's speech to Josiah.[74] As interesting as the speech has turned out to be among later commentators, the word of God to Josiah actually says almost nothing about a scroll found or about its contents. In two short notations (2 Kgs 22:16, 19) the prophecy tangentially mentions that Yahweh has condemned "this people" to desolation and curse and destruction. That's it. There is nothing in it about what the instructions were, what else might have been intended, or that anything was going to stop this disaster from coming.

Indeed, Huldah's speech does not even substantiate that the scroll contained anything except curses. As it appears from her mouth, they seem to be directed against the current populace. At no point does Yahweh, or Huldah for that matter, authenticate the scroll. Moreover, the topic of the coming devastation of the religious world by order of Josiah is not broached. The section is intended to authorize Josiah as a righteous man who fears Yahweh and reacts properly; it does not authorize any religious changes specifically or hint that such action would result in any change of divine wrath and punishment. It does authenticate, however, that the

---

70   It has been suggested that the kings of Judah were also understood to be priests or at least official heads of the religious world: Ahlström, *History of Ancient Palestine*, 476–77; Deenick, "Priest and King," 325, 338–39.

71   See discussion of the Azariah/Uzziah passage in Hamilton, *Handbook on the Historical Books*, 245, 453; Klein, *2 Chronicles*, 377–81, and citations there. Note that in 2 Sam 6:17, David is presented to be acting as a priest and that this passage in Chronicles removes the king from the priestly activity (377).

72   De Vaux (*Ancient Israel*, 175) notes that, in Kings, it is the king who "reforms" the cult, not the clergy. Of course, both Kings and Chronicles are more concerned with kings than priests. See Watts, "Scripturalization and the Aaronide Dynasties," 4.

73   Bertil Albrektson, *History and the Gods: An Essay on the Idea of Historical Events as Divine Manifestations in the Ancient Near East and in Israel*, ConBOT 1 (Lund: Gleerup, 1967), 45; Ahlström, *Royal Administration*, 1–9.

74   Lowell K. Handy, "Role of Huldah," 40; Mathieu, "Recherché du livre retrouvé!," 73.

people are guilty and deserve what is coming—both a religious revolution and a political devastation.[75]

Since the prophecy is perceived to legitimate Josiah and his righteousness in the eyes of Yahweh, the changes required by him in the religious world of Judah may be deemed true and proper (Part F). Up to this point in the narrative, has any information been provided as to what had been going wrong with the cult of Yahweh? Just two wrongs are noted by Yahweh through Huldah: the people have stopped worshiping or believing in Yahweh and they have sacrificed to deities that were not Yahweh. Certainly, nothing is mentioned about what needs to be done to rectify the situation. As the story unfolds, however, reference to the scroll and the words on it become the rationale for the wholesale removal of other deities, their cultic paraphernalia, their cultic personnel, and their devotees from the temple in Jerusalem, the local religious sites of Judah, and throughout the territory of Israel. It is simply taken for granted that what Josiah is recorded as doing is covered in the *torah* read to him from the temple precinct. The summary statement for Josiah's reign before his death scene would seem to correlate this activity with the scroll and with the directives provided in hoary antiquity to wandering Israelites long before there had been a landed populace to incorporate them. So, the 'corrections' Josiah implements correspond not to the proper cult ascribed to David, let alone the improper cult imposed by Solomon, but to a religious reality that up to that point had never been implemented.

Finally, it needs to be emphasized that the actual religious changes in this tale are implemented by cultic personnel (Part G). Granted, these are 'proper' cultic personnel: Hilkiah and the Levites. The Levitical nature of this activity becomes decidedly more pointed in Chronicles than in Kings.[76] However, Josiah does not do any of the burning, firing, desecrating, executing, or destroying; in proper *torah* manner, he keeps his hands off while religious employees do the actual work of changing the cult and entering the temple. The distinction between the religious realm of the priests and the political world of the king is kept very clearly here, even if the command to undertake these religious activities is credited to the king and sanctioned as royal duty by none other than Yahweh.

---

[75] Marianne Grohmann ("Hulda, die Prophetin," 210) emphasizes the textual notation that Josiah inquired of Huldah not only for himself but also for the populace and Judah as a whole.

[76] Zwickel ("Priesthood and the Development of Cult in the Books of Kings," in Lemaire and Halpern, *The Books of Kings*, 424), properly points out that Levitical priests do not make an appearance in Kings at all.

The activities of Josiah in rearranging the religious life of Judah and Israel are set forth in a very short list.[77] How many of these activities are likely to have been implemented by a king of the minor polity of Judah in the last quarter of the seventh century BCE? It is probable that none of them would have made any sense at that time.[78] It is always possible that ruling elites might do strange things for reasons which cannot be discerned, but this list of cultic renovations seems out of place in the political and cultural world that can be reconstructed for Josiah. Limiting worship to the Jerusalem temple alone seems illogical for at least two reasons: 1) it is unclear what exact nature of the traditional religious practice of the populace then being practiced would support such a move;[79] and 2) the texts do not say anything about the temple being the only place to worship, only that a lot of outlying sites were closed down.[80] No doubt Josiah ordered repair work to be carried out on the temple and undoubtedly made changes in the liturgical life of the palace chapel. During a perilous time internationally and an internal political situation of dubious stability, how much would a 'wise' king wish to alienate his core population? Let us begin with the notion that this was the ancient Near East and a small peripheral entity; the king simply was not all-powerful, and Josiah's tale of religious enactments is told without a single military reference. It is all priests and the enthusiastic people who do as they are shown to do by the priests, acting, of course, under the guise of royal orders, derived from a scroll they have heard read a single time.

Simply because it is the least likely aspect of the story, Josiah's control of the religion of Israel is a place to begin. It has been a stock comment among Bible scholars for a century and a half that Josiah implemented his 'reform' upon discovering himself free from Assyrian control.[81] With Judah

---

77   Anderson, *History and Religion of Israel*, 125; Lods, *Prophets and the Rise of Judaism*, 138–39. Traditionally, these events have been written out in expansions of the biblical texts themselves: George Rawlinson, *The Kings of Israel and Judah*, Men of the Bible (New York: Anson D. F. Randolph, 1889), 217–19, 220–21; Miller and Hayes, *History of Ancient Israel and Judah*, 457–60; Dever, "The Silence of the Text: An Archaeological Commentary on 2 Kings 23," in Coogan, Exum, and Stager, *Scripture and Other Artifacts*, 147.

78   In "What Did Josiah Reform?," in *"He Unfurrowed His Brow and Laughed:" Essays in Honour of Professor Nicolas Wyatt*, ed. W. G. E. Watson, AOAT 299 (Münster: Ugarit, 2007), 25, Margaret Barker correctly notes that whether one wishes to divide the religion of Judah into official and country or not, what Josiah was removing was the traditional cult of the region.

79   Maag, "Erwägungen zur deuteronomischen Kultzentralisation," 12.

80   Greenspahn, "Deuteronomy and Centralization," 232, 234.

81   Robinson, *History of Israel*, 416–17; Herrmann, *History of Israel*, 265; Spieckermann, *Juda unter Assur in der Sargonidenzeit*, 307–70; Leuchter, *Josiah's Reform and Jeremiah's Scroll*, 50.

allied to Egypt, it is unlikely that it found itself any less under foreign imperial obligation than when it had been allied to Assyria; this would not have been a time when 'independence' occurred. If any territory found itself suddenly independent, it would have been Israel itself. Formally a province of Assyria for a century, Samerina would have been effectively lost to Assyrian control well before 612 BCE. How much earlier than that is incapable of being determined, but it is unlikely to have preceded the death of Ashurbanipal in 627 BCE. What can be assumed (and it is an assumption) is that the populace of "Israel" did not suddenly find itself dissolved from being part of Assyria and immediately think, "Oh, we must rush down to Josiah in Judah and adhere to that Jerusalemite dynasty!"

If Samerina had continued to have its own regional governing body to the end of direct Assyrian control, it is highly unlikely that those holding political power simply gave it up because the region was now independent of the Assyrian Empire. It is possible that the Assyrian administrators and the Assyrian troops left the area, the former to return to the central Assyrian territory and the latter being desperately needed in defense maneuvers. However, since the Assyrians did not rule the regions of their empire solely by Assyrian nationals, those Israelites and/or ethnic peoples who were moved into Israelite territory by the Assyrians would have continued to maintain some semblance of political control.[82] It is possible, but not likely, that dispossessed descendants opted to move back to Babylon, Cuthah, Avva, Hamath, and Sepharvaim as Ezra-era Judahites did from Babylonia (2 Kgs 17:24).[83] More likely, like most Judeans in Babylonia, the third and fourth generations of 'new' Israelites considered themselves quite at home in Samerina, irrespective of what it was called.[84]

More to the point, when Israel had been an independent minor kingdom it was decidedly more powerful and more important politically and

---

82 Melville ("A New Look," 189) argues that there was little Assyrian effort, governmentally or militarily, to hold a "buffer zone" like Israel. On the population of Samerina having held fairly steady from the time of Israel as a mix of Israelites and importees from elsewhere in the Assyrian periphery, see Liverani, *Assyria*, 193. Certainly, Samaria continued as a regional administrative center of some kind without a major interruption: Gary N. Knoppers, "In Search of Post-exilic Israel: Samaria after the Fall of the Northern Kingdom," in Day, *In Search of Pre-Exilic Israel*, 171.

83 In "A Slip of the Pen? On Josiah's Actions in Samaria (2 Kings 23:15–20)," in *The Moshe Weinfeld Jubilee Volume: Studies in the Bible and the Ancient Near East, Qumran, and Post-Biblical Judaism*, ed. C. Cohen, A. Hurvitz, and S. M. Paul (Winona Lake, IN: Eisenbrauns, 2004), 4, Mordechai Cogan succinctly describes the religious versus ethnic problems with the biblical author's vision of Josiah-era Israel; note that "Israelites" were clearly still inhabiting the region (8).

84 Knoppers ("In Search of Post-exilic Israel," 170–71) posits that the relatively few "outsiders" moved by Assyria into Samerina were assimilated into the Israelite populace and culture.

economically, and was greater in sheer demographic numbers, than Judah to its south. It had its own international relations and, most important for the Josianic narrative, its own religion.[85] It had no need for advice from Jerusalem and would not have accepted it. Indeed, the biblical story in Kings is quite clear that the official religious traditions of Samerina were those of Israel itself, taught by official priests of Israel's own tradition (2 Kgs 17:27–28).[86] There is simply no way in which Josiah would move into Samerina, declare it "Israel," and claim either its population or its territory for his own. It would have been neither Assyria nor Egypt that would have opposed such a move; it would have been Israelites fending off an invasion.

There is nothing to suggest that the newly independent northern kingdom would have submitted to a forced and violent incursion into its territory and culture. Nor would it be reasonable to conclude that tiny Judah had the wherewithal to carry out such a mission against a region as proud and enthusiastic about its new independence as modern scholars blithely attribute to Josiah and a not-nearly-so politically redefined Judah. The northern incursion of religious tampering by Josiah reflects notions of bickering between Jerusalem and Samaria over cultic control within the Persian Empire at the earliest.[87] The story does not reflect a historical Josiah having any control over the northern territory at all.[88]

As a subset of Israel's status as independent of Assyria, Egypt, *and* Judah, it is unclear whether Bethel was in Josiah's domain.[89] If Samerina had not

---

85 Na'aman ("No Anthropomorphic Graven Images," 394–95) stresses the need to view Israel and Judah as separate entities with their own religious traditions.

86 In "The Judean Priesthood during the Neo-Babylonian and Achaemenid Periods: A Hypothetical Reconstruction," *CBQ* 60 (1998): 35, Joseph Blenkinsopp notes that Assyria is represented in the biblical texts as recognizing Bethel as the, or a, center of Israelite religion, and argues it continued as such after the Assyrian conquest and after Josiah (31). Any actual cultic material behind 2 Kings 17, however, has been compromised in the literary and textual tradition of the passage. See Edward Lipinski, "Foreign Cults in Seventh Century Samaria," *PJBR* 15, no. 1 (2016): 32, though Lipinski does try to theorize about possible real religious backgrounds.

87 Knoppers, *Jews and Samaritans*, 98–99. See also Noll ("Did 'Scripturalization' Take Place?," 208), who would argue for a Hasmonean period and the claim of Jerusalem for rule of the Samaritans.

88 See Hermann Michael Niemann, *Herschaft Königtum und Staat: Skizzen zur soziokulturellen Entwicklung im monarchischen Israel*, FAT 6 (Tübingen: Mohr Siebeck, 1993), 221–27, who also suggests (234) that centralized kings in Judah had no control over any cultic activity outside of Jerusalem (contra Ahlström). This is acknowledged by Hardmeier, "King Josiah in the Climax of the Deuteronomic History," in Grabbe, *Good Kings and Bad Kings*, 158.

89 Horsley (*Biblical Criticism*, 1.234) explains that Bethel had been in the territory of Judah since the reign of Abijah (2 Chr 13:19), a theory that still has adherents. The status of Bethel between Israel and Judah, however, remains unknown: Joseph

fallen into total chaos by having the Assyrian Empire collapse around it, it is unlikely that it would give up a major religious temple city of long standing. It has been argued often enough that Josiah took Bethel when Assyria crumbled, but Bethel displays no signs of conquest and certainly would not have surrendered to Judah and Davidic dynastic control without a fight. It is most likely that the suggestion in Kings is correct: Bethel was northern kingdom territory.[90] The entire narrative of Josiah at Bethel is entertaining and symbolic of Jerusalem's notion of itself as the seat of the proper dynasty and cultic traditions, but it makes no sense as a historical event.[91] In the first place, rulers of the ancient world were not in the habit of rolling into foreign territories simply to destroy an altar (if there had been a temple in Bethel, it gets no notice here).[92] Hauling ashes and rubbish from a cult demolition in Jerusalem to Bethel for disposal would have been a massive amount of work for so little symbolic payout as to be nonsense.[93] The trip itself, then, makes little sense. The monument to the apostate prophet is illogical as a historical memorial. Moreover, if there had been a religious tradition of long standing at Mount Gerizim, a tradition claimed to this day by Samaritans, it is bizarre that Josiah would have such a long story about Bethel recorded but not a word about the site 'later' to be claimed as "the place where Yahweh will cause to dwell his name."[94] Indeed, if the Josiah narratives had been written as late as the end of the Persian era, or the beginning of the Seleucid era, Gerizim would

---

Blenkinsopp, "Bethel in the Neo-Babylonian Period," in *Judah and the Judeans in the Neo-Babylonian Period*, ed. O. Lipschits and J. Blenkinsopp (Winona Lake, IN: Eisenbrauns, 2003), 94–95.

90 Gomes (*Sanctuary of Bethel*, 48) observes that there is nothing to substantiate Judah taking *any* territory from "Israel," Bethel included.

91 Klaus Koenen, *Bethel: Geschichte, Kult und Theologie*, OBO 192 (Freiburg: Universitätsverlag, 2003), 53, 55–56. Davies ("Josiah and the Law Book," in Grabbe, *Good Kings and Bad Kings*, 75–76) hypothesizes that a possible reason for Josiah being remembered as a reforming king is that he may have destroyed at least an altar at Bethel, causing him to be in mortal disfavor with Neco, but this is a real stretch.

92 Destroying altars or temples was part and parcel of destroying whole settlements and towns: Brinkman, *Prelude to Empire*, 67–68, 102.

93 Koenen, *Bethel*, 55; Pakkala, "Jeroboam without Bulls," 518; see also Gomes, *Sanctuary of Bethel*, 46–47, who labels the tale as propaganda rather than history of any kind.

94 On the question of Mount Gerizim having been a sacred site at the time of Josiah, see Ferdinand Dexinger, "Limits of Tolerance in Judaism: The Samaritan Example," in *Jewish and Christian Self-Definition*, vol. 2: *Aspects of Judaism in the Greco-Roman Period*, ed. E. P. Sanders (Philadelphia: Fortress, 1981), 92 and 328n21. The archaeological evidence is scant at best and dates no earlier than the Persian Empire: Stern, *Archaeology of the Land of the Bible*, 52; Knoppers, *Jews and Samaritans*, 11, 123–24.

be expected to be in the story.⁹⁵ What is in the story is Bethel, and even if in decline, Bethel appears to have been extant throughout and beyond Josiah's reign, whether there was a significant altar there or not.⁹⁶ The religious cult of Israel/Samerina/Samaria did not change historically at the time of Josiah and would not have done so because of the machinations of an uninspired foreign ruler of minor significance.⁹⁷ Josiah might be a major figure in Jerusalem, Kings, and Chronicles, but he is a nonentity among the Samaritans.⁹⁸

Before leaving the material on Josiah's religious activities in "Israel," there is one last oddity. Perhaps the most extensive literary reflection in Kings, if less pronounced in Chronicles and lacking altogether in First Esdras, is the removal of non-Yahwistic deities from Judah. It is a fascinating textual tradition that puts so much effort into describing the destruction of Samarian sacred sites, but has nothing at all to say about the gods that the book of Kings has enumerated for Israel's past.⁹⁹ The deities mentioned in Josiah's story are all related to the temple in Jerusalem or to the religious world of Judah (2 Kgs 23:24). Israel, no less than Judah, had a number of deities, archaeologically or biblically definable, but they play no part in any of the biblical Josiah stories.¹⁰⁰ Apparently, it was enough

---

95   Noll ("Did Scripturalization Take Place?," 203, 215–16) doubts much, if any, textual authority for the Gerizim temple and definitely not before Hasmonean times. Jan Dushek ("Mt. Gerizim Sanctuary, Its History and Enigma of Origin," *HBAI* 3 [2014]: 132–33) posits Josiah destroying Mount Gerizim as one of the "high places." However, it seems unlikely that it would not have been recorded in some format given the importance of the site for the Samaritans, unless "Bethel" was standing in symbolically for Gerizim.

96   That a 'temple' or sacred site remained in Bethel is possible: Joshua Schwartz, "Jubilees, Bethel and the Temple of Jacob," *HUCA* 56 (1985): 78. In any case, Bethel itself seems to have continued undisturbed from its late Assyrian Empire days into the Persian Empire: Koenen, *Bethel*, 59–64; Knoppers, *Jews and Samaritans*, 34. It has been suggested that the entire story of Josiah and Bethel reflects Persian occupation: Diana V. Edelman, *The Origins of the "Second" Temple: Persian Imperial Policy and the Rebuilding of Jerusalem*, BibleWorld (London: Equinox, 2005), 232.

97   Blenkinsopp ("Bethel in the Neo-Babylonian Period," 95) adroitly notes that even were one to take the Josiah story concerning Bethel seriously as reflecting a historical event, his actions would have had no lasting repercussions.

98   Blenkinsopp (*Judaism*, 147) asserts that it would be "naïve" to assume the extent of Josiah's suppression of religious places and peoples given archaeological data; this should be taken especially seriously for "Israel."

99   Gray (*Christian Workers' Commentary*, 193) observes that Israel was "where that worship had originally arisen." Kings at least stresses the gods of Israel prior to Josiah but then curiously ignores them in the section about Josiah, which Gray does not notice.

100 Ahlström (*Aspects of Syncretism*, 46–57) stresses the reality of "Canaanite" deities as integral to the cults of both Judah and Israel.

to state that Josiah had the sacred precincts destroyed and their priests executed. This only makes sense if the intent of the "Israel" incursion by Josiah in Kings and Chronicles is to verify the authority of Jerusalem; clearly, it was not emphasizing the 'horrid pantheon' of that northern Yahwistic region.

If it is odd that the Josiah narratives fail to comment on deities worshiped in "Israel," it is significant that there are so many gods listed for Judah and Jerusalem in particular. In Kings, the method of ridding the cultic world of them is simply to destroy the images used in worshiping them. Since there was a theological idea that deities and their statues (or other religious symbols signifying their presence) were intimately related,[101] it was possible to damage the deity by damaging the image.[102] Anthropomorphism of divine inhabitants extended as far as gods being capable of dying.[103]

Kings, however, insists that these other deities did not exist; therefore, breaking down, pulverizing, and burning images of them and their ritual vessels could do nothing to them as they were nothing. And 'nothing deities' in the neo-Assyrian period said more about the people worshiping them than about the gods themselves; the worshipers are enemies of the true God and the true ruler.[104] However, such activities would mean something to devotees who saw the images of their gods eradicated. For the theology of the time, it was the death sentence on the gods themselves.[105]

---

101 Christopher Walker and Michael B. Dick, "The Induction of the Cult Image in Ancient Mesopotamia: The Mesopotamian *mis pî* Ritual," in *Born in Heaven, Made on Earth: The Making of the Cult Image in the Ancient Near East*, ed. M. B. Dick (Winona Lake, IN: Eisenbrauns, 1999), 57; David Lorton, "The Theology of Cult Statues in Ancient Egypt," in Dick, *Born in Heaven, Made on Earth*, 179-89.

102 Scurlock, "Josiah: The View from Mesopotamia," BR 51 (2006): 17.

103 Handy, "Realignment," 348-50, 359, though I would not argue for a Josianic date for Psalm 82 now; it contains the ideology of reducing a pantheon but more likely derives from the Second Temple liturgy. See Peter Machinist, "How Gods Die, Biblically and Otherwise: A Problem of Cosmic Restructuring," in Pongratz-Leisten, *Reconsidering the Concept of Revolutionary Monotheism*, 220-23.

104 According to Liverani (*Assyria*, 15), "godless" people may actually worship real gods wrongly or have abandoned gods they should have been worshiping. Kings appears to imply both in the destruction of the images. It is not possible with the data at hand to presuppose that some general shift in theological thought during the Neo-Assyrian Empire caused deity statues to cease to be religiously relevant to large swaths of worshipers or that such a shift would be useful for understanding Josiah. See Seth Richardson, "The Hypercoherent Icon: Knowledge, Rationalization, and Disenchantment at Nineveh," in May, *Iconoclasm and Text Destruction*, 252. The text knows no such cultural movement and relies on there being a divide between Josiah and the idol-addicted worshipers.

105 In "'In Order to Make Him Completely Dead': Annihilation of the Power of

Clearly, the method of removing the non-Yahwistic images came from the cultural climate of the ancient Near East, but it is the literary rendition that remains, and it would conform to some known patterns for completely and indignantly removing unwanted and horrid items. It would also assume that Josiah had believed to that point that they were real deities and he was destroying the gods along with the statues. Were the story in Kings a retelling of actual events, the items could have been merely picked up and removed. The telling of the tale clearly includes the literary reflection of a theology not in line with that of the narrative. Was it a reflection of some historical event? Who knows? History it is not.

Now, if one were attempting to rally the populace to a cause of political and religious independence under the aegis of one king, it probably would not be the most prudent method to declare the entire population to be intolerable apostates. The record of Josiah demolishing all cultic centers that were not the Jerusalemite temple (2 Kgs 23:8–20, 24; 2 Chr 34:3–7, 33) and mandating that all the people in Judah (and Israel) worship only Yahweh and only at Josiah's chapel (the temple in Jerusalem) makes for a nice centralizing tale.[106] However, a proud people who had their own gods and centuries-old local religious traditions at their own venerated altars would generally not find this a rallying cry for accepting the king who insisted on destroying their culture.[107]

There is no textual or archaeological evidence for a political or economic crisis that would have caused the general populace to acquiesce voluntarily to such a policy. Demolishing temples usually symbolized the conquest of a subjected people.[108] The mass execution of regional and

---

Images in Mesopotamia," in *La famille dans le Proche-Orient ancien: réalités, symbolisms, at images: Proceedings of the 55th Recontre Assyriologique Internationale at Paris 6–9 July 2009*, ed. L. Marti (Winona Lake, IN: Eisenbrauns, 2014), 701, Natalie N. May notes that the Assyrians were loath to demolish deity images, reserving the practice for implacable and long-standing rivals. The actual breaking of divine images by Assyrians was known but decidedly rare. See Richardson, "Hypercoherent Icon," 238. Scurlock ("Josiah," 24) demonstrates that the background for the actions taken by Josiah against images would have been seen (even by himself) as the killing of the divine beings themselves.

106 And this is certainly a purpose in telling the story as story. See Maag, "Erwägungen zur deuteronomischen Kultzentralisation," 18, who combines the narratives of Josiah and Hezekiah with notions of Jerusalem after the death of Josiah.

107 That Josiah's measures and methods would not have been popular with the general populations of either Judah or Israel has long been acknowledged: Lohfink, "The Cult Reform of Josiah of Judah," in Miller, Hanson, and McBride, *Ancient Israelite Religion*, 469. More recently phrased in terms of socio-cultural class and idioms of ethnic and political struggle, Nakanose, *Josiah's Passover*, 51–92

108 Handy, "Realignment," 162. Also Scurlock, "Josiah," 20–22, who cites Babylon ransacking Assyrian temples.

traditional priests would suggest the same, though the removal of local leaders would have been more rational.[109]

The argument put forth in Kings is that Josiah is recreating the original culture of the kingdoms of Israel and Judah; however, the reality appears to have been that both territories traditionally had a religious world of many deities and many religious sites and neither state seems to have had centralized control of the outlying shrines.[110] In fact, at no point do the narratives concerning Josiah even suggest that the outlying sanctuaries were intended for any deity other than Yahweh.[111]

For most of the latter half of the twentieth century, scholars held to archaeological evidence of destroyed altars or cultic sites as bolstering an argument for Josianic removal of outlying cultic centers.[112] After a re-evaluation of stratigraphic issues, some of these artifacts have been re-dated to Hezekiah or abandoned completely as markers of cultic closure.[113] Outside the biblical narratives, there is little to suggest that any attempt to reduce the heavenly population of Jerusalem, let alone Judah, took place in the time of Josiah.[114]

---

109 Certainly, Assyria considered the execution of political leaders a significant action in demonstrating a complete victory: Liverani, *Assyria*, 86–87.

110 Niemann, *Herschaft Königtum und Staat*, 192–216.

111 Suggested as early as 1882 by Abraham Kuenen, *Religions and Universal Religions*, Hibbert Lectures 1882 (New York: Scribner's Sons, 1882), 66; Moshe Weinfeld, "Cult Centralization in Israel in the Light of a Neo-Babylonian Analogy," *JNES* 23 (1964): 204.

112 Yohanan Aharoni, "Arad: It's Inscription and Temple," *BA* 31 (1968): 26; Yigael Yadin, "Beer-sheba: The High Place Destroyed by King Josiah," *BASOR* 222 (1976): 7, 14.

113 Yohanan Aharoni, "Notes and News: Tel Beersheba," *IEJ* 24 (1974): 271; Menahem Haran, *Temples and Temple-Service in Ancient Israel: An Inquiry into Biblical Cult Phenomena and the Historical Setting of the Priestly School* (Winona Lake, IN: Eisenbrauns, 1985) 37–38; Finkelstein and Silberman, *Bible Unearthed*, 250; Lisbeth S. Fried, "The High Places and the Reforms of Hezekiah and Josiah: An Archaeological Investigation," *JAOS* 122 (2002): 437–65. See survey in Bibb, "'Be Mindful, Yah Gracious God," 160–62. Ze'ev Herzog ("Perspectives on Southern Israel's Cult Centralization: Arad and Beer-sheba," in Kratz and Spieckermann, *One God—One Cult—One Nation*, 179–95) makes an extensive, if inconclusive, argument for the cult reform of Hezekiah being reflected in these archaeological sites.

114 It has been suggested that the time for a major religious reformulation for Jerusalem would have been when a brand-new temple was built in a brand-new political situation under the Persians. See Edgar Kellenberger ("JHWH und die Götter im globalisierten Perserreich: Anmerkungen zu einigen Thesen von A. de Pury," *CV* 52 [2010]: 137), who suggests the new situation of the Judeans inside Persia would need a new set of identifying norms. At the very least, Persian Yehud is now seen as a time of changing identity for the region. See Ephraim Stern ("The Religious Revolution in Persian-Period Judah," in Lipschits and Oeming, *Judah and the Judeans in the Persian Period*, 199–204), who sees a reduction in deities and religious sites in

Along similar lines, the claim that sacrifice ought to occur solely in the temple of Jerusalem, which is generally extrapolated from the destruction of outlying altars and shrines (2 Kgs 23:8; 2 Chr 34:6–7), would have made absolutely no religious, or domestic, sense. An ancient culture heavily dependent on small livestock for its meat intake would need to have had permission to slaughter and consume fresh flesh rather quickly.[115] If sacrifice were actually a normal practice for butchering and serving meat, having all sacrifice done in Jerusalem would be a silly requirement resulting in almost universal disobedience, widespread veganism, or open revolt.[116] If the practice of sacrifice was solely carried out for respectful devotion to a deity and was not required for ordinary meals, the requirement to abolish sacrifice to any deity other than Yahweh would fit a notion of enforced Yahweh-worship. However, such centralized sacrifice would still make little sense if the local altars had been understood to be dedicated to Yahweh.

Needing to sacrifice lamb daily for use in meals at only one altar for the entire population would have been logistically impossible. Distance, clean-up, and the sheer amount of time necessary to accomplish all this butchering make this requirement ridiculous, *unless* sacrifice was only a restricted ritual event and was not related to mundane livestock slaughtering for consumption. In the end, there is little evidence that Josiah (or anyone else [say, Hezekiah]) ended animal sacrifice outside of Jerusalem in Judah, let alone anywhere else.[117] The contention that Josiah ended child sacrifice actually seems to be a literary ploy to depict as horrific that which the king is claimed to have rectified; it is more literary purple prose than historical memory.[118]

---

the archaeological record of Yehud (but not a marked rise in the importance of Jerusalem); Cynthia Edenburg ("From Covenant to Connubium: Persian Period Developments in the Perception of Covenant in Deuteronomistic History," in *Covenant in the Persian Period: From Genesis to Chronicles*, ed. R. J. Bautch and G. N. Knoppers [Winona Lake, IN: Eisenbrauns, 2015], 135–39, 142), who finds the shift in rewriting or reading the Deuteronomistic History in Persia; James Anderson ("Creating Dialectical Tensions," in Edelman, Fitzpatrick-McKinley, and Guillaume, *Religion in the Achaemenid Persian Empire*, 21), who sees it as a period of shifting and overlapping religious identity from Yahwisms to Judaisms.

115 Consumption of livestock was fairly restricted to sheep, goats, and swine in the archaeological record; larger cattle were seldom slaughtered for consumption, though wild gazelles and deer occasionally appear in excavations: Nathan MacDonald, *What Did the Ancient Israelites Eat? Diet in Biblical Times* (Grand Rapids: Eerdmans, 2008), 32–34.

116 Olmstead ("Reform of Josiah," 569) emphasizes the "secular" result in outlawing peasant mutton consumption by removing sacrifice to the temple.

117 Knowles, *Centrality Practiced*, 52, 122.

118 See Azize ("Was There Regular Child Sacrifice in Phoenicia and Carthage?," in Azize and Weeks, *Gilgameš and the World of Assyria*, 186, 203), who notes that child

On the other hand, the least unlikely aspects of the religious actions credited to Josiah concern changes in the Jerusalem temple.[119] This edifice was, after all, the king's chapel according to the biblical rendition. If the ruling pontiff cannot adapt his own religious space to his own liking, he is not much of a ruler. Though the texts of Kings and Chronicles are concise, certain activities are definitely asserted as having been instigated by Josiah for his chapel (2 Kgs 23:4–7, 11–12; 2 Chr 34:3; 35:2–3). Most of these activities concern removing the cultic objects of a series of deities stated in no uncertain terms to have been located in Josiah's Jerusalemite temple. For the authors of Kings and Chronicles, this is a wholesale clearing out of the pantheon of Judah. Upon what actual activities, if any, of Josiah these tales were made cannot be determined.[120] It is interesting, if of no use for historical reconstruction, that Chronicles is very vague about idols in the temple itself; all the activity is generically expressed to have taken place in Judah and Jerusalem (2 Chr 34:3–5). There is no mention of a non-Yahweh deity of any kind having been in the temple.[121]

Apparently, Chronicles intended to distance the temple from nefarious influences even aside from Josiah's piety. Otherwise, Chronicles restricts Josiah's temple-tinkering to relocating an 'ark' into the temple, rearranging the orders of Levites to serve in the temple, and adding a new and never-before-celebrated Passover religious feast. So, if this material was the recollection of Josiah's temple changes, he did very little and nothing of monotheistic enforcement.[122]

---

sacrifice has been documented for Greece and Rome to a greater extent than for Semitic cultures. In Classical literature, citations of child sacrifice were specifically utilized to demonize enemies with the Roman use of the ritual to define Carthage (201).

119 Hardmeier ("King Josiah in the Climax of the Deuteronomistic History," in Grabbe, *Good Kings and Bad Kings*, 153–59) concludes that the temple activities form the ur-text for the expanded 'reform' narratives and reflects a historical event in a primary source (159). Without arguing for its historicity, Grabbe has suggested the short list of changes to the Jerusalemite temple may have been the original Josianic narrative to which more material was added: Grabbe, *1 & 2 Kings*, 74.

120 And here it is useful to think of 'utopian' literature with regard to Josiah's Jerusalem: Terje Stordalen, "Heaven on Earth—Or Not? Jerusalem as Eden in Biblical Literature," in *Beyond Eden: The Biblical Story of Paradise (Genesis 2–3) and Its Reception History*, ed. K. Schmid and C. Riedweg, FAT 2.34 (Tübingen: Mohr Siebeck, 2008), 38, 43, 46–47. The Jerusalem Josiah was supposedly creating was one that never existed, save in exilic or postexilic memory, Eden and Ezekiel being Stordalen's touchstones.

121 As noted, the decidedly Persian era Chronicles has already removed them under Manasseh: Lynch, *Monotheism and Institutions*, 203.

122 Modern definitions of 'monotheism' would not have been a consideration in the ancient Near Eastern world. Becker ("Von der Staatsreligion zum Monotheismus," 14) assigns its religious derivation behind Kings to early Judaism at the earliest.

The ark passage seems odd in relation to Josiah; where was this object if not in the temple? In order to get the ark out of the temple so that it could be returned by this king, scholars have suggested, despite a lack of supporting textual (or other) evidence, that it had been removed by the Assyrians, Manasseh, or Amon.[123] More logically, it might be a connection invented by the Chronicler which was intended to link Josiah with King David, who was the last king who had moved the ark to the (not yet existing) temple in a different tradition.[124] Some such scenario needs to have taken place, unless the ark were understood to have been in the temple all the time.[125] This would appear to be a late literary idea related to Josiah in theological retrospect that begs the question of whether this ark reference actually conveys a negative observation concerning Josiah—which is a reasonable suggestion.[126] The actual movement of the ark is not mentioned and has led to the suggestion that the Chronicler's reference to Josiah and the ark reflects the ark's disappearance long before Josiah.[127]

As for the Levites, this material has long been assumed to reflect the traditions of the Persian period when Chronicles was written.[128] The

---

Even the notion of a single deity in Judah at the time of Josiah has been seen as an anachronistic anomaly from exilic times at the earliest, though attempts to create a 'history' of this have been unsuccessful; see Bernhard Lang, "Die Jahwe-allein-Bewegung," in *Der einzige Gott: Die Geburt des biblischen Monotheismus*, ed. B. Lang (Munich: Kosel, 1981), 70-74; also Stolz ("Monotheismus in Israel," in Keel, *Monotheismus im Alten Israel und seiner Umwelt*, 179-82), who posits Deutero-Isaiah as the origin of monotheism. Noll ("Was there Doctrinal Dissemination?," 417-18) dismisses Second Isaiah as a possible time for monotheistic thought and posits (427) that, prior to the Hellenistic Age, monolatry and monotheism were "not well known." I would contend they were not known at all in any form moderns think of them.

123 See Glagolev et al., "Vtoraia Kniga Paralipomenon," in Lopukhin, *Tolkovaia Biblia*, 185. Matthew Lynch, *Monotheism and Institutions*, 95-96.

124 The scroll of Samuel contains a tradition that David would have brought the ark into a "house" if there had been one (2 Sam 6:1-11), while Chronicles (1 Chr 15:1) has David create a house (tent) for the ark. More significant is the observation that the ark with David signified Yahweh being with and supporting the king. See Steussy, *David*, 60. 2 Chr 35:3 connects Josiah with Solomon and David and the ark. The relation to David is more closely designated in some readings of the verse than in others: see Myers, *II Chronicles*, 209; also Japhet, *I & II Chronicles*, 1048, who notes that the whole directive to the Levites must be a late (Persian) text.

125 Klein, *2 Chronicles*, 519, who translates with variant manuscripts.

126 Christopher L. Begg, "The Ark in Chronicles," in Graham, McKenzie, and Knoppers, *The Chronicler as Theologian*, 141-42.

127 See Theodore D. Ehrlich ("The Disappearance of the Ark of the Covenant," *JBQ* 40 [2012]: 176-78), who hypothesizes Athaliah and her courtiers destroyed the ark long before Josiah. In any case, the Second Temple certainly contained no such item: Diana V. Edelman, "God Rhetoric," in Zvi, Edelman, and Polak, *A Palimpsest*, 81.

128 De Vaux, *Ancient Israel*, 393; Japhet, *I & II Chronicles*, 1041. However, the Kings

passage clearly understands Levites as officiating priests.[129] The references to a newly instigated Passover might possibly be related to a ritual adaptation of some festival involving a meal or otherwise, but it remains unclear.[130] That such a celebration would have traditionally been a Jerusalemite temple event, however, is highly unlikely.[131] For the Chronicler, a ritual establishment for the future cult tops pantheon removal as the central concern of Josiah's narrative.[132] It needs to be remembered that, in the literary rendition of the history of the Jerusalem temple in Kings and by extension in Chronicles, the entire chronology has been stylized and any historical reconstruction based on it remains suspect.[133] In the end, even the material about religious changes made in the temple would be unlikely to have been instigated by Josiah.

---

passage has often been argued to reflect some centralization of priestly activity, unclearly understood: Ernest Nicholson, "Josiah and the Priests of the High Places (II Reg 23,8a.9)," ZAW 119 (2007): 512–13, seeing the term 'Levite' as a designation for the outlying priests.

129 The argument that Levites were brought into Jerusalem to be judges has no biblical or extra-biblical foundation. See Mark Leuchter, "'The Levites in Your Gates': Deuteronomic Redefinition of Levitical Authority," JBL 126 (2007): 417–36; Nadav Na'aman, "Sojourners and Levites in the Kingdom of Judah in the Seventh Century BCE," ZABR 14 (2009): 261–62n58, though Na'aman does see ur-Deuteronomy to be a product of Levitical scribes in post-Sennacherib Jerusalem.

130 This topic is dealt with in Chapter 7, below.

131 Johannes Pedersen ("Pessahfest und Passahlegende," ZAW 52 [1934]: 163) sees Josiah's Passover as temple-instigated.

132 Lynch, *Monotheism and Institutions*, 204–6.

133 Koenen, *Bethel*, 504; see charts 496 and 498 and the extensive bibliography at 494n1.

CHAPTER SEVEN
AN INVITATION TO DINNER:
JOSIAH AND HIS PASSOVER NARRATIVES[1]

What are the respective Passover narratives doing in the two biblical presentations of Josiah's reign (2 Kgs 23:21-23 and 2 Chr 35:1-19[2])?[3] The simplest answer might be that they are both accurate reports of an event that actually took place during the reign of Josiah.[4] It would be simple, but, for numerous reasons, would not explain the purpose of recording such an event for the reign of Josiah in these two narrative texts. While nothing conforming in ritual praxis to what is celebrated in the modern world as 'Passover' is claimed to have taken place during the reign of Josiah, the

---

1   This chapter is a revised expansion of a paper presented at the annual meeting of the Midwest Regional Society of Biblical Literature, St. Mary of the Lake University, Mundelein, Illinois, February 24, 2002.

2   The Passover is not mentioned in Sir 49:1-4. However, it is the opening narrative in 1 Esd 1:1-20, where the Chronicler's account is elaborated, and Josiah's centrality is reaffirmed if not intensified: Sebastian Grätz, "Das Bild des Königs im Dritten Esrabuch (3.Esr): Beobachtungen zur Gesamtkonzeption des apokryphen Esrabuches," in *Israel zwischen den Mächten: Festschrift für Stefan Timm zum 65. Geburtstag*, ed. M. Pietsch and F. Hartenstein, AOAT 364 (Münster: Ugarit, 2009), 111-13. See now Sebastian Grätz, "The Image of the King(s) in 1 Esdras," in *Was 1 Esdras First? An Investigation into the Priority and Nature of 1 Esdras*, ed. L. S. Fried, AIL 7 (Atlanta: Society of Biblical Literature, 2011), 168-69, a Passover for future celebration.

3   For the purposes of this study, it is acknowledged that 1 Esdras contains the most detailed description of Josiah's Passover (1 Esd 1:1-17), but it should not be taken in any way as reflecting an independent source of information about a historical event: Böhler, *1 Esdras*, 33.

4   The essential historical reliability of the existence of a Passover as ascribed to Josiah in Kings and Chronicles still holds wide support in the academic community. Among others, see Hobbs, *2 Kings*, 337; McKenzie, *The Trouble with Kings*, 149; Nakanose, *Josiah's Passover*, 9; Japhet, *I & II Chronicles*, 1041; Gary N. Knoppers, *Two Nations under God: The Deuteronomistic History of Solomon and the Dual Monarchies*, vol. 2: *The Reign of Jeroboam, the Fall of Israel, and the Reign of Josiah*, HSM 53 (Atlanta: Scholars Press, 1994), 215; Erik Eynikel, *The Reform of King Josiah and the Composition of the Deuteronomistic History*, OtSt 33 (Leiden: Brill, 1996), 320-21, 351; Fretheim, *First and Second Kings*, 217; Brueggemann, *1 & 2 Kings*, 557-58; Hamilton, *Handbook on the Historical Books*, 465-66.

historiographical renditions of a repast play important parts in Kings and Chronicles.⁵ This importance is much less evident in Kings, where the three verses dedicated to the incident are as abstract and devoid of clear content as the comments concerning the rest of the acts of Josiah in the list of activities provided to display his 'cult reform.'⁶ Indeed, it is not even

---

5   What is currently celebrated as Passover and the manner in which it is ritually observed has evolved over millennia. It is most logical to assume that the Passover or Spring Harvest or New Year's festivals in Judah [or Israel] changed meaning and form through the centuries of the existence of the two kingdoms. Moreover, it is highly probable that the celebration had several meanings simultaneously in various locales for different groups of people and in the imaginations of various individuals in the two kingdoms. What the final redactor of Kings meant by Passover may or may not have corresponded to anything that the Judahites or Israelites of the monarchic period had known. An extended discussion, following Molly Zahn's paper on Passover in the biblical calendars at the Midwest Society of Biblical Literature meeting in February 2002, covering the American celebration of Memorial Day/ Remembrance Day/Decoration Day, adequately displayed the variety and shifting meanings of a given national memorial day, even when the establishment of the event was explicit. Memorial Day began as a movement to make certain that Confederate soldiers were honored in the states that had made up the Confederate States of America; it was adopted by General John A. Logan, Commander and Chief of the Grand Army of the Republic, in 1868 to honor Union soldiers, choosing their date of discharge from the service (May 30) to honor the Civil War military dead from the United States of America. At that time, many of the former 'Confederate' states ceased observing Decoration Day since they would not observe any commemoration ordered by the federal government. Exactly what was being honored differed explicitly by locality and more generally between northern and southern states. The holiday has changed markedly over its 150-year existence: it was expanded to include all American war dead; it was extended further to remember all family dead; it was, in some communities, taken as a day to clean up cemeteries in general, in others to display flowers on parents' graves, and in others to have parades. In the late twentieth century, the two major activities of Memorial Day in the general population have been watching the Indianapolis 500 car race and celebrating with picnics the official beginning of Summer (a date accepted by many governmental agencies). Moreover, the date of the holiday has been changed to suit vacationers by officially holding it on a Monday to create a three-day weekend. To assume that Passover in ancient Judah was not as convoluted as this highly specific American commemoration of the dead of the Civil War (War of the Rebellion, War Between the States, War of the Succession, even naming the war remains controversial) would be difficult to defend. More telling, perhaps because it has been more studied, is the shifting meaning and celebration of a religious holiday whose meaning, and the celebration of which, has shifted vastly in a short period of time within one nation. For Christmas in the United States, see Stephen Nissenbaum, *The Battle for Christmas* (New York: Vintage, 1997) and Karal Ann Marling, *Merry Christmas! Celebrating America's Greatest Holiday* (Cambridge, MA: Harvard University Press, 2000).

6   The note on the Josianic Passover/Pesach in Kings (2 Kgs 23:21–23) provides

clear in Kings that this 'Passover' entailed a meal.[7] While many consider Passover to be an integral part of Josiah's reform, there have been—and still are—scholars who view the Passover cited in the Josiah narratives as an anachronism.[8] For the current study, it is immaterial whether or not the Passovers of Kings and Chronicles are late additions to an earlier text or even whether or not they are based on an actual event.[9] What is of concern is what the individual narratives do with their respective Passover descriptions.[10]

Passover appears in the present (MT) Hebrew text of Kings as a constituent item within a list of activities that ends with a note that all of these activities fulfilled the teaching in the scroll found by Hilkiah.[11] This is a literary list compiled to showcase Josiah as a 'good religious ruler.'[12] Several

---

absolutely no information on what this event entailed, as has been reflected in histories of Jewish festivals: Schauss, *Jewish Festivals*, 46; Bloch, *Biblical and Historical Background*, 120.

7   De Vaux (*Ancient Israel*, 486) notes this lack specifically. Noll ("Was there Doctrinal Dissemination?," 400) observes correctly that the 'Passover' mentioned for Elephantine cannot in any way be assumed to be related to that in Persian Yehud.

8   Pedersen, "Passahfest und Passahlegende," 175; Würthwein, "Die Josianische Reform und das Deuteronomium," 408, 425; Hoffmann, *Reform und Reformen*, 264–70, who sees most of Josiah's 'reform' as post-exilic historiography; Karlo Visaticki, *Die Reform des Josija und die religiöse Heterodoxie in Israel*, Dissertationen theologische Reihe 21 (St. Ottilien: EOS, 1987), 267, who sees the Josianic Passover as reflecting the exilic period; or Barrick, *King and the Cemeteries*, 129, who sees the Passover material added as early as during the reign of Jehoiakim.

9   Why Josiah would [re]invent a Passover and even hold one that was remembered at all raises a *lot* of questions that are neither noted nor answered here. Welch (*Post-Exilic Judaism*, 49) posited the wholly unlikely theory that Josiah was celebrating a new liberation from Egypt. That Josiah is represented as creating a new event but giving it a (creative, if dubious) historical past related to Joshua (also a dubious past) would seem to be the intent of the author of this short Kings passage: Wagner, "Ein antike Notiz zur Geschichte des Pesach," 31, 35.

10   Jeon (*Impeccable Solomon?*, 133) emphasizes the wide disparity between Kings and Chronicles in terms of the importance of the Passover as being two different renditions entirely.

11   2 Kgs 23:24, also designated as the "instruction of Moses" in 23:25. Some scholars separate the Passover from the other 'reform' measures in the compilation of the list (Hoffmann, *Reform und Reformen*, 259), though this may not be the case if the entire list was composed at a 'late' date, meaning after Josiah's death.

12   See Eynikel (*Reform of King Josiah*, 360–61), who points out its literary purpose to contrast with the events displayed for earlier kings in the book of Kings. It has also been noted that the events that are presented to show Josiah's 'goodness' are specifically cultic, not pointedly political or cultural in nature: see Joseph Robinson, *The Second Book of Kings*, CBC (Cambridge: Cambridge University Press, 1976), 219; Norbert Lohfink, "The Cult Reform of Josiah of Judah," in Miller, Hanson, and

studies have demonstrated that the items recorded in this list belong to part of a series of literary texts recurring throughout Kings that culminate in the 'Josiah's reform' narrative. However, among the items on this list, Passover is not an event that has previously appeared in the book of Kings; it therefore does not, by itself, reflect a reforming narrative tradition within Kings.[13] It would appear to be an action ascribed to Josiah that was seen by the author of the passage concerning Passover as a good religious activity, but which was derived from sources other than the previous reforms enumerated earlier in Kings. It just as easily could have been excluded from the earlier stories about kings so as to save it for the crowning righteousness of Josiah in Kings.[14] In any case, it is not an item of good royal behavior stressed in the narratives of Kings, making it a unique royal event in this particular biblical work.

What is actually reported in the Kings narrative about the Passover is minimal. A quick review of the text leaves a lot to be known. The preface is short: "And the king commanded all the people" (2 Kgs 23:21a). This is presented as a command from the top down and Passover was not, at least in the Kings rendition, any kind of popular memorial known to the people.[15]

McBride, *Ancient Israelite Religion*, 460–61. For a survey of early twentieth-century studies of chapter 23, see Montgomery, *Critical and Exegetical Commentary*, 528–36; for the latter half of the twentieth century, see Eynikel, *Reform of King Josiah*, 10–31.

13 Several relatively recent volumes have dealt extensively with the study of 'reform' items in relation to the historiography of Kings. Major contributions to the genre include: Zorn, "The Pre-Josianic Reforms of Judah" (1977); Hoffmann, *Reform und Reformen* (1980); Lowery, *Reforming Kings and Society* (1991); and Eynikel, *Reform of King Josiah* (1996), 287–91, who presents the general agreement that the Passover material does not reflect Kings material but narratives from Deuteronomy and/or Joshua.

14 In "Das Pesach ist 'zwischeneingekommen' (Dtn 16,1-8)," *Bib* 91 (2010): 495, after reviewing biblical Passover texts, Volker Wagner suggests that the Pesach actually began with Josiah, using Deut 16:1–16 as a Josianic invention. What is important here is the observation that 'Passover' was not a traditional celebration of the monarchies. There is no way to confirm that even an unleavened bread festival (let alone Passover) was celebrated, though if it were, it would have been a domestic rite and perhaps dedicated to the household deities. See Cynthia Shafer-Elliott, "The Role of the Household in the Religious Feasting of Ancient Israel and Judah," in *Feasting in the Archaeology and the Texts of the Bible and the Ancient Near East*, ed. P. Altmann and J. Fu (Winona Lake, IN: Eisenbrauns, 2014), 215–16, though the evidence for such a ritual exists solely in the biblical texts.

15 The call for a feast unknown to the people at large appears central to the narrative. Note the need to emphasize that this has not taken place in living memory (v. 22). However, many scholars insist on the Passover having been well known to the populace: Montgomery, *Critical and Exegetical Commentary*, 535; Haran, *Temples and Temple Service in Ancient Israel*, 347–48; Niditch, *Ancient Israelite Religion*, 105; J. Alberto Soggin, *Israel in the Biblical Period: Institutions, Festivals, Ceremonies, Rituals,*

The passage presumes that this ritual event was not celebrated by the populace and indeed was unknown to them. The king's authority on this matter, as explained by the text, was not born of his own whim, but came from the "scroll of the covenant." However, this scroll was only recently found, as the narrative explains, and it appears to have condemned the people of Judah and Israel for what they had been doing. All this suggests that the story as told presupposes that what the king was commanding was new information to the people. As far as the populace is concerned, the authority for this 'new' and required celebration is Josiah.

As far as who the people involved were, little can be said. From the context, we know that the king being cited was Josiah, but the extent of the population intended to be addressed by this command is less clear. It says *kl h'm* and, taken literally, would have to mean *all* the people. Whether this meant all the people in Jerusalem (which is the only actual location provided for those partaking in the event), all the people in Judah, all the people in Judah and Israel, all the people in the world, or just all the people physically standing before Josiah at some (undisclosed) juncture, is unclear. The extent of "the people" is not made any clearer by the rest of the passage. There is no particular reason from the text to assume that the people referred to in this pericope extend beyond the adult males of Jerusalem.[16] Certainly, the references to Judah and Israel (v. 22) demark only the non-existence of prior royal celebrations of the event and do not constitute expressions of the extent of Josiah's command populace. Chronicles, as will be seen below, elaborates on the extent of those included.

The command itself, as recorded, is fairly ambiguous and would have been more so for people who had heard the scroll read to them once (unless they were more attentive than modern college students or conference attendees!): "Make Passover to Yahweh your God as written on this scroll of the covenant!" (23:21b). Clearly, the directions for what a Passover was and what making one would entail would have to be reiterated, though this is not stated. It is highly unlikely that the assembled people would have been paying close enough attention to have remembered the

---

trans. J. Bowden (Edinburgh: T&T Clark, 2001), 94. See de Vaux, *Ancient Israel*, 484–93, for a fairly standard reconstruction of the origin and celebration of Passover.

16 The absence of any references to women in this (or even the Chronicler's) passage may not be incidental. Weems ("Huldah, the Prophet," in Strawn and Miller, *A God So Near*, 330) insists that the fact that Huldah is a woman is centrally important to the author since it is mentioned; whether that means that the absence of women in this passage was also important cannot be determined. However, it is possible that this was only an adult male affair. Phyllis A. Bird ("Women in the Ancient Mediterranean World: Ancient Israel," *BR* 39 [1994]: 44–45) cautions about making clear statements about the religious life of women in ancient Israel/Judah since many cultures have gender distinctions in praxis, even when the same event is taking place.

details of one small section of a lengthy document read to them for the first time. The command format would normally suggest that carrying out this festival was not something the people were going to agree to do voluntarily, in which case an entry line like "Let us make a Passover ..." or "Isn't it about time we rejuvenated the practice of having a Passover ..." would have been sufficient and more appropriate. The text seems to suggest that the people were not altogether behind this feast (or, perhaps, the 'reform' altogether); at the very least, it shows that the author wished to convey that the king, not the people, was responsible for doing things correctly and that the ruler directs the population to act properly.

The phrase "Yahweh, your God" appears often in Deuteronomistically influenced texts (and this is one, certainly). It reads oddly in the mouth of Josiah at this junction. Why do the people repeatedly need to be reminded that Yahweh is 'their' deity? Has not the slaughter just described in the narrative suggested rather forcefully that devotees of other divinities were not acceptable to this king?[17] The phrase may be stock language, but the reader knows who Yahweh is, and one assumes that the people in the narrative would have known. But perhaps they did not and the phrasing is more intentional than a surface reading might suggest. That is, according to the text, these people have just stopped worshiping a goodly number of deities on threat of death by this very king, so that the notion of which of their 'former' pantheon they were ordered to worship may not have been at all clear, such that "Yahweh, your God" may be central to their understanding the command.[18] Finally, Josiah seems to be holding, pointing to, or distributing the scroll. For this command, as for Kings' Josiah material in general, this is "this scroll of the covenant," though exactly what

---

17   2 Kgs 23:20. Depending on the account in Chronicles, Barrick (*King and the Cemeteries*, 23), with others, prefers to read the verse without any killing of live persons, though others, equally cautious, accept executions, e.g., Lowery, *Reforming Kings*, 208. That at least some (if not all) other deities were unacceptable to the Josiah portrayed in the passage has been made clear in their destruction along with the paraphernalia of their worship: 2 Kgs 23:4–8, 10–15. That these were real deities of the real Judahite cult is evident enough, but not relevant to the story as narrative: see Dever, "The Silence of the Text," in Coogan, Exum, and Stager, *Scripture and Other Artifacts*, 146–61, and Jacob Milgrom, "The Nature and Extent of Idolatry in Eighth-Seventh Century Judah," *HUCA* 69 (1998): 1–13.

18   The named deities are restricted to Baal, Asherah, Chemosh, Astarte, and Milcom; the "host of heaven" remains debated in that it may refer to a specific group of deities, to all the gods together, or it may have changed meaning through time. See the survey in Herbert Niehr, "Host of Heaven," *DDD* cols. 812–13. Perhaps ghosts and honored dead were also worshipped: 2 Kgs 23:24. Following the Passover material is too suggestive and too ambiguous to be certain of exactly what is being condemned.

covenant this is supposed to refer to is never actually made clear in the entire book of Kings. The use of the phrase in this particular passage, however, heightens the connection of A) the king, B) the people, C) the Passover, and D) its observance for Yahweh (their God). The directions for this particular Passover are lost to us; those in Deuteronomy, by which everyone has to come to Jerusalem to slaughter the main course, do not appear in this rendition of the event. Unquestionably, the later, familiar, ritual celebration of the 'family' Passover had no connection to Josiah's cultic celebration as reported in Kings.[19] The text simply does not allow us to determine what was meant.[20]

The final, long comment in Kings about the Passover is concerned with its uniqueness:

> For such a Passover had not been made from the days of the rulers who ruled Israel and all the days of kings of Israel and kings of Judah except in the eighteenth year of King Josiah was made such a Passover to Yahweh in Jerusalem.
> (23:22-23)

Usually, the passage is interpreted to mean that such a Passover was kept in the time of the early rulers (what we have generally called "judges"), but not in the days of the "kings" of Judah and Israel, though the position that no Passover had been kept in all the days of Israel and Judah's rulers altogether also has its adherents.[21] From possible syntax and from context it would appear that the author intended to mean that no Passover like this had been held since the people had any kind of leader over them while they were in the land; in any case, it clearly excludes the possibility of any similar Passover having taken place under any *mlk*.[22] In addition,

---

19   See Bloch (*Biblical and Historical Background*, 124), who connects the 'family' Passover to chanting the *Hallel* in the Second Temple era, though Bloch relates this to the Levitical singers in 2 Chr 35:15. There are no such personnel in the Kings rendition.

20   The lack of material in Kings to determine what Josiah's Passover entailed has been properly noted: see, for example, Visaticki, *Reform des Josija*, 163, and Lowery, *Reforming Kings*, 163. The disconnection of Josiah's Passover from that in Deuteronomy has long been observed: see Engnell, *Rigid Scrutiny*, 58, 187. The ambiguity of the event is nicely captured in Cohn, *2 Kings*, 160. However, many scholars still assume that Josiah is following Deuteronomy, e.g., de Vaux, *Ancient Israel*, 486. The fact that Josiah holds this event only once would seem to disqualify Deuteronomy as the source of the memorial as presented by Josiah in Kings.

21   Robinson, *Second Book of Kings*, 227, along with the New English Bible translation, included the period of the Judges in the span of time when the Passover was not kept. On the other hand, it is interesting to note that First Esdras follows Chronicles in having the last previous celebration of Passover in the time of Samuel.

22   This would still leave open the possibility of a reference to a Passover under Joshua before the land was conquered (Josh 5:10). However, it is not necessarily the

it is important to note that Josiah only holds the Passover once. The sentence simply says that, in the entire period from the creation of the (for lack of a better word) polity of Israel (and/or Judah) to the destruction of Judah, there was exactly one Passover and it was in the reign of Josiah. It was also in the eighteenth year of Josiah, so Kings wishes it to be clear that this event was tied closely to the finding of the scroll in the temple, to the reaction of Josiah to that scroll, and to the list of religious activities that surround the Passover notice in Kings. It is worth noting that a 'real' Passover had not been kept in Israel nor in Judah. This is significant since Kings tends to downplay Judahite apostasy while foregrounding Israel's.[23]

Finally, this is a Passover in Jerusalem; it is not a Passover in Israel or even in the other cities or rural regions of Judah. As far as 2 Kgs 23:23 is concerned, the Passover of Josiah is an event of the king's city only; no other area is implied by the text. Occasionally, it is claimed on the basis of Deuteronomy (and in conflict with Exodus) that the populace of Judah and Israel all went to Jerusalem to observe Passover on the order of the king.[24] The text, however, says nothing of the kind.[25] The immensity of a lavish feast related to the temple and its deity as in Chronicles would relate Josiah to Yahweh in a significant way, but Kings has no feast recorded.[26]

---

one recorded in Joshua itself, as it is used in the narrative as the stopping point for the wilderness wandering sequence of Israel's existence, making no reference to future requirements for its observance.

23   Whatever modern scholars may think of Israelite Passover practices being adapted for Judah by Josiah, Kings does not, and would not, suggest such a historical relationship. Both Nicholson (*Deuteronomy and Tradition*, 1–17, 83–106) and Gray (*I & II Kings*, 719) present one school of thought, holding that Deuteronomy and its traditions came from Israelites fleeing to Jerusalem. For a ruler being depicted as re-establishing an ancient and proper Judahite cult (especially in the face of Kings' presentation of Israel's corrupted cult), it would be unlikely in the extreme to have the author of Kings present Josiah knowingly using Israelite practices in his reform. The historical reality behind Josiah's Passover remains irretrievable.

24   The idea of the Passover including all of Judah and Israel comes from 2 Chr 35:18 and is then read into the short note of Kings. Building on previous work by N. K. Gottwald and W. E. Claburn, Nakanose (*Josiah's Passover*, 28, 71–77) sees the feast as part of a general centralization of Israel and Judah under the control of the king and as a device for removing local autonomy from peasants. The notion that Josiah ruled over a recreated Davidic empire lies behind this interpretation of the extent of the Passover participation, a notion highly popular in the middle of the twentieth century: Lowery, *Reforming Kings*, 163. However, the recreation of a lost Davidic empire would appear to be a relatively recent nostalgic notion. See Lowell K. Handy, "The Rise and Fall of the *Sogennant* Josianic Empire," PEGLAMBS 21 (2001): 70–73.

25   As correctly noted by J. Maxwell Miller and John H. Hayes, *A History of Ancient Israel and Judah* (Philadelphia: Westminster, 1986), 399.

26   See David B. Weisberg, "A 'Dinner at the Palace' during Nebuchadnezzar's

In summation, the report of the Passover in Kings is a short note, intended to fit into the list of activities undertaken by Josiah upon learning the contents of the scroll. The form of the event is not reported (we only assume it has to do with eating because other references to Passovers in the Hebrew Bible, the New Testament, the Rabbinic literature, and more modern seders all entail eating).[27] Eating is not important here and, in reality, who partakes in the Passover is not important here either. What is important is that Josiah commands it, restoring an 'ancient' but forsaken ritual required by God. Moreover, for a character who is in many ways paired off with Solomon, it is noteworthy that the Passover is not one of the parallel topics. Solomon has a big feast (an extremely large meal/sacrifice) at the founding of the temple in Jerusalem (1 Kgs 8:62–65), but he has no Passover. Neither, it should be noticed by those who see Josiah as some sort of "David redivivus," does David.[28] In this, Josiah is (explicitly, according to Kings) totally unique and he provides only one occasion of said Passover. The extent of the people partaking of Passover is probably intended to be those present in Jerusalem (and maybe only the adult men of Jerusalem at that), but, for the passage, it is quite immaterial who would have taken part. That King Josiah is devoted to Yahweh *is* important; the entire Passover itself is *not*.

The Chronicler's version of Passover is much longer and, despite the comment that this is the first such festival since Samuel (2 Chr 35:18), it follows Hezekiah's Passover (2 Chronicles 30) after the long gap of Manasseh's reign, Amon's being very short. The description of the extent of the celebration is restricted to Jerusalem, and those who are presented as attending appear to be those who were in Jerusalem at the time of its proclamation. This, at least, is true of the Israelites (35:17) who are stated to be those who are present; they also stayed for the seven days of the

---

Reign," in Galil, Geller, and Millard, *Homeland and Exile*, 263–65, for feasts and Nebuchadnezzar.

27 It should also be noted that the Passover in Kings does not entail reading Scripture, a central part of Pesach by the rabbinic period (m. Meg. 3:5); Arie van der Kooij, "The Public Reading of Scriptures at Feasts," in Tuckett, *Feasts and Festivals*, 27. This may only be of interest given the interest of the Josianic passage in written directions; there may be written directions for carrying out a Passover in the story, but not a direction for reading during Passover.

28 Though Josiah and Solomon are in many ways paralleled in Kings, the large sacrifice by Solomon at the dedication of the temple and Josiah's Passover are not among the proper parallels, as noted by Knoppers, *Two Nations under God*, 117 and 117n51. The phrase "David redivivus" is taken from Laato, *Josiah and David Redivivus*. It is also used by Knoppers, *Two Nations under God*, 245.

Feast of Unleavened Bread.[29] Here, unlike in Kings, Passover is presented as a feast and it is connected to a/the Feast of Unleavened Bread.

In Chronicles we are presented with a great deal more of material concerned with the manner in which the Passover was carried out than is the case with the narrative in Kings. It is not terribly surprising, given the Chronicler's concern for proper cult, and proper priests, that the narrative focuses on the Levites and not King Josiah.[30] We are told Josiah made the Passover for Yahweh in Jerusalem and it was done on the fourteenth day of the first month of the eighteenth year. But the king's command here is not made to "all the people," as it is in Kings, but to the Levites:

> Put the holy ark in the house which Solomon, son of David, King of Israel, built; it is not to carry on the shoulders; you will serve Yahweh your God and his people Israel; set yourselves up by houses of your fathers according to your divisions in the writing of David, King of Israel, and in the manuscript of Solomon, his son, and serve in the holy by divisions of the house of the fathers to your brothers, sons of the people and division of the house of the father of the Levites. And slaughter the Passover and sanctify yourselves and establish for your Brothers to do according to the word of Yahweh by the hand of Moses.
> (2 Chr 35:3b–6)

This conforms nicely with the concern for establishing the temple and the ranks of priests detailed in Chronicles for the reign of David.[31] In this aspect, at least, Chronicles is re-establishing the temple and the priests as they were to be properly construed in the first place by David (who, in Chronicles, one needs to remember is not the scoundrel of Samuel or even Kings, but the paradigm of the good ruler).[32] In the arrangements of the temple and priests, Josiah is not shown to be an innovator from the decrees of David and of Solomon. Likewise, he is not an innovator of the Passover, as this is the very mode of celebration given by Yahweh and

---

29 Klein (*2 Chronicles*, 523) emphasizes the lack of any mention of a Feast of Unleavened Bread in the Kings' version of Josiah and yet how it is given even more prominence in the Chronicler's rendition of Hezekiah (2 Chr 30:13, 21–27).

30 The centrality of Levites and proper priestly behavior in the Passover in Chronicles is stressed by Johnstone, *1 and 2 Chronicles*, 246. In a subtle way, this passage delimits the status of Josiah and the Levites as superior to others, which is a common feature of feasts that allow visual observation of status. See Barbara Hold-Cavell, "The Ethological Bases of Status Hierarchies," in *Food and the Status Quest: An Interdisciplinary Perspective*, ed. P. Wiessner and W. Schiefenhövel, AFN 1 (Providence, RI: Berghahn Books, 1996), 19–20, 26–28.

31 Noted often by commentators, e.g., Myers, *II Chronicles*, 212; Klein, *2 Chronicles*, 519–20.

32 See stages of Davidic development in William Franklin Stinespring, "Eschatology in Chronicles," *JBL* 80 (1961): 219. Steussy (*David*, 125) notes the contrast with Samuel's David in the centrality of David as instigator of the cult.

written down by Moses.[33] Unfortunately, the reference to Moses' scrivener work is not elaborated upon here or in the rest of the Josiah passage. What, exactly, this "word of Yahweh" was supposed to have represented in the ideal of the author of Chronicles is unknown, since the ensuing description of the Passover feast is not one for which we have a record in Torah; it conforms neither to Exodus nor Deuteronomy.[34]

What is then described (2 Chr 35:7–18) is a vast royal banquet, not a simple Passover meal as required in Torah.[35] Moreover, the people do not supply the Passover sacrifices according to this rendition; these come from the king, his officers, the N^{e}gidey-byt elohim, and the Levites. This largess would normally designate these people as elites to whom those invited owe allegiance.[36] As described, Josiah is the clear supplier of the bulk of the food, indeed perhaps all of it for the general populace while the rest is reported as coming from religious personnel. The extent of their generosity is duly recorded:

Donor	Small Livestock	Large Livestock
Josiah	30,000	3,000
Officers	?	?
Temple "Chiefs"	2,600	300
Levitical Officers	5,000	500

This totals some 40,400+ head of livestock. Now, of these, the 7,600 sheep and goats and the 800 cows deriving from the priests are delineated for

---

33   The lack of reference to this work as a "book of the covenant" disconnects it from the text described in Kings. Myers (*II Chronicles*, 211) assumes it would be so understood because it is mentioned in the Chronicler's section on Hezekiah's reign, but this is not clearly the case.

34   2 Chr 35:13 appears to be attempting to combine the mutually exclusive presentations of Passover preparation in Exodus and Deuteronomy: so Myers, *II Chronicles*, 211; McKenzie, *Trouble with Kings*, 114. However, it is possible that it simply reflects yet another variant tradition, either textual or ritual.

35   Some assert, however, that the Torah Passover legislation does not reflect the early Passover event, which was, they posit, a temple service all along: Cogan and Tadmor, *II Kings*, 290, basing their work on Haran, *Temples and Temple Service*, 343–48.

36   Michael Dietler, "Feasts and Commensal Politics in the Political Economy: Food, Power and Status in Prehistoric Europe," in Wiessner and Schiefenhövel, *Food and the Status Quest*, 90–91. In *Fillets of Fatling and Goblets of Gold: The Use of Meal Events in the Ritual Imagery in the Ugaritic Mythological and Epic Texts*, GUS 4 (Piscataway, NJ: Gorgias, 2008), 84, 209, Dan Belnap emphasizes the "largess" of the feast displaying the generosity and capability of the host's provision. These feasts in Babylonia were usually restricted to the uppermost levels of society: Weisberg, "Dinner at the Palace," 262. The feast provided by a ruler also implies a stable social situation and displays social standards: Mary Douglas, *In the Active Voice* (London: Routledge, 1982), 85, 111–13.

the consumption by the priests and Levites, while the offerings coming from the stock of the king and the officers are expressly said to be divided among the people and priests (and Levites). For the text, the question of where the priests and Levites got all of this livestock is not one of importance; just be aware that if the priesthood had this much farm produce, there are real questions about the land holdings of the religious establishment.[37]

A little thought about the livestock presented in the story is not unreasonable. The consumption of meat from livestock among the ancient Mediterranean cultures was highly restricted; larger livestock was in relatively short supply and was needed for other products.[38] Animal labor, wool, milk, and other dairy products were the major reasons for raising most livestock and one did not willingly slaughter large numbers of them, particularly since large herds were extremely rare in the classical world.[39] The territory required to have been under royal control in order to produce 3,000 head of cattle for slaughter and 30,000 small head of expendable livestock (presumably sheep and goats unneeded for wool or dairy products) would have been considerable. Exactly how much land would have been needed to be set aside for cattle-raising for this banquet is impossible to determine. One needs to keep in mind that, if Deuteronomy reflects any sort of reality as to sacrifice purity laws, it would take several head of cattle to provide faultless bovines (Deut 17:1); this would

---

37 Nakanose (*Josiah's Passover*, 109–10) reads this information as a manner by which the priestly elite extract yet more power for themselves from the poor peasants. However, he does not address the question of where the priests got this massive amount of livestock, assuming, as he does, that it belongs to them and they extract payment from the populace to make use of it. None of this appears in the Chronicles account, but it can be reconstructed hypothetically from Torah legislation and the Chronicler's narrative. Note that in the Hezekiah narrative in Chronicles (30:24), the priests supply no livestock for the Passover at all.

38 Peter Garnsey, *Food and Society in Classical Antiquity*, Key Themes in Ancient History (Cambridge: Cambridge University Press, 1999), 16; MacDonald, *What Did the Ancient Israelites Eat?*, 62–64; Jodi Magness, "Conspicuous Consumption: Dining on Meat in the Ancient Mediterranean World and Near East," in Altmann and Fu, *Feasting in the Archaeology and Texts of the Bible*, 53.

39 Garnsey, *Food and Society*, 16–17; Judy Urquhart, *Animals on the Farm: Their History from the Earliest Times to the Present Day* (London: MacDonald, 1983), 83. On modern African cattle herding societies, see Gudrun Dahl and Anders Hjurt, *Having Herds: Pastoral Herd Growth and Household Economy*, Stockholm Studies in Social Anthropology 2 (Stockholm: University of Stockholm Press, 1976), 161–62, but note that cattle slaughter is usually restricted to very few animals, and at times when milk production is abnormally low. They also note that, in a communal feast, everyone is expected to contribute (163), rather than one person supplying everything (which is the situation reflected in 2 Chr 31:3–10).

require yet more land. While in the United States an acre of land will suffice for raising a cow in Iowa, it takes 230 acres to raise a cow in Nevada.[40] The ancient Mediterranean lands simply were not on the Iowa arm of this scale.[41] Beef was a prestigious food, usually restricted to the diets of the elite.[42] Moreover, the resources for butchering and serving beef on such a large scale appears to be a literary hyperbole that the Judahite livestock population of the time of Josiah would not have maintained.[43] The enormity of the meat provided is clearly intended to impress the reader with the largess of the priests, Josiah, and Yahweh, but hardly reflects any actual Josianic meal.[44] Recordings of huge feasts are not unusual for the ancient Near East, with massive numbers of livestock on the table.[45] However, these banquets also enumerate a huge amount of other types of

---

40   Laurie Winn Carlson, *Cattle: An Informal Social History* (Chicago: Ivan R. Dee, 2001), 276. However, note that the United States Department of Agriculture recommends two acres of pasture for each dairy cow raised: U.S. Department of Agriculture, Extension Service, *Raising Livestock on Small Farms*, Farmers' Bulletin No. 2224 (Washington, DC: Government Printing Office, 1983), 8; for ewes it is suggested that two acres be supplied for every three to eight head (14).

41   Garnsey, *Food and Society*, 123.

42   Carol Meyers, "Menu: Royal Repasts and Social Class in Biblical Israel," in Altmann and Fu, *Feasting in the Archaeology and Texts of the Bible*, 133, who notes that even among the elite, sheep predominate over cattle; Garnsey, *Food and Society*, 124–25. Note, also that the most common sacrificial animal in the Mediterranean world of Josiah's time was swine (17).

43   MacDonald (*What Did the Ancient Israelites Eat?*, 79) posits a limited amount of useable livestock at the time due to tribute payments to Assyria. Magness ("Conspicuous Consumption," 52) suggests pottery shapes indicate a decline in meat consumption in the area in general in the seventh century BCE.

44   Myers, *II Chronicles*, 212. Belnap (*Fillets of Fatling and Goblets of Gold*, 70) notes the use of large amounts of beef served in feasts is a cliché of the Hebrew Bible. However, note the much lower numbers of actual bones buried in a pit at Ramat Rahel from contemporary feasts: Deidre N. Fulton et al., "Feasting in Paradise: Feast Remains from the Iron Age Palace of Ramat Rahel and Their Implications," *BASOR* 374 (2015): 35.

45   Ashurnasirpal II's Nimrod ten-day feast is often cited, wherein he served 29,200 head of assorted livestock to feed 69,574 people for the ten days and the menu included a vast variety of meats and bread, lots of beer, and unnumbered fruits, nuts, roasted grains, and dairy products. However, this was Assyria at its height, not Judah at its end: Peter Altmann, *Festive Meals in Ancient Israel: Deuteronomy's Identity Politics in Their Ancient Near Eastern Context*, BZAW 424 (Berlin: de Gruyter, 2011), 78–98; Meyers, "Menu," 142. In Athens, a total of 240 bulls was considered an enormous outlay of meat for a civil religious feast: Louise Bruit Zaidman and Pauline Schmitt Pantel, *Religion in the Ancient Greek City*, trans. P. Cartledge (Cambridge: Cambridge University Press, 1992), 30.

food for the attendees.⁴⁶ Interestingly enough, in Josiah's festival what is recorded is only meat. The staples of any eating occasion of the time are all missing: bread, wine, and olive oil.⁴⁷ Clearly, the 'menu' is restricted to the prestige course.

Note that this ceremony, according to the text, is not supplied by the people of the land but by the incoming power structure of Jerusalem. The head of the polity and 'father of the feast' is King Josiah. He is credited with the bulk of the consumable items. The rest of the enumerated foodstuffs are credited to those who align with the king, and who now control the religious aspects of the city and have exclusive rights to that control— the Levites. Josiah reinstates the positions of the cult as required by David, who, in v. 15, is actually given the credit for commanding the singers (and one might infer the gatekeepers and priests) to do their appropriate tasks "on that day."⁴⁸ The royal banquet pictured here is at least as symbolic as it may be a reflection of any actual Passover celebration. The king, as the representative of God, supplies the feast; the people receive it for free. David, Solomon, and Josiah represent the idea of 'kingship' here and really are interchangeable as textual characters. The temple (including its Levitical priesthood) provides both the lavishness of the community banquet and its location. This is not how a real royal feast would have happened, but it is the ideological point of the narrative. As symbolic occurrence, this is all a literary construction and not an elaboration on any event in Josiah's (or any other) reign. For Chronicles, it presents the king as the embodiment of ancient tradition from before the monarchy itself in his provision of a feast in honor of and commitment to Yahweh that henceforth is to be recognized in the Jerusalemite temple and its Levitical priesthood. It is, as Peter Altmann has correctly noted, a Passover in which Josiah is the focal point.⁴⁹

Three meals are divided out by the author: 1) the sacrificial meal to Yahweh, carried out by the Aaronite priests and that took all daylight hours to prepare (this included the blood, unspecified burnt offerings sections, and the fatty portions of the slaughtered carcasses); 2) the meal of the Levites and other priests, all cooked and served by the Levites, setting

---

46   Fulton et al. ("Feasting in Paradise," 34–36) record a wide variety of meat servings, heavy on fowl in addition to sheep, goats, and cattle (also some fish).

47   MacDonald, *What Did the Ancient Israelites Eat?*, 91, a triad now often repeated. Dever, *Lives of Ordinary People*, 170; Leann Pace, "Feasting and Everyday Meals in the World of the Hebrew Bible: The Relationship Reexamined through Material Culture and Texts," in Altmann and Fu, *Feasting in the Archaeology and Texts of the Bible*, 187.

48   It might be noted that these singers, sons of Asaph, are as close as any commentator can come to finding anything like a Seder in this Passover: Bloch, *Biblical and Historical Background*, 124–25. Bloch acknowledges it probably does not predate the Second Temple.

49   Altmann, *Festive Meals*, 191, a very different focus from that in Deuteronomy 16.

them apart socially and religiously from the population in general, so that the other priests could continue their activities uninterrupted; and 3) the massive meat-feast by the king, fed to the people who were present.

The first of the 'meals' is restricted to Yahweh. As a sacrifice, it is intended for the deity whereby Yahweh receives ritual recognition with the splashing of blood and the first serving of the meal itself. This 'first' meal can only be prepared and offered by the proper Levites. In this case, it is stipulated that only the Levites who were descendants of Aaron, the first priest, were to make the sacrifice proper. This was clearly a distinction in social status of some importance to the Chronicler that reflected the strict hierarchy of the priesthood of the Persian period. The focal point of any city's sacrificial meal is the sacrifice relating the community to its god/s. This was a form of 'communication' with the deity that guaranteed divine maintenance of the human community.[50] As the most important aspect of any sacrificial festival in the ancient world, it preceded the consumption by anyone else, allowing the primacy of the god to be the focal point of all in attendance. As with the Greek community sacrificial meal, the deity receives only restricted burnt portions and the fat (2 Chr 35:14).[51] If Yahweh received burned sections of the Paschal lamb, it was from the roasted sacrifice. Boiling the meat was the norm for any meat dish throughout the period in Judah and would have conformed to any fancy meal at any time.[52] That the boiled meat went to the gathered people was no doubt a clear religious and social distinction; that roasted meat was distributed to the tribal families is restricted by the note that this was offering material to be given to Yahweh (2 Chr 35:12). Once the food for Yahweh was taken care of, the general feast could take place.

In Chronicles, the 'second' meal described is that of the Levites. While the Aaronite Levites continued to sacrifice and prepare meat for consumption for Yahweh and the population in general, the Levites prepared their own meals and those for the gatekeepers. Apparently, all priests consumed meat prepared only by Levites. Thus, the special status of the Levites in Chronicles is stressed explicitly in this section, where they form a separate elite dining population.[53] They also roasted and boiled unspecified "sacred offerings" that became the general feast for the congregated populace. It is interesting that, in this Passover passage in Chronicles, the

---

50 Bruit Zaidman and Schmitt Pantel, *Religion*, 29–30, 34.

51 Burkert (*Greek Religion*, 57) notes that the gods get the inedible parts. For Greeks it was the thigh bones and fat: Bruit Zaidman and Schmitt Pantel, *Religion*, 36.

52 Magness, "Conspicuous Consumption," 47–49; MacDonald, *What Did the Ancient Israelites Eat?*, 32.

53 Fulton et al. ("Feasting in Paradise," 44) note archaeological evidence for the segregation by social status at Ramat Rahel.

Levites are given the occupation of skinning the Paschal lamb; a part of the sacrifice with special significance in Greek civil feasts,[54] although it is unclear whether the skins were for the benefit of the Levites or the city treasury in the biblical passage. Neither Leviticus nor Deuteronomy mentions the hides of the Passover sacrifice, so its appearance in Chronicles might suggest some interest in civil feasts beyond Jerusalem (the question of the ritual purity regulations regarding the handling of hides is not broached in this passage).

Finally, the 'third' Passover meal in Chronicles is that of the gathered population. Cooked and served by the Levites, the menu supplied is mutton and beef. That they are roasting and boiling the meat in order to cover at least two *torah* traditions has been sufficiently noted.[55] What is more significant in this section is that the populace supplies nothing for this 'Passover.' This is entirely top down, and the general populace is dependent on the priests and their patron, the king, for the entire Passover; in this case, that includes what to do, the requirement to participate, and everything to be consumed. Both Leviticus and Deuteronomy describe Passover and the Feast of Unleavened Bread as extended family meals centered on the sacrificed lamb, but the importance of bread in both repasts is imperative. There is no bread mentioned in Josiah's meat festival; neither does bread appear for the Feast of Unleavened Bread. That it is missing tends to highlight the absence of women in these feast narratives, since they were traditionally the bread bakers.[56] Moreover, there is significantly more beef here than mutton for a Passover; given that beef was a prestigious food, its serving impresses upon the reader the power of Josiah, the generousness of Yahweh, and the importance of the Jerusalemite population to whom it is served. The Chronicler's Passover is much less a Pesach than a civic festival celebrating the importance of Jerusalem, its God, its priesthood, and its king.

While the Jerusalemites are said to have been there, only the Judahites and Israelites who were present at the moment were in attendance. This is not a Passover for the entirety of Judah, let alone for both Judah and Israel. The Passover as rendered by the Chronicler cannot be taken as a story devised to place Josiah as ruler over Israel (as it has occasionally

---

54   Bruit Zaidman and Schmitt Pantel, *Religion*, 35–36, where the skins in public feasts were sold for the polis funds, but in private feasts, the skins were part of the price paid to the priests.

55   Fishbane, *Biblical Interpretation*, 135. Most commentators make note of the traditions, see Klein, *2 Chronicles*, 522.

56   MacDonald, *What Did the Ancient Israelites Eat?*, 21; Dever, *Lives of Ordinary People*, 160, 164; now Gale A. Yee, "'He Will Take the Best of Your Fields': Royal Feasts and Rural Extraction," *JBL* 136 (2017): 834–35.

been interpreted), nor can it be taken as a narrative about control over even Judah.⁵⁷ The passage can be read as a narrative placing Josiah on the side of the true and righteous David and Solomon against other rulers in the history of Judah. In this, Josiah commands a proper religious festival that is carried out explicitly by the Levites on behalf of the people as well as for the other priests. It is, according to the Chronicler's vision, a meal of religious significance and of religious origin. On the functional level, however, it truly is a civic festival uniting Yahweh with Jerusalem and Yahweh's temple personnel in Jerusalem.

As long as one is fairly warned not to take sociological models too seriously, they can be of service in understanding biblical texts. A number of studies have been made concerning eating and meals in the ancient world, and the Passover of Josiah in Chronicles may be viewed in relation to some of these studies. If Goody's study of the production divisions of meals is considered, one can see how much of the Passover described in Chronicles is intended to display control by the king:⁵⁸

Production (growing food)	King, Officials, Priests and Levites
Storing/Distribution	King, Officials, Priests and Levites
Preparation (cooking)	Levites
Consumption	Priests, Levites, People
Cleaning Up	[Not mentioned]

Simply by issuing a command and inviting a certain populace to partake of the food, the king is presented as forming a community.⁵⁹ All meals in the ancient (or any) world reflected social relationships, and the symbolism of who was allowed to eat with whom at what times set cultural boundaries. The Passover in Chronicles makes this meal one in which Yahweh is the head of the feast, but not its provider. The provision is made by those who symbolically serve Yahweh and Yahweh alone: King Josiah, who has not only taken up the activity of reducing the worshiped divine level to

---

57 On the expansion and contraction of reconstructions of Josiah's 'empire' in scholarly research of the twentieth century, see Handy, "Rise and Fall," 69–77.

58 Jack Goody, *Cooking, Cuisine and Class: A Study in Comparative Sociology* (Cambridge: Cambridge University, 1982), as cited in Alan Beardsworth and Teresa Keil, *Sociology on the Menu: An Invitation to the Study of Food and Society* (London: Routledge, 1996), 47; MacDonald, *What Did the Ancient Israelites Eat?*, 10. It should be noted that all the preparation of this feast is done by males, according to the narrative, as with other feast narratives: Belnap, *Fillets of Fatling and Goblets of Gold*, 69. Of course, the clean-up is not mentioned, leaving the possibility that women were assumed to do this work—we don't know.

59 Beardsworth and Keil, *Sociology on the Menu*, 73–99.

one god but who has managed to make this 'forgotten' Passover meal in the exact manner prescribed by Yahweh through Moses. As an internal literary narrative, this comment can stand; once we try to find Passover as royal banquet in the larger biblical textual tradition, this all falls apart. It is especially the case that there is no Torah-related 'Mosaic' description of Passover that conforms to a huge monarchical feast.

If we assume that this Passover was intended to define the members of some community, it must be those who recognize Jerusalem as the religious and political center of their existence. This would explain the emphasis on the feeding of Jerusalemites and those Judahites and Israelites who were in Jerusalem, not to mention the Levites who now live in Jerusalem. Israel is no more within this circle than would be the Israel of Tobit, where Tobit alone recognizes Jerusalem's centrality (Tob 1:3-9).[60] If one takes a swift look at the civic banquet in Greece as studied by Garnsey, one can see a similar use of sacrificial meals to make a political point regarding who is in and out of the civil community.[61] In this regard, it is interesting to note that, in Athenian polis festivals, the meat was carefully distributed in equal amounts to the adult free males as a sign of their citizenship and to all citizens, if not in carefully equal helpings, during its period of democracy. That the Passover in Chronicles looks like a civic banquet is neither surprising nor particularly insightful. Garnsey's outline of the importance of the Greek and Roman civic banquet looks right at home:[62]

1. Arranged by a political authority
2. Follows a public sacrifice (always a blood sacrifice)
3. Uses sacrificial food as an ingredient of the civic meal
4. Religious aspect (indeed, all meals had some religious aspect)
5. Public event integrated into the life of the city involving more members of the city than any other

Garnsey continues that the meal of the entire polis connects the city into a family relationship, simultaneously binding consumer and community together. Nonetheless, the meal is still a hierarchy, and the meals were financed, supplied, and controlled by the elite of the polis.[63] Being a sociological study, the ideology of the connection of the sacrificial meal with the gods of the city of Athens does not come into play in Garnsey's work; it was, however, a part of the Athenian understanding of the meal, and it

---

60 José Vílchez Líndez, *Tobías y Judit*, NBEN 3 (Estella: Verbo Divino, 2000), 61-63.
61 Garnsey, *Food and Society in Classical Antiquity*, 132-33.
62 Ibid.
63 Ibid., 134; the host uses the feast to solidify authoritative leadership: Belnap, *Fillets of Fatling and Goblets of Gold*, 70, 84.

is clearly central to the Passover in Chronicles.[64] In the context of ancient civic feasts, an actual banquet of the type presented in Chronicles would have bound the partakers into a social (or even political) alliance with the 'host' and this appears to be understood by the author of Chronicles for this feast as well.[65]

In sum, Josiah's Passover in Chronicles is used to demonstrate the loyalty of Josiah to Yahweh, but in a manner in which Josiah becomes the mediator of God to the people in Jerusalem as the proper successor to David and Solomon.[66] Far from representing a general pious recognition of Yahweh as God on the part of the population, the use of a royally provided feast serves to show loyalty (and probably a form of patronage) to the representative of the god providing the feast. Josiah becomes the legitimate and righteous king in his being chosen by, as well as being obedient to, Yahweh and by being recognized and accepted by the people.[67] Jerusalem is Yahweh's city and the Jerusalemites are Yahweh's people.[68] This Passover is a symbolic narrative of the status of Josiah and Jerusalem rather than a record of any historical meal that possibly may have been served during the reign of Josiah. In the end, the story emphasizes the scroll as the authority for the feast, and Passover can and will pass into Jewish tradition devoid of both Josiah and Jerusalem.

---

64 See Burkert (*Greek Religion*, 57–58), who notes the importance for the Greeks of the relationship with the gods in the sacrificial meal, and, that everyone—women, boys, girls—has their part in the repast while for the community it defines that community. Altmann (*Festive Meals*, 122) connects meat itself with the blessing of Yahweh (Deut 12:15).

65 See Aldina da Silva, "La symbolique du repas au Proche-Orient ancien," *Studies in Religion/Sciences religieuses* 24 (1995): 150–52, who raises the question of loyalty and patronage on the part of the 'family' of diners.

66 The importance of the king to represent the god/s and to be of royal lineage was significant throughout Assyrian-controlled territory in Josiah's time (and certainly in biblical tradition thereafter): Radner, "Assyrian and Non-Assyrian Kingship," in Lanfranchi and Rollinger, *Concepts of Kingship in Antiquity*, 25, 30.

67 See Georg Fohrer, "Der Vertrag zwischen König und Volk in Israel," in *Studien zur alttestamentliche Theologie und Geschichte (1949-1966)* (Berlin: de Gruyter, 1969), 342–43.

68 Fulton et al. ("Feasting in Paradise," 29) record the feasting in Ramat Rahel as potentially reflecting the overlordship of Assyria, in which case the emphasis on Jerusalem as the proper place for Yahweh feasts might be a profession of identity, not so much for Assyrian control, but of Persian.

CHAPTER EIGHT
THE POPULAR AFTERLIFE OF JOSIAH:
THE KING IN WORLD HISTORIES[1]

The Josiah of the biblical texts, whether in Kings, Chronicles, First Esdras, or Sirach, was already a remembered literary figure. Each author used the king for their own purposes. These representations of Josiah were merely the starting point for a tradition of understanding Josiah and writing about him that continues to the present. What is cursorily to follow is the path by which this biblical figure of modest record has become a major player in the social evolution of homo sapiens sapiens. This trail is tracked from the anonymous author of Kings[2] to the pivotal study on the rise of monotheism by Jan Assmann.[3] It is a look at King Josiah as a player not in biblical studies themselves, but in reconstructions of the history of the ancient world. The long tradition of Christian chronologies is of little interest for this study as they routinely reproduced minimal chronological data lifted from the biblical text: it would usually suffice that Josiah reigned for thirty-one years and that Jeremiah began his prophetic career in Josiah's thirteenth year, as Alonso de Maldonado repeats in this chronologies tradition in 1624, though it should be pointed out that, in de Maldonado's chronology, he

---

1   This chapter is an augmented version of "Josiah and the History of the World," a presentation in homage to Ralph W. Klein, Chicago Society of Biblical Research, Lutheran School of Theology at Chicago, October 22, 2016. Originally published as Lowell K. Handy, "Josiah and the History of the World," *BR* 62 (2017): 26–47. Used in this extensive adaptation by permission.

2   Neither Huldah nor Jeremiah will do. The former has recently had her supporters: Adrien Janis Bledstein, "Is Judges a Woman's Satire of Men Who Play God?," in *A Feminist Companion to Judges*, ed. A. Brenner, FCB 4 (Sheffield: Sheffield Academic, 1993), 52; Yael Shemesh, "Directions in Jewish Feminist Bible Study," *CurBR* 14 (2016): 391–92; very much less convincing is Preston Kavanagh, *Huldah: The Prophet Who Wrote Hebrew Scripture* (Eugene, OR: Pickwick, 2012); idem, *The Shapan Group: The Fifteen Authors Who Shaped the Hebrew Bible* (Eugene, OR: Pickwick, 2011), 76–78. The rabbinic notion (B. Bat. 15a) that Jeremiah wrote Kings is also not viable, though it, too, has reappeared recently: Richard Elliott Friedman, *Who Wrote the Bible?* (New York: HarperSanFrancisco, 1997), 146–47, 209.

3   Jan Assmann, *Moses der Ägypter: Entzifferung einer Gedächtnisspur* (Munich: Hanser, 1998); idem, *Of God and Gods: Egypt, Israel, and the Rise of Monotheism* (Madison: University of Wisconsin Press, 2008), 27.

noted that there are problems with the biblical chronology.[4] Aside from appearing in lists of Judean kings, these chronologies from Eusebius and Jerome[5] onward (Jerome's was highly influential throughout the Middle Ages) do not, with few exceptions, use Josiah as a historical character so much as a chronological marker. The parallel Roman and Greek material often predominates, but when it does not, Josiah frequently appears solely as the backdrop for prophets: Jeremiah, Zephaniah, and even Huldah.[6] For this investigation, it is not Josiah as date marker but Josiah as historiographical figure that marks him as an actor in history. All such information on Josiah derives eventually from Kings, though most early historians before 1800 assumed three primary sources for Josiah and his reign: Kings, Chronicles, and Josephus; the latter two are now recognized as dependent on Kings.[7]

In Kings, Josiah is a one-dimensional figure. Aside from dying in a fashion that allows endless reflection (even three narrative renditions in biblical texts alone if we count First Esdras),[8] Josiah is a religious figure. "And he did straight in the eyes of Yahweh and walked in all the way of his father David, and did not turn to right or left" (2 Kgs 22:2). This comment at the beginning of Josiah's narrative in Kings pretty much sums up the entire reign as presented in this scroll.[9] Unlike the narratives of the

---

4   Alonso de Maldonado, *Chronica universal de todos las naciones y tiempos* (Madrid: Luis San, 1924), 9–10 [sections XXII–XXIII].

5   Jerome would continue to update his 'translation' of Eusebius' chronicle, but an expansion on the biblical texts is not part of his endeavor. See J. D. N. Kelly, *Jerome: His Life, Writings, and Controversies* (New York: Harper & Row, 1975), 72–75; on his influence throughout the Middle Ages, p. 74.

6   Anthony T. Grafton and Urs. B. Leu, *Henricus Glareanus's (1488–1563) Chronologia of the Ancient World: A Facsimile Edition of a Heavily Annotated Copy in Princeton University Library*, Studies in Medieval and Reformation Traditions 177 (Leiden: Brill, 2014), 76, 78.

7   There are exceptions: A. Graeme Auld, "What Was the Main Source of the Book of Chronicles?," in *The Chronicler as Author: Studies in Text and Texture*, ed. M. P. Graham and S. L. McKenzie, JSOTSup 263 (Sheffield: Sheffield Academic, 1999), 98–99; idem, *Life in Kings: Reshaping the Royal Story in the Hebrew Bible*, AIL 20 (Atlanta: Scholars Press, 2017), 153–54; Person, *The Deuteronomic History and the Book of Chronicles*, 129. All of these authors assume a common source; however, we do not have this source nor can one be reconstructed. See the conclusion by Isaac Kalimi, "Kings *with* Privilege: The Core Source(s) of the Parallel Texts between the Deuteronomistic and Chronistic Histories," *RB* 119 (2012): 517, preceded by his learned response to Auld.

8   Talshir, "Three Deaths of Josiah," 213–36; Delamarter, "Death of Josiah," 29–60, among others. First Esdras has been a canonical text in most Orthodox Christian canons from the era of the early church: Böhler, *1 Esdras*, 21.

9   Steussy (*David*, 94–95) correctly observes that, in Kings, the references to following in the way of David are restricted to religious propriety.

major kings immediately before him (of Hezekiah and Manasseh, given that Amon gets little text), the narratives concerning Josiah in Kings consist of a young man repairing the temple; the inquirer and recipient of a message from Yahweh; a king making cultic changes in Jerusalem's temple and to the religious personnel; and public worship of Jerusalem and Judah. And, of course, apparently the most important event of his reign for Kings' author: Josiah desecrated the temple at Bethel. This is the centerpiece of the author of the book's vision of Josiah; it is the event predicted at the beginning of the scroll's section on the divided monarchy with the impressive line: "Altar, altar, thus says Yahweh: Listen-up! A son will be born to the house of David, Josiah his name, and he will sacrifice the priests of the sanctuaries who burn incense on you and human bones will be burned on you!" (1 Kgs 13:2). This Josiah, already a literary figure, might have been important to Judah and might have been a blip on the screen of Samerina, but a world-shaking figure of major import? One would not suppose so from the text of Kings.

Josiah gains little more character in the Chronicler's retelling of the same material, though he does become even more religiously one-dimensional. This is accomplished by making his extreme piety an aspect of his early childhood. He plans at that young age to restore the religious world of Judah and Samerina. Before encountering the scroll of Moses, his cultic responsibilities exceed those presented in Kings and he is capable of re-empowering the proper Levitical priesthood. These aspects are in addition to his providing a huge Passover that deviates from the Passover in Kings in many ways beyond simple literary extension.[10] It might be noted that Josiah is slightly more active in his own death in Chronicles than he was in Kings, but this appears to be due to Ahab as a literary model.[11] A king to be remembered? Chronicles certainly insists so (2 Chr 35:24–25), where he is remembered in Judah and Israel (explicitly mentioned) to this day; so, again, a major figure of import for the world? Well, certainly in Jewish and Christian historiographies.

If the notion of world history may have begun in Jeremiah, as Konrad Schmid has suggested,[12] Josiah does not appear as part of that. More to the point, in the allegorical history of Judah and Israel as part of an allegorized world history presented in the 'Apocalypse of the Animals,' now a portion

---

10 Klein, *2 Chronicles*, 492–93, 515.
11 Ibid., 527; Japhet, *I & II Chronicles*, 1042–43.
12 Konrad Schmid, "Nebuchadnezzar, the End of Davidic Rule, and the Exile in the Book of Jeremiah," in *The Prophets Speak on Forced Migration*, AIL 21 (Atlanta: Society of Biblical Literature, 2015), 75. Schmid's theory is that the swift shift of ruling powers controlling Jerusalem forced the notion of universal history on the author.

of Enoch (1 En 89:65–67), Josiah is conspicuously absent.[13] It might be derived from this that Josiah was not significant (or, though highly unlikely, known) to the allegorist.[14] Josiah shows up in plenty of early Jewish literature, and whilst these are not histories of the world, they contribute to the Josiah understood to have existed in the writings that came after.[15] The Wisdom of Jesus ben Sirach, probably written in or around Jerusalem about 180 BCE, is a continuation of the biblical wisdom literature tradition.[16] Certainly Yeshua ben Sirach was not imagining a return to monarchic rule, being more concerned with the temple priesthood.[17] In traditional wisdom format with the relevant distinctive characteristics, he wrote that he perceived true wisdom to be embodied in the cult of the Second Temple, especially the sacrificial continuity from ancient times. The truly great leaders of the past included those who were political, military, and judicial, but those of special renown were those who were properly religious (Sirach 44–50). While each of the ancestors highlighted had an office and performed great deeds, Yeshua emphasizes the religious nature of their character, their piety and faithfulness to God, and the resultant fact that God acted on their behalf; indeed, the final and most glorified of the figures is the high priest, Simon ben Onias.[18] Josiah, therefore, makes a perfect king for this selected list of heroes from the past; his memory is recorded in one of the shorter passages (Sir 49:1–3), where he is memorialized as incense and music (features of the cultic liturgy) and a good banquet. What Sirach stresses is Josiah's cultic reform, not the Passover that plays such a large part in Chronicles and First Enoch, suggesting that his authoritative source was Kings, where the destruction of religious abominations throughout

---

13 See Patrick A. Tiller, *A Commentary on the Animal Apocalypse of I Enoch*, EJL 4 (Atlanta: Scholars Press, 1993), 320, 340; George W. E. Nickelsburg, *1 Enoch 1: A Commentary on the Book of 1 Enoch, Chapters 1–36; 81–108*, Hermeneia (Minneapolis: Fortress, 2001), 386. Both argue that Josiah is omitted because he is irrelevant to the history, his reform being a failure in averting the destruction of Judah and Jerusalem.

14 But, then, no king of Judah is mentioned explicitly, and perhaps none are actually referenced in the entire work: Daniel Olson, *A New Reading of the Animal Apocalypse of 1 Enoch: "All Nations Shall be Blessed": with a New Translation and Commentary*, SVTP 24 (Leiden: Brill, 2013), 27. Olson does suggest that perhaps the embarrassment of Josiah's death at the hands of "Egypt" might have an allusion (133). In "The Chronology in the Animal Apocalypse of 1 Enoch 85–90," *JSP* (2016): 11, 13, Antti Laato assumes the unmentioned Josiah and his reform nonetheless provide the pivotal date for the allegorical work.

15 Handy, "Josiah after the Chronicler," 95–102.

16 Alexander A. Di Lella, "Wisdom of Ben-Sira," *ABD* 6.932. On the possible spread of dates for the book, see George W. E. Nickelsburg, *Jewish Literature between the Bible and the Mishnah* (Philadelphia: Fortress, 1981), 64–65.

17 Perdue, *Wisdom Literature*, 218–19.

18 Ibid., 260–61.

the land and the violent reformation of the people to return to Yahweh are extensively described. In Sirach, Josiah is shown as one who, in a culture gone evil, managed against all odds to produce a righteous moment. On the other hand, the founder of righteous religion in Sirach is David, who looks a good deal more like the Chronicles version than the clearly apostate Solomon, whose memory herein derives from the text of Kings (Sir 47:19–23).[19] Sirach presents only David, Hezekiah, and Josiah as moral; all other kings of Judah (and Israel) were evil (Sir 49:4).

Josiah is the opening character in the history recorded in First Esdras. The volume appears to have been composed in the second century BCE.[20] A cursory reading of the Josianic material in First Esdras suffices to demonstrate that the source material for the story comes from Chronicles.[21] As the entire work is concerned with temple and cult, Josiah makes a perfect figure with which to introduce the history of the major reformation made by Ezra in the rest of the narrative. There are two interpolations into the story that are significant. Josiah is described as having ordered the Levites to bring the ark of the Lord into the temple and then to turn to the business of presenting the Passover to the people of the land as a whole (1 Esd 1:3–4). The notion that Josiah has a particular relationship to the care of the ark of the covenant is one that will reappear in later Jewish traditions, though here only the notion that Josiah is responsible for the ark to reside officially in the temple as opposed to being carried around by the Levites is presented. The text is very clear that Josiah was doing this in exact conformity to the orders of David (and of Solomon) but implies that, up to that point in time, it had not been done since the Davidic pronouncement had been made.

The other interpolation of note concerns the death of Josiah. The prophecy by Huldah in Kings apparently promised Josiah a peaceful death; however, he is slain by Neco, leaving the relation between the prophecy and the death confusing.[22] If the Chronicler attempted to make sense of this disparity by putting the words of God in the mouth of Neco, thereby making the pharaoh on a mission from God (2 Chr 35:21–22), it allowed Josiah to be slain for not recognizing the very words of Yahweh even if spoken by the Egyptian pharaoh, who, apparently, was to have

---

19 Rehoboam's brief mention is attached to Solomon's folly. Clearly, Solomon had not raised his heir in a wise fashion ensuing in disastrous results for Israel.

20 Böhler, *1 Esdras*, 13–14; Myers, *I & II Esdras*, 14; William Goodman, "Esdras, First Book of," *ABD* 2.610.

21 Klein, "The Rendering of 2 Chronicles 35–36 in 1 Esdras," in Fried, *Was 1 Esdras First?*, 219–20, with several modifications, likely deriving from different translations and variant manuscripts.

22 Halpern and Vanderhooft ("The Edition of Kings," 221–30) discuss the history of the debate.

been recognized as a true prophet of Yahweh.[23] The author of First Esdras includes this explanation, if somewhat amplified (1 Esd 1:24-25). However, a much more forceful prophetic voice is added to the narrative. It is the warning given Josiah by Jeremiah, which he ignores to his own demise (1 Esd 1:26).[24] The long tradition of wondering why Josiah did not inquire of Jeremiah, or why Jeremiah does not appear in the biblical texts of Josiah's reign, are reflected in this adaptation. In this manner, Josiah ceases to be a perfect paradigm of goodness by failing, if only at the end of his life, as Solomon had (in Kings, not in Chronicles). Clearly, it was apparent to the author that Josiah's disobeying the word of God spoken by Jeremiah carried more weight than his disobeying the word of God spoken by Neco.[25] Finally, First Esdras offers a short notice that Josiah has been remembered precisely because he was pious, when all others alive at this time were evil (1 Esd 1:21-22), a reflection of the theme already seen in Sirach.[26]

Josephus, in retelling his history of the Jewish people in his *Jewish Antiquities*, made use of Kings, Chronicles, and First Esdras, but transforms the Josianic material into a historiographical story narrative. While it is essentially the world history of a single ethnic/religious group, Josephus unravels its continuity from the beginning of the world to his own time, making it a history of the world.[27] Until relatively recent times, his history has not been a highly cited Jewish source for Josiah, but Christian traditions and their offspring have favored Josephus as a historical witness. Josephus's Josiah, rewritten for Jewish, Egyptian, Greek, and Roman audiences in the Hellenistic period, melds biblical material but adapts the ruler to Roman interests.[28] A few additions or, perhaps better, midrashic interpretations deserve notice before entering into the subsequent use of the king by world historians. The extreme youth of Josiah as a pious Jew who purposefully modeled his life on that of the peerless David, the ideal of all kings (*Ant.* 10.49), intends to demonstrate Josiah as a good, classical

---

23 Gottwald, *The Politics of Ancient Israel*, 85. The directive proclaimed by Neco in the Esdras narrative is more clearly the word of Yahweh than it was in Chronicles: Klein, *2 Chronicles*, 526; Böhler, *1 Esdras*, 41.

24 An amplification clearly derived from Chronicles' attempt to explain the narrative of Kings; Pajunen, "The Saga of Judah's Kings Continues," 580, this was then again amplified in 4Q381.

25 Klein, "Rendering of 2 Chronicles," 221; Myers, *I & II Esdras*, 29; Böhler (*1 Esdras*, 41-42) relates the passage to 2 Chr 36:12 and Jeremiah's warnings to Zedekiah.

26 As noted, for example, by Klein, "Rendering of 2 Chronicles," 228.

27 Sylvia Castelli, "Kings in Josephus," in Lemaire and Halpern, *The Books of Kings*, 558-59.

28 See, for extensive examples, Louis H. Feldman, "Josephus' Portrait of Josiah," *LS* 18 (1993): 110-30; Christopher T. Begg, "The Death of Josiah: Josephus and the Bible," *ETL* 64 (1988): 157-63.

ruler who shows his right to rule from his minority and who selects personal characteristics from the lives of the best rulers in order to conform his own behavior and piety. Of course, this has to have been the David of Chronicles, if he is all-good and pious. He posits that Josiah was an incredibly wise man who knew what was needed from the past, what needed to be corrected from tradition, and what needed to be done for the future; he knew to which elderly advisors to listen (*Ant.* 10.50–51). Unlike any passage in biblical stories about Josiah, Josephus hails a militaristic, victorious, and brave Josiah (*Ant.* 10.74–77) that undoubtedly influenced forthcoming notions of the imperialist Josiah. Josephus's portrayal of a warrior Josiah was certainly intended to impress the citizenry of a rapidly expanding Roman Empire. Unlike the ambiguity some scholars see in the biblical accounts, Josephus has Josiah kill the apostate priests; there is no ambiguity here (*Ant.* 10.65). Finally, Josiah was persuasive in convincing the Israelites to give up their idolatrous religious ways; he then helped them clean out the remaining improper cultic materials (*Ant.* 10.68). He is much less violent about it in Josephus than in Kings.[29] For the Egyptian Jewish community, who were recently incorporated into the Roman Empire and who were clearly interested in the Jewish prior incorporation under the Seleucids, that Josiah was fairly beneficent in dealing with Israel's cult reflected a similar desire for Rome to be beneficent to Jewish religious traditions. Since Josephus passed into Christian historiography as a source as reliable as Kings and Chronicles, these changes play into the history of world historical use of Josiah as much as the biblical texts.

Whatever else they might have been, the first-century Christians were a sect of Judaism. The early church's collection of sacred texts at the very least included King Josiah as he appeared in Kings and Chronicles. Clearly, Josiah appeared in earliest Christian literature solely as a single link in the chain of descendants from David to Jesus, though in the canonical or the known non-canonical gospels, Josiah is recorded by name only in Matt 1:10–11 as the son of "Amos" [or "Amon"][30] and the father of Jeconiah and his brothers,[31] with a somewhat ambiguous note that this was the time of the Babylonian Exile. Luke's genealogy (3:23–38) makes no mention of Josiah. For Matthew, this notation is of world-historical importance, since

---

29 Castelli, "Kings in Josephus," 554–55.

30 On the history of theories of the Amos/Amon citation, see Raymond E. Brown, *The Birth of the Messiah: A Commentary on the Infancy Narratives in Matthew and Luke* (Garden City, NY: Doubleday, 1977), 60–61.

31 Brown (*Birth of the Messiah*, 83) notes and provides explanations for the inaccurate rendition of Josiah's family; the apparent error had been noted for a long time. There is evidence for scribal attempts to rectify the citation: Edward Hayes Plumptre, *The Gospel According to St. Matthew*, HC (London: Cassell, Peter, Galpin, 1879), 3–4.

Jesus is the Messiah and a direct descendant of David, but Josiah, as he will be in the innumerable Christian chronologies and the multitude of illustrations of the tree of Jessie,[32] is a mere link in a chronological list, not a player on the world stage.

Among the longer passages on Josiah in Jewish pseudepigraphical literature is that in 2 Baruch 66. The composition was probably written around 100 CE.[33] It forms one segment of an apocalyptic vision as though it had been seen by Baruch. The work as a whole stresses the salvation of Israel by God, who has a special relationship with the Jews even though there have been alternating periods of Jewish obedience and wickedness; God is faithful.[34] In the opening sentences on King Josiah, the author stresses the purity of Josiah amidst evil; as in Sirach, Josiah is seen as the sole righteous man in his time. Following the general outline of Kings, Josiah is presented as violently enforcing proper worship of God upon an impious nation and the destruction of those people who did not so worship. Because of his faithfulness to Torah, the heavenly vision insists Josiah will be raised up with the righteous in the final judgment. The resurrection of Josiah was certainly a new innovation among the extant materials dealing with Josiah. The author believed that the righteous would live forever, as expressed in the Wisdom of Solomon and accepted by some Pharisaic circles and early Christians.

Talmudic material does not record a world history, though Josiah is marginally aggrandized in Talmudic midrash;[35] he was certainly not as central a character as was David, Solomon, or Moses, but the Talmudic material flows into both Jewish and Christian portrayals of Josiah thereafter. Eight significant rabbinic observations concerning Josiah appear in the Talmud.[36] First, it is asserted that it was Josiah who hid the ark of the covenant so that it could not be taken by the Babylonians. This event is

32 Leslie Ross, *Medieval Art: A Topical Dictionary* (Westport, CN: Greenwood, 1996), 144, 248.

33 A. F. J. Klijn, "2 (Syriac Apocalypse of) Baruch (Early Second Century A.D.): A New Translation and Introduction," *OTP* 1:616–17; James H. Charlesworth, "Baruch, Book of 2 (Syriac)," *ABD* 1.620; Nickelsburg, *Jewish Literature*, 287.

34 Klijn, "2 (Syriac Apocalypse of) Baruch," 618; Nickelsburg, *Jewish Literature*, 285.

35 The following material on Josiah in the Talmud is adapted from Handy, "Josiah after the Chronicler," 98–99. A short survey of rabbinic material on Josiah appears in Grohmann, "Hulda, die Prophetin," 214–15.

36 Josiah is understood to be in the background for other Talmudic stories. See, for example, the Hanukkah foundation story in Shabb. 21b; Zvi Ron, "Antecedents of the Hanukkah Oil Story," *RRJ* 18 no. 1 (2015): 70–73. This is true as well for other postbiblical material, see Adam H. Becker, "2 Baruch," in *Outside the Bible: Ancient Jewish Writings Related to Scripture*, ed. L. H. Feldman, J. L. Kugel, and L. H. Schiffman (Philadelphia: Jewish Publication Society of America, 2013), 2.1568.

mentioned several times and appears to have been an established Josianic tradition within rabbinic circles. This action included saving the contents of the ark, including the gold objects sent back with the ark by the Philistines in the time of Samuel. Citing Deut 28:36, the tradition insists that Josiah carried out this protective slight-of-hand by obeying Torah (Hor. 12a; Yoma 52b).[37] The tale provides some later Jewish traditions with the grounds for building a third temple.[38]

Second, Josiah is used as an example of the truth of prophecy. Rabbi Akiba is reported as answering a question about God lengthening a lifespan by citing the prophecy of the coming of Josiah (1 Kgs 13:2) long before Manasseh was born (Yebam. 50a), while Rabbi Johanan cites the same prophecy to show that Josiah ruled over the northern kingdom ('Arak. 33a).[39] There are comments about prophecy and the death of Josiah: Rabbi Jonathan is cited by his student, Samuel ben Nachman, as having explained that because Josiah consulted Huldah rather than the more authoritative and trustworthy Jeremiah, he deserved to die (Ta'an. 22b). Indeed, Jeremiah is said to have overheard Josiah, devotedly pious to the end, declaring with his last breath that this sentence by God was just (Josiah himself citing Lam 1:18).[40] Apparently, there was considerable debate as to why Josiah chose to consult Huldah rather than Jeremiah, but it was agreed by most rabbis that Huldah was one of the seven legitimate prophetesses, was a close relative to Jeremiah, and besides, Jeremiah had gone off to bring back the ten tribes; therefore, Josiah was righteous in seeking her advice (Meg. 14b).[41]

The next two items relate Josiah to foundational tales concerning Jewish liturgy. Third, Josiah's rendition of the Passover was agreed to have been the foundational event for the second day of Passover celebration thereafter (Meg. 31a). Fourth, one may listen to the Hallel and not recite

---

37 Of course, the Talmudic tradition is recognized as late midrash such that alternative reasons for the disappearance of the ark have been mentioned, however dubiously: see Ehrlich ("The Disappearance of the Ark of the Covenant," 176–78), who hypothesizes that Athaliah and her Baalist devotees took or demolished the ark while the reference to Josiah and the ark (2 Chr 35:3) was a Josianic subterfuge given that there was by then no ark. This may come under the category of modern midrash.

38 Ron, "Antecedents of the Hanukkah Oil Story," 73.

39 Midrash Rabbah contains several instances of Josiah being foretold: to Moses (Midrash I Exodus 40.3); to Ruth (Midrash I Ruth 7.2); to David (Midrash I Leviticus 20.1); to Amos (Midrash I Leviticus 30.3).

40 Also attested in Midrash Rabbah Lamentations 1.18.

41 The curses concerning Joab made by David (2 Sam 3:29–30) also came true in the Davidic lineage, Josiah embodying the one who fell by the sword.

it because Josiah heard the scroll read to him, but he did not orally repeat it himself (Sukkah 38b).

Fifth, Jeremiah went on a mission to bring back the northern ten tribes so that Josiah could rule over them and provide them with a proper religious life in place of the evil cult they had at Bethel (Meg. 14b; ʿArak. 33a). Sixth, his body was not just pierced by an arrow, but was riddled like a sieve, which did not conflict with Huldah's prophecy, it is explained, because the temple still stood (Sanh. 48b; Moʿed Qaṭ. 28b). Seventh, Josiah's righteousness was considered remarkable. He was so good that his behavior was sufficient to allow his father Amon to enter into the Life-to-Come despite his own apostasy (Sanh. 104a). Josiah is one of the people on the famous list of Samuel ben Nachman, in the name of his teacher Rabbi Jonathan, of those who should never be said to have sinned. Some argued that Josiah was a penitent (a popular topic in early Judaism)[42] because he changed from evil in his youth to righteousness in his maturity, Samuel arguing that he corrected every wrong he had committed to right before his eighteenth year (Shab. 56b).[43] Eighth, the mourning by Jeremiah and all the people of the land over the death of Josiah becomes the measure by which mourning for all persons may be gauged (Meg. 3a; Moʿed Qaṭ. 25b, 28b).

The History of the Rechabites (± 200 CE) merely uses Josiah as a date for Jeremiah, a role Josiah will fulfill in much subsequent literature. That landmark of Christian historiographical writing, Augustine of Hippo's *De civitate Dei*, cites Josiah only as a date marker for Jeremiah.[44] To be fair, Augustine includes Josiah; the extant *Chronographia* of John Malalas (ca. 574) skips from Manasseh to Eliakim (5.73) in what is assumed to be a lacuna more apt to be a textual copying error than one intentionally made by John, but it is interesting that Josiah is not at present extant in a major and influential Christian chronology at the turn from the ancient world to the medieval one.[45]

Among the first millennium chronologies, not all produced by the Christian tradition were simple lists of dates and chronological correlations. Perhaps the pride of place should go to that of George Synkellos, Byzantine historian, who produced his *Chronography* in the years 808–810.[46]

---

42 Johnson, *Prayer in the Apocrypha and Pseudepigrapha*, 54–61.

43 Midrash I Numbers 19.1 uses Josiah as one example among others of clean coming from the unclean.

44 Augustine, *Civ.* 18.33. Here, Ancus Martius of Rome gets more mention than Josiah even for dating purposes. Zephaniah is dated not by Josiah, but by Jeremiah!

45 John Malalas, *The Chronology of John Malalas*, trans. E. Jeffreys, M. Jeffreys, and R. Scott (Melbourne: Australian Association for Byzantine Studies, 1986), 79n73.

46 George Synkellos, *The Chronography of George Synkellos: A Byzantine Chronicle of Universal History*, trans. William Adler and Pau Tuffin (Oxford: Oxford University Press, 2002), xxix.

218 *Josiah*

In comparison to other chronologies, his section on Josiah is extensive. This chronology lists events in chronological order but expands on the list of kings and makes non-biblical comments to the biblical texts.[47] Of significance for later histories of the world, Synkellos dates the Scythian invasion of Palestine to Josiah's reign (Herodotus' *Historiae*, book 2, serves as his source, via Eusebius). The usual dating of prophets is included, as well as a record of his zeal for God and the cleaning out of the religious establishments and apostate worshipers everywhere, removing both the living and the dead. The list of apostates is prefaced with the observation that Josiah had them all burned, so, like Josephus, there is no ambiguity about their fate. The episode of the encounter with Neco is based on the expanded renditions in Chronicles and First Esdras to include two chariots (2 Chr 35:24; 1 Esd 1:29) after an explicitly unprovoked attack on the Egyptian army. He ends with a non-biblical but good Talmudic legend in which Jeremiah hides the ark of the covenant and other cultic articles rather than Josiah.[48] This will suffice for traditions of chronology dealing with Josiah in the history of the world during the Byzantine era.

If the Christian chronologists were the predominate tellers of world history for the first millennium of the common era, the High Middle Ages produced what was to be considered the first authoritative history of the world. It also happened to be a paraphrase, with marginalia, of the biblical text, but where else would a good Parisian Christian find the history of the world? In roughly the year 1173, Petrus Comestor completed his *Historia scholastica*, a tome to be of use in the teaching of the Bible to students in Paris.[49] The history was an innovative Christian use of the historical-literal meaning of the Bible, a Jewish method of reading which had been recently adapted by the St. Victors.[50] It was destined to become *the* history of the world into the Reformation period. It was famous as a peak of scholastic scholarship to the early twentieth century, when, as Mark Clark explains, it was simply forgotten by everyone save for specialists in medieval Latin studies.[51] Essentially, the section concerning Josiah consists of a rewrite

---

47 Synkellos, *Chronography*. Pages 313–15 contain the Josiah reign; all citations of events that follow here are from these pages.

48 Ibid., 316.

49 Mark. J. Clark, *The Making of the* Historia scholastica, *1150–1200*, Mediaeval Law and Theology 7; TS 198 (Toronto: Pontifical Institute of Medieval Studies, 2015), 51.

50 Jean Châtillon, "La Bible dans les écoles du XIIe siècle," in *Le Moyan Age et la Bible*, ed. P. Riché and G. Lobrichon, BTT4 (Paris: Beauchesne, 1984), 195–96.

51 Châtillon, "Bible dans les écoles," 2. The work remained influential well into the nineteenth century. See Geoffrey Shepherd, "The Vernacular Scriptures: English Versions of the Scriptures before Wyclif," in *Cambridge History of the Bible: The West from the Fathers to the Reformation*, ed. G. H. W. Lampe (Cambridge: Cambridge University Press, 1969), 382–83.

of the biblical text of Kings with some commentary. Of interest here are three items. First, a large section devoted to Josiah is taken up with the prophet Jeremiah, for which there was certainly precedent; second, the 'book' found in the temple is declared to be Deuteronomy, which Moses had written; and third, Ezekiel and Zephaniah are trotted out as witnesses to the irrefutable fact that Josiah's rectification of the religion of Judah did not resonate with the populace for very long.[52] As far as official Church Latin was concerned, this history of the world would stand for centuries as the exemplar. Note, however, that it was a medieval Bible textbook and that it had been written for that purpose rather than as the definitive world history as it was to be treated afterward.

One should turn to the very first recognized world history in a vernacular of the West—that authorized by Alfonso El Sabio (Alfonso X, King of Castile and Leon), the *General estoria* of the mid-thirteenth century.[53] It is not surprising that the Bible plays a singularly central part in the history of the world in this six-part, eight-volume (albeit uncompleted) work; the biblical narrative was, after all, considered the authoritative document of the early world and it had been good enough for Petrus. However, it should be mentioned that, at the same time, Alfonso was having the Bible translated into Castilian.[54] Here, Josiah takes up what might be considered an inordinate amount of space (18 pages of the modern Madrid edition), but then the biblical material needed to be covered. This appears odd only when compared, for example, with the *Chronica sive historia de duabus civitatibus*, written by Bishop Otto of Freising in 1143–1147, a Latin prose narrative chronology, where Josiah is reduced to a single note that he and Hezekiah alone of all the kings of Judah and Israel were not reprobates—less than half a sentence.[55] Of course, Bishop Otto was a renowned pessimist whose chronology illustrated the fallen state of humanity—really, really fallen. However, it is more impressive that Alfonso's Josiah passage far outpaces Petrus's section. In Alfonso's history, Josiah's designated 'chapter' includes not only the entire content of the narratives of Kings and Chronicles but a fair

---

52 A notion repeated by succeeding works noted in this chapter as well as more 'modern' commentaries, e.g., Gray, *Christian Workers' Commentary*, 193.

53 Alfonso X, *General estoria: Tercera parte, Tomo II*, ed. Pedro Sánchez-Prieto Borja, Autores clásicos españoles (Madrid: Biblioteca Castro, 2009), 413–30.

54 Simon R. Doubleday, *The Wise King: A Christian Prince, Muslim Spain, and the Birth of the Renaissance* (New York: Basic Books, 2015), 100; though some consider the *General estoria* the Bible translation itself, in which case it *is* more of a history than a translation!

55 Otto, Bishop of Freising, *The Two Cities: A Chronicle of Universal History to the Year 1146 A.D.*, ed. A. P. Evans and C. Knapp, trans. C. C. Mierow, Records of Western Civilization (New York: Columbia University Press, 2002), 150. It might be added that Alfonso's section on Josiah was at least four times as long as Synkellos' section on Josiah.

amount of the debate raised by the differences between those accounts. In addition, it drew material from Josephus and Petrus Comestor, whose *Historia scholastica* formed the fourth major source after Kings, Chronicles, and Josephus, for this section of the *Estoria*. There is a great emphasis on Josiah's piety from his youth to his death. Here, it is attributed specifically to the priesthood, to Eliaquín, and to his trusted secretary, Safán, both of whom receive good presentations in this rendition. The discovery of the 'book of the law,' or the 'Book of Moses,' is a central concern repeatedly identified with the book of Deuteronomy; obviously the authors did not consult de Wette, like modern scholars, but cited Petrus and, before him, Jerome. Before making the wholesale cleansing of the religious practices of Israel and Samaria, Josiah checked with the prophetess Oldán (the author uses the form of the name provided by Jerome) to ensure that this was the very word of God. The cleansing of the cult included clearing out the baals, the asherahs, the astartes, the tophets, the images of mice (see the ark narrative, 1 Sam 6:8, 17–18), sun idols, chariots to the sun, moon idols, and the complete pulverization of the altar at Bethel.

There is much more in Alfonso's history of Josiah, but three things are significant in the contents: 1) the 'book' is Deuteronomy and there is no question about that here; 2) all the vanities of the previous kings of Judah and Israel, a list expanded beyond the material on Josiah in Kings and Chronicles, are removed and destroyed (and with Josephus, their priests are killed); and 3) the good, pious King Josiah listens to his priest and learned secretary (again, a Josephus background is possible). It needs only be mentioned that Alfonso's father had brought his boy up to remove the Muslims from Granada, all that remained of Muslim Spain, but Alfonso was more taken with learning than fighting (and obviously better at it, but that is another matter). The fact that Josiah was charged by God to rectify the land of Judah and Israel of improper religious relics and personnel, obediently listening to his priest, should not be lost when reading the extensive section on Josiah in Alfonso's *Estoria*.

As the 'Middle Ages' gave way to the 'Modern' world, printed volumes were a defining characteristic. Among the very first published volumes was Hartmann Schedel's *Liber chronicarum* of 1493. A prominent citizen of Nuremberg, then a center of early modern science and philosophy, Schedel was steeped in fifteenth-century German humanism. His history was a collaborative effort by the erudite Nuremberg community. It was also fully illustrated. Josiah appears in the 'Fourth Age of the World' (from David to the Babylonian Captivity) and commands roughly half a page, in which the biblical accounts of Kings and Chronicles are condensed.[56] The

---

56 Hartmann Schedel, *Chronicle of the World: The Complete and Annotated Nuremberg Chronicle of 1493* (Köln: Taschen, 2001), leaf LX recto.

content focuses on his adherence to God and his death at the hands of the Egyptian King. The text is not particularly noteworthy, save that Josiah appeared in two of the very first printed volumes of Europe, one of which was a world history [the other, of course, was the Gutenberg Bible].[57]

A quartet of early modern world histories are of interest. That written in 1614 by Sir Walter Raleigh[58] includes, as would be expected, a section relating the biblical narrative. Raleigh was writing the history of the world for the education of Prince Henry, son of King James I of England with whom Walter was then definitely out of favor. The popular prince was seen by many in England as the bulwark of Protestantism.[59] The entire work was to have demonstrated divine providence in human history, somewhat dependent on the lives of kings and rulers, which should display the manner in which Henry should rule when king.[60] It is interesting in that one can read through the text on Josiah to the Protestant Reformation and especially the ongoing war in the Low Countries between Spain, whose empire then contained the region, and the Protestants, backed by England, seeking both to implement Reformed churches and disengage from Spanish rule. Which of these two causes most inflamed the Dutch Protestants of the time provokes a modern debate, but the political and religious aspects were inseparable during the Dutch Reformation. Josiah had become a biblical role model for many Protestants. His intransigent intolerance for idolatry and idols inspired many a devout Protestant in the Netherlands and England to tear down, chop up, and burn to ashes the idols of the Roman Catholic faith.[61] Raleigh's history makes the obser-

---

57 Guy Bedouelle, "Le tournant de l'impremerie," in *Le temps des Réformes et la Bible*, ed. G. Bedouelle and B. Roussel, BTT 5 (Paris: Beauchesne, 1989), 40–41.

58 Raleigh Trevelyan, *Sir Walter Raleigh* (New York: Henry Holt, 2002), xiii, 427–28, details Raleigh's authorship, with advice from specialists. It was published anonymously and its authorship is actually still debated. Dr. Robert Burhill (Rector of Northwold, Norfolk) served as Raleigh's resource for Hebrew sources. On the debate over authorship, see Christopher M. Armitage, *Sir Walter Raleigh: An Annotated Bibliography* (Chapel Hill: University of North Carolina Press, 1987), 6.

59 Trevelyan, *Sir Walter Raleigh*, 427, 443–45; upon the death of Prince Henry, November 6, 1612, Raleigh ceased work on the history—it was never close to completion.

60 Trevelyan, *Sir Walter Raleigh*, 429.

61 On Henry VIII of England as 'Josiah' demolishing the idols, at that time seen as any Catholic religious art, see Susan Brigden, *New Worlds, Lost Worlds: The Rule of the Tudors, 1485–1603* (New York: Viking, 2001), 130. Upon Henry's death the attack on Catholic art and practices intensified: Eamon Duffy, *The Stripping of the Altars: Traditional Religion in England 1400–1580* (New Haven: Yale University Press, 1992), 448–54. The wholesale attack on Catholic art in the Netherlands came as a revolt against Spanish rule and in reaction to an edict to suppress 'heretics': George H. Williams, *The Radical Reformation* (Philadelphia: Westminster, 1962), 771–72.

vation that one cannot rectify the cultic worship centers of a territory without having first gained political (in this case military) control of that territory. Three centuries later, Cross and Freedman will make the same observation, thereafter cited as having discerned some new insight. Raleigh already saw a Josiah reclaiming the empire of David and imposing a proper religious culture upon the reunited Israel.[62] For Raleigh, Josiah was both a religious reformer and a political strategist. And, not incidentally, the pious king was an apparent Protestant.

On the Roman Catholic side, Bishop Bossuet's 1681 *Discours sur l'histoire universelle* presents an interesting contrast.[63] If Raleigh's Josiah was essentially a devout, victorious leader of his people, Jacques-Bénigne Bossuet's Josiah was pious but ineffectual. This rather slender two-volume work carried a theological import, as was proper for a priest known for his sermonic talent. The narrative on Josiah was embedded in the sequence running from the repentance of Manasseh, which was shared by the people of the land and which was what saved them from Nebuchadnezzar (this history is derived from the book of Judith).[64] However, Josiah, pious as he was in attempting to rectify the impiety of his predecessors, was unable to curb the impiety of the people, who only increased impiety "beyond measure" so that Josiah could only, through his goodness and humility, postpone the punishment on the people.[65] This is essentially a sermon with a preacher's interest in the lives of the congregation: a good ruler will not a good people make; nor will good governance save evil populaces from themselves. True repentance, on the other hand, of king and populace, brings God's protection. As one of the most earnest defenders of the divine right of kings, Bossuet's portrayal of Josiah was clearly related to the seventeenth-century situation of church and state in France.[66]

---

62 Walter Raleigh, *The History of the World*, The Works of Sir Walter Raleigh 4 (Oxford: Oxford University Press, 1829), 785. Cross and Freedman, "Josiah's Revolt against Assyria," 56–58.

63 G. R. Cragg, *The Church and the Age of Reason 1648–1789*, Pelican History of the Church 4 (Baltimore: Penguin Books, 1970), 35–36. Bossuet was the premier Catholic preacher in France and a tenacious defender of traditional Catholicism against both Protestants and Catholic revival movements.

64 In "Un théologien gallican et l'Ecriture sainte: Le 'Projet biblique' de Louis Ellies Du Pin (1657–1719)," in *Le Grand Siècle et la Bible*, ed. Jean-Robert Armogathe, BTT 6 (Paris: Beauchesne, 1989), 258, Jacques Gres-Gayer notes that Bossuet was a strenuous defender of the historicity and authority of the Deuterocanonicals.

65 Jacque-Bénigne Bossuet, *An Universal History, From the Beginning of the World to the Empire of Charlemagne* (Aberdeen: Francis Douglass & William Murry, 1755), 36–37.

66 Jean Delumeau, *Catholicism between Luther and Voltaire: A New View of the Counter-Reformation*, trans. Jeremy Moiser (London: Burns & Oates, 1977), 226.

More interesting is André Guillaume's *Histoire des différens peuples du monde*[67] of 1771, whose world history is defined as one concerned with the religious beliefs and cults of the entire world. A hefty portion of the first volume was dedicated to China. The work clearly builds on the then recent fascination with comparative religions.[68] Unsurprisingly, the section on the Hebrews is mostly concerned with the figure of Moses, but David, Solomon, and a swift generic summary of the kings of Jerusalem continue the history. Josiah, however, appears as an individual at the end of the section in which improper worship has been noted, vis-à-vis Moses (and, to a lesser extent, Solomon); Josiah is credited with "abolishing idolatry; re-establishing the worship of the true God, reigning 31 years and dying in [the year] 3338."[69] It goes on to mention his death at the hands of Neco. That the sole aspect of Josiah's life appearing in this Catholic world history concerns his rectifying the true religion in the face of a world given to idolatry cannot have been an accident in a six-volume history of the world's peoples and their 'superstitions.' The quite extensive information on the religious traditions of the world comes almost exclusively from Catholic missionaries. Like Raleigh's Josiah as good Protestant reformer, Guillaume's Josiah is a good Roman Catholic missionary, bringing the straying peoples of the world back to the true religion and the true God.

For the English-speaking world, George Sale's large 66-volume, *An Universal History*, first published in 1744 and reprinted throughout the nineteenth century, provided the standard reference work for world history.[70] King Josiah of Judah takes up four large pages of this history, since whoever wrote this section (which is unclear) spent considerable time engaging in the then current debates about this ruler. These included such topics as: "Were the deities purged from Judah and Israel Assyrian or Israelite?" The first mention of the topic assumes they were Assyrian, but some four hundred pages later it is assumed they were the impieties of Solomon and assorted successive kings;[71] "Was the book found in the Temple an ancient Deuteronomy, as commonly believed, a Deuteronomy that was a work written at the time of Josiah, as cutting edge scholars of the time were expounding, or some excerpts from the Deuteronomistic text?" It is

---

67   The title, in the mode of that day, is more extensive: André Guillaume, *Histoir des différens peoples du monde, contenant les ceremonies religieuses et civiles, l'origine des religions, leurs sects & superstitions & les moeurs & usages de chacque nation* (Paris: Heissant le Fils, Libraire, 1771).
68   Guy G. Stroumsa, "John Spencer and the Roots of Idolatry," HR 41 (2001): 3–8.
69   André Guillaume, *Histoir des différens peoples du monde...*, 3.277. Translation was my own.
70   Sale, *An Universal History*.
71   Ibid., 1.372, 843.

Deuteronomy;[72] "Was the reform [this was a good Protestant work] successful or was it a surface change that reverted upon Josiah's death?" Just read Zephaniah and, to a lesser extent, Jeremiah!

For this history, the people who hear the scroll of the law and watch Josiah cleanse the worship of Jerusalem, Judah, and Israel are like those who behaved well upon the repentance of Manasseh but reverted instantly on the reign of Amon, so the people under Josiah only showed "outward zeal" but inwardly were as impious as ever: "They were, as their whole history shews, ready for every market."[73] Josiah is supported by God, and in the face of an impossible task of cleaning up the religion of Judah and Israel, can only succeed through divine supernatural backing.

In Sale's rendition, Josiah razes all the cities of Israel to wipe out the idolatrous practices, destroying all idols, and executing all priests who served those idols. The list of cultic cleansing is quite extensive, pulled from several parts of the Hebrew Bible. In relation to the Jerusalem temple repairs, he stripped the temple of all furnishings that were not original and sought out and replaced everything just as it had been when Solomon built it; a decidedly Protestant 'reformation' Christian midrash. The book of the law, it is assumed (aside from being Deuteronomy itself), was a copy written up during the flurry of scribal work done under Hezekiah and then hidden away, perhaps in a private collection kept during the reigns of Manasseh and Amon. The inquiry of Huldah, we are informed, was to discern the fate of both Judah and Israel and of the king (himself) as well as the people. The solution to the age-old problem of Josiah's dying in peace here is simply this: God decided to take Josiah to himself before the destruction of Judah, so he reigned thirty-one years in peace; therefore, Neco's slaying of Josiah, who lives just long enough to die as the chariot enters Jerusalem, is God's way of sparing Josiah the punishment promised (and deserved) by the people of Judah. The convoluted Assyrian/Babylonian/Egyptian/Judahite political relationships contained herein need just as well be passed over; Assyriology was a century away and Sale's historical reconstruction was already in obvious error by the work's latest printings.[74] At least Sale dismisses Judith as a historical text out of hand. In this

---

72 Ibid., 1.843–44nE. The Josephus/Jewish notion that it was the entire Torah is dismissed because that would be too long, though the option that it might have been a summary of the entire Pentateuch is not out of the question. Also, that the scroll consisted solely of Deuteronomy "28, 20 [sic] 30, + 31," a then recently proposed suggestion, is considered possible, especially if Josiah only saw the outermost sections of a rolled-up scroll.

73 Sale, *An Universal History*, 1.845.

74 The confusion of Assyria and Babylonia, especially with the book of Judith being taken as historical, kept the historical reconstructions interesting, if not

history, Josiah is presented as possibly having a legitimate religion, but, again, people are so much harder to correct than inanimate objects.[75]

Until the past couple of decades, modern, western volumes on the history of the ancient world referred to Mesopotamia and Egypt through the Roman Empire, at least until the Christians took over. These histories make some mention of this minor ruler of the minor Judah. In a survey made of several volumes on the ancient world, it was interesting to note that Josiah often appears in short mentions, but not always.[76] In the classic college textbook by Chester Starr, Josiah appears primarily as a religious reformer who eliminates Assyrian religious traditions and non-Yahwistic cults, images, and priests while establishing the centrality of the Jerusalem temple. As a political note, he and his successors are mentioned in passing as mistakenly opposing the rise of Nebuchadnezzar and Babylon.[77] Starr claims the part of the book of Deuteronomy "discovered" by Josiah was merely hidden away during the Assyrian ascendancy. If Starr concentrated on Josiah the reformer and dealt with politics slightly, Susan Bauer's ancient history, on the other hand, concentrates on a political and military Josiah with a short comment on the religious reform, all of which she sees as anti-Assyrian action.[78] Here, Josiah is an aggressive military leader who takes advantage of Assyria's disintegration to reassert Judah's independence and leads raiding parties into former Israel, "getting rid of all traces of Assyrian shrines and cults."[79] Neco II, we are informed, had no interest in Judah or Jerusalem at that time, but Josiah, not wishing Assyria to be replaced by Egypt as ruler of Judah, marched out to fight Neco at Megiddo. Neco, the history explains, found this mostly a tangential annoyance, having no trouble defeating the Judahite force and killing its politically motivated king.

---

accurate; Handy, "Josiah in a New Light," in Holloway, *Orientalism, Assyriology and the Bible*, 415–16.

75 It is of some interest that Diderot's *Encyclopédia* (1780) identifies Josiah's actions as reform ("renouvelle"), s.v. "Josias," *EDRS* 19.30, while the collapse of Assyria is a "revolution," s.v. "Assyrie," *EDRS* 1.282.

76 The references can be quite short, merely mentioning the religious return to the ancient cult as the state of Judah approaches annihilation: Sabatino Moscati, *The Face of the Ancient Orient: A Panorama of Near Eastern Civilization in Pre-Classical Times* (Garden City, NY: Doubleday, 1960), 248.

77 Chester G. Starr, *A History of the Ancient World*, 4th ed. (New York: Oxford University Press, 1991), 151, 156.

78 Susan Wise Bauer, *The History of the Ancient World: From the Earliest Accounts to the Fall of Rome* (New York: Norton, 2007), 415, 440. It is worth noting that Bauer includes a note on the origin of monotheism; that event is related to a historical Moses (128). The anti-Assyrian rendition of Josiah in a history of the ancient world of course appears elsewhere and earlier: William W. Hallo and William Kelly Simpson, *The Ancient Near East: A History* (New York: Harcourt Brace Jovanovich, 1971), 143.

79 Bauer, *History of the Ancient World*, 440.

Note that Carl Roebuck, in his 1966 ancient history, actually has the Josiah-Neco confrontation as part of Josiah's aggressive attempt to expand Judah.[80] These two approaches to Josiah fairly cover his appearance in recent ancient histories; either he is mostly a religious reformer or he is mostly a political warrior.

It is of some interest to mention the *Storia Universale* of 1862 by Cesare Cantù. In the midst of the exertions to unify Italy, he sees Josiah as the re-creator of the national Israel from the Euphrates to the Nile.[81] In addition, Cantù remarks that Manasseh had introduced the foreign Phoenician cult to Judah and that it is this alien cult that Josiah was removing. Indeed, Josiah is restoring the territorial unity of the nation, the traditional culture and its ritual, as well as reviving festivals not celebrated since the time of Samuel. Clearly, if it worked for Judah, it would work for Italy.

A note should be made about Bible education in schools in the English-speaking world of the nineteenth century. It was standard curriculum for elementary level education to include Bible studies and biblical passages as reading assignments. In learning world history, it was assumed that biblical history would form a primer to subsequent ages. For this purpose, numerous class textbooks were composed. A single example will suffice: George Frederick Maclean's *Old Testament History* was published in 1885, the year he was granted the status of honorary Canon of Canterbury Cathedral. He had long been active in British education and his history begins with creation and ends about 413 BCE with the completion of Nehemiah's second term in office. Josiah is covered on two of the 124 pages of text.[82] Maclean has Josiah taking a "tour" of Judah and Israel, where he demolished Jeroboam's chapel before collecting contributions for repairs to the "temple." The reforms are then enumerated and Josiah dies attempting to stop Egypt from taking Carchemish from the Assyrians by blocking the Egyptian army on Israelite soil. The language resounds of parish life among the Church of England in the nineteenth century—no doubt vocabulary intended to sound familiar to the youthful students.

Before turning to the world histories of the twentieth century, a short side-trip to a few late twentieth-century world histories specifically of the Jewish people is in order.[83] Three historical examples and one intellectual

---

80 Carl Roebuck, *The World of Ancient Times* (New York: Scribner's Sons, 1966), 152.

81 Cesare Cantù, *Storia Universale* (Turin: Unione Tipografico-Editrice, 1862), 1.149.

82 George Frederick Maclear, *A Shilling Book of Old Testament History for National and Elementary Schools* (London: Macmillan, 1885), 117–18.

83 This is not to ignore early twentieth-century Zionist Jewish histories like Josef Kastein's [Julius Katzensteain's] history, which reads the Hebrew Bible as a political tract that had been written and rewritten to fit changing conditions in the

history will suffice. The histories are: Leo W. Schwarz's edited volume, *Great Ages and Ideas of the Jewish People* (1956), Daniel Jeremy Silver and Bernard Martin's *A History of Judaism* (1974), and Robert M. Seltzer's *Jewish People, Jewish Thought: The Jewish Experience in History* (1980). The volume of intellectual history is Thomas Cahill's *The Gifts of the Jews* (1998). If the material on Josiah in Leo W. Schwarz's history reads very much like Yehezkel Kaufmann's studies of the religion of ancient Israel, it is because Kaufmann wrote the entry on "The Biblical Age."[84] Josiah is important in Jewish history here for two reasons. First, in his short notation of Josiah, the king is presented as the culmination of the conquest of Canaan; Josiah carried out a "radical Reformation" (a term Moshe Greenberg, the translator, if not Kaufmann himself, certainly used purposefully with Protestant origins in mind) that brought the paganism of Judah and Israel to a virtual end, extending beyond his life to the following rulers. To quote: "He purged the pagan cults, leaving hardly a remnant."[85] Following the book of Kings closely, Kaufmann also has Josiah purge the non-Jerusalem cults altogether in both Judah and Samaria. Second, Josiah makes the book of the Torah "the law of the land."[86] This made Deuteronomy 'canonical' and led directly to the creation of the entire Torah under Ezra and Nehemiah and, thus, to Judaism and the Jewish people.

In Silver's history, Josiah finds the book of Deuteronomy while already being a pious king; the allegations made that either he or his high priest fabricated the scroll are dismissed out of hand, and Josiah re-establishes a covenant between God and God's people, the possible antiquity of which is left, perhaps wisely, uncommented upon.[87] Josiah is also mentioned as "a clear-eyed monarch," politically seeing the demise of Assyria on the horizon and expediently aligning himself with Babylon, only to be crushed by an Egyptian pharaoh (unnamed herein). This caused biblical authors and rabbinic scholars no end of difficulty since Josiah was clearly pious, unlike his perfidious grandfather, Manasseh, whose cult Josiah had thoroughly purified. Manasseh was given the blame, but Silver aligns Josiah

---

ancient world. Josiah is presented as a patriotic Judean called to expand his realm into Samaria in an attempt to recreate David's Israel, all of which pointed forward to the distant future age of the Messiah: Josef Kastein, *History and Destiny of the Jews*, trans. H. Paterson (London: John Lane the Bodley Head, 1933), 61-62 [the German original appeared in 1931]. It should be acknowledged that the notion that biblical history writing was begun early in the united monarchy and rewritten continuously as it proved politically useful continues in academic writing: see, for example, Feinman, *Jerusalem Throne Games*, 156-362.

84 Kaufmann, "The Biblical Age," in Schwarz, *Great Ages and Ideas*, 1-92.
85 Ibid., 56. A two-page expansion of the Josianic reform appears at 71-72.
86 Ibid., 71.
87 Silver, *History of Judaism*, 121.

with the people and their fate as a nation before Egyptians and Babylonians.[88] For Silver, Josiah comes across as an insightful if inept politician whose sole enduring accomplishment was the raising of Deuteronomy to a viable authoritative level in the Judahite cult.

Seltzer's volume presents a much more assertive Josiah. First, Josiah forcibly annexed territories from the failing Assyrian Empire, in the mode of Sir Walter Raleigh's Josiah, restoring the united monarchy under his rule and purging it of any religious sites or activities which were not in concert with Deuteronomy.[89] This law book was the product of a group who were perhaps working during the reign of Hezekiah, but, citing Jeremiah, were quite possibly composing Deuteronomy under the auspices of Josiah himself.[90] Interestingly, like Augustine, Seltzer mostly uses Josiah as a date marker for activities of a literary nature: the writing of Deuteronomy, Judges through Kings, and Jeremiah.[91] Indeed, in like manner, Cahill stresses the same importance of Josiah as the ruler whose reign gives rise to Deuteronomy, Joshua, Judges, Samuel, Kings, and Jeremiah by laying the foundational religious groundwork in the abolition of the worship of the deities Baal, Astarte, and Molech, who "are the gods of human desires" removed now that it is determined that the rich are the idolaters who sacrifice children while the poor are righteous.[92] In these world histories that are specifically centered on Jewish history and culture, it may not be surprising to find Josiah, though his minor role in such specialized works is interesting.

The general world histories of the first half of the twentieth century found Josiah to be a major player in world histories as part and parcel of Israel.[93] Two examples will suffice: John A. Hammerton's *Universal History of the World* (1927–1929) and Walter Goetz's *Das Erwachen der Menschheit* (1931). Both are parts of multivolume histories of the world with specialized authors for each section of each volume. Hammerton's author for the ancient Israelite section is the well-known Bible scholar Theodore

---

88   Ibid., 129–30.

89   Robert M. Seltzer, *Jewish People, Jewish Thought: The Jewish Experience in History* (New York: Macmillan, 1980), 31.

90   Ibid., 41–42, 96.

91   Ibid., 41, 96, 100, 103.

92   Thomas Cahill, *The Gifts of the Jews: How a Tribe of Desert Nomads Changed the Way Everyone Thinks and Feels* (New York: Anchor Books, 1998), 222–23.

93   In *The Passing of the Empires*, ed. A. H. Sayce, trans. M. L. McClure (New York: D. Appleton, 1900), 510–14 [this was a translation of volume 3 of *Histoire ancienne des Peuples de l'Orient classique*, Paris, 1897], Gaston Maspero expends much text on Josiah as an important figure, closely adhering to the biblical accounts, while Wells (*The Outline of History*, 209) notes Josiah in passing as the ruler of a "little country in between" who chose the wrong side and was slain by Neco.

H. Robinson, whose section on Josiah is heavily overlaid with the then famous "Scythian Invasion" as represented by interpreted passages in Zephaniah and Jeremiah. It is in this "ruined countryside" that Josiah set out to revive the religion as well as the political state of Judah and Israel.[94] He removed all foreign influences and aligned the cult of Jerusalem with the teachings of the eighth-century prophets. While Assyria saw this activity as a rebellion, it chose not to interfere, whereas Egypt took this as an intolerable attempt at independence from its ally Assyria, and acting in the cause of Assyrian defense of its tributary put down the rebellion, slaying Josiah in the process. Neco called Josiah to Megiddo to face the king of Egypt serving as Assyria's subordinate, and he put the Judean king to death for treason. This may sound familiar from quite recent presentations in the field, but, clearly, it is not a new idea.

As for Goetz's history, the author of the Israelite section is the equally famous, if not as infamous as his son Gerhard,[95] Rudolf Kittel. In his history, Josiah plays a large part in the story of Neco, which he claims to have adapted from Josephus rather than the biblical texts themselves, but there is very little material in Kittel's history on the actual reign of Josiah. Let it suffice that Josiah militarily annexed Samaria as Assyria collapsed while the fight with Egypt was for control of this territory. Perhaps more interesting for that time and place, Kittel contends that Josiah moved against the religion and the thought of the people (*Religion und Denken der Volker*).[96] In the early thirties, these would have been fighting words as the National Socialists appraised Judaism, from the biblical period forward, as a group detrimental to culture and world history altogether.[97] Indeed, Josiah could be seen as an example of leaders interfering in religion, even

---

94 Theodore H. Robinson, "Israel in the Light of History," in *Universal History of the World*, vol. 2: *From the Hittite Empire to Fifth Century Athens*, ed. John Alexander Hammerton (London: Amalgamated, 1927), 832–33.

95 Horst Junginger, *Die Verwissenschaftlichung der "Judenfrage" im Nationalsozialismus* (Darmstadt: Wissenschaftliche Buchgesellschaft, 2011), 134, 240. The antisemitism of Rudolf Kittel cannot be divorced from the worldview of his more examined son, Gerhard. See Susannah Heschel, *The Aryan Jesus: Christian Theologians and the Bible in Nazi Germany* (Princeton: Princeton University Press, 2008), 2, 180–89. Rudolf Kittel's Kings commentary was an internationally influential work through most of the twentieth century: *Die Bücher der Könige: Übersetzt und erklärt*, HAT (Göttingen: Vandenhoek & Ruprecht, 1900).

96 Rudolf Kittel, "Die Völker des vorderen Orients," in *Das Erwachen der Menschheit: De Kulturen de Urzeit, Ostastiens, und des vordern Orients*, ed. Wlater Goetz, Propyläen: Welgeschichte 1 (Berlin: Propyläen, 1931), 534; citation on Josiah's religious moves against the people at p. 502. However, the notion was not new: Kuenen, *Religions and Universal Religions*, 61.

97 Gerhard Lindemann, "Theologische Forschung über das Judentum in unterschiedlichen politischen Kontexten am Beispiel von Karl Georg Kuhn," *KZ* 17 (2004):

taking it over and remaking it into something to their own liking in parallel to the National Socialists recreating the German church.[98] So, between Robinson and Kittel there is a wide divide: Josiah as a righteous prefigure of moral and religious propriety or Josiah as the evil prefigure of royal oppression of the people, and a Jewish one at that. That contrast is to reappear in the present approaches to Josiah; both are currently popular academic positions.

In modern 'world' histories (post-mid-twentieth century), Josiah does not appear with the prevalence of the pre-twentieth-century volumes,[99] yet, often enough, he gets as much or more text than those specialized texts mentioned on Jewish world history. William Langer's 1952 history introduces him via Neco's defeat of Josiah at Megiddo and the Egyptian conquest of Judea in 609 as part of Egypt's restoration of its Asiatic empire.[100] In 638, Josiah himself, we are informed, reformed the worship of Judah, centralizing it in the temple cult of Jerusalem.[101] William McNeill's 1963 history, *The Rise of the West*, devotes a few sentences to King Josiah, managing in this terse space to avow that his reign intersected religion and politics when the "Party of Religious Reform" came to power,[102] that this group "launched an energetic campaign to purify the religion of Yahweh," and that this group probably created Deuteronomy. Note that McNeill, like Petrus Comestor, manages in this short passage to cite Ezekiel as proof that the reform did not include the behavior of the general population.[103] Derrik Mercer's *Chronicle of the World* (1996) contains more

---

335, concerning the Berlin lecture (1938) published as a pamphlet by Karl Georg Kuhn, *Die Judenfrage als weltgeschichtliches Problem* (Hamburg: Hanseatische, 1939).

98 See Aaron Schart, "Martin Noth," in Wagner, Vieweger, and Erlemann, *Kontexte*, 246–48, 249–50.

99 Several survey volumes of world history skip any mention of Josiah by name or event. For examples, see: J. M. Roberts and Odd Arne Westad, *The History of the World* (London: Dorling Kindersley, 1996); Welsh, *The History of the World*, 42, who does manage to mention Hezekiah as an ally of Egypt; Joanne Suter, *Globe Fearson's World History*, 3rd ed. (Upper Saddle River, NJ: Globe Fearson, 1999), the last intended as a textbook.

100 William L. Langer, *An Encyclopedia of World History: Ancient, Medieval, and Modern, Chronologically Arranged*, rev. ed. (Boston: Houghton Mifflin, 1952), 24.

101 Langer, *Encyclopedia of World History*, 31.

102 It probably does not need to be mentioned given the transparent source for this topic of the popularity in Hebrew Bible Studies at the time that McNeill was writing of the idea of a political action committee in Jerusalem, most widely known in its later formation in Morton Smith, *Palestine Parties and Politics that Shaped the Old Testament* (New York: Columbia University Press, 1971). The notion of some collection of scribes, prophets, and priests pushing Josiah's reform was decidedly older: Wellhausen, *Prolegomena to the History of Ancient Israel* (1957), 26.

103 William H. McNeill, *The Rise of the West: A History of the Human Community* (Chicago: University of Chicago Press, 1963), 162–63.

8 The Popular Afterlife of Josiah 231

Josianic data than any of the four Jewish history volumes mentioned. Aside from noting that the boy Josiah became king at the age of 8, the book centers on Assyria's loss of a political grip on Judah.[104] The youngster takes advantage of this to restore pure Yahwistic religion by removing the trappings of sixty years of "pagan worship" (these historians inaccurately and anachronistically use the term 'pagan').[105] This was done by use of the book discovered that was supposedly written by Yahweh the deity himself: "He has purified the temple, destroying everything in it that was related to pagan gods. All the pagan holy places which have grown up around the country have been suppressed: temples have been desecrated, idols destroyed and priests stripped of their religious authority! It is now illegal to practice divination."[106] Note that, unlike Josephus, these priests get fired; they are not burned. Josiah loses his life as Egypt restores its Asian empire. Usually, as with Gilbert Lafforgue, Josiah is dedicated a couple of sentences, while, here, he has just enough to list the works of his reign: Joshua, Judges, Samuel, Kings, with the beginnings of Jeremiah, and the note that Josiah detested Assyria who is replaced by Babylonia.[107] Sometimes the reference in such works is much shorter. Bernard Grun's, for example: "King Josiah revives Yahweh worship in Jerusalem."[108]

In popular multi-volume histories of the world, Josiah has continued to make his appearance. The once highly popular Time-Life book series of the 1960s and 1970s produced its Emergence of Man series, spanning the time from hominoid origins to the classical world. Among its titles was *The Israelites*, whose consultants were Baruch A. Levine and James B. Pritchard.[109] In this 159-page volume which was heavily illustrated and intended for a general audience interested primarily in the history of humanity, Josiah finds small but interesting space. He is cited as taking territory from Assyria and his repairs to the temple are reported as leading to the finding of the book of Moses. The priests already knew the content of this

---

104 Derrik Mercer, ed., *Chronicle of the World* (London: Dorling Kindersley, 1996), 76.

105 The term 'pagan' continues to be used to draw a clean and clear distinction between 'Israel's' religion and everything else: Yehezel Kaufmann, *The Religion of Israel: From Its Beginnings to the Babylonian Exile*, trans. M. Greenberg (Chicago: University of Chicago Press, 1960), 2. However, the term derives from Latin and simply refers to rural life, which hardly suits religion/s in ancient Judah. Also, the clear distinction made by Kaufmann and others cannot have represented Judahite (or Israelite) religious reality: Collins, *Bible after Babel*, 100–101.

106 Mercer, *Chronicle of the World*, 78.

107 Gilbert Lafforgue, "La haute antiquité," in *Histoire universelle: Des origines à la fin des grands empires*, ed. M. Guillemot (Paris: Larousse-Bordas, 1998), 378.

108 Bernard Grun, *The Timetables of History: A Horizontal Linkage of People and Events*, 4th ed. (New York: Touchstone Books, 2005), 8.

109 Charles Osborne, ed., *The Israelites*, The Emergence of Man (New York: Time-Life Books, 1975).

book, but the book itself had been unknown by them. Here, it is stated that the book was already 100 years old when it was found; however, it had not acquired its later aspect of being a sacred text so that those who found it then rewrote it into the current book of Deuteronomy. The Moses authorial tradition is assumed. Finally, Josiah appears as a "religious reformer" who centralized the Judean cult in Jerusalem by abolishing all other sanctuaries, but this last is important for the text solely as background to Jeremiah.[110] As a historiographical narrative, this work presents Josiah as a political expansionist and an opponent of "paganism" (the term used).

A decidedly more erudite series aimed at the general public was that by Will and Ariel Durant, of which the first volume presents a Josiah taken into a Yahwistic priestly movement based on the tactics of earlier successful prophets.[111] The secret archives of the temple were "discovered" by Hilkiah, who had Josiah proclaim the priestly text of Moses to all the elders, priests, and prophets endorsing the book of Deuteronomy (or, perhaps, Exodus 20–23) essentially to close and "put down" idolatrous (meaning non-Yahwistic) altars and cultic personnel.[112] For Durant, Josiah was not only a religious figure but a political ruler whose importance derived solely from the religious establishment of Jerusalem, whose status, or, as currently popular in humanities, 'power,' is insured by Josiah's royal patronage. For Durant's history, Josiah's lasting importance is not monotheism but the religiously based construction of Persian Yehud.[113]

Recently, Josiah has returned to the center of a world history philosophical storm. It began innocently enough. Jan Assmann, falling into step with the then current rage for works on 'Orientalism,' after the dissemination of Said's volume and the interest in memory as a major aspect of history as a received tradition, wrote an interesting, if popular, volume on the image of ancient Egypt and how it has been colored by the figure of the biblical Moses.[114] Heavily influenced by Freud's *Moses and Monotheism*, as well as Karl Jasper's "axial age," Assmann laid out his theory of the origins of monotheism as a counterpoint to the polytheism of Egypt, and its ramifications on the psyche of the people that came after in the Jewish, Christian, and Islamic (not to mention other religious, scientific,

---

110 Ibid., 10, 14–15, 143.

111 Will Durant, *Our Oriental Heritage*, The Story of Civilization 1 (New York: Simon and Schuster, 1954), 320.

112 Ibid., 323. Note that the prophetic backing of this movement is provided by Huldah (333).

113 Ibid., 328.

114 Edward W. Said, *Orientalism* (New York: Vintage, 1978). Jan Assmann, *Moses the Egyptian: The Memory of Egypt in Western Monotheism* (Cambridge, MA: Harvard University Press, 1997).

and political) traditions.¹¹⁵ At the end of the work, Assmann throws out a comment on the postmodernist return to Egyptian thought as earlier traditions have recovered found pasts before: "History is full of forgotten knowledge that returned in the discovery of a book, from legendary discoveries such as the unearthing of the book of Deuteronomy during restoration work in the temple of Jerusalem."¹¹⁶ This minor reference to the unnamed Josiah has an afterlife in the firestorm that the volume produced about monotheism and its fanatic followers as the purveyors of violence from that day to the present.¹¹⁷ Assmann carefully responded that neither Moses nor monotheism, *per se*, were violent or in any particular necessity producers of violence, but its implementation necessitated the "destruction" of the older perception of reality and this can be traced to the "bloody" reforms of Josiah, here named, as the cultic founder of violent monotheism.¹¹⁸ Early twenty-first-century religious revivals (Jewish, Christian, Muslim, Hindu, Buddhist) have provided a backdrop for the popularization of Assmann's work as proof of organized (as opposed to 'indigenous') religion as violent. Apparently, Josiah has had tremendous influence on modern civilization.¹¹⁹

In summary, then, it is necessary merely to point out that, for historians, Josiah has been as malleable a figure as he has always been for biblical scholars (as well as clergy). The medieval historians, here Petrus and Alfonso, were primarily concerned with biblical history. Modern historians have found the Josiah they seek, whether warrior (read 'power' to be current), pious (read 'spiritual' to be current), irrelevant ('critical thought' to be current), or a monotheistic fanatic (irreligious thought as well as Assmann interpreters). It is of some interest to note that the twentieth-century world histories that deal with ancient Israel often appear

---

115 Auffarth ("Justice, the King and the Gods," in Kratz and Spieckermann, *One God—One Cult—One Nation*, 421–25) critiques Assmann's position and prefers to replace Moses with Plato as the founder of 'monotheism.' Of course, Auffarth's specialty is Greek thought, not ancient Israelite.

116 Assmann, *Moses the Eqyptian*, 218.

117 This notion derived from Assmann appears in some very non-historical, non-biblical places. For example: Mariano Delgado, "Die Gewaltfrage im interreligiösen Dialog," *Zeitschrift für Missionswissenschaft und Religionswissenschaft* 99 (2015): 3; or, Jan-Heiner Tück, "'Bei Gott gibt es keine Gewalt': Was Jan Assmanns Monotheismuskritik theologisch zu denken gibt," *TP* 86 (2011): 222–53, wherein the role of Josiah as a central figure is noted (228).

118 Assmann, *Of God and Gods*, 27; Idem, *The Price of Monotheism*, trans. R. Savage (Stanford: Stanford University Press, 2010), 21.

119 Albertz ("Monotheism and Violence," in van Ruiten and de Vos, *The Land of Israel*, 383–84) argues that Josiah's religious impositions were not violent, but "internalized by law, education, and self-commitment" ... well, except maybe at Bethel.

simply to turn the material over to biblical scholars when such histories deal at length with ancient Judah at all.

Let us end with the observation that Josiah does not currently appear in world histories with the frequency of years of yore. Aside from the obvious, there is more history every minute, there is more of an effort to cover more regions and peoples (though it would be a disservice to André Guillaume to suggest such efforts are new or even better rendered), and there is a marked movement to avoid being occidentally biased, which includes not focusing on Judaism and Christianity. Small sections, often one or two pages long, now cover the entirety of ancient Judah, Israel, and the 'biblical' world and these with few names, often only Moses (and that raises questions about the 'historicity' of the history in these modern general histories [reference to Alfonso El Sabio intended]). Sometimes, of course, the absence is philosophically and/or politically motivated, as, for example, Chris Harman's Marxist *A People's History of the World*, where non-iron producing Judah and Israel are entirely ignored (well, to be fair, modern Israel gets a Cold War treatment).[120] Perhaps a biblical scholar, if not an author, might yet be useful still, however. Let us end with a quotation from the fairly recent world history by Alex Woolf: "As Assyrian power began to wane in the 630s, Judah regained its independence under Joshua (reigned 640–609) and expanded its territory to include the former kingdom of Israel. But after Joshua's death in battle against the Egyptians at Megiddo, Egypt briefly occupied Judah."[121] An entire chapter could be composed on the problems with that reference to Josiah *cum* Joshua, but enough said.

---

120 Chris Harman, *A People's History of the World: From the Stone Age to the New Millennium* (London: Verso, 2008) [first published 1999]. Assyria gets coverage since it used and produced new technology; the entirety of the Old Testament is dismissed in a portion of one sentence (40).

121 Woolf, *History of the World*, 33.

CHAPTER NINE
ART OF THE STORY OF THE KING[1]

Josiah, like most rulers in the biblical texts, is never physically described.[2] In addition, there are no known examples of Josiah in illustrations from the ancient Near East.[3] However, biblical narratives have a long history of depiction and Josiah's religious adventures are no exception, not to mention that a good death in a chariot makes an excellent action portrait. There have been a wide range of portrayals of Huldah, given that she also has no description in the biblical texts; however, in her case, since no age is given for her, she has been illustrated as everything from a young girl to an aged crone.[4] Josiah tends to appear as a young adult, and these portrayals of the king and his reign have traditionally concentrated on a limited number of scenes. In portraying these scenes from the story of Josiah, artists have reconceived the appearance of costumes, implements, and backgrounds for the central characters such that a history of representing the king in visual form through the centuries can be made. Most of the existing illustrations of Josiah are one-off pictures of a single selected scene from his life; however, illustrated continuums rendering a pictorial narrative also exist. How Josiah has been presented in a select number of these illustrated narrative presentations forms the finale of this chapter.

There is a long, multicultural history of biblical art; needless to say, Josiah has not been one of the major focal points of this branch of

1   The first part of this chapter is expanded from a section on "Josiah's Image" in Handy, "Josiah in a New Light," in Holloway, *Orientalism, Assyriology and the Bible*, 430–35. For a short, informative survey of Josiah in Christian art to the Reformation, see Aston, *The King's Bedpost*, 37–81. This chapter will concentrate on a select few modern Bible illustrations and the creation of visual continuity retellings of Josiah's narrative.
2   Avioz, "Motif of Beauty," 359.
3   A pot shard line drawing from Ramat Rahel has occasionally been suggested as a depiction of one of the last of the Judean kings, usually Jehoiakim, though Josiah and Jehoahaz have been mentioned: Aharoni and Avi-Yonah, *Macmillan Bible Atlas*, 105, and Isserlin, *The Israelites*, 271, Fig. 77. It is a seated human figure, but what, let alone who, it was remains unknown. That it would have been Josiah is unlikely in the extreme.
4   Handy, "Reading Huldah as Being a Woman," 35–38.

illustration. Even the illustrations in Bibles, having a long, global history of their own, including the many 'people's Bibles' whose mass of illustrations often correlate otherwise seemingly disparate narratives, do not represent Josiah with any regularity. Though he has not been prevalent in the genre, Josiah Bible illustrations of the fifteenth and sixteenth centuries have been well discussed by Margaret Aston.[5]

Medieval illustrations related to Josiah's narrative tend toward a limited number of scenes.[6] While depictions of the discovery of the book of Deuteronomy occur, they lack a portrayal of Josiah because he was not present for the event. Josiah does appear in three other common depictions. The first depicts the scroll of the law, usually rendered as a large book, as it is read to King Josiah, who tends to be either pensively absorbing the text in regal fashion or tearing his garment in humility and mourning for his failure to keep the law of Moses. Continuing a popular theme from earlier art, the second portrays Josiah as he leads the people in his mass destruction of idols. Since classical times, these idols tended to be depicted as Greek and Roman gods ablaze in huge bonfires. Josiah, as a regal and usually bearded king, looks on approvingly as others toss idols into the flames. The third is that of Josiah setting out the Passover for the general population which puts the king before a large assembly of people attending the sacrifice and the accompanying feast provided by the king. This last was often an illustration for the book of First Esdras.[7]

More generic representations of Josiah appeared throughout the Middle Ages. The two most common depictions were of Josiah as king of Israel, and Josiah as an ancestor of Jesus. Cathedral doors often had carved lintels with assembled personages of specific character types. Saints and apostles were common enough, but the line of kings in Jerusalem from the Christian 'Old Testament' formed a particular recurring motif. Among the rather nondescript male figures usually lined up in a row would be a figure of Josiah, not obviously differentiated from any of the other rulers depicted, all of whom wore crowns. The illustration of Israelite kings as a continuity was not restricted to portals; in the *Liber chronicarum* of 1493 Nuremberg, Josiah's portrait appears in a sequence of many pages including all the kings mentioned in the books of Samuel and Kings. Josiah's image is that of an elderly man with a divided, reddish-brown beard and holding an orb in his left hand and a scepter in his right; the crown on his head designates him as the king.[8] As far as the accouterments he

---

5   Aston, *The King's Bedpost*, 37–48.
6   Ibid., 49.
7   Eléonore Fournié, *L'iconographie de la Bible historiale*, RILMA 2 (Turnhout: Brepols, 2012), 61 and Fig. 78.
8   Schedel, *Chronicle of the World*, leaf LX recto.

is depicted with, he is not distinguished from the other illustrations of either biblical or classical kings in the volume; however, all are drawn as individuals with their own physical characteristics.

Alternatively, in artistic representation of various media, was the popular "Tree of Jesse" that presented in word or figure the ancestors of Jesus as recorded in Matt 1:2–16 and/or Luke 3:23–38.[9] The vine-like branches of the tree carried either names or illustrations of the lineage of kings; again, the individual rulers were not clearly distinguished.[10] In some cases, patrons or royal figures were used as models for the kings.[11] The introduction of several kingly ancestors of Jesus to the art of the Tree of Jesse came with the twelfth century; previously, the objects of major concern were the Virgin Mary and the prophets who had foretold her miraculous child.[12] A late innovation of the motif was to have all the kings playing instruments.[13] Josiah could be depicted as an individual Old Testament ruler in stained glass, who was not engaged in any activity; such is the Trinity Chapel window at Canterbury Cathedral, where Josiah appears in portrait mode holding an unrolled scroll representing the law of Moses.[14]

With the coming of the Reformation, Protestants adapted Josiah to themselves. The Roman Catholic Church continued illustrating Josiah in the medieval manner. Protestants came to view Josiah as the embodiment

---

9   For the Tree of Jesse window in Canterbury Cathedral, Luke's genealogy was followed with the interpolation of some kings taken from Matthew's Gospel: Madeline Harrison Caviness, *The Early Stained Glass of Canterbury Cathedral circa 1175–1220* (Princeton: Princeton University Press, 1977), 107–8. Arthur Watson, *The Early Iconography of the Tree of Jesse* (Oxford: Oxford University Press; London: Humphrey Milford, 1934), 1–2, notes that, while earlier art motifs were incorporated, the Tree of Jesse popularity arose in the eleventh century and reached its peak in the twelfth century. Ross, *Medieval Art*, 248; on Josiah, p. 144.

10   It is interesting, if not necessarily intentional, that the sole surviving stained glass portrait of a king from the Tree of Jesse window at Canterbury Cathedral is that of Josiah, preserved in a private collection from the mid-nineteenth century. As the cathedral shifted from Catholic to Anglican, only Josiah and Mary survived: Jeffrey Weaver and Madeline Harrison Caviness, *The Ancestors of Christ Windows at Canterbury Cathedral* (Los Angeles: J. Paul Getty Museum, 2013), 76, Fig. 53. Watson, *Early Iconography*, pls. XXVII, XXVIII, XXXII (and others) presents Tree of Jesse renderings in glass, manuscripts, and paintings; Aston (*The King's Bedpost*, 50, Fig. 34) prints a title page illustration of the Tree of Jesse from a 1578 prayer book.

11   Caviness (*Early Stained Glass*, 74) notes that it has been suggested that King Richard I of England was used for the model of Josiah in the Canterbury Cathedral Tree of Jesse.

12   Watson, *Early Iconography*, 9, 112–13.

13   Watson (*Early Iconography*, 170–71) points out that this was an expansion on early pictures of David playing a harp. See Fournié, *Iconographie de la Bible*, 61, 85–86, and Fig. 131.

14   Caviness, *Early Stained Glass*, 115.

of all they perceived themselves to be. At times this was depicted quite literally, as when Martin Luther and Frederick the Wise were illustrated respectively as Hilkiah and Josiah for an illustration in a Lutheran Bible.[15] Perhaps the most reproduced of all Protestant (Lutheran) depictions of Josiah is that by Julius Schnorr von Carolsfeld for his picture Bible of 1860.[16] Protestant stained-glass church windows allowed the figure of Josiah. These depictions included him as part of a tree of Jesse, as destroyer of idols, and as the exemplar of the righteous and pious king. Josiah was a natural choice as a role model for iconoclast Protestants and, purportedly, the first illustration of Josiah by a Protestant artist appears in an ink design for stained glass.[17] Niklaus Manuel Deutsch's Josiah window survives, displaying a regal Josiah ordering the destruction of the idols in the temple with a tip of his scepter; a text is fully imprinted in the window, which was a standard early Protestant artistic conventional reference to the importance of text, in this case Scripture, in biblical illustration.[18] Manuel Deutsch was a Protestant convert active in a variety of artistic fields, but himself engaged in Protestant Reformation iconoclasm, which explains why Josiah forms one of only two biblical window designs he composed.[19]

The identification of biblical figures with contemporary political and religious persons was widely represented in biblical illustrations of the time. A fine example of this is an illustration of Josiah hearing the law that was printed in a seventeenth-century French Catholic edited version of the Bible.[20] Here, a regal King Josiah, clothed in a combination of clas-

15 Aston, *The King's Bedpost*, 42, Fig. 30 (1572 Luther Bible illustration).
16 Julius Schnorr von Carolsfeld, *Das Buch der Büchen in Bildern: 240 Darstellungen erfunden und gezeichnet* (Leipzig: Georg Wigand, 1908), pl. 123. Interestingly, the nominally Catholic Gustave Doré's illustration of *King Josiah Destroying the Idols of Baal*, which includes a Baal priest being killed by a soldier to the fore left and the smashed idol of Baal (very classical) to the fore right, does not include the king and simply was not one of the illustrations often used in Doré Bibles.
17 Aston (*The King's Bedpost*, 51–52, Fig. 35) reproduces Niklaus Manuel Deutsch's 1527 ink design for a 1530 window showing Josiah directing the destruction of assorted anthropomorphic idols. A color plate of the window can be found in Barbara Butts and Lee Hendrix, *Painting on Light: Drawings and Stained Glass in the Age of Dürer and Holbein* (Los Angeles: J. Paul Getty Museum; St. Louis: St. Louis Art Museum, 2000), 275, pl. 275 (the window has been tentatively ascribed to Joseph Gösler, 274). On the primacy of Josiah in Protestant art, see Glenn Ehrstine, *Theater, Culture, and Community in Reformation Bern: 1523–1555*, SMRT 85 (Leiden: Brill, 2002) 208.
18 Ehrstine, *Theater, Culture and Community*, 209.
19 Butts and Hendrix, *Painting on Light*, 274. On Niklaus Manuel Deutsch's graphic and literary activity, see Ehrstine, *Theater, Culture and Community*, 205–14.
20 Nicolas Fontaine, *The History of the Old Testament and New Testament, Extracted out of Sacred Scripture and Writings of the Fathers: To Which Are Added the Lives, Travels and Sufferings of the Apostles: With a Large and Exact Historical Chronology of all the*

sical Roman and medieval Gallic attire, sits rather calmly on his French canopied throne pointing to a bearded Shaphan.[21] It might be noted that Josiah is represented in a very European fashion, relaying the medieval European notion that there was some direct link between 'Israel's' royal lineage and that of the European royal houses; however, Shaphan is drawn as a Jewish figure. Shaphan reads the 'book,' a sizeable bound volume located on a lectern either placed on the back of a serf or acolyte (perhaps on a stand carved to look like one). Given that there are at least three volumes at Shaphan's disposal, it would appear that Josiah is listening to the entire Torah. Shaphan is clothed in a flowing robe with the peaked hat that had been a staple of Christian artistic renditions of Jews. Behind Shaphan sit men looking at each other with serious expressions while beside the king stand a trio of militarily-clad men before a massive assembly of robed figures. Beyond the assembly is the exterior, where men with long poles are tending a small fire; to the left of the flames, a man approaches carrying a human image, no doubt an idol. The picture manages to include in one scene the hearing of the law by Josiah, the reading of the law to the amassed elders, and the results of the hearing of the law in the destruction of idolatry.

Beginning in the nineteenth century, especially after the publication in Europe of the dramatic reports of impressive remains of the Assyrian and Babylonian empires, attempts to include Mesopotamian artistic elements in biblical illustrations became common. There was clearly a fascination among illustrators with the newly discovered images of Assyrian chariots that these artists chose to display in exciting death scenes for Josiah. The Josiah death scene included in a 1905 Russian Bible Commentary, among other places of publication, includes a number of Assyrian relief motifs.[22] Josiah wears Assyrian royal garb and is coiffed with Assyrian relief-inspired hair and beard, having just dropped his Assyrian-style shield.[23] This rendition of Josiah's death was based on that which appears in 2 Chr 35:23–24. There were numerous Assyrian chariot death illustrations for King Josiah.[24] It should be noted that the illustrations of Josiah's destruction of idols began to incorporate images of excavated deities and demons as well.[25]

Affairs and Actions Related in the Bible, 2nd ed. (London: S. and J. Sprint, C. Brome, J. Nicholson, J. Pero, & Benj. Toeke, 1699), pl. 129 (between 164–65).

21 Handy, "Josiah in a New Light," 431, 432, Fig. 56.

22 Aleksander Glagolev et al., *Tolkovaia Biblia*, 188.

23 Handy, "Josiah in a New Light," 433–34 (this description of the illustration was written with the help of Steven W. Holloway).

24 Note, for example, Frank E. Wright's *Josiah Killed by the Egyptians* chariot scene in *The New Illuminated Bible* (Philadelphia: American Bible House, 1897).

25 Clearly useful for children's books illustrations: note images of Pazuzi, Thoth, and 'Baal' being hammered to pieces in Trevor Barnes, *The Kingfisher's Children's Bible*

The popular watercolors of William Brassey Hole (1846–1917) exemplify the biblical illustration of Josiah for the Assyriology-influenced late nineteenth and early twentieth centuries.[26] Hole had been a religiously devout Protestant since his youth and sought in his art to combine religious life and common life. A close friend of Robert Louis Stevenson, the two wrote and acted Sunday School theatricals together, and he was a distinguished member of the Royal Scottish Academy.[27] Hole considered it a religiously edifying endeavor to illustrate sacred scriptures as well as the land of Palestine. His illustrated biblical history appeared after his death in 1925.

He devoted three watercolors to dramatic presentations of Josiah's reign in his posthumously published book of Bible illustrations.[28] While two of these illustrations have been widely reproduced, the first of the three plates in the volume for the section on Josiah has seen less interest. A very atmospheric, eerie scene entitled *The Sin of Witchcraft* looks as though it might have started life as a vision of the Witch of Endor; however, it wound up as a description of the necromancy that Josiah ended.[29] In a gloomy, bluish painting, a deathly almost white-grey elderly woman sits staring blindly (pupilless eyes) toward the viewer, clearly in the act of speaking. The entire scene is illuminated solely by a brazier flame placed in the lower center of the illustration. Above, in the center, the ghost is represented by a pale human face with a body that slowly disappears into the background as one scans downward. To the right foreground, two men shrink back in terror before the apparition. The men are dressed in classic Orientalism cloaks and headgear. The illustration is a classic of its time. Spiritualism was immensely popular in England from the mid-nineteenth century until the Second World War.[30] Though often condemned by the established church as witchcraft, necromancy held the popular imagination as well as that of a sizeable portion of the intellectual community,

---

(New York: Kingfisher, 2001), 121, as well as Thomas Donaghy, *New Catholic Children's Bible*, St. Joseph Junior Books (Totowa, NJ: Catholic Book Publishing, 2005), 112.

26   Steven W. Holloway ("Introduction: Orientalism, Assyriology and the Bible," in Holloway, *Orientalism*, 8–26) outlines the cultural obsession in Europe, England in particular, with Assyrian art and history in the nineteenth century, publications with illustrations being then both popular and lucrative.

27   Mrs. William Hole, *Memories of William Hole, R.S.A.* (London: W. & R. Chambers, 1920), 7, 48–49, 75, 95. Hole was devoted to parish church work being also a Sunday School teacher (80).

28   William Hole, *Old Testament History: Retold and Illustrated* (London: Eyre & Spottiswoode, 1925), 124–30, contains the text on Josiah; the plates are unpaginated inserts.

29   Hole, *Old Testament History*, pl. 65 (between 124–25).

30   Warren Sylvester Smith, *The London Heretics 1870–1914* (New York: Dodd, Mead, 1968), 141–68.

some of whom found it compatible with the teachings of the church.³¹ Hole's illustration reflects the burgeoning clamor for visual representations of séances, mediums, and actual ghosts. His evocative watercolor reflects the contemporary doctored photographs of such spirit encounters right down to the clearer head and disappearing body of the called-upon spirit beside and behind the medium.³² In the event, Hole's fantasy creation is more dramatic than the photographs.

The following two plates center on episodes in the Josiah narrative itself. In *King Josiah Cleansing the Land of Idols*, a vividly red conflagration lights up an enormous seated ram-horned idol in Mesopotamian royal sculpture relief form.³³ The idol rises high above the people surrounding it on a throne decorated with a striding bovine. Josiah stands, his back to the viewer, directing the demolition of the religious object. Men to the left pull at ropes that will clearly topple the unwanted item. A man to the right hauls a smaller idol toward the fire. The colors are bright, but the scene presents solely the destruction of a single item to convey the universal removal of idols from Josiah's kingdom. The magnitude of the task is symbolized by the size of the idol. A much busier panorama scene by Hole is *The Death of King Josiah at Megiddo*.³⁴ Here, a more subtle coloring scheme portrays the moment that Josiah is slain. The Nubian Egyptian archers appear front and center, aiming directly at the white horse-drawn chariot upon which Josiah falls backward from the arrow in his chest. Attacking soldiers surround him and fill the background as Megiddo goes up in flames in the upper right background. The city is defended by a phalanx of Egyptian white-robed archers behind another row of shield-bearing warriors. Hole's visits to the Near East provided him with a Megiddo based on Syro-Palestinian urban architecture and his human figures are painted in garments derived from archaeological reliefs and his own modern life

---

31 Rather typical of the mainline church's response to spiritualism was George Baldwin's condemnation of spiritualism as a whole in relation to the witch of Endor: George C. Baldwin, *Representative Women: From Eve, the Wife of the First, to Mary, the Mother of the Second Adam* (New York: Sheldon, Lamport and Blakeman, 1856), 190–91. The highly influential William T. Stead, however, was obsessed with the spiritualist movement and believed it was acceptable within Christianity: Smith, *London Heretics*, 164–68.

32 Andreas Fischer, "'The Most Disreputable Camera in the World': Spirit Photography in the United Kingdom in the early Twentieth Century," in *The Perfect Medium: Photography and the Occult*, ed. J.-L. Champion, trans. T. Selous (New Haven: Yale University Press, 2004), 72–75; photos 1-right; and 82–83 photos 28 [24 examples].

33 Hole, *Old Testament History*, pl. 66 (between 126–27).

34 Ibid., pl. 67 (between 128–29).

242   *Josiah*

sketches.³⁵ The two Josiah illustrations epitomize the era of Orientalism in European art and biblical illustration. Hole himself observed on his travels that "now we find ourselves right in the midst of a thousand years ago" in the world of the 1001 Nights and the Bible.³⁶ The theory was that this manner of presentation would more accurately describe the historical events in the Bible. In fact, it managed to provide a window into an imagined European vision of the ancient biblical world, making it more domestic to the West, and displayed how foreign the biblical world was in the then current notion of 'the East.'

Bible illustrations of the twentieth century tended to drop the orientalist leanings of the nineteenth century. For the popular vernacular English Bible, the Good News Bible, Annie Vallotten created some 500 illustrations. Her image for 2 Kgs 23:4, the sole illustration concerned with Josiah, shows the bonfire outside Jerusalem into which four shawled men are depositing a pillar (Asherah?).³⁷ The stylized collection of items being burned include a wheel (chariot of the sun?), a human image (Baal?), a figure of a goat (*se'irim*?),³⁸ and assorted broken pots and rolled scrolls (the paraphernalia of the temple's unwanted deities). Designated by a stylized royal crown, King Josiah, slightly off balance to the right of the flames, stands with folded arms watching passively as the non-Yahwistic cultic material is destroyed by fire. As a line drawing, it is less than clear how old the man is supposed to be, though he has a slight beard. The picture may be of significance as that of a woman contracted to illustrate an entire Christian Bible for use in popular family devotions.

Barry Moser was a ubiquitous book illustrator in the late twentieth century. His style was a fairly distinctive rendition of classical engraving art. Over the years, he re-illustrated a number of literary classics from Lewis Carroll's Alice books, through *Great Ghost Stories*, to Herman Melville's *Moby Dick*. For his portrait of Josiah included in the illustrated Authorized Version of 1999, Moser rendered the head of a young boy whom only the text allows one to know is King Josiah.³⁹ The inspiration for Josiah was a photograph of a Jewish child taken in a German Nazi concentra-

---

35 Mrs. Hole, *Memories*, 100–122, contains Hole's description of his 1901 trip to Palestine; pages 147–87 reproduce his diary from his 1912 journey through Palestine.

36 Quoted in Mrs. Hole, *Memories*, 101.

37 Annie Vallotten, illus., *Good News Bible: The Bible in Today's English Version* (New York: American Bible Society, 1976), 434.

38 Münnich ("What Did the Biblical Goat-Demons Look Like?," 526–29) theorizes *se'irim* refers to demons with some form of goat appearance or that were even simply understood to look like a goat; so also Monroe, "A 'Holiness' Substratum," 46–49. That is apparently what is pictured in this fire.

39 Barry Moser, illus., *The Holy Bible: Containing All the Books of the Old and New Testaments: King James Version* (New York: Penguin Books, 1999), 408.

tion camp. In this way, Moser keeps the memory of this unknown victim of the Shoah alive in an illustration that will clearly have staying power. The artist thereby integrates Josiah, the king who re-established the faith, with those who have died for it. The continuation of Jewish life and tradition is embodied in a small rendition of Josiah.[40]

Picture-laden presentations of biblical narratives were not uncommon book subjects, though Josiah was not among the usual topics. For the character of Josiah, the most renowned example of a picture book is *History of Josiah* produced by Phillipe Galle (1537-1612) in 1569.[41] The production and acquisition of illustrated texts was a fashion of the time in the Netherlands, as it was in much of Northern Europe. It has been noted that this art was drawn overwhelmingly by males for a male clientele; this is certainly true in the cases of Bible illustration and formal painting. In this particular graphic rendition of Josiah in a series of eight numbered engravings, the biblical story of the king is related. The plates were reproductions, as was the custom of the time, of formal art works; the series of Josiah paintings, now lost, were by the contemporary famous Dutch artist Martin van Heemskerk (1498-1574), who was the first and foremost Dutch artist for the graphics trade.[42] Van Heemskerk had studied extensively in Italy, making several sketches and paintings of classical architecture, which he incorporated into his art after returning to the Netherlands.[43] The sixteenth and seventeenth centuries had a fascination with classical culture, with Roman art and architecture in particular favor; the use of Roman ruins in biblical illustrations was common at the time.[44] All eight of van Heemskerk's Josiah pictures used his Roman archi-

---

40   Catherine Madsen, "A Terrible Beauty: Moser's Bible," *CrCur* 50 (2000): 139.

41   Jan Garff, *Tegninger af Maerten van Heemskerck: Illustreret Katalog* (Copenhagen: Statens Museum for Kunst, 1971), pls. 102-109; note that these graphics have been printed in reverse of most imprints and the following descriptions describe the more common imprint. Aston (*The King's Bedpost*, 67-81) devotes an entire chapter to Heemskerk's art and Galle's graphics; pages 78-79 reproduce half of the engravings [the remaining four were easily found on multiple sites on the internet]. Text on both renditions of the engravings demonstrate they were sold in both formats.

42   Ilja Veldman, *Maarten van Heemskerck and Dutch Humanism in the Sixteenth Century* (Amsterdam: Meulenhoff, 1977), 16; Leon Preibisz, *Martin van Heemskerck: Ein Beitrag zur Geschichte des Romanismus in der Niederländiscen Malerei des XVI-Jahrhunderts* (Leipzig: Klinkhardt und Biermann, 1911), 52-55.

43   Veldman, *Maarten van Heemskerck*, 11-12.

44   The popular artistic culture of the time in Northern Europe relied heavily on Renaissance classical depictions and related imagery of the nude. For the highly lucrative trade in demonic/witchcraft illustration, see Lyndal Roper, *The Witch in the Western Imagination* (Charlottesville: University of Virginia Press, 2012), 15; and for illustrating the 'new' Amerindians, often imagined by artists who had never seen a native of the Americas but who knew classical art images, see Olive P. Dickason,

tectural interest to create their settings. Van Heemskerk was noted for his depictions of the seven ancient wonders of the world, and his output included an extensive production of biblical scenes of destruction.[45] The destruction of idols was a common enough topic in these illustrations, which is of interest given that he worked in the early years of the Protestant Reformation, when the question of Catholic images as idols was a central concern. Van Heemskerk was Catholic, a member of the Guild of Saint Luke (patron saint of painters), such that his depiction of 'idols' continued the Catholic Christian tradition of depicting these items as those of the classical world (pls. 4-6). A Catholic deacon and churchwarden for the last third of his life, he consciously continued late medieval artistic theory that illustrations should be didactic and should encourage morals; he designed much work for church interiors.[46] He was, however, a prominent member of the Haarlem intelligentsia.[47] Galle's religious affiliation is more difficult to determine, but his engravings have a decided emphasis on destruction and idol-smashing.[48] It needs to be remembered that one did not need to be a Protestant in sixteenth-century Europe to have considered images either idolatrous or over emphasized.

The eight engravings of Galle's *History of Josiah* do not represent the complete biblical narrative of Josiah but a select section of the account expressly taken from the book of Kings. The subject is the restitution of the proper religion of Jerusalem; or, perhaps more descriptively, the destruction of the improper religion of Israel. The first scene depicts the moment that Josiah realizes he and his religious world have been in error for generations (2 Kgs 22:10-11). Shaphan, piously staged with hand to breast, reads from a moderately sized book held by two acolytes while Josiah, clothed in royal raiment of a medieval European king, grasps his garment to rend it. Appropriately, Josiah's eyes are not cast downward upon Shaphan (properly staged on a lower level than the king on his raised throne, signifying his status *vis-à-vis* the king), but upward toward the god he has been offending. The eight-year-old Josiah and his early religious reforms, not

---

The Myth of the Savage: And the Beginnings of French Colonialism in the Americas (Edmonton: University of Alberta Press, 1997), 15-16. A confluence of both classical art and the nude are found in van Heemskerk's Josiah series. 'Busy' illustrations and violent action so prevalent in 'New World' depictions also define these works, though Galle's Josiah engravings avoid supernatural depictions so common in the 'witch' art of the time.

45 Aston, *The King's Bedpost*, 58, 63-64, 70.
46 Garff, *Tegninger af Maerten van Heemskerck*, 2 [unpaginated]; and Veldman, *Maarten van Heemskerck*, 13-16, 32.
47 Veldman, *Maarten van Heemskerck*, 32.
48 Aston, *The King's Bedpost*, 56. Galle was also a member of the Guild of Saint Luke, but at home in the Dutch Humanist circles, amiable to English Protestants.

to mention Josiah's death at the hands of Neco, make no appearance in this narrative. In this rendition, there are numerous men standing around listening and commenting on the book being read. The reading of the law is continued in the second engraving (2 Kgs 23:1–3). Here, the two acolytes hold the book upright for a very agitated priest (Hilkiah?) to read the book of the law of the Lord to a group of eight people gathered in the foreground. Josiah stands as royal authority before a pillar of the temple with a large scepter, gesturing to the crowd upon which he gazes with a serious expression. A classical depiction of temple pillars forms the backdrop before which Josiah stands,[49] with the portico to the right topped with those horses to the sun dedicated by Josiah's royal forefathers. Given the depiction of Yachin and Boaz in the eighth engraving, these pillars would appear to be simple, standard, classical, temple pillar architecture.

Second Kings 23:4–5 provides the text for the third engraving. With this engraving a series of five illustrations of directed destruction begins. The first picture depicts the cleaning out of the accouterments of the worship of Baal. Josiah appears top center directing the demolition, striding masterfully forward, sword by his side but not drawn. In his right hand his scepter admonishes the priest who reacts with left hand on heart and right hand gesturing toward the destruction underway. The destruction itself is carried out by others who are all males. Far in the right background a circle of men feed a huge bonfire, the contents of which are not recognizable. In the left middle-ground, a Zeus/Jupiter-like statue of Baal is being smashed with adzes (or sledge hammers); the base of the idol is being attacked in the illustration, the statue's left hand having already been broken away. From left to right across the foreground a priest of Baal is slain by sword, vessels are hauled away, weapons are left abandoned on the ground, a priest of Baal is slain by a scimitar, and a vessel is hauled off by a running, clearly aggrieved young man. Conflagration, vandalism, homicide, and looting—this was a portrait for the times as Protestants took to the streets of the Netherlands to demolish Catholic artworks while Catholics and Reformers entered into armed conflict.

The fourth engraving illustrates the destruction of the horses and chariots dedicated to the sun (2 Kgs 23:11). From the roof of the portico of the rather Pantheon-like temple, men pull the statues of horses to the

---

49 Raymond Apple ("The Pillars of the Temple," *JBQ* 42 [2014]: 225–27) describes the uncertainty of the positions of the pillars Yachin and Boaz as well as their appearance, but notes that early churches and synagogues in Europe often included them as free-standing pillars before the buildings. Such replication of the pillars in Christian church architecture is noted in Simon Goldhill, *The Temple of Jerusalem* (Cambridge, MA: Harvard University Press, 2005), 29. The classical art of van Heemskerk explains their depiction in these illustrations.

ground with ropes, the chariots already having fallen and carted off. The broken pieces of chariots can be seen on the level area before the portico being consumed by the bonfire depicted in the lower right register of the engraving. In the fire, clearly drawn, is the head of some idol (crowned young male, not the bearded head of Baal from the third engraving; perhaps Apollo given the context) and pieces of the head and leg of another horse. Center front and to the left stand a group of soldiers and, as they have cowls, perhaps priests watching the destruction; to their immediate left (illustration right) two men pry the broken rear of a horse statue into smaller pieces. Josiah stands to the left of the action in this scene, pointing with his scepter toward the bonfire while looking backward to the priest (Hilkiah?) who appears to be giving the king directions. This would pictorially change the flow of authority from the biblical account where the king, on the authority of the scroll, directs the priests; however, it may well reflect political theology of a Catholic in the Counter-Reformation.

Turning to the destruction of the idolatrous behavior of Solomon, the fifth engraving presents the destruction of the cults of the abominations "Astoroth, Chamos and Melchon" (2 Kgs 23:13-14). The impiety of Solomon had been illustrated by van Heemskerk before (1559).[50] Here, that apostasy receives its pictorial end. The edifice, built by Solomon for the many gods of his wives, is being demolished by men with mallets in the background of the illustration, even as the statues/idols are being destroyed in that same background. To the left, men with ropes are pulling a fully depicted elderly deity's standing statue down while other men hammer away at the statue and its base.[51] To the foreground of that statue lies the already toppled idol of a young male. Perhaps Milcom is represented by the elderly figure and Chemosh by the younger. Around the circular interior of the temple are a series of niches in some of which are standing female figures; before others lie toppled and broken naked feminine statues. From those still upright in their niches, it can be determined that these are the idols of Astarte. As with the revival of classical art and architecture, the sixteenth century saw a proclivity for artistic representations of the unclothed female figure; here, several nice nude female figures are related to the worship of Astarte, to whom sexuality was generally attributed. To the far right stands King Josiah, scepter raised as he gazes across the open area to the destruction of the two male idols (one wonders if it was

50 Aston, *The King's Bedpost*, 60, Fig. 41.
51 It might be observed that the same method of destroying an unwanted religious symbol appears in Antonio de Herrera y Tordesillas' *Histoire génerale des voyages et conquests des Castillans...* (1659-1571), where Guarionex on Hispaniola topple a large Spanish cross in the same pictorial manner, with ropes and axes; illustration reproduced in Dickason, *Myth of the Savage*, 127.

intentional that the 'good' king does not stare steadily at the naked female figures; it might be supposed that the purchasers of the print may have nonetheless).[52] Behind him Hilkiah and Shaphan (?) watch. In the upper far background, men haul the dead bodies of the priests and devotees of this trio of deities off into the woods. It is clear from this representation that van Heemskerk and Galle envisioned Solomon's worship places for his wives as lavish temples to rival the one dedicated to Yahweh.

Josiah's trip to Bethel (2 Kgs 23:15-20) forms the content of the sixth scene. Josiah stands with his companions center stage. Looking to the left of the picture at the tomb of the unnamed prophet, Josiah holds his scepter out to stop the man wielding a sledge-hammer from attacking the elaborate tomb. A fascination with Egyptian antiquities is reflected in this graphic. The massive tomb monument is here illustrated complete with an impressive lengthy inscription as well as constructed with Egyptian sphinxes at its corners. Meanwhile, the exhumation of the graves around and about the area is being carried out, and in the background towards the right the bodies are hauled to the altar of Bethel upon which the dead priests of Bethel are being burned in a great conflagration. To the right a man hammers away at a lion-faced monument while to the rear left a nice Egyptian obelisk is being toppled. A pictorial display of death, the skeletons and disarticulated bones fill the lower register; tombs surround the king and his three companions, while the sparing of the unnamed prophet's tomb highlights the destruction filling the remaining space in the composition. It is not unreasonable to posit that the Egyptian identification with Bethel here reflects a notion of Jeroboam's Israel as connected to the Egypt from which Israel should have escaped and which symbolized for many the land of death from which one escaped to life.

Completing the engravings of massive destruction, scene seven showcases the slaughter of the priests of Israel (2 Kgs 23:20). In this engraving, Josiah is depicted as the largest human figure, set off in the illustration in the left foreground pointing with his scepter toward the altar on which three priests are being executed. A fourth in the right foreground is being brought by two soldiers behaving not too gently, the soldier to the right jabbing his spear shaft into the man's back, while the other soldier pulls the priest's hair and kicks him in his rear. These are brutal, vicious executions. The edifice in which all of this is taking place would seem to be another temple even as it is being dismantled from the roof and the walls. The altar on which the offending priests are being killed, on the orders of Josiah, has Greek sphinxes at its corners, clearly demarking it as an idolatrous altar. The execution of the priests is more central to the illustration

---

52 Roper (*The Witch in the Western Imagination*, 115) comments on the confluence of sex as fascination and as abhorrence in demonic illustrations of the time.

than the destruction of the temple, while the altar itself is not undergoing any damage. King Josiah performs none of the punishing action, but directs uniformed soldiers and essentially naked laymen in carrying out the elimination of the priests of non-Yahwistic cults.

The eighth and final engraving depicts the great Passover called for by Josiah. While, no doubt, 2 Chr 35:1–19 and 1 Esd 1:1–17 were known to van Heemskerk, the illustration explicitly depicts 2 Kgs 23:21–23. Since the engraving includes the sheep and cattle, Passover material from Chronicles and First Esdras has clearly been incorporated. In this picture, King Josiah, far right under the royal canopy, oversees the great feast, his left hand on the Pascal lamb. Apparently, the Passover meal is being served alongside the queen. On the upper register, priests sacrifice upon a large altar which is dedicated to Yahweh as another sheep is being taken to them from a pair of animals awaiting processing. Beneath the arch that holds up the sacrificial altar are men boiling meat in a cauldron. On both levels, cattle are being herded onto the scene along with a ram above and a sheep carried from below to the upper level. Small braziers of fire appear on the floor in the foreground separating the diminutive group to the left, who are apparently eating off bones, and the much larger group at the king's table to the right, who seemingly taste small morsels. All of the figures to the front of the illustration carry long poles signifying the staffs ready for the Exodus. The highly ornate temple background on which this activity is displayed reflects van Heemskerk's illustrations of classical architecture. The two pillars before the temple have massive figures of naked people climbing up their swerving columns, reflecting medieval Jewish and Christian legendary readings of the free-standing pillars before the temple, Yachin and Boaz.[53]

In considering Galle's engravings of van Heemskerk's illustrations, certain aspects stand out. To begin, there is a decided lack of women in the entire series; Huldah, so important to the biblical narratives, does not appear. A queen seems to attend the Passover with Josiah, but otherwise all eight depictions concern the activities of males. In all cases Josiah is a king who commands; he directs the actions of others, and the scepter, representing royal authority, is prominent in all of the scenes save for the Passover, where the king joins with the men in bearing a ceremonial pole/staff. Unquestionably, the central concern of relating this Josiah sequence is the removal of spurious religion and its practitioners. Whether one was Catholic or Protestant in the Netherlands, the Reformation provided a point at which the violent removal of those deemed sacrilegious entailed violent means and highly emotional action. For humanistic Catholics, the

---

53 Sweeney (*I & II Kings*, 121) explains the unusual descriptions given for the two pillars before the temple, including that they may have been "twisted work."

concept of idolatry was as strong an anathema as it was to the Protestants and for Galle and van Heemskerk, both having Humanist tendencies, the vast destruction displayed on these engravings would mark them neither as Protestant nor as Catholic. In these depictions the king is in control, reflecting the right of sovereignty to dictate the religious convictions of the kingdom as a whole; portraying a monarch as ultimately responsible for executing proper religious conformity even by violent means would also not differentiate a Roman Catholic from a Dutch Reformed Protestant at the time.

Galle's publication may be taken as an early example of a much later common picture publication format. Comic books, known later as graphic novels in a somewhat higher quality format, have often been used to introduce children and young people to a variety of subjects, the Bible among them.[54] At first, newspaper comic strips were simply reprinted in book format in a process that continues to this day. Cheap paper periodical comic books originated in 1929 in the United States in a very short-lived venture called simply *The Funnies*.[55] A short time later, smaller comic books on newsprint in slick covers were produced and proliferated. Sold to children and youths, there was a decided trend towards adventure, drama, super heroes, science fiction, and horror; it was what caught the attention of the young, at least when parents were not at hand.[56] So omnipresent were these juvenile periodicals that adult public reaction strove to remove them and their assumed baneful influence from society.[57] However, the comic book format was one that church education leaders saw as a way to interest children in the biblical narrative.

---

54   No doubt the best-known series for introducing children to literature was "Classics Illustrated," which published a series of comic-adapted literary texts from 1941-1962 (American series published by three successive publishers: Elliot; Giberton; Frawley). Innumerable comic books were published to introduce children to specific topics as varied as arithmetic and energy conservation: *Donald in Mathmagic Land* (Dell Four Color 1198, 1961) and *Mickey Mouse and Goofy Explore Energy* (Burbank, CA: Walt Disney Educational Media Company, 1976).

55   Nicky Wright, *The Classic Era of American Comics* (Chicago: Contemporary Books, 2000), 13-14; Michael Barrier and Martin Williams, *A Smithsonian Book of Comic-Book Comics* (New York: Smithsonian Institution and Harry N. Abrams, 1981), 9.

56   Art Spiegelman and Françoise Mouly, *The Toon Treasury of Classic Children's Comics* (New York: Abrams, 2009), 9; Wright, *The Classic Era of American Comics*, 32-103, 174-201; artwork featuring gore, scantily-clad women, murder, and monsters were abundant.

57   The United States adopted a Comics Code in October of 1954 that put a decided damper on comic book content after a Senate investigation of lurid story lines. Needless to say, comic books have outlasted the code; Barrier and Williams, *Smithsonian Book*, 15-16; the process in outlined in Wright, *The Classic Era of American Comics*, 204-16.

In any Bible comic attempting to render the First Testament, Josiah makes at least a minor appearance.[58] Four examples will suffice in order to comment on the manner in which this biblical figure and his story have been drawn for youthful readers. *The Story of Josiah*, written by Montgomery Mulford and illustrated by Dom Cameron, was an early (1943) rendition of Josiah in comic book form.[59] This Bible comic book was one of numerous illustrated renditions of all kinds published by the first successful comic book promoter, Maxwell Charles Gaines, and his "Picture Stories from the Bible" series was one of the few ideas he was allowed to retain when he was bought out a few years preceding his death in 1947.[60] Josiah is not amongst the four Bible stories featured on the cover of the comic; these are eye-catching action poses.[61] The first four panels of the Josiah story deal with the youth of the king and his piety. He is depicted as an eight-year-old boy who, interestingly, receives his admonition to kingship from his mother, advice he is urged to follow by an advisor at his side. Here is a Bible comic book urging a child to obey his mother. Finding this in Kings or Chronicles would be futile; however, Gaines's household was highly regulated by parents. In the second panel, little Josiah thinks to himself that he must seek wisdom as had his ancestors; a light-beam-exuding cloud, that one must assume represents the deity, tells him to "rule as had King David," which is a good variation of biblical text. The next two panels show little Josiah ordering the "return to worship of the true God" by means of the destruction of idolatry, while in the background a pile of rubbish, topped with an oversized anthropomorphic figure, is attacked with a sledgehammer by three men. The discovery of the scroll in the walls of the temple, while it is being repaired, occupies a quarter of the story. A workman finds the scroll (and it is a scroll) but being illiterate turns it over to Hilkiah, who turns it over to Shaphan, who reads it to a fully adult Josiah. Both Hilkiah and Shaphan know this is the "long lost" scroll of Deuteronomy and its authenticity is made known to Josiah by

---

58   There have been plenty of comic strip versions of biblical stories including Josiah narratives among those consulted but not commented upon here: Iva Hoth, *The Picture Bible* (Elgin, IL: David C. Cook, 1978), 429–34; Libby Weed, ed., *Read-n-Grow Picture Bible* (Fort Worth, TX: Sweet, 1984), 162–63.

59   Montgomery Mulford, *Picture Stories from the Bible: Complete Old Testament* (New York: M. C. Gaines, 1943): 174–77. With thanks to Robert Mowery for lending me his copy. The story of Josiah explicitly makes use of Kings and Chronicles/Paralipomenon as they appear in the King James, Jewish Publication Society of America, and Douay Versions.

60   Wright, *The Classic Era of American Comics*, 3, 11–12, 154.

61   The cover includes Moses decking the Egyptian with a right cross; David slicing off Goliath's head; Abraham stopped short of sacrificing Isaac; and (the sole peaceful illustration) Elijah being fed by a raven in flight. Art by Don Cameron.

Shaphan. The truth of the scroll is here disclosed by a male official such that Huldah is consulted for guidance as to what should be done, already knowing the scroll is authentic. This means she begins, wholly divergent from the biblical text, with "If what you say is true..." as though she needed to be told. Huldah merely informs Josiah that the impious population will be destroyed but not he; she functions as a prophet in the form of a teller of the future. When the adult Josiah reads the scroll to the people, he does so in the course of a great banquet, explicitly described as supplied by Josiah's largess, celebrating the return of the temple to the true worship and a renewal of the Passover.

Chronicles clearly produces the timeline for this rendition; there are no panels concerned with the massive destruction or removal of impious items or people. Instead, as befits a comic before the Comic Code, the final quarter of the story illustrates the battle in which Josiah gallantly defends Israel against a mighty Egyptian attack. This engagement begins with Josiah receiving news that "a vast army" of Egyptians is attacking so that a very determined clenched-fisted Josiah frowns out his determination to "meet them." A nice double-panel spread shows racing horses pulling Josiah in his chariot before two more chariots charging directly toward the reader (there is a lot of dust!). This highly charged panel is followed by Josiah inside the fort at Megiddo, giving the order for his troops to hold "here" even as the Egyptians attack the fort. But, in the next panel, the Israelites despair: "The king is struck," and the outnumbered troops are burst upon by the victorious Egyptians. Josiah, appearing rather surprised, stands with the arrow that kills him extending from his chest.[62] This picture is a classic example of a battle scene for war comics of pre-current times (a bloodless arrow in the heart) or innumerable B-movie westerns of the time. It is also effective in portraying the sudden and deadly end to the life of Josiah. In the end of the tale, Jehoahaz takes the throne and promises to keep Josiah's laws, so "right shall rule." However, his reign is cut short by Pharaoh Neco. That the comic appeared in the early years of America's entrance into World War II no doubt has some relation to the extended battle coverage and the insistence that Josiah stands for goodness as God defines it.

If Gaines was primarily a secular comic book publisher, the following three editions are all products of conservative, Bible-based Christian publishing houses. The intent in each case is to make the Bible exciting and interesting to young readers at the same time as presenting church teachings according to the author of the comic-book text. All three were produced after the demise of the Comic Code.

---

62 Bob Mowery passed on the comment that, as a boy, he was particularly impressed with this illustration of Josiah's death.

252   *Josiah*

The Coming Storm, by Ben Avery and illustrated by Mat Broome, is a 2007 graphic novel in Zondervan's series of creative narratives loosely based on biblical texts.[63] The central figure in this picture Bible story is Iddo, the prophet, a character (probably) of the Chronicler's imagination (2 Chr 9:29; 12:15; 13:22).[64] The book is a very nonlinear retelling of the biblical accounts of Josiah as if through the life of Iddo, whose existence here is entirely of Avery's creation.[65] As a portion of the Former Prophets, it may not be too strange to find that the prophets Isaiah and Jeremiah have extended roles to play, but the tale relates the non-biblically based prophetic activity of Iddo. Indeed, the "Prologue" consists of Isaiah's confrontation with Hezekiah and stresses the kingship not of Davidic rulers but of "the Lord," and the capacity of God to bring peace to the faithful.[66] The book ends with Iddo remarking upon King Jehoahaz's misunderstanding that war would be a disaster; only God brings peace.[67]

Intermixed with the Iddo narrative is that of Josiah. The first chapter of the graphic novel proper is a visually harsh and repetitive rendition of Josiah as a berserk warrior.[68] Good 'action shots' of Josiah on a chariot, dressed in disguise so his troops follow him solely because of his military prowess, play on for sixteen pages. This opening volley in the story is actually, of course, the end of the narrative of Josiah. It is an impressive series of sword and swagger panels with very little dialogue aside from a very menacing "HRM?" as the battle ramps up.[69] Certainly, this warrior Josiah is intended to capture the attention of the young lads who open the comic book. A very angry Josiah (also an angry horse) roars, spear drawn, across the opening page of a chapter that ends with Josiah being struck by arrows (some continuity editing on how many and where they hit might have allayed some confusion in these death scenes). The battle

---

63   Ben Avery, *The Coming Storm*, Kingdoms: A Biblical Epic (Grand Rapids: Zondervan, 2007). The biblical quotations used in this comic are taken from the New International Version.

64   Jonker, "The Chronicler and the Prophets," in Ben Zvi and Edelman, *What Was Authoritative for Chronicles?*, 148, 160; Steven J. Schweitzer, "Judging a Book by Its Citations: Sources and Authority in Chronicles," in Ben Zvi and Edelman, *What Was Authoritative for Chronicles?*, 60n77.

65   Iddo has been attached to Josiah's story in Kings in the past: Stanley, *Lectures on the History of the Jewish Church*, 430.

66   Avery, *Coming Storm*, 15, 20 [unpaginated].

67   Ibid., 147–48 [unpaginated].

68   A very unbiblical description is given to Josiah after he has been struck by an arrow: "HE WAS LIKE AN ANGEL OF DEATH!" (39, capitalization in the original).

69   Readers without any Hebrew knowledge would not grasp the clear reference to the ḥerem all-out warfare being commanded by Josiah the warrior. As the sole war cry in the sequence, it is obviously deemed a serious notion; however, it is totally lacking in any biblical account of Josiah.

9 *Art of the Story of the King*   253

is lost but not because of the plans of Josiah; how was he to know the Egyptians would deploy archers?[70] The dying king is to be dispatched to Jerusalem but his actual death is not pictured. Josiah is introduced as a mighty, super-hero-like warrior, capable of fighting it out with the best of them. This is decidedly not the central aspect of Josiah in Kings, Chronicles, or (least likely) First Esdras. Josephus would barely recognize his classical world warrior Josiah.

A long chapter on Iddo's family leads to the third chapter, in which Josiah's nanny/nurse/surrogate mother, Dalia, regales eight-year-old Josiah with tales of great King David for 12 pages, even as the palace assassination of his father, who forbids such tales be told to young Josiah, takes place 'off stage.' Jedidah and Josiah hope that, like Manasseh, Amon will repent and become a pious Yahwist but it is too late as the coup is complete. For reasons unknown, the assassins inform Jedidah that, obviously, she and her son will not be harmed. This young mother assures Josiah and the reader that she cares not for what has happened because Amon was an evil guy; she is concerned only about what her son, the new king, will do. This Josiah looks more like a gangling, young teenager than a boy of eight and is portrayed as grimly determined to walk "in the ways of David his forefather" (p. 111) and not to cry for his evil father. A slightly older Josiah (the addition of a mustache and beard age him) sends for Shaphan, who, we learn, was selected by Jedidah as her son's trusted official, and as such is entrusted with the purge of Judah and Jerusalem in Josiah's twelfth year (pp. 118–19). There must be a clearing out of the enemy in the midst of the country (p. 120) lest all are as guilty as the evil ones among them. This announcement is followed by a few pages of tearing down and breaking up faintly anthropomorphic images.

Having cleared out the "false gods," but unable to change his subjects' hearts, Josiah sets out to repair the temple. Hilkiah finds the scroll of the book of the law of Moses. He does not need to have it explained to him; he knows what it is when he hands it to Shaphan, who reads it to a despairing Josiah (swiftly displayed as pensive, anguished, and distraught). Interestingly, here again Huldah is consulted only to find out what Josiah is to do now; "Some prophetess. Didn't even know we were coming," says one of the members of the committee. However, for the young readers of the comic, Huldah is a very attractive, raven-haired young woman, who serves bread of high quality while advising doom for Judah but an escape from the destruction for Josiah. In other words, Huldah becomes a beautiful

---

70 Seriously, that's the line put in the mouth of the dying Josiah. It would have succeeded if not for the archers! This is a graphic novel geared towards impressive illustrations for emotional effect, not intelligent military strategy.

domestic with future-telling powers. One suspects the intended audience is pre-teen boys.

The chapter ends with Josiah proclaiming the proper allegiance to Yahweh for all the people, and that, for as long as he lives, they will remain true. However, a messenger arrives to announce the coming of the Egyptians. A serious looking Josiah interprets the Egyptians as an invading force and, against Iddo's warning, sets out to attack Neco. Josiah is disguised by shaving off his little beard; it is about as convincing as Superman as Clark Kent. In purple prose, he rides off in his chariot declaring himself to be the arrow that will fly to the heart of the Egyptians (p. 138); since the reader already knows the outcome, this is irony lacking any subtlety.

In the Avery/Broome rendition of Josiah, the need for conversion plays a central role. The enemies are within and without. The enemy within needs conversion, although in the text the violence is restricted to the idols and places of worship; the people are convinced to worship properly by the words of the king taken from tradition. Evangelizing the unrepentant seems clearly behind this section of the story, and the implication that failing to properly convert the populace reflects sin upon the preacher is clearly stated. The militaristic violence for the enemy without is overt, even though the book as a whole claims it is only by God's plan that peace may come. Interestingly, Josiah does not understand that aspect of theology, nor does he understand that foreigners can be used by Yahweh, and should be accepted as doing so. The Josiah material also pounds home that there should be neither tolerance nor tears for those who are evil, while much mourning and respect is the proper response for those who walk in the way of David. There are personal relationships more important than those of family ties; this is the case here where, due to an evil father, Josiah's mother sustains the parental relation in the story. For a volume with such a spoken emphasis on God's bringing peace, the picture of Josiah is one of movie-level war hero.

Two Josiah tales appear in *The Action Bible* graphic novel. Sergio Cariello's "A Righteous King and a Reluctant Prophet" focuses more on Jeremiah than on Josiah.[71] The opening panel shows a very young Josiah gazing wistfully out of a window while Hilkiah stands to the side; the priest is raising the boy. On the second page, Josiah stands, glaring straight forward amidst the ruins of the temple (and, here, they are actual ruins) as he declares that it will be rebuilt immediately. Beside him stand four older men, Hilkiah among them. Interestingly, the temple ruins contain, amid the broken pottery, an overturned table and an almost perfect cross (on the right), both of which seem to reflect Christian temple stories in the

---

71 Sergio Cariello, *The Action Bible: God's Redemptive Story*, ed. Doug Mauss (Colorado Springs: David C. Cook, 2110), 446–48.

New Testament. It is among a pile of stones that Hilkiah finds a scroll that he recognizes immediately as the "long lost Torah." When read to Josiah, who is now a young man, he frowns deeply as he declares Judah and Jerusalem doomed. One aide inquires whether one can just act as if the scroll had never been found, but pious Josiah says that is not an option; one cannot ignore God's word. The delegation to Huldah, who is a severe-looking young woman, hear her declare that there is nothing that can be done at this point but that the coming destruction will not happen while Josiah is king. Hoping for God's forgiveness, Josiah reads the scroll to the people while celebrating Passover. Apparently, Josiah does not take Huldah's prophetic capacities very seriously.

This is followed by "Why Do Bad Things Happen to Good People?"[72] Here, Josiah and Jeremiah work together to rid Judah and Israel of idol worship. However, more of the story is concerned with Josiah's refusal to listen to Jeremiah with regard to warfare. Against Yahweh's warning through Jeremiah, Josiah insists on leading a contingent of soldiers to defend Megiddo. In classic movie *mano-a-mano* cliché, Pharaoh Neco faces off against Josiah and kills him. The body is returned to Jerusalem in a very modern casket on the shoulders of his troops. There Jeremiah greets them. In these two snippets of Josiah stories, we find a youthful Josiah brought up by Hilkiah, not his father or mother, and devoted to the worship of Yahweh, but not particularly interested in the prophets of Yahweh, though the prophets get decent play in the stories.

Highly popular comic presentations of the late twentieth and early twenty-first centuries are the manga volumes. Modern manga publications were derived from the combination of traditional Japanese art scrolls with American comic books and animated cartoons following World War II. Dedicated manga readers became a world-wide phenomenon. Ryo Azumi, a noted manga writer and artist, believed the medium was a perfect way to introduce young people to biblical stories. His rendition of the Josiah story appears as "Josiah's Reformation" in his volume on the prophets, *Manga Messengers*.[73] Ryo begins the story of Josiah with his grandfather, Manasseh. Here, he is presented as a pliant client of Assyria and an inclusive ruler, welcoming all cults and including them in his temple, even including the "Asherah poles." He is quoted saying, "in my mind, the gods of Assyria seem as good as any others."[74] Shifting sources to Chronicles, Manasseh is captured by the Assyrians and imprisoned. He then realizes the error of his thought: "Lord, now I see that you are the true God." But it

---

72 Cariello, *Action Bible*, 449–50.
73 Ryo Azumi, *Manga Messengers*, Manga Bible (Carol Stream, IL: Tyndale House, 2011), 160–69.
74 Ibid., 160.

was too late. Judah had joyously reverted to idolatry; Amon carried on in the mode of the day.

Josiah appears as a very baby-faced boy being crowned by an official (apparently Hilkiah) who believes the lad is too young to rule; however, Josiah, big manga grey-blue eyes shining, informs one and all that he is not like his father or grandfather but will serve only God and will need their help. They are all happy and in the next panel Josiah, the young man astride a white horse (bad historical military rendition, but classic American western movies cliché),[75] slashes and smashes idols, with pieces flying in all directions as his subjects cheer. Josiah is portrayed as an older teenager with unkempt hair (everyone else in this section of the comic would seem to have used combs) surrounded with a simple gold band for a crown. Having broken the idols, Josiah turns to repairing the temple, which is presented as more in need of a lot of plastering than anything else. There are two pages devoted to Hilkiah's finding of the scroll and to Shaphan's reading of it, while crying, to a stunned Josiah, who has a single tear dropping from his left eye. Turning to Hilkiah, Josiah demands that a prophet of the Lord be found so that they might know what to do. They "find" Huldah. Here, she is a middle-aged, brown-haired, brown-eyed woman who informs the two-man delegation of Hilkiah and Shaphan that they are to tell the king that all the destruction in the book of the law will happen and that the deity will not turn back on it. However, God will wait until Josiah is dead because he wept. An angry-looking Josiah attempts to change God's mind by reading the scroll to the elders, having them repent, and promise to do everything in the scroll. There is then a full page with a splash panel of Josiah furiously commanding everyone to purify themselves and return to the Lord; the destruction is not vividly displayed but is only mentioned. With the exception, one assumes, of the slain priests, on the next page everyone cheers "Hip, Hip, Hooray" for Josiah, a king like no other. The rest of the two-and-a-half pages display the reaction of Josiah to news that the Egyptians are coming near the borders of Judah on their way to aid Assyria. Since Hezekiah was an ally of Babylon, Josiah refuses to acknowledge Neco's message that God has spoken to him and he leads out a column of foot soldiers to confront Neco. This comic contains a single panel of battle before the panel of an arrow piercing Josiah's armor as he rides in his chariot. It takes

---

75 Unless Judah's king had taken up cavalry bareback riding, which would explain the horse-and-rider figurines: Raz Kletter and Katri Saarelainen. "Horses and Riders and Riders and Horses," in Albertz, Nakhal, Olyan, and Schmitt, *Family and Household Religion*, 213–14, who note that Assyria had fairly rudimentary cavalry units, but none are discernible in "Palestine." See still Yigael Yadin, *The Art of Warfare in Biblical Lands: In the Light of Archaeological Study*, trans. M. Pearlman (New York: McGraw-Hill, 1963), 2.297–302.

three double panels for the king to expire, giving him time to tell God that the deity has kept his word and Josiah is okay with the divine will, before asking for God's mercy on the people. Taken to Jerusalem, Josiah dies and is mourned; interestingly, these events are told solely via text without illustrations. The story ends with a vivid yellow and red-attired portrait of Nebuchadnezzar II.

Azumi's Josiah adheres more closely to the combined narratives of Kings and Chronicles than do the other Christian graphic renditions considered here. However, in this work the central emphasis is placed on the need to adhere to the worship of the one Lord. Josiah is presented as overtly pious from his youth, as well as consulting with, but not educated by, Hilkiah. The destruction of idols and false priests is mentioned but not violently portrayed. In Azumi's depiction, he is no military warrior and, interestingly, the refusal of Josiah to acknowledge the word of God from Neco is emphasized. Nonetheless, Josiah is to be remembered and venerated for being loyal to one single deity and cult, forcing his people to do likewise, and for *not* being open to multiculturalism in opposition to the openness of his grandfather Manasseh in his evil days. In the early twenty-first century, tolerance toward other cultures' religions as the harbinger of death and disaster sets the Manga Bible on the hardcore conservative Evangelistic Protestant side of the 'culture wars.' This topic is a central emphasis in this story which is not pressed in the other modern renditions.

Finally, children's Bibles and Bible storybooks are replete with illustrations. Josiah, as a young boy who became king, has been a popular subject. Certainly, Protestants have long presented Josiah as a particularly suitable model for children to imitate: "A good pattern is no small help for young beginners, Josiah sets his father David before him, not Ammon, not Manasseh" [1614].[76] Josiah has appeared in illustrations often enough as a very young child. Isabella Child's *The Child's Picture Bible* from 1855 provides a good example of nineteenth-century illustration which attempts both to make the Bible at home with European children and to display the eastern foreignness of the Judahite world. Child's Josiah is a very young boy attired in European princely garb but attended by his priest Hilkiah, who is illustrated as a stereotypical oriental sage in oversized turban and flowing gown.[77] Recent distinct renditions of the child-king include a book intended for very young children that has a pleasingly cartoonish Josiah illustrated by Herb Halpern Productions, who, for 28 pages, demonstrate what a "good boy" ought to do, while fitting in some references to the

---

76 Hall, *Contemplations of the Historical Passages of the Old and New Testaments*, 112.
77 Isabella Child, *The Child's Picture Bible* (New York: J.Q. Preble, 1855), 82. Discussed in Handy, "Josiah in a New Light," 432–33.

biblical narrative as well.[78] For a child's first Bible picture book, Gloria Oostema's very young boy in an oversized royal purple robe, wearing a slipping oversized gold crown, carries a large wooden mallet and points authoritatively off to his left; the colorful picture is clearly intended to illustrate the short passage regarding the eight year old's order to "fix God's house."[79] The story deals only with the child-king's desire to rebuild the place of worship. Shawna J. C. Tenney's book for children pictures eight-year-old Josiah as a somewhat older child, attired in purple with a plain gold band about his head and a medallion about his neck that provides continuity throughout the illustrations of his adulthood.[80] The picture book concentrates on the finding of the scroll and the burning of idols; the latter is portrayed in simplified forms recognizable from excavated deity statues of Mesopotamian, Egyptian, and Syro-Palestinian extraction (p. 10). It is worth noting that this children's book has the Passover being served in Josiah's presence not by Levitical priests, but entirely by women; no doubt this is intended as a nod to twenty-first century cultural desires to include women in both Bible studies and children's books.[81] Tim O'Connor illustrates Stephen Elkins's short children's story, *Josiah: A Teenager Finds a Treasure*, with a beardless older youth worriedly reading a scroll, though the text has Shaphan reading it to him.[82] The short rendition focuses on forgiveness and a rather ambiguous promise to obey the law of Moses. The moral for the child to learn, however, is: "I will read my Bible each day!" This fits with Josiah doing the reading and explains the illustration of a boy who is actually old enough to read. In these illustrated Josiah depictions intended for children, the presentations render him at every age from a toddler to a teenaged youth.

A multitude of other pictures of Josiah appear, from formal portraits with scepter (as in that of an unrecorded seventeenth-century artist for the Sankta Maria Kyrka, Åhus, Sweden)[83] to sketchy picture book illustrations (as in Eric Thomas and Amy Burch's pictures for *The Children's Illustrated Bible*, 2004).[84] Like figures in all biblical illustrations, Josiah's appearance reflects the culture in which the art is produced. Western European artists

---

78 Marquardt, *Good Little Josiah*; book provided by Elaine Ramshaw.

79 Tracy L. Harrast, *My Baby and Me Story Bible* (Grand Rapids: Zonderkidz, 1995), 76–77. Discussed in Handy, "Josiah in a New Light," 435.

80 Kristin R. Nelson, *King Josiah and God's Book*, Arch Books 59v2216 (St. Louis: Concordia, 2008), 2, 4 [unpaginated]; book provided by Elaine Ramshaw.

81 Nelson, *King Josiah*, 12–13 [unpaginated].

82 Stephen Elkins, *Children in the Bible*, Word&Song, Greatest Bible Stories Ever Told 9 (Nashville: Broadman and Holman, 2002), 26.

83 Image available on Wikimedia Commons.

84 Selina Hastings, *The Children's Illustrated Bible* (New York: Dorling and Kindersley, 2004), 156–57.

picture a European king, often with medieval European royal accouterments, though attempts to produce 'historical' verisimilitude tend toward classic orientalism creations. As long as visual adaptations of the Bible remain popular, Josiah will continue to be reimagined. The text, however, provides not an iota of information about the physical appearance of this Judahite king. So, the story lines will continue to provide the action of any artistic representations. Reproductions of earlier works will no doubt continue to account for most Josiah illustrations.[85]

---

[85] Note the reproduction of a classic "Josiah defiles the heathen altars by burning on them the bones of men" illustration for the children's story Bible: Turner Hodges, *The Bible Story Library*, vol. 3: *From Solomon to the Roman Conquest* (New York: Educational Book Guild, 1956), 461. And the popularly reproduced Schnorr von Carolsfeld's image of Shaphan reading the law to Josiah appears in many works, popular and academic.

CHAPTER TEN
CREATING MEMORIES OF JOSIAH

No one remembers Josiah. After all, he died over two and a half millennia ago. No one alive today, or who ever published a book, spoke with him. More significantly, no one who wrote his story in any form that exists to this day had known him. Yeshua ben Sirach revered him as a memory.[1] It is generally assumed that Sirach remembered Simon ben Onias from personal encounter.[2] However, he could only recollect a memory of Josiah from traditions written about him by earlier writers. These writers created the memory of Josiah.

The author of Kings provides highly select episodes attributed to the life of Josiah but explicitly emphasizes that, should one wish to know about the king, one needs to inquire elsewhere.[3] What the "scroll of the words of the days of the kings of Judah" (2 Kgs 23:28) refers to, we have no idea.[4] It is pos-

---

1   Reading with the Hebrew text of Sir 49:1.
2   It has long been assumed that the author of Sirach had seen the high priest Simon officiating at the temple: George Herbert Box and William Oscar Emil Oesterley, "The Book of Sirach," *APOT* 1.293; Victor Tcherikover, *Hellenistic Civilization and the Jews*, trans. S Applebaum (Philadelphia: Jewish Publication Society of America, 1959; repr., New York: Antheneum, 1970), 80. Martin Hengel assumes the high priest Simon II, whose death was perhaps only a decade before the composition of Sirach's poem: Martin Hengel, *Judaism and Hellenism: Studies in Their Encounter in Palestine during the Early Hellenistic Period*, trans. J. Bowden (Philadelphia: Fortress, 1974), 1.131.
3   George Savran insists that these off-hand references demonstrate that the authors have intentionally produced highly biased literary historical records: George Savran, "1 and 2 Kings," in *The Literary Guide to the Bible*, ed. R. Alter and F. Kermode (Cambridge, MA: Belknap, 1987), 146.
4   It has been the general understanding for centuries that the references to written records that appear throughout Kings signify scrolls of some antiquity and reliability that were used by the author. See, for example, Alan R. Millard, "Books and Writing in Kings," in Lemaire and Halpern, *The Books of Kings*, 155, 159–60. It is interesting that many modern commentaries skip any notation on 2 Kgs 23:28, moving on to the more expandable death scene. Those who make note of the reference to the previous scroll tend to view it as a source used by the author for composing Kings (e.g., Gray, *I & II Kings*, 746–47). The text says nothing about this 'scroll' having been used for the composition at hand. From what is recorded, it could just as well have been a composition contemporary to Kings from the same scribal circles.

sible that this was the same text referred to by the Chronicler as the "scroll of the Kings of Israel and Judah" (2 Chr 35:27) and again in First Esdras as the "book of the Kings of Israel and Judah" (1 Esd 1:31). The Chronicler included a source reference because he used the book of Kings and since his source included such a reference, so did he. The problem is that, as far as we know, we have nothing from either of these alleged materials. In fact, it is unclear whether Chronicles had any source other than Kings; the title of the referred-to scroll could certainly describe the book of Kings. The literary work cited in 2 Kgs 23:28 is not described. There is no way of knowing whether such a text existed, and, if it did, what it was. To assume it was an official archive or chronicle is wishful thinking.[5] It may as well have been a chronology, a study tablet, a fictitious narrative, or a collection of legendary events. What it is not, and cannot be used for, is a memory of Josiah.

The modern memory of Josiah is a creation of four authors: the writers of Kings, Chronicles, First Esdras, and Flavius Josephus (*Jewish Antiquities*). They wrote at different times and for different reasons. More importantly, none of them wrote specifically about Josiah. The narrative of each of the four compositions produced by these men includes Josiah as a character within a larger vision. Josiah serves their agenda and his memory is entangled with their greater purposes. Those purposes themselves help determine the Josiah they provide. These authors form a chronological chain leading backward from Josephus through First Esdras, through Chronicles, to Kings. Each memory was dependent on the memory imagined by the one preceding it.

The book of Kings is the foundational text for the memory of Josiah. As it is now known, it begins with a swiftly deteriorating King David and a quickly escalating disaster concerned with the succession to the throne. More of the text deals with the tale of how Solomon followed David on the throne than for the entire narrative concerned with Josiah. The final scene of the scroll is not of Josiah but of his son, Jehoiachin. This descendent of David, a royal scion of the Davidic dynasty, sits as a captive of a foreign king in his foreign land, totally dependent on him. The work moves from a king no longer able to rule his kingdom to a king who no longer rules any kingdom. The tale told is of a tempestuous period when Judah was once an independent polity, from a time when it was, in its own eyes, a favored territory being a kingdom of great kings. Throughout the scroll the reader is reminded that David was once a great king, though this is never explained or described; Solomon is explained and described as the very model of the perfect philosopher-king, wise and in control, but for a short period of

---

5   Robert Alter (*The Art of Biblical Narrative*, 34–35) provides the traditional argument that the referred-to 'chronicle' had been a court record without a theological aspect. This cannot be presumed from the text of Kings.

time. The majority of the story deals with two kingdoms, neither of which is portrayed in anything approaching greatness or glory.[6] In the narrative, Josiah forms one small segment of this anguished loss of political identity but his is a significant episode in the retention of religious identity.

Two central concerns shape the book of Kings. On the one hand, it is a highly "fictionalized history" of the sequence of kings in Judah and Israel.[7] On the other, it is a "sermon" on how Judahites ought to have lived but did not. The author of Kings presents what is believed to be a full slate of ruling persons for two territories involved in the worship of the deity Yahweh.

The amount of narrative expended on each of these rulers differs widely. A lack of detailed information is reasonable for some of these kings: King Zechariah of Israel reigned six months and was assassinated (2 Kgs 15:8); King Shallum of Israel lasted just one month (2 Kgs 15:13); King Zimri of Israel managed seven days (1 Kgs 16:15); and Tibni never became king, according to the text, even though he had as large a following as Omri, who eventually defeated him, and despite his people wishing to make him king (1 Kgs 16:21–22). No doubt, he was the king as far as they were concerned.[8] For these short-reigning men there is little text. At the same time, however, there is not a great deal of material recorded for King Jehoshaphat of Judah during his reign of twenty-five years (1 Kgs 22:41–50).[9] The central concern of the book of Kings is not, therefore, a rendition of the events during the reigns of the kings of Judah and Israel. The record of their names and that they ruled preserves their memory, but there is not much specifically recalled about the majority of them. Being a king in

---

6   Although some biblical historians find that, during the reign of the Omrides, Israel had been an important kingdom in the ancient Near East, this view is not reflected in Kings: Miller and Hayes (*History of Ancient Israel and Judah*, 251–52, 265–71) conclude that the author of Kings discounts Omri and Ahab since they do not fit his "theological principles" but these were the historical high points of either Judah or Israel as independent kingdoms.

7   Alter, *Art of Biblical Narrative*, 25. Alter assumes the author of Kings had source material but creatively fictionalized the historiography of Israel and Judah, including in such works actual events, legendary tales, and invented situations.

8   Miller and Hayes (*History of Ancient Israel and Judah*, 265–66) note the lack of useful information about Tibni and his backers, even though the narrative in Kings insists that his contingent was as large as Omri's, and both armies assumed they were backing the ruler. Kenneth H. Cuffey ("Tibni," *ABD* 6.551) surveys theories about the origins, movement, and death of Tibni. The struggle with Omri was a long one (four years, apparently), with both sides fighting for their leader to be king; it is unrealistic to assume that these embattled men did not accept their leader as 'king' during this civil war.

9   The reign of Jehoshaphat receives a significantly larger description from the Chronicler (2 Chr 17:1–21:1).

these two kingdoms was not sufficient to be considered important, only to have been set down for readers to notice.

There are kings who have major parts to play in the story presented in Kings. The first of these is King Solomon of Israel. He is, at least, the king of Israel as a literary figure in the narrative; whether Solomon ruled anything in reality is not germane here. In Kings he is an invented memory and, as that, he had an impressive empire. He set the stage both for the rise of the kingdom of Israel and for the continuation of the dynasty of David in Judah. The disruption of his glorious reign in the rendition of the book of Kings was his many foreign wives. His counterpart in terms of literary significance is Ahab, who, like Solomon, rules Israel under the fatal guidance of his foreign wife, Jezebel. The destruction of Israel contrasted with the salvation of Jerusalem under Hezekiah.[10] In this short rendition of the two kingdoms, Josiah provides the finale to the independent kingdom of Judah. For the author of Kings, Josiah was a closure to the polity of Judah as a kingdom with proper cultus and independence from foreign empires. As for history, the material on Josiah reflects literary imagination.

As a repository of the names of rulers, Kings makes use of Judah and Israel to define their respective kings as either good or bad. In this endeavor, all rulers of Israel are evil. Rulers of Judah can be one or the other, with bad kings outnumbering good ones. Josiah is not only one of the good ones but the best of them (2 Kgs 22:2; 23:25). Significantly, the designation of a ruler as either 'good' or 'bad' rests not on how they ruled, whether they enlarged the territory, or if their populace was well fed, happy, or under attack; it depends in all cases on whether or not the king was a loyal devotee of the God Yahweh. As far as being a proper king is concerned, Josiah was in all ways a "good" ruler for the author of this tale. He was of direct Davidic lineage.[11] He was a man.[12] He dwelt in Jerusalem as king of Judah. He consulted Yahweh through a legitimate prophet.[13] He

---

10   The interpretation of 'salvation' of Jerusalem under Hezekiah is a heavily propagandistic memory of Sennacherib's attack on Judah, itself not well understood: Elayi, *Sennacherib, King of Assyria*, 69–88.

11   For Savran ("1 and 2 Kings," 158–59), the promise to David of a continuing dynasty is the first of the major themes of Kings. This aspect of Josiah's Davidic heritage, however, is mentioned in passing.

12   This was apparently important enough that the author excluded Athaliah as a legitimate ruler, being neither of the Davidic lineage nor a man. Her illegitimate role has been commented on by, e.g., Phyllis A. Bird, *Missing Persons and Mistaken Identities*, 91–92. The fact that she was related to Ahab and Jezebel probably had something to do with her demonized portrayal by the author of Kings: Handy, "Speaking of Babies in the Temple," 155. In Kings, she "rules" (2 Kgs 11:3) but is not really the monarch; that designation belongs to Joash.

13   Savran ("1 and 2 Kings," 161) takes oracles and their fulfillment to be the

264   Josiah

organized his cultic world around the single deity, Yahweh, and through royal authority led his subjects to engage properly in approved cultic activities. He was free from any foreign dominance.[14] In this literary portrait, Josiah is a worthy king and his memory provides later readers with a model for an enthusiastic piety and a religious identity. That none of these characteristics in the text may reflect a historical Josiah does not affect the memory Kings has created.

If Kings provides a historiographical delineation of monarchs, allowing for the retention of the names and memory of long-gone rulers, the thrust of the scroll as a whole is that of a 'sermon.' Like other ancient historiographical documents, Kings is didactic.[15] In the case of Kings this edifying intent is concerned with the proper worship of Yahweh and the identity of those who ought to be his devotees; in later liturgical situations, such religiously oriented expositions may fairly be defined as 'sermons.' This sermonic presentation in Kings does not look backward to the lost kingdoms of Judah and Israel; they form the backdrop to the message. Yahweh is God and Judahites and Israelites are defined by allegiance to this deity, to the proper cultus properly observed, and to directives from an active deity concerned that devotees acknowledge the behavior demanded of them by their God. Such political situations as appear in Kings receive a religious twist from the author; Yahweh sides with or against kings to their victory or defeat according to their adherence to Yahweh. This aspect of Kings runs throughout the several prophetic passages in the work and culminates in Josiah and the last prophetic incident. It is this sermonic theme that makes Josiah an important figure in the work as a whole. If we remember Josiah at all, it is because the author of Kings drew a Josiah who was true to Yahweh.

Near the beginning of the narrative in Kings, King Solomon built a temple in Jerusalem that was the religious center of a vast kingdom incorporating all the minor polities surrounding it.[16] He made a speech at the dedication of the temple that explicated the terms of being a good Israelite

---

third of his major themes in Kings. Huldah's prediction of the destruction of Judah is the climax of these prophetic oracles.

14   The absence of any reference to Assyria, Egypt, Babylonia, or any other foreign political power during Josiah's reign is obviously a literary choice that does not reflect any possible historical Josianic period. The resultant misleading portrait of Josiah's international status appears to have been intentionally crafted: Grabbe, *Ancient Israel*, 214; Moore and Kelle, *Biblical History and Israel's Past*, 320.

15   Emphasized for Chronicles, Josephus, and Genesis by Brettler, *The Creation of History in Ancient Israel*, 41, 78. Emphasized for Kings by Handy, "Historical Probability and the Narrative of Josiah's Reform in 2 Kings," in Holloway and Handy, *The Pitcher Is Broken*, 259.

16   Savran ("1 and 2 Kings," 159–60) assumes the temple in Jerusalem is the

(1 Kgs 8:12–61). Central to that cultic institution was the notion that there was only one deity who was Yahweh, the temple being dedicated was the god's one house, and apostasy from these conditions would result in disaster. All the political alliances and all the wisdom displayed for Solomon went for naught. His many foreign wives led him from Yahweh, from the temple, and into ruin. In parallel with Josiah, that ruin is presented as coming after Solomon has left the narrative; inherited thrones did not carry inherited promise.[17] So the tale of Israel as the northern kingdom begins in the ashes of the character of the first heir to the throne of David. Josiah is the end of that line of ruling potentates. Solomon begins in righteousness but fails to maintain it, building innumerable temples to innumerable deities for 1,000 wives, concubines, and their plethora of divine inhabitants. Josiah begins his reign in silence concerning the eighteen years of his rule devoted to the religious world inherited from his father, Amon. His story explodes upon his eighteenth year on the throne with a destruction of the very temples to the deities that Solomon had introduced. Josiah is portrayed as the antithesis of Solomon; he rectifies for one last, brief moment the acceptable cultus envisioned by the author of Kings that had been established by Solomon before being desecrated by him.

What is deemed worthy of memory for Josiah is not that he ruled eighteen years over a kingdom devoted to Asherah, Baal, and a myriad of other divinities; this is never mentioned. The memory of Josiah is dependent on his rejecting all other deities and all other religious sites aside from Yahweh and the Yahwistic temple in Jerusalem. All his recorded actions prior to his concise death notice are religiously oriented.[18] His death is noted without emphasis. He is memorialized in Kings for religious aspects. He repairs the Jerusalemite temple even before he becomes aware of needing to "clean out" the religious world. And the need to force the northern territory to the Yahwism of Jerusalem is elaborated and central to the intentions of the author of Kings. Upon hearing the scroll found by Hilkiah, he mourns. This emotion is emphasized with the tearing of his clothes, the tear from his eye, and the immediate order to double-check the contents of the scroll. He consults with Yahweh, although it should be

---

second major theme of Kings. In this, Josiah plays the part of "the ideal of the good king," restoring the exclusivity of worship in the temple.

17   There were understood limits to the promises made by Yahweh to rulers, priests, and prophets, including David: Handy, "Characters of Heirs," 21–22.

18   2 Kgs 23:29–30a does not constitute a death narrative; it barely constitutes a death notice. The elongated narrative of Josiah's encounter with Neco appears in 2 Chr 35:20–25. The elaboration of Josiah's death and its meaningful consequences are dependent on the memory of Josiah's demise in Chronicles, First Esdras, and Josephus.

noticed that the author does not elaborate on the reception of Huldah's prophecy from Yahweh as it is repeated to Josiah (2 Kgs 22:20b).

It is not Josiah who is central to this prophetic encounter; it is Yahweh's proclamation. That proclamation emphasizes two things: the place and its inhabitants will be destroyed because they have not been acting in accord with the requirements of Solomon's temple speech, and Josiah will not live to see the promised desolation because he was humble, repentant, and wept on hearing whatever the scroll read to him had recorded. Significantly, Judah, Israel, and Jerusalem are never mentioned in this prophecy of doom; Judah and Israel appear only in relation to King Josiah and his avoidance of that catastrophe. Josiah then reads the scroll to the elders and to all the people of Judah and Jerusalem, and ends by the cutting of a covenant between all of them and Yahweh. Josiah is memorialized for destroying sacred sites outside the temple of Jerusalem; especially important is the burning down of the shrine or temple at Bethel and ruining its altar. That this last is the most significant item to be passed on is emphasized by its connection to the man from Judah, recorded for the reign of Jeroboam and the false prophet related there to Samaria (1 Kgs 13:32). Early Persian-era controversies between Jerusalem and Samaria for recognition by Persian authority would seem to have existed in the mind of the author of Kings.[19]

For a text from the early Persian period, Kings records a Josiah who is long gone. By the time of its composition, there are no kings in Judah. There is no kingdom of Judah. The scroll concludes with Jehoiachin as a captive far from Jerusalem. Josiah marks the end of the kingdom of Judah; however, he represents the polity at its religious best as far as the author of Kings is concerned. More important, Josiah pays attention to written instructions left in the care of religious leaders. The exact composition of that text is left to the imagination of the reader but demonstrates that king, priest, and people are now under the guidance of written religious instruction. The identity of Yehudites is tied up in something older than they are, greater than they are, and consultable. It is not the entity of Judah. It is the temple of Jerusalem as commandeered by Josiah from its former polytheistic past. In an empire stretching from South Asia to Nubia, with a welter of sacred sites, multitudes of pantheons, and hundreds of thousands of worshipers of pantheons without Yahweh, one will be a "Judahite" by being like Josiah. This is a Josiah for the Jewish diaspora. Ultimate allegiance is not to Persian bureaucracy, or Achaemenid kings, or even Judahite kings; one owes obedience to Yahweh. There may be a plethora of places to pray, sing, and record one's allegiance to Yahweh, but there is only one site that can legitimately serve as *the* temple to Yahweh; sacrifice

---

19 Sweeney, *I & II Kings*, 182.

in Jerusalem is the only sacrifice that matters. A memory of Josiah is an affirmation of who one is.

The Chronicler continued a tradition of rewriting the memory of an independent Judah. In doing this reconstruction of memory, he made use of "an astonishing freedom in the expansion and adaptation of the received historical tradition" as he emphasized the justice of God in dealing with Judahite kings and the populace in his narrative.[20] He used the source material in Kings to invent a slightly different memory of Josiah. One very obvious re-imagining deals with the right of Jerusalem to reign over the northern kingdom. The control of Judah over its northern neighbor is important in Chronicles. King Hezekiah is written about as though he immediately filled the void when Assyria imploded—at least, he is presented as concerned with the cultic life of the Israelites.[21] For this reason, Josiah's activities to the north did not need to be recorded; Judah already controlled the core territory of the former kingdom of Israel.[22]

Interestingly, the Chronicler both increases the religious life of Josiah and lessens it. If the Josiah of Kings had an enlightenment moment in the eighteenth year of his reign (2 Kgs 22:3),[23] the Josiah of Chronicles became a pious devotee of Yahweh in the eighth year of his reign, "when he was still a boy" (2 Chr 34:3).[24] For the Chronicler, Josiah implements a cultus for his single deity at the age of twenty, demonstrating his devotion much earlier than in Kings; also, this chronology displays a Josiah with a knowledge to clear out Asherahs, Baals, and innumerable sacred sites without the need for prodding by a scroll, a prophetess, or even Yahweh. Most importantly for the Chronicler, the Judahite religious service remains corrupted for a very short period of time in his work as opposed to the span of time in Kings. Since Manasseh had repented and rectified the worship of Yahweh, the religious world of deities and multiple religious sites lasted

---

20 Hengel, *Judaism and Hellenism*, 100. Hengel places the Chronicler, Jason of Cyrene, Justice of Tiberias, and Flavius Josephus in this historiographical tradition.

21 Finkelstein, *Hasmonean Realities*, 146–47.

22 Finkelstein, *Hasmonean Realities*, 150. Finkelstein dates this material to the time of John Hyrcanus, which is not necessary for an imagined past.

23 The year provided in Kings is almost universally taken to be the year of his reign, not his age; John Rogerson, *Chronicle of the Old Testament Kings*, 146; Sweeney, *I & II Kings*, 443.

24 Klein (*2 Chronicles*, 495–96) provides a summary of positions on the rather strange date that appears in the Chronicler's chronology of Josiah. He is certainly correct that the young age provided is connected to the desire for good kings in Chronicles to have been pious from their minority. That Josiah is shown not doing anything particularly noteworthy for four years would raise questions were it not that the age of twenty was a significant age. There is more reason to assume both 8 and 12 are literary creations of the Chronicler.

a mere ten years. Only for the two years of Amon's reign and the first eight years of the reign of Josiah could the proper worship of Yahweh have been corrupted before Josiah re-set the legitimate religion as defined by David and Solomon, previously purified from error in quick succession by Hezekiah and Manasseh before Josiah. More impressive is the lack of narrative on the "cleansing" of the temple of Yahweh that appeared in Kings; there is only one oblique reference to the "house" with a single comment that it had been rectified along with the land (2 Chr 34:8).

By dropping Israel from his history, the Chronicler eliminated most of the evil rulers who filled the narrative of Kings. Instead, there is an emphasis on the tradeoff between good and bad rulers in Judah. Since the Chronicler depicted only David, Solomon, and three other kings as pristine in their righteousness, the need for the temple cult in Jerusalem to be recurrently overseen by a righteous ruler required some literary reworking. While nine of the rulers are depicted by the Chronicler as totally evil, he managed to present eight as fluctuating between the good-bad polarity.[25] This way, the temple never quite reaches the abysmal state that it had in Kings. For the Josianic narrative in Chronicles, Josiah's father and sons all fall into the 'constantly evil' category, leaving Josiah as the last good king in this scroll. Even so, he also falls away from Yahweh at the very end of the Chronicler's rendition.

For the Chronicler it was no longer the case that Josiah was the reverse of Solomon because Solomon never 'went bad.' Josiah reinstates the proper temple worship that David and Solomon had established. The temple's religious world had had a checkered career in Chronicles with the various kings alternating between upholding proper worship and corrupting it. There is no memory passed on in the Chronicler's Josianic text of the impiety of the previous kings of Judah. Solomon, Ahaz, and Manasseh were all named in Kings as Judahite monarchs who perverted the proper worship of Judah that Josiah corrected; they are absent as such from the Chronicler's rendition.[26] More significantly, Jeroboam, who, in Kings, is a heretic king because of his attempt to set up a rival altar at Bethel, makes no appearance in the Chronicler's Josianic narrative, nor does Bethel. In Chronicles, Josiah is the ideal religious ruler written about by David and Solomon, both of whom were sterling individuals. The Jerusalemite temple is presented in Chronicles as the acknowledged center of Yahweh worship by all Yahweh devotees, north or south (2 Chr 34:9). With such enthusiastic support for the temple in Jerusalem, one might wonder why

---

25   The schema is presented in table format in Hamilton, *Handbook on the Historical Books*, 481–82.

26   Solomon appears as the perfect source for Josiah's restoration of the cultus; however, Ahaz and Manasseh disappear altogether.

the kings of Judah had let its repairs go until it was in need of major reconstruction; however, that is not broached in the Chronicler's story. Josiah is the king of Judah who repairs the temple and staffs it with proper personnel, consulting the very words of David and Solomon. Those who had gone astray are not the former kings but the people themselves (2 Chr 34:25), especially those of the Northern Kingdom (2 Chr 34:33).[27] Josiah is the one who brings them all into conformity with proper Yahweh worship.

The primary memorial event in Jewish liturgical calendars to this day remains the observance of Pesach. According to the Chronicler, this event existed in some hoary, forgotten past until Josiah enacted one in his eighteenth year exactly as it had been written down by David and by Solomon, two kings whom the Chronicler assures us never celebrated it (2 Chr 35:18–19). Great detail is provided for this feast; however, it is only recorded as having been celebrated once in Josiah's time. Nonetheless, Josiah is to be remembered in Chronicles for having instigated the commemoration for all those who came after.

In Chronicles, Josiah does not go out with the glory with which he reigned. Despite the repetition of the "report card" provided in 2 Kgs 22:2, in 2 Chr 35:22 Josiah is depicted going against Yahweh's wishes at his death. Having heard the prophet Huldah and having read the scroll from the temple to the assembled populace, Josiah could not hear the word of Yahweh in the mouth of King Neco of Egypt. Neco's simple speech explains why Josiah should leave the Egyptian army alone and concludes with the warning that God will destroy the disobedient king should he insist on confronting Neco. Josiah defies the word of Yahweh and is slain. In this way, the Chronicler allows the death of Josiah to be the fulfillment of a divine prophecy countering that delivered by Huldah. The narrative of Neco's prophecy also allows Josiah's death to be a case of obstinate disregard of a direct command given by Yahweh to Josiah himself. Through this rendition of his death, Josiah provided the Chronicler with a lesson about adhering to Yahweh for those who would later read this edifying tale.

The Chronicler was fully aware that Josiah was long dead and that the readers of his scroll would know this about Josiah. This rendition of the Josianic narrative ends not with Josiah's death but with an emphasis on memory. His subjects mourned over their loss (2 Chr 35:24c–25). It is a notation not made by the Chronicler for any other dead king of Judah.[28] The

---

27 Klein (*2 Chronicles*, 507) notes that the addition by the Chronicler sets the entire population within the "lands" of Israel under Josiah's religious orthodoxy.

28 Klein, *2 Chronicles*, 528; Pietsch, *Die Kultreform Josias*, 465. 1 Chr 29:28 and 2 Chr 32:33 note only that the population of Judah and Jerusalem honored David and Hezekiah at the time of their deaths. Solomon, Abijah, and Jotham—the remaining 'all good' kings—have no note of being honored, lamented, or remembered.

prophet Jeremiah, who has made no appearance in this tale to this point, suddenly is at hand breaking out in lament. By attaching the name of this major prophet to the recollection of this king, Josiah is raised in status above other Judahite rulers who were never lamented by the prophets of Yahweh. The Chronicler goes on to insist, or invent, a liturgical tradition that singers composed laments about Josiah that were sung in some fashion as a regular tradition. Unfortunately, there is no record as to what was supposed to have been sung about Josiah. The context implies nothing concerning the Josiah being lamented. This leaves the memory created by the Chronicler as the Josiah commemorated in this literary postmortem.

Whereas Kings and Chronicles end with Josiah, First Esdras begins with him. Heavily dependent on the Josiah recorded in Chronicles, the author of First Esdras focuses on only two events in Josiah's life.[29] The great Passover event opens the scroll, placing the centrality of the proper ritual of the Jerusalemite cultus squarely in the monarchic era of the long-gone Judah.[30] It is curious that the ritual imposed by Josiah is now one of significant memory in that the aspect of commemorating any past event is decidedly absent from this account. Only the fact that David and Solomon recorded that it should be observed connects Passover to the past. For the author of First Esdras, Josiah represents the king of Judah who ruled over the correct temple world. The focus of First Esdras is not on Josiah; it is on Ezra.[31] Ezra codifies the biblical instruction and, with marginal help from Nehemiah, shores up the territorial integrity of Yehud within the Persian Empire.[32] Central to Ezra's importance is the reconstruction of the temple and compiling of *torah*; however, an emphasis on Davidic kingship distinguishes First Esdras from Ezra-Nehemiah.[33] Josiah provides two important events presaging the narrative of Ezra. He prepares and celebrates the

---

29 Böhler (*1 Esdras*, 33) sees the Josianic material translated unchanged from Chronicles. Klein ("The Rendering of 2 Chronicles 35–36 in 1 Esdras," in Fried, *Was I Esdras First?*, 220) concisely compares texts showing the variations. Zipora Talshir posits a common tradition but two separate textual traditions in *I Esdras: From Origin to Translation*, SCS 47 (Atlanta: Society of Biblical Literature, 1999), 115.

30 Erich S. Gruen, *Heritage and Hellenism: The Reinvention of Jewish Tradition*, HCS 30 (Berkeley: University of California Press, 1998), 161; Böhler, *1 Esdras*, 14.

31 Myers, *I & II Esdras*, 9. It is a truism of biblical studies that First Esdras is a variation on the scroll of Ezra-Nehemiah: Böhler, *1 Esdras*, 16–20. That the scroll seems to begin in the middle of copying Chronicles and ends with an unfinished sentence is immaterial here; the book has been saved in this form for two millennia.

32 Gruen (*Heritage and Hellenism*, 161) emphasizes the downplaying of Nehemiah in First Esdras, concentrating instead on the cooperation between Zerubbabel and Ezra.

33 Michael Bird, *1 Esdras: Introduction and Commentary on the Greek Text in Codex Vaticanus*, SeptCom (Leiden: Brill, 2012), 111; Böhler, *1 Esdras*, 20–21.

proper Passover as directed long ago by David and Solomon (1 Esd 1:4, 14),[34] and his death ends the independence of Judah, setting the stage for the mission of Ezra under the auspices of Persia.

The return of the temple to its correct ritual observance is embodied in the person of Ezra, who is foreshadowed by Josiah. The king acts in proper fashion; it is Josiah who instigated the Passover (1 Esd 1:1, 7, 18). The cleansing of the religious world of Judah and Israel is not pertinent in this work and does not occur. Josiah does not rectify a totally corrupt religious world in First Esdras because what Ezra needs is to reinstate the proper temple ritual. In this case, it is not a religious world gone widely off course that needs correcting; it is a destroyed temple and its ritual that needs reestablishing. Josiah embodies the proper monarch ensuring the proper temple services from the first temple as originally prescribed by David and Solomon. The unquestioned piety of Josiah in relation to the worship of Yahweh and the restoration of proper ritual predominates.[35] The additional passage in 1 Esd 1:21–22 concentrates on the righteousness of Josiah, not the actions accredited to him.[36] As Josiah had performed correctly, Ezra will oversee that the traditions of correct ritual will be maintained. Now that the monarchy no longer exists, it is the written directives that will legitimate cultic calendars and feasts. Therefore, in First Esdras the use of explicit directions deriving from David and Solomon take on extra significance (1 Esd 1:4, 14) while the very written instructions of Moses were consulted by Josiah (1 Esd 1:10). That Ezra compiled instructions just as Josiah had conformed to them makes Josiah's Passover an appropriate opening to the scroll.

Unique to this narrative, the author places blame for the evil behavior as understood by God squarely on the populace, who are designated as the greatest sinners of any ancient people (1 Esd 1:22). Josiah is declared fully righteous (1 Esd 1:21). If nothing else, this contrast makes clear that people need to obey the instructions provided by God; it will not suffice to count on rulers or other leaders to be righteous. As it turns out, even Josiah can fail. First Esdras highlights the depths of depravity related to the severity of God's judgment and counters it with the possibility of the enormity of God's mercy; the possibility of actually being good is demonstrated with

---

34 The numbering system for First Esdras follows that of the Göttingen edition, it being readily available in the Böhler commentary, *1 Esdras*. Note that it differs by a few verses from most modern European language translations.

35 Talshir, *I Esdras*, 13; Bird, *1 Esdras*, 109.

36 Talshir (*I Esdras*, 15) sees the addition as a proof that the scroll intended to begin with Josiah; see also Bird, *1 Esdras*, 114; Böhler, *1 Esdras*, 32.

Josiah, before his death in battle, and by Ezra providing the means for Hellenistic Jews to maintain God's mercy.[37]

First Esdras follows the Chronicler in the rendition of Josiah's death at the hands of Neco. Neco explains his mission to Josiah as one ordained by the Lord God. If the Chronicler found that sufficient, First Esdras did not; the prophet Jeremiah is added to Neco in declaring how ill-advised Josiah's planned military activity is, but to no avail. Here, Josiah disobeys two prophets, one foreign and one Judahite. The result was his death. Like the Chronicler, the author of First Esdras concluded his section on Josiah with an emphasis on memory. Josiah is to be remembered in written record and in perpetual ritual (1 Esd 1:30). It seems to have been a literary flourish since, elsewhere, no references to this commemoration appear.[38]

Flavius Josephus made use of the previous three sources to construct a Josiah who would be admired in the cultured circles of the Roman Empire, whether Jewish, Greek, or Roman.[39] He used the intertwined classical genres of history and biography to develop models of virtuous and impious kings.[40] In this way, Josephus created an apology of the Jews for a classical world that marginalized them.[41] To attain this transformation of the Judahite King Josiah into a model Hellenistic pious hero and philosopher king, several minor adjustments to the biblical texts were necessary. These included expansions and deletions of existing Josianic material.

Plato posited five virtues for such rulers: wisdom, courage, temperance, justice, and piety.[42] Josephus emphasized each as aspects of King Josiah.[43] Josiah's restructure of the religious world of Judah (*Ant.* 10.50–51) is presented as a rational, wise decision, implementing both his knowledge and his capacity to use that knowledge.[44] Since, in the three biblical texts, Josiah displays neither overt courage nor militaristic prowess, Josephus had to create these pretty much *ex nihilo* extrapolating tangential material from the meager tales of Josiah at his disposal. The death scenes with chariots provided a perfect opportunity to invent a warrior

---

37 Bird, *1 Esdras*, 30, 33; Gruen, *Heritage*, 161.
38 Josephus (*Ant.* 10.78) insists that Jeremiah's lament still existed in his day but makes no comment about any official remembrance of the king.
39 Feldman, "Josephus' Portrait," 110, 113–14. Feldman's article adequately compares the biblical texts with the changes made in Josephus's *Jewish Antiquities* and is followed here with his citations.
40 Castelli, "Kings in Josephus," in Lemaire and Halpern, *The Books of Kings*, 542.
41 Hengel, *Judaism and Hellenism*, 70.
42 Feldman, "Josephus' Portrait," 113.
43 Castelli, "Kings in Josephus," in Lemaire and Halpern, *The Books of Kings*, 554.
44 See Feldman, "Josephus' Portrait," 117, who notes that this aspect of the 'reform' is entirely Josephus's invention.

Josiah with military daring and personal bravado (*Ant.* 10.76).⁴⁵ Temperance could only be inferred from Josiah's efforts (*Ant.* 10.50) to convince his subjects to act reasonably, which is a creation of Josephus.⁴⁶ Josiah as practitioner and promoter of law (*Ant.* 10.50–51) made him a pinnacle of justice for a Roman Empire enthusiastic about legalities.⁴⁷ Finally, Josiah's piety is stretched from his twelfth year of age to his last dying breath; it also informs all his wise decisions.⁴⁸

As with all good heroic men of classical biographies, Josiah is a natural leader from his minority. If the Chronicler presented him as pious from the twelfth year of his reign, Josephus made him pious from his twelfth year of age.⁴⁹ As a young lad, Josiah knows whom to imitate: the great King David. He also knows how to teach and persuade his people and raise funds for his temple.⁵⁰

Writing in an empire of many and various polytheistic peoples but with a view to impressing the philosophically elite, the Josiah of the book of Kings was something of a problem for Josephus. While it was intellectually current to dismiss idols as nothings, and even to see pantheons as the imaginative realm of the unenlightened or to assume that all gods were really one deity, it was not acceptable to go smashing, breaking, and burning temples and divine statuary.⁵¹ Since this kind of activity constituted a major portion of the story of Josiah in Kings, Josephus omitted the violent destruction of idols, shrines, necromancers, and other such personnel in accordance with First Esdras. He included the slaying of priests but clears

---

45 Feldman ("Portrait of Josiah," 122–23) notes the clear decision to delete the cowardly disguise worn by Josiah when going out to meet Neco as well as envisioning a zealous soldier bounding from one end of the (unrecorded in the sources) battlefield to the other. Josiah is also cool, brave, and self-controlled even as he dies.

46 Feldman, "Josephus' Portrait," 123.

47 Ibid., 123–24; Castelli ("Kings in Josephus," in Lemaire and Halpern, *The Books of Kings*, 555) notes that the religious reforms in Josephus are connected to judicial reforms.

48 Feldman ("Josephus' Portrait," 125) sees piety as Josephus's central quality in Josiah.

49 Ibid., 115–16, 124.

50 Ibid., 118.

51 Robert M. Grant outlines various approaches to pantheons by contemporary philosophers, and notes that to assume a single deity was an acceptable practice among them: Robert M. Grant, *Gods and the One God*, LEC 1 (Philadelphia: Westminster, 1986), 75–83. Feldman ("Josephus' Portrait," 126–27) notes that this might well be true, but philosophers do not demolish the gods' accessories. Ogilvie (*Romans and Their Gods*, 3, 19–20) observes that, while Stoics could philosophize a single world-spirit sort-of-deity, they were tolerant of the vast number of gods and rituals; Jews were deemed suspect on this ground as they did not accept the multitudes of "other" deities or the cultic implements that accompanied them.

Josiah of wanton manslaughter by noting that the slain were not Aaronides and, therefore, were performing improper worship; sacrilege was also a serious offense in Rome.[52]

The interaction displayed in the biblical texts between Josiah and Yahweh via Huldah takes several turns in Josephus (*Ant.* 10.60–61). Significantly, Josiah sends his delegation directly to Huldah, unlike in Kings or Chronicles where he issues a command to consult Yahweh. Moreover, his intent in doing so is to win favor with God in an attempt to avoid his subjects being exiled; Josephus perceives the prophetess to be a mediator capable of changing the deity's intentions.[53] None of the information Josiah relates to Huldah derives from Josephus's biblical sources. Clearly, he felt no compunction to record the prophetic words of the prophetess; rather than reproduce a quotation of Huldah's oracle, he creates his own prophetic message in descriptive prose. For Josephus, Huldah's proclamation is one of unswerving divine destruction of the people because of their long-standing disobedience; there is no way to deter this punishment. In this way, Josephus has Huldah answer Josiah's plea to her in the negative. The conclusion of Huldah's response emphasizes that God must keep the promise made and must not back down from the punishment related to the infringement performed. Only Josiah's total righteousness allows him to die in advance of the devastation to come. In Josephus's rendition, the report from his delegation led directly to Josiah's calling all his people of every age to Jerusalem to hear the holy books and to vow to be righteous (*Ant.* 10.62). However, though Josiah sees Huldah as a way out of the destruction of his people, God does not.[54]

The obvious disobedience to the word of Yahweh in Josiah's death story as told in Chronicles and First Esdras was not amenable to the vision of Josiah being proffered by Josephus. A good, wise, and pious ruler does not willfully act in direct contradiction to the revelation of his own god, as Josiah had done.[55] Therefore, Josephus chose to make use of the narrative in Kings where Josiah meets a Neco who says nothing to him. It is clear that Josephus was familiar with the stories of Josiah's death in Chronicles and First Esdras; he derives his vision of Josiah as a great military leader from them. Nonetheless, the warnings made by Neco in the narratives of Chronicles and First Esdras are not recorded. Instead of a prophet of

---

52 Feldman, "Josephus' Portrait," 127, 128. However, Roman religious tradition did not include the existence of priestly families, a far different cultural situation from that of the strict observance of family inheritance of Jewish priesthood. See Ogilvie, *Romans and Their Gods*," 106.
53 Handy, "Reading Huldah as Being a Woman," 9.
54 Feldman, "Josephus' Portrait," 124.
55 Begg, "Death of Josiah," 163; followed by Feldman, "Josephus' Portrait," 120.

Yahweh, Neco becomes an invading enemy wishing to extend his kingdom over Asia.⁵⁶ Had Josephus retained the word of God in the mouth of Neco, Josiah would have been disobedient before an Egyptian king who was obedient to Josiah's deity.⁵⁷ Josephus's location of the confrontation between Neco and Josiah in Mende, an Egyptian town explicitly declared to be in Josiah's kingdom (*Ant.* 10.75), may be the result of confused textual transmission, but it serves to present Josiah as a valiant defender rather than an active aggressor.

The Josiah of Josephus's retelling of Jewish history had a major influence on later Christian reconstructions of Josiah. The memory of Josiah as the restorer of the temple worship in Jerusalem was not important to the Church, but the more abstract notion of Josiah as the embodiment of the righteous devotee of God who rids worship of any unnecessary and impious aspects was found highly amenable. The iconographic controversy of the first millennium that so influenced certain strands of Islam can be traced back to the pious activities of Josiah reenacted in the elimination of idols by the Church once it became the religion of the Roman Empire. For an empire, the memory of Josephus's Josiah provided a useful blend of Jewish and Roman backgrounds. Josiah could be a model for monastic piety, royal submission to priestly admonishment, public participation in proper religious celebration, and militaristic service to God. Throughout the succeeding millennia, the memory of Josiah has been and continues to be refashioned from this variety of sources according to the memory of Josiah useful at a given time or place.

---

56 Feldman, "Josephus' Portrait," 120.
57 Begg, "Death of Josiah," 161.

Bibliography

Achtelstetter, Karin. "Huldah at the Table: Reflections on Leadership and the Leadership of Women." *CurTM* 37 (2010): 176–84.

Ackerman, Susan. *Under Every Green Tree: Popular Religion in Sixth-Century Judah*. HSM 46. Atlanta: Scholars Press, 1992.

Aguiler, Grace. *The Women of Israel: Or Characters and Sketches from the Holy Scriptures and Jewish History*. 8th ed. London: Groombridge and Sons, 1873.

Aharoni, Yohanan. "Arad: Its Inscriptions and Temple." *BA* 31 (1968): 2–32.

–. *The Archaeology of the Land of Israel from the Prehistoric Beginnings to the End of the First Temple Period*. Edited by Miriam Aharoni. Translated by Anson F. Rainey. Philadelphia: Westminster, 1982. https://doi.org/10.1177/014610798301300208

–. "Notes and News: Tel Beersheba." *IEJ* 24 (1974): 270–72.

Aharoni, Yohanan, and Michael Avi-Yonah. *The Macmillan Bible Atlas*. New York: Macmillan, 1968. https://doi.org/10.2307/3210503

Ahlström, Gösta W. "Administration of the State in Canaan and Ancient Israel." Pages 587–603 in *Civilizations of the Ancient Near East*. Vol. 1. Edited by Jack M. Sasson. New York: Scribner's Sons, 1995.

–. *An Archaeological Picture of Iron Age Religions in Ancient Palestine*. StudOr 55/3. Helsinki: Societas Orientalis Fennicae, 1984.

–. *Aspects of Syncretism in Israelite Religion*. Translated by Eric J. Sharpe. HoSo 5. Lund: Gleerup, 1963.

–. *The History of Ancient Palestine from the Palaeolithic Period to Alexander's Conquest*. Edited by Diana V. Edelman. JSOTSup 146. Sheffield: JSOT Press, 1993. https://doi.org/10.1017/s0036930600048225

–. *Royal Administration and National Religion in Ancient Palestine*. SHANE 1. Leiden: Brill, 1982.

Alberi, Mary. "'Like the Army of God's Camp': Political Theology and Apocalyptic Warfare at Charlemagne's Court." *Viator* 41, no. 2 (2010): 1–20. https://doi.org/10.1484/j.viator.1.100789

Albertz, Rainer. *A History of Israelite Religion in the Old Testament Period*. Translated by John Bowden. 2 vols. OTL. Louisville: Westminster John Knox, 1994.

–. "Introduction." Pages 1–29 in *Family and Household Religion in Ancient Israel and the Levant*. Edited by Rainer Albertz and Rüdiger Schmitt. Winona Lake, IN: Eisenbrauns, 2012. https://doi.org/10.5615/neareastarch.77.2.0154

–. "Methodological Reflections." Pages 21–56 in *Family and Household Religion in Ancient Israel and the Levant*. Edited by Rainer Albertz and Rüdiger Schmitt. Winona Lake, IN: Eisenbrauns, 2012. https://doi.org/10.5615/neareastarch.77.2.0154

–. "Monotheism and Violence: How to Handle a Dangerous Biblical Tradition." Pages 373–87 in *The Land of Israel in Bible, History, and Theology: Studies in Honour of Ed Noort*. Edited by Jacques van Ruiten and J. Cornelis de Vos. VTSup 124. Leiden: Brill, 2009. https://doi.org/10.1163/ej.9789004175150.i-474.134

–. "Personal Names and Family Religion." Pages 245–386, 534–609, in *Family and Household Religion in Ancient Israel and the Levant*. Edited by Rainer Albertz and Rüdiger Schmitt. Winona Lake, IN: Eisenbrauns, 2012. https://doi.org/10.5615/neareastarch.77.2.0154

–. "A Possible *terminus ad quem* for the Deuteronomistic Legislation: A Fresh Look at Deut 17:16." Pages 271–96 in *Homeland and Exile: Biblical and Ancient Near Eastern Studies in Honour of Busteney Oded*. Edited by Gershon Galil, Mark Geller, and Alan Millard. VTSup 130. Leiden: Brill, 2009. https://doi.org/10.1163/ej.9789004178892.i-648.85

–. "The Relevance of Hebrew Name Seals for Reconstructing Judahite and Israelite Family Religion." Pages 33–52 in *Family and Household Religion: Toward a Synthesis of Old Testament Studies, Archaeology, Epigraphy, and Cultural Studies*. Edited by Rainer Albertz, Beth Alpert Nakhal, Saul M. Olyan, and Rüdiger Schmitt. Winona Lake, IN: Eisenbrauns, 2014. https://doi.org/10.3764/ajaonline1201.muller

–. "Why a Reform like Josiah's Must Have Happened." Pages 27–46 in *Good Kings and Bad Kings*. Edited by Lester L. Grabbe. LHBOTS 393. ESHM 5. London: T&T Clark, 2005.

Albertz, Rainer, and Rüdiger Schmitt. *Family and Household Religion in Ancient Israel and the Levant*. Winona Lake, IN: Eisenbrauns, 2012. https://doi.org/10.5615/neareastarch.77.2.0154

Albrektson, Bertil. *History of the Gods: An Essay on the Idea of Historical Events as Divine Manifestations in the Ancient Near East and in Israel*. ConBOT 1. Lund: Gleerup, 1967. https://doi.org/10.1017/s0041977x00126151

Albright, William Foxwell. *From the Stone Age to Christianity: Monotheism and the Historical Process*. 2nd ed. Garden City, NY: Doubleday Anchor Books, 1957. https://doi.org/10.1163/156853657x00077

Alfonso X, King of Castile and Leon. *General estoria: Tercera parte, Tomo II*. Edited by Pedro Sánchez-Prieto Borja. Autores clásicos españoles. Madrid: Biblioteca Castro, 2009.

Allen, Leslie C. *The Books of Joel, Obadiah, Jonah and Micah*. NICOT. Grand Rapids: Eerdmans, 1976.

Alter, Robert. *The Art of Biblical Narrative*. New York: Basic Books, 1981.

Althann, Robert. "Josiah." *ABD* 3.1015–18.

Altmann, Peter. *Festive Meals in Ancient Israel: Deuteronomy's Identity Politics in Their Ancient Near Eastern Context*. BZAW 424. Berlin: de Gruyter, 2011. https://doi.org/10.1515/9783110255379

Anderson, George Wishart. *The History and Religion of Israel*. NCBOT. Oxford: Oxford University Press, 1966.

Anderson, James. "Creating Dialectical Tensions: Religious Developments in Persian-Period Yehud Reflected in Biblical Texts." Pages 9–23 in *Religion in the Achaemenid Persian Empire: Emerging Judaisms and Trends*. Edited by Diana V. Edelman, Anne Fitzpatrick-McKinley, and Philippe Guillaume. ORA 17. Tübingen: Mohr Siebeck, 2016. https://doi.org/10.1628/978-3-16-154690-7

Andreasen, Niels-Erik A. "The Role of the Queen Mother in Israelite Society." *CBQ* 45 (1983): 179–94.

Andrews, Herbert T. "The Letter of Aristeas." *APOT* 2.83–122.

Angel, Hayyim J. *Revealed Texts, Hidden Meanings: Finding the Religious Significance in Tanakh*. Jersey City, NJ: Ktav, 2009. https://doi.org/10.5508/jhs.2009.v9.r69

Ansberry, Christopher B., and Jerry Hwang. "No Covenant before the Exile? The

Deuteronomic Torah and Israel's Covenant Theology." Pages 74-94 in *Evangelical Faith and the Challenge of Historical Criticism*. Edited by Christopher M. Hays and Christopher B. Ansberry. Grand Rapids: Baker Academic, 2013. https://doi.org/10.1177/0040571x14522949n

Antoni, Klaus. "Creating a Sacred Narrative: *Kojiki* Studies and Shinto Nationalism." *JapanRel* 36 (2011): 3-30.

Apple, Raymond. "The Pillars of the Temple." *JBQ* 42 (2014): 221-28.

Armitage, Christopher M. *Sir Walter Raleigh: An Annotated Bibliography*. Chapel Hill: University of North Carolina Press, 1987.

Arneth, Martin. "Die antiassyrische Reform Josias von Juda: Überlegungen zur Komposition und Intention von 2 Reg 23,4-15." *ZABR* 7 (2001): 189-216.

Arnold, Bill T. "Deuteronomy 12 and the Law of the Central Sanctuary *noch einmal*." *VT* 64 (2014): 236-48. https://doi.org/10.1163/15685330-12341150

Assmann. Jan. *Ägypten-Theologie und Frömigkeit einer frühen Hochkultur*. Stuttgart: Kohlhammer, 1984.

-. "Amun." *DDD* cols. 47-54.

-. *Moses der Ägypter: Entzifferung einer Gedächtnisspur*. Munich: Hanser, 1998. https://doi.org/10.1515/arbi.2000.18.1.25

-. *Moses the Egyptian: The Memory of Egypt in Western Monotheism*. Cambridge, MA: Harvard University Press, 1997. https://doi.org/10.1086/ahr/104.3.1039

-. *Of God and Gods: Egypt, Israel, and the Rise of Monotheism*. Madison: University of Wisconsin Press, 2008.

-. *The Price of Monotheism*. Translated by Robert Savage. Stanford, CA: Stanford Univerity Press, 2010.

Aston, Margaret. *The King's Bedpost: Reformation and Iconography in a Tudor Group Portrait*. Cambridge: Cambridge University Press, 1993. https://doi.org/10.2307/3169725

Auffarth, Christoph. "Justice, the King and the Gods: Polytheism and Emerging Monotheism in the Ancient World." Pages 421-53 in *One God—One Cult—One Nation: Archaeological and Biblical Perspectives*. Edited by Reinhard G. Kratz and Hermann Spieckermann. BZAW 405. Berlin: de Gruyter, 2010. https://doi.org/10.1515/9783110223583.421

Auld, A. Graeme. *Life in Kings: Reshaping the Royal Story in the Hebrew Bible*. AIL 20. Atlanta: Scholars Press, 2017. https://doi.org/10.2307/j.ctt1p0vk08

-. "What Was the Main Source of the Book of Chronicles?" Pages 91-99 in *The Chronicler as Author: Studies in Text and Texture*. Edited by M. Patrick Graham and Steven L. McKenzie. JSOTSup 263. Sheffield: Sheffield Acadamic Press, 1999.

Avery, Ben. *The Coming Storm*. Kingdoms: A Biblical Epic 1. Grand Rapids: Zondervan, 2007.

Avioz, Michael. "Josiah's Death in the Book of Kings: A New Solution to an Old Theological Conundrum." *ETL* 83 (2007): 359-66.

-. "The Motif of Beauty in the Books of Samuel and Kings." *VT* 59 (2009): 341-59. https://doi.org/10.1163/156853309x445025

-. "What Happened at Megiddo? Josiah's Death as Described in the Book of Kings." *BN* 142 (2009): 5-11.

Azevido, Joaquim. "El concepto de lo malo en la teodicea del cronista." *Theologika* 28 (2013): 2-35.

Azize, Joseph J. "Was There Regular Child Sacrifice in Phoenicia and Carthage?" Pages 185-205 in *Gilgameš and the World of Assyria: Proceedings of the Conference*

Held at Mandelbaum House, The University of Sydney, 21-23 July 2004. Edited by Joseph Azize and Noel Weeks. ANESSup 21. Leuven: Peeters, 2007. https://doi.org/10.5508/jhs.2007.v7.r26

Azumi, Ryo. *Manga Messengers*. Manga Bible. Carol Stream, IL: Tyndale House, 2011.

Bagg, Ariel M. "Palestine under Assyrian Rule: A New Look at the Assyrian Imperial Policy in the West." *JAOS* 133 (2013): 119-44. https://doi.org/10.7817/jameroriesoci.133.1.0119

Bahar, Shlomo. "'He Erected Altars to the Baal' (2Kgs 21,3): The Absence of Iconic Objects in Cultic Sites for 'Other Gods' in the Biblical Narrative." *BN* 145 (2010): 25-36.

Bailey, Lloyd R., Sr. *Biblical Perspectives on Death*. OBT. Philadelphia: Fortress, 1979.

Bakon, Shimon. "Egypt: The Nemesis of Israel and Judah." *JBQ* 40 (2012): 9-14.

Baldwin, George C. *Representative Women: From Eve, the Wife of the First, to Mary, the Mother of the Second Adam*. New York: Sheldon, Lamport, and Blakeman, 1856.

Baly, Denis. *The Geography of the Bible*. New and rev. ed. New York: Harper and Row, 1974.

Barker, Margaret. *The Hidden Tradition of the Kingdom of God*. London: SPCK, 2007.

–. "What Did Josiah Reform?" Pages 11-33 in *"He Unfurrowed His Brow and Laughed": Essays in Honour of Professor Nicolas Wyatt*. Edited by Wilfred G. E. Watson. AOAT 299. Münster: Ugarit, 2007.

Barlow, George. *A Homiletical Commentary on the Book of Kings*. PCHCOT. New York: Funk & Wagnalls, 1892.

Barnes, Trevor. *The Kingfisher's Children's Bible*. New York: Kingfisher, 2001.

Barrick, W. Boyd. "Burning Bones at Bethel: A Closer Look at 2 Kings 23,16a." *SJOT* 14 (2000): 3-16.

–. "Dynastic Politics, Priestly Succession, and Josiah's Eighth Year." *ZAW* 112 (2000): 564-82. https://doi.org/10.1515/zatw.2000.112.4.564

–. *The King and the Cemeteries: Toward a New Understanding of Josiah's Reform*. VTSup 88; Leiden: Brill, 2002.

–. "Loving too Well: The Negative Portrayal of Solomon and the Composition of the King's History." *EstBib* 59 (2001): 419-50.

–. "What Do We Really Know about 'High Places'?" *SEÅ* 45 (1980): 50-57.

–. "The Word *bmh* in the Old Testament." Ph.D. diss., University of Chicago, 1977.

Barrier, Michael, and Martin Williams, eds. *A Smithsonian Book of Comic Book Comics*. New York: Smithsonian Institution and Harry N. Abrams, 1981.

Bartelmus, Alexa, and Jon Taylor. "Collecting and Connecting History: Nabonidus and the Kassite Rebuilding of the E(ul)maš of (Ištar)-Annunitu in Sippar-Annunitu." *JCS* 66 (2014): 113-28. https://doi.org/10.5615/jcunestud.66.2014.0113

Barth, Hermann. *Die Jesaja-Worte in der Josiazeit: Israel und Assur als Thema einer produktiven Neuinterpretation der Jesajaüberlieferung*. WMANT 48. Neukirchen-Vluyn: Neukirchener, 1977.

Basser, Herbert W. "The Butchering of Jewish Texts to Feed the Masses." Pages 233-41 in *Judaism in Late Antiquity. Part 3: Where We Stand: Issues and Debates in Ancient Judaism. Volume One*. Edited by Jacob Neusner and Alan J. Avery-Peck. HdO 40/3.1. Leiden: Brill, 1999. https://doi.org/10.1163/9789004294097

Basson, Alec. "Death as Deliverance in Job 3:11-26." Pages 66-80 in *"From Ebla to Stellenbosch": Syro-Palestinian Religions and the Hebrew Bible*. Edited by Izak Cornelius and Louis Jonker. ADPV 37. Wiesbaden: Harrassowitz, 2008.

Bauckham, Richard. *The Fate of the Dead: Studies on the Jewish and Christian Apocalypses.* NovTSup 93. Atlanta: Society of Biblical Literature, 1998.

Bauer, Susan Wise. *The History of the Ancient World: From the Earliest Accounts to the Fall of Rome.* New York: Norton, 2007.

Beardsworth, Alan, and Teresa Keil. *Sociology on the Menu: An Invitation to the Study of Food and Society.* London: Routledge, 1996.

Beaulieu, Paul-Alain. "Nabonidus the Mad King: A Reconsideration of His Steles from Harran and Babylon." Pages 137–66 in *Representations of Political Power: Case Histories from Times of Change and Dissolving Order in the Ancient Near East.* Edited by Marlies Heinz and Marian H. Feldman. Winona Lake, IN: Eisenbrauns, 2007. https://doi.org/10.1017/s0041977x0800013x

–. *The Reign of Nabonidus, King of Babylon 556–539 B.C.* YNER 10. New Haven: Yale University Press, 1989. https://doi.org/10.2307/j.ctt2250wnt

Becker, Adam H. "2 Baruch." Pages 1565–85 in *Outside the Bible: Ancient Jewish Writings Related to Scripture.* Edited by Louis H. Feldman, James L. Kugel, and Lawrence H. Schiffman. Philadelphia: Jewish Publication Society of America, 2013. https://doi.org/10.1163/15685179-12341380

Becker, Uwe. "Von der Staatsreligion zum Monotheismus: Ein Kapital israelitisch-jüdischer Religionsgeschichte." *ZTK* 102 (2005): 1–16. https://doi.org/10.1628/004435405774520280

Becking, Bob. "The Enigmatic Garden of Uzza: A Religio-Historical Footnote to 2 Kings 21:18, 26." Pages 383–91 in *Berührungspunkte: Studien zur Sozial- und Religionsgeschichte Israels und seiner Umwelt: Festschrift für Rainer Albertz zu seinem 65. Geburtstag.* Edited by Ingo Kottsieper, Rüdiger Schmitt, and Jakob Wöhrle. AOAT 350. Münster: Ugarit, 2008. https://doi.org/10.1515/9783110897005

–. "The Return of the Deity: Iconic or Aniconic?" Pages 53–62 in *Essays on Ancient Israel in Its Near Eastern Context: A Tribute to Nadav Na'aman.* Edited by Yairah Amit, Ehud Ben Zvi, Israel Finkelstein, and Oded Lipschits. Winona Lake, IN: Eisenbrauns, 2006. https://doi.org/10.1086/basor25067068

Bedouelle, Guy. "Le tournant de l'impremerie." Pages 39–52 in *Le temps des Réformes et la Bible.* Edited by Guy Bedouelle and Bernard Roussel. BTT 5. Paris: Beauchesne, 1989. https://doi.org/10.14375/np.9782701010922

Begg, Christopher T. "The Ark in Chronicles." Pages 133–45 in *The Chronicler as Theologian: Essays in Honor of Ralph W. Klein.* Edited by M. Patrick Graham, Steven L. McKenzie and Gary N. Knoppers. JSOTSup 371. London: T&T Clark, 2003. https://doi.org/10.1086/521770

–. "The Death of Josiah: Josephus and the Bible." *ETL* 64 (1988): 157–63.

Belnap, Dan. *Fillets of Fatling and Goblets of Gold: Use of Meal Events in the Ritual Imagery of the Ugaritic Mythological and Epic Texts.* GUS 4. Piscataway, NJ: Gorgias, 2008. https://doi.org/10.31826/9781463216139

Ben-Barak, Zafrira. "The Status and Right of the *Gebira*." *JBL* 110 (1991): 23–34.

Ben-Dor Evian, Shirly. "Egypt and Israel: The Never-Ending Story." *NEA* 80 (2017): 30–39. https://doi.org/10.5615/neareastarch.80.1.0030

Ben-Zion, Sigalit. *A Roadmap to the Heavens: An Anthropological Study of Hegemony among Priests, Sages, and Laymen.* JJL. Boston: Academic Studies Press, 2009. https://doi.org/10.1515/9781618110374

Ben Zvi, Ehud. "Are There Any Bridges Out There? How Wide Was the Conceptual Gap between the Deuteronomistic History and Chronicles?" Pages 59–86 in *Community Identity in Judean Historiography: Biblical and Comparative Perspectives.*

Edited by Gary N. Knoppers and Kenneth A. Ristau. Winona Lake, IN: Eisenbrauns, 2009. https://doi.org/10.31826/9781463235505-062
–. *A Historical-Critical Study of the Book of Zephaniah*. BZAW 198. Berlin: de Gruyter, 1992.
–. "Imagining Josiah's Book and the Implications of Imagining It in Early Persian Yehud." Pages 193–212 in *Berührungspunkte: Studien zur Sozial- und Religionsgeschichte Israels und seiner Umwelt: Festschrift für Rainer Albertz zu seinem 65. Geburtstag*. Edited by Ingo Kottsieper, Rüdiger Schmitt, and Jakob Wöhrle. AOAT 350. Münster: Ugarit, 2008. https://doi.org/10.1515/9783110897005
–. "Josiah and the Prophetic Books: Some Observations." Pages 47–64 in *Good Kings and Bad Kings*. Edited by Lester L. Grabbe. LHBOTS 393. ESHM 5. London: T&T Clark, 2005.
–. "Observations on Josiah's Account in Chronicles and Implications for Reconstructing the Worldview of the Chronicler." Pages 89–106 in *Essays on Ancient Israel in Its Near Eastern Context: A Tribute to Nadav Na'aman*. Edited by Yairah Amit, Ehud Ben Zvi, Israel Finkelstein, and Oded Lipschits. Winona Lake, IN: Eisenbrauns, 2006. https://doi.org/10.1086/basor25067068
–. "The Secession of the Northern Kingdom in Chronicles: Accepted 'Facts' and New Meanings." Pages 61–88 in *The Chronicler as Theologian: Essays in Honor of Ralph W. Klein*. Edited by M. Patrick Graham, Steven L. McKenzie, and Gary N. Knoppers. JSOTSup 371. London: T&T Clark, 2003. https://doi.org/10.1086/521770
–. *Signs of Jonah: Reading and Rereading in Ancient Yehud*. JSOTSup 367. London: Sheffield Academic, 2003.
Berry, George Richter. "The Code Found in the Temple." *JBL* 39 (1920): 44–51.
–. "The Date of Deuteronomy." *JBL* 59 (1940): 133–39.
Bewer, Julius A. *The Literature of the Old Testament*. Revised by Emil G. Kraeling. 3rd ed. RCSS 5. New York: Columbia University Press, 1962.
Bibb, Bryan D. "'Be Mindful, Yah Gracious God': Extra-biblical Evidence and Josiah's Religious Reforms." *Koinonia* 12 (2000): 156–74.
Bird, Michael. *1 Esdras: Introduction and Commentary on the Greek Text in Codex Vaticanus*. SeptCom. Leiden: Brill, 2012. https://doi.org/10.1177/0014524613481180t
Bird, Phyllis A. "The End of the Male Cult Prostitute: A Literary-Historical and Exigetical Analysis of Hebrew *qadeš/qedešim*." Pages 37–80 in *Congress Volume Cambridge 1995*. Edited by John A. Emerton. VTSup 66. Leiden: Brill, 1997. https://doi.org/10.1163/9789004275904_004
–. *Missing Persons and Mistaken Identities: Women and Gender in Ancient Israel*. OBT. Minneapolis: Fortress, 1997.
–. "Women in the Ancient Mediterranean World: Ancient Israel." *BR* 39 (1994): 31–45.
Bledstein, Adrien Janis. "Is Judges a Woman's Satire of Men Who Play God?" Pages 34–54 in *A Feminist Companion to Judges*. Edited by Athalyah Brenner. FCB 4. Sheffield: Sheffield Academic, 1993.
Blenkinsopp, Joseph. "Bethel in the Neo-Babylonian Period." Pages 93–107 in *Judah and the Judeans in the Neo-Babylonian Period*. Edited by Oded Lipschits and Joseph Blenkinsopp. Winona Lake, IN: Eisenbrauns, 2003. https://doi.org/10.2307/3268055
–. *David Remembered: Kingship and National Identity in Ancient Israel*. Grand Rapids: Eerdmans, 2013. https://doi.org/10.15695/hmltc.v39i1.3944
–. *A History of Prophecy in Israel*. Philadelphia: Westminster, 1983.

–. *Judaism: The First Phase: The Place of Ezra and Nehemiah in the Origins of Judaism*. Grand Rapids: Eerdmans, 2009. https://doi.org/10.1093/jts/flq054

–. "The Judean Priesthood During the Neo-Babylonean and Achaemenid Periods: A Hypothetical Reconstruction." *CBQ* 60 (1998): 25–43.

–. *The Pentateuch: An Introduction to the First Five Books of the Bible*. ABRL. New York: Doubleday, 1992.

Bloch, Abraham P. *The Biblical and Historical Background of the Jewish Holy Days*. New York: Ktav, 1978.

Bloch-Smith, Elizabeth. "Death in the Life of Israel." Pages 139–43 in *Sacred Time, Sacred Place: Archaeology and the Religion of Israel*. Edited by Barry M. Gitten. Winona Lake, IN: Eisenbrauns, 2002.

–. "From Womb to Tomb: The Israelite Family in Death as in Life." Pages 122–31 in *The Family in Life and Death: The Family in Ancient Israel: Sociological and Archaeological Perspectives*. Edited by Patricia Dutcher-Walls. LHBOTS 504. New York: T&T Clark, 2009. https://doi.org/10.1111/j.1467-9418.2010.00629.x

–. *Judahite Burial Practices and Beliefs about the Dead*. JSOTSup 123. Sheffield: JSOT Press, 1992. https://doi.org/10.2307/3210452

–. "Solomon's Temple: The Politics of Ritual Space." Pages 83–94 in *Sacred Time, Sacred Place: Archaeology and the Religion of Israel*. Edited by Barry M. Gitten. Winona Lake, IN: Eisenbrauns, 2002.

–. "'Who Is the King of Glory?' Solomon's Temple and Its Symbolism." Pages 18–31 in *Scripture and Other Artifacts: Essays on the Bible and Archaeology in Honour of Philip J. King*. Edited by Michael D. Coogan, J. Cheryl Exum, and Lawrence E. Stager. Louisville: Westminster John Knox, 1994. https://doi.org/10.2307/3210504

Block, Daniel I. *The Gods of the Nations: Studies in Ancient Near Eastern National Theology*. 2nd ed. Grand Rapids: Baker Academic, 2000.

–. "Transformation of Royal Ideology in Ezekiel." Pages 208–46 in *Transforming Visions: Transformations of Text, Tradition, and Theology in Ezekiel*. Edited by William A. Tooman and Michael A. Lyons. PTMS 127. Eugene, OR: Pickwick, 2010. https://doi.org/10.1177/0014524613480108l

Boda, Mark J. "Identity and Empire, Reality and Hope in the Chronicler's Perspective." Pages 249–72 in *Community Identity in Judean Historiography: Biblical and Comparative Perspectives*. Edited by Gary N. Knoppers and Kenneth A. Ristau. Winona Lake, IN: Eisenbrauns, 2009.

Bodel, John. "Death, the Afterlife, and Other Last Things: Rome." Pages 489–92 in *Religions of the Ancient World: A Guide*. Edited by Sarah Iles Johnston. Cambridge, MA: Belknap, 2004.

Boer, Roland. *Marxist Criticism of the Bible*. London: T&T Clark, 2003.

–. "National Allegory in the Hebrew Bible." *JSOT* 74 (1997): 106–12.

–. *Rescuing the Bible*. BlMan. Malden, MA: Blackwell, 2007.

Böhler, Dieter. *1 Esdras*. Translated by Linda M. Maloney. IECOT. Stuttgart: Kohlhammer, 2016.

Borowski, Oded. *Agriculture in Iron Age Israel*. Boston: American Schools of Oriental Research, 2002.

Bossuet, Jacque-Bénigne. *An Universal History, From the Beginning of the World to the Empire of Charlemagne*. Aberdeen: Francis Douglass & William Murry, 1755.

Box, George Herbert, and William Oscar Emil Oesterley. "The Book of Sirach." *APOT* 1.268–517.

Bradshaw, Christopher. "David or Josiah? Old Testament Kings as Exemplars in Edwardian Religious Polemic." Pages 77–90 in *Protestant History and Identity in Sixteenth-Century Europe*. Vol. 2 of *The Later Reformation*. StASRH. Edited by Bruce Gordon. Aldershot: Ashgate, 1996.

Breen, John, and Mark Teeuwen. *A New History of Shinto*. BBHR. Chichester: Wiley-Blackwell, 2010.

Bremmer, Jan N. "From Holy Books to Holy Bible: An Itinerary from Ancient Greece to Modern Islam via Second Temple Judaism and Early Christianity." Pages 327–60 in *Authoritative Scriptures in Ancient Judaism*. Edited by Mladen Popovic. JSJSup 141. Leiden: Brill, 2010. https://doi.org/10.1163/ej.9789004185302.i-402.75

Brenner, Athalya. "Gender in Prophecy, Magic and Priesthood: From Sumer to Ancient Israel." Pages 3–18 in *Embroidered Garments: Priests and Gender in Biblical Israel*. Edited by Deborah W. Rooke. HBM 25. Sheffield: Sheffield Phoenix, 2009.

Brettler, Marc Zvi. *The Creation of History in Ancient Israel*. London: Routledge, 1995.

Brewer-Boydston, Ginny. *Good Queen Mothers, Bad Queen Mothers: The Theological Presentation of the Queen Mother in 1 and 2 Kings*. CBQMS 54. Washington, DC: Catholic Biblical Association of America, 2016.

Brichto, Herbert Chanan. *The Problem of "Curse" in the Hebrew Bible*. Corrected repr. JBLMS 13. Atlanta: Society of Biblical Literature, 1968.

Brigden, Susan. *New Worlds, Lost Worlds: The Rule of the Tudors, 1485–1603*. New York: Viking, 2001.

Bright, John. *A History of Israel*. Philadelphia: Fortress, 1959.

–. *Jeremiah: A New Translation with Introduction and Commentary*. AB 21. Garden City, NY: Doubleday, 1965.

Brinkman, John A. *Prelude to Empire: Babylonian Society and Politics, 747–626 B.C.* OPBF 7. Philadelphia: Babylonian Fund, University Museum, 1984.

Brooks, Beatrice A. "Fertility Cult Functionaries in the Old Testament." *JBL* 60 (1941): 227–53.

Brown, Raymond E. *The Birth of the Messiah: A Commentary on the Infancy Narratives in Matthew and Luke*. Garden City, NY: Doubleday, 1977.

Brown, Sally. "2 Kings 23:1–20." *Int* 60 (2006): 68–70.

Brueggemann, Walter. *1 & 2 Kings*. SHBC 8. Macon, GA: Smyth & Helwys, 2000.

–. *Truth Speaks to Power: The Countercultural Nature of Scripture*. Louisville: Westminster John Knox, 2013. https://doi.org/10.1111/rsr.12937

Brueggemann, Walter, and Davis Hankins. "The Affirmation of Prophetic Power and Deconstruction of Royal Authority in the Elisha Narratives." *CBQ* 76 (2014): 58–76.

Bruit Zaidman, Louise, and Pauline Schmitt Pantel. *Religion in the Ancient Greek City*. Translated by Paul Cartledge. Cambridge: Cambridge University Press, 1992. https://doi.org/10.1017/s0963926800010749

Brunet, Adrien-M. "Le Chroniste et ses Sources." *RB* 61 (1954): 349–86.

Budin, Stephanie L. "A Reconsideration of the Aphrodite-Ashtart Syncretism." *Numen* 51 (2004): 95–145. https://doi.org/10.1163/156852704323056643

Burkert, Walter. *Greek Religion*. Cambridge, MA: Harvard University Press, 1985.

Burkitt, Francis C. "The Code Found in the Temple." *JBL* 40 (1921): 166–67.

Busink, Theodor A. *Der Tempel von Jerusalem von Salomo bis Herodes: Eine archäologische Studie unter Berücksichtigung des westsemitischen Tempelbaus*. SFSMD 3. Leiden: Brill, 1970–1980.

Buttenweiser, Moses. *The Psalms: Chronologically Treated with a New Translation*. Chicago: University of Chicago Press, 1938.
Butting, Klara. *Prophetinnen gefragt: Die Bedeutung der Prophetinnen im Kanon aus Tora und Prophetie*. ERH 3. Wittingen: Erev-Rav, 2001.
Butts, Barbara, and Lee Hendrix. *Painting on Light: Drawings and Stained Glass in the Age of Dürer and Holbein*. Los Angeles: J. Paul Getty Trust, 2000. https://doi.org/10.3202/caa.reviews.2001.70
Cahill, Thomas. *The Gifts of the Jews: How a Tribe of Desert Nomads Changed the Way Everyone Thinks and Feels*. New York: Anchor Books, 1998. https://doi.org/10.1097/00005053-199907000-00017
Cantù, Cesare. *Storia Universale*. Turin: Unione Tipografico-Editrice, 1862.
Cariello, Sergio. *The Action Bible: God's Redemptive Story*. Edited by Doug Mauss. Colorado Springs, CO: David C. Cook, 2010.
Carlson, Laurie Winn. *Cattle: An Informal Social History*. Chicago: Ivan R. Dee, 2001.
Carroll, Robert P. *Jeremiah: A Commentary*. OTL. Philadelphia: Westminster, 1986.
Cassuto, Umberto. *The Goddess Anath: Canaanite Epics of the Patriarchal Age*. Translated by Israel Abrahams. Jerusalem: Magnes, 1971. https://doi.org/10.1093/jts/xxvi.1.125
Castelli, Silvia. "Kings in Josephus." Pages 541–59 in *The Books of Kings: Sources, Composiiton, Historiography, and Reception*. Edited by André Lemaire and Baruch Halpern. TSup 129. Atlanta: Society of Biblical Literature, 2010. https://doi.org/10.5508/jhs.2017.v17.r21
Cathcart, Kevin J. "Nahum, Book of." *ABD* 4.998–1000.
Caviness, Madeline Harrison. *The Early Stained Glass of Canterbury Cathedral circa 1175-1220*. Princeton: Princeton University Press, 1977. https://doi.org/10.2307/3164899
Chalcraft, David J. "Sociology and the Book of Chronicles: Risk, Ontological Security, Moral Panics, and Types of Narrative." Pages 201–27 in *What Was Authoritative for Chronicles?* Edited by Ehud Ben Zvi and Diana V. Edelman. Winona Lake, IN: Eisenbrauns, 2011. https://doi.org/10.1515/olzg-2015-0165
Charlesworth, James H. "Baruch, Book of 2 (Syriac)." *ABD* 1.620–21.
Châtillon, Jean. "La Bible dans les écoles du XIIe siècle." Pages 163–97 in *Le Moyan Age et la Bible*. Edited by Pierre Riché and Guy Lobrichon. BTT 4. Paris: Beauchesne, 1984. https://doi.org/10.2307/3165429
Chen, Ching-Wen. "The Asylum Cities: A Reconsideration." *TwnJTh* 20 (1998): 103–22.
Cheyne, Thomas Kelley. *The Decline and Fall of the Kingdom of Judah*. London: Black, 1908.
Child, Isabella. *The Child's Picture Bible*. New York: J.Q. Preble, 1855.
Childs, Brevard S. *The Book of Exodus: A Critical, Theological Commentary*. OTL. Louisville: Westminster John Knox, 1994.
Christensen, Duane L. "Huldah and the Men of Anathoth: Women in Leadership in the Deuteronomistic History." *SBLSP* 23 (1984): 399–404.
–. *Transformations of the War Oracle in Old Testament Prophecy: Studies in the Oracles Against the Nations*. HDR 3. Missoula, MT: Scholars Press, 1975.
–. "Zephaniah 2:4-15: A Theological Basis for Josiah's Program of Political Expansion." *CBQ* 46 (1984): 669–82.
Christiansen, Birgit, and Elena Devecchi. "Die hethitischen Vasallenverträge und die biblische Bundeskonzeption." *BN* 156 (2013): 63–87.

Chrysikopoulos, Vassilis I. "The Statue of Padihor, General of the Army of Psammetichus I, at the National Archaeological Museum of Athens." Pages 157–68 in *Moving across Borders: Foreign Relations, Religion and Cultural Interactions in the Ancient Mediterranean*. Edited by Panagiotis Kousoulis and Konstantinos Magliveras. OLA 159. Leuven: Peeters, 2007.

Chun, S. Min. *Ethics and Biblical Narrative: A Literary and Discourse-Analytical Approach to the Story of Josiah*. OTRM. Oxford: Oxford University Press, 2014. https://doi.org/10.1093/acprof:oso/9780199688968.001.0001

Chuzho, Husazulu. "Women as Agents of Transformation." *UBS Journal* 4, no. 1 (2005): 43–56.

Claburn, W. Eugene. "The Fiscal Basis of Josiah's Reforms." *JBL* 92 (1973): 11–22.

Clark, Mark J. *The Making of the* Historia scholastica, *1150–1200*. Mediaeval Law and Theology 7. TS 198. Toronto: Pontifical Institute of Medieval Studies, 2015. https://doi.org/10.1086/703908

Clark, Stuart. *Thinking with Demons: The Idea of Witchcraft in Early Modern Europe*. Oxford: Oxford University, 1997.

Clements, Ronald E. "Deuteronomy and the Jerusalem Cult Tradition." *VT* 15 (1965): 300–312.

–. "A Dialogue with Gordon McConville on Deuteronomy: I. The Origins of Deuteronomy: What Are the Clues?" *SJT* 56 (2003): 508–16. https://doi.org/10.1017/s0036930603211212

–. *Isaiah 1–39*. NCB. Grand Rapids: Eerdmans, 1980.

Cochell, Trevor. "The Religious Establishments of Jeroboam I." *SCJ* 8 (2005): 85–97.

Cogan, Mordecai [Morton]. *1 Kings: A New Translation with Introduction and Commentary*. AB 10. New York: Doubleday, 2001.

–. *Imperialism and Religion: Assyria, Judah and Israel in the Eighth and Seventh Centuries B.C.E.* SBLMS 19. Missoula, MT: Scholars Press, 1974.

–. "A Slip of the Pen? On Josiah's Actions in Samaria (2 Kings 23:15–20)." Pages 3–8 in Sefer Moshe: *The Moshe Weinfeld Jubilee Volume: Studies in the Bible and the Ancient Near East, Qumran, and Post-Biblical Judaism*. Edited by Chaim Cohen, Avi Hurvitz, and Shalom M. Paul. Winona Lake, IN: Eisenbrauns, 2004. https://doi.org/10.1086/671437

Cogan, Mordecai, and Hayim Tadmor. *II Kings: A New Translation with Introduction and Commentary*. AB 11. Garden City: Doubleday, 1988.

Cohn, Robert L. "Characterization in Kings." Pages 89–105 in *The Books of Kings: Sources, Composiiton, Historiography, and Reception*. Edited by André Lemaire and Baruch Halpern. VTSup 129. Atlanta: Society of Biblical Literature, 2010. https://doi.org/10.5508/jhs.2017.v17.r21

–. *2 Kings*. Berit Olam. Collegeville, MN: Liturgical Press, 2000.

Collins, John J. *The Bible after Babel: Historical Criticism in a Postmodern Age*. Grand Rapids: Eerdmans, 2005.

–. "Death, the Afterlife, and Other Last Things: Israel." Pages 480–83 in *Religions of the Ancient World: A Guide*. Edited by Sarah Iles Johnston. Cambridge, MA: Belknap, 2004.

Conrad, Diethelm. "Der Gott Reschef." *ZAW* 83 (1971): 157–83.

Conti, Marco, ed. *1–2 Kings, 1–2 Chronicles, Ezra, Nehemiah, Esther*. ACCSOT 5. Downers Grove, IL: InterVarsity Press, 2008.

Cook, Gregory D. "Naqia and Nineveh in Nahum: Ambiguity and the Prostitute Queen." *JBL* 136 (2017): 895–904. https://doi.org/10.15699/jbl.1364.2017.198627

Cook, Stanley Arthur. "Biblical Criticism 'Moderate' and 'Advanced.'" *JQR* 20 (1907): 158–65.

—. "The 'Evolution' of Biblical Religion." *ModC* 24 (1934): 471–84.

—. "Josiah." *EncBrit*[11] 15.520.

—. "Kings, First and Second Books of." *EncBrit*[11] 15.810–15.

—. *Samuel to the Captivity*. Vol. 2 of *Lectures on the History of the Jewish Church*. New Edition. New York: Scribner's Sons, 1901.

Cook, Stephen L. "Death, Kinship, and Community: Afterlife and the חסד ideal in Israel." Pages 106–21 in *The Family in Life and Death: The Family in Ancient Israel: Sociological and Archaeological Perspectives*. Edited by Patricia Dutcher-Walls. LHBOTS 504. New York: T&T Clark, 2009. https://doi.org/10.1111/j.1467-9418.2010.00629.x

Cornell, Collin, "Cult Statuary in the Judean Temple at Yeb." *JSJ* 47 (2016): 291–309. https://doi.org/10.1163/15700631-12340446

Cortese, Enzo. "I tentative di una teologia (Cristiana) dell'Antico Testamento." *LASBF* 56 (2006): 9–28. https://doi.org/10.1484/j.la.2.303636

Cragg, G. R. *The Church and the Age of Reason*. Pelican History of the Church 4. Baltimore: Penguin Books, 1970.

Crain, Jeanie C. *Reading the Bible as Literature: An Introduction*. Cambridge: Polity, 2010.

Crenshaw, James L. *Ecclesiastes: A Commentary*. OTL. Philadelphia: Westminster, 1987.

—. *Education in Ancient Israel: Across the Deadening Silence*. ABRL. New York: Doubleday, 1998.

Cross, Frank Moore. *Canaanite Myth and Hebrew Epic: Essays in the History of the Religion of Israel*. Cambridge, MA: Harvard University Press, 1973. https://doi.org/10.1086/ahr/79.4.1149

Cross, Frank Moore, and David Noel Freedman. "Josiah's Revolt against Assyria." *JNES* 12 (1953): 56–58.

Crouch, Carly L., "Funerary Rites for Infants and Children in the Hebrew Bible in Light of Ancient Near Eastern Practice." Pages 15–26 in *Feasts and Festivals*. Edited by Christopher Tuckett. CBET 53. Leuven: Peeters, 2009.

—. *Israel and the Assyrians: Deuteronomy, the Succession Treaty of Esarhaddon, and the Nature of Subversion*. SBLANEM 8. Atlanta: Society of Biblical Literature, 2014. https://doi.org/10.2307/j.ctt1287mx4

Cruz, Hieronomous. "Centralisation of Cult by Josiah: A Biblical Persepctive in Relation to Globalisation." *Jeevadhora* 55 (1995): 65–71.

Cuffey, Kenneth H. "Tibni." *ABD* 6.550–51.

Cunchillos, Jesus Luis. *Cuando los angeles eran dioses*. Salamanca: Universidad Pontificia, 1976.

—. "Étude philologique de *mal'ak*: Perspectives sur le *mal'ak* de la divinité dans la Bible hébraïque." Pages 30–51 in *Congress Volume: Vienna, 1980*. Edited by John A. Emerton. VTSup 32. Leiden: Brill, 1981. https://doi.org/10.1163/9789004275553_004

Dahl, Gudrun, and Anders Hjurt. *Having Herds: Pastoral Herd Growth and Household Economy*. SSSA 2. Stockholm: University of Stockholm Press, 1976. https://doi.org/10.1525/aa.1979.81.2.02a00670

Dahood, Mitchell. "Ancient Semitic Deities in Syria and Palestine." Pages 65–94 in *Le Antiche Divinita Semitiche*. Edited by Sabatino Moscati. Rome: Centro di Studi Semitici, 1958.

Dalley, Stephanie. "Near Eastern Patron Deities of Mining and Smelting in the Late

Bronze and Early Iron Ages." Pages 61–66 in *Report of the Department of Antiquities, Cyprus, 1987*. Nicosia: Zavallis, 1987.

Dandamayev, Mukhammed A. "State and Temple in Babylonia in the First Millennium B.C." Pages 589–96 in *State and Temple Economy in the Ancient Near East*. Vol. 2. Edited by Edward Lipinski. OLA 6. Leuven: Depertement Orientalistiek, 1979.

Da Riva, Rocio. "Dynastic Gods and Favourite Gods in the Neo-Babylonian Period." Pages 45–61 in *Concepts of Kingship in Antiquity: Proceedings of the European Science Foundation Exploratory Workshop: Held in Padova, November 28th–December 1st, 2007*. Edited by Giovanni B. Lanfranchi and Robert Rollinger. HANE/M 11. Padua: S.A.R.G.O.N. Editrice e Libereria, 2010.

Davies, Philip R. "1 Samuel and the 'Deuteronomistic History.'" Pages 105–18 in *Is Samuel among the Deuteronomists? Current Views on the Place of Samuel in a Deuteronomistic History*. Edited by Cynthia Edenburg and Juha Pakkala. AIL 16. Atlanta: Society of Biblical Literature, 2013. https://doi.org/10.2307/j.ctt5hjh2n

–. *In Search of 'Ancient Israel'*. JSOTSup 148. Sheffield: Sheffield Academic, 1995.

–. "Josiah and the Law Book." Pages 65–77 in *Good Kings and Bad Kings*. Edited by Lester L. Grabbe. LHBOTS 393. ESHM 5. London: T&T Clark, 2005.

–. "Urban Religion and Rural Religion." Pages 104–17 in *Religious Diversity in Ancient Israel and Judah*. Edited by Francesca Stavrakopoulou and John Barton. London: T&T Clark, 2010.

Day, Edward. "The Promulgation of Deuteronomy." *JBL* 21 (1902): 197–213.

Day, John. "Asherah." *ABD* 1.483–87.

–. "Asherah in the Hebrew Bible and Northwest Semitic Literature." *JBL* 105 (1986): 385–408. https://doi.org/10.2307/3260509

–. *Molech: A God of Human Sacrifice in the Old Testament*. UCOP 41. Cambridge: Cambridge University Press, 1989. https://doi.org/10.1017/s0036930600037509

Dearman, J. Andrew. *Religion and Culture in Ancient Israel*. Peabody, MA: Hendrickson, 1992.

Deenick, Karl. "Priest and King: Or Priest-King in 1 Samuel 2:35." *WTJ* 73 (2011): 325–39.

Deist, Ferdinand E. "Conservative Rebound in Deuteronomy: A Case Study in Social Values." *JNSL* 22 (1996): 17–30.

Delamarter, Steve. "The Death of Josiah in Scripture and Tradition: Wrestling with the Problems of Evil?" *VT* 54 (2004): 29–60. https://doi.org/10.1163/156853304772932924

Delcor, Matthias. "Les cultes éstrangers en Israël au moment de la réforme de Josias d'après 2R 23: D'Étude de religions sémitiques compares." Pages 91–123 in *Mélanges bibliques et orientaux en l'honneur de M. Henri Cazelles*. Edited by André Caquot and Matthias Delcor. AOAT 212. Kevelaer: Butzon & Bercker; Neukirchen-Vluyn: Neukirchener, 1981. https://doi.org/10.1163/157006386x00167

Delgado, Mariano. "Die Gewaltfrage im interreligiösen Dialog." *Zeitschrift für Missionswissenschaft und Religionswissenschaft* 99 (2015): 3–4.

Delumeau, Jean. *Catholicism between Luther and Voltaire: A New View of the Counter-Reformation*. Translated by Jeremy Moiser. London: Burns & Oates, 1977. https://doi.org/10.1017/s0360966900016303

Dempster, Stephen. "'A Light in a Dark Place': A Tale of Two Kings and Theological Interpretation of the Old Testament." *SBJT* 14, no. 2 (2010): 18–26.

Dever, William G. *Did God Have a Wife? Archaeology and Folk Religion in Ancient Israel*. Grand Rapids: Eerdmans, 2005. https://doi.org/10.5508/jhs.2006.v6.r27

–. "Folk Religion in Ancient Israel: The Disconnect between Text and Artifact." Pages 425–39 in *Berührungspunkte: Studien zur Sozial- und Religionsgeschichte Israels und seiner Umwelt: Festschrift für Rainer Albertz zu seinem 65. Geburtstag*. Edited by Ingo Kottsieper, Rüdiger Schmitt, and Jakob Wöhrle. AOAT 350. Münster: Ugarit, 2008. https://doi.org/10.1515/9783110897005

–. *The Lives of Ordinary People in Ancient Israel: Where Archaeology and the Bible Intersect*. Grand Rapids: Eerdmans, 2013. https://doi.org/10.5508/jhs.2013.v13.r32

–. *Recent Archaeological Discoveries and Biblical Research*. Seattle: University of Washington Press, 1990.

–. "The Silence of the Text: An Archaeological Commentary on 2 Kings 23." Pages 143–68 in *Scripture and Other Artifacts: Essays on the Bible and Archaeology in Honour of Philip J. King*. Edited by Michael D. Coogan, J. Cheryl Exum, and Lawrence E. Stager. Louisville: Westminster John Knox, 1994. https://doi.org/10.2307/3210504

Dexinger, Ferdinand. "Limits of Tolerance in Judaism: The Samaritan Example." Pages 88–114 in *Jewish and Christian Self-Definition*. Vol. 2 of *Aspects of Judaism in the Greco-Roman Period*. Edited by E. P. Sanders. Philadelphia: Fortress, 1981. https://doi.org/10.1017/s0360966900022787

Dickason, Olive P. *The Myth of the Savage: And the Beginnings of French Colonialism in the Americas*. Edmonton: University of Alberta Press, 1997. https://doi.org/10.1086/ahr/90.4.1000-a

Dickinson, Colby. "Canons and Canonicity: Late Modern Reflections on Cultural and Religious Canonical Texts." *ASE* 30 (2013): 369–92.

Dietler, Michael. "Feasts and Commensal Politics in the Political Economy: Food, Power and Status in Prehistoric Europe." Pages 87–125 in *Food and the Status Quest: An Interdisciplinary Perspective*. Edited by Polly Wiessner and Wulf Schiefenhövel. AFN 1. Providence: Berghahn Books, 1996.

Dietrich, Manfred, Oswald Loretz, and Joaquín Sanmartín. "Die ugaritischen Totengeister *rpu(m)* und die biblischen Rephaim." *UF* 8 (1976): 45–52.

Dietrich, Walter. "Josia und das Gesetzbuch (2 Reg. XXII)." *VT* 27 (1977): 13–35. https://doi.org/10.1163/156853377x00023

Di Lella, Alexander A. "Wisdom of Ben-Sira." *ABD* 6.931–45.

Dion, Paul-Eugène. "La Religion des papyrus d'Éléphantine: un reflet de Juda d'avant l'exil." Pages 243–54 in *Kein Land für sich allein: Studien zum Kulturkontakt in Kanaan, Israel/Palästina und Ebirnâri für Manfred Weippert zum 65. Geburtstag*. Edited by Ulrich Hübner and Ernst Axel Knauf. OBO 186. Freiburg: Universitätsverlag; Göttingen: Vandenhoeck & Ruprecht, 2002. https://doi.org/10.1086/498369

Dobbins, Frank. "Music in French Theatre of the Late Sixteenth Century." *EMH* 13 (1994): 85–122. https://doi.org/10.1017/s0261127900001315

Donagay, Thomas. *The Catholic Children's Bible*. St. Joseph Junior Books. Totowa, NJ: Catholic Book Publishing, 2005.

Doubleday, Simon R. *The Wise King: A Christian Prince, Muslim Spain, and the Birth of the Renaissance*. New York: Basic Books, 2015.

Douglas, Mary. *In the Active Voice*. London: Routledge, 1982.

Driver, Samuel Rolles. *The Book of Exodus*. Cambridge Bible for Schools and Colleges. Cambridge: Cambridge University Press, 1918.

Droge, Arthur J. "'The Lying Pens of the Scribes': Of Holy Books and Pious Frauds." *MTSR* 15 (2003): 117–47.

Duffy, Eamon, *The Stripping of the Altars: Traditional Religion in England 1400–1580*. New Haven: Yale University, 1992. https://doi.org/10.2307/4051332
Durant, Will. *Our Oriental Heritage*. The Story of Civilization 1. New York: Simon and Schuster, 1954.
Dushek, Jan. "Mt. Gerizim Sanctuary, Its History and Enigma of Origin." *HBAI* 3 (2014): 111–33. https://doi.org/10.1628/219222714X13994465496749
Eakin, Frank E., Jr. "Yahwism and Baalism before the Exile." *JBL* 84 (1965): 407–14. https://doi.org/10.2307/3264867
Edelman, Diana V. "Cultic Sites and Complexes beyond the Jerusalem Temple." Pages 82–103 in *Religious Diversity in Ancient Israel and Judah*. Edited by Francesca Stavrakopoulou and John Barton. London: T&T Clark, 2010. https://doi.org/10.4324/9781315710891
–. "From Prophets to Prophetic Books: The Fixing of the Divine Word." Pages 29–54 in *The Production of Prophecy: Constructing Prophecy and Prophets in Yehud*. Edited by Diana V. Edelman and Ehud Ben Zvi. BibleWorld. London: Equinox, 2009.
–. "God Rhetoric: Reconceptualizing YHWH Sebaot as YHWH Elohim in the Hebrew Bible." Pages 81–107 in *A Palimpest: Rhetoric, Ideology, Stylistics, and Language Relating to Persian Israel*. Edited by E. Ben Zvi, D. V. Edelman, and F. Polak. PHSC 5. Piscataway, NJ: Gorgias, 2009. https://doi.org/10.31826/9781463216740-007
–. "Hezekiah's Alleged Cultic Centralization." *JSOT* 32 (2008): 395–434.
–. "Huldah the Prophet—of Yahweh or Asherah?" Pages 231–50 in *A Feminist Companion to Samuel and Kings*. Edited by Athalya Brenner. FCB 5. Sheffield: Sheffield Academic, 1994.
–. *The Origins of the 'Second' Temple: Persian Imperial Policy and the Rebuilding of Jerusalem*. BibleWorld. London: Equinox, 2005. https://doi.org/10.5508/jhs.2007.v7.r12
–. "Solomon's Adversaries Hadad, Rezon and Jeroboam: A Trio of 'Bad Guy' Characters Illustrating the Theology of Immediate Retribution." Pages 166–91 in *The Pitcher Is Broken: Memorial Essays in Honor of Gösta W. Ahlström*. Edited by Steven W. Holloway and Lowell K. Handy. JSOTS 190. Sheffield: Sheffield Academic, 1995. https://doi.org/10.1086/468675
Edenburg, Cynthia. "From Covenant to Connubium: Persian Period Developments in the Perception of Covenant in the Deuteronomistic History." Pages 131–49 in *Covenant in the Persian Period: From Genesis to Chronicles*. Edited by Richard J. Bautch and Gary N. Knoppers. Winona Lake, IN: Eisenbrauns, 2015. https://doi.org/10.1515/olzg-2017-0047
Ehrlich, Theodore D. "The Disappearance of the Ark of the Covenant." *JBQ* 40 (2012): 174–78.
Ehrstine, Glenn. *Theater, Culture, and Community in Reformation Bern: 1523–1555*. SMRT 85. Leiden: Brill, 2002. https://doi.org/10.1017/s002204690384719x
Eissfeldt, Otto, *The Old Testament: An Introduction*. Translated by P. R. Ackroyd. New York: Harper & Row, 1965.
Elayi, Josette. *Sennacherib, King of Assyria*. ABS 24. Atlanta: Society of Biblical Literature, 2018.
Eliav, Yaron Z. *God's Mountain: The Temple Mount in Time, Place, and Memory*. Baltimore: Johns Hopkins University, 2005.
Elkins, Stephen. *Children in the Bible*. Word&Song, Greatest Bible Stories Ever Told 9. Nashville: Broadman and Holman, 2002.

Ellis, Richard S. *Foundation Deposits in Ancient Mesopotamia*. YNER 2. New Haven: Yale University Press, 1968.

Emerton, John A. "The Biblical High Place in the Light of Recent Study." *PEQ* 129 (1997): 116–32.

—. "New Light on Israelite Religion: The Implications of the Inscriptions from Kuntillet Ajrud." *ZAW* 94 (1982): 2–20. https://doi.org/10.1515/zatw.1982.94.1.2

Emmerson, Grace I. *Hosea: An Israelite Prophet in Judean Perspective*. JSOTSup 28. Sheffield: JSOT Press, 1984.

—. "Women in Ancient Israel." Pages 371–94 in *The World of Ancient Israel: Sociological, Anthropological and Political Perspectives*. Edited by Roland E. Clements. Cambridge: Cambridge University Press, 1989.

Engnell, Ivan. *A Rigid Scrutiny: Critical Essays on the Old Testament*. Nashville: Vanderbilt, 1969.

—. *Studies in Divine Kingship in the Ancient Near East*. Oxford: Blackwell, 1967.

Erickson, Lois Nordling. *Huldah*. Hagerstown, MD: Review and Herald, 1991.

Esler, Philip F. "Prototypes, Antitypes and Social Identity in *First Clement*: Outlining a New Interpretive Model." *ASE* 24 (2007): 125–46.

Evans, Carl D. "Jeroboam 1." *ABD* 3.742–45.

Eynikel, Erik. *The Reform of King Josiah and the Composition of the Deuteronomistic History*. OtSt 33. Leiden: Brill, 1996.

—. "The Reform of King Josiah 2 Kings 23:1–24." Pages 394–425 in *Die Septuaginta—Texte, Kontexte, Lebenswelten: Internatinale Fachtagung veranstaltet von Septuaginta Deutsch (LXX.D), Wuppertal 20.-23. Juli 2006*. Edited by Martin Karrer and Wolfgang Kraus. WUNT 219. Tübingen: Mohr Siebeck, 2008. https://doi.org/10.5840/mayeutica2008347725

Faure, Bernard. *The Fluid Pantheon*. Vol. 1 of *Gods of Medieval Japan*. Honolulu: University of Hawai'i Press, 2016.

—. *Protectors and Predators*. Vol. 2 of *Gods of Medieval Japan*. Honolulu: University of Hawai'i Press, 2016.

Faust, Avraham. "The Shephelah in the Iron Age: A New Look on the Settlement of Judah." *PEQ* 145 (2013): 203–29.

Feinman, Peter. *Jerusalem Throne Games: The Battle of Bible Stories after the Death of David*. Oxford: Oxbow, 2017. https://doi.org/10.2307/j.ctt1v2xtf0

Feldman, Louis H. "Josephus' Portrait of Josiah." *LS* 18 (1993): 110–30.

Felton, Debbie. *Haunted Greece and Rome: Ghost Stories from Classical Antiquity*. Austin: University of Texas Press, 1999.

Finegan, Jack. *Handbook of Biblical Chronology: Principles of Time Reckoning in the Ancient World and Problems of Chronology in the Bible*. Rev. ed. Peabody, MA: Hendrickson, 1998. https://doi.org/10.2307/3264077

Finkelstein, Israel. "The Archaeology of the Days of Manasseh." Pages 169–87 in *Scripture and Other Artifacts: Essays on the Bible and Archaeology in Honour of Philip J. King*. Edited by Michael D. Coogan, J. Cheryl Exum, and Lawrence E. Stager. Louisville: Westminster John Knox, 1994. https://doi.org/10.2307/3210504

—. "The Expansion of Judah in II Chronicles: Territorial Legitimation for the Hasmoneans?" *ZAW* 127 (2015): 669–95. https://doi.org/10.1515/zaw-2015-0035

—. *The Forgotten Kingdom: The Archaeology and History of Northern Israel*. SBLANEM 5. Atlanta: Society of Biblical Literature, 2013.

—. "A Great United Monarchy? Archaeological and Historical Perspectives." Pages 3–28 in *One God—One Cult—One Nation: Archaeological and Biblical Perspectives*.

Edited by Reinhard G. Kratz and Hermann Spieckermann. BZAW 405. Berlin: de Gruyter, 2010. https://doi.org/10.1515/9783110223583.1
–. *Hasmonean Realities behind Ezra, Nehemiah, and Chronicles: Archaeological and Historical Perspectives*. AIL 34. Atlanta: Society of Biblical Literature, 2018. https://doi.org/10.2307/j.ctv5jxq51
–. "Rehoboam's Fortified Cities (II Chr 11,5–12): A Hasmonean Reality?" *ZAW* 123 (2011): 92–107. https://doi.org/10.1515/zaw.2011.007
–. "State Formation in Israel and Judah: A Contrast in Context, A Contrast in Trajectory." *NEArch* 62 (1999): 35–52. https://doi.org/10.2307/3210721
Finkelstein, Israel, and Neil Asher Silberman. *The Bible Unearthed: Archaeology's New Vision of Ancient Israel and the Origin of Its Sacred Texts*. New York: Free Press, 2001. https://doi.org/10.1111/j.1949-3606.2001.tb00429.x
Finsterbusch, Karin. "Modelle schriftgestützten religiösen Lehrens und Lernens in der Hebräischen Bibel." *BZ* 52 (2008): 223–41.
Finucane, Ronald C. *Ghosts: Appearances of the Dead and Cultural Transformation*. Amherst, NY: Prometheus Books, 1996.
Fischer, Andreas. "'The Most Disreputable Camera in the World': Spirit Photography in the United Kingdom in the early Twentieth Century." Pages 72–91 in *The Perfect Medium: Photography and the Occult*. Edited by Jean-Loup Champion. Translated by Trista Selous. New Haven: Yale University Press, 2004.
Fishbane, Michael. *Biblical Interpretation in Ancient Israel*. Oxford: Clarendon, 1985.
Flower, Michael Attyah. *The Seer in Ancient Greece*. Berkeley: University of California Press, 2008. https://doi.org/10.1111/j.1540-6563.2010.00267_50.x
Foakes-Jackson, Frederick John. *The Biblical History of the Hebrews to the Christian Era*. 3rd enlarged edition. New York: George H. Doran, 1920.
Focken, Friedrich-Emanuel. "Joschijas Gesetzesschrift: Eine literarkritische und redaktionsgeschichtliche Analyse von 2Kön 22,1–23,3; 23,21–30." *BN* 163 (2014): 25–43.
Fohrer, Georg. *History of Israelite Religion*. Translated by David E. Green. Nashville: Abingdon, 1972.
–. "Der Vertrag zwischen König und Volk in Israel." Pages 330–51 in *Studien zur alttestamentliche Theologie und Geschichte (1949–1966)*. Berlin: de Gruyter, 1969. https://doi.org/10.1515/9783110827095-019
Fontaine, Carole R. "Josiah." *WB*[2018] 11.169.
Fontaine, Nicolas. *The History of the Old and New Testament, Extracted out of Sacred Scripture and Writings of the Fathers: To Which Are Added the Lives, Travels and Sufferings of the Apostles: with a Large and Exact Historical Chronology of All the Affairs and Actions Related in the Bible*. 2nd corrected ed. London: S. and J. Sprint, C. Brome, J. Nicholson, J. Pero, and Benj. Tooke, 1699.
Fournié, Eléonore. *L'iconographie de la Bible historiale*. RILMA 2. Turnhout: Brepols, 2012.
Frankena, Rintje. "The Vassal-Treaties of Esarhaddon and the Dating of Deuteronomy." *OtSt* 14 (1965): 122–54.
Freed, Alexander. "The Code Spoken of in II Kings 22–23." *JBL* 40 (1921): 76–81.
Freedman, David Noel. "Between God and Man: Prophets in Ancient Israel." Pages 57–87 in *Prophecy and Prophets*. Edited by Yehoshua Gitay. SemeiaSt. Atlanta: Scholars Press, 1997.
–. "Yahweh of Samaria and His Asherah." *BA* 50 (1987): 241–49.

Fretheim, Terence E. *First and Second Kings*. WBCom. Louisville: Westminster John Knox, 1999.
–. *What Kind of God? Collected Essays of Terence Fretheim*. Edited by Michael J. Chan. SLTHS 14. Winona Lake, IN: Eisenbrauns, 2015. https://doi.org/10.5508/jhs.2017.v17.r30
Fried, Lisbeth S. "The High Places and the Reforms of Hezekiah and Josiah: An Archaeological Investigation." *JAOS* 122 (2002): 437–65. https://doi.org/10.2307/3087515
Friedman, Richard Elliott. *Who Wrote the Bible?* New York: HarperSanFrancisco, 1997.
Friedman, Richard Elliott, and Shawna Dolansky Overton. "Death and Afterlife: The Biblical Silence." Pages 35–59 in *Judaism in Late Antiquity. Part 4: Where We Stand: Issues and Debates in Ancient Judaism. Volume One*. Edited by Alan Avery-Peck and Jacob Neusner. HdO 1 49/4. Leiden: Brill, 2000. https://doi.org/10.1163/9789004294059_001
Frisch, Amos. "Comparison with David as a Means of Evaluating Character in the Book of Kings." *JHS* 11 (2001). https://doi.org/10.5508/jhs.2011.v11.a7
Frost, Stanley Brice. "The Death of Josiah: A Conspiracy of Silence." *JBL* 87 (1968): 369–82.
Frymer-Kensky, Tikva. *In the Wake of the Goddess: Women, Culture, and the Biblical Transformation of Pagan Myth*. New York: Free Press, 1992.
Fulco, William J. *The Canaanite God Reshep*. AOS 8. New Haven: American Oriental Society, 1976.
Fulton, Deirdre N., Yuval Gadot, Assaf Kleiman, Liora Freud, Ombi Lernau, and Oded Lipschits. "Feasting in Paradise: Feast Remains from the Iron Age Palace of Ramat Rahel and Their Implications." *BASOR* 374 (2015): 29–48. https://doi.org/10.5615/bullamerschoorie.374.0029
Gadd, C. J. *The Fall of Nineveh*. London: British Museum, 1923.
Gafney, Wilda C. *Daughters of Miriam: Women Prophets in Ancient Israel*. Minneapolis: Fortress, 2008. https://doi.org/10.1111/j.1748-0922.2008.00322_1.x
Galil, Gershon. *The Chronology of the Kings of Israel and Judah*. SHCANE 9. Leiden: Brill, 1996.
Galvin, Garrett. *David's Successors: Kingship in the Old Testament*. Collegeville, MN: Liturgical Press, 2016.
Gane, Roy. "The End of the Israelite Monarchy." *JATS* 10 (1999): 333–56.
Garbini, Giovanni. *History and Ideology in Ancient Israel*. Translated by John Bowden. New York: Crossroad, 1988. https://doi.org/10.1086/ahr/95.5.1500
Garff, Jan, ed. *Tegninger af Maerten van Heemskerck: Illustreret Katalog*. Copenhagen: Statens Museum for Kunst, 1971.
Garnsey, Peter. *Food and Society in Classical Antiquity*. KTAH. Cambridge: Cambridge University Press, 1999.
Gaß, Erasmus. "Hosea zwischen Tradition und Innovation am Beispiel von Hos 2,16f." *ZAW* 122 (2010): 169–84. https://doi.org/10.1515/zaw.2010.013
Geike, Cunningham. *Old Testament Characters*. New York: James Pott, 1885.
Gelb, Norman. *Kings of the Jews: The Origins of the Jewish Nation*. Philadelphia: Jewish Publication Society of America, 2010.
Geobey, Ronald A. "The Jeroboam Story in the (Re)Formulation of Israelite Identity: Evaluating the Literary-Ideological Purposes of 1 Kings 11–14." *JHS* 16 (2016). https://doi.org/10.5508/jhs.2016.v16.a2

Geoghegan, Jeffrey C. "The Levites and the Literature of the Late-Seventh Century." *JHS* 7 (2007): 30–41. doi:10.5508/jhs.2007.v7.a10.

Gerstenberger, Erhard S. "Persian-Empire Spirituality and the Genesis of Prophetic Books." Pages 111–30 in *The Production of Prophecy: Constructing Prophecy and Prophets in Yehud*. Edited by Diana V. Edelman and Ehud Ben Zvi. BibleWorld. London: Equinox, 2009. https://doi.org/10.4324/9781315710891

Geva, Hillel. "Western Jerusalem at the End of the First Temple Period in Light of the Excavations in the Jewish Quarter." Pages 183–208 in *Jerusalem in Bible and Archaeology: The First Temple Period*. Edited by Andrew G. Vaughn and Ann E. Killebrew. SBLSymS 18. Atlanta: Society of Biblical Literature, 2003. https://doi.org/10.1086/586679

Gillingham, Susan E. *The Poems and Psalms of the Hebrew Bible*. Oxford Bible Series. Oxford University Press, 1994. https://doi.org/10.1163/1568533972651315

Gin Lum, Kathryn. *Damned Nation: Hell in America from the Revolution to Reconstruction*. Oxford: Oxford University Press, 2014. https://doi.org/10.1093/acprof:oso/9780199843114.001.0001

Glagolev, Aleksander Aleksandovich, Archimandrite Joseph, Aleksandr Vasilievich Petrovskii, and Vladimir Petrovich Rybinskii. "Vtoraia Kniga Paralipomenon." Pages 89–196 in *Tolkovaia Biblia: ili Kommentariy na vse knigi Sv. Pisania Vetkhago I Novago Zaveta*. Edited by Aleksandr Pavlovich Lopukhin. St. Petersburg: 1904–1913. Repr. Stockholm: Institute of Bible Translation, 1987.

Glagolev, Aleksander Aleksandovich, Theodore Gerasimovich Eleonskii, Vasilii Ivanovich Protopopov, and Ivan Gavrilovich Troitskii. "Chetvertaia Kniga Tsarstv." Pages 479–582 in *Tolkovaia Biblia: ili Kommentariy na vse knigi Sv. Pisania Vetkhago I Novago Zaveta*. Edited by Aleksandr Pavlovich Lopukhin. St. Petersburg: 1904–1913. Repr. Stockholm: Institute of Bible Translation, 1987.

Glassner, Jean-Jacques. *Mesopotamian Chronicles*. Edited by Benjamin R. Foster. SBLWAW 19. Atlanta: Society of Biblical Literature, 2004.

Glatt-Gilad, David A. "Revealed and Concealed: The Status of the Law (Book) of Moses within the Deuteronomistic History." Pages 185–99 in *Mishneh Todah: Studies in Deuteronomy and Its Cultural Environment in Honor of Jeffrey H. Tigay*. Edited by Nili SacherFox, David A. Glatt-Gilad, and Michael J. Williams. Winona Lake, IN: Eisenbrauns, 2009. https://doi.org/10.1111/j.1748-0922.2010.01487_9.x

–. "The Role of Huldah's Prophecy in the Chronicler's Portrayal of Josiah's Reform." *Bib* 77 (1986): 16–31.

Goff, Beatrice L. "Syncretism in the Religion of Israel." *JBL* 58 (1939): 151–61.

Goldhill, Simon. *The Temple of Jerusalem*. Cambridge, MA: Harvard University Press, 2005.

Goldstein, Jonathan A. *II Maccabees: A New Translation with Introduction and Commentary*. AB 41A. Garden City, NY: Doubleday, 1983.

–. *Peoples of an Almighty God: Competing Religions in the Ancient World*. ABRL. New York: Doubleday, 2002.

Gomes, Jules Francis. *The Sanctuary of Bethel and the Configurations of Israelite Identity*. BZAW 368. Berlin: de Gruyter, 2006.

Goodman, William R. "Esdras, First Book of." *ABD* 2.609–11.

Goody, Jack. *Cooking, Cuisine and Class: A Study in Comparative Sociology*. TSS. Cambridge: Cambridge University Press, 1982.

Gottwald, Norman K. *The Politics of Ancient Israel*. LAI. Louisville: Westminster John Knox, 2001.

–. T*The Tribes of Yahweh: A Sociology of the Religion of Liberated Israel 1250-1050 B.C.E.* Maryknoll, NY: Orbis, 1979. https://doi.org/10.1177/030908928000501813

Grabbe, Lester L. *1 and 2 Kings: History and Story in Ancient Israel.* TTCSGOT 5. London: Bloomsbury T&T Clark, 2017.

–. *Ancient Israel: What Do We Know and How Do We Know It?* London: T&T Clark, 2007. https://doi.org/10.21697/ct.2018.88.1.10

–. "The Kingdom of Judah from Sennacherib's Invasion to the Fall of Jerusalem: If We Had only the Bible…" Pages 78–122 in *Good Kings and Bad Kings.* Edited by Lester L. Grabbe. LHBOTS 393. ESHM 5. London: T&T Clark, 2005. https://doi.org/10.1111/j.1748-0922.2008.00298_5.x

–. *Priests, Prophets, Diviners, Sages: A Socio-historical Study of Religious Specialists in Ancient Israel.* Valley Forge, PA: Trinity Press, 1995. https://doi.org/10.1177/030908929602107211

–. "Sup-urbs or only Hyp-urbs? Prophets and Populations in Ancient Israel and Socio-Historical Method." Pages 95–123 in *'Every City Shall Be Forsaken': Urbanism and Prophecy in Ancient Israel and the Near East.* Edited by Lester L. Grabbe and Robert D. Haak. JSOTSup 330. Sheffield: Sheffield Academic, 2001.

Graetz, Heinrich. *From the Earliest Period to the Death of Simon the Maccabee (135 B.C.E.).* Vol. 1 of *History of the Jews.* Philadelphia: Jewish Publication Society of America, 1891.

Grafton, Anthony T., and Urs. B. Leu. *Henricus Glareanus's (1488–1563) Chronologia of the Ancient World: A Fascsimile Edition of a Heavily Annotated Copy in Princeton University Library.* Studies in Medieval and Reformation Traditions 177. Leiden: Brill, 2014. https://doi.org/10.1163/9789004261761_002

Grant, Deena E. *Divine Anger in the Hebrew Bible.* CBQMS 52. Washington, DC: Catholic Biblical Association of America, 2014. https://doi.org/10.5508/jhs.2015.v15.r8

Grant, Robert M. *Gods and the One God.* LEC 1. Philadelphia: Westminster, 1986.

Grätz, Sebastian. "Das Bild des Königs im Dritten Esrabuch (3.Esr): Beobachtungen Zur Gesamtkonzeption des apokryphen Esrabuches." Pages 109–20 in *Israel zwischen den Mächten: Festschrift für Stefan Timm zum 65. Geburtstag.* Edited by Michael Pietsch and Freidhelm Hartenstein. AOAT 364. Münster: Ugarit, 2009.

–. "The Image of the King(s) in 1 Esdras." Pages 167–77 in *Was 1 Esdras First? An Investigation into the Priority and Nature of 1 Esdras.* Edited by Lisbeth S. Fried. AIL 7. Atlanta: Society of Biblical Literature, 2011.

Graupner, Axel. "Exodus 18,13–27: Ätiologie einer Justireform in Israel?" Pages 11–26 in *Recht und Ethos im Alten Testamen—Gestalt und Wirkung: Festschrift für Horst Seebass zum 65, Geburtstag.* Edited by Stefan Beyerle, Günter Mayer and Hans Strauß. Neukirchen-Vluyn: Neukirchener, 1999. https://doi.org/10.1515/9783110800388.127

Gray, James M. *Christian Workers' Commentary on the Old and New Testaments.* New York: Fleming H. Revell, 1915.

Gray, John. *I & II Kings: A Commentary.* OTL. 2nd ed. Philadelphia: Westminster, 1970.

Greenspahn, Frederick E. "Deuteronomy and Centralization." *VT* 64 (2014): 227–35.

Gres-Gayer, Jacques. "Un théologien gallican et l'Escriture sainte: Le 'Projet biblique' de Louis Wllies Du Pin (1657–1719)." Pages 255–75 in *Le Grand Siècle et la Bible.* Edited by Jean-Robert Armogathe. BTT 6. Paris: Beauchesne, 1989. https://doi.org/10.14375/np.9782701011561

Grohmann, Marianne. "Hulda, die Prophetin (2Kön 22,14–20)." *CV* 45 (2003): 209–16.

Grosby, Steven. *Biblical Ideas of Nationality: Ancient and Modern*. Winona Lake, IN: Eisenbrauns, 2002.

Grottanelli, Cristiano. *Kings and Prophets: Monarchic Power, Inspired Leadership, and Sacred Text in Biblical Narrative*. New York: Oxford University Press, 1999. https://doi.org/10.1086/490720

Gruen, Eric S. *Heritage and Hellenism: The Reinvention of Jewish Tradition*. HCS 30. Berkeley: University of California Press, 1998. https://doi.org/10.1086/ahr/105.2.593

Grun, Bernard. *The Timetables of History: A Horizontal Linkage of People and Events*. 4th ed. New York: Touchstone Books, 2005.

Guibbory, Achsah. "Israel and English Protestant Nationalism: 'Fast Sermons' During the English Revolution." Pages 115-38 in *Early Modern Nationalism and Milton's England*. Edited by David Loewenstein and Paul Stevens. Toronto: University of Toronto Press, 2008. https://doi.org/10.3138/9781442687943-006

Guillaume, André. *Histoir des différens peoples du monde: contenant les ceremonies religieuses et civiles, l'origine des religions, leurs sects et superstitions et les moeurs et usages de chacque nation*. Paris: Heissant le Fils, Libraire, 1771. https://doi.org/10.5479/sil.306893.39088000723049

Guillaume, Philippe. "Did Moses Die before Entering Canaan?" *ThRev* 24 (2003): 41-54.

Gulde, Stefanie Ulrike. *Der Tod als Herrscher in Ugarit und Israel*. FAT 22. Tübingen: Mohr Siebeck, 2007. https://doi.org/10.1111/j.1748-0922.2009.01362_17.x

Haak, Robert D. *Habakkuk*. VTSup 44. Leiden: Brill, 1992.

Habel, Norman C. *Yahweh versus Baal: A Conflict of Religious Cultures*. New York: Bookman, 1964.

Hackett, JoAnn. "Can a Sexist Model Liberate Us? Ancient Near Eastern 'Fertility' Goddesses." *JFSR* 5 (1989): 65-76.

Hadley, Judith M. *The Cult of Asherah in Ancient Israel and Judah: Evidence for a Hebrew Goddess*. Cambridge: Cambridge University Press, 2000. https://doi.org/10.1086/498361

Hagedorn, Anselm C. "When Did Zephaniah Become a Supporter of Josiah's Reform?" *JTS* 62 (2011): 453-75. https://doi.org/10.1093/jts/flr103

Hall, Joseph. *Contemplations of the Historical Passages of the Old and New Testaments*. 2 vols. The Christian's Family Library 3. Glasgow: Blackie and Sons, 1835.

Hallo, William W., and William Kelly Simpson. *The Ancient Near East: A History*. New York: Harcourt Brace Jovanovich, 1971.

Halpern, Baruch. "Between Elective Autocracy and Democracy: Formalizing Biblical Constitutional Theory." Pages 165-83 in *Literature as Politics, Politics as Literature: Essays on the Ancient Near East in Honor of Peter Machinist*. Edited by David S. Vanderhooft and Abraham Winitzer. Winona Lake, IN: Eisenbrauns, 2013.

–. *The First Historians: The Hebrew Bible and History*. San Francisco: Harper & Row, 1988. https://doi.org/10.1086/ahr/95.5.1500-a

–. "Why Manasseh Is Blamed for the Babylonian Exile: The Evolution of a Biblical Tradition." *VT* 48 (1998): 473-514. https://doi.org/10.1163/156853398774228417

Halpern, Baruch, and David S. Vanderhooft. "The Editions of Kings in the 7th-6th Centuries B.C.E." *HUCA* 62 (1991): 179-244.

Hamilton, Victor P. *Handbook on the Historical Books: Joshua, Judges, Ruth, Samuel, Kings, Chronicles, Ezra-Nehemiah, Esther*. Grand Rapids: Baker Academic, 2001.

Hammer, Jill. *Sisters at Sinai: New Tales of Biblical Women*. Philadelphia: Jewish Publication Society of America, 2001.

Hammond, Joseph. *The Boys and Girls of the Bible: Sermons to Children and Adults*. Vol. 1 of *Old Testament*. London: Skeffington & Son, 1898.

Hamori, Esther J. "Childless Female Diviners in the Bible and Beyond." Pages 169–91 in *Prophets Male and Female: Gender and Prophecy in the Hebrew Bible, the Eastern Medierranean, and the Ancient Near East*. Edited by Jonathan Stökl and Corrine L. Carvalho. AIL 15. Atlanta: Society of Biblical Literature, 2013. https://doi.org/10.2307/j.ctt16wdmbj.12

–. "The Prophet and the Necromancer: Women's Divination for Kings." *JBL* 132 (2013): 827–43. https://doi.org/10.1353/jbl.2013.0061

–. *Women's Divination in Biblical Literature: Prophecy, Necromancy, and Other Arts of Knowledge*. AYBRL. New Haven: Yale University Press, 2015. https://doi.org/10.2307/j.ctvggx4g3

Handy, Lowell K. *Among the Host of Heaven: The Syro-Palestinian Pantheon as Bureaucracy*. Winona Lake, IN: Eisenbrauns, 1994.

–. "The Characters of Heirs Apparent in the Book of Samuel." *BR* 38 (1993): 5–22.

–. "The Good, Bad, Insignificant, Indispensible King Josiah: A Brief Historical Survey of Josiah Studies in the Church." Pages 41–56 in *Restoring the First-Century Church in the Twenty-first Century: Essays on the Stone-Campbell Restoration Movement in Honor of Don Haymes*. Edited by Warren Lewis and Hans Rollmann. StHCWC. Eugene, OR: Wipf & Stock, 2005.

–. "Hezekiah's Unlikely Reform." *ZAW* 100 (1988): 111–15.

–. "Historical Probability and the Narrative of Josiah's Reform in 2 Kings." Pages 252–75 in *The Pitcher Is Broken: Memorial Essays for Gösta W. Ahlström*. Edited by Steven W. Holloway and Lowell. K. Handy. JSOTSup 190. Sheffield: Sheffield Academic, 1995. https://doi.org/10.1086/468675

–. *Jonah's World: Social Science and the Reading of Prophetic Story*. BibleWorld. London: Equinox, 2007. https://doi.org/10.5508/jhs.2009.v9.r34

–. "Josiah." *EDB* 471.

–. "Josiah after the Chronicler." *PEGLAMBS* 14 (1994): 95–103.

–. "Josiah and the History of the World." *BR* 62 (2017): 26–47.

–. "Josiah as Religious Peg for Persian Period Jews and Judaism." Pages 72–90 in *Religion in the Achaemenid Persian Empire: Emerging Judaisms and Trends*. Edited by Diana V. Edelman, Anne Fitzpatrick-McKinley, and Philippe Guillaume. ORA 17. Tübingen: Mohr Siebeck, 2016. https://doi.org/10.1628/978-3-16-154690-7

–. "Josiah in a New Light: Assyriology Touches the Reforming King." Pages 415–35 in *Orientalism, Assyriology and the Bible*. Edited by Steven W. Holloway. HBM 10. Sheffield: Sheffield Academic, 2006.

–. "Reading Huldah as Being a Woman." *BR* 55 (2010): 5–44.

–. "A Realignment in Heaven: An Investigation into the Ideology of the Josianic Reform." Ph.D. diss., University of Chicago, 1987.

–. "Rehabilitating Manasseh: Remembering King Manasseh in the Persian and Hellenistic Periods." Pages 221–35 in *Remembering Biblical Figures in the Late Persian and Early Hellenistic Periods: Social Memory and Imagination*. Edited by Diana V. Edelman and Ehud Ben Zvi. Oxford: Oxford University Press, 2013. https://doi.org/10.1093/acprof:oso/9780199664160.003.0011

–. "The Rise and Fall of the *sogennant* Josianic Empire." *PEGLAMBS* 21 (2001): 69–79.

–. "The Role of Huldah in Josiah's Cult Reform." *ZAW* 106 (1994): 40–53.

–. "Serpent, Bronze." *ABD* 5.1117.

–. "Sounds, Words and Meanings in Psalm 82." *JSOT* 47 (1990): 51–66.

–. "Speaking of Babies in the Temple." *PEGLAMBS* 8 (1988): 155–65.
Haran, Menahem. *Temples and Temple Service in Ancient Israel: An Inquiry into Biblical Cult Phenomena and the Historical Setting of the Priestly School*. Oxford: Clarendon, 1978. Repr. with corrections. Winona Lake, IN: Eisenbrauns, 1985. https://doi.org/10.2307/1517626
Hardacre, Helen. *Shinto and the State, 1868–1988*. StCS. Princeton: Princeton University Press, 1989. https://doi.org/10.1093/jcs/32.3.631
Hardmeier, Christof. "King Josiah in the Climax of the Deuteronomic History (2 Kings 22–23) and the Pre-Deuteronomic document of a cult reform at the place of residence (23.4–15*): Criticism of Sources, Reconstruction of Literary Pre-Stages and the Theology of History in 2 Kings 22–23." Translated by Anja-Marleen Krause. Pages 123–63 in *Good Kings and Bad Kings*. Edited by Lester L. Grabbe. LHBOTS 393. ESHM 5. London: T&T Clark, 2005. https://doi.org/10.1111/j.1748-0922.2008.00298_5.x
Harman, Chris. *A People's History of the World: From the Stone Age to the New Millennium*. London: Verso, 2008.
Harrast, Tracy L. *My Baby and Me Story Bible*. Grand Rapids: Zonderkidz, 1995.
Hastings, Selina. *The Children's Illustrated Bible*. New York: Dorling Kindersley, 2004.
Hauser, W. A. *The Fabulous Gods Denounced in the Bible: Translated from John Seldon's "Syrian Deities."* Philadelphia: Lippincott, 1880.
Hayes, John H., and Paul K. Hooker. *A New Chronology for the Kings of Israel and Judah and Its Implications for Biblical History and Literature*. Atlanta: John Knox, 1988. https://doi.org/10.2307/1518901
Hays, Christopher B. *A Covenant with Death: Death in the Iron Age II and Its Rhetorical Uses in Proto-Isaiah*. Grand Rapids: Eerdmans, 2015. https://doi.org/10.1111/rsr.12672
Healey, John F. "Mot." *DDD* cols. 1122–32.
Healey, Joseph P. "Am ha'areṣ." *ABD* 1.168–69.
Heaton, E. W. *The Hebrew Kingdoms*. NCBOT 3. London: Oxford University Press, 1968.
–. *The School Tradition of the Old Testament*. Bampton Lectures 1994. Oxford: Oxford University Press, 1994.
–. *Solomon's New Men: The Emergence of Ancient Israel as a National State*. New York: Pica, 1974.
Hehn, Johannes. *Die biblische und die babylonische Gottesidee*. Leipzig: Hinrichs, 1913.
Heider, George C. *The Cult of Molek: A Reassesment*. JSOTSup 43. Sheffield: JSOT Press, 1985.
Heltzer, Michael. "Some Questions Concerning the Economic Policy of Josiah, King of Judah." *IEJ* 50 (2000): 105–108.
Hengel, Martin. *Judaism and Hellenism: Studies in Their Encounter in Palestine during the Early Hellenistic Period*. Translated by John Bowden. Philadelphia: Fortress, 1974. https://doi.org/10.1177/004057367503200323
Henige, David. "Found but Not Lost: A Skeptical Note on the Document Discovered in the Temple under Josiah." *JHS* 7 (2007). https://doi.org/10.5508/jhs.2007.v7.a1
Hepner, Gershon. "Three's a Crowd in Shunem: Elisha's Misconduct with the Shunamite Reflects a Polemic against Prophetism." *ZAW* 122 (2010): 387–400. https://doi.org/10.1515/zaw.2010.027
Herr, Bertram. "Jhwh und die Götter: Ein Querschnitt durch die Forschung zum syrisch-palästinischen Gottesversändnis." *ZRGG* 52 (2000): 167–75. https://doi.org/10.1163/157007300x00250

Herrmann, Siegfried. *A History of Israel in Old Testament Times*. Translated by John Bowden. Philadelphia: Fortress, 1975.

Herzog, Ze'ev. "Perspectives on Southern Israel's Cult Centralization: Arad and Beer-sheba." Pages 169–99 in *One God—One Cult—One Nation: Archaeological and Biblical Perspectives*. Edited by Reinhard G. Kratz and Hermann Spieckermann. BZAW 405. Berlin: de Gruyter, 2010. https://doi.org/10.1515/9783110223583.169

Heschel, Susannah. *The Aryan Jesus: Christian Theologians and the Bible in Nazi Germany*. Princeton: Princeton University Press, 2008. https://doi.org/10.1177/004057360906600314

Hess, Richard S. *Israelite Religions: An Archaeological and Biblical Survey*. Grand Rapids: Baker Academic, 2007.

Hilber, John W. "Royal Cultic Prophecy in Assyria, Judah, and Egypt." Pages 161–86 in *"Thus Speaks Ishtar of Arbela": Prophecy in Israel, Assyria, and Egypt in the Neo-Assyrian Period*. Edited by Robert P. Gordon and Hans M. Barstad. Winona Lake, IN: Eisenbrauns, 2013. https://doi.org/10.1111/rsr.12151_9

Hillers, Delbert R. *Lamentations: A New Translation with Introduction and Commentary*. 2nd rev. ed. AB 7. New York: Doubleday, 1992.

–. *Micah*. Hermeneia. Philadelphia: Fortress, 1984.

Hobbs, R. Gerald. "Bucer's Use of King David as Mirror of the Christian Prince." *RRR* 5 (2003): 102–28.

Hobbs, T. Raymond. *2 Kings*. WBC 13. Waco, TX: Word, 1985.

Hodges, Turner. *From Solomon to the Roman Conquest*. Vol. 3 of *The Bible Story Library*. New York: Educational Book Guild, 1956.

Hoffman, Yair. "The Deuteronomistic Concept of the Herem." *ZAW* 111 (1999): 196–210.

Hoffmann, Hans-Detlef. *Reform und Reformen: Untersuchungen zu einem Grundthema der deuteronomistischen Geschichtsschreibung*. ATANT 66. Zurich: Theologische, 1980. https://doi.org/10.2307/3260761

Hold-Cavell, Barbara. "The Ethological Bases of Status Hierarchies." Pages 19–31 in *Food and the Status Quest: An Interdisciplinary Perspective*. Edited by Polly Wiessner and Wulf Schiefenhövel. AFN 1. Providence: Berghahn Books, 1996.

Hole, William B. *Old Testament History: Retold and Illustrated*. London: Eyre & Spottiswoode, 1925.

Hole, William, Mrs. *Memories of William Hole*. London: W. & R. Chambers, 1920.

Holladay, John S., Jr. "Religion in Israel and Judah under the Monarchy: An Explicitly Archaeological Approach." Pages 249–99 in *Ancient Israelite Religion*. Edited by Patrick D. Miller, Jr., Paul D. Hanson, and S. Dean McBride. Philadelphia: Fortress, 1987. https://doi.org/10.1086/487929

Holladay, William Lee. *Jeremiah 1*. Hermeneia. Philadelphia: Fortress, 1986.

Holloway, Steven W. *Aššur Is King! Aššur Is King! Religion in the Exercise of Power in the Neo-Assyrian Empire*. CHANE 10. Leiden: Brill, 2002.

–. "Introduction: Orientalism, Assyriology and the Bible." Pages 1–41 in *Orientalism, Assyriology and the Bible*. Edited by Steven W. Holloway. HBM 10. Sheffield: Sheffield Phoenix, 2006. https://doi.org/10.1515/ebr.assyriologyandbiblicalstudies

–. "Sargon II and His Redactors Repair Eanna of Uruk." *BR* 43 (1998): 22–53.

–. "Smart Mobs, Bad Crowds, Godly People and Dead Priests: Crowd Symbols in the Josianic Narrative and Some Mesopotamian Parallels." *BR* 51 (2006): 25–52.

Holm, Iva. *The Picture Bible*. Elgin, IL: David C. Cook, 1973.

Hölscher, Gustav. "Komposition und Ursprung des Deuteronomiums." *ZAW* 40 (1922): 161–255. https://doi.org/10.1515/zatw.1922.40.1.161

Hoppe, Leslie J. "The Death of Josiah and the Meaning of Deuteronomy." *LASBF* 48 (1998): 31–47.

–. "Vengeance and Forgiveness: The Two Faces of Psalm 79." Pages 1–22 in *Imagery and Imagination in Biblical Literature: Essays in Honor of Aloysius Fitzgerald, F.S.C.* Edited by Lawrence Boadt and Mark S. Smith. CBQMS 32. Washington, DC: Catholic Biblical Association of America, 2001.

Horsley, Samuel. *Biblical Criticism on the First Fourteen Historical Books of the Old Testament: Also, On the First Nine Prophetical Books.* Vol. 1. 2nd ed. London: Longman, Brown, Green, & Longmans, 1844.

Horton, Robert F. *Women of the Old Testament: Studies in Womanhood.* New York: E. R. Herrick, 1897.

Houtman, Cornelis, "Queen of Heaven." *DDD* cols. 1278–83.

Howard, David M., Jr. "David." *ABD* 2.41–49.

Hughes, Jeremy. *Secrets of the Times: Myth and History in Biblical Chronology.* JSOTSup 66. Sheffield: JSOT Press, 1990.

Hulster, Isaak de. "Figurines from Persian Period Jerusalem." *ZAW* 124 (2012): 73–88. https://doi.org/10.1515/zaw-2012-0005

Ilan, Tal. "Huldah, the Deuteronomic Prophetess of the Book of Kings." *LDif* 10, no. 1 (2010). http://www.lectio.unibe.ch/10_1/ilan.html.

Ions, Veronica. *Egyptian Mythology.* 2nd ed. London: Hamlyn, 1968.

Irwin, Brian Paul. "Baal and Yahweh in the Old Testament: A Fresh Examination of the Biblical and Extra-biblical Data." Ph.D. diss., Toronto School of Theology, 1999.

Irwin, William A. "An Objective Criterion for the Dating of Deuteronomy." *AJSL* 56 (1939): 337–49.

Ishida, Tomoo. *The Royal Dynasties in Ancient Israel: A Study of the Formation and Development of Royal-Dynastic Ideology.* BZAW 142. Berlin: de Gruyter, 1977. https://doi.org/10.1515/9783110853766

Isserlin, B. S. J. *The Israelites.* Minneapolis: Fortress, 2001.

James, Anne. *Poets, Players, and Preachers: Remembering the Gunpowder Plot in Seventeenth-Century England.* Toronto: University of Toronto, 2016. https://doi.org/10.1086/696461

Janzen, David. "The Sins of Josiah and Hezekiah: A Synchronic Reading of the Final Chapters of Kings." *JSOT* 37 (2013): 349–70.

Japhet, Sara. *I & II Chronicles: A Commentary.* OTL. Louisville: Westminster John Knox, 1993.

Jarick, John. "The Stings in the Tales of the Kings of Judah." Pages 226–36 in *Far from Minimal: Celebrating the Work and Influence of Philip R. Davies.* Edited by Duncan Burns and John William Rogerson. LHBOTS 484. London: T&T Clark, 2012.

Jensen, Kjold. "Om de moaiske Lovskrifters Alder." *DTT* 5 (1942): 1–14.

Jeon, Yong Ho. *Impeccable Solomon? A Study of Solomon's Faults in Chronicles.* Eugene, OR: Pickwick, 2013.

Jepsen, Alfred. *Die Quellen des Königsbuches.* Halle: Max Niemeyer, 1953.

Jewel, John. *View of a Seditious Bull Sent into Englande, from Pius Quintus of Rome, anno, 1569.* Pages 1128–60 in *Works of John Hewel.* Edited by John Ayre. Cambridge: Cambridge University Press, 1850.

Jirku, Anton. *Altorientalischer Kommentar zum Alten Testament*. Leipzig: A. Deichert, 1923.

Job, John Brian. *Jeremiah's Kings: A Study of the Monarchy in Jeremiah*. SOTSMS. Aldershot: Ashgate, 2006. https://doi.org/10.1177/00145246081190061109

Jöcken, Peter. *Das Buch Habakuk: Darstllung der Geschichte seiner kritischen Erforschung mit einer eigenen Beurteilung*. BBB 48. Cologne: Peter Hanstein, 1977. https://doi.org/10.1163/157006378x00157

Johnson, Norman Burrows. *Prayer in the Apocrypha and Pseudepigrapha*. SBLMS 2. Philadelphia: Society of Biblical Literature and Exegesis, 1948.

Johnston, Philip S. *Shades of Sheol: Death and Afterlife in the Old Testament*. Downers Grove, IL: InterVarsity Press, 2002.

Johnstone, William. *2 Chronicles 10–36: Guilt and Atonement*. Vol. 2 of *1 and 2 Chronicles*. JSOTSup 254. Sheffield: Sheffield Academic, 1997.

Jonker, Louis C. "The Chronicler and the Prophets: Who Were His Authoritative Sources?" Pages 145–64 in *What Was Authoritative for Chronicles?* Edited by Ehud Ben Zvi and Diana V. Edelman. Winona Lake, IN: Eisenbrauns, 2011. https://doi.org/10.1515/olzg-2015-0165

–. *Reflections of King Josiah in Chronicles: Late Stages of the Josiah Reception in 2 Chr 34f*. TSHB 2. Gütersloh: Gütersloher, 2003.

Joseph, Alison L. *Portrait of the Kings: The Davidic Prototype in Deuteronomistic Poetics*. Minneapolis: Fortress, 2015. https://doi.org/10.2307/j.ctt9m0txn

Junginger, Horst. *Der Verwissenschaftlichung der "Judenfrage" im Nationalsozialismus*. VFLUS 19. Darmstadt: Wissenschaftliche Buchgesellschaft, 2011. https://doi.org/10.1093/hgs/dcu049

Junod, Samuel. "'Maintenant moi, Jérémie': De l'exposition de Jérémie a l'exploitation de Jérémie." Pages 171–90 in *Las paraphrases bibliques aux XVIe et XVIIe siècles: Actes du Colloque de Bordeaux des 22, 23 et 24 septembre 2004*. Edited by Véronique Ferrer and Anne Mantero. Geneva: Droz, 2006. https://doi.org/10.1353/ren.2007.0238

Kahn, Dan'el. "The Historical Setting of Zephaniah's Oracles against the Nations (Zeph 2:4–15)." Pages 439–53 in *Homeland and Exile: Biblical and Ancient Near Eastern Studies in Honour of Busteney Oded*. Edited by Gershon Galil, Mark Geller and Alan Millard. VYSup 130. Leiden: Brill, 2009. https://doi.org/10.1163/ej.9789004178892.i-648.123

–. "Judean Auxilliaries in Egypt's Wars against Kush." *JAOS* 127 (2007): 507–16.

Kaiser, Otto. *Gott, Mensch und Geschichte: Studien zum Verständnis des Menschen und seiner Geschichte in der klassischen, biblischen und nachbiblischen Literatur*. BZAW 413. Berlin: de Gruyter, 2010. https://doi.org/10.1515/9783110228106

Kalimi, Isaac. "Kings with Privilege: The Core Source(s) of the Parallel Texts between the Deuteronomistic and Chronistic Histories." *RB* 119 (2012): 498–517.

–. *The Reshaping of Ancient Israelite History in Chronicles*. Winona Lake, IN: Eisenbrauns, 2005.

Kam, Rose Sallberg. *Their Stories, Our Stories: Women of the Bible*. New York: Continuum, 1995.

Kapelrud, Arvid S. "Temple Building, A Task for Gods and Kings." Pages 184–90 in *God and His Friends in the Old Testament*. Oslo: Universitetsforlaget, 1979.

Kastein, Josef. *History and Destiny of the Jews*. Translated by Huntley Paterson. London: John Lane the Bodley Head, 1933.

Katz, Dina. "Death, the Afterlife, and Other Last Things: Mesopotamia." Pages 477–79 in *Religions of the Ancient World: A Guide*. Edited by Sarah Iles Johnston. Cambridge, MA: Belknap, 2004.

Kaufmann, Yehezkel. "The Bible and Mythological Polytheism." Translated by Moshe Greenberg. *JBL* 70 (1951): 179–97. https://doi.org/10.1086/371689

–. "The Biblical Age." Translated by Moshe Greenberg. Pages 1–92 in *Great Ages and Ideas of the Jewish People*. Edited by Leo W. Schwarz. New York: Modern Library, 1956.

–. *The Religion of Israel: From Its Beginnings to the Babylonian Exile*. Translated by Moshe Greenberg. Chicago: University of Chicago Press, 1960.

Kavanagh, Preston. *Huldah: The Prophet Who Wrote Hebrew Scripture*. Eugene, OR: Pickwick, 2012.

–. *The Shapan Group: The Fifteen Authors Who Shaped the Hebrew Bible*. Eugene, OR: Pickwick, 2011.

Keel, Othmar, and Christoph Uehlinger. *Gods, Goddesses, and Images of God: In Ancient Israel*. Translated by T. H. Trapp. Minneapolis: Fortress, 1998.

Kelle, Brad E. "Judah in the Seventh Century: From the Aftermath of Sennacherib's Invasion to the Beginning of Jehoiakim's Rebellion." Pages 350–82 in *Ancient Israel's History: An Introduction to Issues and Sources*. Edited by Bill T. Arnold and Richard S. Hess. Grand Rapids: Baker Academic, 2014. https://doi.org/10.1111/rsr.12302

Kellenberger, Edgar. "JHWH und die Götter im globalisierten Perserreich: Anmerkungen zu einigen Thesan von A. de Pury." *CV* 52 (2010): 136–43.

Kelly, J. D. N. *Jerome: His Life, Writings, and Controversies*. New York: Harper & Row, 1975.

Kelso, James A. "Theodoret and the Law Book of Josiah." *JBL* 22 (1903): 51.

Kelso, James L. "Bethel." *NEAEHL* 1.194.

Kenyon, Kathleen M. *Jerusalem: Excavating 3000 Years of History*. London: Thames & Hudson, 1967. https://doi.org/10.1017/s0003598x00034347

Killebrew, Ann E. "Biblical Jerusalem: An Archaeological Assessment." Pages 329–45 in *Jerusalem in Bible and Archaeology: The First Temple Period*. Edited by Andrew G. Vaughn and Ann E. Killebrew. SBLSymS 18. Atlanta: Society of Biblical Literature, 2003. https://doi.org/10.1086/586679

Kim, Uriah Y. *Decolonizing Josiah: Toward a Postcolonial Reading of the Deuteronomic History*. BMW 5. Sheffield: Sheffield Phoenix, 2006. https://doi.org/10.2104/bc070047

King, Philip J. *Amos, Hosea, Micah: An Archaeological Commentary*. Philadelphia: Westminster, 1988.

Kinns, Samuel. *Graven in the Rock: or, The Historical Accuracy of the Bible Confirmed by Reference to the Assyrian and Egyptian Monuments in the British Museum and Elsewhere*. London: Cassell, 1891.

Kitagawa, Joseph M. *Religion in Japanese History*. New York: Columbia University Press, 1966.

Kitchen, Kenneth A. *On the Reliability of the Old Testament*. Grand Rapids: Eerdmans, 2003.

–. *The Third Intermediate Period in Egypt (1100–650 BC)*. 2nd ed. Warminster: Aris & Phillips, 1986.

Kittel, Rudolf. *Die Bücher der Könige: Übersetzt und erklärt*. HAT. Göttingen: Vandenhoek & Ruprecht, 1900.

–. "Die Völker des vorderen Orients." Pages 407–568 in *Das Erwachen der Menschheit: De Kulturen de Urzeit, Ostastiens, und des vordern Orients*. Edited by Wlater Goetz. Propyläen. Welgeschichte 1. Berlin: Propyläen, 1931. https://doi.org/10.1524/klio.1936.29.29.298

Klein, Ralph W. "The Rendering of 2 Chronicles 35–36 in 1 Esdras." Pages 225–35 in *Was 1 Esdras First? An Investigation into the Priority and Nature of 1 Esdras*. Edited by Lisbeth S. Fried. AIL 7. Atlanta: Society of Biblical Literature, 2011.

–. *2 Chronicles: A Commentary*. Hermeneia. Minneapolis: Fortress, 2012.

Kletter, Raz. "Pots and Politics: Material Remains of Late Iron Age Judah in Relation to Its Political Borders." *BASOR* 314 (1999): 19–54. https://doi.org/10.2307/1357450

Kletter, Raz, and Katri Saarelainen. "Horses and Riders and Riders and Horses." Pages 197–224 in *Family and Household Religion: Toward a Synthesis of Old Testament Studies, Archaeology, Epigraphy, and Cultural Studies*. Edited by Rainer Albertz, Beth Alpert Nakhal, Saul Olyan, and Rüdger Schmitt. Winona Lake, IN: Eisenbrauns, 2014. https://doi.org/10.3764/ajaonline1201.muller

Klijn, A. F. J. "2 (Syriac Apocalypse of) Baruch (Early Second Century A.D.): A New Translation and Introduction." *OTP* 1.615–52.

Knauf, Ernst Axel. "L'"Historiographie deutéronomiste' (DTRG) exist-t-elle?" Pages 409–18 in *Israël construit son histoire: L'historigraphie deutéronomiste à la lumière des recherches récentes*. Edited by Albert de Pury, Thomas Römer, and Jean-Daniel Macchi. MdB 34. Genève: Labor et Fides, 1996.

–. "Kings among the Prophets." Pages 131–49 in *The Production of Prophecy: Constructing Prophecy and Prophets in Yehud*. Edited by Diana V. Edelman and Ehud Ben Zvi. BibleWorld. London: Equinox, 2009. https://doi.org/10.4324/9781315710891

–. *Die Umwelt des Alten Testaments*. NSKAT 29. Stuttgart: Katholisches Bibelwerk, 1994.

–. "'You Shall Have No Other Gods': Eine notwendige Notiz zu einer überflüssigen Diskussion." *DBAT* 26 (1989–1990): 238–45.

Knauf, Ernst Axel, and Philippe Guillaume. *A History of Biblical Israel: The Fate of the Tribes and Kingdoms from Merenptah to Bar Kochba*. WANEM. Sheffield: Equinox, 2016. https://doi.org/10.1515/olzg-2017-0161

Knoppers, Gary N. "'The City Yhwh Has Chosen': The Chronicler's Promotion of Jerusalem in Light of Recent Archaeology." Pages 307–26 in *Jerusalem in Bible and Archaeology: The First Temple Period*. Edited by Andrew G. Vaughn and Ann E. Killebrew. SBLSymS 18. Atlanta: Society of Biblical Literature, 2003. https://doi.org/10.1086/586679

–. "Democratizing Revelation? Prophets, Seers and Visionaries in Chronicles." Pages 391–409 in *Prophecy and Prophets in Ancient Israel: Proceedings of the Oxford Old Testament Seminar*. Edited by John Day. LHBOTS 531. New York: T&T Clark, 2010. https://doi.org/10.1111/j.1467-9418.2011.00770.x

–. "The Deuteronomist and the Deuteronomic Law of the King: A Reexamination of a relationship." *ZAW* 108 (1996): 329–46.

–. "Ethnicity, Genealogy, Geography, and Change: The Judean Communities of Babylon and Jerusalem in the Story of Ezra." Pages 147–71 in *Community Identity in Judean Historiography: Biblical and Comparative Perspectives*. Edited by Gary N. Knoppers and Kenneth A. Ristau. Winona Lake, IN: Eisenbrauns, 2009. https://doi.org/10.31826/9781463235505-062

–. "History and Historiography: The Royal Reforms." Pages 557–78 in *Israel's Past in*

Present Research: Essays on Ancient Israelite Historiography. Edited by V. Philips Long. SBTS 7. Winona Lake, IN: Eisenbrauns, 1999.

–. "In Search of Post-Exilic Israel: Samaria after the Fall of the Northern Kingdom." Pages 150–80 in *In Search of Pre-Exilic Israel: Proceedings of the Oxford Old Testament Seminar*. Edited by John Day. JSOTSup 406. London: T&T Clark, 2004. https://doi.org/10.1111/j.1468-2265.2009.00438_17.x

–. *Jews and Samaritans: The Origins and History of Their Relations*. Oxford: Oxford University Press, 2013.

–. *The Reign of Jereboam, the Fall of Israel, and the Reign of Josiah*. Vol. 2 of *Two Nations under God: The Deuteronomistic History of Solomon and the Dual Monarchies*. HSM 53. Atlanta: Scholars Press, 1994. https://doi.org/10.1163/9789004369696

–. *The Reign of Solomon to the Rise of Jeroboam*. Vol. 1 of *Two Nations under God: The Deuteronomistic History of Solomon and the Dual Monarchies*. HSM 52. Atlanta: Scholars Press, 1993. https://doi.org/10.1163/9789004369689

–. "Yhwh's Rejection of the House Built for His Name: On the Significance of Anti-temple Rhetoric in the Deuteronomistic History." Pages 221–38 in *Essays on Ancient Israel in Its Near Eastern Context: A Tribute to Nadav Na'aman*. Edited by Yairah Amit, Ehud Ben Zvi, Israel Finkelstein, and Oded Lipschits. Winona Lake, IN: Eisenbrauns, 2006. https://doi.org/10.1086/basor25067068

Knowles, Melody D. *Centrality Practiced: Jerusalem in the Religious Practice of Yehud and the Diaspora in the Persian Period*. ABS 16. Atlanta: Society of Biblical Literature, 2006. https://doi.org/10.1086/661082

Koch, Klaus. *Der Gott Israels und die Götter des Orients: Religionsgeschichtliche Studien zwei: zum achtzigsten Geburtstag von Klaus Koch*. Edited by Friedhelm Hartenstein and Martin Rösel. FRLANT 216. Göttingen: Vandenhoeck & Ruprecht, 2007. https://doi.org/10.1111/j.1748-0922.2009.01362_28.x

–. *The Prophets: The Assyrian Period*. Translated by M. Kohl. Philadelphia: Fortress, 1982.

Köckert, Matthias. "YHWH in the Northern and Southern Kingdom." Pages 357–94 in *One God—One Cult—One Nation: Archaeological and Biblical Perspectives*. Edited by Reinhard G. Kratz and Hermann Spieckermann. BZAW 405. Berlin: de Gruyter, 2010. https://doi.org/10.1515/9783110223583.357

Koenen, Klaus. "1200 Jahre von Abrahams Geburt bis zum Tempelbau." ZAW 126 (2014): 494–505. https://doi.org/10.1515/zaw-2014-0030

–. *Bethel: Geschichte, Kult und Theologie*. OBO 192. Freiburg: Universitätsverlag, 2003.

Kofoed, Jens Bruun. *Text and History: Historiography and the Study of the Biblical Text*. Winona Lake, IN: Eisenbrauns, 2005. https://doi.org/10.2104/bc070044

Kooij, Arie van der. "The Public Reading of Scriptures at Feasts." Pages 27–44 in *Feasts and Festivals*. Edited by Christopher Tuckett. CBET 53. Leuven: Peeters, 2009.

Kratz, Reinhard G. "The Idea of Cultic Centralization and Its Supposed Ancient Near Eastern Analogies." Pages 121–44 in *One God—One Cult—One Nation: Archaeological and Biblical Perspectives*. Edited by Reinhard G. Kratz and Hermann Spieckermann. BZAW 405. Berlin: de Gruyter, 2010. https://doi.org/10.1515/9783110223583.119

Kroger, Joseph, and Patrizia Granziera. *Aztec Goddesses and Christian Madonnas: Images of the Divine Feminine in Mexico*. Farnham: Ashgate, 2012. https://doi.org/10.1111/blar.12273

Krueger, Derek. "The Old Testament and Monasticism." Pages 199–221 in *The Old Testament in Byzantium*. Edited by Paul Magdaline and Robert Nelson. Washington, DC: Dumbarton Oaks Research Library and Collection, 2010. https://doi.org/10.1017/s0038713412002497

Kselman, John S. "Zephaniah, Book of." *ABD* 6.1077–80.

Kuenen, Abraham. *The Religion of Israel to the Fall of the Jewish State*. London: Williams and Norgate, 1875.

–. *Religions and Universal Religions*. Hibbert Lectures 1882. New York: Scribner's Sons, 1882.

Kuhn, Karl Georg. *Die Judenfrage als weltgeschichtliches Problem*. Hamburg: Hanseatische, 1939.

Kuhrt, Amélie. "Cyrus the Great of Persia: Images and Realities." Pages 137–66 in *Representations of Political Power: Case Histories from Times of Change and Dissolving Order in the Ancient Near East*. Edited by Marlies Heinz and Marian H. Feldman. Winona Lake, IN: Eisenbrauns, 2007. https://doi.org/10.1017/s0041977x0800013x

Kuntz, J. Kenneth. "'In Sheol Who Can Give You Praise?': Death and 'Immortality' in the Hebrew Psalter." *PCS* (2000): 71–85.

Laato, Antti. "Beloved and Lovely! Despised and Rejected: Some Reflections on the Death of Josiah." Pages 115–28 in *Houses Full of All Good Things: Essays in Memory of Timo Veijola*. Edited by Juha Pakkala and Martti Nissinen. PFES 95. Helsinki: Finnish Exegetical Society; Göttingen: Vandenhoeck & Ruprecht, 2008.

–. "The Chronology in the Animal Apocalypse of 1 Enoch 85–90." *JSP* 26 (2016): 3–19.

–. *History and Ideology in the Old Testament Prophetic Literature: A Semiotic Approach to the Reconstruction of the Proclamation of the Historical Prophets*. ConBOT 41. Stockholm: Almquist & Wiksell, 1996. https://doi.org/10.2307/3266405

–. *Josiah and David Redivivas: The Historical Josiah and the Messianic Expectations of Exilic and Postexilic Times*. ConBOT 33. Stockholm: Almqvist & Wiksell, 1992. https://doi.org/10.2307/3266796

Laffey, Alice L. *First and Second Kings*. NCBC 9. Collegeville, MN: Liturgical Press, 2011.

–. *Wives, Harlots and Concubines: The Old Testament in Feminist Perspective*. London: SPCK, 1990. https://doi.org/10.2307/1518512

Lafforgue, Gilbert. "La haute antiquité." Pages 135–440 in *Histoire universelle: Des origines à la fin des grands empires*. Edited by Michell Guillemot. Paris: Larousse-Bordas, 1998.

Lambert, Wilfred G. "Mesopotamian Sources and Pre-Exilic Israel." Pages 352–63 in *In Search of Pre-Exilic Israel: Proceedings of the Oxford Old Testament Seminar*. Edited by John Day. JSOTSup 406. London: T&T Clark, 2004. https://doi.org/10.1111/j.1468-2265.2009.00438_17.x

Lang, Bernhard. "Die Jahwe-allein-Bewegung." Pages 47–83 in *Der einzige Gott: Die Geburt des biblischen Monotheismus*. Edited by Bernhard Lang. Munich: Kosel, 1981.

–. *Monotheism and the Prophetic Minority*. SWBA 1. Sheffield: Almond Press, 1983.

Langer, William L. *An Encyclopedia of World History: Ancient, Medieval, and Modern, Chronologically Arranged*. Rev. ed. Boston: Houghton Mifflin, 1952.

Larsson, Gerhard, "The Documentary Hypothesis and the Chronological Structure of the Old Testament." *ZAW* 97 (1985): 316–33.

Lee, Kyung Sook. "Books of Kings: Images of Women without Women's Reality." Pages 159–77 in *Feminist Biblical Interpretation: A Compendium of Bible and Related*

Literature. Edited by Luise Schottroff and Marie-Theres Wacker. Grand Rapids: Eerdmans, 2012. https://doi.org/10.1177/0040571x13511042k

Lemaire, André. *The Birth of Monotheism: The Rise and Disappearance of Yahwism*. Edited and translated by Jack Meinhardt. Washington, DC: Biblical Archaeology Society, 2007. https://doi.org/10.1086/661084

—. "Levantine Literacy ca. 1000–750 BCE." Pages 11–45 in *Contextualizing Israel's Sacred Writings: Ancient Literacy, Orality, and Literary Production*. Edited by Brian Schmidt. AIL 22. Atlanta: Society of Biblical Literature, 2015. https://doi.org/10.2307/j.ctt1647cmz.5

—. Remarques sur la datation des estamilles lmlk." *VT* 25 (1975): 678–82. https://doi.org/10.1163/156853375x00106

Lemche, Niels Peter. *Ancient Israel: A New History of Israelite Society*. Translated by Fred Cryer. BibSem 5. Sheffield: JSOT Press, 1990.

—. "Did a Reform like Josiah's Happen?" Pages 11–19 in *The Historian and the Bible: Essays in Honour of Lester L. Grabbe*. Edited by Philip R. Davies and Diana V. Edelman. LHBOTS 530. New York: T&T Clark, 2010. https://doi.org/10.1111/rsr.12056_8

—. "Historie og kulturel erindring I Det Gamle Testamente." *DTT* 76 (2013): 18–31. https://doi.org/10.7146/dtt.v76i1.105650

—. "On Doing Sociology with 'Solomon'." Pages 312–35 in *The Age of Solomon: Scholarship at the Turn of the Millennium*. Edited by Lowell K. Handy. SHCANE 11. Leiden: Brill, 1997.

Lepore, Luciano. "La storicità del 'manifesto' di Giosia." *BeO* 45 (2003): 3–33.

—. "L'umanità in camino dall'enoteismo al monoteismo: l'evoluzione della religione di Israele." *BeO* 47 (2005): 23–54.

Leuchter, Mark. "Jeroboam the Ephratite." *JBL* 125 (2006): 51–72. https://doi.org/10.2307/27638346

—. *Josiah's Reform and Jeremiah's Scroll: Historical Calamity and Prophetic Response*. HBM 6. Sheffield: Sheffield Phoenix, 2006. https://doi.org/10.1177/001452460811900070402

—. "'The Levites in Your Gates': The Deuteronomic Redefinition of Levitical Authority." *JBL* 126 (2007): 417–36. https://doi.org/10.2307/27638446

—. "Tyre's '70 Years' in Isaiah." *Bib* 87 (2006): 412–16.

Levenson, Jon D. *Resurrection and the Restoration of Israel: The Ultimate Victory of the God of Life*. New Haven: Yale University Press, 2006. https://doi.org/10.1086/656637

—. "Who Inserted the Book of the Torah?" *HTR* 68 (1975): 203–33.

Levin, Christoph. "Die Frömmigkeit der Könige von Israel und Juda." Pages 129–68 in *Houses Full of All Good Things: Essays in Memory of Timo Veijola*. Edited by Juha Pakkala and Martti Nissinen. PFES 95. Helsinki: Finnish Exegetical Society; Göttingen: Vandenhoeck & Ruprecht, 2008.

—. "Das synchronistische Exzerpt aus den Annalen der Könige Israel und Juda." *VT* 61 (2011): 616–28. https://doi.org/10.1163/156853311x560772

Levinson, Bernard M. "Die neuassyrischen Ursprünge der Kanonformel in Deuteronomium 13,1." Pages 23–59 in *Viele Wege zu dem Einen: Historische Bibelkritik—Die Vitalität der Glaubensüberlieferung in der Moderne*. Edited by Stefan Beyerle, Axel Graupner, and Udo Rütersworden. BibThS 121. Neukirchen-Vluyn: Neukirchener Theologie, 2012.

Lewis, Theodore J. "Dead, Abode of the." *ABD* 2.101–5.

–. "Syro-Palestinian Iconography and Divine Images." Pages 69–107 in *Cult Image and Divine Representation in the Ancient Near East*. Edited by Neal H. Walls. ASORBS 10. Boston: American Schools of Oriental Research, 2005.

Licht, Jacob. "Biblical Historicism." Pages 107–20 in *History, Historiography and Interpretation: Studies in Biblical and Cuneiform Literatures*. Edited by Hayim Tadmor and Moshe Weinfeld. Jerusalem: Magnes, 1986.

Lindblom, Johannes. *Prophecy in Ancient Israel*. Philadelphia: Fortress, 1962.

Lindemann, Gerhard. "Theologische Forschung über das Judentum in unterschiedlichen politischen Kontexten am Beispiel von Karl Georg Kuhn." *KZ* 17 (2004): 331–38.

Linville, James Richard. *Israel in the Book of Kings: The Past as a Project of Social Identity*. JSOTSup 272. Sheffield: Sheffield Academic, 1998.

Lipinski, Edward. "Forgotten Cults in Seventh Century Samaria." *PJBR* 15, no. 1 (2016): 25–33.

–. *Resheph: A Syro-Canaanite Deity*. OLA 181. StPhon 19. Louvain: Peeters, 2009.

Lipschits, Oded. *The Fall and Rise of Jerusalem: Judah under Babylonian Rule*. Winona Lake, IN: Eisenbrauns, 2005. https://doi.org/10.28977/jbtr.2018.10.43.326

–. "On Cash-Boxes and Finding or Not Finding Books: Jehoash's and Josiah's Decisions to Repair the Temple." Pages 239–54 in *Essays on Ancient Israel in Its Near Eastern Context: A Tribute to Nadav Na'aman*. Edited by Yairah Amit, Ehud Ben Zvi, Israel Finkelstein, and Oded Lipschits. Winona Lake, IN: Eisenbrauns, 2006. https://doi.org/10.1086/basor25067068

Liverani, Mario. *Assyria: The Imperial Mission*. Translated by Andrea Trameri and Jonathan Valk. MC 21. Winona Lake, IN: Eisenbrauns, 2017.

–. *Israel's History and the History of Israel*. Translated by Chiara Peri and Philip R. Davies. BibleWorld. London: Equinox, 2005.

Lloyd, Alan B. "The Late Period (664–332 BC)." Pages 369–94 in *The Oxford History of Ancient Egypt*. Edited by Ian Shaw. Oxford: Oxford University Press, 2000.

Lods, Adolphe. *The Prophets and the Rise of Judaism*. Translated by S. Hooke. London: Kegal Paul, Trench, Trubner, 1937.

–. *La Religion d'Israël*. HRel. Paris: Librairie Hachette, 1939.

Lohfink, Norbert. "Die Bundesurkunde des Königs Josias (Eine Frage an die Deuteronomiumsforschung)." *Bib* 44 (1963): 261–88, 461–98.

–. "The Cult Reform of Josiah of Judah: 2 Kings 22–23 as a Source for the History of Israelite Religion." Pages 459–75 in *Ancient Israelite Religion*. Edited by Patrick D. Miller, Jr., Paul D. Hanson, and S. Dean McBride. Philadelphia: Fortress, 1987. https://doi.org/10.1086/487929

–. "Die Gattung der 'Historischen Kurzgeschichte' in den letzten Jahren von Judah und in der Zeit des Babylonischen Exils." *ZAW* 90 (1978): 319–47. https://doi.org/10.1515/zatw.1978.90.3.319

–. "Gott und die Götter im Alten Testament." *ThA* 6 (1969): 50–71.

–. "Zur neuen Diskussion über 2 Kön 22–23." Pages 24–48 in *Das Deuteronomium: Entstehung, Gestalt und Botschaft*. Edited by Norbert Lohfink. BETL 68. Leuven: Leuven University Press; Peeters, 1985. https://doi.org/10.1177/030908928601103510

Long, Burke O. *1 Kings with an Introduction to Historical Literature*. FOTL 9. Grand Rapids: Eerdmans, 1984.

Lopasso, Vincenzo. "La riforma di Giosia nel nord." *BeO* 199 (1999): 29–40.

Lorton, David. "The Theology of Cult Statues in Ancient Egypt." Pages 123–210 in

Born in Heaven, Made on Earth: The Making of the Cult Image in the Ancient Near East. Edited by Michael B. Dick. Winona Lake: IN: Eisenbrauns, 1999.

Lowery, Richard H. *The Reforming Kings and Society in First Temple Judah.* JSOTSup 120. Sheffield: JSOT Press, 1991.

Lynch, Matthew. *Monotheism and Institutions in the Book of Chronicles: Temple, Priesthood, and Kingship in Post-Exilic Perspective.* FAT 2.64. Tübingen: Mohr Siebeck, 2014.

Maag, Victor. "Erwägungen zur deuteronomischen Kultzentralisation." *VT* 6 (1956): 10–18. https://doi.org/10.2307/1516022

MacDonald, Nathan. *What Did the Ancient Israelites Eat? Diet in Biblical Times.* Grand Rapids: Eerdmans, 2008. https://doi.org/10.1177/0014524611420353

Machinist, Peter. "How Gods Die, Biblically and Otherwise: A Problem of Cosmic Restructuring." Pages 189–240 in *Reconsidering the Concept of Revolutionary Monotheism.* Edited by Beate Pongratz-Leisten. Winona Lake, IN: Eisenbrauns, 2011. https://doi.org/10.1163/15685276-12341269

Maclear, George Frederick. *A Shilling Book of Old Testament History for National and Elementary Schools.* London: Macmillan, 1885.

McKane, William. *Introduction and Commentary on Jeremiah I–XXXV.* Vol. 1 of *A Critical and Exegetical Commentary on Jeremiah.* ICC. Edinburgh: T&T Clark, 1986. https://doi.org/10.1017/s0036930600040886

McKay, John W. *Religion in Judah under the Assyrians 732–609 B.C.* SBT^2 26. Naperville, IL: Allenson, 1973.

McKenzie, Steven L. *The Trouble with Kings: The Composition of the Book of Kings in the Deuteronomistic History.* VTSup 42. Leiden: Brill, 1991. https://doi.org/10.1017/s0364009400006371

McKinlay, Judith E. "Gazing at Huldah." *BCT* 1, no. 3 (2005). https://doi.org/10.2104/bc050015

McLaughlin, John L. *What Are They Saying about Ancient Israelite Religion?* WATSA. New York: Paulist, 2016.

McNeill, William H. *The Rise of the West: A History of the Human Community.* Chicago: University of Chicago Press, 1963.

Madsen, Catherine. "A Terrible Beauty: Moser's Bible." *CrCur* 50 (2000): 136–45.

Magness, Jodi. "Conspicuous Consumption: Dining on Meat in the Ancient Mediterranean World and Near East." Pages 33–59 in *Feasting in the Archaeology and Texts of the Bible and the Ancient Near East.* Edited by Peter Altmann and Janling Fu. Winona Lake, IN: Eisenbrauns, 2014.

Malalas, John. *The Chronology of John Malalas.* Translated by Elizabeth Jeffreys, Michael Jeffreys, and Roger Scott. Melbourne: Australian Association for Byzantine Studies, 1986. https://doi.org/10.1163/9789004344600

Malamat, Abraham. "The Historical Background of the Assassination of Amon." *IEJ* 3 (1953): 26–29.

–. "The Last Kings of Judah and the Fall of Jerusalem: An Historical-Chronological Study." *IEJ* 18 (1968): 137–56.

–. "The Twilight of Judah in the Egyptian-Babylonian Maelstrom." Pages 123–45 in *Congress Volume: Edinburgh 1974.* Edited by G. W. Anderson (with International Organization for the Study of the Old Testament). VTSup 28. Leiden: Brill, 1975. https://doi.org/10.1163/9789004275515_010

Malandra, William W. *An Introduction to Ancient Iranian Religion: Readings from the Avesta and the Achaemenid Inscriptions.* Minneapolis: University of Minnesota Press, 1983. https://doi.org/10.2307/601567

Maldonado, Alonso de. *Chronica universal de todos las naciones y tiempos*. Madrid: Luis San, 1924.

Mallau, Hans Harald. "Las diversas reacciones al mensaje profético en Israel y su Ambiente: Una contribución al problema de los profetas verdaderos y los profetas falsos." *CTh* 2 (1972): 35–57.

Mandell, Alice, and Jeremy Smoak. "Reading and Writing in the Dark at Khirbet el-Qom: The Literacies of Ancient Subterranean Judah." *NEArch* 80 (2017): 188–95. https://doi.org/10.5615/neareastarch.80.3.0188

Manor, Dale W. "Gates and Gods: High Places in the Gates." *SCJ* 2 (1999): 235–53.

Marble, Annie Russell. *Women of the Bible: Their Services in Home and State*. New York: Century, 1923.

Margalit, Baruch. "The Meaning and Significance of Asherah." *VT* 40 (1990): 264–97.

Mariottini, Claude F. "The Trial of Jeremiah and the Killing of Uriah the Prophet." *JBQ* 42 (2014): 27–35.

Marling, Karal Ann. *Merry Christmas! Celebrating America's Greatest Holiday*. Cambridge, MA: Harvard University Press, 2000. https://doi.org/10.1086/ahr/107.1.182

Marquardt, Melvin. *Good Little King Josiah*. Arch Books. St. Louis: Concordia, 1978.

Martin-Archard, Robert. *La Mort en face: Selon la Bible hébraïque*. EssBib 15. Geneva: Labor et Fides, 1988.

Maspero, Gaston. *The Passing of the Empires 850 B.C. to 330 B.C.* Edited by Archibald Henry Sayce. Translated by M. L. McClure. New York: D. Appleton, 1900.

Mastin, Brian A. "Yahweh's Asherah, Inclusive Monotheism and the Question of Dating." Pages 326–51 in *In Search of Pre-Exilic Israel: Proceedings of the Oxford Old Testament Seminar*. Edited by John Day. JSOTSup 406. London: T&T Clark, 2004.

Mathieu, Yvan. "À la recherché du livre retrouvé: Le 'Livre de la Loi' et son autorité en 2 R 22–23." Pages 65–81 in *Écritures et réécritures: La preprise interpretative des traditions foundatrices par la literature biblique et extra-biblique*. Edited by Claire Clivaz, Corina Combet-Galland, Jean-Daniel Macchi, and Chistophe Nihan. BETL 248. Leuven: Peeters, 2012. https://doi.org/10.1163/9789004266544_007

Mathys, Hans-Peter. "Wilhelm Martin Lebrecht de Wettes *Dissertatio critico-exegetica* von 1805." Pages 171–211 in *Biblische Theologie und historisches Denken: Wissenschafsgeschichtliche Studiesn*. Edited by Martin Kessler and Martin Wallraff. SGWB 5. Basel: Schwabe, 2008.

Matsunaga, Daigan, and Alicia Matsunaga. *The Aristocratic Age*. Vol. 1 of *Foundation of Japanese Buddhism*. Los Angeles: Buddhist Books International, 1974.

–. *The Mass Movement (Kamakura and Muromachi Period)*. Vol. 2 of *Foundation of Japanese Buddhism*. Los Angeles: Buddhist Books International, 1974.

Mattingly, Gerald L. "Chemosh." *ABD* 1.895–97.

Maxey, Trent. "The Crisis of 'Conversion' and Search for National Doctrine in Early Meiji Japan." Pages 3–26 in *Converting Cultures: Religion, Ideology and Transformations of Modernity*. Edited by Dennis Washburn and A. Kevin Reinhart. SSA 14. Leiden: Brill, 2007. https://doi.org/10.1163/ej.9789004158221.i-507.5

May, Natalie N. "'In Order to Make Him Completely Dead': Annihilation of the Power of Images in Mesopotamia." Pages 701–28 in *La famille dans le Proche-Orient ancien: réalités, symbolisms, at images: Proceedings of the 55th Rencontre Assyriologique Internationale at Paris 6–9 July 2009*. Edited by Lionel Marti. Winona Lake, IN: Eisenbrauns, 2014.

Mays, James Luther. *Amos: A Commentary*. OTL. Philadelphia: Westminster, 1969.

–. *Micah: A Commentary*. OTL. Philadelphia: Westminster, 1976.

Mazar, Amihai. "Archaeology and the Biblical Narrative: The Case of the United Monarchy." Pages 29–58 in *One God—One Cult—One Nation: Archaeological and Biblical Perspectives*. Edited by Reinhard G. Kratz and Hermann Spieckermann. BZAW 405. Berlin: de Gruyter, 2010. https://doi.org/10.1515/9783110223583.29
–. *Archaeology of the Land of the Bible: 10,000–586 B.C.E.* ABRL. New York: Doubleday, 1992.
Medina, Richard W. "Life and Death Viewed as Physical and Lived Spaces: Some Preliminary Thoughts from Proverbs." *ZAW* 122 (2010): 199–211. https://doi.org/10.1515/zaw.2010.015
Meier, Samuel A. "Granting God a Passport: Transporting Deities across International Boundaries." Pages 185–208 in *Moving across Borders: Foreign Relations, Religion and Cultural Intyeractions in the Ancient Mediterranean*. Edited by Panagikotis Kousoulis and Konstantinos Magliveras. Louvain: Peeters, 2007.
Melville, Sarah C. "A New Look at the End of the Assyrian Empire." Pages 179–201 in *Homeland and Exile: Biblical and Ancient Near Eastern Studies in Honour of Busteney Oded*. Edited by Gershon Galil, Mark Geller, and Alan Millard. VTSup 130. Leiden: Brill, 2009. https://doi.org/10.1093/jts/flq151
Mendenhall, George E. "Covenant Forms in Israelite Tradition." *BA* 17 (1954): 50–75.
–. "The Worship of Baal and Asherah: A Study in the Social Bonding Functions of Religious Systems." Pages 147–58 in *Biblical and Related Studies Presented to Samuel Iwry*. Edited Ann Kort and Scott Morschauser. Winona Lake, IN: Eisenbrauns, 1985. https://doi.org/10.1177/030908928601103642
Menn, Esther. "Inner-Biblical Exegesis in the Tanak." Pages 55–79 in *The Ancient Period*. Vol. 1 of *A History of Biblical Interpretation*. Edited by Alan J. Hauser and Duane F. Watson. Grand Rapids: Eerdmans, 2003.
Mercer, Derrik, ed. *Chronicle of the World*. London: Dorling Kindersley, 1996.
Mettinger, Tryggve N. D. "A Conversation with My Critics: Cultic Image or Aniconism in the First Temple?" Pages 273–96 in *Essays on Ancient Israel in Its Near Eastern Context: A Tribute to Nadav Na'aman*. Edited by Yairah Amit, Ehud Ben Zvi, Israel Finkelstein, and Oded Lipschits. Winona Lake, IN: Eisenbrauns, 2006. https://doi.org/10.1086/basor25067068
–. *No Graven Image? Israelite Aniconism in Its Ancient Near Eastern Context*. ConBOT 42. Stockholm: Almqvist & Wiksell, 1995. https://doi.org/10.1086/468681
Meyers, Carol. "Menu: Royal Repasts and Social Class in Biblical Israel." Pages 129–47 in *Feasting in the Archaeology and Texts of the Bible and the Ancient Near East*. Edited by Peter Altmann and Janling Fu. Winona Lake, IN: Eisenbrauns, 2014.
Michael, Matthew. "The Prophet, the Witch and the Ghost: Understanding the Parody of Saul as a 'Prophet' and the Purpose of Endor in the Deuteronomistic History." *JSOT* 38 (2014): 315–46. https://doi.org/10.1177/0309089214527208
Michener, James A. *The Source*. New York: Fawcett Crest, 1967.
Milgrom, Jacob. "Did Josiah Control Megiddo?" *Beit Mikrah* 16 (1971): 23–27. [Hebrew].
–. "The Nature and Extent of Idolatry in Eighth-Seventh Century Judah." *HUCA* 69 (1998): 1–13.
Millard, Alan R. "Books and Writing in Kings." Pages 155–60 in *The Books of Kings: Sources, Composition, Historiography, and Reception*. Edited by André Lemaire and Baruch Halpern. VTSup 129. Atlanta: Society of Biblical Literature, 2010. https://doi.org/10.5508/jhs.2017.v17.r21
Miller, Geoffrey P. *The Ways of a King: Legal and Political Ideas in the Bible*. JAJSup 7. Göttingen: Vandenhoeck & Ruprecht, 2011.

Miller, J. Maxwell. *The Old Testament and the Historian.* GBSOT. Philadelphia: Fortress, 1976.

Miller, J. Maxwell, and John H. Hayes. *A History of Ancient Israel and Judah.* 2nd ed. Louisville: Westminster John Knox, 2006. https://doi.org/10.5508/jhs.2007.v7.r28

Miller, J. Maxwell, and Gene M. Tucker. *The Book of Joshua.* CBC. Cambridge: Cambridge University Press, 1974.

Mitchell, Christine. "The Ironic Death of Josiah in 2 Chronicles." *CBQ* 68 (2006): 421–35.

Mohol, Eliya. "Prophetic and Popular Responses to Religious Pluralism in Jeremiah 44." *UBSJ* 6, no. 2 (2009): 31–55.

Molin, Georg. "Die Stellung der Gebira im Staate Juda." *TZ* 10 (1954): 161–75.

Monroe, Lauren A. S. "A 'Holiness' Substratum in the Deuteronomistic Account of Josiah's Reform." *JHS* 7 (2007): 42–53. doi:10.5508/jhs.2007.v7.a10.

–. *Josiah's Reform and the Dynamics of Defilement: Israelite Rites of Violence and the Making of a Biblical Text.* Oxford: Oxford University, 2011. https://doi.org/10.5508/jhs.2013.v13.r7

Montgomery, James A. *A Critical and Exegetical Commentary on the Books of Kings.* Edited by H. S. Gehman. ICC. Edinburgh: T&T Clark, 1951.

Moore, Megan Bishop, and Brad E. Kelle, *Biblical History and Israel's Past: The Changing Study of the Bible and History.* Grand Rapids: Eerdmans, 2011. https://doi.org/10.1111/rsr.12033_17

Morenz, Siegfried. *Egyptian Religion.* Translated by Ann E. Keep. Ithaca, NY: Cornell University Press, 1973.

Morgan, Sydney. *Woman and Her Master.* Philadelphia: Carey and Hart, 1840.

Morris, Ellen F. "Sacrifice for the State: First Dynasty Royal Funerals and the Rites at Macramallah's Rectangle." Pages 15–37 in *Performing Death: Social Analyses of Funerary Traditions in the Ancient Near East and Mediterranean.* Edited by Nicola Laneri. OIS 3. Chicago: Oriental Institute of the University of Chicago, 2007.

Morrow, William S. "The Paradox of Deuteronomy 13: A Post-Colonial Reading." Pages 227–39 in *"Gerechtigkeit und Recht zu üben" (Gen 18,19): Studien zur altorientalischen und Biblischen Rechtsgeschichte, zur Religionsgeschichte Israels und zur Religionssoziologie: Festschrift für Eckart Otto zum 65. Geburtstag.* Edited by Reinhard Achenbach and Martin Arneth. BZABR 13. Wiesbaden: Harrassowitz, 2009. https://doi.org/10.5508/jhs.2010.v10.r76

–. "Were There Neo-Assyrian Influences in Manasseh's Temple? Comparative Evidence from Tel-Miqne/Ekron." *CBQ* 75 (2013): 53–73.

Moscati, Sabatino. *The Face of the Ancient Orient: A Panorama of Near Eastern Civilizations in Pre-Classical Times.* Garden City: Doubleday, 1960. https://doi.org/10.1086/ahr/66.1.112

Moser, Barry. Illustrator. *The Holy Bible: Containing all the Books of the Old and New Testaments: King James Version.* New York: Penguin Books, 1999.

Mulford, Montgomery. *Picture Stories from the Bible: Complete Old Testament Edition.* New York: M. C. Gaines, 1943.

Müller, Hans-Peter. "Chemosh." *DDD* cols. 356–62.

Münnich, Maciej M. *The God Resheph in the Ancient Near East.* ORA 11. Tübingen: Mohr Siebeck, 2013. https://doi.org/10.5615/neareastarch.78.1.0054

–. "What Did the Biblical Goat-Demons Look Like?" *UF* 38 (2006): 525–35.

Murdock, Graeme. "Death, Prophecy and Judgement in Transylvania." Pages 206–23 in the *Place of the Dead: Death and Remembrance in Late Medieval and Early Modern Europe*. Edited by Bruce Gordon and Peter Marshall. Cambridge: Cambridge University Press, 2000. https://doi.org/10.1017/s0009640700096505

Myers, Jacob M. *I & II Esdras: A New Translation with Introduction and Commentary*. AB 42. Garden City: Doubleday, 1974.

–. *II Chronicles: A New Translation with Introduction and Commentary*. AB 13. Garden City: Doubleday, 1965.

Na'aman, Nadav. "The 'Discovered Book' and the Legitimation of Josiah's Reform." *JBL* 130 (2011): 47–62. https://doi.org/10.2307/41304187

–. "Dismissing the Myth of a Flood of Israelite Refugees in the Late Eighth Century BCE." *ZAW* 126 (2014): 1–14. https://doi.org/10.1515/zaw-2014-0001

–. "The Exodus Story: Between Historical Memory and Historiographical Composition." *JANER* 11 (2011): 39–69.

–. "Hezekiah's Fortified Cities and the *lmlk* Stamps." *BASOR* 261 (1986): 5–21.

–. "The Israelite-Judahite Struggle for the Patrimony of Israel." *Bib* 91 (2010): 1–23.

–. "Josiah and the Kingdom of Judah." Pages 189–247 in *Good Kings and Bad Kings*. Edited by Lester L. Grabbe. LHBOTS 393. ESHM 5. London: T&T Clark, 2005.

–. "The King Leading Cult Reforms in His Kingdom: Josiah and Other Kings in the Ancient Near East." *ZABR* 12 (2006): 131–68.

–. "The Kingdom of Judah under Josiah." *TA* 18 (1991): 3–71.

–. "Literacy in the Negev in the Late Monarchical Period." Pages 47–70 in *Contextualizing Israel's Sacred Writings: Ancient Literacy, Orality, and Literary Production*. Edited by Brian Schmidt. AIL 22. Atlanta: Society of Biblical Literature, 2015. https://doi.org/10.2307/j.ctt1647cmz.6

–. "No Anthropomorphic Graven Images: Notes on the Assumed Anthropomorphic Cult Statues in the Temples of YHWH in the Pre-Exilic Period." *UF* 31 (1999): 391–415.

–. "Notes on the Temple 'Restorations' of Jehoash and Josiah." *VT* 63 (2013): 640–51. https://doi.org/10.1163/15685330-12341130

–. "Queen Mothers and Ancestors Cult in Judah in the First Temple Period." Pages 479–90 in *Berührungspunkte: Studien zur Sozial- und Religionsgeschichte Israels und seiner Umwelt: Festschrift für Rainer Albertz zu seinem 65. Geburtstag*. Edited by Ingo Kottsieper, Rüdiger Schmitt, and Jakob Wöhrle. AOAT 350. Münster: Ugarit, 2008. https://doi.org/10.1515/9783110897005

–. "The Sanctuary of the Gibeonites Revisited." *JANER* 9 (2009): 101–24.

–. "A Sapiential Composition from Horvat 'Usa." *HeBAI* 2, no. 2 (2013): 221–233.

–. "Sojourners and Levites in the Kingdom of Judah in the Seventh Century BCE." *ZABR* 14 (2008): 237–79.

Nakanose, Shigeyuki. *Josiah's Passover: Sociology and the Liberating Bible*. BLib. Maryknoll: Orbis, 1993.

Nam, Roger S. *Portrayals of Economic Exchange in the Book of Kings*. BibIntS 112. Leiden: Brill, 2012.

Naveh, Joseph. "The Excavations at Mesad Hashavyahu: Preliminary Report." *IEJ* 12 (1962): 89–113.

Nel, Philip J. "Social Justice as Religious Responsibility in Near Eastern Religions: Historical Ideal and Ideological Illusion." *JNSL* 26, no. 2 (2000): 143–53.

Nelson, Kristin R. *King Josiah and God's Book*. Arch Books 59-2216. St. Louis: Concordia, 2008.

Nelson, Richard D. *Historical Roots of the Old Testament (1200–63 BCE)*. BibEnc 13. Atlanta: Society of Biblical Literature, 2014. https://doi.org/10.2307/j.ctt9qh1r8

–. "Josiah in the Book of Joshua." *JBL* 100 (1981): 531–40.

Neumann, Erich. *The Great Mother: An Analysis of the Archetype*. Translated by Ralph Manheim. 2nd ed. Bollingen Seroes 47. Princeton: Princeton University Press, 1963.

Nicholson, Ernest W. "The Centralization of the Cult in Deuteronomy." *VT* 13 (1963): 380–89.

–. *Deuteronomy and the Judean Diaspora*. Oxford: Oxford University Press, 2014.

–. *Deuteronomy and Tradition*. Philadelphia: Fortress, 1967.

–. *Jeremiah 1–25*. CBC. Cambridge University Press, 1973.

–. "Josiah and the Priests of the High Places (II Reg 23,8a.9)." *ZAW* 119 (2007): 499–513.

–. "Reconsidering the Provenance of Deuteronomy." *ZAW* 124 (2012): 528–40.

Nickelsburg, George W. E. *1 Enoch 1: A Commentary on the Book of 1 Enoch, Chapters 1–36; 81–108*. Hermenaeia. Minneapolis: Fortress, 2001. https://doi.org/10.2307/j.ctvb9373x.5

–. *Jewish Literature between the Bible and the Mishnah*. Philadelphia: Fortress, 1981.

Niditch, Susan. *Ancient Israelite Religion*. New York: Oxford University, 1997.

–. "Experiencing the Divine: Heavenly Visits, Earthly Encounters and the Land of the Dead." Pages 11–22 in *Religious Diversity in Ancient Israel and Judah*. Edited by Francesca Stavrakopoulou and John Barton. London: T&T Clark, 2010.

Niehr, Herbert. "Host of Heaven." *DDD* cols. 811–14.

–. "'Israelite Religion' and 'Canaanite' Religion." Pages 23–36 in *Religious Diversity in Ancient Israel and Judah*. Edited by Francesca Stavrakopoulou and John Barton. London: T&T Clark, 2010.

–. "Die Reform des Jeschija: Methodische, historische und religionsgeschichtliche Aspekte." Pages 33–55 in *Jeremia und die "deuteronomistische Bewegung*. Edited by Walter Groß. BBB 98. Weinheim: Beltz Athenäum, 1995.

–. "The Rise of YHWH in Judahite and Israelite Religion: Methodological and Religio-Historical Aspects." Pages 45–72 in *The Triumph of Elohim: From Yahwisms to Judaisms*. Edited by Diana V. Edelman. Grand Rapids: Eerdmans, 1995. https://doi.org/10.1163/1568533972651306

Niemann, Hermann Michael. *Herrschaft, Königtum und Staat: Skizzen zur soziokulturellen Entwicklung im monarchischen Israel*. FAT 6. Tübingen: Mohr Siebeck, 1993. https://doi.org/10.2307/605562

Nihan, Christophe. "'Moses and the Prophets': Deuteronomy 18 and the Emergence of the Pentateuch as Torah." *SEÅ* 75 (2010): 21–55.

Nissenbaum, Stephen. *The Battle for Christmas*. New York: Vintage, 1997.

Nissinen, Marti. *References to Prophecy in Neo-Assyrian Sources*. SAAS 7. Helsinki: Neo-Assyrian Text Corpus Project, 1998.

Nocquet, Dany. *Le 'livre noir de Baal': La polémique contre le dieu Baal dans la Bible hébraïque et lancien Israël*. ARech. Geneva: Labor et Fides, 2004. https://doi.org/10.2307/3642399

Nodet, Étienne Nodet, "On the Biblical 'Hidden' Calendar." *ZAW* 124 (2012): 583–97.

Noegel, Scott B. "Phoenicia, Phoenicians." Pages 792–98 in *Dictionary of the Old Testament: Historical Books*. Edited by Bill T. Arnold and H. G. M. Williamson. Downers Grove, IL: InterVarsity Press, 2005. https://doi.org/10.1108/09504120710719400

Noll, Kurt L. "Did 'Scripturalization' take place in Second Temple Judaism?" *JSOT* 25 (2011): 201–16. https://doi.org/10.1080/09018328.2011.608541
–. "Is the Scroll of Samuel Deuteronomistic?" Pages 119–48 in *Is Samuel among the Deuteronomists? Current Views on the Place of Samuel in a Deuteronomistic History*. Edited by Cynthia Edenburg and Juha Pakkala. AIL 16. Atlanta: Society of Biblical Literature, 2013. https://doi.org/10.2307/j.ctt5hjh2n
–. "Was there Doctrinal Dissemination in Early Yahweh Religion?" *BibInt* 16 (2008): 395–427. https://doi.org/10.1163/156851508x288986
Noort, Edward. "Der Tod und die Gerechtigkeit im alten Israel." Pages 369–81 in *Berührungspunkte: Studien zur Sozial- und Religionsgeschichte Israels und seiner Umwelt: Festschrift für Rainer Albertz zu seinem 65. Geburtstag*. Edited by Ingo Kottsieper, Rüdiger Schmitt, and Jakob Wöhrle. AOAT 350. Münster: Ugarit, 2008. https://doi.org/10.1515/9783110897005
North, Christopher R. "The Religious Aspects of Hebrew Kingship." *ZAW* 50 (1932): 8–38.
North, Robert. "The Theology of the Chronicler." *JBL* 82 (1963): 369–81.
Noth, Martin. *The History of Israel*. 2nd rev. ed. Translated by P. R. Ackroyd. New York: Harper & Row, 1960.
–. *Überlieferungsgeschichtliche Studien I: Die sammelnden und bearbeitenden Geschichtswerke im Alten Testament*. Halle: Max Niemeyer, 1943.
Novotny, Jamie. "'I Did Not Alter the Site Where That Temple Stood': Thoughts on Esarhaddon's Rebuilding of the Assur Temple." *JCS* 66 (2014): 91–112. https://doi.org/10.5615/jcunestud.66.2014.0091
Oden, Robert A, Jr. "The Persistence of Canaanite Religion." *BA* 39 (1976): 31–36.
Oded, Bustenay, "Judah and the Exile." Pages 435–88 in *Israelite and Judaean History*. Edited by John H. Hayes and J. Maxwell Miller. OTL. Philadelphia: Westminster, 1977. https://doi.org/10.1017/s0360966900014717
O'Donovan, Joan Lockwood. "The Church of England and the Anglican Communion: A Timely Engagement with the National Church Tradition?" *SJT* 57 (2004): 313–37. https://doi.org/10.1017/s0036930604000237
Ogilvie, Robert Maxwell, *The Romans and Their Gods in the Age of Augustus*. Ancient Culture and Society. New York: Norton, 1969.
Ogunkunle, Caleb O. "Josiah's Reform as a Model for Religious and Political Rebranding in Nigeria." *IJOURELS* 2 (2012): 1–15.
Ojo, Jonathan Ola. "Prophetess Huldah as a Prinicipal Strategist of Josiah's Reforms (2 Kings 22): Lessons for Women in Political and Religious Leadership in Africa." *AJBS* 31 (2013): 117–34.
Olmo Lete, Gregorio del. "Antecedentes y concomitantes del culto hebreo-bíblico." Pages 115–32 in *Los caminos inexhauribles de la Palabra (Las relecturas creativas en la Biblia y de la Biblia): Homenaje de colegas y discipulos a J. Severino Croatto en sus 70 años de vida, 40 de magisterio, y 25 en el ISEDET*. Edited by Guillermo Hansen. Buenos Aires: Lumen-ISEDET, 2000. https://doi.org/10.31819/9783865279668-003
–. *Mitos y leyendas de Canaan segun la tradicion de Ugarit: Textos, version y estudio*. FCBib 1. Madrid: Cristiandad, 1986. https://doi.org/10.1086/373241
–. "La religion cananea de los antiguos hebreos." Pages 223–350 in *Mitología y religion del oriente antiguo. II/2: Semiticas occidentales (Emar, Ugarit, Hebreos, Fenicios, Arameos, Árabes)*. Edited by Daniel Arnaud, François Bron, Gregorio del Olmo Lete, and Javier Teixidor. EstOr 9. Sabadell: AUSA, 1995. https://doi.org/10.1515/9781614514923

Olmstead, Albert Ten Eyck. "The Reform of Josiah and Its Secular Aspects." *AHR* 20 (1915): 566–70.

Olson, Daniel. *A New Reading of the Animal Apocalypse of 1 Enoch: "All Nations Shall be Blessed": with a New Translation and Commentary*. SVTP 24. Leiden: Brill, 2013. https://doi.org/10.1111/rsr.13029

Olyan, Saul M. *Asherah and the Cult of Yahweh in Israel*. SBLMS 34. Atlanta: Scholars Press, 1988.

–. "Problems in the History of the Cult and Priesthood in Ancient Israel." PhD diss., Harvard University, 1985.

–. "Theorizing Circumstantially Dependent Rites in and out of War Contexts." Pages 15–24 in *Warfare, Ritual, and Symbol in Biblical and Modern Contexts*. Edited by Brad E. Kelle, Frank Ritchel Ames, and Jacob L. Wright. AIL 18. Atlanta: Society of Biblical Literature, 2014. https://doi.org/10.2307/j.ctt6wqb3g.5

Oppenheimer, Aharon. *The 'am ha-aretz: A Study in the Social History of the Jewish People in the Hellenistic-Roman Period*. Translated by Israel H. Levine. ALGHJ 8. Leiden: Brill, 1977. https://doi.org/10.1163/157006378x00445

Orlinsky, Harry M. *Ancient Israel*. The Development of Western Civilization. 2nd ed. Ithaca: Cornell University Press, 1960.

Osborne, Charles, ed. *The Israelites*. The Emergence of Man. New York: Time-Life Books, 1975.

Osborne, James F. "Secondary Mortuary Practice and the Bench Tomb: Structure and Practice in Iron Age Judah." *JNES* 70 (2011): 35–53. https://doi.org/10.1086/658476

Östreicher, Theodor. *Das deuteronomische Grundgesetz*. BFCT 27.4. Gütersloh: Bertelsmann, 1923.

Otto, Bishop of Freising. *The Two Cities: A Chronicle of Universal History to the Year 1146 A.D.* Translated by Charles Christopher Mierow. Edited by Austin P. Evans and Charles Knapp. Records of Western Civilization. New York: Columbia University Press, 2002. https://doi.org/10.1086/ahr/34.3.566

Ouellette, Jean. "The Basic Structure of Solomon's Temple and Archaeological Research." Pages 1–20 in *The Temple of Solomon: Archaeological fact and Medieval Tradition in Christian, Islamic and Jewish Art*. Edited by J. Gutmann. RelArts 3. Missoula, MT: Scholars Press, 1976. https://doi.org/10.2307/3049720

Pace, Leann. "Feasting and Everyday Meals in the World of the Hebrew Bible: The Relationship Reexamined through Material Culture and Texts." Pages 179–98 in *Feasting in the Archaeology and Texts of the Bible and the Ancient Near East*. Edited by Peter Altmann and Janling Fu. Winona Lake, IN: Eisenbrauns, 2014.

Pajunen, Mika S. "The Saga of Judah's Kings Continues: The Reception of Chronicles in the Late Second Temple Period." *JBL* 136 (2017): 565–84. https://doi.org/10.15699/jbl.1363.2017.3131

Pakkala, Juha. "The Date of the Oldest Edition of Deuteronomy." *ZAW* 121 (2009): 388–401.

–. "Jeroboam without Bulls." *ZAW* 120 (2008): 501–25.

–. "Why the Cult Reforms in Judah Probably Did Not Happen." Pages 201–35 in *One God—One Cult—One Nation: Archaeological and Biblical Perspectives*. Edited by Reinhard G. Kratz and Hermann Spieckermann. BZAW 405. Berlin: de Gruyter, 2010. https://doi.org/10.1515/9783110223583.201

Park, Song-Mi. *Hezekiah and the Dialogue of Memory*. EmSch. Minneapolis: Fortress, 2015.

Parpola, Simo. *Assyrian Prophecies.* SAA 9. Helsinki: Helsinki University Press, 1997.
Paton, Lewis B. "Ashtart (Astoreth), Astarte." *ERE* 1.115–18.
–. "Baal, Beel, Bel." *ERE* 2.283–98.
–. "The Religion of Judah from Josiah to Ezra." *BibW* 11 (1898): 410–21.
Patrick, Dale. *Old Testament Law.* Atlanta: John Knox, 1985.
–. *The Rendering of God in the Old Testament.* OBT. Philadelphia: Fortress, 1981.
Paul, Shalom M. "Two Notes on Biblical and Mesopotamian Imagery." Pages 171–77 in *Built by Wisdom, Established by Understanding: Essays on Biblical and Near Eastern Literature in Honor of Adele Berlin.* Edited by Maxine L. Grossman. Bethesda: University Press of Maryland, 2013.
Pedersen, Johannes. *Israel: Its Life and Culture, III–IV.* Translated by A. I. Fausbøll. London: Oxford University Press, 1940.
–. "Passahfest und Passahlegende." *ZAW* 52 (1934): 161–75.
Penchansky, David. *Twilight of the Gods: Polytheism in the Hebrew Bible.* Louisville: Westminster John Knox, 2005. https://doi.org/10.5508/jhs.2006.v6.r14
Perdue, Leo G. *Wisdom Literature: A Theological History.* Louisville: Westminster John Knox, 2007.
Person, Raymond F., Jr. *The Deuteronomic History and the Book of Chronicles: Scribal Works in an Oral World.* AIL 6. Atlanta: Society of Biblical Literature, 2010. https://doi.org/10.1111/rsr.12033_19
Pettey, Richard J. "Asherah: Goddess of Israel?" PhD. diss., Marquette University, 1985.
Pfeiffer, Charles F. *Old Testament History.* Grand Rapids: Baker Books, 1973.
Pfeiffer, Richard J. "The Polemic against Idolatry in the Old Testament." *JBL* 43 (1924): 229–40.
Pietsch, Michael. *Die Kultreform Josias: Studien zur Religionsgeschichte Israels in der späten Königszeit.* FAT 86. Tübingen: Mohr Siebeck, 2013. https://doi.org/10.5508/jhs.2013.v13.r67
–. "Prophetess of Doom: Hermeneutical Reflections on the Huldah Oracle (2 Kings 22)." Pages 71–80 in *Soundings in Kings: Perspectives and Methods in Contemporary Scholarship.* Edited by Mark Leuchter and Klaus-Peter Adam. Minneapolis: Fortress, 2010. https://doi.org/10.2307/j.ctt22nm7cc.8
Pitard, Wayne T. "Tombs and Offerings: Archaeological Data and Comparative Methodology in the Study of Death in Israel." Pages 145–67 in *Sacred Time, Sacred Place: Archaeology and the Religion of Israel.* Edited by Barry M. Gitten. Winona Lake, IN: Eisenbrauns, 2002.
Plumptre, Edward Hayes. *The Gospel According to St. Matthew.* HC. London: Cassell, Peter, Galpin, 1879.
Porath, Renatus. "Dois textos, duas leituras: Um diálogo crítico entre a exegese e a arqueologia." *VS* 13 (2005): 57–67.
Porter, Barbara Nevling. *Trees, Kings, and Politics: Studies in Assyrian Iconography.* OBO 197. Fribourg: Academic; Göttingen: Vandenhoeck & Ruprecht, 2003. https://doi.org/10.1086/649617
Powell, Joseph. *The Death of Good Josiah Lamented: A Sermon Occasioned by the Death of Our Late Most Gracious Soveraign Queen Mary, of Ever Blessed Memory, Preach'd at Balsham in Cambridgshire, March 3, 1695.* London: Three Crowns, 1695. https://doi.org/10.1163/2214-8264_dutchpamphlets-kb1-kb16481
Preibisz, Leon. *Martin van Heemskerck: Ein Beitrag zur Geschichte des Romanismus in der*

Niederländiscen Malerei des XVI-Jahrhunderts. Leipzig: Klinkhardt und Biermann, 1911.

Price, Ira Maurice, Ovid R. Sellers, and E. Leslie Carlson. *The Monuments and the Old Testament: Light from the Near East on the Scriptures*. Rev. ed. Philadelphia: Judson, 1958.

Priest, John. "Huldah's Oracle." *VT* 30 (1980): 366–68.

Provera, Mario. "Il culto lunare nella tradizione biblica e profana." *BeO* 33 (1991): 65–68.

Quack, Joachim Friedrich. "The Interaction of Egyptian and Aramaic Literature." Pages 375–401 in *Judah and the Judeans in the Achaemenid Period: Negotiating Identity in an International Context*. Edited by Oded Lipschits, Gary N. Knoppers, and Manfred Oeming. Winona Lake, IN: Eisenbrauns, 2011. https://doi.org/10.1086/658973

–. "Postulated and Real Efficacy in Late Antique Divination Rituals." *JRitSt* 24 (2010): 45–59.

Quack, Johannes, and Paul Töbelmann. "Questioning 'Ritual Efficacy.'" *JRitSt* 24 (2010): 13–28.

Rabbinowitz, Joseph, trans. *Midrash Rabbah: Deuteronomy*. 3rd ed. London: Soncino, 1983.

Radner, Karen. "Assyrian and Non-Assyrian Kingship in the First Millennium BC." Pages 25–34 in *Concepts of Kingship in Antiquity: Proceedings of the European Science Foundation Exploratory Workshop: Held in Padova, November 28th–December 1st, 2007*. Edited by Giovanni B. Lanfranchi and Robert Rollinger. HANE/M 11. Padua: S.A.R.G.O.N. Editrice e Libereria, 2010.

Raleigh, Walter. *The History of the World*. Oxford: Oxford University Press, 1829.

Ramis Darder, Francesc. *Qué se sabe de Los profetas*. QS. Estella: Verbo Divino, 2010.

Rapp, Claudia. "Old Testament Models for Emperors in Early Byzantium." Pages 175–97 in *The Old Testament in Byzantium*. Edited by Paul Magdaline and Robert Nelson. Washington, DC: Dumbarton Oaks Research Library and Collection, 2010. https://doi.org/10.1017/s0038713412002497

Rawlinson, George. *The Kings of Israel and Judah*. Men of the Bible. New York: Anson D. F. Randolph, 1889.

Reade, Julian. *Assyrian Sculpture*. Cambridge, MA: Harvard University Press, 1983.

Redford, Donald B. *Akenaten: The Heretic King*. Princeton: Princeton University Press, 1984. https://doi.org/10.1086/ahr/92.4.932

–. *Egypt, Canaan, and Israel in Ancient Times*. Princeton: Princeton University Press, 1992. https://doi.org/10.1086/ahr/98.3.841

–. "Some observations on the Traditions Surrounding 'Israel in Egypt'." Pages 279–364 in *Judah and the Judeans in the Achaemenid Period: Negotiating Identity in an International Context*. Edited by Oded Lipschits, Gary N. Knoppers, and Manfred Oeming. Winona Lake, IN: Eisenbrauns, 2011. https://doi.org/10.1086/658973

Reed, William L. *The Asherah in the Old Testament*. Fort Worth: Texas Christian University Press, 1949.

Renan, Ernest. *From the Time of Hezekiah till the Return from Babylon*. Vol. 3 of *History of the People of Israel*. Boston: Roberts Brothers, 1896.

–. "The History of the People of Israel." Pages 107–48 in *Studies of Religious History and Criticism*. Translated by O. B. Frothingham. New York: Carleton, 1864.

Rendtorff, Rolf. "The Jewish Bible and Its Anti-Jewish Interpretation." *CJR* 16 (1983): 3–20.

—. *The Problem of the Process of Transmission in the Pentateuch.* JSOTSup 89. Sheffield: Sheffield Academic, 1990.

Riaud, Jean. "Les Anciens." Pages 23–47 in *Les Élites dans le monde biblique*. Edited by Jean Riaud. BEJH 32. Paris: Honoré Champion, 2008.

Richardson, H. Neil, "The Historical Reliability of Chronicles." *JBR* 26 (1958): 9–12.

Richardson, Seth. "The Hypercoherent Icon: Knowledge, Rationalization, and Disenchantment at Nineveh." Pages 231–58 in *Iconoclasm and Text Destruction in the Ancient Near East and Beyond*. Edited by Natalie Naomi May. OIS 8. Chicago: Oriental Institute of the University of Chicago, 2012.

Richter, Sandra. "Eighth-Century Issues: The World of Jeroboam II, the Fall of Samaria, and the Reign of Hezekiah." Pages 319–49 in *Ancient Israel's History: An Introduction to Issues and Sources*. Edited by Bill T. Arnold and Richard S. Hess. Grand Rapids: Baker Academic, 2014. https://doi.org/10.1111/rsr.12302

Ringgren, Helmer. *Israelite Religion*. Translated by David E. Green. Philadelphia: Fortress, 1966.

—. *Religions of the Ancient Near East*. Translated by John Sturdy. Philadelphia: Westminster, 1973. https://doi.org/10.1086/462704

Ristau, Kenneth A. "Reading and Rereading Josiah: The Chronicler's Representation of Josiah for the Postexilic Community." Pages 219–47 in *Community Identity in Judean Historiography: Biblical and Comparative Perspectives*. Edited by Gary N. Knoppers and Kenneth A. Ristau. Winona Lake, IN: Eisenbrauns, 2009. https://doi.org/10.31826/9781463235505-062

Ritner, Robert K. *The Libyan Anarchy: Inscriptions from Egypt's Third Intermediate Period*. Edited by Edward Wente. SBLWAW 21. Atlanta: Society of Biblical Literature, 2009. https://doi.org/10.1093/jss/fgr041

Roberts, J. J. M. *Nahum, Habakkuk, and Zephaniah: A Commentary*. OTL. Louisville: Westminster John Knox, 1991. https://doi.org/10.1177/004057369204900111

—. "Nebuchadnezzar I's Elamite Crisis in Theological Perspective." Pages 182–87 in *Essays on the Ancient Near East in Memory of Jacob Joel Finkelstein*. Edited by Maria de Jong Ellis. MCAAS 19. Hamden, CT: Archon Books, 1977.

Roberts, J. M., and Odd Arne Westad. *The History of the World*. London: Dorling Kindersley, 1996.

Robinson, Donald W. B. *Josiah's Reform and the Book of the Law*. London: Tyndale Press, 1951.

Robinson, Joseph. *The First Book of Kings*. CBC. Cambridge: Cambridge University Press, 1972.

—. *The Second Book of Kings*. CBC. Cambridge: Cambridge University Press, 1976.

Robinson, Theodore H. *From the Exodus to the Fall of Jerusalem, 586 B.C.* Vol. 1 of *A History of Israel*. Oxford: Clarendon, 1932.

—. "Israel in the Light of History." Pages 809–34 in *From the Hittite Empire to Fifth Century Athens*. Vol. 2 of *Universal History of the World*. Edited by John Alexander Hammerton. London: Amalgamated, 1927.

Rochberg, Francesca. "'The Stars Their Likenesses': Perspectives on the Relation between Celestial Bodies and Gods in Ancient Mesopotamia." Pages 41–91 in *What Is a God? Anthropomorphic and Non-Anthropomorphic Aspects of Deity in Ancient Mesopotamia*. Edited by Barbara Nevling Porter. TCBAI 2. Winona Lake, IN: Eisenbrauns, 2009. https://doi.org/10.7208/chicago/9780226789408.003.0002

Roebuck, Carl. *The World of Ancient Times*. New York: Scribner's Sons, 1966.

Rofé, Alexander. "The Scribal Concern for the Torah as Evidenced by the Textual

Witnesses of the Hebrew Bible." Pages 185–99 in *Mishneh Todah: Studies in Deuteronomy and Its Cultural Environment in Honor of Jeffrey H. Tigay*. Edited by Nili Sacher Fox, David A. Glatt-Gilad, and Michael J. Williams. Winona Lake, IN: Eisenbrauns, 2009. https://doi.org/10.1111/j.1748-0922.2010.01487_9.x

Rogerson, John W. *Chronicle of the Old Testament Kings: The Reign-by-Reign Record of the Rulers of Ancient Israel*. London: Thames and Hudson, 1999. https://doi.org/10.1108/rr.2002.16.1.49.56

–. *The So-called Deuteronomistic History: A Sociological, Historical and Literary Introduction*. London: T&T Clark, 2007.

–. *W. M. L. de Wette, Founder of Modern Biblical Criticism: An Intellectual Biography*. JSOTSup 126. Sheffield: JSOT Press, 1992. https://doi.org/10.1163/1568533952663314

Rollston, Christopher A. "Scribal Curriculum During the First Temple Period: Epigraphic Hebrew and Biblical Evidence." Pages 71–101 in *Contextualizing Israel's Sacred Writings: Ancient Literacy, Orality, and Literary Production*. Edited by Brian Schmidt. AIL 22. Atlanta: Society of Biblical Literature, 2015. https://doi.org/10.2307/j.ctt1647cmz.7

Römer, Thomas. "L'Autorité du livre dans les trois parties de la Bible Hébraïque." Pages 83–102 in *Écritures et réécritures: La preprise interpretative des traditions foundatrices par la literature biblique et extra-biblique*. Edited by Claire Clivaz, Corina Combet-Galland, Jean-Daniel Macchi, and Chistophe Nihan. BETL 248. Leuven: Peeters, 2012. https://doi.org/10.4000/books.pulm.405

–. "The Formation of the Book of Jeremiah as a Supplement to the So-called Deuteronomistic History." Pages 168–83 in *The Production of Prophecy: Constructing Prophecy and Prophets in Yehud*. Edited by Diana V. Edelman and Ehud Ben Zvi. BibleWorld. London: Equinox, 2009. https://doi.org/10.4324/9781315710891

–. *The So-Called Deuteronomistic History: A Sociological, Historical and Literary Introduction*. London: T&T Clark, 2007. https://doi.org/10.5508/jhs.2009.v9.a17

–. "Transformations in Deuteronomistic and Biblical Historiography: On 'Book-Finding' and Other Literary Strategies." *ZAW* 109 (1997): 1–11.

–. "Von Maulwürfen und verhinderten Propheten: Einige Anmerkungen zum prophetischen Buch." *CV* 51 (2009): 173–83.

Ron, Zvi. "Antecedents of the Hanukkah Oil Story." *RRJ* 18 (2015): 63–74.

Roper, Lyndal. *The Witch in the Western Imagination*. SEMGH. Charlottesville: University of Virginia, 2012. https://doi.org/10.1515/hzhz-2014-0058

Ross, Leslie. *Medieval Art: A Topical Dictionary*. Westport, CN: Greenwood, 1996.

Rost, Leonard. *The Succession to the Throne of David*. Translated by Michael D. Rutter and David M. Gunn. HTIBS 1. Sheffield: Almond Press, 1982.

Rouillard, Hedwige. "Rephaim." *DDD* cols. 1307–24.

Routledge, Robin L. "Death and Afterlife in the Old Testament." *JEBS* 9 (2008): 22–39.

Rowlett, Lori. "Inclusion, Exclusion and Monarchy in the Book of Joshua." Pages 372–80 in *Social-Scientific Old Testament Criticism*. Edited by David J. Chalcraft. BibSem 47. Sheffield: Sheffield Academic, 1997.

Rowley, H. H. *The Growth of the Old Testament*. Hutchinson University Library. London: Hutchinson, 1950. Repr. Cloister Library. New York: Harper & Row, 1963.

–. "Zadok and Nehushtan." *JBL* 58 (1939): 113–41.

Rowton, Michael B. "Jeremiah and the Death of Josiah." *JNES* 10 (1951): 128–30.

Rudolph, Wilhelm. "Problems of the Books of Chronicles." *VT* 4 (1954): 401–9.

Rütersworden, Udo. "Die Prophetin Hulda." Pages 234–42 in *Meilenstein: Festgabe für*

Herbert Donner zum 16. Februar 1995. Edited by M. Weippert and S. Timm. ÄAT 30. Wiesbaden: Harrassowitz, 1993.

Ryle, Herbert Edward. *The Canon of the Old Testament: An Essay on the Gradual Growth and Formation of the Hebrew Canon of Scripture*. 2nd ed. London: Macmillan, 1914. https://doi.org/10.1086/471058

Sabourin, Leopold. *The Psalms: Their Origin and Meaning*. Staten Island, NY: Alba House, 1969.

Sahagún, Bernadino de. *General History of the Things of New Spain. Book 1: The God*. Translated by Arthur J. O. Anderson and Charles E. Dibble. 2nd ed. MASR 14.2. Santa Fe, NM: School of American Research and University of Utah, 1970. https://doi.org/10.2307/276589

Said, Edward W. *Orientalism*. New York: Vintage, 1978.

Sale, George. *An Universal History, from the Earliest Account of Time to the Present: Compiled from Original Authors*. 66 vols. Dublin: George Faulkner, 1744.

Sasson, Jack M. *Jonah: A New Translation with Introduction, Commentary, and Interpretation*. AB 24B. New York: Doubleday, 1990.

—. *Ruth: A New Translation with a Philological Commentary and a Formalist-Folklorist Interpretation*. JHNES. Baltimore: Johns Hopkins University, 1979. https://doi.org/10.1177/030908928000501611

Savran, George. "1 and 2 Kings." Pages 146–64 in *The Literary Guide to the Bible*. Edited by Robert Alter and Frank Kermode. Cambridge, MA: Belknap, 1987. https://doi.org/10.1017/s0360966900039785

Schart, Aaron. "Martin Noth: Auf dem Hintergrund der NS-Zeit gelesen." Pages 235–52 in *Kontexte: Biografische und forschungsgeschichtliche Schnittpunkte der alttestamentlichen Wissenschaft: Festschrift für Jochen Boecker zum 80. Geburtstag*. Edited by Thomas Wagner, Dieter Vieweger, and Kurt Erlemann. Neukirchen-Vluyn: Neukirkener, 2008.

Schaudig, Hanspeter. "Cult Centralization in the Ancient Near East? Conceptions of the Ideal Capital in the Ancient Near East." Pages 145–68 in *One God—One Cult—One Nation: Archaeological and Biblical Perspectives*. Edited by Reinhard G. Kratz and Hermann Spieckermann. BZAW 405. Berlin: de Gruyter, 2010. https://doi.org/10.1515/9783110223583.145

—. "Death of Statues and Rebirth of Gods." Pages 123–49 in *Iconoclasm and Text Destruction in the Ancient Near East and Beyond*. Edited by Natalie Naomi May. OIS 8. Chicago: Oriental Institute of the University of Chicago, 2012.

Schauss, Hayyim. *The Jewish Festivals: History and Observance*. Translated by Samuel Jaffe. New York: Schocken Books, 1962.

Schearing, Linda S. "Models, Monarchs and Misconceptions: Athaliah and Joash of Judah." PhD diss., Emory University, 1992.

—. "Queen." *ABD* 5.583–86.

—. "A Wealth of Women: Looking Behind, Within, and Beyond Solomon's Story." Pages 428–56 in *The Age of Solomon: Scholarship at the Turn of the Millennium*. Edited by Lowell K. Handy. SHCANE 11. Leiden: Brill, 1997.

—. "Zeruah." *ABD* 6.1084.

Schedel, Hartmann. *Chronicle of the World: The Complete and Annotated Nuremberg Chronicle of 1493*. Köln: Taschen, 2001.

Schipper, Bernd Ulrich. *Israel und Ägypten in der Königszeit: Die kulturellen Kontakte von Salomo bis zum Fall Jerusalems*. OBO 170. Freiburg: Universitätsverlag; Göttingen: Vandenhoeck & Ruprecht, 1999.

Schmid, Hans Heinrich. *Der sogenannte Jawhist: Beobachtungen und Fragen zur Pentateuchforschung.* Zurich: Theologischer, 1976.

Schmid, Konrad. "Nebuchadnezzar, the End of Davidic Rule, and the Exile in the Book of Jeremiah." Pages 63–76 in *The Prophets Speak on Forced Migration.* AIL 21. Atlanta: Society of Biblical Literature, 2015. https://doi.org/10.2307/j.ctt1b7x6cn.10

Schmidt, Brian B. "Canaanite Magic vs. Israelite Religion: Deuteronomy 18 and the Taxonomy of Taboo." Pages 242–59 in *Magic and Ritual in the Ancient World.* Edited by Paul Mirecki and Marvin Meyer. RGRW141. Leiden: Brill, 2002. https://doi.org/10.1163/9789047400400_014

Schmitt, Rüdiger. "Elements of Domestic Cult in Ancient Israel." Pages 57–219 in *Family and Household Religion in Ancient Israel and the Levant.* Edited by Rainer Albertz and Rüdiger Schmitt. Winona Lake, IN: Eisenbrauns, 2012. https://doi.org/10.5615/neareastarch.77.2.0154

–. "Kultinventare aus Wohnhäusern als materielle Elemente familiärer Religion im Alten Israel." Pages 441–77 in *Berührungspunkte: Studien zur Sozial- und Religionsgeschichte Israels und seiner Umwelt: Festschrift für Rainer Albertz zu seinem 65. Geburtstag.* Edited by Ingo Kottsieper, Rüdiger Schmitt, and Jakob Wöhrle. AOAT 350. Münster: Ugarit, 2008. https://doi.org/10.1515/9783110897005

–. "Typology of Iron Age Cult Places." Pages 220–44 in *Family and Household Religion in Ancient Israel and the Levant.* Edited by Rainer Albertz and Rüdiger Schmitt. Winona Lake, IN: Eisenbrauns, 2012. https://doi.org/10.5615/neareastarch.77.2.0154

Schmitz, Philip C. "Queen of Heaven." *ABD* 5.586–88.

Schneider, Tammi J. *An Introduction to Ancient Mesopotamian Religion.* Grand Rapids: Eerdmans, 2011.

Schniedewind, William M. "Jerusalem, the Late Judahite Monarchy, and the Composition of the Biblical Texts." Pages 375–93 in *Jerusalem in Bible and Archaeology: The First Temple Period.* Edited by Andrew G. Vaughn and Ann E. Killebrew. SBLSymS 18. Atlanta: Society of Biblical Literature, 2003. https://doi.org/10.1086/586679

–. "Prophets and Prophecy in the Books of Chronicles." Pages 204–24 in *The Chronicler as Historian.* Edited by M. Patrick Graham, Kenneth G. Hoglund, and Steven L. McKenzie. JSOTSup 238. Sheffield: Sheffield Acadamic, 1997. https://doi.org/10.1163/1568533982721758

Schnorr von Carolsfeld, Julius. *Das Buch der Bücher in Bildern: 240 Darstellungen erfunden und gezeichnet.* Leipzig: Georg Wigand, 1908.

Schütte, Wolfgang. "Wie wurde Juda israelitisiert?" *ZAW* 124 (2012): 52–72. https://doi.org/10.1515/zaw-2012-0004

Schwartz, Joshua. "Jubilees, Bethel and the Temple of Jacob." *HUCA* 56 (1985): 63–85.

Schweitzer, Steven J. "Judging a Book by Its Citations: Sources and Authority in Chronicles." Pages 37–65 in *What Was Authoritative for Chronicles?* Edited by Ehud Ben Zvi and Diana V. Edelman. Winona Lake, IN: Eisenbrauns, 2011. https://doi.org/10.1515/olzg-2015-0165

Scibona, Rocco. "Betel e le tradizioni cananaiche e orientali dell'Antico Testamento anteriore." *BeO* 40 (1998): 65–98.

Scot, Reginald. *The Discoverie of Witchcraft.* London: John Rodker, 1930. Repr., New York: Dover, 1972.

Scurlock, JoAnn. "Josiah: The View from Mesopotamia." *BR* 51 (2006): 9–24.

–. *Magico-Medical Means of Treating Ghost-Induced Illnesses in Ancient Mesopotamia*. AMD 3. Leiden: Brill, 2006. https://doi.org/10.1017/s0041977x11000863

–. "Sins of Omission or Commission or What Can Assyrian Scribes Teach Us about the Bible as an Edited Book." Paper presented at the Spring Meeting of the Chicago Society of Biblical Research. Chicago, 7 April 2018.

Sellin, Ernst, and Georg Fohrer. *Introduction to the Old Testament*. Translated by David E. Green. Nashville: Abingdon, 1968.

Seltzer, Robert M. *Jewish People, Jewish Thought: The Jewish Experience in History*. New York: Macmillan, 1980.

Sensenig, Peter M. "Chariots on Fire: Military Dominance in the Old Testament." *HBT* 34 (2012): 73–80. https://doi.org/10.1163/187122012x627812

Shafer, Bryon E. "Temples, Priests, and Rituals: An Overview." Pages 1–30 in *Temples of Ancient Egypt*. Edited by Bryon E. Shafer. Ithaca, NY: Cornell University, 1997.

Shafer-Elliott, Cynthia. "The Role of the Household in the Religious Feasting of Ancient Israel and Judah." Pages 199–221 in *Feasting in the Archaeology and Texts of the Bible and the Ancient Near East*. Edited by Peter Altmann and Janling Fu. Winona Lake, IN: Eisenbrauns, 2014.

Shemesh, Yael. "Directions in Jewish Feminist Bible Study." *CurBR* 14 (2016): 372–406.

Shepherd, Geoffrey. "The Vernacular Scriptures: English Versions of the Scriptures before Wyclif." Pages 362–87 in *Cambridge History of the Bible: The West from the Fathers to the Reformation*. Edited by G. H. W. Lampe. Cambridge: Cambridge University Press, 1969. https://doi.org/10.1017/s0022046900057572

Shipp, Mark R. "The First Restoration Movement: The Chronicler's Program of Restoration and Churches of Christ." *ChrSt* 27 (2015): 21–29.

Silberman, Neil Asher. "Archaeology, Ideology, and the Search for David and Solomon." Pages 395–405 in *Jerusalem in Bible and Archaeology: The First Temple Period*. Edited by Andrew G. Vaughn and Ann E. Killebrew. SBLSymS 18. Atlanta: Society of Biblical Literature, 2003. https://doi.org/10.1086/586679

Silva, Aldina da. "La symbolique du repas au ProcheOrient ancien." *SR* 24 (1995): 147–57.

Silver, Daniel Jeremy. *From Abraham to Maimonides*. Vol. 1 of *A History of Judaism*. New York: Basic Books, 1974.

Simpson, William Kelly. "Reshep in Egypt." *Or* 29 (1960): 63–74.

Skehan, Patrick, and Alexander Di Lella. *The Wisdom of Ben Sira: A New Translation with Notes*. AB 39. New York: Doubleday, 1987. https://doi.org/10.1163/157006388x00453

Skjærvø, Prods Oktor. "Zarathustra: A Revolutionary Monotheist?" Pages 317–50 in *Reconsidering the Concept of Revolutionary Monotheism*. Edited by B. Pongratz-Leisten. Winona Lake, IN: Eisenbrauns, 2011. https://doi.org/10.1163/15685276-12341269

Smith, Louise Pettibone, and Ernest R. Lacheman. "The Authorship of the Book of Zephaniah." *JNES* 9 (1950): 137–42.

Smith, Mark S. *The Early History of God: Yahweh and the Other Deities in Ancient Israel*. 2nd ed. Bible Resource Series. Grand Rapids: Eerdmans, 2002. https://doi.org/10.1086/524165

Smith, Morton. *Palestine Parties and Politics that Shaped the Old Testament*. New York: Columbia University Press, 1971.

Smith, W. Robertson. *The Religion of the Semites: The Fundamental Institutions*. New York: Schocken Books, 1972.

Smith, Warren Sylvester. *The London Heretics: 1870-1914*. New York: Dodd, Mead, 1968.
Soggin, J. Alberto. *Israel in the Biblical Period: Institutions, Festivals, Ceremonies, Rituals*. Translated by John Bowden. Edinburgh: T&T Clark, 2001.
—. *Joshua: A Commentary*. Translated by R. A. Wilson. OTL. Philadelphia: Westminster, 1972.
Solvang, Elna K. *A Woman's Place Is in the House: Royal Women of Judah and Their Involvement in the House of David*. JSOTSup 349. London: Sheffield Academic, 2003. https://doi.org/10.1086/505004
Soza, Joel A. "Jeroboam." Pages 544-47 in *Dictionary of the Old Testament: Historical Books*. Edited by Bill T. Arnold and H. G. M. Williamson. Downers Grove, IL: InterVarsity Press, 2005. https://doi.org/10.1108/09504120710719400
Spieckermann, Hermann. "God and His People: The Concept of Kingship and Cult in the Ancient Near East." Pages 341-56 in *One God—One Cult—One Nation: Archaeological and Biblical Perspectives*. Edited by Reinhard G. Kratz and Hermann Spieckermann. BZAW 405. Berlin: de Gruyter, 2010. https://doi.org/10.1515/9783110223583.339
—. *Juda unter Assur in der Sargonidenzeit*. FRLANT 129. Göttingen: Vandenhoeck & Ruprecht, 1982. https://doi.org/10.13109/9783666538001
—. "YHWH Bless You and Keep You: The Relation of History of Israelite Religion and Old Testament Theology Reconsidered." *SJOT* 23 (2009): 165-82. https://doi.org/10.1080/09018320903303520
Spiegelman, Art, and Françoise Mouly. *The Toon Treasury of Classic Children's Comics*. New York: Abrams, 2009
Spronk, Klass. *Beatific Afterlife in Ancient Israel and in the Ancient Near East*. AOAT 219. Kevelaer: Butzon und Bercker; Neukirchen-Vluyn: Neuchirchener, 1986.
Stadelmann, Rainer. *Syrisch-Palästinensische Gottheiten in Ägypten*. PAe 5. Leiden: Brill, 1967.
Stanley, Arthur Penrhyn. *Samuel to the Captivity*. Vol. 2 of *Lectures on the History of the Jewish Church*. New Ed. New York: Scribner's Sons, 1901.
Stanton, Elizabeth Cady. *The Woman's Bible. Part II: Comments on the Old and New Testaments from Joshua to Revelation*. New York: European Publishing, 1898.
Starr, Chester G. *A History of the Ancient World*. 4th ed. New York: Oxford University Press, 1991.
Stavrakopoulou, Francesca. "'Popular' Religion and 'Official' Religion: Practice, Perception, Portrayal." Pages 37-58 in *Religious Diversity in Ancient Israel and Judah*. Edited by Francesca Stavrakopoulou and John Barton. London: T&T Clark, 2010.
Steinberg, Naomi. "Exodus 12 in Light of Ancestral Cult Practices." Pages 89-105 in *The Family in Life and Death: The Family in Ancient Israel: Sociological and Archaeological Perspectives*. Edited by P. Dutcher-Walls. LHBOTS 504. New York: T&T Clark, 2009.
Stern, Ephraim. *The Assyrian, Babylonian, and Persian Periods (732-332 B.C.E.)*. Vol. 2 of *Archaeology of the Land of the Bible*. ABRL. New York: Doubleday, 2001.
—. "The Eastern Border of the Kingdom of Judah in Its Last Days." Pages 399-409 in *Scripture and Other Artifacts: Essays on the Bible and Archaeology in Honour of Philip J. King*. Edited by Michael D. Coogan, J. Cheryl Exum, and Lawrence E. Stager. Louisville: Westminster John Knox, 1994. https://doi.org/10.2307/3210504
—. "From Many Gods to the One God: The Archaeological Evidence." Pages 395-403 in *One God—One Cult—One Nation: Archaeological and Biblical Perspectives*. Edited by

Reinhard G. Kratz and Hermann Spieckermann. BZAW 405. Berlin: de Gruyter, 2010. https://doi.org/10.1515/9783110223583.395
–. "The Religious Revolution in Persian-Period Judah." Pages 199–205 in *Judah and Judeans in the Persian Period*. Edited by Oded Lipschits and Manfred Oeming. Winona Lake, IN: Eisenbrauns, 2006. https://doi.org/10.1086/658973
Steussy, Marti J. *David: Biblical Portraits of Power*. SPOT. Columbia: University of South Carolina Press, 1999.
Stevens, Marty E. *Temples, Tithes, and Taxes: The Temple and the Economic Life of Ancient Israel*. Peabody, MA: Hendrickson, 2006.
Stinespring, William Franklin. "Eschatology in Chronicles." *JBL* 80 (1961): 209–19.
Stipp, Hermann-Josef. "Die sechste und siebte Fürbitte des Tempelweihegebets (1 Kön 8,44–51) in der Diskussion um das deuteronomistische Geschichtswerk." *JNSL* 24 (1998): 193–216. https://doi.org/10.3726/978-3-653-00800-5/2
Stökl, Jonathan, "Deborah, Huldah, and Innibana: Constructions of Female Prophecy in the Ancient Near East and the Hebrew Bible." *JAJ* 6 (2016): 320–34. https://doi.org/10.13109/jaju.2015.6.3.320
Stolz, Fritz. "Monotheismus in Israel." Pages 143–89 in *Monotheismus im Alten Israel und seiner Umwelt*. Edited by Othmar Keel. BibB 14. Fribourg: Schweizerisches Katholisches Bibelwerk, 1980. https://doi.org/10.2307/3260452
Stordalen, Terje. "Heaven on Earth—Or Not? Jerusalem as Eden in Biblical Literature." Pages 28–57 in *Beyond Eden: The Biblical Story of Paradise (Genesis 2–3) and Its Reception History*. Edited by K. Schmid and C. Riedweg. FAT 2.34. Tübingen: Mohr Siebeck, 2008. https://doi.org/10.1177/00145246101210080810
–. "Imagined and Forgotten Communities: Othering in the Story of Josiah's Reform (2 Kings 23)." Pages 182–200 in *Imagining the Other and Constructing Israelite Identity in the Early Second Temple Period*. Edited by Ehud Ben Zvi and Diana V. Edelman. LHBOTS 456. London: Bloomsbury, 2014. https://doi.org/10.5040/9780567659163.ch-010
Stott, Katherine. "Finding the Lost Book of the Law: Re-Reading the Story of 'The Book of the Law' (Deuteronomy–2 Kings) in Light of Classical Literature." *JSOT* 30 (2005): 153–69. https://doi.org/10.1177/0309089205052685
Strange, John. "Solomon and His Empire: Fact or Fiction?" *SJOT* 29 (2015): 11–21.
Street, J. S. *French Sacred Drama from Bèze to Corneille: Dramatic Forms and Their Purposes in the Early Modern Theatre*. Cambridge: Cambridge University Press, 1983. https://doi.org/10.1093/fs/38.3.334
Stroumsa, Guy G. "John Spencer and the Roots of Idolatry." *HR* 41 (2001): 1–23.
Suriano, Matthew J. *The Politics of Dead Kings: Dynastic Ancestors in the Book of Kings and Ancient Isreal*. FAT 2.48. Tübingen: Mohr Siebeck, 2010.
–. "Sheol, the Tomb, and the Problem of Postmortem Existence." *JHS* 16 (2016). https://doi.org/10.5508/jhs.2016.v16.a11
Suter, Joanne. *Globe Fearson's World History*. 3rd ed. Upper Saddle River, NJ: Globe Fearson, 1999.
Suzuki, Yoshihide. "Deuteronomic Reformation in View of the Centralization of the Administration of Justice." *AJBI* 13 (1987): 22–58.
–. "A New Aspect on Occupation Policy by King Josiah." *AJBI* 18 (1992): 31–61.
Sweeney, Marvin A. *I & II Kings: A Commentary*. OTL. Louisville: Westminster John Knox, 2007.
–. "Ezekiel's Debate with Isaiah." Pages 555–74 in *Congress Volume Ljubljana 2007*.

Edited by André Lemaire. VTSup 133. Leiden: Brill, 2010. https://doi.org/10.1163/ej.9789004179776.i-640.124

—. *Isaiah 1-39 with an Introduction to Prophetic Literature*. FOTL 16. Grand Rapids: Eerdmans, 1996.

—. "Josiah." Pages 575-79 in *Dictionary of the Old Testament: Historical Books*. Edited by Bill T. Arnold and H. G. M. Williamson. Downers Grove, IL: InterVarsity Press, 2005. https://doi.org/10.1108/09504120710719400

—. *King Josiah of Judah: The Lost Messiah of Israel*. Oxford: Oxford University, 2001.

—. *The Origins of Kingship in Israel and Japan: A Comparative Analysis*. OPIAC 33. Claremont, CA: Institute for Antiquity and Christianity, 1995.

Swidler, Arlene. "In Search of Huldah." *TBT* 98 (1978): 1780-85.

Synkellos, George. *The Chronography of George Synkellos: A Byzantine Chronicle of Universal History*. Translated by William Adler and Pau Tuffin. Oxford: Oxford University, 2002. https://doi.org/10.1086/524174

Syros, Vasileios. "Founders and Kings versus Orators: Medieval and Early Modern Views on the Origins of Social Life." *Viator* 42 (2011): 383-408. https://doi.org/10.1484/j.viator.1.102015

Talshir, Zipora. *I Esdras: From Origin to Translation*. SCS 47. Atlanta: Society of Biblical Literature, 1999.

—. "The Three Deaths of Josiah and the State of Biblical Historiography (2 Kings xxiii 29-30, 2 Chronicles xxxv 20-25, 1 Esdras i 23-31)." *VT* 46 (1996): 213-36. https://doi.org/10.1163/1568533962580793

Tatum, Lynn. "Jerusalem in Conflict: The Evidence for the Seventh-Century B.C.E. Religious Struggle over Jerusalem." Pages 291-306 in *Jerusalem in Bible and Archaeology: The First Temple Period*. Edited by Andrew G. Vaughn and Ann E. Killebrew. SBLSymS 18. Atlanta: Society of Biblical Literature, 2003. https://doi.org/10.1086/586679

Taylor, John. "Death, the Afterlife, and Other Last Things: Egypt." Pages 471-75 in *Religions of the Ancient World: A Guide*. Edited by Sarah Iles Johnston. Cambridge, MA: Belknap, 2004.

Tcherikover, Victor. *Hellenistic Civilization and the Jews*. Translated by S Applebaum. Philadelphia: Jewish Publication Society of America, 1959. Repr., New York: Antheneum, 1970. https://doi.org/10.1086/ahr/65.4.872

Teeter, Emily. *Religion and Ritual in Ancient Egypt*. Cambridge: Cambridge University Press, 2011.

Terry, Milton S. *Commentary on the Old Testament: Kings to Esther*. Whedon's Commentary 4. New York: Phillips & Hunt, 1875.

Thames, John Tracy, Jr. "A New Discussion of the Meaning of the Phrase 'am ha'areṣ in the Hebrew Bible." *JBL* 130 (2011): 109-25.

Thompson, Thomas L. *The Mythic Past: Biblical Archaeology and the Myth of Israel*. New York: Basic Books, 1999.

Thon, Johannes. "Das Grab des 'Lügenpropheten' im Dienste Wahrheit (1 Kön 13,11-32; 2 Kön 23,15-18)." Pages 467-75 in *Die unwiderstehliche Wahrheit: Studien zur alttestamentlichen Prophetie: Festschrift für Arndt Meinhold*. Edited by Rüdiger Lux and Ernst-Joachim Waschke. ABG 23. Leipzig: Evangelische, 2006.

Throntveit, Mark A. "The Chronicler's Speeches and Historical Reconstruction." Pages 225-45 in *The Chronicler as Historian*. Edited by M. Patrick Graham, Kenneth G. Hoglund, and Steven L. McKenzie. JSOTSup 238. Sheffield: Sheffield Academic, 1997. https://doi.org/10.1163/1568533982721758

–. "The Relationship of Hezekiah to David and Solomon in the Books of Chronicles." Pages 104–21 in *The Chronicler as Theologian: Essays in Honor of Ralph W. Klein*. Edited by M. Patrick Graham, Steven L. McKenzie, and Gary N. Knoppers. JSOTSup 371. London: T&T Clark, 2003. https://doi.org/10.1086/521770
Tigay, Jeffrey H. *Deuteronomy*. JPSTC. Philadelphia: Jewish Publication Society of America, 1996.
–. ""Israelite Religion: The Onomastic and Epigraphic Evidence." Pages 157–94 in *Ancient Israelite Religion*. Edited by Patrick D. Miller, Jr., Paul D. Hanson, and S. Dean McBride. Philadelphia: Fortress, 1987. https://doi.org/10.1086/487929
–. "The Torah Scroll and God's Presence." Pages 323–40 in *Built by Wisdom, Established by Understanding: Essays on Biblical and Near Eastern Literature in Honor of Adele Berlin*. Edited by Maxine L. Grossman. Bethesda: University Press of Maryland, 2013.
–. *You Shall Have No Other Gods: Israelite Religion in the Light of Hebrew Inscriptions*. HSS 31. Atlanta: Scholars Press, 1986. https://doi.org/10.1163/9789004360440_002
Tiller, Patrick A. *A Commentary on the Animal Apocalypse of I Enoch*. EJL 4. Atlanta: Scholars Press, 1993.
Toorn, Karel van der. *From Her Cradle to Her Grave: The Role of Religion in the Life of the Israelite and the Babylonian Woman*. Translated by Sara J. Denning-Bolle. BSS 23. Sheffield: JSOT Press, 1994. https://doi.org/10.2307/605210
–. "L'Oracle de victoire comme expression prophétique au Proche-Orient ancient." *RB* 94 (1987): 63–97.
–. "Sun." *ABD* 6.237–39.
Townsend, Joan B. "The Goddess: Fact, Fallacy and Revitalization Movement." Pages 179–203 in *Goddesses in Religion and Modern Debate*. Edited by Larry W. Hurtado. UMSR 1. Atlanta: Scholars Press, 1990.
Toy, Crawford H. "The Triumph of Yahwism." *JBL* 24 (1905): 91–106.
Trevelyan, Raleigh. *Sir Walter Raleigh*. New York: Henry Holt, 2002.
Trible, Phyllis. "Huldah's Holy Writ: On Women and Biblical Authority." *Touchstone* 3 (1985): 6–13.
Trimmer, Sarah. *Sacred History, Selected from the Holy Scriptures; with Annotations and Reflections, Particularly to Facilitate the Study of the Bible in Schools and Families*. 9th ed. London: J. G. F. & J. Rivington, 1840.
Tück, Jan-Heiner. "'Bei Gott gibt es keine Gewalt': Was Jan Assmanns 'onotheismuskritik theologisch zu denken gibt." *TP* 86 (2011): 222–53.
Uehlinger, Christoph. "Was There a Cult Reform under King Josiah? The Case for a Well-grounded Minimum." Pages 279–316 in *Good Kings and Bad Kings*. Edited by Lester L. Grabbe. LHBOTS 393. ESHM 5. London: T&T Clark, 2005.
Ulmer, Rivka. "The Egyptian Gods in Midrashic Texts." *HTR* 103 (2010): 181–204.
United States Department of Agriculture: Extension Service. *Raising Livestock on Small Farms*. Farmers' Bulletin 2224. Washington, DC: Government Printing Office, 1983.
Urquhart, Judy. *Animals on the Farm: Their History from the Earliest Times to the Present Day*. London: MacDonald, 1983.
Ussishkin, David. *The Conquest of Lachish by Sennacherib*. Tel Aviv: Tel Aviv University Press, 1982. https://doi.org/10.1179/033443577792432890
–. "Solomon's Jerusalem: The Texts and the Facts on the Ground." Pages 103–15 in *Jerusalem in Bible and Archaeology: The First Temple Period*. Edited by Andrew G.

Vaughn and Ann E. Killebrew. SBLSymS 18. Atlanta: Society of Biblical Literature, 2003. https://doi.org/10.1086/586679

Valerio, Adriana. Il profetismo femminile Cristiano nel II secolo: Bilancio storiografico e questioni aperte. Pages 159–72 in *Profeti e profezia: Figure profetiche cristianesimo del II secolo*. Edited by Anna Carfora and Enrico Cattaneo. Oi Christianoi 6. Trapani: Pozzo di Giacobbe, 2007. https://doi.org/10.5840/agstm201353118

Vallotten, Annie. Illustrator. *Good News Bible: The Bible in Today's English Version*. New York: American Bible Society, 1976.

Van Seters, John. "The Deuteronomist—Historian or Redactor? From Simon to the Present." Pages 359–75 in *Essays on Ancient Israel in Its Near Eastern Context: A Tribute to Nadav Na'aman*. Edited by Yairah Amit, Ehud Ben Zvi, Israel Finkelstein, and Oded Lipschits. Winona Lake, IN: Eisenbrauns, 2006. https://doi.org/10.1086/basor25067068

–. *The Edited Bible: The Curious History of the 'Editor' in Biblical Criticism*. Winona Lake, IN: Eisenbrauns, 2006. https://doi.org/10.1086/604681

–. *In Search of History: Historiography in the Ancient World and the Origins of Biblical History*. New Haven: Yale University Press, 1983. https://doi.org/10.1086/ahr/89.2.412

Vaux, Roland de. *Religious Institutions*. Vol. 2 of *Ancient Israel*. New York: McGraw-Hill, 1965.

Veldman, Ilja. *Maarten van Heemskerck and Dutch Humanism in the Sixteenth Century*. Amsterdam: Meulenhoff, 1977.

Vermeylen, Jacques. *Du prophète Isaïe à l'apocalyptique: Isaïe 1–35*. EBib. Paris: Gabalda, 1977–1978.

–. "L'unité du livre d'Isaïe." Pages 11–53 in *The Book of Isaiah*. BETL 81. Edited by J. Vermeylen. Leuven: Leuven University Press, 1989.

Viezel, Eran. "Un precedent juif de De Wette: Un commenteire attribué à Rashi sur le livre de Chroniques, autour du livre trouvé au Temple par le prêtre Hilkiyyahou." Translated by Rony Klein. *REJ* 170 (2011): 521–32.

Vílchez Líndez, José. *Tobias y Judit*. NBEN 3. Estella: Verbo Divino, 2000.

Visaticki, Karlo. *Die Reform des Josija und die religiöse Heterodoxie in Israel*. Dissertationen theologische Reihe 21. St. Ottilien: EOS, 1987.

Vriezen, Karel J. H. "Cakes and Figurines: Related Women's Cultic Offerings in Ancient Israel?" Pages 251–63 in *On Reading Prophetic Texts: Gender-Specific and Related Studies in Memory of Fokkelien van Dijk-Hennes*. Edited by Bob Becking and Meindert Dijkstra. BibIntS 18. Leiden: Brill, 1996. https://doi.org/10.1093/jts/50.1.197

Vriezen, Theodoor Christiaan. *The Religion of Ancient Israel*. Translated by Hubert Hoskins. Philadelphia: Westminster, 1967.

Wacker, Marie-Theres. "'Kultprostitution' im Alten Israel? Forschungsmythen, Spuren, Thesen." Pages 55–84 in *Tempelprostitution im Altertum: Fakten und Fiktionen*. Edited by T. S. Scheer. ÖSAW 6. Berlin: Antike, 2009.

Wagner, Volker. "Eine antike Notiz zur Geschichte des Pesach (2 Kön 23,21–23)." *BZ* 54 (2010): 20–35. https://doi.org/10.1163/25890468-054-01-90000002

–. "Das Pesach ist 'zwischeneingekommen' (Dtn 16,1–8)." *Bib* 91 (2010): 481–98.

Walker, Christopher, and Michael B. Dick. "The Induction of the Cult Image in Ancient Mesopotamia: The Mesopotamian *mis pî* Ritual." Pages 55–121 in *Born in Heaven, Made on Earth: The Making of the Cult Image in the Ancient Near East*. Edited by Michael B. Dick. Winona Lake: IN: Eisenbrauns, 1999. https://doi.org/10.1086/380353

Walsh, Jerome T. "Nebat." *ABD* 4.1054.
Warburton, David A. "The Importance of the Archaeology of the Seventh Century." Pages 317–35 in *Good Kings and Bad Kings*. Edited by Lester L. Grabbe. LHBOTS 393. ESHM 5. London: T&T Clark, 2005.
Warhurst, Amber K. "The Chronicler's Use of the Prophets." Pages 165–81 in *What Was Authoritive for Chronicles?* Edited by Ehud Ben Zvi and Diana V. Edelman. Winona Lake, IN: 2011.
Watson, Arthur. *The Early Iconography of the Tree of Jesse*. Oxford: Oxford University Press; London: Humphrey Milford, 1934.
Watts, James W. "Scripturalization and the Aaronide Dynasties." *JHS* 13 (2013). https://doi.org/10.5508/jhs.2013.v13.a6
Watts, John D. W. *The Books of Joel, Obadiah, Jonah, Nahum, Habakkuk and Zephaniah*. CBC. Cambridge: Cambridge University Press, 1975.
Weaver, Jeffrey, and Madeline H. Caviness. *The Ancestors of Christ Windows at Canterbury Cathedral*. Los Angeles: J. Paul Getty Museum, 2013. https://doi.org/10.1017/s0038713414002218
Weed, Libby, ed. *Read-and-Grow Picture Bible*. Fort Worth, TX: Sweet, 1984.
Weems, Renita J. "Huldah, the Prophet: Reading a (Deuteronomistic) Woman's Identity." Pages 321–39 in *A God So Near: Essays on Old Testament Theology in Honour of Patrick D. Miller*. Edited by Brent A. Strawn and Nancy R. Bowen. Winona Lake, IN: Eisenbrauns, 2003.
Weinfeld, Moshe. "Cult Centralization in Israel in the Light of a Neo-Babylonian Analogy." *JNES* 23 (1964): 202–12. https://doi.org/10.1086/371773
–. *Deuteronomy and the Deuteronomic School*. Winona Lake, IN: Eisenbrauns, 1992.
Weippert, Helga. "Die 'deuteronomistischen' Beurteilungen der Könige von Israel und Juda und das Problem der Redaktion der Königbucher." *Bib* 53 (1972): 301–39.
Weippert, Manfred. "Fragen des israelitischen Geschichtsbewustseins." *VT* 23 (1973): 415–42.
Weisberg, David B. "A 'Dinner at the Palace' during Nebuchadnezzar's Reign." Pages 261–68 in *Homeland and Exile: Biblical and Ancient Near Eastern Studies in Honour of Bustenay Oded*. Edited by Gershon Galil, Mark Geller and Alan Millard. VTSup 130. Leiden: Brill, 2009. https://doi.org/10.1093/jts/flq151
Welch, Adam C. *The Code of Deuteronomy: A New Theory of Its Origin*. London: James Clarke, 1924.
–. "The Death of Josiah." *ZAW* 43 (1925): 255–60.
–. *Deuteronomy: The Framework to the Code*. London: Oxford University Press, 1932.
–. *Post-Exilic Judaism*. Edinburgh: William Blackwood & Sons, 1935.
–. "When Was the Worship of Israel Centralized at the Temple?" *ZAW* 43 (1925): 250–55.
–. *The Work of the Chronicler: Its Purpose and Its Date*. Schweich Lectures 1938. London: Oxford University Press, 1939.
Welch, Eric Lee. "The Roots of Anger: An Economic Perspective on Zephaniah's Oracle Against the Philistines." *VT* 63 (2013): 471–85. https://doi.org/10.1163/15685330-12341125
Wellhausen, Julius. *Prolegomena to the History of Ancient Israel*. Translated by Sutherland Black and Allan Menzies. Cleveland: Meridian Books, 1957.
Wells, H. G. *Prehistory to the Roman Empire*. Vol. 1 of *The Outline of History*. Barnes & Noble Library of Essential Reading. New York: Macmillan, 1920. Repr., Barnes and Noble, 2004.

Welsh, Frank. *The History of the World: From the Dawn of Humanity to the Modern Age.* London: Quercus, 2011.

White, Ellen. *Yahweh's Council: Its Structure and Membership.* FAT 2, Riehe 65. Tübingen: Mohr Siebeck, 2014.

Whitley, C. F. "The Date of Jeremiah's Call." *VT* 14 (1964): 467–83.

Whybray, R. N. "Wisdom Literature in the Reigns of David and Solomon." Pages 13–26 in *Studies in the Period of David and Solomon and Other Essays.* Edited by Tomoo Ishida. Winona Lake, IN: Eisenbrauns, 1982. https://doi.org/10.4324/9781315233970-26

Widengren, Geo. "The Persians." Pages 312–57 in *Peoples of Old Testament Times.* Edited by Donald J. Wiseman. Oxford: Clarendon, 1973.

Wiggins, Steve A. "The Myth of Asherah: Lion Lady and Serpent Goddess." *UF* 23 (1991): 383–94.

–. *A Reassessment of 'Asherah': A Study according to the Textual Sources of the First Two Millennia B.C.E.* AOAT 235. Kevelaer: Butzon & Bercker; Neukirchen Vluyn: Neukirchener, 1993. https://doi.org/10.1163/1568533952662289

Wikander, Ola. "Finding Indra, Finding Torah: The Story of Shibamata Taishakuten and Josiah's Renovation," *SEÅ* 80 (2015): 69–77.

Wilcoxen, Jay A. "The Political Background of Jeremiah's Temple Sermon." Pages 151–66 in *Scripture in History and Theology: Essays in Honor of J. C. Rylaarsdam.* Edited by Arthur L. Merrill and Thomas W. Overholt. PittTM 17. Pittsburgh: Pickwick, 1977. https://doi.org/10.1086/486696

Williams, Donald L. "The Date of Zephaniah." *JBL* 82 (1963): 77–88.

Williams, George H. *The Radical Reformation.* Philadelphia: Westminster, 1962.

Williamson, H. G. M. "The Death of Josiah and the Continuing Development of the Deuteronomic History." *VT* 32 (1982): 242–48.

–. "Prophetesses in the Hebrew Bible." Pages 65–80 in *Prophecy and Prophets in Ancient Israel: Proceedings of the Oxford Old Testament Seminar.* Edited by John Day. LHBOTS 531. New York: T&T Clark, 2010.

Wilson, Leslie S. *The Serpent Symbol in the Ancient Near East.* SJud. Lanham, MD: University Press of America, 2001.

Wilson, Robert R. "Deuteronomy, Ethnicity, and Reform: Reflections on the Social Setting of the Book of Deuteronomy." Pages 107–23 in *Constituting the Community: Studies on the Polity of Ancient Israel in Honor of S. Dean McBride Jr.* Edited by John T. Strong and Steven S. Tuell. Winona Lake, IN: Eisenbrauns, 2005.

–. *Prophecy and Society in Ancient Israel.* Philadelphia: Fortress, 1980.

Wiseman, Donald J. *1 and 2 Kings: An Introduction and Commentary.* TOTC 9. Leicester: Inter-Varsity Press, 1993.

Wolff, Hans Walter. *Amos the Prophet: The Man and His Background.* Translated by F. R. McCurley. Philadelphia: Fortress, 1973.

–. *Joel and Amos.* Translated by W. Janzen, S. D. McBride, Jr., and C. A. Muenchow. Hermeneia. Philadelphia: Fortress, 1977. https://doi.org/10.1177/004057367803500215

Wood, W. Carleton. *The Religion of Canaan: From the Earliest Times to the Hebrew Conquest.* Ontario: Newmarket, 1916.

Woolf, Alex. *A History of the World: The Story of Mankind from Prehistory to the Modern Day.* London: Arcturus, 2015.

Wright, Nicky. *The Classic Era of American Comics.* Chicago: Contemporary Books, 2000.

Würthwein, Ernst. "Die Josianische Reform und das Deuteronomium." *ZTK* 73 (1976): 395–423.

Wyatt, Nicolas. "Asherah." *DDD* cols. 183–96.
–. "Astarte." *DDD* cols. 203–13.
–. *The Mythic Mind: Essays on Cosmology and Religion in Ugaritic and Old Testament Literature.* BibleWorld. London: Equinox, 2005. https://doi.org/10.5508/jhs.2006.v6.r25
–. "Royal Religion in Ancient Judah." Pages 61–81 in *Religious Diversity in Ancient Israel and Judah.* Edited by Francesca Stavrakopoulou and John Barton. London: T&T Clark, 2010.
Xella, Paolo. "Death and the Afterlife in Canaanite and Hebrew Thought." Translated by G. Faith Richardson. Pages 2059–70 in *Civilizations of the Ancient Near East:* III. Edited by Jack M. Sasson. New York: Scribner's Sons, 1995.
–. "Resheph." *DDD* cols. 1324–30.
Yadin, Yigael. *The Art of Warfare in Biblical Lands: In the Light of Archaeological Study.* Translated by M. Pearlman. New York: McGraw-Hill, 1963.
–. "Beer-sheba: The High Place Destroyed by King Josiah." *BASOR* 222 (1976): 5–17. https://doi.org/10.2307/1356295
Yamauchi, Edwin M. *Africa and the Bible.* Grand Rapids: Baker Academic, 2004.
Yee, Gale A. *Composition and Tradition in the Book of Hosea: A Redaction Critical Investigation.* SBLDS 102. Atlanta: Scholars Press, 1987.
–. "'He Will Take the Best of Your Fields': Royal Feasts and Rural Extraction." *JBL* 136 (2017): 821–38. https://doi.org/10.15699/jbl.1364.2017.310569
Youngberg, Brendan G. "Identity Coherence in the Chronicler's Narrative: King Josiah as a Second David and a Second Saul." *JHS* 17 (2017). https://doi.org/10.5508/jhs.2017.v17.a4
Younger, K. Lawson. "Another Look at an Aramaic Astral Bowl." *JNES* 71 (2012): 209–30.
Zamora García, Pedro. *Reyes I: La fuerza de la narración.* NBEH. Estella: Verbo Divino, 2011.
Zehnder, Markus. "Building on Stone? Deuteronomy and Esarhaddon's Loyalty Oaths (Part 1): Some Preliminary Observations." *BBR* 19 (2009): 341–74.
–. "Building on Stone? Deuteronomy and Esarhaddon's Loyalty Oaths (Part 2): Some Additional Observations." *BBR* 19 (2009): 511–35.
Zevit, Ziony. "Deuteronomy in the Temple: An Exercise in Historical Imagining." Pages 201–18 in *Mishneh Torah: Studies in Deuteronomy and Its Cultural Environemnt in Honor of Jeffrey H. Tigay.* Edited by Nili Sacher Fox, David Glatt-Gilad, and Michael J. Williams. Winona Lake, IN: Eisenbrauns, 2009. https://doi.org/10.1111/j.1748-0922.2010.01487_9.x
–. "The Khirbet el-Qôm Inscription Mentioning a Goddess." *BASOR* 255 (1984): 39–47. https://doi.org/10.2307/1357074
–. *The Religions of Ancient Israel: A Synthesis of Parallactic Approaches.* New York: Continuum, 2001. https://doi.org/10.1017/s0364009405210097
–. "The Textual and Social Embeddedness of Israelite Family Religion: Who Were the Players? Where Were the Stages?" Pages 287–314 in *Family and Household Religion: Toward a Synthesis of Old Testament Studies, Archaeology, Epigraphy, and Cultural Studies.* Edited by Rainer Albertz, Beth Alpert Nakhal, Saul M. Olyan, and Rüdiger Schmitt. Winona Lake, IN: Eisenbrauns, 2014. https://doi.org/10.3764/ajaonline1201.muller
Zimmerli, Walther. *Ezekiel 1.* Translated by Ronald E. Clements. Hermeneia. Philadelphia: Fortress, 1979.

Zorn, Jeffrey R. "The Burials of the Judean Kings: Sociohistorical Considerations and Suggestions." Pages 801–20 in *"I Will Speak the Riddles of Ancient Times": Archaeological and Historical Studies in Honor of Amihai Mazar on the Occasion of His Sixtieth Birthday*. Edited by Aren M. Maier and Pierre de Miruschedji. Winona Lake, IN: Eisenbrauns, 2006. https://doi.org/10.1086/basor25067066

Zorn, Ronny M. "The Pre-Josianic Reforms of Judah." Ph.D. diss., Southern Baptist Theological Seminary, 1977.

Zwickel, Wolfgang, "Priesthood and the Development of Cult in the Books of Kings." Pages 401–26 in *The Books of Kings: Sources, Composition, Historiography, and Reception*. Edited by André Lemaire and Baruch Halpern. VTSup 129. Atlanta: Society of Biblical Literature, 2010. https://doi.org/10.5508/jhs.2017.v17.r21

INDEX OF SCRIPTURE REFERENCES

Exodus		6:1–11	187	12:29–13:1	131
20–23	232	6:17	175	12:30	90
32	131	7:11–16	80	12:31	131
		8:2	146	12:32–13:10	102
Leviticus		12:25	80	12:32	85
21:1–4	36	12:26–31	148	13	99
				13:1–2	104
Numbers		*First Kings*		13:2	17, 18, 35,
5:2–4	36	1–2	71		77, 82, 210,
16:40	175	2:3	172		216
21:6–9	163	4:21	147	13:3	118
		4:24	147	13:6	118
Deuteronomy		5–7	159	13:8–9	118
5–28	66	5:3	127	13:11	32
13	67	6:1–7:51	127	13:16–17	118
16	66, 202	7:8	159	13:20–22	105
16:1–16	192	8:12–61	265	13:21–26	17, 37
17:1	200	8:22–53	128	13:21–22	118
17:14–20	66	8:44–51	128	13:22	118
17:15	66	8:62–65	197	13:26	118
18	66	9:4–9	74	13:29–31	17, 31, 32
19–25	66	11:1–10	165	13:32	266
19:1–13	67	11:1–8	63	13:33	83, 118
20	67	11:1	147	14:4	84
28:29–31	224	11:3–8	126	14:6–14	22
28:36	216	11:5	145, 146	14:7–14	86
34:10–12	66	11:7	145, 147	14:9	82, 86
		11:8	145	14:13	81
Joshua		11:11	145	14:17	84
5:10	195	11:14–40	78	15:27–28	22
		11:28	78, 79	16:1–4	22
First Samuel		11:30–37	83	16:9–10	22
6:8	220	11:31–39	81	16:15	262
6:17–18	220	11:33	84	16:21–22	262
28:7–20	32	12:20	82, 86	16:30	92
		12:25	84	18	144
Second Samuel		12:26–27	88	21:19–22	94
3:29–30	216	12:28–29	83	21:20–29	87
5:24	143	12:28	84, 88	21:25–26	96

332 *Josiah*

21:25	97	22:8	64, 157		104, 145, 147
22:5–28	105	22:10–11	244		
22:17	22	22:11	64, 92–93, 94	23:14	146, 147
22:29–38	22			23:15–20	132, 246
22:41–50	262	22:12–13	116	23:15	26, 131, 132
		22:13–20	116	23:16–18	17, 32, 82, 104
Second Kings		22:13	64		
2:24	37	22:14–20	99, 106	23:16–17	17
8:26–27	25	22:14	112, 116	23:16	18, 35
9:1–10	22	22:15–20	53, 94, 111	23:17	131, 132
9:3–10	22	22:15	109, 116	23:18	32, 35
9:14–27	22	22:16–17	17, 117, 119	23:19	132
9:27	22	22:16	37, 38, 64, 175	23:20	35, 247
9:27–28	22			23:21–23	85, 189, 190, 248
11:1–3	21	22:18–19	37		
11:3	263	22:18	109, 116	23:21	64, 192, 193
13:20–21	31	22:19	37, 92, 95, 175	23:22–23	195
14:6	172			23:22	26, 69, 130, 192, 193
14:25	47	22:19–20	38, 81, 93, 117		
15:8	262			23:23	196
15:12	22	22:20	17, 22, 69, 92, 266	23:24	155, 181, 183, 191, 194
15:13	262				
16:2–3	74	23:1–3	38, 245		
16:3	74	23:1–25	63	23:25	55, 61, 64, 69, 86, 92, 94, 158, 171, 191, 263
16:17–18	74	23:2–3	88		
17	179	23:2	64		
17:19	90	23:4–8	194		
17:21–23	90	23:4–7	186	23:26–27	74
17:24	178	23:4–5	104, 245	23:26	69
17:27–28	179	23:4	129, 242	23:27	26
18:3	25, 70	23:5	18, 35, 69, 129, 148, 149, 150, 153	23:28	69, 260, 261
19:35–37	27			23:29–30	22, 265
20:6	61			24:13	72
21:2	25				
21:3–5	74	23:6	129, 140	*First Chronicles*	
21:6	74	23:7	129, 153, 154	12:1–2	103
21:20–22	133			15:1	187
21:23	18	23:8–20	183	28:3	72
21:24	19	23:8	18, 35, 83, 185	29:1–5	127
21:26–23:30	57			29:28	269
21:26–22:1	17	23:9	35, 140		
22:1	63, 140, 157	23:10–15	194	*Second Chronicles*	
22:2–3	82	23:10	74, 147	3:1–5:1	127
22:2	25, 61, 70, 77, 82, 86, 92, 209, 263, 269	23:11–12	186	3:1	127
		23:11	69, 149, 245	7:17–22	74
		23:12	69, 149	9:29	252
		23:13–14	246	11	61
22:3	63, 127, 267	23:13	72, 73, 84,	12:15	252

13:4–12	99, 103	35:13	199	7:18	151	
13:19	179	35:14	203	26:18	49	
13:22	252	35:15	195, 202	30–31	51	
17:1–21:1	262	35:17	197	44:17	151	
17:3–5	114	35:18–19	269	44:18	152	
26:16–21	175	35:18	70, 130, 196, 197	*Lamentations*		
29:5	164			1:18	216	
29:16	164	35:20–25	265			
30	197	35:20–24	92	*Ezekiel*		
30:6–9	166	35:21–22	102, 212	17–18	100	
30:13	198	35:22	24, 269	19:1–14	76	
30:21–27	198	35:23–24	23, 24, 239			
30:24	200	35:24–25	33, 210, 269	*Hosea*		
31:3–10	200	35:24	70	2:16	49	
32:33	269	35:25	34, 101			
33:24	18	35:27	70, 261	*Amos*		
33:25–34:1	17	36:12	213	1:1	104	
34:1	63, 157			4:4–13	48	
34:2	71, 269	*Psalms*		7:10–15	104	
34:3–7	183	8	60			
34:3–5	186	19–21	60	*Micah*		
34:3	63, 158, 186, 267	42–49	60	1–3	49	
		78	60	4–6	49	
34:5	18, 35	82	60, 182			
34:6–7	185	104	60	*Nahum*		
34:8	158, 268			1:1	46	
34:9	268	*Proverbs*		3:8	46	
34:11	69	25:1	54			
34:14	158, 172			*Habakkuk*		
34:19	95	*Isaiah*		3:5	150	
34:22–28	99, 106	2–32	48			
34:24	37, 38	5–12	48	*Zephaniah*		
34:24–25	17, 119	10:27	48	1:1	43, 100	
34:25	269	14–23	48	2:4–15	45	
34:27	37, 95	14:18	34	2:4	45	
34:28	17–18, 38, 70	27–32	48	2:5–15	45	
		36–37	48			
34:29–35:19	63			*Tobit*		
34:29–32	38	*Jeremiah*		1:3–9	206	
34:32	38, 132	1–3	49			
34:33	183, 269	1:2	51, 100	*Sirach*		
35:1–19	189, 248	1:4–10	51	44–50	211	
35:2–3	186	2:1–37	51	47:19–23	212	
35:3–6	198	3:1–4:4	51	49:1–4	189	
35:3	72, 216	3:6–10	51	49:1–3	211	
35:6	119	3:6	51	49:1	260	
35:7–18	199	3:12	50	49:4	212	
35:12	203	4–6	49			

Josiah

Second Maccabees		1:18	271	Second Baruch	
6:4	153	1:21–22	133, 213, 271	66	125
First Esdras		1:21	271	Matthew	
1:1–20	189	1:22	271	1:2–16	237
1:1–17	189, 248	1:24–25	102, 213	1:10–11	214
1:1	271	1:26	100, 213		
1:3–4	212	1:29	218	Luke	
1:4	271	1:30	33, 101, 272	2:1–5	38
1:7	271	1:31	261	3:23–38	214, 237
1:10	271				
1:14	271	Enoch			
1:18–19	119	89:65–67	211		

Index of Authors

Achtelstetter, K. 109, 115
Ackerman, S. 151, 152
Aguiler, G. 108
Aharoni, Y. 10, 79, 83, 127, 184, 235
Ahlström, G. W. 18, 53, 56, 57, 62, 86, 115, 121, 159, 171, 173, 175, 179, 181
Alberi, M. 5
Albertz, R. 9, 56, 64, 121, 122, 131, 139, 144, 145, 149, 150, 171, 233
Albrecktson, B. 175
Albright, W. F. 121
Alfonso X, King 219
Allen, L. C. 47
Alter, R. 71, 261, 262
Althann, R. 2
Altmann, P. 201, 202, 207
Anderson, G. W. 161, 177
Anderson, J. 121, 185
Andreasen, N.-A. 142
Andrews, H. T. 10
Angel, H. J. 87, 115
Ansberry, C. B. 56
Antoni, K. 13
Apple, R. 245
Armitage, C. M. 221
Arneth, M. 163, 169
Arnold, B. T. 59
Assmann, J. 12, 80, 208, 232-33
Aston, M. 5, 6, 235-38, 243, 244, 246
Auffarth, C. 8, 233
Auld, A. G. 209
Avery, B. 252
Avioz, M. 21, 39, 55, 135
Avi-Yonah, M. 10, 235
Azevido, J. 28
Azize, J. J. 148, 185
Azumi, R. 255

Bagg, A. M. 26
Bahar, S. 165
Bailey, L. 28, 29, 35
Bakon, S. 23
Baldwin, G. 241
Baly, D. 79
Barker, M. 152, 177
Barlow, G. 71, 75
Barnes, T. 239
Barrick, W. B. 2, 8, 35, 36, 85, 125, 132, 165, 191, 194
Barrier, M. 249
Bartelmus, A. 12
Barth, H. 48
Basser, H. W. 87
Basson, A. 28, 29
Bauckham, R. 30
Bauer, S. W. 225
Beardsworth, A. 205
Beaulieu, P.-A. 12
Becker, A. H. 215
Becker, U. 53, 186
Becking, B. 31, 128, 150
Bedouelle, G. 221
Begg, C. T. 187, 213, 274, 275
Belnap, D. 199, 201, 205, 206
Ben-Barak, Z. 142
Ben-Dor Evian, S. 123
Ben-Zion, S. 20
Ben Zvi, E. 3, 40, 44, 47, 52, 68, 100, 103, 115, 174
Berry, G. R. 115
Bewer, J. A. 46, 47, 51, 53
Bibb, B. D. 138, 158, 184
Bird, M. 270, 271, 272
Bird, P. A. 91, 141, 154, 155, 193, 263
Bledstein, A. J. 208
Blenkinsopp, J. 59, 68, 71, 79, 99, 153, 179-80, 181

Bloch, A. P. 130, 191, 202
Bloch-Smith, E. 29, 33, 34, 127, 128
Block, D. I. 100, 122, 124
Boda, M. J. 25, 27
Bodel, J. 34
Boer, R. 28, 87
Böhler, D. 100, 101, 102, 133, 165, 189, 209, 212, 213, 270, 271
Borowski, O. 139
Bossuet, J.-B. 222
Box, G. H. 260
Bradshaw, C. 5, 157
Breen, J. 13, 136
Bremmer, J. N. 174
Brenner, A. 112
Brettler, M. Z. 4, 264
Brewer-Boydston, G. 76, 141
Brichto, H. C. 117
Brigden, S. 221
Bright, J. 11, 51, 125, 161, 162
Brinkman, J. A. 36, 163, 180
Brooks, B. A. 154
Brown, R. E. 124
Brown, S. 89
Brueggemann, W. 17, 19, 40, 90, 92, 97, 111, 189
Bruit Zaidman, L. 201, 203, 204
Brunet, A.-M. 73, 127
Budin, S. L. 125, 146, 154
Burkert, W. 32, 203, 207
Burkitt, F. C. 66
Businck, T. A. 127
Buttenwieser, M. 60
Butting, K. 108
Butts, B. 238

Cahill, T. 228
Cantù, C. 226
Cariello, S. 254–5
Carlson, E. L. 23
Carlson, L. W. 201
Carroll, R. P. 50, 51
Cassuto, U. 137
Castelli, S. 213, 214, 272, 273
Cathcart, K. J. 46
Caviness, M. H. 237
Chalcraft, D. J. 39, 79
Charlesworth, J. H. 215

Châtillon, J. 218
Chen, C.-W. 57, 67
Cheyne, T. K. 161
Child, I. 257
Childs, B. S. 64
Christensen, D. L. 40, 45, 46, 107, 109
Christiansen, B. 162
Chrysikopoulos, V. I. 168
Chun, S. M. 70
Chuzho, H. 7
Claburn, W. E. 9, 15, 196
Clark, M. J. 218
Clark, S. 6
Clements, R. E. 48, 66, 67, 167
Cochell, T. 131
Cogan, M. 24, 35, 37, 74, 77, 95, 105, 106, 125, 154, 178, 199
Cohn, R. L. 26, 37, 77, 92, 108, 195
Collins, J. J. 29, 141, 231
Conrad, D. 151
Conti, M. 108
Cook, G. D. 46, 113
Cook, S. A. 52, 114
Cook, S. L. 30, 31
Cornell, C. 122, 128
Cortese, E. 122
Cragg, G. R. 222
Crain, J. C. 107, 115
Crenshaw, J. L. 42, 76, 130
Cross, F. M. 54, 60, 71, 88, 161, 222
Crouch, C. L. 29, 162
Cruz, H. 7
Cuffy, K. H. 262
Cunchillos, J. L. 152, 153

Dahl, G. 200
Dahood, M. 124
Dalley, S. 151
Dandamayev, M. A. 129, 157
Da Riva, R. 138
Davies, P. R. 4, 26, 52, 55, 56, 67, 139, 171, 180
Day, E. 56
Day, J. 142, 143, 147
Dearman, J. A. 129, 149
Deenick, K. 71, 175
Deidre, N. 201
Deist, F. E. 13

Delamarter, S. 21, 209
Delcor, M. 124
Delgado, M. 233
Delumeau, J. 222
Dempster, S. 74
Devecchi, E. 162
Dever, W. G. 122, 137, 142, 149, 177, 194, 202, 204
Dexinger, F. 180
Dick, M. B. 182
Dickason, O. P. 243, 246
Dickinson, C. 52
Dietler, M. 199
Dietrich, M. 29
Dietrich, W. 64, 106
Di Lella, A. A. 33, 211
Dion, P.-E. 122
Dobbins, F. 5
Donagay, T. 240
Doubleday, S. R. 219
Douglas, M. 199
Driver, S. R. 86, 131
Droge, A. J. 53, 65
Duffy, E. 221
Durant, W. 232
Dushek, J. 181

Eakin, F. E., Jr. 144
Edelman, D. V. 44, 78, 107, 114, 126, 129, 154, 164, 181, 187
Edenburg, C. 185
Ehrlich, T. D. 187, 216
Ehrstine, G. 238
Eissfeldt, O. 46, 51
Elayi, J. 164, 263
Eliav, Y. Z. 73, 127
Elkins, S. 258
Ellis, R. S. 174
Emerton, J. A. 125, 141, 152
Emmerson, G. 49, 108, 111, 117
Engnell, I. 115, 142, 157, 195
Erickson, L. N. 75
Esler, P. F. 1
Evans, C. D. 77
Eynikel, E. 132, 189, 191, 192

Faure, B. 135
Faust, A. 11

Feinman, P. 42, 145, 227
Feldman, L. H. 213, 272, 273, 274, 275
Felton, D. 32
Finegan, J. 1
Finkelstein, I. 2, 9, 26, 59, 71, 72, 77, 78, 83, 132, 133, 166, 184, 267
Finsterbusch, K. 2, 57, 76
Finucane, R. C. 32
Fischer, A. 241
Fishbane, M. 43, 162, 204
Flower, M. A. 113
Foakes-Jackson, F. J. 28, 108
Focken, F.-E. 112, 132
Fohrer, G. 46, 47, 125, 207
Fontaine, C. R. 2
Fontaine, N. 238
Fournié, E. 236, 237
Frankena, R. 162
Freed, A. 115
Freedman, D. N. 60, 88, 105, 137, 161, 222
Fretheim, T. E. 17, 37, 77, 97, 117, 119, 189
Fried, L. S. 184
Friedman, R. E. 28, 34, 208
Frisch, A. 70
Frost, S. B. 25
Frymer-Kensky, T. 154
Fulco, W. J. 150, 151
Fulton, D. N. 201, 202, 203, 207

Gadd, C. J. 23
Gafney, W. C. 75, 100, 107, 108, 112, 116
Galil, G. 1
Galvin, G. 4, 69, 76
Gane, R. 123
Garbini, G. 58, 69, 123, 127, 129, 147
Garff, J. 243, 244
Garnsey, P. 200, 201, 206
Gaß, E. 49
Geike, C. 47, 160
Gelb, N. 160–61
Geobey, R. A. 102, 103, 104
Geoghegan, J. C. 58
Gerstenberger, E. S. 116
Geva, H. 139
Gillingham, S. E. 60
Gin Lum, K. 156

Glagolev, A. A. 33, 39, 59, 116, 149, 160, 173, 187, 239
Glassner, J.-J. 62
Glatt-Gilad, D. A. 58, 99
Goff, B. L. 140
Goldhill, S. 245
Goldstein, J. 48, 103, 153
Gomes, J. F. 159, 180
Goodman, W. R. 212
Goody, J. 205
Gottwald, N. K. 90, 138, 196, 213
Grabbe, L. L. 7, 8, 10, 11, 23, 99, 139, 153, 158, 186, 264
Graetz, H. 108, 160, 161
Grafton, A. T. 209
Grant, D. E. 119
Grant, R. M. 273
Granziera, P. 135
Grätz, S. 189
Graupner, A. 59
Gray, J. 17, 26, 53, 79, 85, 97, 102, 149, 154, 155, 163, 196, 260
Gray, J. M. 116, 159, 181, 219
Greenspahn, F. E. 6, 177
Gres-Gayer, J. 222
Grohmann, M. 40, 108, 108, 112, 176, 215
Grosby, S. 8
Grottanelli, C. 111
Gruen, E. S. 270, 272
Grun, B. 231
Guibbory, A. 6
Guillaume, A. 223
Guillaume, P. 57–58, 67, 123, 125, 164
Gulde, S. U. 30

Haak, R. D. 50, 150–51
Habel, N. C. 144
Hackett, J. 137
Hadley, J. M. 143
Hagedorn, A. C. 44, 45
Hall, J. 102, 257
Hallo, W. W. 225
Halpern, B. 3, 56, 69, 103, 106, 110, 145, 212
Hamilton, V. P. 7, 175, 189, 268
Hammer, J. 114
Hammond, J. 158

Hamori, E. J. 32, 106, 107, 112, 113, 114, 115, 155
Handy, L. K. 2, 3, 6, 7, 9, 12, 20, 21, 26, 30, 37, 41, 45, 47, 55, 57, 60, 64, 75, 76, 83, 94, 100, 107, 111, 113, 115, 123, 133, 141, 144, 145, 149, 150, 152, 159, 163, 164, 173, 175, 182, 183, 196, 205, 208, 211, 215, 225, 235, 239, 257, 258, 263, 264, 265, 274
Hankins, D. 40
Haran, M. 184, 192, 199
Hardacre, H. 14
Hardmeier, C. 109, 154, 179, 186
Harman, C. 234
Harrast, T. L. 258
Hastings, S. 258
Hauser, W. A. 136
Hayes, J. H. 1, 18, 86, 128, 131, 140, 161, 167, 177, 196, 262
Hays, C. B. 23, 29, 30
Healey, J. F. 30
Healey, J. P. 19
Heaton, E. W. 42, 72, 128, 131
Hehn, J. 136, 137
Heider, G. C. 147
Heltzer, M. 2, 20
Hendrix, L. 238
Hengel, M. 260, 267, 272
Henige, D. 52
Hepner, G. 69
Herr, B. 122
Herrmann, S. 145, 161, 177
Herzog, Z. 184
Heschel, S. 229
Hess, R. S. 29, 142
Hilber, J. W. 114
Hillers, D. R. 49, 101
Hjurt, A. 200
Hobbs, R. G. 5
Hobbs, T. R. 26, 32, 70, 75, 80, 86, 92, 149, 154, 189
Hodges, T. 259
Hoffman, Y. 67, 93
Hoffmann, H.-D. 65, 191, 192
Hold-Cavell, B. 198
Hole, W. B. 240–41
Hole, W., Mrs. 240, 242

Holladay, J. S., Jr. 138
Holladay, W. L. 51
Holloway, S. W. 15, 19, 20, 125, 240
Hölscher, G. 56
Hooker, P. K. 1, 167
Hoppe, L. J. 21, 60
Horsley, S. 143, 179
Horton, R. F. 109
Hoth, I. 250
Houtman, C. 152
Howard, D. M. 70
Hughes, J. 1
Hulster, I. de 126
Hwang, J. 56

Ilan, T. 100
Ions, V. 37
Irwin, B. P. 144
Irwin, W. A. 115
Ishida, T. 126
Isserlin, B. S. J. 160, 162, 235

James, A. 101, 157
Janzen, D. 28, 70, 92
Japhet, S. 24, 35, 38, 39, 63, 71, 99, 127, 132, 158, 187, 189, 210
Jarick, J. 10
Jensen, K. 56
Jeon, Y. H. 158, 191
Jewel, J. 6
Jirku, A. 173
Job, J. B. 27, 51, 101
Jöcken, P. 50
Johnson, N. B. 97
Johnston, P. S. 33
Johnstone, W. 109, 198
Jonker, L. C. 70, 101, 252
Joseph, A. L. 71, 73, 76, 88
Junginger, H. 229
Junod, S. 5

Kahn, D. 10, 45
Kaiser, O. 66
Kalami, I. 92-93, 114, 209
Kam, R. S. 116
Kapelrud, A. S. 159
Kastein, J. 227
Katz, D. 30, 32

Kaufmann, Y. 57, 122, 227, 231
Kavanaugh, P. 208
Keel, O. 121, 123, 150
Keil, T. 205
Kelle, B. E. 10, 11, 140, 149, 264
Kellenberger, E. 184
Kelly, J. D. N. 209
Kelso, J. A. 61
Kelso, J. L. 55
Kenyon, K. M. 126
Killebrew, A. E. 139
Kim, U. Y. 7, 18
King, P. J. 49
Kinns, S. 23, 173
Kitagawa, J. M. 14, 90
Kitchen, K. A. 2, 7, 168
Kittel, R. 229
Klein, R. W. 24, 35, 38, 39, 63, 73, 75, 99, 102, 103, 132, 157, 164, 175, 187, 198, 204, 210, 212, 213, 267, 269, 270
Kletter, R. 61, 256
Klijn, A. F. J. 215
Knauf, E. A. 9, 27, 28, 55, 57-8, 64, 122, 123, 125, 164, 172
Knoppers, G. N. 38, 66, 74, 93, 101, 102, 106, 109, 132, 153, 165, 166, 167, 169, 178, 179, 180, 181, 189, 197
Knowles, M. 143, 185
Koch, K. 43, 124
Köckert, M. 141
Koenen, K. 1, 180, 181, 188
Kofoed, J. B. 3
Kooij, A. van der 197
Kratz, R. G. 12
Kroger, J. 135
Krueger, D. 5
Kselman, J. S. 44
Kuenen, A. 184, 229
Kuhn, K. G. 230
Kuhrt, A. 12
Kuntz, J. K. 31

Laato, A. 27, 34, 71, 72, 75, 165, 197, 211
Lacheman, E. R. 44
Laffey, A. 19, 40, 85, 92, 154
Lafforgue, G. 231, 231
Lambert, W. G. 3

Lang, B. 187
Langer, W. L. 230
Larsson, G. 59
Lee, K. S. 108, 116, 117, 141
Lemaire, A. 9, 61, 143, 148
Lemche, N. P. 2, 4, 13, 43, 129, 171
Lepore, L. 7, 70
Leu, U. B. 209
Leuchter, M. 2, 48, 88, 101, 177, 188
Levenson, J. D. 33, 172
Levin, C. 54, 70, 77
Levinson, B. M. 55, 162
Lewis, T. J. 29, 128, 155, 164
Licht, J. 4
Lindblom, J. 31, 105
Lindemann, G. 229
Linville, J. R. 6, 13, 73, 117
Lipinski, E. 150, 151, 179
Lipschits, O. 10, 11, 127, 166, 169, 173
Liverani, M. 10, 11, 24, 46, 77, 83, 128, 178, 182, 184
Lloyd, A. B. 10, 168
Lods, A. 138, 159, 160, 177
Lohfink, N. 41, 51, 56, 66, 106, 115, 121, 183, 191
Long, B. O. 17, 31, 84, 102, 103
Lopasso, V. 132, 133
Loretz, O. 29
Lorton, D. 182
Lowery, R. H. 41, 98, 192, 194, 195, 196
Lynch, M. 102, 186, 187, 188

Maag, V. 163, 177, 183
Machinist, P. 182
Maclear, G. F. 226
MacDonald, N. 185, 200, 201, 202, 203, 204, 205
McKane, W. 51
McKay, J. W. 125, 148, 149, 150
McKenzie, S. L. 54, 93, 189, 199
McKinlay, J. E. 109, 114
McLaughlin, J. L. 123, 141
McNeill, W. H. 230
Madsen, C. 243
Magness, J. 200, 201, 203
Malalas, J. 217
Malamat, A. 18, 20
Malandra, W. W. 12

Maldonado, A. de 209
Mallau, H. H. 156
Mandell, A. 31
Manor, D. W. 126
Marble, A. R. 75
Margalit, B. 143
Mariottini, C. F. 50
Marling, K. A. 190
Marquardt, M. 158
Martin-Archard, R. 29
Maspero, G. 228
Mastin, B. A. 142
Mathieu, Y. 172, 173, 175
Mathys, H.-P. 55, 56
Matsunga, A. 135
Matsunga, D. 135
Mattingly, G. L. 146
Maxey, T. 14
May, N. N. 183
Mays, J. L. 48, 49, 50
Mazar, A. 126, 127
Medina, R. W. 25, 33, 36
Meier, S. A. 30, 125, 152
Melville, S. C. 161, 178
Mendenhall, G. E. 138, 162
Menn, E. 115
Mercer, D. 231
Mettinger, T. N. D. 128, 129, 171
Meyers, C. 201
Michael, M. 6, 69
Milgrom, J. 11, 194
Millard, A. R. 260
Miller, G. P. 20
Miller, J. M. 4, 18, 57, 86, 128, 131, 140, 161, 177, 196, 262
Mitchell, C. 25, 70
Mitchner, J. A. 28
Mohol, E. 152
Molin, G. 141
Monroe, L. A. S. 2, 38, 71, 115, 147, 242
Montgomery, J. A. 23, 24, 53, 80, 84, 102, 128, 131, 149, 192
Moore, M. B. 10, 140, 264
Morenz, S. 36, 37
Morgan, S. 108, 116
Morris, E. F. 40
Morrow, W. S. 67, 125
Moscati, S. 225

Mouly, F. 249
Mulford, M. 250
Müller, H.-P. 146
Münnich, M. M. 150, 151, 242
Murdock, G. 4
Myers, J. M. 71, 99, 100, 102, 132, 187, 198, 199, 201, 212, 270

Na'aman, N. 9, 23, 53, 57, 58, 61, 88, 113, 114, 127, 129, 132, 142, 160, 167, 169, 173, 179, 188
Nakanose, S. 7, 17, 19, 89, 183, 189, 196, 200
Nam, R. S. 15, 92
Naveh, J. 61
Nel, P. J. 9, 123
Nelson, K. R. 258
Nelson, R. D. 19, 23, 58, 168
Neuman, E. 137, 143
Nicholson, E. W. 51, 65, 67, 164, 188, 196
Nickelsburg, G. W. E. 211, 215
Niditch, S. 29, 121, 123, 192
Niehr, H. 28, 122, 140, 168, 194
Niemann, H. M. 179, 184
Nihan, C. 66, 67, 112
Nissenbaum, S. 190
Nissinen, M. 111
Nocquet, D. 144
Nodet, É. N. 163
Noegel, S. B. 146
Noll, K. L. 9, 38, 55, 66, 116, 174, 179, 181, 187, 191
Noort, E. 30, 37
North, C. R. 130
North, R. 25
Noth, M. 54, 57, 64, 161
Novotny, J. 159

Oded, B. 19
Oden, R. A., Jr. 137
O'Donovan, J. L. 6
Oesterley, O. E. 260
Ogilvie, R. M. 34, 273, 274
Ogunkunle, C. O. 7
Ojo, J. O. 7, 115, 116, 117
Olmo Lete, G. del 29, 36, 124, 137
Olmstead, A. T. E. 15, 89, 185

Olson, D. 211
Olyan, S. M. 36, 141, 143
Oppenheimer, A. 20
Orlinsky, H. M. 162
Osborne, C. 231-2
Osborne, J. F. 31, 34
Östreicher, T. 125, 148, 158
Otto, Bp. of Freising 219
Ouellette, J. 127
Overton, S. D. 28, 34

Pace, L. 202
Pajunen, M. S. 97, 213
Pakkala, J. 56, 77, 134, 162, 180
Park, S.-M. 70, 72
Paton, L. B. 136, 137, 160
Patrick, D. 56, 117, 158
Paul, S. M. 31
Pedersen, J. 65, 67, 188, 191
Penchansky, D. 133, 141
Perdue, L. G. 42, 211
Person, R. F., Jr. 20, 209
Petty, R. J. 141, 143
Pfeiffer, C. F. 23, 158
Pfeiffer, R. J. 134
Pietsch, M. 53, 112, 117, 269
Pitard, W. T. 34
Plumptre, E. H. 214
Porath, R. 134, 159
Porter, B. N. 143, 159
Powell, J. 5, 65
Preibisz, L. 243
Price, I. M. 23
Priest, J. 108, 112
Provera, M. 150

Quack, J. 110
Quack, J. F. 110, 123

Rabbinowitz, J. 21
Radner, K. 79, 207
Raleigh, W. 222
Ramis Darder, F. 100, 112
Rapp, C. 1
Rawlinson, G. 177
Reade, J. 11
Redford, D. B. 12, 20, 59, 62, 77, 140, 160, 168, 174

Reed, W. L. 141
Renan, E. 7, 44
Rendtorff, R. 58, 166
Riaud, J. 113
Richardson, H. N. 7
Richardson, S. 182, 183
Richter, S. 11, 141
Ringgren, H. 146, 147, 159
Ristau, K. A. 18, 27, 110
Ritner, R. K. 168
Roberts, J. J. M. 12, 43, 44, 46, 50
Roberts, J. M. 230
Robinson, D. W. B. 1, 117
Robinson, J. 35, 84, 85, 103, 191, 195
Robinson, T. H. 100, 131, 160, 161, 177, 229
Rochberg, F. 148
Roebuck, C. 226
Rofé, A. 112
Rogerson, J. W. 1, 54, 55, 267
Rollston, C. A. 9
Römer, T. 37, 52, 53, 173
Ron, Z. 215, 216
Roper, L. 243, 247
Ross, L. 215, 237
Rost, L. 80
Rouillard, H. 29
Routledge, R. L. 28, 34
Rowlett, L. 58
Rowley, H. H. 46, 50, 163
Rowton, M. B. 39, 52, 101
Rudolph, W. 75
Rütersworden, U. 107, 111, 116
Ryle, H. E. 65

Saarelainen, K. 256
Sabourin, L. 60
Sahagún Bernardino de 134
Said, E. W. 232
Sale, G. 19, 45, 56, 223–24
Sanmartín, J. 29
Sasson, J. M. 47
Savran, G. 260, 263, 264
Schart, A. 165, 230
Schaudig, H. 129
Schauss, H. 130, 191
Schearing, L. 25, 76, 79, 126
Schedel, H. 220, 236

Schipper, B. U. 169
Schmid, H. H. 58
Schmid, K. 210
Schmidt, B. B. 148, 155
Schmitt, R. 121, 126, 134, 145, 149
Schmitt Pantel, P. 201, 203, 204
Schmitz, P. C. 151, 152
Schneider, T. J. 157, 159
Schniedewind, W. M. 54, 56, 116
Schnorr von Carolsfeld, J. 238
Schütte, W. 167
Schwartz, J. 181
Schweitzer, S. J. 252
Scibona, R. 131
Scot, R. 155
Scurlock, J. 15, 30, 36, 182, 183
Sellers, O. M. 23
Sellin, E. 46, 47
Seltzer, R. M. 228
Sensenig, P. M. 24, 149
Shafer, B. E. 91
Shafer-Elliott, C. 192
Shemesh, Y. 208
Shepherd, G. 218
Shipp, M. R. 7
Silberman, N. A. 2, 59, 83, 166, 184
Silva, A. de 207
Silver, D. J. 111, 227, 128
Simpson, W. K. 151, 225
Skehan, P. 33
Skjærvø, P. O. 13
Smith, L. P. 44
Smith, M. 230
Smith, M. S. 30, 121, 141, 144, 147, 148, 149, 151
Smith, W. R. 136
Smith, W. S. 240
Smoak, J. 31
Soggin, J. A. 57, 192
Solvang, E. K. 141, 142, 147
Soza, J. A. 78
Spieckermann, H. 34, 122, 125, 128, 139, 141, 156, 157, 163
Spiegelman, A. 249
Spronk, K. 151
Stadelmann, R. 125
Stanley, A. P. 23, 65, 89, 160, 252
Stanton, E. C. 108

Starr, C. G. 225
Stavrakopoulou, F. 142
Steinberg, N. 29, 66
Stern, E. 11, 83, 123, 124, 125, 180, 184
Steussy, M. J. 71, 80, 81, 127, 187, 198, 209
Stevens, M. E. 129, 130
Stinespring, W. F. 198
Stipp, H.-J. 128
Stökl, J. 101, 116
Stolz, F. 121, 187
Stordalen, T. 2, 8, 186
Stott, K. 173
Strange, J. 2
Street, J. S. 5
Stroumsa, G. G. 223
Suriano, M. J. 21, 29, 30, 33, 36, 108
Suter, J. 230
Suzuki, Y. 9, 16
Sweeney, M. A. 2, 13, 25, 26, 38, 43, 44, 45, 48, 51, 52, 53, 71, 79, 84, 85, 86, 93, 97, 100, 106, 131, 144, 149, 154, 155, 157, 163, 248, 266, 267
Swidler, A. 107, 111
Synkellos, George 217–218
Syros, V. 5

Tadmor, H. 24, 35, 74, 77, 106, 154, 199
Talshir, Z. 21, 209, 270, 271
Tatum, L. 158, 164
Taylor, J. 12, 30
Tcherikover, V. 260
Teeter, E. 12, 36, 124
Teeuwen, M. 13, 136
Terry, M. S. 111
Thames, J. T., Jr. 20
Thompsin, T. L. 2
Thon, J. 32, 102
Throntveit, M. A. 72, 73, 110
Tigay, J. H. 14, 65, 122, 124, 167
Tiller, P. A. 211
Töbelmann, P. 110
Toorn, K. van der 100, 107, 111, 149, 154
Townsend, J. B. 137
Toy, C. H. 121, 123, 163
Trevelyan, R. 221
Trible, P. 107, 1212

Trimmer, S. 117
Tück, J.-H. 233
Tucker, G. M. 57

Uehlinger, C. 8, 121, 123, 143, 149, 150, 170
Ulmer, R. 124
Urquhart, J. 200
Ussishkin, D. 11, 127

Valerio, A. 107
Vanderhooft, D. S. 106, 212
Van Seters, J. 7, 43, 54, 80
Vaux, Roland de 172, 175, 187, 191, 193, 195
Veldman, I. 243
Vermeylen, J. 48
Viezel, E. 55
Vílchez Líndez, J. 206
Visaticki, K. 191, 195
Vriezen, K. J. H. 152
Vriezen, T. C. 148, 153

Wacker, M.-T. 153, 154
Wagner, V. 130, 191, 192
Walker, C. 182
Walsh, J. T. 79
Warburton, D. A. 166
Warhurst, A. K. 101
Watson, A. 237
Watts, J. D. W. 43, 44, 46
Watts, J. W. 59, 174, 175
Weaver, J. 237
Weed, L. 250
Weems, R. J. 107, 109, 116, 193
Weinfeld, M. 56, 162, 184
Weippert, H. 53
Weippert, M. 71
Weisberg, D. B. 196, 199
Welch, A. C. 21, 64, 72, 92, 125, 159, 163, 191
Welch, E. L. 45
Wellhausen, J. 64, 230
Wells, H. G. 10, 228
Welsh, F. 10, 230
Westad, O. A. 230
White, E. 123, 141, 143
Whitley, C. F. 51

Whybray, R. N. 42
Widengren, G. 160
Wiggins, S. A. 137, 143
Wikandr, O. 14, 173
Wilcoxen, J. A. 8, 10, 18
Williams, D. L. 68, 160
Williams, G. H. 221
Williams, M. 249
Williamson, H. G. M. 92, 99, 101
Wilson, L. S. 163
Wilson, R. R. 57, 107, 109
Wiseman, D. J. 109
Wolff, H. W. 48
Wood, W. C. 30
Woolf, A. 58, 234
Wright, N. 249, 250
Würthwein, E. 92, 191
Wyatt, N. 29, 88, 131, 141, 143, 145, 146

Xella, P. 29, 150, 151

Yadin, Y. 184, 256
Yamauchi, E. M. 46, 168
Yee, G. A. 49, 204
Youngberg, B. G. 72
Younger, K. L. 148

Zahn, M. 190
Zamora García, P. 17, 63, 104, 126, 131, 144
Zehnder, M. 162
Zevit, Z. 30, 65, 80, 112, 121, 122, 123, 126, 141, 142, 154, 173
Zimmerli, W. 167
Zorn, J. R. 24, 33
Zorn, R. M. 41, 98, 192
Zwickel, W. 130, 176

Index of Subjects

Aaron 131, 153, 203
Abijah 99, 103, 179, 269
Abraham 250
Achbor 95, 111, 119
Adaiah 79
Africa 7, 200
Ahab 22, 24, 25, 70, 76, 87, 92-97, 144, 210, 262, 263
Ahaz 69, 73, 74, 75, 149, 268
Ahaziah 22-23, 24, 25
Ahijah (father of Baasha) 94
Ahijah (prophet) 81-82, 84
Ahikam 111, 119
Akhenaton 11-12
Akiba, Rabbi 216
Alfonso X, King of Castile 55, 219-20, 232, 234
Alt, Albrecht 57
altars 18, 35, 37, 73-74, 82, 92, 103-6, 118, 131-32, 149, 153, 180, 184, 185, 210, 220, 232, 247-48, 266, 268
Amarna 124
Amaziah 21, 25
Amerindians 243-44, 246
Ammon 148
Ammut 37
Amon 8, 9-10, 18, 19-20, 21, 26, 31, 43, 63, 69, 75, 79, 133-34, 142, 169, 171, 174, 187, 197, 210, 217, 224, 253, 256, 257, 265, 268
Amon (deity) 10, 80
Amos 104, 216
Amos, Book of 48-49, 60
amulets 156
Anat 137, 138, 152
Ancus Martius 217
angels 27, 118, 152-53
aniconography 86, 128-29
Antiochus IV 153
Aphrodite 146

Apocalypse of the Animals 210-11
Apollo 246
Arabia 161
Arad 184
Aram 22, 78, 140
archaeology 2-4, 9, 34, 58, 61, 72, 83, 121-23, 126, 134, 142, 144, 150, 166, 180, 184, 239
Aristophanes 4
ark of the covenant 173, 186, 187, 198, 212, 215-16
Asaiah 95, 111, 119
Ashdod 62
Asherah 35, 114, 124, 129, 134, 137, 138, 141-43, 144, 145, 149, 152, 154, 158, 194, 220, 242, 255, 265, 267
Ashes 105, 180
Ashurbanipal 11, 26, 48, 62, 161, 167, 168, 178
Ashurnasirpal 201
Assmann, Jan 232-33
Assyria 9, 10, 11, 18, 19, 20, 23, 26, 27, 28, 39, 45, 46, 48, 61, 62, 64, 65, 74, 83, 113, 123, 124, 125, 140, 147, 149, 158, 159, 160, 161-64, 165, 166-69, 178-80, 181, 183, 184, 187, 201, 207, 223, 224, 225, 226, 227-28, 229, 231, 234, 239, 240, 255, 256, 264, 267
Astarte 73, 124, 137, 145-46, 152, 194, 220, 228, 246
Aten (deity) 12
Athaliah 21, 24-25, 126, 187, 216, 263
Athens 201, 206
Augustine of Hippo 217, 228
Avery, Ben 252-54
Avva 178
Azariah/Uzziah 175
Aztecs 134-35
Azumi, Ryo 255-57

Josiah

Baal 35, 92, 114, 124, 129, 134, 136, 137, 138, 139, 144–45, 158, 216, 220, 228, 238, 239, 242, 245, 265, 267
Baasha 94
Babylonia 11, 25, 26, 27, 39, 40, 50, 53, 61–62, 70, 101, 113, 123, 124, 157, 160, 161, 163, 178, 199, 215, 227, 231, 239, 256, 264
Baldwin, George C. 241
barley 139
Bauer, Susan Wise 225
bears 37
beer 201
Beer Sheba 83
Benjamin (tribe) 38, 132
Bes 123–24
Bethel 26, 32, 34, 35, 37, 48, 49, 51, 64, 82, 83–85, 86, 89–90, 103–5, 118, 131, 132–33, 179–81, 210, 220, 233, 247, 266, 268
bones 18, 31, 35–37, 91, 201, 210, 247
Bossuet, Jacques-Bégnine 222
Bozkath 79
bread 201, 202, 204, 253
Broome, Mat 252–54
Buddhism 14, 135, 233
Burch, Amy 258
Burges, Cornelius 6
Burhill, Robert 221
burning 35–37, 50, 176, 182, 210, 231, 247, 258, 266, 273

Cahill, Thomas 227, 228
calendar 104, 130, 190, 271
Cameron, Don 250
Canterbury Cathedral 226, 237
Cantù, Cesare 226
Carchemish 226
Cariello, Sergio 254–55
Carroll, Lewis 242
Carthage 186
Cassius Dio 73
Catholicism 221, 222–23, 237–38, 244, 248–49
cattle 199, 201, 202, 204, 241, 248
Chaldeans 51
chariots 23, 24, 149–50, 220, 224, 235, 239, 241, 242, 245, 246, 251, 252, 254, 156, 272

Charlemagne 5
Charles IX, King of France 5
Chemosh 73, 146–47, 194, 246
Child, Isabella 257
China 135, 223
Christmas 190
Chronicles, Book of 2–3, 7, 8, 13, 20, 21, 24, 28, 69, 157–59, 163–65, 197–207, 209, 210, 212, 261, 267–70
Cicero 5
comic books 249–57
courtiers 54, 89, 97, 113, 114, 169, 187
covenant 38, 58, 80, 88, 167, 194–95, 199, 227, 266
Cranmer, Thomas 5
Cutha 178
Cyprus 146, 151
Cyrus 12, 102

Dalia (Josiah's nursemaid) 253
Damascus 78
Dan 49, 83–85, 86, 89–90, 131
David 1, 6, 13, 25, 27, 33, 42–43, 54, 57, 61, 66, 69, 705, 26, 32, 70–73, 77, 78, 80–83, 127, 128, 131, 145, 146, 147, 158, 171, 174, 176, 187, 197, 198, 202, 205, 207, 209, 212, 213–15, 216, 222, 223, 237, 250, 253, 254, 257, 261, 263, 265, 268, 269, 271, 273
death 17–41, 72, 86–87, 105, 151, 190, 194, 247, 257
deer 185
Deuteronomistic author 17, 19, 40, 54–58, 64, 66, 68, 69, 70, 127, 185
Deuteronomy 6, 8, 9, 13, 16, 44, 49, 54–75, 59, 64–67, 115, 161–62, 175, 192, 195, 196, 219, 220, 223–25, 227, 228, 230, 232, 232, 236, 250
Deutsch, Niklaus Manuel 238
Diderot, Denis 225
Divination 110–13, 156, 231
dogs 94, 96
Donne, John 101, 157
Doré, Gustave 238
Durant, Will 232
Durant, Ariel 232

Ecclesiastes, Book of 42, 47
Eden 186

Edom 78
education 76, 112, 130–31, 226, 233, 249
Egypt 9–11, 18, 20, 23, 25–27, 28, 36–37, 39, 40, 45, 59, 61, 78, 79, 91, 123–24, 128, 131, 140, 146, 148, 157, 163, 168, 178, 179, 191, 211, 213–14, 225, 226, 227–28, 229, 230, 231, 232–34, 241, 247, 251, 253, 254, 256, 258, 264, 274
Ekron 125
El 122, 144
Elah 22
Elam 168
Elephantine 122, 128, 191
Elijah 92, 93–96, 144, 250
Elisha 22
Elizabeth I, Queen of England 5, 6
Elkins, S. 258
empire, Josianic 10–11, 27, 57, 60–61, 71, 72, 132, 196, 205, 216, 222
Endor, Woman of 32, 240–41
England 221, 226, 240
Ephraim (tribe) 79
Esarhaddon 48, 113, 173
Euphrates River 169, 226
Euripides 4
Eusebius 209
Exodus, the 88
Ezekiel 64, 100, 134, 186, 219, 230
Ezekiel, Book of 167
Ezra 38, 53, 212, 227, 270–72

Feast of Weeks 66
fires/bonfires 118, 236, 239, 241, 242, 246, 247
First Esdras, Book of 3, 8, 20, 21, 24, 28, 39, 133–34, 165, 209, 212–13, 236, 245, 251, 270–72, 273
fish 202
food 10
fowl 202
France 222, 239
Frederick III, Elector of Saxony 238
Freud, Sigmund 232
fruits 201

Gaines, Maxwell Charles 250, 251
Galle, Phillipe 243–49
Garnsey, Peter 206
gatekeepers 202, 203
gazelles 185
Gebah 83
Gedaliah 21
Gerizim, Mount 66, 180–81
Germany 229–30, 242–43
ghosts 30–32, 95, 155, 194, 240–41, 242
Gilead 83
goats 185, 199–200, 202, 242
goddesses 124, 136, 139, 140–43, 145–46
Goetz, Walter 228–29
golden calves 85–86, 103, 131
Goliath 250
Goody, Jack 205
Gösler, Joseph 238
grains, roasted 201
Granada 220
graphic novels 249, 252–57
Greece 32, 113, 143, 146, 186, 203–4, 206, 207, 209, 213, 236, 247, 272
Greenberg, Moshe 227
Grun, Bernard 231
Guild of Saint Luke 244
Guillaume, André 223, 233

Habakkuk 100
Habakkuk, Book of 50–51, 60
Hadad 78–79
Hamath 178
Hammerton, John A. 228
Hamutal 75–76
Hanukkah 215
Harman, Chris 234
Hasmoneans 9, 153, 179, 181
Hathor 124
Hearn, Lafcadio 13
Heemskerk, Martin van 243–49
Henry VIII, King of England 221
Henry, Prince (son of James I) 221
Herodotus 160, 161
Herrera y Tordesillas, Antonio de 246
Hezekiah 25, 26, 33, 47, 54, 56, 57, 61, 62, 65, 68, 70, 72, 73, 77, 122, 133, 163, 164–66, 171, 183, 184, 185, 197, 199, 200, 210, 212, 219, 224, 228, 230, 232, 252, 256, 263, 267, 268, 269

348   *Josiah*

Hilkiah 55, 59, 65, 95, 111, 116, 119, 129, 159–61, 172–74, 176, 191, 209, 220, 238, 245, 246, 247, 250, 253, 254–55, 256–57, 265
Hinduism 233
Hiram, King of Tyre 127
history/historiography 1, 3–4, 7–11, 14–16, 62–63, 93, 110, 170–76, 208–35, 260, 262, 272
Hittites 113, 142
Hobbs, John 55
Hole, William Brassey 240–42
Holiness Code 115
Holloway, Steven W. 239
horses 149, 245, 246, 251, 256
Hosea 65
Hosea, Book of 49–50, 60
Hoshea 21
host of heaven 129, 134, 148, 194
Huguenots 5
Huldah 17, 22, 28, 37–40, 53, 55, 65, 69, 81, 87, 88, 93–97, 99–100, 106–17, 155, 161, 175–76, 193, 208, 212, 216, 217, 220, 224, 235, 248, 251, 253, 254, 256, 264, 266, 269, 274

iconoclasm 6, 221, 236, 238, 239, 241, 244–46, 250, 253, 256, 275
Iddo 252–54
idols/images 4, 80, 81, 83, 85, 86, 128–29, 133, 147, 155, 158, 171, 181–83, 186, 220, 221, 223, 224, 225, 231, 232, 236, 238, 241, 244, 246, 255, 258, 273
India 135
Indianapolis 500 190
Iowa 201
Isaac 250
Isaiah 25, 61, 252
Isaiah, Book of 47–48, 60, 64, 187
Isho'dad of Merv 108
Islam 233
Israel 1, 10, 15, 21, 22, 24, 25, 28, 35, 61, 63–64, 65, 72, 76–98, 104, 121–25, 131–33, 144, 161–62, 165, 177–84, 220, 224, 225, 226, 234, 236, 247, 262–63, 265, 266, 267, 268
Ištar 143, 152, 166–67, 169
Italy 226, 243

James I, King of England 221
Japan 13–14, 135–36
Jason of Cyrene 267
Jasper, Karl 232
Jedidah 8, 75–76, 79–80, 112, 253
Jehoahaz 27, 69, 74–76, 235, 251, 252
Jehoiachin 27, 66, 70, 261, 266
Jehoiakim 50, 69, 74–76, 191, 235
Jehoash 21, 127, 132
Jehoshaphat 6, 114, 262
Jehu 22–23
Jeremiah 5, 24, 34, 39, 50, 51, 63, 99, 101, 109, 117, 160, 161, 208, 209, 210, 213, 216, 217, 218, 224, 232, 252, 254–55, 270, 272
Jeremiah, Book of 45, 51–52, 74, 75, 99, 228, 229, 231
Jeroboam I 21, 70, 76–92, 94, 96, 99, 103–5, 118, 119, 131, 132, 171, 226, 247, 266, 268
Jeroboam II 47, 102
Jerome 55, 101, 209, 220
Jerusalem 11, 18, 23, 24, 25, 30, 32, 33, 35, 37, 38, 44, 48, 53, 63–64, 74, 82, 83, 85, 87, 101, 114, 119, 131, 133, 139, 164, 166, 171, 179, 180, 181, 183, 184, 196–97, 206–7, 232, 252, 255, 256, 263, 266
Jesus ben Joseph 214–15, 236–37
Jezebel 76, 94, 96–97, 144, 263
Jimmu, Emperor of Japan 13
Joash 159
Joab 78, 216
Job, Book of 47
Joel, Book of 43
Johanan, Rabbi 216
John Chrysostom 55
John Hyrcanus 83, 267
Jonah, Book of 46–47, 60, 117
Jonathan, Rabbi 216, 217
Joram 22, 24
Joseph (tribe) 79, 83
Josephus, Flavius 3, 27, 34, 101, 209, 213–14, 220, 224, 229, 231, 261, 267, 272–75
Joshua 6, 7, 38, 58, 191, 195, 234
Joshua, Book of 7, 42–43, 54–55, 57–58, 60, 192, 228, 231
Josiah 1–16, 17–28, 31–41, 43–68,

69–98, 99–116, 121, 122, 125, 127, 129–30, 140, 145–49, 151–56, 157–88, 189–99, 201–7, 208–75
Jotham 269
Judah 1, 3, 9–11, 13, 15, 17, 18, 21, 22, 25–28, 35, 37, 38, 40, 43, 62, 69, 74, 104, 117, 119, 121–56, 157–88, 164, 166, 169, 177, 261–63, 266, 267
Judaism, Early 227–28
Judith, Book of 222, 224
Judges, Book of 42, 54–55, 60, 228, 231
Jupiter (deity) 245
Justice of Tiberias 267

Kastein, Josef 226
Kaufmann, Yehezkel 227
Khirbet el-Qom 141
Kings, Book of 2–3, 7, 8, 11, 13, 17, 20, 21, 28, 40, 52–55, 60, 69, 93, 157–60, 164–65, 190–97, 209–10, 228, 231, 236, 260–67
Kinoshita Iwao 13
Kittel, Gerhard 229
Kittel, Rudolf 229–30
Kojiki (book) 13–14
Korea 135
Kuntillet 'Ajrud 141

Lachish 11
Lafforgue, Gilbert 231
Lamentations, Book of 39, 101
laments 34, 101, 269–70, 272
Langer, William L. 230
Levine, Baruch A. 231
Levites 38, 39, 86, 90–91, 109, 164, 167, 176, 186, 187–88, 195, 198, 199–200, 202, 203–5, 210, 212
libraries 174, 232
lions 17, 37, 105, 118, 247
literacy 9
Logan, John A. 190
Lukás, Georg 28
Luther, Martin 238

Maclear, George Frederick 226
McNeill, William H. 230
magic 31, 130, 139, 155–56, 163
Malalas, John 217
Maldonado, Alfonso de 208–9

Martin, B. 227
man of God, the 17, 31–32, 34, 35, 37, 82, 99–100, 102–6, 116, 118–19
Manasseh 8, 10, 11, 19, 20, 25, 26, 31, 61, 63, 65, 73, 74, 75, 133–34, 142, 166, 168, 171, 174, 186, 187, 197, 210, 216, 222, 224, 226, 227, 253, 255, 257, 257, 266, 267, 268
Manasseh (tribe) 79
Mary II, Queen of England 5
Mary, Mother of Jesus 135, 237
meals 118, 152, 165, 186, 188, 190, 197–207, 248, 251, 271
meat 185, 201–4, 206, 207, 248
Medes 161
mediums 155, 240–41
Megiddo 11, 23, 33, 92, 225, 229, 230, 234, 241, 251, 255
Meiji Era 13–14, 90, 136
Melville, Herman 242
Memorial Day 190
memory 4, 13, 18, 33, 232, 264–65, 267, 268, 269–70, 275
Mende 274
Mercer, Derrik 230–31
mercy (divine) 38–40, 118, 119, 257, 271–72
Merneptah inscription 77
Mesha stele 146
Meshullemeth 10
Mesopotamia 3, 20, 30, 32, 113, 128, 129, 130, 131, 146, 148, 157, 163, 173, 225, 239, 241, 258
Mexico 134–5
Mezad Hashavyahu 11
Micah, Book of 49–50, 60
mice 220
Milcom [*see* Molech]
milk 200
Moab 146–84
Molech/Milcom 73, 74, 124, 147–48, 194, 228, 246
monks 5, 275
Moser, Barry 242–43
Moses 5, 6, 37, 38, 55, 61, 66, 67, 77, 78, 81, 84, 88, 94, 112, 158, 161, 163, 172, 198, 199, 206, 215, 216, 219, 223, 225, 232, 233, 234, 236, 250, 271

Mot 30, 124
Motoori Norinaga 13
Mowery, Robert L. 250
Mulford, Montomery 250
Mursili II 113
Muslims 220, 275

Nabonidus 11, 12, 113, 173
Nabopolassar 62
Naboth 94
Nadab 22
Nahum 100
Nahum, Book of 43, 46, 60, 68
Nathan 80
Nebat 78, 94
Nebuchadnezzar I 11
Nebuchadnezzar II 11, 197, 222, 225, 257
Neco II, King of Egypt 11, 22, 23, 24, 26, 33, 39, 45, 87, 102, 180, 212-13, 223, 224, 225-26, 228, 229, 230, 245, 251, 254, 255, 256, 265, 269, 272, 273, 274-75
Necromancy 15, 32, 155, 240-41, 273
Nehemiah 226, 227, 270
Nehustan 163-64
Nergal 151
Netherlands 221, 243, 248
Nevada 201
Nile River 226
Nimrod 201
Nineveh 11, 46-47, 62
Nubia 59, 62, 168, 241, 266
nudes 243-44, 246-47, 248
Nuremberg 220
nuts 201

O'Connor, Tim 258
Oho no Yasumaro 13
olive oil 202
Omri 25, 92, 147, 262
Oostema, Gloria 258
Otto, Bp of Freisin 219

Passover 58, 66, 69, 72, 85, 119, 130, 133, 165, 186, 188, 189-207, 210, 216-17, 236, 248, 251, 255, 258, 269, 270, 271
Pazuzi 239

Pentateuch 58-60
Penuel 84
Persia 13, 57, 122, 123, 126, 128, 153, 163, 167, 179, 180, 181, 184, 232, 266, 270-71
Petrus Comestor 218-20, 230, 233
Philistia 160, 216
Philone 5
Phoenicia 124, 140, 146, 160, 168, 226
pillars 242, 245, 248
Plato 233, 272
priestesses 91, 112, 141, 146, 154
Priest, High 90, 113, 130, 172, 227
priests 17, 18, 19, 20, 35, 37, 39, 63, 65, 82, 86, 90-91, 104, 129, 130, 138, 153-54, 167, 175-77, 179, 182, 184, 188, 198-204, 210, 211, 213, 220, 224, 225, 230, 231, 232, 238, 245, 246, 247-48, 256, 266, 273-74, 275
Pritchard, James B. 231
prophecy 17, 21-22, 37, 39, 40, 53, 82, 87, 93-94, 99-120, 212-13, 216, 269
Protestantism 5-6, 157, 221, 224, 237-38, 244, 248-49
Proverbs, Book of 42-43
Psalms, Book of 42, 59-60
Psamtik I, King of Egypt 10, 11, 59, 62, 161, 168, 169
Psamtik II, King of Egypt 10

queen mother 75-76, 141-43
Queen of Heaven 151-52

Raleigh, Walter 55, 221, 223, 228
Ramat Rahel 11, 83, 139, 201, 203, 207, 235
Ramshaw, Elaine J. 258
Ramoth-Gilead 92
Rechabites, History of 217
Reformation, Protestant 5-6, 157, 218, 245, 248
refugees 27, 78-79
Rehoboam 21, 79, 81, 82, 83, 99, 103, 212
repentance 5, 50, 76, 92-97, 115, 119, 133, 217, 222, 253, 256, 266
Resheph 124, 150-51
resurrection 125
Rezon 78-79

Richard I, King of England 237
ritual 14, 18, 31, 33, 36, 40, 110, 119, 124, 129-30, 138-40, 147, 153, 192-93, 203, 216-17, 226, 269, 271, 273, 275
Robinson, Theodore H. 228-30
Roebuck, Carl 226
Rome 34, 124, 157, 186, 206, 209, 213-14, 225, 236, 239, 243, 272-74, 275
Ruth 216
Ruth, Book of 42, 47, 60

sacrifice 18, 35, 104, 129-30, 147, 148, 152, 185-86, 197, 199, 202, 203, 206, 210, 211, 228, 236, 248, 266-67
Said, Edward W. 232
Sale, George 223-25
Samaria 3, 65, 92, 128, 132, 166, 179-81, 220, 227, 229, 266
Samaritans 179, 180-81
Samerina 26, 62, 63, 104, 123, 132-33, 161-62, 166-67, 178-79, 181, 210
Samuel 32, 84, 195, 197, 216, 226
Samuel ben Nachman 216, 217
Samuel, Book of 54-55, 60, 71, 75, 187, 228, 231, 236
Sankta Maria Kyrka 258
Saul 25, 69, 72, 82
scepters 238, 245, 246, 247, 248, 258
Schedel, Hartmann 220
Schmid, Konrad 210
Schnorr von Carolsfeld, Julius 238, 259
Schwarz, Leo W. 227
scribes 3, 4, 9, 15, 19, 31, 43, 48-50, 52-53, 59-60, 66, 113, 138, 140, 230
scroll (found in temple) 2, 6, 16, 25, 37-40, 53, 55-56, 59, 64-67, 85, 92, 93, 94, 97, 111, 114, 115, 158, 159-60, 172-75, 191, 193, 196, 220, 223, 224, 231-33, 236, 239, 250, 253, 254, 256, 258, 265, 269
Scythians 160-61, 229
Second Baruch 215
seders 197, 202
Seldon, John 136
Seltzer, Robert M. 227, 228
Selucids 180, 214
Sennacherib 11, 27, 61, 164, 263
Sepharvaim 178

sermons 4, 5-6, 73, 222, 264
serpents 37, 163-64
Shallum 109, 112, 262
Shaphan 95, 111, 115, 159-60, 174, 220, 239, 244, 247, 250, 251, 253, 256, 258, 259
Shasu 77
Shechem 84, 89
sheep 185, 199-201, 202, 203-4, 248
Shemaiah 81
Shemesh 35, 129, 149
Sheol 28-32, 36, 149, 151
Shiloh 84
Shinto 14, 136
shrines [see temples]
Sidon 140, 146
signet rings 2
Silver, Daniel Jeremy 227-28
Simon ben Onias 211, 260
Sin (deity) 12
singers 195, 202
Sin-shar-ish-kun 11
Siraiah 172
Smith, Morton 230
soldiers 10, 23, 58, 122, 190, 238, 241, 246, 247-48, 251, 253, 256, 272-73, 275
Solomon 1, 42-3, 54, 61, 63, 69, 72-74, 78-85, 88, 104, 126-28, 131, 137, 145-48, 159, 164-65, 171, 176, 187, 197, 198, 202, 205, 207, 212, 213, 215, 223-24, 246-47, 261, 262, 264-66, 268, 269, 270, 271
Song of Songs, Book of 42
South Asia 266
Spain 135, 157, 220, 221
speeches, biblical 17, 39, 53, 103, 118, 128, 166, 264, 266
spiritualism 240-41
stained glass 237, 238
Starr, Chester G. 225
Stead, William T. 241
Stevenson, Robert Louis 240
Stoics 273
swine 185, 201
Synkellos, George 217-18, 219

Tabernacle 64
Tabernacles, Feast of 85

Talmud 101, 131, 208, 215–17
Taoism 135
Temple, Jerusalem 1, 16, 28, 32, 40, 64, 72, 73, 74, 83–84, 88, 90, 124, 126–30, 140, 144, 147, 149, 157, 159, 169, 171–74, 177, 185, 186, 187–88, 198, 202, 205, 210, 211, 212, 224, 230, 231, 248, 253, 254, 256, 264–66, 268–71
temples/shrines 11, 31, 35, 36, 49, 63, 73, 80, 83–86, 89, 91, 125–26, 130, 131, 140, 147, 153, 159, 164, 171, 181, 182, 184, 185, 210, 225, 226, 227, 228, 231, 232, 247–48, 265, 267, 273
Tenney, Shawna J. C. 258
Tenskwatawa (Shawnee prophet) 156
Thebes 46
Thomas, Eric 258
Thoth 239
Tibni 262
Tirzah 78, 84
Tobit, Book of 66, 206
tombs 17, 24, 31, 32, 33, 34, 87, 103, 180, 247
treaties 162
tree of Jessie 215, 237, 238
trees 142, 143
Tukulti-Ninurta I 11, 173
Tyre 146

Ugarit 30, 142, 144, 150, 161
Unleavened Bread, Feast of 192, 198, 204

Vallotten, Annie 242
veganism 185
violence in art 238, 244–45, 247

war 19, 22–23, 36, 61, 67, 103, 151, 161, 168, 190, 245, 251, 252–54, 255, 272–73

Welch, Adam C. 6
Wellhausen, Julius 64
Wette, Wilhelm M. L. de 55, 56, 64, 220
wheat 139
Whybray, Norman 42
wine 202
Wisdom of Jesus ben Sirach 211–12
Wisdom of Solomon 125
witches 6, 155, 240, 243–44
wool 200
Woolf, Alex 234
wrath (divine) 37–40, 74, 94, 96, 116, 117–20, 175
Wright, Frank E. 239

Xerxes I 11, 173

Yahweh 6, 11, 15–16, 17, 22, 24, 25, 27, 30, 31, 37–40, 47, 50, 80, 85, 86, 88, 92–97, 111–20, 122, 126, 131, 138, 140, 141, 144, 147, 150, 157–58, 160–62, 175–76, 184, 187, 194–95, 198–99, 201–2, 203, 205, 206, 207, 209, 230–21, 248, 263–66, 268, 271, 274
Yareah 129, 150
Yeshua ben Sirach 211, 260

Zarathustra 12, 13
Zebidah 75–76
Zechariah (king) 22, 262
Zedekiah 213
Zerubbabel 270
Zephaniah 63, 100, 160, 161, 209, 219, 224
Zephaniah, Book of 43–45, 46, 60, 68, 229
Zeus 245
Zimri 262
Zobah 78
Zoroastrianism 153

www.ingramcontent.com/pod-product-compliance
Lightning Source LLC
Chambersburg PA
CBHW051627230426
43669CB00013B/2203